T0368446

EVERLASTING EGYPT

Kemetic Rituals for the Gods

RICHARD J. REIDY

EVERLASTING EGYPT
KEMETIC RITUALS FOR THE GODS

Copyright © 2018 Richard J. Reidy.

Cover Image: Ritual scene from the Temple of Hathor at Deir el Medina. Ptolemaic Period. © Matthew Whealton, 2018.'

All rights reserved. No part of this book may be used or reproduced by any means, graphic, electronic, or mechanical, including photocopying, recording, taping or by any information storage retrieval system without the written permission of the author except in the case of brief quotations embodied in critical articles and reviews.

iUniverse books may be ordered through booksellers or by contacting:

iUniverse
1663 Liberty Drive
Bloomington, IN 47403
www.iuniverse.com
1-800-Authors (1-800-288-4677)

Because of the dynamic nature of the Internet, any web addresses or links contained in this book may have changed since publication and may no longer be valid. The views expressed in this work are solely those of the author and do not necessarily reflect the views of the publisher, and the publisher hereby disclaims any responsibility for them.

Any people depicted in stock imagery provided by Thinkstock are models, and such images are being used for illustrative purposes only. Certain stock imagery © Thinkstock.

ISBN: 978-1-5320-3200-4 (sc)
ISBN: 978-1-5320-3201-1 (hc)
ISBN: 978-1-5320-3199-1 (e)

Library of Congress Control Number: 2017916143

Library of Congress Cataloging-in-Publication Data
Reidy, Richard J.
Everlasting Egypt: Kemetic Rituals for the Gods 1. Rituals and ceremonies—Egypt. 2. Egyptian Reconstructionist—religion. 3. Ancient Egypt—Spirituality 4. Magic—Egypt. 5. Neopaganism—Egyptian. I. Reidy, Richard James). II. Title. Includes bibliographical references.

Print information available on the last page.

iUniverse rev. date: 07/18/2018

Contents

ANNUAL FESTIVAL RITUALS

MONTHLY LUNAR RITUALS

Foreword

On November 22nd, 2015 Richard Reidy, the author of this book flew to the West. The book that lies before you was very nearly complete at that time, with all the rituals written and a good portion of the master file assembly built. We, the members of various Temples begun by Rich or with his guidance, have completed the book to the best of our abilities according to his wishes. There are only very minimal changes in the body of the text apart from new reconstructed pronunciations for the portions of the rituals in Ancient Egyptian. Rich had requested those changes from Matt Whealton a few days before his death, so we have edited them into the text. Otherwise, we have preserved his writing as we found it. We hope the few inconsistencies that have resulted are not too distracting. A Key to these pronunciations is found in Appendix 1 and a very approximate version of them is present in-line in the text. You may choose to use the English, 'approximate Egyptian', or full reconstructed Egyptian in your own rituals. The versions are meant to allow you to access the texts in the way that works for you, not be a barrier to applying them in your own life. The Gods and Goddesses will hear; no matter how you say these rituals.

Richard Reidy's first book, Eternal Egypt, has had influence in Kemetic and Theurgic communities across continents. May he and the Gods and Goddesses smile upon this new book, and may you, dear reader, find it useful to your own path.

Acknowledgments

A book like this takes a great deal of research—sifting through hundreds of scholarly volumes and articles, translating both from Middle Egyptian, Late Egyptian as well as modern languages, compiling the needed citations, and finally assembling the rituals for our gods so that they can be worshipped in accord with ancient precedent.

Many people supported this project in various ways. In particular I wish to acknowledge the superb translation work of Matthew Whealton, without whose assistance this book would not have been possible. I also wish to thank HiC Luttmers and Lisa Pedersen for their translation work as well as Thomas Taylor, Mary Beth Crawford, and Bridget Blasius for their help in crafting rituals for specific gods. I also wish to acknowledge the support given to me by Allan Phillips, one of the founding members of the Temple of Ra. His encouragement and assistance over the past two decades has been instrumental in the creation of this book.

Finally, I wish to acknowledge my everlasting debt to the priests and scribes of ancient Egypt. These men and women served our gods as well as having created the great treasure of deeply theological ritual texts that we use today. We stand on their shoulders, inspired and guided by their words. To them I dedicate this volume.

"And the memory of those who wrote such books shall last to the end of time and for eternity." Hymn on the Immortality of Writers, Egypt

ca. 2100 BCE. John Lawrence Foster, *Ancient Egyptian Literature: An Anthology* (University of Texas Press, 2001), p. 226.

Richard J. Reidy
San Francisco, 2016

INTRODUCTION

Individuals and groups who worship the great gods and goddesses of ancient Egypt often are at a loss for authentic ritual texts to use in their ritual service to these deities. This is because of the near absence of reliable books or websites offering authentic ancient texts for ritual and prayer. As a Kemetic Reconstructionist I wish to remedy that situation with the present offering of ritual texts intended for use in the worship of a number of different gods and goddesses.

Most ancient temples have essentially disappeared due to intentional destruction first by fanatical Christians and later by Moslems aimed at obliterating what they regarded as symbols of a pagan past. In spite of such efforts, a relatively few temples did manage to survive. Some had images on walls defaced or covered over with whitewash—eventually being turned into Coptic Christian churches. Others vanished under the sands after local populations had moved away.

Interest in ancient Egyptian history, religion, and antiquities began to increase with the discovery of the Rosetta stone in 1799. French scholar Jean-François Champollion's decipherment of this stone resulted in the publication of its first translation in 1822. Thus began the lengthy two-century's long process of refining our understanding of ancient Egyptian texts, whether in hieroglyphic, Demotic, or hieratic—three closely related forms of ancient Egyptian.

Fortunately for us today, many ritual texts were inscribed in stone on the walls of the surviving temples. From them we can reconstruct some of the rituals that the ancient priesthood originally performed. It must be said that this is a work in progress. Not all such texts have been translated or made available to the general public. Many translations, either whole or partial, may exist in German, French, or some language other than English. Many ancient texts are still in hieroglyphic form and have not been translated at all up to this point in time. Hence the need for individuals conversant with those languages as well as with hieroglyphics.

In the contemporary Kemetic temples with which I am affiliated we have members competent in one or several of those modern languages or quite able to translate the original hieroglyphic texts themselves, whether those texts are from Middle Egyptian or from the later form known as Ptolemaic. From the Temple of Ra in San Francisco we have the translation work of Matthew Whealton who works with hieroglyphic texts as well as both German and French scholarly works. In the Kemetic Temple of San Jose we have HiC Luttmers and in the Kemetic Temple of Sacramento we have Lisa Pedersen. Each brings a level of expertise in one or more foreign languages. Of course, we have other members who work with academic publications in English. Our intent is to revive and restore those ancient rituals. I think I speak for all members of these and our other Reconstructionist temples when I say that we have a strong sense that those ancient rituals contain a profound and powerful theology capable of transforming our modern world. We also maintain that those rituals have an inherent power to bring us into a direct and transformative contact with our gods. As polytheists we affirm the existence of many deities, each being separate and unique. Our own focus is on the gods of ancient Egypt. We feel their call. We affirm their beauty and relevance for today.

We assess the situation thusly. The temples of many of our gods have mostly vanished, with scant remains that often only indicate their location, size, and purpose. However, in those temples that do remain, we possess a treasure trove of ritual texts, all of which display common features in structure and purpose. Examples include the three main temples at Karnak, the temple of Horus at Edfu, the temple of Hathor at Dendera, the temple of Khnum at Esna, the temple of Sobek and Horus the Elder at Kom Ombo, the temple of Isis at Philae, the huge temple complex at Medinet Habu, the temple of Amun at Hibis in the el-Khargeh Oasis, the mortuary temple of Seti I in Abydos, the great temples of Amun, Mut, and Khonsu near Luxor, the twin temples at Abu Simbel, the mortuary temple of Hatshepsut, and the great temple of Osiris at Abydos. This is merely a partial list of extant temples containing hieroglyphic texts of importance for Kemetic Reconstructionists today.

Our task as Reconstructionists is to reassemble the ancient rituals and present them in such a way that we and others can celebrate those rites in this modern era. We are under no illusion that we can duplicate rites in every detail today that once involved large groups of priests, chantresses, and assistants in the larger temples. But most temples in ancient times were small, often with a single priest, helped perhaps by a son or daughter, serving a small village community. Evidence of those village temples is often limited because their stones had been scattered and used for other purposes over the centuries. Restoration work, however, continues to discover and rebuild some of those smaller sites, providing conclusive evidence that local village priests performed rites modeled on those in the larger temples.

In my previous book, *Eternal Egypt: Ancient Rituals for the Modern World*, I presented eleven major and three brief rituals for use today.

Since its publication in 2010 I have received numerous requests for ritual texts for specific gods and goddesses that were not included in that first collection. Consequently, I assembled in this present work as many texts as our team of translators and assistants have created over the years since the founding of the first temple in 1998 in San Francisco. I could not have undertaken these projects without the assistance and encouragement of our members. To them I owe a debt of gratitude.

In creating an authentic and meaningful ritual for today we face a number of challenges. First, our temple families do not necessarily have a specific building or room permanently set aside for ritual. We often meet in members' homes and set up our altars there. A member will have his or her own shrine but that room may not lend itself to group ritual. Therefore, we must literally construct or set up our sacred space within a secular room. In ancient times private persons typically had a home shrine, but this likely would have been for individual family use and not for the community as a whole which would have had one or more small temples in the immediate vicinity. Our solution is to set up the god's shrine and altar in a room and then sanctify the space with natron and spring water, using the appropriate purification ritual. In ancient times the priests did a preliminary cleansing and purification ritual of the consecrated temple before the daily ritual began. We regard our preliminary rite of cleansing and consecrating to be in imitation of those earlier temple rites.

The order of the ritual texts that we use reflects the pattern found in the ancient temples. The texts themselves are based on the ancient texts as much as possible. Typically, the rites follow a certain sequence: temple entrance, lamp lighting, opening of the *Naos/* shrine, attending to the god's statue, purification and consecration rites, offering incense, various rites of homage and adoration, offering Ma'at, libations, offerings of various kinds including food and flowers as well as several symbolic offerings, hymns of praise, and a time for meditation, followed by rites for leaving the temple chamber. A brief concluding rite involves the removal of the food offerings so they form a repast for the temple's members.

The central ritual for the day was the morning rite which occurred at the break of dawn. Egyptologists agree that all the temples of Egypt celebrated a very similar although not identical morning rite, with ritual actions and recitations occurring in a similar sequence. Thus, when we composed our own rituals for the various gods, we maintained this sequence of actions and recitations. We relied as much as possible on ancient prototypes, including both sequence of actions and actual wording of the various recitations. We did this in the conviction that those ancient rituals—rituals that had been repeated throughout the temples of Egypt for thousands of years— actually held great and enduring power, not only because they had been repeated many thousands of times but also because in them is to be found a rich theology for our own era. This reservoir of energy and power is also available to us today in the words and actions of those ancient rites.

It is important to note that we do not enact every single ritual action that may have been performed in ancient times. Episodes involving the intricate daily dressing and ornamenting of the divine statue with precious jewelry and insignia, as well as the many repetitive lustrations and censings are reduced in number. So, too, are the large array of offerings including precious oils, makeup, fabrics, crowns, scepters, a variety of meat offerings and the abundant kinds of produce of the land including different fruits, vegetables and grains. Today we are not state-run and state-subsidized temples. This means that we had to closely examine the nature of the offerings and our own very modest capabilities. We had to focus on what we came to understand are the central offerings for the gods and their significance within the overall purpose of authentic Reconstructionist ritual. We are not an antiquarian society attempting to mimic practices of a bygone era. We are attempting to worship and serve our gods in a way that genuinely reflects ancient practice without slavishly copying extraneous or impossible-to-achieve details.

In all ritual texts and actions, we use the words of the ancient rites. We do not adopt anything from other religious traditions or rituals. We do this because we see the ancient rites—and the ancient theology—as whole and complete, in need of no importation of non-Egyptian elements. I wish to make it clear, though, that this does not serve to disparage or criticize others who do worship our gods with non-Egyptian rites. Our path is a Reconstructionist one. As long as love and respect motivate others' rituals and worship, then surely that is sufficient and worthy of blessing. The gods can be served in many ways.

In an Egyptian temple a variety of rituals were performed each day, with the morning rite being the most elaborate. A midday and evening ritual would round out the day. Larger temples had many more rites throughout the day and in many cases the night as well. Today we have scant information about those rituals.

The modern situation means that either we serve our gods in a solitary manner or in a small group. Perhaps it is all the more important that today we can look back to our ancient priestly precursors for guidance, support, and inspiration. When we enact an ancient rite, the priests and priestesses who celebrated those rites in ancient times join us in spirit. Those rituals are their enduring gift to us.

In this present collection you will find rituals for a variety of the major gods and goddesses—specifically those deities that had their own temples and priesthoods. Those selected represent a cross section of the many deities of ancient Egypt. Some of the gods represented here have no extant temple. That means we could not have recourse to the inscribed texts that may have been found on their walls. In those cases we have fallen back on the prototypical ritual model found at the great temples at Karnak and Abydos, a model repeated in other extant temples throughout Egypt. Certain papyri giving the text of the daily ritual were used as well. This included a papyrus from Thebes, known as the *Berlin Papyrus (no. 3055)*, and "The Ritual of Amenophis I," translated by Alan H. Gardiner in *Hieratic Papyri in the British Museum*. Other temple texts for the morning rite appear in *Religious Ritual at Abydos* by A. Rosalie David. A fourth excellent source for understanding the sequence and types of ritual actions is Katherine Eaton's *Ancient Egyptian Temple Ritual: Performance, Pattern, and Practice* (New York: Routledge Studies in Egyptology, 2013). The present work reflects all key points of ritual from the Abydos Liturgy, the Theban Liturgy, and the Karnak Liturgy. The result has been that I have been able to use the series of ritual formulae that reflect essential actions of the ancient rite.

We also had the resource of prayers and hymns to some of these gods found on papyrus. In addition we scoured the many volumes of collected epithets for each god and goddess. Such works provide a rich source of material for crafting our rites for these gods. Epithets represent a reliable resource for deepening our understanding of how worshippers experienced these deities in ancient times. The principle but not the only source for divine epithets is the eight-volume work *Lexikon der ägyptischen Götter und Götterbezeichnungen* ("Dictionary of Egyptian Gods and God-Names"), abbreviated *LGG*. In these volumes the epithets of each deity typically number in the hundreds. The names of the gods as well as the epithets themselves are written in hieroglyphs, and the source of each epithet is provided. In our work on constructing a ritual for a god, we included only those epithets found in ancient sources. The impressive wealth of epithets shows the multi-aspected nature of our gods.

EPITHETS

An epithet is a characterizing word or phrase added to or used in place of the name of a god or person. Examples include "Ptah, Giver of Shape and Form," and "Sekhmet, Lady of Life." Epithets can reveal the deities' special characteristics, their relation to other gods, their relation to humans, their manifest powers and abilities, their relation to specific places, and other types of information that help us understand the unique character of these divine beings. By pronouncing or writing an epithet we begin to enter into relationship with that deity. In thoughtfully saying 'Ra, Lord of Life" we help ourselves to better understand that god. We also draw nearer to him by virtue of our knowledge. In numerous magical texts the reciter claims to *know* the name of one or another god, thereby enabling that person to interact with and influence that deity. The same technique occurs in spells addressed to evil forces. The reciter announces that he knows the name of that entity and claims thereby to have power over that being by virtue of that special knowledge. Of course, when calling a god, it is not about having power *over* him, but rather calling on that particular aspect of the deity named.

All the ancient ritual texts include numerous examples of divine epithets. They form an important part of both liturgical and magical writings. It is evident, therefore, that if we wish to reconstruct rituals for the gods, then we can do no better than follow that ancient precedent. It is striking to see the large quantity of epithets for each god and goddess. They are not merely honorific or overblown titles: rather, they pinpoint and provide important information about the gods. More importantly, they form a genuine means of connecting with the gods on more than simply an intellectual level. Examples of ancient prayers, hymns, litanies, praises, and other religious writings show the frequent use of epithets whose evident purpose is to connect with those gods. By uttering the name and epithet the person draws closer to that deity. The name and epithet form a bridge between the reciter and the divine being.

All epithets for the gods and goddesses in this book are capitalized for ease in recognition. In that this book is Kemetic Reconstructionist all epithets come from ancient sources, not from any sort of UPG (Unverified Personal Gnosis). This is not intended to discredit or disparage UPG; it simply is to clarify the approach used in crafting the present book.

For personal practice, I suggest finding several of your special deity's epithets and slowly repeating them, focusing on the god's name and epithets. Example:

> *"Praise be to Ra, rising in the East. Praise be to Ra Khepera.*
> *Praise be to Ra, rising in the East. Praise be to Ra Horakhty.*
> *Praise be to Ra, rising in the East. Praise be to Amun-Ra.*
> *Praise be to Ra, rising in the East. Praise be to Ra, Lord of Ma'at.*
> *Praise be to Ra, rising in the East. Praise be to Ra, Lord of Life.*
> *Praise be to Ra, rising in the East. Praise be to Ra, Lord of Joy.*
> *Praise be to Ra, rising in the East. Praise be to Ra, Lord to the Limit.*
> *Praise be to Ra, rising in the East. Praise be to Ra, the Hearing One."*

Then repeat this four times—one for each of the directions—while focusing on the words. Extend your arms in an attitude of praise while reciting these words. You can start with repeating just two or three phrases and increase the number only if and when you feel ready. Create such a series for your own special deity. Follow the recitations with prayers in your own words. This practice can be an excellent way to begin your day. This brief exercise is particularly true for anyone who is very rushed in the morning.

RITUALS FOR TODAY

The focus of all the rituals in this collection is to present rites that not only accurately reflect key elements of their ancient predecessors, but give readers rituals that they can actually perform today. All the Reconstructionist temples with which I am affiliated have performed these rites for many years. We have found them to be not only doable but also inspiring. The words of the ancient priesthood are filled with a power and beauty that continue to guide and inspire us today.

The question arises about who exactly should or can do these rituals? Do they need to be "ordained" by someone "in authority"? What requirements are there for doing such rites? The answer to the first question is any person who in his or her heart wishes to worship and serve the gods through sacred ritual. Any such person. No one need be ordained or authorized by anyone else. Today we need neither a pharaoh nor a high priest to tell us we are qualified. The gods themselves speak to us in the stillness of our own hearts. In ancient times it was only natural for a societal structure to be established in order to organize the priesthood and temple staff; otherwise tasks might have been left undone, and the lack of organization would have significantly hampered temple life. In ancient Egypt its large, fully functioning temples needed an established hierarchy of responsibility. Today we no longer require it. Today we often are solitary in our worship or relatively few in number in any given region. Today people are educated. They can read and write—a skill that was quite rare in ancient times. If the gods call us in the quiet of our hearts to celebrate the ancient rites, then that should be sufficient justification to validate our intent to serve the gods through sacred ritual. Today it is the gods themselves who call us to this special form of service, and not any human authority.

In regard to requirements for celebrating these rituals, the people involved should familiarize themselves with the rite so that it progresses as smoothly as possible. The celebrants should perform a preliminary purification rite consisting in bathing or at least washing thoroughly and thoughtfully. In addition, the mouth should be cleansed with water and natron. If natron is not available, a simple mixture of salt and baking soda can suffice until natron becomes available. The celebrants may use the Morning Rite for Bathing found in my companion volume *Eternal Egypt*, pp. 199-200, which also provides a recipe for making natron. In that text it is Ra himself who is our model and bathes "in the waters of the Lake of Rushes." We emulate Ra in cleansing ourselves. Just as Ra was not spiritually dirty or unclean, neither are we as his children. So, then, what does such ritual bathing actually accomplish? It helps transport us to what the Egyptians called *Zep Tepi,* the First Time, the mythic "in the beginning." We enter into that era of perfection, a time of ma'at. Ritual bathing also begins to prepare our minds to set aside all earthly cares and focus on the sacred rite we are about to celebrate.

Personal purification is very important for all who celebrate sacred ritual. In the temple of Heru (Horus) at Edfu this idea is expressed in the following words:

> *"Beware of entering in impurity, for the Netjer loves purity more than millions of offerings, more than hundreds of thousands of electrum; he sates himself with ma'at [truth]; he is satisfied therewith, and his heart is satisfied with great purity."* [1]

---

[1] From Émile Chassinat, *Le temple d'Édfu*, vol. VI, p. 349, lines 5-6; quoted in "A Scene of the Offering of Truth in the Temple of Edfu," by H. W. Fairman, appearing in *MDAIK*, Vol. 16 (1958), p. 89. *MDAIK* is

If purity was so important for the ancient priesthood, it should be important for us as well. Please refer to pp. 210-211 in *Eternal Egypt* for more on this important topic.

I speak of *celebrating* sacred ritual rather than conducting or performing ritual. It is a joy-filled form of service for it joins us humans with the gods. As the Hermetic text, the Emerald Tablet, observes,

> *Ascend from earth to heaven*
> *and descend again from heaven to earth,*
> *and unite together the power*
> *of things superior and inferior.* [2]

Sacred ritual does precisely that; it unites the powers of heaven and earth. That is why our preparation for ritual should always be completed first. We continue the ancient priestly practice of preparing our bodies and minds for a truly sacred event. It is the necessary prelude to an encounter with the divine.

Some Kemetics are concerned about a taboo that prevents menstruating women from celebrating ritual. I refer the reader to my article "Taboo in Ancient Egypt" on our website *kemetictemple.org*. In brief, we have found no good or clear evidence for such a rule in use throughout all Egypt's nomes. We also have the Knot of Isis, known as the *Tiet* or *Tet* amulet. It has been conjectured by scholars that the *Tiet* represents menstrual blood or a ritual tampon. The amulet was made of red jasper, carnelian, or red glass. There is a famous passage

---

the abbreviation for *Mitteilungen des Deutschen Archaologischen Instituts, Abteilung Kairo.*

[2] Quoted by Alison Roberts, *My Heart, My Mother: Death and Rebirth in Ancient Egypt* (Rottingdean, East Sussex, England: Northgate Publishers, 2005), p. 221.

from the *Book of Coming Forth by Day,* commonly called the *Book of the Dead,* giving us the magical formula for empowering the *Tiet:*

> *Spell for a knot-amulet of red jasper. "You have your blood, O Isis; you have your power, O Isis; you have your magic, O Isis. The amulet is a protection for this Great One (the deceased) which will drive away whoever would commit a crime against him."*
>
> *"To be said over a knot-amulet of red jasper. . . . As for him for whom this is done, the power of Isis will be the protection of his body, and Horus son of Isis will rejoice over him when he sees him; no path will be hidden from him, and one side of him will be towards the sky and the other towards the earth. A true matter; you shall not let anyone see it in your hand, for there is nothing equal to it."* [3]

Tiet amulet, Metropolitan Museum of Art, Dynasty 18, from Abydos. Image in public domain[4]

---

[3] *Spell 156,* Book of Coming Forth by Day; the Papyrus of Ani

[4] http://www.metmuseum.org/art/collection/search/548207, accessed 29 May 2017, by mjwhealton

The *Tiet* amulet is protective. Neither this spell nor any ancient writing connects a woman's menstrual blood with anything unclean or impure. Certainly, the blood of Isis was most pure! It is true that in Judaism as well as among the Eastern Orthodox and Oriental Christian churches women's menstrual period is disparaged as a time of uncleanness. We do not agree. In ancient Egypt sexuality and the human body were deemed to be very good—unlike those other traditions that seem to be uncomfortable and suspicious of both sexuality and the desires of the human body.

Clothing for ritual can range from a clean set of street clothes to a special ritual garment. Robes of natural linen or cotton are preferred, either simple or elaborate in design. Whatever attire you choose, make sure you set it aside for ritual use only. Like members of the ancient priesthood, participants ideally should be clothed in white linen or, if necessary, white cotton. No item made of animal products such as leather or wool is to be worn. Linen represents a pristine product of the earth whereas leather and wool come from humankind's domination of the animals, a domination that becomes part of the "natural order" only *after* the First Time when the *Netjeru* and humans and animals lived in peace and harmony. Just as the Morning Ritual harkens back to that First Time (*Zep Tepi*), so every temple rite re-presents mythic prototypes that occurred "in the beginning," that is, in that time before time. Even the sandals worn by the god's servants were made of white papyrus. This avoidance of animal products by the priesthood fits well with the fact that the ritualist acts as a *Netjer* and verbally asserts that he or she is a *Netjer*. The ancient priesthood understood this.

Incense for the gods should be pure frankincense, myrrh, or *kapet*, also called *Kyphi* (the evening incense made of many natural ingredients). Avoid commercial incense sticks because nowadays they often contain synthetic ingredients. Some powdered incense contains saltpeter, a very combustible ingredient made of potassium (or sodium) nitrate as well as artificial dyes. The smell is often rather acrid even when combined with other, more pleasant scents. It has been reported that some cheap incense sticks from India contain cow dung and/or urea, both of which make such incense unsuitable for a Kemetic altar. The ancient priesthood regarded incense as revelatory of the god's own pleasant odor. A recitation for the offering of incense to the king of the gods gives us insight into how the Egyptians regarded the nature and purpose of incense:

"Peace be to you, O Amun-Ra. Let your heart expand [in joy], for I have brought to you the Eye of Heru, so that you may be great through that which your heart has received, and through that which your nostrils inhale at this censing. . . . The fragrance thereof comes to you; the fragrance of the Eye of Heru is to you, O Amun-Ra, lover of incense." [5]

The incense is identified as the Eye of Heru (i.e., Horus), itself that perfect offering.

In her excellent book, *Sacred Luxuries,* Lise Manniche explains:

"Scents were believed to originate from the gods in the first place, to have sprung from their eyes or their bones, in particular the eye of the sun-god Ra. Many plant ingredients were known as 'fruits of the eye of Ra'. . . . Scent became identified with the eye of the god [Horus] which was restored to its owner: when the burning incense drifted towards the statue it re-enacted the occasion when Thoth [Djehuty], god of magic, presented

---

[5] *Eternal Egypt,* p. 30

Horus with his eye, healed and sound. The act was considered significant for all gods, not only Horus." (p. 34)

The timing of such purification rituals is based on either of two considerations. First, the rising of the sun at dawn, in addition to being the beginning of a new day, is a time for new beginnings. The object being purified begins its new life as something sacred and dedicated to divine service. In addition, according to instructions that accompanied various ancient magic spells the Egyptian priest-magicians regarded dawn as an ideal time to perform magic. The dawning of the first light harkens back to the 'First Time' of creation.

The other consideration regarding the timing of a magical or purificatory rite is midday; that is, the astrological midpoint for day light. The sun is at its zenith and its radiant power is at its maximum. A purification rite, therefore, is best conducted either at dawn or midday.

ALTAR SETUP

All items used in ritual should be reserved exclusively for that purpose. Typically, they include a statue or image of the deity, a votive candle holder, a bowl and pitcher for water, a bowl or container for natron, cups or glasses for liquid offerings, a plate or dish for the bread offering, and a plate or two for other food offerings, and, finally, an incense burner and small bowl for grains of incense. An altar need not have every item. For example if a person cannot use incense for any reason, an aromatherapy diffuser may be substituted. A few drops of high quality essential oil of frankincense or myrrh would be fine. If a person is allergic to scent, then refrain from using either item. An altar may also contain an ankh or *Ib* heart. The admonition "less is more" applies to our altars. Do not clutter them with non-essential items or images of gods from other pantheons.

Placement of the altar should be in a location not visited by others. Your altar is a holy place, set aside for service to a god or goddess. If this is impossible and the altar must be in a public place, then be sure to cover the statue with a linen or cotton cloth—cloth used only for that purpose. In Egypt the statues of the gods in the temples were concealed from the general public. When processions took the image of the deity outside the sanctuary and onto the temple grounds, the images were concealed in a portable shrine, in some cases being surrounded by a curtain. Your statue is a manifestation of and a dwelling place for a god. It is not merely decorative. No one but you should touch the sacred image or the items on your altar.

In our secular Western culture statues are seen as either symbolic of something or someone absent or merely as decorative however inspiring they may be. In ancient Egypt, however, the statue was understood to be the actual dwelling place for a deity. The god was *present* in the statue and *present* in the divine representations on the temple's walls. The ancient Opening of the Mouth (Egyptian *wp.t-r3*) ritual opened the image to a deity's living presence. The reader can refer to my book *Eternal Egypt* for the text of this important rite together with a detailed explanation of its component parts. Today Hindus and many sects of Buddhism also see their deities as present in consecrated statues of divine beings. Catholic, Orthodox, and Oriental Churches also teach the living presence of Jesus Christ in the consecrated elements of bread and wine of their Eucharist. Scholarly evidence reveals that statues were regarded as abodes of the living gods in Greece, Mesopotamia, Assyria, and throughout the ancient Mediterranean world.

Unfortunately, today there are not readily available statues for the wide variety of gods we worship. It may be relatively easy to acquire images of Isis, Osiris, Anubis and perhaps a dozen other gods and goddesses. But in lieu of a statue a picture or photo of a drawing of the god can be used. The internet has many good images of the gods who today lack statues. It is simply a matter of printing the image and securing it to a firm background such as poster board or even cardboard. Then by laminating the image you will have a sturdy as well as a permanent representation for that deity. In our view, together with the ancient Egyptians, the gods actively desire to be embodied in the divine image crafted by human hands. For both priest and layperson there was and is today a firm commitment to the embodiment of the gods. In fact, our personal relationship with a deity is enhanced as a consequence of divine embodiment. The vast majority of the ancient Egyptian population had simple and inexpensive images of their gods. Clay and faience sufficed. Today it might be a picture or photo of an image that we install on our altars. The gods are not restricted to gold or silver.

PURIFYING RITUAL ITEMS

Unlike in ancient times, today non-Kemetics usually manufacture the statues of the gods, so impure hands may have touched the statues when they were gilded or painted. My suggestion is to lay the image in a large container of natron (or natural salt if natron is not available in a large enough quantity). The purpose is to allow impurity/negativity to flow out of the statue. Place it in sunlight (best either at early dawn when the world is renewed) or midday when the sun is at its height. Then bathe the statue, or at least wipe it down, with water mixed with natron. Wash it again with spring water to remove any salts that may have accidentally adhered. As you do this, you can recite aloud a simple spell in the ancient Kemetic manner such as:

> I come as Djehuty, Thrice-Great in Heka Power and Lord of Sacred Words, and I do cleanse and purify this image from all impurity and unworthiness. The radiant light of Ra does cleanse this image. This image is bathed in the waters of Nun. It rises pure and clean. It rises pure and clean.

Using myrrh incense, waft the image over the smoke, once more saying words such as:

> The incense comes. The incense comes. The odor of the Netjer (god) comes. The breath of the Netjer comes. The grains of incense come. The moisture which drops from the Netjer comes, and the smell thereof is upon you, O (name of the god). The Eye of Heru hides you in the tears thereof . . . . You are purified. You are purified.[6]

---

[6] See *Eternal Egypt*, p. 30.

One final action would be to **anoint the statue with frankincense oil** *and say:*

> **Hail, O (name of god)! I have filled you with the Eye of Heru (Horus) . . . . It renews your strength, and it adorns you in its name of 'Wedjat.' Its odor pleases you in its name of 'Sweet Odor.' The Eye of Ra, which is Sekhmet, burns up your enemies for you. Geb has given you his inheritance. Your word is law against your enemies. Wepwawet has opened the roads for you against your enemies.[7]**

Upon finishing, **place the statue on your altar.**

Other items for the altar should undergo a similar rite. The words to be spoken can be the following:

> **I come as Djehuty, Thrice-Great in Heka Power, and I do cleanse and purify this (name of item) from all impurity and unworthiness. The radiant light of Ra does cleanse this (name of item). It is bathed in the waters of Nun. It rises pure and clean. It rises pure and clean for the service of the Netjeru (i.e. the gods).**

---

[7] from the anointing ritual in the temple of Amun-Ra at Karnak, in *Eternal Egypt*, p. 37

BRIEF DAILY RITUAL

Many readers will want to celebrate a brief ritual frequently or even daily. Our busy schedules can often mean that we have very little time to do a longer ritual. Therefore, I suggest doing the following ritual as time permits.

One of the purposes of this or any rite is to build a relationship with a particular deity. After all, friendships and all good relationships take time to develop and need to be nourished. This is what ritual can do.

We begin a brief morning service with the traditional call to "awake in peace," followed by the name of the *Netjer* and the recitation of those epithets of that *Netjer* we intend to invoke. Here is an example:

> **Awake in peace! May you awake well and in peace!**
> **Awake, O Sekhmet, in life and in peace!**
> **Awake in peace, O Lady of Life.**
> **May you awake in peace.**
> **Awake in peace, O Lady of Protection.**
> **May you awake in peace.**
> **Awake in peace, O Beautiful Sekhmet.**
> **May you awake in peace.**

We then open the doors of our shrine, or remove the cloth over the sacred image. We extend our right hand and touch the left shoulder of the statue or image. With our left hand, we touch the right wrist of the *Netjer.* Doing this we say:

> **Djehuty has come to you. Awake when you hear his words. I have come as the envoy of Atum. My two arms are upon you like those of Heru. My two hands are upon you like**

those of Djehuty. **My fingers are upon you like those of Anpu** (Anubis). **Homage be to you. I am a living servant of** *(name of deity).* [8]

This ritual embrace is a vehicle for transferring life force (*Ka*) into the sacred image. The priest or priestess is the conduit for the life-renewing and life-creating energy of the primordial creator Atum. The Ritualist functions as envoy of Atum and, as a consequence, the words of this Utterance coupled with the ritual actions effectively reanimate the sacred image.

The third action for this brief rite is the offering of a water libation. Water is the universal symbol of the power to sustain and invigorate life itself. With the pouring of water, the Ritualist repeats the following Utterance identifying the libation water with Nile water coming from the great river's mythical source at Elephantine (known as *Abu* in Ancient Egyptian):

I bring to you these libations which have come forth from Abu, from 'Place-of-Refreshment'[9]. Nun satisfies you. I have brought to you these libations so that your heart may be refreshed. [10]

The rite concludes with the offering of bread and "of all things good and pure." For the Egyptians bread epitomized the "staff of

---

[8] Taken from Section 44, "Chapitre de mettre ses deux bras sur le dieu," 167-169, in Alexandre Moret, *Le Rituel du Culte Divin Journalier* (Paris: Annales du Musée Guinet, Bibliotheque d'Etudes 14, Ernest Leroux, Editeur, 1902).

[9] *Kebhu*, the region of the First Cataract

[10] Taken from the Ritual of Amenophis I, in *Hieratic Papyri in the British Museum,* Vol. I. TEXT, edited by Alan H. Gardiner (London: British Museum, 1935), 81.

life." Made from grain grown from seed, and then through human industry ground into flour, mixed with life-giving water and, finally, baked to become the food staple for every level of society, bread represents the collaborative effort of the *Netjer*, nature, and humankind. What better gift to present to *Netjer*?

O (name of *Netjer*), come to this your bread. Come to this your bread which I give to you. All life is with you, all stability is with you, all health is with you, all joy is with you. [11]

Extending a hand, palm downward, over the offerings, the rite concludes with the *"Peret er kheru"*[12] offering formula:

May offerings of every kind come forth in abundance, like the things which come forth from the mouth of the god (goddess).

piryá pírit ar hiráw mi purú:riat ma rá' ni nátar (natárat). (**4 times**) [13]

---

[11] Ibid., 84.

[12] Mjwhealton note: The formula used here is a creative adaptation of material found in Budge (see the succeeding note), but ultimately derives from an example of an 'Address to the Living' found in the Dynasty 18 tomb of Paheri at El-Kab, and so does not correspond to any specific "Peret er Kheru" offering forumula. For the Paheri source, see Lichtheim, M. (1976). Ancient Egyptian Literature: A Book of Readings. London, University of California Press. Volume II: The New Kingdom, 20.

[13] Taken from E. A. Wallis Budge, Chapter I: The Doctrine of Offerings, in *The Liturgy of Funerary Offerings* (originally published in 1909; reprinted by Dover Publications, New York, 1944), 24-28. Mjwhealton emendation and additions: The italicized pronunciation guides are the work of Matthew Whealton and are based on Egyptological vocalic reconstruction research.

[approximately pronounced *peer-YA PEER-it ar khi-RAU mee pu-ROOR-iat ma RA nee NAH-tchar (nah-TCHAR-at)*]

At this point we may want to speak with the deity in our own words, presenting petitions or offering thanksgiving and asking for guidance for the upcoming day. We may also offer incense or other wholesome food offerings—fruit, flowers, etc.—as long as those foods will not spoil over the course of the day. If they would spoil, then remove them after having left them on the altar for a brief period. When we remove such items, we recite the following:

O (name of *Netjer*), **these your divine offerings revert to your servant for life, for stability, for health and for joy! May the Eye of Heru flourish for you eternally.**[14]

Junk food and foods filled with chemicals and additives should be avoided. If ultimately such foods are not healthy for us, then they are not worthy of being offered to the gods.

The offerings of bread and water may remain before the *Netjer* until evening when they also should be reverted for our own use. The water may also be used for any plants in the house or garden.

Unlike some modern pagan groups, the ancient Egyptians did not invoke deity into a sacred image only to dismiss or bid farewell to that divine being at the conclusion of the ritual. The continuous

---

An initial verb form was also added to the formula to better reflect the English formula. Any errors are the sole responsibility of Matthew Whealton.

[14] Adapted from Harold H. Nelson, "Certain Reliefs at Karnak and Medinet Habu and the Ritual of Amenophis I," *Journal of Near Eastern Studies,* 8 (1949), 315-317.

beneficent presence of the *Netjer* was a major objective for the Egyptian cult. The living presence of deity in this world was one of the main purposes for the daily rites in the temples.

In the Egyptian tradition we experience the god or goddess not as a lord/lady *in absentia*, or as one who upon occasion visits this world, but rather as a numinous and powerful *present* divine reality. This is the reason that a morning/sunrise ritual is so important. Every day is experienced as a new creation, as an awakening to new life. Every day is a miracle of divine immanence that invites us to be co-creators and co-participants in the cosmic drama. If you find it impossible to celebrate ritual at dawn or in the early morning, then select a time that does work for you. Better to celebrate ritual at some point than to not celebrate it at all. Through sacred ritual we enter into and make present that "time before time," and in so doing we reveal the world to be holy and noble and a manifestation of overflowing love.

TEMPLE GROUPS

Some of us may have others with whom we celebrate rituals as a group. Based on some eighteen years of experience moderating such groups, I have found the following practices helpful in building and maintaining a vibrant temple community.

- [ ] Seek input from all members about all temple matters.
- [ ] Establish well in advance times and dates for coming together for ritual.
- [ ] Avoid having just one person responsible for all or most things.
- [ ] Share and rotate responsibilities.
- [ ] If possible, change the location for ritual so as many members as possible share the job of hosting in their homes.
- [ ] Have all members clean up after ritual. Do not burden the host with this.
- [ ] Have all members bring the various food offerings and foods for the meal after ritual. Rotate assignments of specific foods and beverages so each member spends approximately the same amount of money for these items.
- [ ] Include an educational component each time the group meets in which members discuss a pre-assigned reading, topic, or project.
- [ ] Avoid negativity or criticism of fellow members or other spiritual/religious groups.
- [ ] Allow and even celebrate the fact that some members may also have a current interest in other spiritualities—Wicca, Ceremonial Magic, Shinto, etc. As the Chinese proverb states, "There are many paths to the top of the mountain." We are not fundamentalists who insist that theirs is the only way to the divine.

If possible, develop a pattern of monthly gatherings for ritual. By setting dates at least several months in advance members have the opportunity to build such meeting dates into their own schedules. It is important to be flexible so as many members as possible can participate. It also is very helpful if someone takes responsibility for sending out email reminders two weeks and then one week in advance of a ritual date. Rotate food and beverage assignments so each member gets to bring some specific items for every meeting. A shared meal enables members to chat, build relationships, and share ideas and information about Kemetic topics.

Be sure your meetings/presentations/discussions are safe space for others to express their opinions without fear. All of us, including the founders of temples, are growing in knowledge and understanding. So be kind in your replies and make sure no one assumes a know-it-all posture in your group. Any one of us may come up with an idea that the others take objection to for any variety of reasons; nevertheless, it is important that respect for the other person guides our response. This will make your gatherings truly safe and a positive experience for everyone.

When it comes time to do your first group ritual (even if it is a group of two), prepare beforehand so things do not feel rushed or slapdash. Have each person take an active part in the ritual, both with reciting the recitations as well as doing the ritual actions that accompany those recitations. Our Reconstructionist temples avoid titles such as high-priest or lector-priest. Titles, we find, can lead to the temptation of self-aggrandizement. In ancient Egypt its large, fully functioning temples needed an established hierarchy of responsibility. Today we no longer require it. Our temples are small. Each of us can share responsibilities for our ritual gatherings. We have found that this egalitarian approach avoids the pitfalls of hierarchy and positively encourages ownership in all our temple work. No members should find themselves simply standing and watching while others perform the ritual. All should actively participate in both worship and service.

Membership

Before a candidate for membership is formally accepted into the temple, it is important to have that person participate in a series of meetings with one temple member—often that candidate's sponsor—so the candidate understands the nature and purpose of our rituals, our basic theology, the responsibilities of membership, and the ability to complete assigned readings and projects. Merely the desire to "see" an ancient ritual is not sufficient for actual membership. Neither is it sufficient to seek a spiritual high or to get a "rush" out of ritual. Typically, this takes six months or more of regular meetings, readings, and completion of assignments. As Kemetics our goal is one of service to the gods. The ancient name for a Kemetic priest is *hem netjer*—"servant of the god." Our members make the following pledge on the day of their formal admittance into the temple.

Pledge for Admittance into the Temple

The one being admitted faces the members of the temple.

"I, the *Netjer's* servant, (state your name), make this pledge before the *Netjeru* and *Netjerut* of ancient Kemet and before the priesthood of this temple that to the best of my ability. . .

"I will work to preserve, establish, and restore *ma'at* in this world. In so doing I acknowledge the privilege of being, together with the *Netjeru*, a co-creator and a co-restorer of *ma'at*. This I do solemnly pledge.

"I also pledge to support the work of this temple by participating regularly and faithfully in its rituals and projects to the best of my ability.

"I pledge to continue studying the theology of ancient Kemet so that I might have an ever deeper understanding and appreciation of this great and sacred tradition.

"I pledge my silence regarding those matters which by common consent of the temple are to be kept confidential, including personal information about fellow members.
"Lastly, I pledge to support the members of this temple with prayers and counsel, as well as with such financial and material support as I am able and as may be requested of me from time to time for this temple and its members.

"These things I do solemnly pledge, without mental reservation and with firm conviction."

"I do now ask the members of this temple that I be admitted into the great *Netjer*'s service for the up-building of *ma'at* and for the service of the *Netjeru* [gods]."

The one being admitted kneels before the members of the temple.

*The members of the temple **place their hands on the head of the one being admitted** and **recite an appropriate prayer for their admission.***

*The new member is **anointed with myrrh oil for purification** and then **anointed with sacred oil (olive oil—sacred to Ra)** for strength in the service of the Netjeru.*

After this, the officiating members help the new member to his/her feet and welcome him/her into full membership.

CONTINUING EDUCATION

Both as individuals as well as a group we can enrich our understanding of Kemetic spirituality and religion by preparing for our ritual gatherings with reading assignments from pertinent books or magazines on various topics. Today it is so easy to make copies for distribution. Such reading material can be made available before the next gathering to give sufficient time for members to complete the readings. The assigned readings can be the topic for discussion as members enjoy a meal after ritual. This will enable members to deepen their understanding as well as serve to inspire them in our religion.

Members may also like to report on something they have read. This can be an important way to familiarize others with relevant information. Not everyone may have the time or inclination to do extensive reading. Therefore, any activity that helps others grow in knowledge can be incorporated into the hours shared after ritual. That time together can be a valuable means of cementing our fellowship together. After many years of doing this, we have found it to be an effective way of strengthening our temples.

OUTREACH

When pagan, neopagan, occult, and other alternative or earth-based religions began to emerge in the nineteenth and twentieth centuries in Western Christian nations, many of them developed the practice of keeping secret their societies' rules, rituals, and membership. This was in response to public prejudice and, in some cases, laws punishing such behavior. Fear and lack of understanding among the public made it essential to protect members' identities and everything else pertaining to such groups. Today many of us still need to exercise great caution about sharing our beliefs and practices with our families, friends, and employers. Some of us have the good fortune not to need to carry the burden of secrecy.

Although our monthly ritual gatherings are closed to non-members, it is not from the desire for secrecy. We find that in order to create a safe environment for members so they feel comfortable together and can discuss matters openly, it is best to restrict our meetings to members. In ancient times the temples were not intended for casual observers. Entrance to the temple grounds, not to mention the shrines within, was severely restricted. We continue this tradition today.

From time to time we accept invitations from other groups to discuss our beliefs and celebrate ritual in their presence. Every year we also host a Hospitality Suite at PantheaCon, the major West Coast convention of pagans, reconstructionists, and nature religions— currently the largest in the United States, with some 2,600 attendees. We celebrate ritual, answer questions, and share refreshments with others from a variety of traditions. We also have a temple member serving as our representative with a regional interfaith group. Three of our members participated in the Parliament of the World's Religions in 2015. We find outreach to be a valuable and effective means of building understanding. Secrecy, we believe, can foster misunderstanding and even fear leading to intolerance.

Our temples encourage others to study and use our rituals for honoring the gods. So many Kemetics—whether or not they are Reconstructionist—are not connected with any other Kemetic group. We want to provide them with well-researched rituals and information that can help them in their own spiritual lives.

THE NATURE OF KEMETIC RITUAL

The ancient Egyptian priesthood understood that the rituals they performed involved the interaction of god and god—not solely human and god. This is a unique perspective that can easily escape the modern reader's attention. Several examples from ritual illustrate this.

1) In the first Utterance before the Closed Doors of the Temple we read, "I am [the god] Shu. I flood his/her offering table (*i.e., with an abundance of offerings*)."

2) In the next recitation the priest exclaims, "I am Heru [Horus] in the height of heaven."

3) In the Offering of Ma'at, the celebrant exclaims, "I have come to you as Djehuty [Thoth] whose two hands are joined together under Ma'at."

4) In the closing rite of Removing the Foot [prints], the priest states, "I am Djehuty who reconciles the *Netjeru* [the gods], who makes offerings in their correct form."

5) In the final Reversion of Offerings the officiant states, "I am Djehuty. I come to perform this rite for (*name of god or goddess for whom the ritual was performed*)."

At the same time the human celebrant is still aware that he or she is human. In several places the priest exclaims, "I am pure." This assertion, in fact, may be repeated four times in sequence as if to stress this critical requirement. In the initial Utterance we also read a series of statements in which the priest states that he/she has not broken various taboos: "I have not shown partiality in judgement. I have not consorted with the strong. I have not reproached the lowly. I have not stolen things. I have not diminished the constituents of the Eye of Ra. I have not disturbed the Balance. . . ." The effect of these assertions is that the celebrant claims to be worthy to perform the sacred rite—to enter into the presence of the living god.

In today's world—at least in secular Western societies—we may have to struggle in order to recapture this sense of the holy, this sense of the 'otherness' of our gods. They are not our 'buddies.' They are in every sense superior in the best meaning of that word. They are, however, deeply beneficent and quick to forgive our failings or missteps when we change bad behavior. In the Cairo Hymn to Amun-Ra we find the following theological insights:

> "Hail to you, O Ra, lord of Ma'at!
> Amun hidden in His shrine, yet lord of the Netjeru,
> Khepri in the midst of His barque,
> Who gave commands and the Netjeru came into being.
> Atum, who created humankind,
> Distinguished their natures, made them alive,
> And made their features differ, one from the other.
> Who hears the prayer of him who is in captivity.
> Gracious of Heart to whomever calls on him.
> Saving the fearful from the terrible of heart,
> Rendering judgment on behalf of the weak and the injured."

Later in the same hymn we read,

> "Unique One, alone with many hands,
> Who spends the night wakeful, while all humanity sleeps,
> Seeking benefit for His creatures.
> O Amun, enduring in all things, Atum and Harakhty—
> Praises are yours when they all say,
> 'Jubilation to you because you weary yourself with us!
> Homage to you because you have created us!
> Hail to you for all creatures!

Jubilation to you for every foreign country. . . .'" [15]

When we celebrate a ritual for one of our gods, we engage in a divine/human interaction. This can be no casual or haphazard affair. It is quite literally entering into that 'First Time' when gods and humans worked in harmony. Through sacred ritual that harmony is restored and renewed. Therefore, it is only right and proper that we celebrate ritual with care, with full attention, and with reverence. In that way we "restore the Balance."

---

[15] The Cairo Hymn to Amun-Ra (also spelled Amon-Ra) is a composition preserved on the Papyrus Boulaq 17 in the Cairo Museum, dating from the Eighteenth Dynasty (1550-1350 B.C.). It is reproduced in *Hymns, Prayers, and Songs,* translated by John L. Foster (Atlanta, Georgia: Scholars Press, 1995), pp. 58-65.

PERSONAL PRACTICE AND SACRED RITUAL

The gods can be approached at any time and in a variety of ways. Reconstructionist ritual is one of those ways. You may decide to do a complete ritual from time to time or you may select those portions of the rites that speak to you, that move or inspire you in a special way. You can start small and add elements to your ritual when you feel ready. You may decide to focus on one or another god or goddess. The important factor is that you do so in a spirit of confidence that your service will be accepted by the deity. Do not be concerned about not having every ritual item or not having a ritual garment. The gods are beneficent. They are not rigorists, nor do they demand a 'perfect' ritual performance. Just do your best and that in itself is worthy of a blessing.

As you read through the dozens of rituals for various gods and goddesses, you will notice that some of them contain more and longer recitations for that particular deity. That is because so many gods' temples have been destroyed, and we no longer have the complete ritual texts for them. In other cases we do possess substantial texts. In those cases the recitations are fuller and more complete. As a Reconstructionist my goal is to provide the best up-to-date material for rituals for our gods. No doubt as time passes new texts will become available as Egyptologists continue their important work of discovery, translation, and commentary.

The benefit of celebrating a ritual with ancient origins is that you are joining in rituals that have been enacted for over three millennia in the temples of ancient Egypt. These rituals contain a certain inherent power built up with over thirty centuries of usage. By repeating those rites, by reciting those words of power, we tap into an ancient grid of psychic and spiritual energy capable of enriching and nourishing our own spiritual development. In addition, these

1

sacred rituals enable us to cross an expanse of time that takes us back not simply to ancient Egypt, but to what the Egyptians called the First Time, the time before time, the mythic "in the beginning," when humans and gods shared a common spiritual landscape, that is, when deities and human beings communed in a harmonious peace. By employing the ancient words and images, we reconnect to that mythic universe of ancient Egypt. Setting aside our preoccupations with everyday life, we break through to an ageless spiritual dimension that is at once both mythic and real, invisible and yet genuinely manifest to those who take the time to look.

A further reason for recovering and using the ancient rites is for the important spiritual lessons these rituals can teach us. As members of a contemporary Western society, we breathe, as it were, an atmosphere permeated with secular, materialistic assumptions. We live in a society preoccupied with changing styles and mutable values. But the rituals of ancient Egypt take us into a dimension where values are eternal and mythic truths unchanging. The sacred texts—profoundly symbolic and steeped in ancient myths—call us to ever deeper levels of spiritual comprehension. They invite us to lay aside the cares of the moment and enter into that mythic time of gods and goddesses whose acts had, and still have, cosmic significance. Every action, then, becomes charged with divine energy. Every recitation reveals an eternal mythic dimension capable of transforming our own understanding of what is important in life.

As you read the ancient prayers and recitations you will begin to see how the ancient Egyptians perceived and experienced their gods. They were very much present and approachable. The natural world was a palette upon which the invisible gods made manifest their presence, their power, and their love for humankind.

The Purpose of Sacred Ritual

Ritual serves many important purposes. For the Kemetic Reconstructionist it is our attempt to give thanks to the gods for all the good things in our lives. It also is a time to renew the bonds between ourselves and the gods. Third, it is an opportunity to receive from them the gifts of life, health and healing, courage, guidance, and so much more. Our friendship with the gods is renewed. And perhaps most important of all, the gods have a dwelling place here made for them by human hands. The statues and images become the incarnation of the gods. They are 'enfleshed' and dwell among us.

The gods are not to be outdone with generosity. All our gifts to them—prayers, praises, litanies, and offerings—all prompt the gods to bless us and renew our lives. They were—and are—not just the passive recipients of our offerings. It is clear from every offering scene inscribed on temple walls that the gods responded to each item offered with a gift of their own which was written down in the exchange between the human celebrant and the god. In our rituals as done in the past we offer incense, water, beer, wine, foods including bread, meat, and the produce of the land as well as a variety of symbolic offerings specific to one or another god or goddess.

Sacred ritual can help to lift us out of our daily preoccupations. It can give us a 'break' from the worries and concerns that occupy so much of our time and energy. In our temples some members may have started out tired, burdened by the cares of the day, or not feeling much energy and by the end of ritual they are feeling a sense of uplift, relief, and hope. Those are gifts from the gods. This is further enhanced by the time we spend in fellowship after ritual.

But most important of all, ritual can deepen our understanding and appreciation of life itself.

The Role of Ma'at

The central and most fundamental offering in ancient ritual is the offering of Ma'at to the god. Ma'at cannot be translated by only one word. It contains within itself the concepts of right balance, truth, justice, beauty, harmony, the right order of the universe, and finally the very food of the gods. In the lengthy offering recitation in the ritual for Amun-Ra the Utterance reads in part

> *"Ma'at has come that she may be with you. Ma'at is in every place of yours so that you may rest upon her. You are provided with Ma'at, Creator of things which are, Maker of things which shall be. You are the beneficent God, Beloved One. You go onward in Ma'at. You live in Ma'at. You unite your members to Ma'at, you cause Ma'at to rest upon your head, and she makes her seat upon your brow. You renew your youth when you see your daughter Ma'at, and you live by her fragrance. . . . The Netjeru serve you, and they offer gifts to you in Ma'at for they know her worth. Truly the Netjeru and Netjerut who are in you possess Ma'at, and they know that you live in her. . . ."* [16]

This understanding of Ma'at prompts us who celebrate these rites to put Ma'at into our own lives, influencing our behavior and our

---

[16] Alexandre Moret, *Le Rituel du Culte Divin Journalier* (Paris: Annales du Musée Guimet, Bibliotheque d'Études 14, Ernest Leroux, Editeur, 1902), pp. 138-147. Also see E. A. Wallis Budge, The Book of Opening the Mouth: The Egyptian Texts with English Translations (London: 1909. Reissued in 1980 by Arno Press, New York), p. 221. The second half of Budge's book contains a translation of the Morning Temple Liturgy. See also *Eternal Egypt* for the full offering text, pp. 31-32.

own unique way of embracing life. If the creator god him/herself lives in Ma'at, so too must we.

THE DESIGN OF THIS BOOK

This book is designed so that each ritual is complete in itself. There is no need to flip back and forth for instructions or ritual texts. Once you have read this Introduction, you can proceed directly to the ritual of your choice. All rituals follow a similar model just as was generally done in ancient times. Several rituals have special sections for a festival specific to that god or goddess. If there is a special sort of offering to a particular deity, it is named at the beginning of text for that god. For example, a special offering for Min is lettuce, and for Hathor it is two mirrors. Most deities, however, receive the standard food offerings of a water libation, bread, beer, wine, meat, and the produce of the earth. Some deities are presented with symbols specific to them. For example, Setekh is presented with a three-dimensional representation of his Testicles, a *WAS* scepter, and the Opening of the Mouth instrument known as an Adze. The god Khnum is presented with a representation of a Potter's Wheel. If you are unable to craft the actual item, then you can substitute a drawing of the item along with its written name. Just be sure to consecrate and purify any such item whether two or three dimensional. These, after all, are offerings to the gods and deserve our care.

Each of the deities whose rituals appear here received a temple cult in ancient times. However, due simply to limitations of space, not every god or goddess who had a chapel or received a temple cult could be represented in this volume. By carefully studying the design of the rituals in this book the interested reader can seek out academic resources to help in crafting a ritual for their special deity.

This book is a companion book to *Eternal Egypt*. Please refer to that volume for a detailed explanation of each ritual action as well as more background information. If you have questions or suggestions, I invite you to contact me at rjreidy@hotmail.com or through our temples' website, kemetictemple.org. May your service to the gods bring you into a closer relationship with them and give you joy of heart.

RITUALS FOR THE NETJERU

The General Ritual For Amun

The hymns, prayers, and epithets for Amun come from David Klotz'
excellent book, *Adoration of the Ram: Five Hymns to Amun-Re from
Hibis Temple* (Yale Egyptological Studies, 2006).

Like members of the ancient priesthood, participants should be
clothed in white linen. No item made of animal products such as
leather or wool is to be worn. Linen represents a pristine product
of the earth whereas leather and wool come from humankind's
domination of the animals, a domination that becomes part of
the "natural order" only *after* the First Time when the *Netjeru*
and humans and animals lived in peace and harmony. Just as the
Morning Ritual harkens back to that First Time (*Zep Tepi*), so every
temple rite re-presents mythic prototypes that occurred "in the
beginning," that is, in that time before time. Even the sandals worn
by the god's servants were made of white papyrus. This avoidance
of animal products by the priesthood fits well with the fact that the
ritualist acts as a *Netjer* and verbally asserts that he or she is a *Netjer*.

As with all Egyptian rituals begin with your purification – washing
of hands and cleansing of mouth with Natron. This preliminary rite
helps us to lay aside the cares of the day and to become mindful
of the fact that we will encounter a divine being. If Natron is not
available, then use a natural sea salt in its place until you make
your own Natron.

If two or more persons are participating, then one person, impersonating
the Netjer *Djehuty*, **purifies each person by sprinkling each with**
water while exclaiming:

1

I purify you with the water of all life and good fortune, all stability, all health and happiness.[17]

*Afterwards **each person rinses his mouth with Natron and places a small amount of Natron or sea salt in his mouth while saying:***

I wash my mouth; I chew natron so that I may extol the might of Amun, Lord of All that Exists, the Pure One.[18]

*Participants **assemble outside the Temple Chamber** and begin by softly rattling sistra.*

This time—several minutes or more—is used to focus minds and intention so that distracting thoughts are left behind. The sound of the sistrum was said to placate the deity, purifying the atmosphere in preparation for encountering divinity. The sistrum was associated with Hutheru and also with her and Heru's son Ihy, and thus has connotations of joy, celebration, and dancing. According to Plutarch (A.D. 46-120), the sound of sistra was also reputed to drive away Setekh. But this was of very late date. It may have been that since by that time Setekh had been demonized, the general apotropaic function of the sistrum against evil entities was extended to include this *Netjer* as well.

---

[17] Taken from Aylward M. Blackman's article "Purification (Egyptian)" in Hastings Encyclopedia 10/1918/ 476-82. This article is reprinted in Gods, Priests, and Men, Studies in the Religion of Pharaonic Egypt, edited by Alan B. Lloyd (Kegan Paul International, 1998), p. 9.

[18] Adapted from a temple inscription taken from "The Myth of Horus at Edfu—II" by A. M. Blackman and H. W. Fairman, appearing in Gods, Priests and Men, Studies in the Religion of Pharaonic Egypt, p. 283.

*Standing **before the closed doors**, the Ritualist **recites the entrance spell:***

UTTERANCE BEFORE THE CLOSED DOORS OF THE TEMPLE

*The ritualist **raises hands in adoration** (dua position-arms stretched out in front of the body and raised up to face level, with palms facing outward). The following shall be said:*

O you Netjeru of this Temple, you guardians of the great portal, great Netjeru of mysterious abode, who sanctify the Netjer in his shrine, who consecrate his oblation, who receive the offerings in his presence in the Hall of the Ennead: I have made my way and I enter into your presence. I am one of you. I am Shu, the eldest son of his father, the senior wab servant-priest of Amun. Do not repulse me on the Netjer's path. My feet are not impeded. I am not turned back from the court of the great portal so that I may conduct the divine service, that I may present offerings to him that made them, that I may give bread to Amun. I have come on the way of the god. I have not shown partiality in judgment. I have not consorted with the strong. I have not reproached the lowly. I have not stolen things. I have not diminished the constituents of the Eye of Ra. I have not disturbed the Balance. I have not tampered with the requirements of the Sacred Eye. O Council of the Great Netjer in this Temple, behold, I have come to you to offer Ma'at to the Lord of Ma'at, to content the Sound Eye for its lord. I am Shu; I flood his offering table. I present his offerings, Sekhmet consorting with me, that I may adore Amun at his festivals, that I may kiss the earth so great is his majesty, that I may endow his image with life. I am pure. I am purified.

Richard J. Reidy

*The ritualist **opens the doors to the Temple Chamber,** or, if there are no doors, makes a gesture of opening unseen doors, and steps forward as if crossing over a threshold. The following is said:*

O you Ba-souls of Waset (Thebes) if you are strong, I am strong. If I am strong, you are strong. If your Ka-spirits are strong, my Ka-spirit is strong at the head of the living. As they are living so shall I live . . . . Amun, Bull of his Mother, has given to me life, stability, and serenity round about my members, which Djehuty has gathered together for life. I am Heru in the height of heaven, the beautiful one of awe, Lord of Victory, mighty one of awe, exalted one of the two plumes, great one in Waset, I am pure.

*All temple members **chant:***

Awake in peace, O Amun, Foremost of Ipet Sut (Karnak),
may you awaken in peace.
Awake in peace, O Amun, Tall of Plumes and Lord of Creation,
may you awaken in peace.
Awake in peace, O Amun, Lord of the Firmament,
may you awaken in peace.
Awake in peace, O Amun, Protector of the Divine Order,
may you awaken in peace.
May you awake beautifully at the top of the morning,
through that which the entirety of Netjeru say to you.

*Enter, **close the double doors and stand in front of the Kar-shrine and altar. All bow, touching their hands to their knees.***

*The ritualist slowly opens the two doors of the Kar-shrine housing the sacred image. All others **bow, touching their hands to their knees.** The following is said:*

4

The doors of the sky are open; the doors of the earth are unlocked. This House is open for its Lord. Let me come forth as he shall come forth. Let me enter in as he shall enter in. Amun, the Limitless One, the Mysterious Ba, is exalted upon his Great Seat. The Great Company of the Netjeru are exalted upon their seat.

I have seen the Netjer, and the Netjer sees me. The Netjer rejoices at seeing me. I have gazed upon the statue of the Lord of Everything That Is, the sacred image of Lord of the Netjeru.[19]

Right hand on left shoulder of statue; left hand on right wrist of statue:

Djehuty has come to you. Awake when you hear his words. I have come as the envoy of Atum. My two arms are upon you like those of Heru. My two hands are upon you like those of Djehuty. My fingers are upon you like those of Anpu. Homage be to you. I am a living servant of Amun.

*All present **recite the hymn** honoring Amun:*

Happy is the temple and happy are the priests
And happy are the watchers of the day.
For the Netjer of Heaven has entered his shrine
And the people bow down in homage.

For Amun is all mighty and Amun is all love,
And the poor and the lowly are his care.
He shines like the sun in Ipet-Sut, his city.

---

[19] Based on the temple text found in "Worship and Festivals in an Egyptian Temple," a lecture by H. W. Fairman (publ. by The John Rylands Library, 1954), p. 180.

O Beautiful Face, O Mighty One, O Lover,
Upon whom the Netjeru desire to look
As the Mighty One who comes forth from heaven.

All people, all people of Amun's temple, come and adore,
For Amun the Netjer is here!
And the love that he extends to beggar and to prince
Is the love that casts our fear.

Loud are the shouts that ascend to the sky,
That he hears as he passes on his way,
For happy are the people and happy are the priests,
And happy are the watchers of the day! [20]

*The Ritualist **holds up the bowl of water** in which he/she will be mixing the Natron. The following is said:*

O water may you remove all evil,
As Ra who bathes in the Lake of Rushes,
May Heru wash my flesh,
May Djehuty cleanse my feet,
May Shu lift me up and Nut take my hand!
May Set be my strength, and may Sekhmet be my healing!
And may Amun-Ra be my life and my prospering!

*The bowl of water is set aside and the **container of Natron is lifted up**. The following is said:*

It is pure, it is pure.

---

[20] A hymn to Amun in Margaret A. Murray's *Egyptian Religious Poetry* (London, 1949), pp. 93-94. Original source, *The Journal of Egyptian Archaeology*, vol. xvi (1930), p. 57.

My Natron is the Natron of Heru and the Natron of Heru is
my Natron.
My Natron is the Natron of Setekh and the Natron of Setekh
is my Natron.
My Natron is the Natron of Djehuty, and the Natron of
Djehuty is my Natron.
My Natron is the Natron of Geb and the Natron of Geb is
my Natron.

My mouth is the mouth of a milking calf on the day that I
was born.

*Four pinches of Natron are mixed into the water as this Utterance
is recited:*

I give you essential water, a tide in your time.
I bring the flood waters to purify your sanctuary.
I bring you the flood waters to purify your Temple and your
statue in its place, the primordial water that purifies as in
the First Time!

The Ritualist **places an index finger into the water** *and* **moves it in
a circular direction four times** *as the following is said:*

Amun, Lord of the Thrones of the Two Lands,
does purify this water;
Amun, Foremost of 'Most Select of Places' (Ipet Sut; Karnak
temple),
does cleanse this water;
Amun, who made himself into millions,
does sanctify this water;
Amun himself

does endow this water with power and with life.

*The **Bowl of Natron-infused water** is then taken up and the Ritualist*
sprinkles this lightly in front of and around the statue or image
of Amun, applying some of this water to the base of the image, as the
Utterance is recited:

I come close to you, O Pure One, Mysterious Ba, great Lord
of the Firmament. I bring the water of rejuvenation that
flows from the Two Caverns. I sprinkle the water, purifying
your image and your Temple from all impurity!

*The Ritualist picks up the bowl of Natron and **sprinkles a small***
***amount in each of the four directions** as the following is recited:*

The *Netjer* Amun Himself
does cleanse and purify this, His Temple to the South.
The *Netjer* Amun Himself
does cleanse and purify this, His Temple to the North.
The *Netjer* Amun Himself
does cleanse and purify this, His Temple to the West.
The *Netjer* Amun Himself
does cleanse and purify this, His Temple to the East.

Replacing the Natron on the altar, the Ritualist takes up the bowl of
water, sprinkling a small amount in each of the four directions.
The following Utterance is recited:

The *Netjer* Amun Himself does sanctify and consecrate this,
His Temple to the South.
The *Netjer* Amun Himself does sanctify and consecrate this,
His Temple to the North.
The *Netjer* Amun Himself does sanctify and consecrate this,

His Temple to the West.
The *Netjer* Amun Himself does sanctify and consecrate this,
His Temple to the East.

The Temple of the *Netjer* Amun is established.
It is established for millions of years.

*The Ritualist returns to the altar and **lights the candle or oil lamp** while the following is said:*

Come, come in peace, O glorious Eye of Heru,
Be strong and renew your youth in peace.
For the flame shines like Ra on the double horizon.
The enemies of Ra are defeated. They are defeated.
I am pure, I am pure, I am pure, I am pure.

*The Ritualist **places incense on the burner** and **censes each sacred image** beginning with the statue of Amun while the following is recited:*

The fire is laid, the fire shines;
The incense is laid on the fire, the incense shines.
> Your perfume comes to me, O Incense;
> May my perfume come to you, O Incense.
Your perfume comes to me, you *Netjeru*;
May my perfume come to you, You *Netjeru*.
> May I be with you, you *Netjeru*;
> May you be with me, you *Netjeru*.
May I live with you, you *Netjeru*;
May you live with me, you *Netjeru*.
> I love you, you *Netjeru*;
> May you love me, you *Netjeru*.

*Standing in front of the image of Amun the Ritualist **offers the burning incense** and says:*

>Take the incense, O Lord of Life.
>Its essence is for you.
>Its smoke permeates your shrine, bringing life!
>Take the incense,
>Its essence is for you.
>Your Majesty is appeased with the incense.
>This Eye of Heru,
>This essence of the Eye of Heru comes to you.

At this point the following is said:

>Greetings Amun, O sole *Netjer*, who made himself into millions.
>Whose length and breadth are without limit,
>One powerful and skilled who bore himself.
>Serpent, Giant of Fire, Great of Magic.
>One remote to visible forms, the Mysterious *Ba*.[21]

>Yours is the sky,
>Yours is the earth,
>Yours is the netherworld,
>Yours are the waters,
>And yours is the air which is within them.

>That which is made acclaims you, without tiring.

>O protector of that which is and that which is not,

---

[21] David Klotz, *Adoration of the Ram: Five Hymns to Amun-Re from Hibis Temple* (Yale Egyptological Studies, 2006), p. 136.

You support them as you create them.
Thus their tribute is apportioned for your *Ka*.

O Amun, Lord of Everything that is,
Strong of Heart, Festive of Chest.[22]

*The Ritualist **places more incense on the charcoal** and again and again **slowly raises and lowers the incense cup** as the following is recited:*

O Amun, may you advance with your *Ka*.
Who hides himself in his iris, the arm of your *Ka* is before you,
The arm of your *Ka* is behind you.
O Lord of Heaven, the foot of your *Ka* is before you,
The foot of your *Ka* is behind you.
O Sacred one who cannot be known,
Amun, this incense is offered to you,
May your face be filled as this essence spreads itself over you.

*All present **perform the Henu Rite**—Embrace the Earth, the Fourfold Salute to the God, Embrace the Earth. The bodily gestures are performed alternately four times.*

For Embracing the Earth, all present prostrate themselves, face down, upon the floor. During the Fourfold Salute, all present rise upon one knee, and alternately raise their hands and arms into the *Dua* (praise) position with palms facing outward, followed by the *Sahu* (obedience) gesture, made by striking the chest with a closed fist and raising the other arm (also with closed fist) at a ninety-degree

---

[22] Op. Cit., p. 129.

angle. The *Dua* position is accompanied by the words **"Adoration be to Amun,"** followed by the *Sahu* gesture accompanied with the words, **"Hail to the Lord of Life!"**

*Following this **all present again prostrate themselves** before the god. This is a sign and symbol of total submission and adoration before the Netjer.*

The following is said:

> **Homage to Amun, Chief of the** *Netjeru,*
> **who is established on the Great Seat!**
> **I have placed myself on the floor in awe of you.**
> **I embrace the earth before you as before the Lord of All Powers.**
> **I have come that I might kiss the earth,**
> **that I might worship my Lord,**
> **For I have seen his Strength;**
> **I give praise to Amun,**
> **For I have seen his Power.**
> **His form is more distinguished than the** *Netjeru;*
> **His arm is more powerful than the** *Netjeru.*
> **I am pure, I am pure, I am pure, I am pure!**

*Everyone **stands up.***

*The Ritualist holds **in the palm of one hand the image of Ma'at** and with **the other hand open and raised over the image as if sheltering it,** repeats the following:*

> **I have come to you as Djehuty, whose two hands are joined together under Ma'at. She comes to be with you, for she is everywhere. You are provided with Ma'at. You move in**

Ma'at, you live in Ma'at. She fills your body, she rests in your head, she makes her seat upon your brow; the breath of your body is of Ma'at, your heart does live in Ma'at. All that you eat, all that you drink, all that you breathe is of Ma'at. Djehuty presents Ma'at to you, his two hands are upon her beauty before your face.

The Ritualist **places the image of Ma'at near the divine statue.** *Then he/she* **holds up before the image of Amun a pitcher of water** *and* **pours the water slowly into an offering bowl** *as the following Utterance is recited:*

This libation is for you, O Hidden One.
This libation is for you, O Amun, Lord of All Eternity.
I have brought to you this offering of water,
That your heart may be refreshed.
I have brought to you this Eye of Heru,
Placing this at your feet.
I present to you that which flows forth from you,
That your heart shall continue to beat.
For it is with you that all comes forth at the sound of the voice.

The offering bowl is placed on the altar. The Ritualist **lightly sprinkles sand on the floor in front of the altar** *saying:*

O Amun, who resides in *Waset* (Thebes),
Take to yourself the Eye of Heru.
You have rescued it, O Protector of the Divine Order.
You have sprinkled with sand the Eye of Heru.

Lifting the wine offering *before the sacred image, the Ritualist repeats the following:*

13

mn n.k irp irt ḥrw w3dt

[*"mán-nik 'úrip írat ḥáru wá'dat"*; approximately pronounced *MAHN-neek OO-rip EE-raht HAH-roo WAH-jat*]

Take to yourself wine, the green Eye of Heru,
which I offer to your *Ka.*[23]
O Ruler, how beautiful is your beauty!
May you drink it; may your heart rejoice;
may anger be removed from your face.
It is pure.
[*iw.w wʿb* pronounced *"uwú wáʿib"*; approximately *oo-WOO WAH-ib*]

The Ritualist **places myrrh on the fire** *and* **lifts up the smoking incense** *while at the same time he* **lifts up the meat-offering** *before the Netjer, and says the following:*

The scent of myrrh is for your nose. It fills your nostrils; your heart receives the meat-portions on its scent.[24]

Slowly **elevating the food offerings four times before the image** *of Amun, the Ritualist repeats the following:*

I offer to Amun, Tall of Plumes, Lord of Creation.
All life emanates from you,
All health emanates from you,
All stability emanates from you,
All good fortune emanates from you,

---

[23] Refer to pp. 92, 93, 99, and 105 in Mu-Chou Poo's *Wine and Wine Offerings in Ancient Egypt* (London & New York: Kegan Paul International, 1995).

[24] Quoted in "Worship and Festivals in an Egyptian Temple," by H. W. Fairman (publ. by The John Rylands Library, 1954), p. 191.

O Great One of Heka-u, Amun, forever.

The Ritualist places the food offering before the divine image, and then all present extend one hand, palm down, over the offerings and recite the following:

May offerings of every kind come forth in abundance,
like the things which come forth from the mouth of the
Netjer.

piryá pírit ar ḫiráw mi purú:riat ma rá' ni náṭar. (*4 times*)
[approximately pronounced *peer-YA PEER-it ar khi-RAU mee pu-ROOR-iat ma RA nee NAH-tchar*]

May offerings of every kind come forth in abundance, like
the things that come forth from the mouth of the Netjer.

Holding the Ankh before Amun, the Ritualist says:

Live, O Amun, Lord of the Netjeru,
live for all time and for eternity!

ʿánaḫ niḥáḫ ḏát.
[approximately pronounced *AH-nakh nee-HAH JAHT*]

The Ankh is placed next to the image of the Netjer.

Holding the Ib (the golden heart) before Amun, the Ritualist says:

Hail to you, O Amun, Ithyphallic Scarab. I have brought
to you your heart to set it in its place. Let me draw near
to you with your heart, so that you may have pleasure
through me, and so that by means of me you may have

power over your body. Ascend, O Lord of the double crown, radiant, rejuvenating, equipped as a Netjer. Live, O Lord of the Phallus, live forever and ever!

*After placing the **Ib** near the sacred image, **everyone sings or chants the hymn to Amun**. Participants may wish to alternate the singing of verses.*

Amun, Lord of the *heh-Netjeru*[25] who support the *Netjeru*.
Most primeval of the *Netjeru*,
Eldest of the primeval ones,
Builder of builders,
Renenet of Renenets,
Khnum, who made the Creator *Netjeru,*
Effective counsel,
Open and sharp of face,
Lord of all that exists,
Who predetermined every event.

Bull of his Mother, Begetter of his Father,
Who destroyed A/pep when he manifests manifestations,

Just as he wept mankind from his divine eyes,
So did he spit out the *Netjeru* from his mouth.[26]

Amun is he who smells sweet as a *Netjer,*
Who magnified his cult image in order to carry his 'perfection,'

---

[25] The eight *heh*-gods are members of the Ogdoad of Hermopolis. In the Book of the Heavenly Cow they hold up the Heavenly Cow upon the back of whom Ra travels. Ref. p. 137 in Klotz.
[26] Klotz, p. 142.

Having crafted his form to his desire.

He made himself gracious through the charm of his love,
His prestige, splendor, and dignity
are in excess of all the *Netjeru*.

He created himself through that which created himself,
He conceived himself as the great composite image:
Fatherless, his own phallus engendered him:
Motherless, his own seed was pregnant with him.
The august Winged Scarab,
who makes himself emerge as a *Netjer*.
Father of Fathers, Mother of Mothers.[27]

Your name shall protect against panic.
Fear of you is great in all limbs,
They are protected through recalling of you.
Your name alone shall protect the body of anyone—
Recalling your name is good in a moment of troubles.[28]
May your name be a protection for us who serve you, O Amun.

At this point **perform the meditation or magical action** *or, if it is a special feast, add the appropriate prayers.*

Afterwards **all present back out of the Temple Chamber with heads slightly bowed** *while the Ritualist performs the "removing the foot."*

With the **broom** *the Ritualist, as the last person to exit,* **ritually sweeps the area beginning at the altar.** *(This is known as "removing the foot.") While performing this action the Ritualist recites the following:*

---

[27] Op. Cit., p. 145.
[28] Op. Cit., pp. 145-147.

17

The distress that causes confusion has been driven away, and all the Netjeru are in harmony. I have given Heru his Eye; I have placed the Wedjat-Eye in the correct position. I have given Setekh his Testicles, so that the two lords are content through the work of my hands.

I know the sky, I know the earth;
I know Heru, I know Setekh.
Heru is appeased with his Eyes;
Setekh is appeased with his Testicles.
I am Djehuty, who reconciles the Netjeru,
who makes offerings in their correct form.

*The **double doors are solemnly closed** as the Ritualist says the following:*

Djehuty has come.
He has filled the Eye of Heru;
He has restored the Testicles of Setekh.
No evil shall enter this Temple.
Ptah has closed the door,
Djehuty has set it fast.
The door is closed, the door is set fast with the bolt.

All bow, touching the palms of their hands to their knees.

THE REVERSION OF OFFERINGS

*One ritualist and as many assistants as necessary enter the Temple Chamber a final time. **Lift up the offerings before the sacred image** as the ritualist says:*

O Amun, your enemy[29] withdraws for you. Heru has turned himself to his Eye in its name of 'Reversion-of-Offerings.' I am Djehuty. I come to perform this rite for Amun, Lord of the Netjeru. These, your divine offerings revert, they revert to your servants for life, for stability, for health and for joy! O that the Eye of Heru may flourish for you eternally!

Everyone withdraws, **carrying away all food offerings except for one loaf of bread and a bowl of pure water.** *These last items remain until evening. If this ritual is celebrated after sunset, these items would also be removed.*

After the candle has burned down, a servant-priest enters and closes the doors of the Kar-shrine. **Extinguishing the candle or oil lamp,** *he/she exclaims:*

This is the Eye of Heru by which you have become great, by which you live, and by which you have power, O Amun. This is the Eye of Heru which you consume and through which you enchant your body. The Wedjat-Eye now enters into the West, into Manu, but it shall return. Truly, the Eye of Heru returns in peace![30]

---

[29] Meat offerings held a two-fold meaning for the ancient priesthood. Since meat necessarily came from slain animals, it signified the defeated or slain enemies of the Netjeru. At the same time, the meat offering represented the produce of the land which ultimately was a gift of the Netjeru.

[30] It is important to consume the food offerings after the ceremony. Water used should either be drunk or poured onto the earth. If it is mixed with natron, dilute it very greatly and then you can pour in onto the earth without harming any plantings.

General Ritual for Amun-Ra

The many beautiful hymns, prayers, epithets and glorifications for Amun-Ra come from David Klotz' excellent book, *Adoration of the Ram: Five Hymns to Amun-Re from Hibis Temple* (Yale Egyptological Studies, 2006). This collection is a valuable resource for understanding the nature of this, the king of the *Netjeru*.

Like members of the ancient priesthood, participants should be clothed in white linen. No item made of animal products such as leather or wool is to be worn. Linen represents a *pristine* product of the earth whereas leather and wool come from humankind's domination of the animals, a domination that becomes part of the "natural order" only *after* the First Time when the *Netjeru* and humans and animals lived in peace and harmony. Just as the Morning Ritual harkens back to that First Time (*Zep Tepi*), so every temple rite re-presents mythic prototypes that occurred "in the beginning," that is, in that time before time. Even the sandals worn by the *Netjer*'s servants were made of white papyrus. This avoidance of animal products by the priesthood fits well with the fact that the ritualist acts as a *Netjer* and verbally asserts that he or she is a *Netjer*.

As with all Egyptian rituals begin with your purification—washing of hands and cleansing of mouth with Natron. This preliminary rite helps us to lay aside the cares of the day and to become mindful of the fact that we will encounter a divine being. If Natron is not available, then use a natural sea salt in its place until you make your own Natron.

If two or more persons are participating, then one person, impersonating the Netjer *Djehuty,* **purifies each person by sprinkling each with water** *while exclaiming:*

> **I purify you with the water of all life and good fortune, all stability, all health and happiness.**[31]

Afterwards each person **rinses their mouth** *and* **places a small amount of Natron or sea salt in their mouth** *while saying the following:*

> **I wash my mouth; I chew natron so that I may extol the might of Amun-Ra, Lord of All Powers and King of the Netjeru.**[32]

Participants **assemble outside the Temple Chamber** *and begin by softly rattling sistra.*

This time—several minutes or more—is used to focus minds and intention so that distracting thoughts are left behind. The sound of the sistrum was said to placate the deity, purifying the atmosphere in preparation for encountering divinity. The sistrum was associated with Hutheru and also with her and Heru's son Ihy, and thus has connotations of joy, celebration, and dancing. According to Plutarch (A.D. 46-120), the sound of sistra was also reputed to drive away Setekh. But this was of very late date. It may have been that since

---

[31] Taken from Aylward M. Blackman's article "Purification (Egyptian)" in Hastings Encyclopedia 10/1918/ 476-82. This article is reprinted in Gods, Priests, and Men, Studies in the Religion of Pharaonic Egypt, edited by Alan B. Lloyd (Kegan Paul International, 1998), p. 9.

[32] Adapted from a temple inscription taken from "The Myth of Horus at Edfu—II" by A. M. Blackman and H. W. Fairman, appearing in Gods, Priests and Men, Studies in the Religion of Pharaonic Egypt, p. 283.

by that time Setekh had been demonized, the general apotropaic function of the sistrum against evil entities was extended to include this *Netjer* as well.

Standing before the closed doors, *the Ritualist recites the entrance spell:*

UTTERANCE BEFORE THE CLOSED DOORS OF THE TEMPLE

*The ritualist **raises hands in adoration** (dua position-arms stretched out in front of the body and raised up to face level, with palms facing outward). The following shall be said:*

O you Netjeru of this Temple, you guardians of the great portal, great Netjeru of mysterious abode, who sanctify the Netjer in his shrine, who consecrate his oblation, who receive the offerings in his presence in the Hall of the Ennead: I have made my way and I enter into your presence. I am one of you. I am Shu, the eldest son of his father, the senior wab servant-priest of Amun-Ra, Lord of Hibis, Mighty of Scimitar. Do not repulse me on the Netjer's path. My feet are not impeded. I am not turned back from the court of the great portal so that I may conduct the divine service, that I may present offerings to him that made them, that I may give bread to Amun-Ra. I have come on the way of the Netjer. I have not shown partiality in judgment. I have not consorted with the strong. I have not reproached the lowly. I have not stolen things. I have not diminished the constituents of the Eye of Ra. I have not disturbed the Balance. I have not tampered with the requirements of the Sacred Eye. O Council of the Great Netjer in this Temple, behold, I have come to you to offer Ma'at to the Lord of Ma'at, to content the Sound Eye for its lord. I am Shu; I flood his offering table. I present his offerings, Sekhmet consorting with me, that I may adore Amun-Ra at his festivals, that I may kiss the earth so great is his majesty, that I may endow his image with life. I am pure. I am purified.

*At this point the ritualist **opens the doors to the Temple Chamber**, or, if there are no doors, **makes a gesture of opening unseen doors**, and steps forward as if crossing over a threshold. The following is said:*

O you Ba-souls of Waset (Thebes) if you are strong, I am strong. If I am strong, you are strong. If your Ka-spirits are strong, my Ka-spirit is strong at the head of the living. As they are living so shall I live . . . . Amun-Ra, Bull of his Mother, has given to me life, stability, and serenity round about my members, which Djehuty has gathered together for life. I am Heru in the height of heaven, the beautiful one of awe, Lord of Victory, mighty one of awe, exalted one of the two plumes, great one in Waset (Thebes), I am pure.

All temple members chant:

Awake in peace, O Amun-Ra, the Hearing One,
may you awaken in peace.
Awake in peace, O Amun-Ra mes m ka-ref (the Child in His Shrine),
may you awaken in peace.
Awake in peace, O Amun-Ra, neb ankh (Lord of Life),
may you awaken in peace.
Awake in peace, O Amun-Ra, neb er djer (Lord to the Limit),
may you awaken in peace.

May you awake beautifully at the top of the morning, through that which the entirety of Netjeru say to you.

Hail Amun-Ra, Horakhty, Atum, Khepri,
Heru who ferries across the sky,
Great falcon, with breast decorated for festival,
Perfect of Face with the Great Double Plume.
May you awake perfect upon daybreak
At what the assembled Nine Netjeru say to you.
Jubilation resounds for you in the evening,
Kenmut[33] glorifies you.
One who sleeps conceived, you at whose birth dawn breaks.
Your mother (Nut) absorbs you every full day.

May Ra live and the enemy die.
You are set firm, your opponent (A/pep) is felled.
You cross the sky in life and power,
You make the sky festive in the Morning Barque.
You pass the day in your sacred boat, your heart being sweet.
Ma'at has appeared upon your brow.

Rise, Ra, Shine as Akhty [the horizon god],
Dark god, light of form,
The crew of Ra is jubilant, heaven and earth rejoice,
The great Ennead makes jubilation for you.
Amun-Ra Horakhty is emerged 'True-of-Voice.[34]

---

[33] Kenmut is one of and here represents all thirty-six gods of the decans. The first three decan gods each have some form of the name Kenmut. The first decan takes place during the first ten-day period beginning with Wep Renpet (i.e., New Year). The Egyptian week consisted of ten days, each with a decan god as protector.

[34] According to Egyptologist Stephen Quirke this hymn "is the only example found in original papyrus manuscripts used for the daily liturgy, from the temples at Karnak." It also appears on the walls of the Khonsu

Enter, close the double doors and *stand in front of the Kar-shrine and altar. All bow, touching their hands to their knees.*

The ritualist slowly opens the two doors of the Kar-shrine housing the sacred image. All others bow, touching their hands to their knees. The following is said:

> The doors of the sky are open; the doors of the earth are unlocked. This House is open for its Lord. Let me come forth as he shall come forth. Let me enter in as he shall enter in. Amun-Ra, the Limitless One, Mysterious Ba, is exalted upon his Great Seat. The Great Company of the Netjeru are exalted upon their seat.

> I have seen the Netjer, and the Netjer sees me. The Netjer rejoices at seeing me. I have gazed upon the statue of the Hidden One, the sacred image of the Lord of the Firmament.[35]

Right hand on left shoulder of statue; left hand on right wrist of statue:

> Djehuty has come to you. Awake when you hear his words. I have come as the envoy of Atum. My two arms are upon you like those of Heru. My two hands are upon you like those of Djehuty. My fingers are upon you like those of Anpu. Homage be to you. I am a living servant of Amun-Ra.

The Ritualist holds up the bowl of water in which he/she will be mixing the Natron. The following is said:

---

temple and the Hibis temple. See Stephen Quirke, *The Cult of Ra: Sun-Worship in Ancient Egypt* (New York: Thames & Hudson, 2001), p.70.

[35] Based on a passage in "Worship and Festivals in an Egyptian Temple," a lecture by H. W. Fairman (publ. by The John Rylands Library, 1954) p.180.

O water may you remove all evil,
As Ra who bathes in the Lake of Rushes,
May Heru wash my flesh,
May Djehuty cleanse my feet,
May Shu lift me up and Nut take my hand!
May Setekh be my strength, and may Sekhmet be my healing!
May Amun-Ra be my life and my prospering!

*The bowl of water is set aside and the **container of Natron is lifted up**. The following is said:*

It is pure, it is pure.
My Natron is the Natron of Heru
and the Natron of Heru is my Natron.
My Natron is the Natron of Setekh
and the Natron of Setekh is my Natron.
My Natron is the Natron of Djehuty,
and the Natron of Djehuty is my Natron.
My Natron is the Natron of Geb
and the Natron of Geb is my Natron.

My mouth is the mouth of a milking calf on the day that I was born.

Four pinches of Natron are mixed into the water as this Utterance is recited:

I give you essential water, a tide in your time.
I bring the flood waters to purify your sanctuary.
I bring you the flood waters to purify your Temple and your statue in its place, the primordial water that purifies as in the First Time!

*The Ritualist **places an index finger into the water** and **moves it in
a circular direction four times*** *as the following is said:*

> Amun-Ra, Sweet of Love,
> does purify this water;
> Amun-Ra, foremost of Ipet Sut (Karnak),
> does cleanse this water;
> Amun-Ra, who made himself into millions,
> does sanctify this water;
> Amun-Ra himself
> does endow this water with power and with life.

*The **Bowl of Natron-infused water** is then taken up and the Ritualist
sprinkles this lightly in front of and around the statue or image
of Amun-Ra, applying some of this water to the base of the image, as
the Utterance is recited:*

> I come close to You, O Pure One, Lord of the Firmament.
> I bring the water of rejuvenation
> that flows from the Two Caverns.
> I sprinkle the water,
> purifying your image and your Temple from all impurity!

*The Ritualist picks up the bowl of **Natron** and **sprinkles a small
amount in each of the four directions** as the following is recited:*

> The Netjer Amun-Ra himself
> does cleanse and purify this, his Temple to the South.
> The Netjer Amun-Ra himself
> does cleanse and purify this, his Temple to the North.
> The Netjer Amun-Ra himself
> does cleanse and purify this, his Temple to the West.

The Netjer Amun-Ra himself
does cleanse and purify this, his Temple to the East.

*Replacing the Natron on the altar, the Ritualist takes up the **bowl of**
water, sprinkling a small amount in each of the four directions.*
The following Utterance is recited:

The Netjer Amun-Ra himself
does sanctify and consecrate this, his Temple to the South.
The Netjer Amun-Ra himself
does sanctify and consecrate this, his Temple to the North.
The Netjer Amun-Ra himself
does sanctify and consecrate this, his Temple to the West.
The Netjer Amun-Ra himself
does sanctify and consecrate this, his Temple to the East.

The Temple of the Netjer Amun-Ra is established.
It is established for millions of years.

*The Ritualist returns to the altar and **lights the candle or oil lamp**
while the following is said:

Come, come in peace, O glorious Eye of Heru,
Be strong and renew your youth in peace.
For the flame shines like Ra on the double horizon.
The enemies are Ra are defeated. They are defeated.
The lie is abolished!
I am pure, I am pure, I am pure, I am pure.

*The Ritualist **places incense on the burner** and **censes each sacred***
***image** beginning with the statue of the god while the following is*
recited:

The fire is laid, the fire shines;
The incense is laid on the fire, the incense shines.
    Your perfume comes to me, O Incense;
    May my perfume come to you, O Incense.
Your perfume comes to me, you Netjeru;
May my perfume come to you, You Netjeru.
    May I be with you, you Netjeru;
    May you be with me, you Netjeru.
May I live with you, you Netjeru;
May you live with me, you Netjeru.
    I love you, you Netjeru;
    May you love me, you Netjeru.

*Standing in front of the image of Amun-Ra the Ritualist **offers the burning incense** and says:*

Take the incense, O Lord of the *Netjeru*.
Its essence is for you.
Its smoke permeates your shrine, bringing life!
Take the incense,
Its essence is for you.
Your Majesty is appeased with the incense.
This Eye of Heru,
This essence of the Eye of Heru comes to you.

At this point the following is said:

Hail to you, Amun-Ra, O Sole Netjer,
who made himself into millions
Whose length and breadth are without limit,
One powerful and skilled,
Who bore himself.

Serpent, giant of fire, great of magic.
One remote to visible forms, Mysterious Ba.[36]

Yours is the sky,
Yours is the earth,
Yours is the duat,
Yours are the waters,
And yours is the air within them.
That which is made acclaims you without tiring.
O Protector of that which is and that which is not,
You support them as you create them.
Thus their tribute is apportioned for your Ka.
O Amun-Ra, Lord of Everything that is,
Strong of Heart, Festive of Chest.[37]

Netjer of hearts and minds,
heaven and earth are under your designs.
The Netjeru are in your hands,
humankind rests at your feet.
Great Listener, in the Temple of the Ram-of-Rams (Karnak),
who is open of ears.[38]
As for me, may I live eternally,
beloved of Amun-Ra,
may you save me as son/daughter of Ra
from every knife and every arrow!
May your heart be content with that which I have done.

---

[36] David Klotz, Adoration of the Ram: Five Hymns to Amun-Re from Hibis Temple (Yale Egyptological Studies, 2006), p. 211.
[37] Op. Cit., pp. 207-209.
[38] Op. Cit., p. 169.

*The Ritualist **places more incense on the charcoal** and again and again slowly raises and lowers the incense cup as the following is recited:*

O Amun-Ra, may you advance with your Ka.
Who Hides Himself in his Iris, the arm of your Ka is before you,
The arm of your Ka is behind you.
O Lord of Heaven, the foot of your Ka is before you,
The foot of your Ka is behind you.
O Sacred One who cannot be known, Amun-Ra,
this incense is offered to you,
May your face be filled as this essence spreads itself over you.

*All present **perform the Henu Rite**—Embrace the Earth, the Fourfold Salute to the God, Embrace the Earth. The bodily gestures are performed alternately four times.*

For Embracing the Earth, all present prostrate themselves, face down, upon the floor. During the Fourfold Salute, all present rise upon one knee, and alternately raise their hands and arms into the *Dua* (praise) position with palms facing outward, followed by the *Sahu* (obedience) gesture, made by striking the chest with a closed fist and raising the other arm (also with closed fist) at a ninety-degree angle. The *Dua* position is accompanied by the words **"Adoration be to Amun-Ra,"** followed by the *Sahu* gesture accompanied with the words, **"Hail to the Lord of Heaven!"** The bodily gestures are performed alternately four times.

*Following this all present again **prostrate themselves before the Netjer**. This is a sign and symbol of total submission and adoration before the Netjer. The following is said:*

31

Homage to Amun-Ra, chief of the Netjeru, Sweet of Love,
who is established on the Great Seat!
I have placed myself on the floor in awe of you.
I embrace the earth before you as before the Lord of All
Powers.
I have come that I might kiss the earth,
that I might worship my Lord,
who illuminates by means of his flame
For I have seen his Strength;
I give praise to Amun-Ra,
For I have seen his Power.
His form is more distinguished than the Netjeru;
His arm is more powerful than the Netjeru.
I am pure, I am pure, I am pure, I am pure!

Everyone stands up.

*The Ritualist **holds in the palm of one hand the image of Ma'at** and
with **the other hand open and raised over the image** as if sheltering
it, repeats the following:*

I have come to you as Djehuty, whose two hands are joined
together under Ma'at. She comes to be with you, for she
is everywhere. You are provided with Ma'at. You move in
Ma'at, you live in Ma'at. She fills your body, she rests in
your head, she makes her seat upon your brow; the breath
of your body is of Ma'at, your heart does live in Ma'at. All
that you eat, all that you drink, all that you breathe is of
Ma'at. Djehuty presents Ma'at to you, his two hands are
upon her beauty before your face.

*The Ritualist **places the image of Ma'at near the divine statue.**
Then he/she holds up before the image of Amun a **pitcher of water***

and ***pours the water slowly into an offering bowl*** *as the following Utterance is recited:*

> This libation is for you, O Hidden One.
> This libation is for you, O Amun-Ra, Lord of all Eternity.
> I have brought to you this offering of pure water,
> That your heart may be refreshed.
> I have brought to you this Eye of Heru,
> Placing this at your feet.
> I present to you that which flows forth from you,
> That your heart shall continue to beat.
> For it is with you
> that all comes forth at the sound of the voice.

The offering bowl is placed on the altar. At this point the Ritualist ***lightly sprinkles sand on the floor in front of the altar*** *as the following is recited:*

> O Amun-Ra, who resides in Waset (Thebes),
> Take to yourself the Eye of Heru.
> You have rescued it,
> O Protector of that which is and that which is not.
> You have sprinkled with sand the Eye of Heru.

Lifting the wine offering *before the sacred image, the Ritualist repeats the following:*

> mn n.k irp irt ḥrw wȝḏt
> [*"mán-nik 'úrip írat ḥáru wá'ḏat"*; approximately pronounced *MAHN-neek OO- rip EE-raht HAH-roo WAH-jat*]

> *Take to yourself wine, the green Eye of Heru,*

which I offer to your *Ka*.[39]
O Amun-Ra, lord of everything that is,
strong of heart, festive of chest,
May you drink it; may your heart rejoice;
may anger be removed from your face.
It is pure.
[iw.w w'b pronounced "uwú wá'ib"; approximately oo-
WOO WAH-ib]

*The Ritualist **places myrrh on the fire** and **lifts up the smoking
incense** while at the same time he **lifts up the meat-offering** before
the Netjer, and says the following:*

The scent of myrrh is for your nose. It fills your nostrils;
your heart receives the meat-portions on its scent.[40]

*Slowly **elevating the food offerings four times** before the image of
the Netjer, the Ritualist repeats the following:*

I offer to Amun-Ra, Lord of Creation.
Yours is the sky,
yours is the earth,
yours is the Duat,
yours are the waters,
and yours are the air within them.
That which is made acclaims you without tiring.
O Protector of that which is and that which is not,

---

[39] Refer to pp. 92, 93, 99, and 105 in Mu-Chou Poo's *Wine and Wine
Offerings in Ancient Egypt* (London & New York: Kegan Paul International,
1995).

[40] Quoted in "Worship and Festivals in an Egyptian Temple," by H. W.
Fairman (publ. by The John Rylands Library, 1954), p. 191.

You support them as you create them,
Thus, their tribute is apportioned for your Ka.[41]
All life emanates from you.
All health emanates from you.
All stability emanates from you.
All good fortune emanates from you,
O Great One, Lord of All Eternity forever."

The Ritualist **places the food offering before the divine image,** *and then all present* **extend one hand, palm down, over the offerings** *and recite the following:*

May offerings of every kind come forth in abundance,
like the things which come forth from the mouth of the
Netjer.

piryá pírit ar ḫiráw mi purú:riat ma rá' ni náṭar. (4 times)
[approximately pronounced *peer-YA PEER-it ar khi-RAU mee pu-ROOR-iat ma RA nee NAH-tchar*]

May offerings of every kind come forth in abundance, like
the things that come forth from the mouth of the Netjer.

Holding the **Ankh** *before the Netjer the Ritualist says:*

Live, O Amun-Ra, Lord of the Netjeru,
live for all time and for eternity!

ʿánaḫ niḥáḫ ḍát.
[approximately pronounced *AH-nakh nee-HAH JAHT]*

---

[41] David Klotz, pp. 207-208.

The **Ankh is placed next to the image** of the Netjer.

*Holding the **Ib (the golden heart)** before the Netjer, the Ritualist says:*

Hail to you, O Amun-Ra, brilliant of visible forms, mysterious one, whose secrets cannot be known. I have brought to you your heart to set it in its place. Let me draw near to you with your heart, so that you may have pleasure through me, and so that by means of me you may have power over your body. Ascend, O Bull who ejaculates Nun, radiant, rejuvenating, equipped as a Netjer. Live, O Lord of the Phallus, live forever and ever!

*After placing the **Ib** near the sacred image, **everyone sings or chants** the hymn to Amun-Ra. Participants may wish to alternate the singing of verses.*

Amun-Ra, Lord of the heh-Netjeru who support the Netjeru,
Most primeval of the Netjeru,
Eldest of the primeval ones,
Builder of builders,
Renenutet of Renenutets,[42]
Khnum, who made the Creator Netjeru (i.e., the Ogdoad),
Effective of counsel,
Open and sharp of face,
Lord of all that exists,
Who foresees every event.

Bull of his Mother, Begetter of his Father,
Who destroyed A/pep when he manifests manifestations.

---

[42] the one who builds the bodies of those who build the bodies of people

Just as he wept mankind from his divine Eyes,
So did he spit out the Netjeru from his mouth.[43]

Amun-Ra is he whose odor is sweet as a Netjer,
Who magnified his cult image in order to carry his 'perfection,'
Having crafted his form to his desire.

He made himself gracious through the charm of his love,
His prestige, splendor, and dignity
are in excess of all the Netjeru.

He created himself through that which he created himself;
He conceived himself as the great composite image:
Fatherless, his own phallus engendered him:
Motherless, his own seed was pregnant with him.
The august Winged Scarab,
who makes himself emerge as a Netjer.
Father of Fathers, Mother of Mothers.[44]

Lord of Manifestations, plentiful of colors,
Who conceals himself in the Wedjat-Eye from his children.
Great Netjer that sits in the flame, who is in the midst of the flame.
O Amun-Ra, the Ithyphallic-Scarab, lord of the Wedjat-Eyes:
Fierce-of-iris" is your name.[45]

---

[43] Op. Cit., pp. 141-142.

[44] Op. Cit., p. 145.

[45] Op. Cit., p. 177. Amun-Ra combines the 'hiddenness' of Amun with the visibility of the sun (i.e., Ra). This very physical image points to a deep theological truth.

Richard J. Reidy

*At this point perform the **meditation or magical action** or, if it is a special feast, add the appropriate prayers.*

*Afterwards **all present back out of the Temple Chamber with heads slightly bowed** while the Ritualist performs the "**removing the foot.**"*

*With the **broom** the Ritualist, as the last person to exit, **ritually sweeps the area beginning at the altar**. (This is known as "removing the foot.") While performing this action the Ritualist recites the following:*

The distress that causes confusion has been driven away, and all the Netjeru are in harmony. I have given Heru his Eye; I have placed the Wedjat-Eye in the correct position. I have given Setekh his Testicles, so that the two lords are content through the work of my hands.

I know the sky, I know the earth;
I know Heru, I know Setekh.
Heru is appeased with his Eyes;
Setekh is appeased with his Testicles.
I am Djehuty, who reconciles the Netjeru,
who makes offerings in their correct form.

*The **double doors are solemnly closed** as the Ritualist says the following:*

Djehuty has come.
He has filled the Eye of Heru;
He has restored the Testicles of Setekh.
No evil shall enter this Temple.
Ptah has closed the door,
Djehuty has set it fast.
The door is closed, the door is set fast with the bolt.

*All **bow, touching the palms of their hands to their knees**.*

THE REVERSION OF OFFERINGS

*One ritualist and as many assistants as necessary enter the Temple Chamber a final time. **Lift up the offerings before the sacred image** as the ritualist says:*

> O Amun-Ra, your enemy[46] withdraws for you. Heru has turned himself to his Eye in its name of 'Reversion-of-Offerings.' I am Djehuty. I come to perform this rite for Amun-Ra, Lord of the Netjeru. These, your divine offerings revert, they revert to your servants for life, for stability, for health and for joy! O that the Eye of Heru may flourish for you eternally!

*Everyone withdraws, **carrying away all food offerings except for one loaf of bread and a bowl of pure water**. These last items remain until evening. If this ritual is celebrated after sunset, these items would also be removed.*

*After the candle has burned down, a servant-priest enters and closes the doors of the Kar-shrine. **Extinguishing the candle or oil lamp**, he/she exclaims:*

> This is the Eye of Heru by which you have become great, by which you live, and by which you have power, O Amun-Ra.

---

[46] Meat offerings held a two-fold meaning for the ancient priesthood. Since meat necessarily came from slain animals, it signified the defeated or slain enemies of the Netjer. At the same time, the meat offering represented the produce of the land which ultimately was a gift of the Netjeru.

This is the Eye of Heru which you consume and through which you enchant your body. The Wedjat-Eye now enters into the West, into Manu, but it shall return. Truly, the Eye of Heru returns in peace! [47]

---

[47] It is important to consume the food offerings after the ceremony. Water used should either be drunk or poured onto the earth. If it is mixed with natron, dilute it very greatly and then you can pour in onto the earth without harming any plantings.

The General Ritual for Anpu

All epithets of the god are based on those found in the *Lexikon der ägyptischen Götter und Götterbezeichnungen* (Dictionary of Egyptian Gods and God-Names"), eight volumes. The epithets are capitalized in order to facilitate identification.

Like members of the ancient priesthood, participants should be clothed in white linen. No item made of animal products such as leather or wool is to be worn. Linen represents a pristine product of the earth whereas leather and wool come from humankind's domination of the animals, a domination that becomes part of the "natural order" only *after* the First Time when the *Netjeru* and humans and animals lived in peace and harmony. Just as the Morning Ritual harkens back to that First Time (*Zep Tepi*), so every temple rite re-presents mythic prototypes that occurred "in the beginning," that is, in that time before time. Even the sandals worn by the god's servants were made of white papyrus. This avoidance of animal products by the priesthood fits well with the fact that the ritualist acts as a *Netjer* and verbally asserts that he or she is a *Netjer*.

As with all Egyptian rituals begin with your purification—washing of hands and cleansing of mouth with Natron. This preliminary rite helps us to lay aside the cares of the day and to become mindful of the fact that we will encounter a divine being. If Natron is not available, then use a natural sea salt in its place until you make your own Natron.

If two or more persons are participating, then one person, impersonating the Netjer *Djehuty,* **purifies each person by sprinkling each with water while exclaiming**:

> **I purify you with the water of all life and good fortune, all stability, all health and happiness.**[48]

Afterwards each person **rinses his mouth with Natron** *and places a small amount of Natron or sea salt in his mouth* while saying:

> **I wash my mouth; I chew natron so that I may extol the might of Anpu, Lord of Purification and Lord of the Scale.**[49]

Participants **assemble outside the Temple Chamber** *and begin by softly rattling sistra.*

This time—several minutes or more—is used to focus minds and intention so that distracting thoughts are left behind. The sound of the sistrum was said to placate the deity, purifying the atmosphere in preparation for encountering divinity. The sistrum was associated with Hutheru and also with her and Heru's son Ihy, and thus has connotations of joy, celebration, and dancing. According to Plutarch (A.D. 46-120), the sound of sistra was also reputed to drive away Setekh. But this was of very late date. It may have been that since by that time Setekh had been demonized, the

---

[48] Taken from Aylward M. Blackman's article "Purification (Egyptian)" in Hastings Encyclopedia 10/1918/ 476-82. This article is reprinted in Gods, Priests, and Men, Studies in the Religion of Pharaonic Egypt, edited by Alan B. Lloyd (Kegan Paul International, 1998), p. 9.

[49] Based on a temple inscription taken from the scholarly article "The Myth of Horus at Edfu—II" by A. M. Blackman and H. W. Fairman, appearing in Gods, Priests and Men, Studies in the Religion of Pharaonic Egypt (Kegan Paul International, 1998) p. 283.

general apotropaic function of the sistrum against evil entities was extended to include this *Netjer* as well.

*Standing **before the closed doors**, the Ritualist **recites the entrance spell**:*

UTTERANCE BEFORE THE CLOSED DOORS OF THE TEMPLE

*The ritualist **raises hands in adoration** (dua position-arms stretched out in front of the body and raised up to face level, with palms facing outward). The following shall be said:*

O you *Netjeru* of this Temple, you guardians of the great portal, great *Netjeru* of mysterious abode, who sanctify the god in his shrine, who consecrate his oblation, who receive the offerings in his presence in the Hall of the Ennead: I have made my way and I enter into your presence. I am one of you. I am Shu, the eldest son of his father, the senior *wab* servant-priest of Anpu. Do not repulse me on the *Netjer's* path. My feet are not impeded. I am not turned back from the court of the great portal so that I may conduct the divine service, that I may present offerings to him that made them, that I may give bread to Anpu. I have come on the way of the *Netjer*. I have not shown partiality in judgment. I have not consorted with the strong. I have not reproached the lowly. I have not stolen things. I have not diminished the constituents of the Eye of Ra. I have not disturbed the Balance. I have not tampered with the requirements of the Sacred Eye. O Council of the Great *Netjer* in this Temple, behold, I have come to you to offer Ma'at to the Great One of the *Duat* [netherworld], to content the Sound Eye for its lord. I am Shu; I flood his offering table. I present his offerings, Sekhmet consorting with me, that I may adore

43

Anpu at his festivals, that I may kiss the earth so great is his majesty, that I may endow his image with life. I am pure. I am purified.

*At this point the ritualist **opens the doors to the Temple Chamber**, or, if there are no doors, makes a gesture of opening unseen doors, and **steps forward as if crossing over a threshold**. The following is said:*

O you *Ba*-souls of *Hardai* [Cynopolis[50]] if you are strong, I am strong. If I am strong, you are strong. If your *Ka*-spirits are strong, my *Ka*-spirit is strong at the head of the living. As they are living so shall I live . . . . Anpu, the Splendid Jackal, has given to me life, stability, and serenity round about my members, which Djehuty has gathered together for life. I am Heru in the height of heaven, the beautiful one of awe, Lord of Victory, mighty one of awe, exalted one of the two plumes, great one in Thebes, I am pure.

*Enter, **close the double doors** and **stand in front of the Kar-shrine and altar**. All **bow, touching their hands to their knees**.*

All recite the following:

Awake, awake in peace, O Splendid Jackal.
May you awake in peace.
Awake, awake in peace, O Son of Ausir.
May you awake in peace.
Awake, awake in peace, O Perfect Protector of Your Father.
May you awake in peace.

---

[50] Cynopolis, the Greek name for the ancient Egyptian town of Hardai, located in the 17th Nome of Upper Egypt. It was the cult center for the Netjer Anpu.

Awake, awake in peace, O Anpu, Lord of the Hidden
Chamber.
May you awake in peace.

May you awake beautifully at the top of the morning,
through that which the entirety of Netjeru say to you.

*The ritualist slowly opens the two doors of the Kar-shrine housing the
sacred image. All others bow, touching their hands to their knees. The
following is said:*

The doors of the sky are open; the doors of the earth are
unlocked. This House is open for the Seer of Hearts. Let me
come forth as he shall come forth. Let me enter in as he
shall enter in. Anpu, First Lector Priest of the Seat of Ma'at
is exalted upon his Great Seat. The Great Company of the
Netjeru are exalted upon their seat.

I have seen the Netjer, and the Netjer sees me. The Netjer
rejoices at seeing me. I have gazed upon the statue of the
Guardian of the Duat, the sacred image of the Reckoner of
Hearts.[51]

Right hand on left shoulder of statue; left hand on right wrist of statue:

Djehuty has come to you. Awake when you hear his words. I
have come as the envoy of Atum. My two arms are upon you
like those of Heru. My two hands are upon you like those

---

[51] Based on the temple text found in "Worship and Festivals in an Egyptian
Temple," a lecture by H. W. Fairman (publ. by The John Rylands Library,
1954), p. 180.

of Djehuty. My fingers are upon you like those of Heka.
Homage be to you. I am a living servant of Anpu.

*The Ritualist holds up the **bowl of water** in which he/she will be mixing the Natron. The following is said:*

O water may you remove all evil,
As Ra who bathes in the Lake of Rushes,
May Heru wash my flesh,
May Djehuty cleanse my feet,
May Shu lift me up and Nut take my hand!
May Setekh be my strength, and may Sekhmet be my healing!
And may Amun-Ra be my life and my prospering!

*The bowl of water is set aside and the **container of Natron is lifted up**. The following is said:*

It is pure, it is pure.
My Natron is the Natron of Heru,
and the Natron of Heru is my Natron.
My Natron is the Natron of Setekh,
and the Natron of Setekh is my Natron.
My Natron is the Natron of Djehuty,
and the Natron of Djehuty is my Natron.
My Natron is the Natron of Geb,
and the Natron of Geb is my Natron.

My mouth is the mouth of a milking calf
on the day that I was born.

Four pinches of Natron are mixed into the water as this Utterance is recited:

I give you essential water, a tide in your time.
I bring the flood waters to purify your sanctuary,
O Powerful One of the West.
I bring you the flood waters
to purify your Temple and your statue in its place,
the primordial water that purifies as in the First Time!

The Ritualist places an index finger into the water and moves it in a circular direction four times as the following is said:

Anpu, Son of Hesat[52] and Offspring of the Mnevis Bull, does purify this water;
Anpu, Foremost of the Pure Place, does cleanse this water;
Anpu, Who Drives out Enemies, does sanctify this water;
Anpu himself does endow this water with power and with life.

The Bowl of Natron-infused water is then taken up and the Ritualist sprinkles this lightly in front of and around the statue or image of Anpu, applying some water to the base of the image, as the Utterance is recited:

I come close to you, O Lord of Purification.
I bring the water of rejuvenation
that flows from the Two Caverns.

---

[52] Hesat is a goddess taking the form of a white cow, with sun disk between her horns. She provides humankind with milk (referred to as "the beer of Hesat"). In Heliopolis she and Ra in his earthly animal form as the Mnevis Bull, were worshipped as the parents of Anpu.

I sprinkle the water,
purifying your image and your Temple from all impurity!

*The Ritualist **picks up the bowl of Natron** and **sprinkles a small amount in each of the four directions** as the following is recited:*

The *Netjer* Anpu himself does cleanse and purify this,
his Temple to the South.
The *Netjer* Anpu himself does cleanse and purify this,
his Temple to the North.
The *Netjer* Anpu himself does cleanse and purify this,
his Temple to the West.
The *Netjer* Anpu himself does cleanse and purify this,
his Temple to the East.

*Replacing the Natron on the altar, the Ritualist takes up **the bowl of water, sprinkling a small amount in each of the four directions.** The following Utterance is recited:*

The *Netjer* Anpu himself does sanctify and consecrate this,
his Temple to the South.
The *Netjer* Anpu himself does sanctify and consecrate this,
his Temple to the North.
The *Netjer* Anpu himself does sanctify and consecrate this,
his Temple to the West.
The *Netjer* Anpu himself does sanctify and consecrate this,
his Temple to the East.

The Temple of the *Netjer* Anpu is established.
It is established for millions of years.

*The Ritualist returns to the altar and **lights the candle or oil lamp** while the following is said:*

Come, come in peace, O glorious Eye of Heru,
Be strong and renew your youth in peace.
For the flame shines like Ra on the double horizon.
The enemies of Ra are defeated. They are defeated.
I am pure, I am pure, I am pure, I am pure.

*The Ritualist **places incense on the burner** and **censes each sacred image** beginning with the statue of the Netjer while the following is recited:*

The fire is laid, the fire shines;
The incense is laid on the fire, the incense shines.
    Your perfume comes to me, O Incense;
    May my perfume come to you, O Incense.
Your perfume comes to me, you *Netjeru*;
May my perfume come to you, You *Netjeru*.
    May I be with you, you *Netjeru*;
    May you be with me, you *Netjeru*.
May I live with you, you *Netjeru*;
May you live with me, you *Netjeru*.
    I love you, you *Netjeru*;
    May you love me, you *Netjeru*.

*Standing in front of the image of Anpu the Ritualist **offers the burning incense** and says:*

Take the incense, O Great One of the *Duat* [netherworld].
Its essence is for you.
Its smoke permeates your shrine, bringing life!

Take the incense,
Its essence is for you.
Your Majesty is appeased with the incense.
This Eye of Heru,
This essence of the Eye of Heru comes to you.

At this point the following is said:

Hail to you, Anpu, True Guardian of the *Duat* [netherworld],
O Lord of the Scale and Balance Keeper,
you lead the dead before the Judge.
You place the heart on the pan of the Scale.
Truly you are the Reckoner of Hearts.
May you be present for me on the day of my burial,
O Lord of the Necropolis.
May you find my heart in balance with the feather of Ma'at.
May you find my soul blameless
on the day of the weighing of the heart.
May you take my hand and lead me forth to the throne of
Ausir.
O Powerful One, hear me now and watch over me in peace.
In peace.

*The Ritualist places **more incense on the charcoal** and again and
again **slowly raises and lowers the incense cup** as the following is
recited:*

O Anpu, may you advance with your *Ka.*
O Powerful One, the arm of your *Ka* is before you,
The arm of your *Ka* is behind you.
O Great Strong One of the *Wedjat*-Eye,
the foot of your *Ka* is before you,
The foot of your *Ka* is behind you.

O True Guardian of the Gate of the *Duat*,
this incense is offered to you,
May your face be filled as this essence spreads itself
over you.

All present **perform the Henu Rite** *— Embrace the Earth, the Fourfold Salute to the God, Embrace the Earth. The bodily gestures are performed alternately four times.*

For Embracing the Earth, all present prostrate themselves, face down, upon the floor. During the Fourfold Salute, all present rise upon one knee, and alternately raise their hands and arms into the *Dua* (praise) position with palms facing outward, followed by the *Sahu* (obedience) gesture, made by striking the chest with a closed fist and raising the other arm (also with closed fist) at a ninety-degree angle. The *Dua* position is accompanied by the words **"Adoration be to Anpu,"** followed by the *Sahu* gesture accompanied with the words, **"Hail to the Guardian of the *Duat*!"** The bodily gestures are performed alternately four times.

Following this all present again **prostrate themselves before the divine image.** *This is a sign and symbol of total submission and adoration before the Netjer. The following is said:*

Homage to Anpu, Victorious of Arm,
who is established on the Great Seat!
I have placed myself on the floor in awe of you.
I embrace the earth before you
as before the Reckoner of Hearts.
I have come that I might kiss the earth,
that I might worship my Lord,
the Perfect Protector of His Father Ausir.
For I have seen his Strength;

I give praise to Anpu,
For I have seen his Power.
His form is more distinguished than the *Netjeru*;
His arm is more powerful than the *Netjeru*.
I am pure, I am pure, I am pure, I am pure!

Everyone stands up.

The Ritualist holds in the palm of one hand **the image of Ma'at** *and* **with the other hand open and raised over the image as if sheltering it,** *repeats the following:*

I have come to you as Djehuty, whose two hands are joined together under Ma'at. She comes to be with you, for she is everywhere. You are provided with Ma'at. You move in Ma'at, you live in Ma'at. She fills your body, she rests in your head, she makes her seat upon your brow; the breath of your body is of Ma'at, your heart does live in Ma'at. All that you eat, all that you drink, all that you breathe is of Ma'at. Djehuty presents Ma'at to you, his two hands are upon her beauty before your face.

The Ritualist places the image of Ma'at near the divine statue. Then he/she holds up before the image of Amon a **pitcher of water** *and* **pours the water slowly into an offering bowl** *as the following Utterance is recited:*

This libation is for you, O Lord of Libations.
This libation is for you, O Anpu, Who Tests the Heart.
I have brought to you this offering of water,
That your heart may be refreshed.
I have brought to you this Eye of Heru,
Placing this at your feet.

I present to you that which flows forth from you,
That your heart shall continue to beat.
For it is with you that all comes forth at the sound of the
voice.

The offering bowl is placed on the altar. At this point the Ritualist **lightly sprinkles sand on the floor in front of the altar** *as the following is recited:*

O Anpu, who resides in *Rosetau* [the necropolis near the Giza pyramids],
Take to yourself the Eye of Heru.
You have rescued it, O Powerful One of the West.
You have sprinkled with sand the Eye of Heru.

Lifting the wine offering *before the sacred image, the Ritualist repeats the following:*

mn n.k irp irt ḥrw wȝdt
["*mán-nik 'úrip írat ḥáru wá'ḏat*"; approximately pronounced *MAHN-neek OO- rip EE-raht HAH-roo WAH-jat*]

Take to yourself wine, the green Eye of Heru,
which I offer to your *Ka*. [53]
O Beloved One, how beautiful is your beauty!
May you drink it; may your heart rejoice;
may anger be removed from your face.
It is pure.

---

[53] Refer to pp. 92, 93, 99, and 105 in Mu-Chou Poo's *Wine and Wine Offerings in Ancient Egypt* (London & New York: Kegan Paul International, 1995).

[*iw.w w'b* pronounced *"uwú wá'ib"*; approximately *oo-WOO WAH-ib*]

The Ritualist places myrrh on the fire and lifts up the smoking incense while at the same time he lifts up the meat-offering before the Netjer, and says the following:

The scent of myrrh is for your nose. It fills your nostrils; your heart receives the meat-portions on its scent.[54]

Slowly elevating the food offerings four times before the image of the Netjer, the Ritualist repeats the following:

I offer to Anpu, Lord of Offering.
All life emanates from you,
All health emanates from you,
All stability emanates from you,
All good fortune emanates from you,
O Beloved One, forever.

The Ritualist places the food offering before the divine image, and then all present extend one hand, palm down, over the offerings and recite the following:

May offerings of every kind come forth in abundance,
like the things which come forth from the mouth of the
Netjer.

piryá pírit ar ḫiráw mi purú:riat ma rá' ni nátar. (4 times)
[approximately pronounced *peer-YA PEER-it ar khi-RAU mee pu-ROOR-iat ma RA nee NAH-tchar*]

---

[54] Quoted in "Worship and Festivals in an Egyptian Temple," by H. W. Fairman (publ. by The John Rylands Library, 1954), p. 191.

May offerings of every kind come forth in abundance, like the things that come forth from the mouth of the Netjer.

*Holding the **Ankh** before the image of Anpu, the Ritualist says:*

Live, O Anpu, Great One of Power,
live for all time and for eternity!

ʿánaḫ niḥáḥ ḏát
[approximately pronounced *AH-nakh nee-HAH JAHT*]

*The **Ankh** is placed next to the Netjer.*

*Holding the **Ib (the golden heart)** before the Netjer, the Ritualist says:*

Hail to you, O Anpu, Reckoner of Hearts. I have brought to you your heart to set it in its place. Let me draw near to you with your heart, so that you may have pleasure through me, and so that by means of me you may have power over your body. Ascend, O Guardian of the *Duat* [netherworld], radiant, rejuvenating, equipped as a *Netjer*. Live, O Powerful One of the West, live forever and ever!

*After placing the **Ib** near the sacred image, **everyone sings or chants** the hymn to Anpu. Participants may wish to alternate the singing of verses.*

Praise be to you, O Splendid Jackal.
You are the True Guardian of the Gate of the *Duat*.
You are the Aggressive *Ba*
and the Protection of your Father Ausir.
May you protect me from the Eater of the Dead.
May I receive the pectoral from your hands,

and may you make my body divine in the God's Booth
so that I might eat loaves in the presence of the *Netjer*
by the Great Staircase of the Lord of the Ennead.

May I turn from there to the place where the *Netjer* is
in the midst of the high tribunal of judges.
May I move about freely among them,
being a friend to the Followers of Heru.
May I come and go unhindered
and not be turned back from the doors of the otherworld.
May the gates of heaven be opened to me,
and the very doorbolts unlock by themselves.
May I enter the Hall of the Two Truths
and may the *Netjer* who is in it honor me.

May I go forth from the tomb each dawn
and find my way back each evening.
May a taper be kindled for me at night
until the sun shines upon my breast.
Let it be said to me,
'Welcome, welcome to your house of the Ever-Living One!'

May I gaze upon Ra in the circuit of heaven
and glimpse Amun when he shines.
May I be mindful of beauty every day,
may all that impedes me be driven to earth.
May I spend eternity in gladness of heart,
esteemed by the *Netjer* within me.

May my heart be with me; it will never abandon me,
and may my provisions endure in their place.
O Anpu Who Restores and Makes Proficient the Body,

may you make perfect my body so that I may join those
True-of-Voice in the Great Hall of Ausir.[55]

At this point perform the **meditation or magical action** *or, if it is a special feast, add the appropriate prayers.*

Afterwards **all present back out of the Temple Chamber with heads slightly bowed** *while the Ritualist performs the* **"removing the foot."**

With the **broom** *the Ritualist, as the last person to exit,* **ritually sweeps the area beginning at the altar.** *(This is known as* **"removing the foot.")** *While performing this action the Ritualist recites the following:*

The distress that causes confusion has been driven away, and all the Netjeru are in harmony. I have given Heru his Eye; I have placed the Wedjat-Eye in the correct position. I have given Setekh his Testicles, so that the two lords are content through the work of my hands.

I know the sky, I know the earth;
I know Heru, I know Setekh.
Heru is appeased with his Eyes;
Setekh is appeased with his Testicles.
I am Djehuty, who reconciles the Netjeru,
who makes offerings in their correct form.

The **double doors are solemnly closed** *as the Ritualist says the following:*

---

[55] The preceding paragraphs are based on a prayer in *Hymns, Prayers, and Songs: An Anthology of Ancient Egyptian Lyric Poetry* by John L. Foster (Atlanta, Georgia: Scholars Press, 1995), pp. 128-9.

Djehuty has come.
He has filled the Eye of Heru;
He has restored the Testicles of Setekh.
No evil shall enter this Temple.
Ptah has closed the door,
Djehuty has set it fast.
The door is closed, the door is set fast with the bolt.

*All **bow, touching the palms of their hands to their knees**.*

THE REVERSION OF OFFERINGS

*One priest or priestess and as many assistants as necessary enter the Temple Chamber a final time. While he/she and any assistants **lift up the offerings** before the sacred image the ritualist shall say:*

O Anpu, your enemy[56] withdraws for you. Heru has turned himself to his Eye in its name of 'Reversion-of-Offerings.' I am Djehuty. I come to perform this rite for Anpu, Lord of Offering. These, your divine offerings revert, they revert to your servants for life, for stability, for health and for joy! O that the Eye of Heru may flourish for you eternally!

*Everyone withdraws, **carrying away all food offerings except for one loaf of bread and a bowl of pure water**. These last items remain until evening. If this ritual is celebrated after sunset, these items would also be removed.*

---

[56] Meat offerings held a two-fold meaning for the ancient priesthood. Since meat necessarily came from slain animals, it signified the defeated or slain enemies of the Netjer. At the same time, the meat offering represented the produce of the land which ultimately was a gift of the Netjeru.

*After the candle has burned down, a servant-priest enters and closes the doors of the Kar-shrine. **Extinguishing the candle or oil lamp,** he/she exclaims:*

This is the Eye of Heru by which you have become great, by which you live, and by which you have power, O Anpu. This is the Eye of Heru which you consume and through which you enchant your body. The *Wedjat*-Eye now enters into the West, into *Manu*, but it shall return. Truly, the Eye of Heru returns in peace![57]

---

[57] It is important to consume the food offerings after the ceremony. Water used should either be drunk or poured onto the earth. If it is mixed with Natron, dilute it very greatly and then you can pour in onto the bare earth.

General Ritual for Aset

All epithets for this *Netjeret* (goddess) as well as all major hymns to her come from *Hymns to Isis in Her Temple at Philae*, by Louis V. Zabkar (Brandeis University Press, 1988) as well as other scholarly sources including the eight-volume *Lexikon der ägyptischen Götter und Götterbezeichnungen (Dictionary of Egyptian Gods and God-Names)*. No attempt has been made to fabricate or "make up" epithets for this great *Netjeret*. The ancient sources are sufficiently rich in themselves. The inscriptions at the temple at Philae are of late date, and, consequently, some show a marked syncretistic tendency to identify Aset with all other *Netjerut* (goddesses), ultimately claiming that all *Netjerut* are one. This is in contradiction to the genuinely polytheistic theology of Pharaonic Egypt. Therefore, I have been very careful not to repeat this tendency in the present ritual. Aset is magnificent enough on her own. She does not need an inflated, syncretistic approach in ritual.

Please do not feel that you must either do the entire ritual or nothing at all. If certain elements of the ritual speak to you and have special meaning, then please just do those particular elements. However, in my own experience I have found that as I repeat the ritual a few times, I am pleasantly surprised with 'aha!' moments where some new insight comes to light. The ritual's words have special meaning and power, and so may not be evident on first reading. Be patient and I believe the *Netjeru* will reward your effort.

Special Food Offering for Aset: milk. The offerings also should include the regular food and beverage offerings.

Like members of the ancient priesthood, participants should be clothed in white linen. No item made of animal products such as leather or wool is to be worn. Linen represents a pristine product of the earth whereas leather and wool come from humankind's domination of the animals, a domination that becomes part of the "natural order" only *after* the First Time when the *Netjeru* and humans and animals lived in peace and harmony. Just as the Morning Ritual harkens back to that First Time (*Zep Tepi*), so every temple rite re-presents mythic prototypes that occurred "in the beginning," that is, in that time before time. Even the sandals worn by the god's servants were made of white papyrus. This avoidance of animal products by the priesthood fits well with the fact that the ritualist acts as a *Netjer* and verbally asserts that he or she is a *Netjer*.

As with all Egyptian rituals begin with your purification—washing of hands and cleansing of mouth with Natron. This preliminary rite helps us to lay aside the cares of the day and to become mindful of the fact that we will encounter a divine being. If Natron is not available, then use a natural sea salt in its place until you make your own Natron.

If two or more persons are participating, then one person, impersonating the Netjer *Djehuty,* **purifies each person by sprinkling each with water while exclaiming:**

I purify you with the water of all life and good fortune, all stability, all health and happiness.[58]

---

[58] Taken from Aylward M. Blackman's article "Purification (Egyptian)" in Hastings Encyclopedia 10/1918/ 476-82. This article is reprinted in Gods, Priests, and Men, Studies in the Religion of Pharaonic Egypt, edited by Alan B. Lloyd (Kegan Paul International, 1998), p. 9.

*Afterwards each person **rinses his mouth** and **places a small amount of Natron or sea salt in his mouth** while saying:*

I wash my mouth; I chew natron so that I may extol the might of Aset, the Pure One and Mother of Heru.[59]

*Participants **assemble outside the Temple Chamber** and begin by **softly rattling sistra**.*

This time—several minutes or more—is used to focus minds and intention so that distracting thoughts are left behind. The sound of the sistrum was said to placate the deity, purifying the atmosphere in preparation for encountering divinity. The sistrum was associated with Hutheru and also with her and Heru's son Ihy, and thus has connotations of joy, celebration, and dancing. According to Plutarch (A.D. 46-120), the sound of sistra was also reputed to drive away Setekh. But this was of very late date. It may have been that since by that time Setekh had been demonized, the general apotropaic function of the sistrum against evil entities was extended to include this *Netjer* as well.

*Standing **before the closed doors**, the Ritualist **recites the entrance spell**:*

UTTERANCE BEFORE THE CLOSED DOORS OF THE TEMPLE

*The ritualist **raises hands in adoration** (dua position-arms stretched out in front of the body and raised up to face level, with palms facing outward). The following shall be said:*

---

[59] Based on a temple inscription taken from "The Myth of Horus at Edfu—II" by A. M. Blackman and H. W. Fairman, appearing in Gods, Priests and Men, Studies in the Religion of Pharaonic Egypt (Kegan Paul International, 1998) p. 283.

O you Netjeru of this Temple, you guardians of the great portal, great Netjeru of mysterious abode, who sanctify the Netjeret (goddess) in her shrine, who consecrate her oblation, who receive the offerings in her presence in the Hall of the Ennead: I have made my way and I enter into your presence. I am one of you. I am Shu, the eldest son of his father, the senior wab servant-priest of Aset. Do not repulse me on the Netjeret's path. My feet are not impeded. I am not turned back from the court of the great portal so that I may conduct the divine service, that I may present offerings to her that made them, that I may give bread to Aset. I have come on the way of the Netjeret. I have not shown partiality in judgment. I have not consorted with the strong. I have not reproached the lowly. I have not stolen things. I have not diminished the constituents of the Eye of Ra. I have not disturbed the Balance. I have not tampered with the requirements of the Sacred Eye. O Council of the Great Netjeret in this Temple, behold, I have come to you to offer Ma'at to the Queen of the Netjeru, to content the Sound Eye for its mistress. I am Shu; I flood her offering table. I present her offerings, Sekhmet consorting with me, that I may adore Aset at her festivals, that I may kiss the earth so great is her majesty, that I may endow her image with life. I am pure. I am purified.

At this point the ritualist **opens the doors to the Temple Chamber,** *or, if there are no doors,* **makes a gesture of opening unseen doors,** *and* **steps forward as if crossing over a threshold.** *The following is said:*

O you Ba-souls of Pi-lak (i.e., Philae[60]), if you are strong, I am strong. If I am strong, you are strong. If your Ka-spirits

---

[60] Pi-lak (Greek, Philae) is the cult center for Aset just beyond the southernmost border of Egypt..

are strong, my Ka-spirit is strong at the head of the living. As they are living so shall I live . . . . Sekhmet, the great Netjeret, beloved of Ptah, has given to me life, stability, and serenity round about my members, which Djehuty has gathered together for life. I am Heru in the height of heaven, the beautiful one of awe, Lord of Victory, mighty one of awe, exalted one of the two plumes, great one in Abdju (Abydos) I am pure.

Enter, close the double doors and stand in front of the Kar-shrine and altar. All bow, touching their hands to their knees.

All recite the following:

Awake, awake in peace, O Aset, Lady of Heaven.
May you awake in peace.
Awake, awake in peace, O Mistress of the Universe.
May you awake in peace.
Awake, awake in peace, O Lady of Life.
May you awake in peace.
Awake, awake in peace, O Aset,
Great Royal Spouse of Wennofer.
May you awake in peace.

May you awake beautifully at the top of the morning,
through that which the entirety of Netjeru say to you.

*The ritualist **slowly opens the two doors of the Kar-shrine** housing the sacred image. All others **bow, touching their hands to their knees**. The following is said:*

The doors of the sky are open; the doors of the earth are unlocked. This House is open for its Mistress. Let me come forth as she shall come forth. Let me enter in as she shall enter in. Aset, Lady of Heaven, Beloved of Ausir, is exalted upon her Great Seat. The Great Company of the Netjeru are exalted upon their seat.

I have seen the Netjeret, and the Netjeret sees me. The Netjeret rejoices at seeing me. I have gazed upon the statue of the Lady of Life, the sacred image of the Queen of Heaven.[61]

Right hand on left shoulder of statue; left hand on right wrist of statue:

Djehuty has come to you.
Awake when you hear his words.
I have come as the envoy of Atum.
My two arms are upon you like those of Heru.
My two hands are upon you like those of Djehuty.
My fingers are upon you like those of Anpu.
Homage be to you.
I am a living servant of Aset.

*The Ritualist holds up the **bowl of water** in which he/she will be mixing the Natron. The following is said:*

O water may you remove all evil,
As Ra who bathes in the Lake of Rushes,
May Heru wash my flesh,
May Djehuty cleanse my feet,

---

[61] Based on a passage in "Worship and Festivals in an Egyptian Temple," a lecture by H. W. Fairman (publ. by The John Rylands Library, 1954), p. 180.

May Shu lift me up and Nut take my hand!
May Setekh be my strength, and may Sekhmet be my healing!
And may Amun-Ra be my life and my prospering!

The bowl of water is set aside and the container of **Natron** *is lifted up. The following is said:*

It is pure, it is pure.
My Natron is the Natron of Heru,
and the Natron of Heru is my Natron.
My Natron is the Natron of Setekh,
and the Natron of Setekh is my Natron.
My Natron is the Natron of Djehuty,
and the Natron of Djehuty is my Natron.
My Natron is the Natron of Geb,
and the Natron of Geb is my Natron.

My mouth is the mouth of a milking calf
on the day that I was born.

Four pinches of Natron are mixed into the water as this Utterance is recited:

I give you essential water, a tide in your time.
I bring the flood waters to purify your sanctuary.
I bring you the flood waters
to purify your Temple and your statue in its place,
the primordial water that purifies as in the First Time!

The Ritualist **places an index finger into the water** *and* **moves it in a circular direction four times** *as the following is said:*

Aset, the Netjer's Mother, does purify this water;
Aset, Lady of Heaven, does cleanse this water;
Aset, Queen of the Netjeru, does sanctify this water;
Aset herself, Great of Magic,
    does endow this water with power and with life.

*The **Bowl of Natron-infused water** is then taken up and the Ritualist sprinkles this lightly in front of and around the statue or image of Aset, applying some water to the base of the image, as the Utterance is recited:*

I come close to You, O Pure One, Lady of the Waters of Life.
I bring the water of rejuvenation
that flows from the Two Caverns.
I sprinkle the water,
    purifying your image and your Temple from all impurity!

*The Ritualist picks up the bowl of **Natron** and **sprinkles a small amount in each of the four directions** as the following is recited:*

The Netjeret Aset herself does cleanse and purify this,
her Temple to the South.
The Netjeret Aset herself does cleanse and purify this,
her Temple to the North.
The Netjeret Aset herself does cleanse and purify this,
her Temple to the West.
The Netjeret Aset herself does cleanse and purify this,
her Temple to the East.

*Replacing the Natron on the altar, the Ritualist takes up the bowl of **water, sprinkling a small amount in each of the four directions.** The following Utterance is recited:*

The Netjeret Aset herself does sanctify and consecrate this,
her Temple to the South.
The Netjeret Aset herself does sanctify and consecrate this,
her Temple to the North.
The Netjeret Aset herself does sanctify and consecrate this,
her Temple to the West.
The Netjeret Aset herself does sanctify and consecrate this,
her Temple to the East.
The Temple of the Netjeret Aset is established.
It is established for millions of years.

*The Ritualist returns to the altar and **lights the candle or oil lamp**
while the following is said:*

Come, come in peace, O glorious Eye of Heru,
Be strong and renew your youth in peace.
For the flame shines like Ra on the double horizon.
The enemies of Ra are defeated. They are defeated.
I am pure, I am pure, I am pure, I am pure.

*The Ritualist **places incense on the burner** and **censes each sacred
image** beginning with the statue of the Netjeret while the following is
recited:*

The fire is laid, the fire shines;
The incense is laid on the fire, the incense shines.
   Your perfume comes to me, O Incense;
   May my perfume come to you, O Incense.
Your perfume comes to me, you Netjeru;
May my perfume come to you, You Netjeru.
   May I be with you, you Netjeru;
   May you be with me, you Netjeru.

May I live with you, you Netjeru;
May you live with me, you Netjeru.
   I love you, you Netjeru;
   May you love me, you Netjeru.

Standing in front of the image of Aset the Ritualist **offers the burning incense** *and says:*

Take the incense,
Its essence is for you, O Lady of Heaven and Earth.
Its smoke permeates your shrine, bringing life!
Take the incense,
Its essence is for you.
Your Majesty is appeased with the incense.
This Eye of Heru,
This essence of the Eye of Heru comes to you.

At this point the following is said:

Hail to you, Aset, Great of Magical Power,
The eldest in the womb of her mother, Nut,
Mighty in Heaven before Ra.

Adoration to you in the night-barque,
jubilation to you in the day-barque,
You who gave birth to Heru.

I have come before you, Lady of Life,
On this day on which you have gloriously appeared,
To tie onto you the Uraeus-Diadem,
To fasten onto you the Mighty One.

May your Ka be in peace, O Lady of Life,
On this day on which you have gloriously appeared,
You whom the Netjeru have propitiated.

O beloved of Ra who are in his barque,
Repelling A/pep with the effectiveness of your utterance,
Behold, I have come before you,
So that, purified, I may adore your beauty.[62]

May you come to your House to join your Image,
Your radiance inundating our faces,
Like the radiance of Ra when he shows himself in the
morning.

You are the Female Heru, beloved of the great Heru,
Mother of Heru, created by Atum,
Great Royal Spouse, united with Ra,
Who protects her brother Ausir.

O Aset the Great, Netjer's Mother, Lady of Pi-lak [Philae],
Mother of Heru, daughter of Ra, beloved of his very heart,
Lady of appearances, Worshipped in your sanctuaries.

Make enduring our years.
Establish us like the Falcon upon the Serekh.
Make us to endure eternally, like Ra.[63]

---

[62] From Hymn VIII, in Hymns to Isis in Her Temple at Philae, by Louis V. Zabkar (Brandeis University Press, 1988), p. 119.
[63] Op. Cit., from Hymn V, pp. 58-59.

*The Ritualist **places more incense on the charcoal** and again and again **slowly raises and lowers the incense cup** as the following is recited:*

> O Aset, may you advance with your Ka.
> O Lady of love, the arm of your Ka is before you,
> The arm of your Ka is behind you.
> O Queen of Heaven, the foot of your Ka is before you,
> The foot of your Ka is behind you.
> O Beautiful Aset, this incense is offered to you,
> May your face be filled as this essence spreads itself over you.

*All present **perform the Henu Rite**—Embrace the Earth, the Fourfold Salute to the God, Embrace the Earth. The bodily gestures are performed alternately four times.*

For Embracing the Earth, all present prostrate themselves, face down, upon the floor. During the Fourfold Salute, all present rise upon one knee, and alternately raise their hands and arms into the *Dua* (praise) position with palms facing outward, followed by the *Sahu* (obedience) gesture, made by striking the chest with a closed fist and raising the other arm (also with closed fist) at a ninety-degree angle. The *Dua* position is accompanied by the words **"Adoration be to Aset,"** followed by the *Sahu* gesture accompanied with the words, **"Hail to the Mother of Heru!"** The bodily gestures are performed alternately four times.

*All present perform the **Henu Rite**—Embrace the Earth, the Fourfold Salute to Aset, Embrace the Earth—and then the following is said:*

> Homage be to Aset, who opens the New Year, Sopdet,
> who is established on the Great Seat!

I have placed myself on the floor in awe of you.
I embrace the earth before you
as before the Lady of Heaven and Earth.
I have come that I might kiss the earth,
that I might worship my Mistress,
for I have seen her Beauty;
I give praise to Aset,
for I have seen her Power.
Her form is more distinguished than the Netjeru;
Her arm is more powerful than the Netjeru.
I am pure, I am pure, I am pure, I am pure!

Everyone stands up.

*The Ritualist holds **in the palm of one hand the image of Ma'at** and **with the other hand open and raised over the image as if sheltering it**, repeats the following:*

I have come to you as Djehuty, whose two hands are joined together under Ma'at. She comes to be with you, for she is everywhere. You are provided with Ma'at. You move in Ma'at, you live in Ma'at. She fills your body, she rests in your head, she makes her seat upon your brow; the breath of your body is of Ma'at, your heart does live in Ma'at. All that you eat, all that you drink, all that you breathe is of Ma'at. Djehuty presents Ma'at to you, his two hands are upon her beauty before your face.

*The Ritualist places the image of Ma'at near the divine statue. Then he/she holds up before the image of Aset a **pitcher of water** and **pours the water slowly into an offering bowl** as the following Utterance is recited:*

This libation is for you, O Lady of Love.

This libation is for you, O Aset.

I have brought to you this offering of water,

That your heart may be refreshed.

I have brought to you this Eye of Heru,

Placing this at your feet.

I present to you that which flows forth from you,

That your heart shall continue to beat.

For it is with you that all comes forth at the sound of the voice.

The offering bowl is placed on the altar. At this point the Ritualist lightly sprinkles sand on the floor in front of the altar as the following is recited:

O Aset, who resides in Pi-lak, [Philae]

Take to yourself the Eye of Heru.

You have rescued it, O Mistress of the Universe.

You have sprinkled with sand the Eye of Heru.

*Lifting the **offering of milk**, the following is said:*

Take to yourself this white and sweet milk, created by your mother Nut.

May you live on it, may you be healthy on account of it. May your body be refreshed every day.[64]

*Lifting the **wine offering** before the sacred image, the Ritualist repeats the following:*

---

[64] Amr, Aber, The Central Hall in the Egyptian Temples of the Ptolemaic Period, Durham theses, Durham University. (2009) Available at Durham E-Theses Online: http://etheses.dur.ac.uk/88/ This offering formula occurs in the central hall of the temple at Edfu. See p. 454 in the dissertation.

mn n.t irp irt ḥrw wȝdt

["mán-niṯ 'úrip írat ḥáru wá'ḏat"; approximately pronounced
MAHN-neetch OO-rip EE-raht HAH-roo WAH-jat]

Take to yourself wine, the green Eye of Heru,
which I offer to your Ka.[65]
O Queen, how beautiful is your beauty!
May you drink it; may your heart rejoice;
may anger be removed from your face.
It is pure.

[iw.w w'b pronounced "uwú wá'ib"; approximately oo-WOO
WAH-ib]

The Ritualist **places myrrh on the fire** *and* **lifts up the smoking
incense while at the same time he lifts up the meat-offering** *before
the Netjeret, and says the following:*

The scent of myrrh is for your nose. It fills your nostrils;
your heart receives the meat-portions on its scent.[66]

Slowly **elevating the food offerings four times** *before the image of
the Netjeret, the Ritualist repeats the following:*

I offer to Aset, Foremost of Netjerut (goddesses).
All life emanates from you,
All health emanates from you,
All stability emanates from you,
All good fortune emanates from you,

---

[65] Refer to pp. 92, 93, 99, and 105 in Mu-Chou Poo's Wine and Wine
Offerings in Ancient Egypt (London & New York: Kegan Paul International,
1995).

[66] Quoted in "Worship and Festivals in an Egyptian Temple," by H. W.
Fairman (publ. by The John Rylands Library, 1954), p. 191.

O Aset, Lady of Life, forever.

The Ritualist places the food offering before the divine image, and then all present extend one hand, palm down, over the offerings and recite the following:

May offerings of every kind come forth in abundance, like the things which come forth from the mouth of the Netjeret.

piryá pírit ar ḫiráw mi purú:riat ma rá' ni naṯárat. (4 times) [approximately pronounced *peer-YA PEER-it ar khi-RAU mee pu-ROOR-iat ma RA nee nah-TCHAR-at*]

May offerings of every kind come forth in abundance, like the things that come forth from the mouth of the Netjeret.

*Holding the **Ankh** before the Netjeret, the Ritualist says:*

Live, O Aset, Lady of Love, live for all time and for eternity!

ʿánaḫ niḥáḫ ḏát. [approximately pronounced *AH-nakh nee-HAH JAHT*]

*The **Ankh** is placed next to the Netjeret.*

*Holding the **Ib** (the golden heart) before the Netjeret, the Ritualist says:*

Hail to you, O Aset, Mistress of All. I have brought to you your heart to set it in its place. Let me draw near to you with your heart, so that you may have pleasure through me, and so that by means of me you may have power over your body. Ascend, O Great of Magic, radiant, rejuvenating, equipped as a Netjeret. Live, O Excellent of Tongue whose speech cannot fail, live forever and ever!

*After placing the **Ib** near the sacred image, **everyone sings or chants** the hymn to Aset. Begin by **slowly playing the sistra**. Participants may wish to alternate the singing of verses.*

I play the sistra before your beautiful face,
Aset, Giver of Life, residing in the Sacred Mound,
Who has no equal in heaven.

I play the sistra for you,
Great of Love, Mistress of Women,
Who fills heaven and earth with your beauty,
Divine mother of Kamutef (i.e., Heru, Bull of His Mother),
Great Royal Spouse of Wennefer.

August one, Great Lady in the Hall of the Prince,
Mighty One in the mansion of the sacred benben stone,
One who moves freely in the barque of millions,
Who governs the divine barque.[67]

May your beautiful face be gracious to us who honor you.
O Mistress of Joy, Sweet of Love, Great of Praise, Lady of Charm,
Whose face enjoys the trickling of fresh myrrh.[68]
O Giver of Life, be gracious, be gracious to us who serve you.

*At this point perform the **meditation or magical action** or, if it is a special feast, add the appropriate prayers.*

---

[67] Op. Cit., Hymn VII, p. 107.
[68] Op. Cit., Hymn III, p. 42.

*Afterwards **all present back out of the Temple Chamber with heads slightly bowed** while the Ritualist performs the "removing the foot."*

*With the **broom** the Ritualist, as the last person to exit, **ritually sweeps the area beginning at the altar.** (This is known as "removing the foot.") While performing this action the Ritualist recites the following:*

The distress that causes confusion has been driven away, and all the Netjeru are in harmony. I have given Heru his Eye; I have placed the Wedjat-Eye in the correct position. I have given Setekh his Testicles, so that the two lords are content through the work of my hands.

I know the sky, I know the earth;
I know Heru, I know Setekh.
Heru is appeased with his Eyes;
Setekh is appeased with his Testicles.
I am Djehuty, who reconciles the Netjeru,
who makes offerings in their correct form.

*The **double doors are solemnly closed** as the Ritualist says the following:*

Djehuty has come.
He has filled the Eye of Heru;
He has restored the Testicles of Setekh.
No evil shall enter this Temple.
Ptah has closed the door,
Djehuty has set it fast.
The door is closed, the door is set fast with the bolt.

*All **bow, touching the palms of their hands to their knees.***

THE REVERSION OF OFFERINGS

*One priest or priestess and as many assistants as necessary enter the Temple Chamber a final time. While he/she and any assistants **lift up the offerings** before the sacred image the ritualist shall say:*

O Aset, your enemy[69] withdraws for you. Heru has turned himself to his Eye in its name of 'Reversion-of-Offerings.' I am Djehuty. I come to perform this rite for Aset, Queen of the Netjeru. These, your divine offerings revert, they revert to your servants for life, for stability, for health and for joy! O that the Eye of Heru may flourish for you eternally!

*Everyone withdraws, **carrying away all food offerings except for one loaf of bread and a bowl of pure water**. These last items remain until evening. If this ritual is celebrated after sunset, these items would also be removed.*

*After the candle has burned down, a servant-priest enters and closes the doors of the Kar-shrine. **Extinguishing the candle or oil lamp**, he/she exclaims:*

This is the Eye of Heru by which you have become great, by which you live, and by which you have power, O Aset. This is

---

[69] Meat offerings held a two-fold meaning for the ancient priesthood. Since meat necessarily came from slain animals, it signified the defeated or slain enemies of the Netjeret. At the same time, the meat offering represented the produce of the land which ultimately was a gift of the Netjeru.

the Eye of Heru which you consume and through which you enchant your body. The *Wedjat*-Eye now enters into the West, into *Manu*, but it shall return. Truly, the Eye of Heru returns in peace![70]

---

[70] It is important to consume the food offerings after the ceremony. Water used should either be drunk or poured onto the earth. If it is mixed with Natron, dilute it very greatly and then you can pour in onto the bare earth.

The General Ritual for Ausir

Like members of the ancient priesthood, participants should be clothed in white linen. No item made of animal products such as leather or wool is to be worn. Linen represents a pristine product of the earth whereas leather and wool come from humankind's domination of the animals, a domination that becomes part of the "natural order" only *after* the First Time when the *Netjeru* and humans and animals lived in peace and harmony. Just as the Morning Ritual harkens back to that First Time (*Zep Tepi*), so every temple rite re-presents mythic prototypes that occurred "in the beginning," that is, in that time before time. Even the sandals worn by the god's servants were made of white papyrus. This avoidance of animal products by the priesthood fits well with the fact that the ritualist acts as a *Netjer* and verbally asserts that he or she is a *Netjer*.

Special Food Offerings for Ausir: dates. The offerings also should include the regular food and beverage offerings.

Like members of the ancient priesthood, participants should be clothed in white linen. No item made of animal products such as leather or wool is to be worn. Linen represents a pristine product of the earth whereas leather and wool come from humankind's domination of the animals, a domination that becomes part of the "natural order" only *after* the First Time when the *Netjeru* and humans and animals lived in peace and harmony. Just as the Morning Ritual harkens back to that First Time (*Zep Tepi*), so every temple rite re-presents mythic prototypes that occurred "in the beginning," that is, in that time before time. Even the sandals worn by the god's servants were made of white papyrus. This avoidance of animal products by the priesthood fits well with the fact that the ritualist acts as a *Netjer* and verbally asserts that he or she is a *Netjer*.

As with all Egyptian rituals begin with your purification—washing of hands and cleansing of mouth with Natron. This preliminary rite helps us to lay aside the cares of the day and to become mindful of the fact that we will encounter a divine being. If Natron is not available, then use a natural sea salt in its place until you make your own Natron.

If two or more persons are participating, then one person, impersonating the Netjer *Djehuty*, **purifies each person by sprinkling each with water while exclaiming:**

I purify you with the water of all life and good fortune, all stability, all health and happiness.[71]

*Afterwards each person **rinses his mouth** and **places a small amount of Natron or sea salt in his mouth** while saying:*

I wash my mouth; I chew natron so that I may extol the might of Ausir, Lord of Eternity, Holy of Forms.[72]

*Participants **assemble outside the Temple Chamber** and begin by **softly rattling sistra.***

---

[71] Taken from Aylward M. Blackman's article "Purification (Egyptian)" in Hastings Encyclopedia 10/1918/ 476-82. This article is reprinted in Gods, Priests, and Men, Studies in the Religion of Pharaonic Egypt, edited by Alan B. Lloyd (Kegan Paul International, 1998), p. 9.
[72] Based on a temple inscription taken from "The Myth of Horus at Edfu—II" by A. M. Blackman and H. W. Fairman, appearing in Gods, Priests and Men, Studies in the Religion of Pharaonic Egypt (Kegan Paul International, 1998) p. 283.

This time—several minutes or more—is used to focus minds and intention so that distracting thoughts are left behind. The sound of the sistrum was said to placate the deity, purifying the atmosphere in preparation for encountering divinity. The sistrum was associated with Hutheru and also with her and Heru's son Ihy, and thus has connotations of joy, celebration, and dancing. According to Plutarch (A.D. 46-120), the sound of sistra was also reputed to drive away Setekh. But this was of very late date. It may have been that since by that time Setekh had been demonized, the general apotropaic function of the sistrum against evil entities was extended to include this *Netjer* as well.

*Standing **before the closed doors**, the Ritualist **recites the entrance spell:***

UTTERANCE BEFORE THE CLOSED DOORS OF THE TEMPLE

*The ritualist **raises hands in adoration** (dua position-arms stretched out in front of the body and raised up to face level, with palms facing outward). The following shall be said:*

O you Netjeru of this Temple, you guardians of the great portal, great Netjeru of mysterious abode, who sanctify the Netjer in his shrine, who consecrate his oblation, who receive the offerings in his presence in the Hall of the Ennead: I have made my way and I enter into your presence. I am one of you. I am Shu, the eldest son of his father, the senior wab servant-priest of Ausir. Do not repulse me on the Netjer's path. My feet are not impeded. I am not turned back from the court of the great portal so that I may conduct the divine service, that I may present offerings to him that made them, that I may give bread to Ausir. I have come on the way of the Netjer. I have not shown partiality

in judgment. I have not consorted with the strong. I have not reproached the lowly. I have not stolen things. I have not diminished the constituents of the Eye of Ra. I have not disturbed the Balance. I have not tampered with the requirements of the Sacred Eye. O Council of the Great Netjer in this Temple, behold, I have come to you to offer Ma'at to the Judge of Ma'at, to content the Sound Eye for its Lord. I am Shu; I flood his offering table. I present his offerings, the great Netjeret Sekhmet consorting with me, that I may adore Ausir at his festivals, that I may kiss the earth so great is his majesty, that I may endow his image with life. I am pure. I am purified.

At this point the ritualist **opens the doors to the Temple Chamber,** *or,* *if there are no doors,* **makes a gesture of opening unseen doors,** *and* **steps forward as if crossing over a threshold.** *The following is said:*

O you Ba-souls of Abdju (i.e., Abydos), if you are strong, I am strong. If I am strong, you are strong. If your Ka-spirits are strong, my Ka-spirit is strong at the head of the living. As they are living so shall I live, Sekhmet, the great Netjeret, beloved of Ptah, has given to me life, stability, and serenity round about my members, which Djehuty has gathered together for life. I am Heru in the height of heaven, the beautiful one of awe, Lord of Victory, mighty one of awe, exalted one of the two plumes, great one in Abdju I am pure.

All recite the following:

Awake, awake in peace, O Ausir.
May you awake in peace.
Awake, awake in peace, O Ram of Eternity.

May you awake in peace.
Awake, awake in peace, O Bull of the West.
May you awake in peace.
Awake, awake in peace, O Ausir, Kindly of Countenance.
May you awake in peace.

May you awake beautifully at the top of the morning,
through that which the entirety of Netjeru say to you.

Enter, close the double doors and stand in front of the Kar-shrine and altar. All bow, touching their hands to their knees.

The ritualist slowly opens the two doors of the Kar-shrine housing the sacred image. All others bow, touching their hands to their knees. The following is said:

The doors of the sky are open; the doors of the earth are unlocked. This House is open for its Lord. Let me come forth as he shall come forth. Let me enter in as he shall enter in. Ausir, beloved of Aset, first born of Nut and Geb, is exalted upon his Great Seat. The Great Company of the Netjeru are exalted upon their seat.

I have seen the Netjer, and the Netjer sees me. The Netjer rejoices at seeing me. I have gazed upon the statue of the Foremost of the Westerners, the sacred image of the Heir of Geb.[73]

Right hand on left shoulder of statue; left hand on right wrist of statue:

---

[73] Based on a passage in "Worship and Festivals in an Egyptian Temple," a lecture by H. W. Fairman (publ. by The John Rylands Library, 1954; p.180).

Djehuty has come to you. Awake when you hear his words. I have come as the envoy of Atum. My two arms are upon you like those of Heru. My two hands are upon you like those of Djehuty. My fingers are upon you like those of Anpu. Homage be to you. I am a living servant of Ausir.

*The Ritualist holds up the **bowl of water** in which he/she will be mixing the Natron. The following is said:*

O water may you remove all evil,
As Ra who bathes in the Lake of Rushes,
May Heru wash my flesh,
May Djehuty cleanse my feet,
May Shu lift me up and Nut take my hand!
May Setekh be my strength,
and may Sekhmet be my healing!
And may Amun-Ra be my life and my prospering!

*The bowl of water is set aside and the container of **Natron** is lifted up. The following is said:*

It is pure, it is pure.
My Natron is the Natron of Heru,
and the Natron of Heru is my Natron.
My Natron is the Natron of Setekh,
and the Natron of Setekh is my Natron.
My Natron is the Natron of Djehuty,
and the Natron of Djehuty is my Natron.
My Natron is the Natron of Geb,
and the Natron of Geb is my Natron.

Richard J. Reidy

My mouth is the mouth of a milking calf on the day that I
was born.

*Four pinches of Natron are mixed into the water as this Utterance is
recited:*

I give you essential water, a tide in your time.
I bring the flood waters to purify your sanctuary.
I bring you the flood waters
to purify your Temple and your statue in its place,
the primordial water that purifies as in the First Time!

*The Ritualist **places an index finger into the water** and **moves it in
a circular direction four times** as the following is said:*

Ausir, who brings forth the Nile from its cavern,
does purify this water.
Ausir, Lord of the Silent Land,
does cleanse this water;
Ausir, Lord of the Living,[74]
does sanctify this water;
Ausir himself does endow this water
with power and with life.

*The **Bowl of Natron-infused water** is then taken up and the Ritualist
sprinkles this lightly in front of and around the statue or image of
Ausir, applying some water to the base of the image, as the Utterance
is recited:*

---

[74] Erik Hornung, Conceptions of God in Ancient Egypt (Ithaca, NY: Cornell
Univ. Press, 1996), p. 233. In ancient Egypt, the Blessed Dead were often
referred to as "The Living Ones."

I come close to you, O Ausir Wennefer,[75]
who passes eternity repeatedly,[76]
I bring the water of rejuvenation
that flows from the Two Caverns.
I sprinkle the water,
    purifying your image and your Temple from all impurity!

*The Ritualist picks up the bowl of **Natron** and **sprinkles a small amount in each of the four directions** as the following is recited:*

The Netjer Ausir himself does cleanse and purify this,
his Temple to the South.
The Netjer Ausir himself does cleanse and purify this,
his Temple to the North.
The Netjer Ausir himself does cleanse and purify this,
his Temple to the West.
The Netjer Ausir himself does cleanse and purify this,
    his Temple to the East.

*Replacing the Natron on the altar, the Ritualist takes up the bowl of **water, sprinkling a small amount in each of the four directions**. The following Utterance is recited:*

The Netjer Ausir himself does sanctify and consecrate this,
his Temple to the South.
The Netjer Ausir himself does sanctify and consecrate this,

---

[75] Faulkner, R. O., The Egyptian Book of the Dead: The book of going forth by day. (San Francisco, 1996);
introductory hymn to Ausir. "Wennefer" is a title for Ausir, specifically associated with resurrection and renewal.

[76] Faulkner, op. cit., chapter 185. Unfortunately, Faulkner does not include page numbers, so it is only possible to make reference to chapter numbers in this otherwise excellent work.

his Temple to the North.

The Netjer Ausir himself does sanctify and consecrate this, his Temple to the West.

The Netjer Ausir himself does sanctify and consecrate this, his Temple to the East.

The Temple of the Netjer Ausir is established.
It is established for millions of years.

*The Ritualist returns to the **altar and lights the candle or oil lamp** while the following is said:*

Come, come in peace, O glorious Eye of Heru.
Be strong and renew your youth in peace.
For the flame comes like Ra on the double horizon,
and the enemies of Ra are defeated. They are defeated.
I am pure, I am pure, I am pure, I am pure.

*The Ritualist **places incense on the burner** and **censes each sacred image beginning with the statue** of the Netjer while the following is recited:*

The fire is laid, the fire shines;
The incense is laid on the fire, the incense shines.
    Your perfume comes to me, O Incense;
    May my perfume come to you, O Incense.
Your perfume comes to me, you Netjeru;
May my perfume come to you, You Netjeru.
    May I be with you, you Netjeru;
    May you be with me, you Netjeru.
May I live with you, you Netjeru;
May you live with me, you Netjeru.
    I love you, you Netjeru;
    May you love me, you Netjeru.

*Standing in front of the image of Ausir the Ritualist **offers the burning incense** and says:*

> Take the incense,
> Its essence is for you.
> Its smoke permeates your shrine, bringing life!
> Take the incense,
> Its essence is for you.
> Your Majesty is appeased with the incense.
> This Eye of Heru,
> This essence of the Eye of Heru comes to you.

At this point the following is said:

THE GREAT HYMN TO OSIRIS

Hail to you Ausir, Lord of Eternity, King of the *Netjeru*, of many names, of Holy Forms, of secret rites in the temples! Noble of *Ka*, you preside in *Djedu*. You are rich and sustainable in Sekhem. Lord of Acclaim in *Andjety*. Foremost in offerings in *Iunu*. Lord of remembrance in the hall of Ma'at. Secret *Ba* of the lord of the Cavern. Holy in the White Wall. You are the *Ba* of Ra and his very body, who reposes in *Henes*, who is worshipped in the *Naret* tree that grew up to bear your *Ba*. Lord of the palace of Khmun, much revered in *Shashotep*. Eternal Lord who presides in *Abdju*, who dwells distant in the Western Valley, whose name endures in people's mouths.

Most Ancient in the joined Two Lands, Nourisher before the nine *Netjeru*. Potent Spirit among spirits. Nun has given you your waters. The North Wind journeys south for you. The sky makes wind before your nose, so that your heart might be satisfied. Plants sprout at your wish. Earth grows its food for you. The sky and its stars obey you. The great portals open for you. Lord of acclaim in the southern sky, sanctified in the northern sky. The imperishable stars are under your rule. The unwearying stars are your abode. One offers to you by Geb's command. The nine *Netjeru* adore you. Those in the *Duat* embrace the Earth before you. The *Akhu* rejoice to see you. They are in awe of you.

The two joined lands adore you when your majesty approaches. Mightiest noble among nobles, first of rank, of lasting rule. Benevolent leader of the Nine *Netjeru*, gracious and lovely to behold, awe inspiring to all lands. May your name be foremost. All make offerings to you, lord of remembrance in Heaven and Earth. Rich in acclaim at the *Wag* feast, hailed in unison by the Two Lands. Foremost of your brothers, eldest of the Nine *Netjeru*, you have set Ma'at in its place. Lauded by your father Geb, Beloved of your mother Nut, mighty when you fell the rebel, strong-armed when you slay your foe. You cast fear on your enemy. You vanquish the evil plotters. Your heart is firm when you crush the rebels.

You are Geb's heir in kingship of the two lands. Seeing your worth, he gave them to you. You lead the lands to good fortune. Geb placed this land into your hand, its water, its wind, its plants, its cattle. All that flies, all that alights, its reptiles and its desert game. All these things have been given to the Son of Nut, and the two lands are content. You appear on your father's throne, like Ra when he arises. You place light above the darkness. You light the shade with your plumes. You flood the two lands like Aten at dawn. Your crown is among the stars. It pierces the sky. You are the leader of all the *Netjeru*. Effective is your word and command. The great Ennead praises you. The small Ennead loves you.[77]

The Ritualist places more incense on the charcoal and again and again slowly raises and lowers the incense cup as the following is recited:

O Ausir, may you advance with your *Ka*.
O Far-Strider Who Crosses the Sky,
the arm of your *Ka* is before you.
The arm of your *Ka* is behind you.
O Starry One in *Iunu*, the foot of your *Ka* is before you,
The foot of your *Ka* is behind you.
O Glorious Ausir, this incense is offered to you.
May your face be filled as this essence spreads itself over you.

All present perform the Henu Rite—Embrace the Earth, the Fourfold Salute to the God, Embrace the Earth. The bodily gestures are performed alternately four times.

For Embracing the Earth, all present prostrate themselves, face down, upon the floor. During the Fourfold Salute, all present rise upon one knee, and alternately raise their hands and arms into the *Dua* (praise) position with palms facing outward, followed by the *Sahu* (obedience) gesture, made by striking the chest with a closed fist and raising the other arm (also with closed fist) at a ninety-degree angle. The *Dua* position is accompanied by the words **"Adoration be to Ausir,"** followed by the *Sahu* gesture accompanied

---

[77] Miriam Lichteim, Ancient Egyptian Literature, Vol. II, pp. 81-83. Taken from the Stela of Amenmose.

with the words, **"Hail to the Bull of the West!"** The bodily gestures are performed alternately four times.

Following this all present again prostrate themselves before the god. This is a sign and symbol of total submission and adoration before the Netjer. The following is said:

Homage to Ausir, Kindly of Countenance,
who is established on the Great Seat.
I have placed myself on the floor in awe of you.
I embrace the earth before you
as before the Foremost of the Westerners.
I have come that I might kiss the earth
that I might worship my Lord.
For I have seen his beauty.
I give praise to Ausir for I have seen his power.
His form is more distinguished than the *Netjeru*;
His arm is more powerful than the *Netjeru*.
I am pure, I am pure, I am pure, I am pure!

Everyone stands up.

*The Ritualist **holds in the palm of one hand the image of Ma'at** and with **the other hand open and raised over the image as if sheltering it,** repeats the following:*

I have come to you as Djehuty, whose two hands are joined together under Ma'at. She comes to be with you, for she is everywhere. You are provided with Ma'at. You move in Ma'at, you live in Ma'at. She fills your body, she rests in your head, she makes her seat upon your brow; the breath of your body is of Ma'at, your heart does live in Ma'at. All that you eat, all that you drink, all that you breathe is of Ma'at.

Djehuty presents Ma'at to you, his two hands are upon her beauty before your face.

*The Ritualist places the image of Ma'at near the divine statue. Then he/ she holds up before the image of Ausir a **pitcher of water** and **pours the water slowly into an offering bowl** as the following Utterance is recited:*

This libation is for you, O Bull of the West.
This libation is for you, O Ausir.
I have brought to you this offering of water,
that your heart may be refreshed.
I have brought to you this Eye of Heru,
placing this at your feet.
I present to you that which flows forth from you,
that your heart shall continue to beat.
For it is with you that all comes forth at the sound of the voice.

*The libation bowl is placed on the altar. At this point the Ritualist **lightly sprinkles sand on the floor in front of the altar** as the following is recited:*

O Ausir, who resides in *Abdju,*
Take to yourself the Eye of Heru,
You have rescued it, O Lord of Truth.
You have sprinkled with sand the Eye of Heru.

***Lifting the wine offering** before the sacred image, the Ritualist repeats the following:*

mn n.k irp irt ḥrw wꜣdt
[*"mán-nik 'úrip írat ḥáru wá'dat"*; approximately pronounced *MAHN-neek OO-rip EE-raht HAH-roo WAH-jat*]

Take to yourself wine, the green Eye of Heru,
which I offer to your *Ka*.[78]
O Lord of Earth, how green is your kingdom.
May you drink this wine. May your heart rejoice.
May anger be removed from your face.
It is pure.
[*iw.w wᶜb* pronounced *"uwú wáᶜib"*; approximately *oo-WOO WAH-ib*]

*Lifting up **an offering of dates**, the Ritualist pronounces the following:*

I present to you this receptacle of dates. Take these, the emanations of Geb. The secret substances from your body gather together and protect you. They are brought together by your sister Aset in order to reunite your body.[79]

*The Ritualist **places myrrh on the fire** and **lifts up the smoking incense** while at the same time he **lifts up the meat-offering** before the Netjer, and says the following:*

The scent of myrrh is for your nose. It fills your nostrils; your heart receives the meat-portions on its scent.[80]

*Slowly **elevating the remaining food offerings four times** before the image of the Netjer, the Ritualist repeats the following:*

---

[78] Refer to pp. 92, 93, 99, and 105 in Mu-Chou Poo's Wine and Wine Offerings in Ancient Egypt (London & New York: Kegan Paul International, 1995).

[79] Émile Chassinat et al., Le temple de Dendara, Vols. II, p. 145, and XII, p. 279.

[80] Quoted in "Worship and Festivals in an Egyptian Temple," by H. W. Fairman (publ. by The John Rylands Library, 1954), p. 191.

I offer to Ausir, whose flesh enriched the Sacred Land.
All life emanates from you,
All health emanates from you,
All stability emanates from you,
all good fortune emanates from you,
who presides over the Field of Reeds forever.

The Ritualist places the food offering before the divine image, and then all present extend one hand, palm down, over the offerings and recite the following:

May offerings of every kind come forth in abundance,
like the things which come forth from the mouth of the
Netjer.

piryá pírit ar ḫiráw mi purú:riat ma rá' ni náṯar. (4 times)
[approximately pronounced *peer-YA PEER-it ar khi-RAU mee pu-ROOR-iat ma RA nee NAH-tchar*]

May offerings of every kind come forth in abundance, like
the things that come forth from the mouth of the Netjer.

*Holding the **Ankh** before the Netjer, the Ritualist says:*

Live, O Ausir, who comes forth rejuvenated in his time.
Live for all time and for eternity!

ʿánaḫ niḥáḫ ḏát.
[approximately pronounced *AH-nakh nee-HAH JAHT*]

*The **Ankh** is placed next to the Netjer.*

*Holding the **Ib (the golden heart)** before the Netjer, the Ritualist says:*

Hail to you, O Ausir, Ram of Eternity. I have brought to you your heart to set it in its place. Let me draw near to you with your heart, so that you may have pleasure through me, and so that by means of me you may have power over your body. Ascend, Lord of the *Naret* Tree, radiant, rejuvenating, equipped as a *Netjer*. Live, O Sovereign Lord, live forever and ever!

*After placing the **Ib** near the sacred image, **everyone sings or chants** the hymn to Ausir. Participants may wish to alternate the singing of verses.*

Those who exist are with you, both *Netjeru* and humans. You prepare their places in the Realm of the Dead, and they beseech your *Ka*. They come by the millions and millions. In the end there is the landing in your presence.

Those in their mother's womb already have their faces turned toward you, and there is no delaying in Kemet. They are in your hands; they all come to you, great and small. Yours is what lives on earth. All the world comes to you. You are their lord; there is none other than you. All this—it belongs to you.[81]

Earth lies upon your arm, and its corners are upon you, as well as the four supports of the sky. When you quiver, the land trembles. The inundation comes forth from the sweat of your hands.

---

[81] Jan Assmann, Death and Salvation in Ancient Egypt (Ithaca, NY: Cornell Univ. Press, 2005), pp. 125-126.

If canals are built...if one builds homes and temples, moves monuments, plants fields, excavates tombs—they are built upon you. They endure upon your back and you do not say, 'I am burdened.'[82]

Whether one sails upstream or downstream in the course of a lifetime, morning by morning, your Majesty is there like Ra. All that is and is not follows you.

I have come to you, knowing your will. I am aware of your role in the Duat. You sit in judgment, Ma'at being before you. You judge the hearts on the Scale. Here I am, before you. There is no lie in my heart. My heart is filled with Ma'at.

I pray to your might for you are strong. I soothe the Ennead who surround you. I give praise to you and rejoice before you. I kiss the ground tirelessly before you.[83]

At this point **perform the meditation or magical action** *or, if it is a special feast, add the appropriate prayers.*

Afterwards **all present back out of the Temple Chamber with heads slightly bowed** *while the Ritualist performs the* **"removing the foot."**

With the **broom** *the Ritualist, as the last person to exit,* **ritually sweeps the area beginning at the altar.** *(This is known as "removing the foot.") While performing this action the Ritualist recites the following:*

[82] Alison Roberts, My Heart, My Mother:Death and Rebirth in Ancient Egypt (Northgate Publishers, 2000), pp. 33-34.
[83] Assmann, op. cit., p. 126.

The distress that causes confusion has been driven away, and all the Netjeru are in harmony. I have given Heru his Eye; I have placed the Wedjat-Eye in the correct position. I have given Setekh his Testicles, so that the two lords are content through the work of my hands.

I know the sky, I know the earth;
I know Heru, I know Setekh.
Heru is appeased with his Eyes;
Setekh is appeased with his Testicles.
I am Djehuty, who reconciles the Netjeru,
who makes offerings in their correct form.

*The **double doors are solemnly closed** as the Ritualist says the following:*

Djehuty has come.
He has filled the Eye of Heru;
He has restored the Testicles of Setekh.
No evil shall enter this Temple.
Ptah has closed the door,
Djehuty has set it fast.
The door is closed, the door is set fast with the bolt.

*All **bow, touching the palms of their hands to their knees.***

THE REVERSION OF OFFERINGS

*One priest or priestess and as many assistants as necessary enter the Temple Chamber a final time. While he/she and any assistants **lift up the offerings** before the sacred image the ritualist shall say:*

O Ausir, your enemy[84] withdraws for you. Heru has turned himself to his Eye in its name of 'Reversion-of-Offerings.' I am Djehuty. I come to perform this rite for Ausir, Lord of All. These, your divine offerings revert, they revert to your servants for life, for stability, for health and for joy! O that the Eye of Heru may flourish for you eternally!

Everyone withdraws, **carrying away all food offerings except for one loaf of bread and a bowl of pure water.** These last items remain until evening. If this ritual is celebrated after sunset, these items would also be removed.

After the candle has burned down, a servant-priest enters and closes the doors of the Kar-shrine. **Extinguishing the candle or oil lamp,** *he/she exclaims:*

This is the Eye of Heru by which you have become great, by which you live, and by which you have power, O Ausir. This is the Eye of Heru which you consume and through which you enchant your body. The *Wedjat-***Eye now enters into the West, into** *Manu,* **but it shall return. Truly, the Eye of Heru returns in peace![85]**

---

[84] Meat offerings held a two-fold meaning for the ancient priesthood. Since meat necessarily came from slain animals, it signified the defeated or slain enemies of the Netjeret. At the same time, the meat offering represented the produce of the land which ultimately was a gift of the Netjeru.

[85] It is important to consume the food offerings after the ceremony. Water used should either be drunk or poured onto the earth. If it is mixed with Natron, dilute it very greatly and then you can pour in onto the bare earth.

The General Ritual for Bastet

Bastet reveals herself as loving mother and powerful protector, as well as a goddess both sensuous and formidable. Her early iconography shows Bastet as a lioness. In our own era this great goddess is often connected with cats due to her feline appearance, an iconography that occurred much later in Egypt. However, in the ritual below the reader will find no epithets or titles connecting Bastet with cats. The reason is that nowhere in the academic sources is she so connected. Since this present rite is Reconstructionist in purpose this writer did not deem it appropriate to create feline epithets when none exist in the available ancient writings. The primary source for her epithets is the eight-volume *Lexikon der ägyptischen Götter und Götterbezeichnungen* (i.e., "Dictionary of Egyptian Gods and God-Names"). In the hundreds of beautiful epithets for this goddess there is no reference to her relationship to domestic cats.

This lack of such epithets may very well be due to the relatively total destruction of her great temple in Bubastis. Her temple may certainly have contained epithets, hymns and other references to her association with cats. We do know that cats were mummified and offered to the goddess, eventually being buried in a cemetery near her temple. The private worshipper is, of course, free to create meaningful epithets for Bastet according to his or her own insight and experience. My goal is simply to throw light on those other epithets of hers that do occur in existing ancient sources. In no way do I wish to minimize the experience or insights of her contemporary worshippers. My goal is simply to adhere to a Reconstructionist methodology. This has been my approach with epithets and titles for all of our gods.

Like members of the ancient priesthood, participants should be clothed in white linen. No item made of animal products such as leather or wool is to be worn. Linen represents a pristine product of the earth whereas leather and wool come from humankind's domination of the animals, a domination that becomes part of the "natural order" only *after* the First Time when the *Netjeru* and humans and animals lived in peace and harmony. Just as the Morning Ritual harkens back to that First Time (*Zep Tepi*), so every temple rite re-presents mythic prototypes that occurred "in the beginning," that is, in that time before time. Even the sandals worn by the god's servants were made of white papyrus. This avoidance of animal products by the priesthood fits well with the fact that the ritualist acts as a *Netjer* and verbally asserts that he or she is a *Netjer*.

As with all Egyptian rituals begin with your purification—washing of hands and cleansing of mouth with Natron. This preliminary rite helps us to lay aside the cares of the day and to become mindful of the fact that we will encounter a divine being. If Natron is not available, then use a natural sea salt in its place until you make your own Natron.

If two or more persons are participating, then one person, impersonating the Netjer *Djehuty,* **purifies each person by sprinkling each with water while exclaiming**:

I purify you with the water of all life and good fortune, all stability, all health and happiness.[86]

---

[86] Taken from Aylward M. Blackman's article "Purification (Egyptian)" in Hastings Encyclopedia 10/1918/ 476-82. This article is reprinted in Gods, Priests, and Men, Studies in the Religion of Pharaonic Egypt, edited by Alan B. Lloyd (Kegan Paul International, 1998), p. 9.

*Afterwards each person **rinses his mouth** and **places a small amount of Natron or sea salt in his mouth** while saying:*

I wash my mouth; I chew natron so that I may extol the might of Bastet, Lady of Life and Mistress of the *Netjeru.*[87]

*Participants **assemble outside the Temple Chamber** and **begin by softly rattling sistra.***

This time—several minutes or more—is used to focus minds and intention so that distracting thoughts are left behind. The sound of the sistrum was said to placate the deity, purifying the atmosphere in preparation for encountering divinity. The sistrum was associated with Hutheru and also with her and Heru's son Ihy, and thus has connotations of joy, celebration, and dancing. According to Plutarch (A.D. 46-120), the sound of sistra was also reputed to drive away Setekh. But this was of very late date. It may have been that since by that time Setekh had been demonized, the general apotropaic function of the sistrum against evil entities was extended to include this *Netjer* as well.

*Standing **before the closed doors,** the Ritualist **recites the entrance spell:***

UTTERANCE BEFORE THE CLOSED DOORS OF THE TEMPLE

*The ritualist **raises hands in adoration** (dua position-arms stretched out in front of the body and raised up to face level, with palms facing outward). The following shall be said:*

---

[87] Based on a temple inscription taken from "The Myth of Horus at Edfu—II" by A. M. Blackman and H. W. Fairman, appearing in Gods, Priests and Men, Studies in the Religion of Pharaonic Egypt (Kegan Paul International, 1998) p. 283.

O you *Netjeru* of this Temple, you guardians of the great portal, great *Netjeru* of mysterious abode, who sanctify the *Netjeret* in her shrine, who consecrate her oblation, who receive the offerings in her presence in the Hall of the Ennead: I have made my way and I enter into your presence. I am one of you. I am Shu, the eldest son of his father, the senior *wab* servant-priest of Bastet. Do not repulse me on the *Netjeret's* path. My feet are not impeded. I am not turned back from the court of the great portal so that I may conduct the divine service, that I may present offerings to her that made them, that I may give bread to Bastet. I have come on the way of the *Netjeret*. I have not shown partiality in judgment. I have not consorted with the strong. I have not reproached the lowly. I have not stolen things. I have not diminished the constituents of the Eye of Ra. I have not disturbed the Balance. I have not tampered with the requirements of the Sacred Eye. O Council of the Great *Netjeret* in this Temple, behold, I have come to you to offer Ma'at to the Lady of Ma'at, to content the Sound Eye for its mistress. I am Shu; I flood her offering table. I present her offerings, Sekhmet consorting with me, that I may adore Bastet at her festivals, that I may kiss the earth so great is her majesty, that I may endow her image with life. I am pure. I am purified.

At this point the ritualist **opens the doors to the Temple Chamber,** *or, if there are no doors,* **makes a gesture of opening unseen doors,** *and* **steps forward as if crossing over a threshold.** *The following is said:*

O you *Ba*-souls of *Per Bastet* (i.e., Bubastis[88]), if you are strong, I am strong. If I am strong, you are strong. If your *Ka*-spirits are strong, my *Ka*-spirit is strong at the head of the living. As they are living so shall I live . . . . Sekhmet, the great *Netjeret*, beloved

---

[88] Per Bastet (Greek, Bubastis) is the cult center for Bastet.

of Ptah, has given to me life, stability, and serenity round about my members, which Djehuty has gathered together for life. I am Heru in the height of heaven, the beautiful one of awe, Lord of Victory, mighty one of awe, exalted one of the two plumes, great one in *Abdju* (Abydos) I am pure.

All temple members chant:

Awake in peace, O Bastet, Daughter of Ra,
may you awaken in peace.
Awake in peace, O Bastet, Lady of Joy,
may you awaken in peace.
Awake in peace, O Bastet, Foremost of *Netjerut* [goddesses],
may you awaken in peace.
Awake in peace, O Bastet, Lady of Transformations,
may you awaken in peace.

**May you awake beautifully at the top of the morning,
through that which the entirety of *Netjeru* say to you.**

Enter, **close the double doors** *and* **stand in front of the Kar-shrine and altar. All bow, touching their hands to their knees.**

The ritualist **slowly opens the two doors of the Kar-shrine** *housing the sacred image. All others* **bow, touching their hands to their knees.** *The following is said:*

The doors of the sky are open; the doors of the earth are unlocked. This House is open for its Mistress. Let me come forth as she shall come forth. Let me enter in as she shall enter in. Bastet, Daughter of Ra and Lady of Light, is exalted upon her Great Seat. The Great Company of the *Netjeru* are exalted upon their seat.

I have seen the *Netjeret,* and the *Netjeret* sees me. The *Netjeret* rejoices at seeing me. I have gazed upon the statue of the Lady of Light, the sacred image of the Eye of Ra.[89]

Right hand on left shoulder of statue; left hand on right wrist of statue:

Djehuty has come to you. Awake when you hear his words. I have come as the envoy of Atum. My two arms are upon you like those of Heru. My two hands are upon you like those of Djehuty. My fingers are upon you like those of Anpu. Homage be to you. I am a living servant of Bastet.

The Ritualist holds up the **bowl of water** *in which he/she will be mixing the Natron. The following is said:*

O water may you remove all evil,
As Ra who bathes in the Lake of Rushes,
May Heru wash my flesh,
May Djehuty cleanse my feet,
May Shu lift me up and Nut take my hand!
May Setekh be my strength, and may Sekhmet be my healing!
And may Amun-Ra be my life and my prospering!

The bowl of water is set aside and the container of **Natron** *is lifted up. The following is said:*

It is pure, it is pure.
My Natron is the Natron of Heru,

---

[89] Based on the temple text found in "Worship and Festivals in an Egyptian Temple," a lecture by H. W. Fairman (publ. by The John Rylands Library, 1954), p. 180.

and the Natron of Heru is my Natron.
My Natron is the Natron of Setekh,
and the Natron of Setekh is my Natron.
My Natron is the Natron of Djehuty,
and the Natron of Djehuty is my Natron.
My Natron is the Natron of Geb,
and the Natron of Geb is my Natron.

My mouth is the mouth of a milking calf on the day that I was born.

Four pinches of Natron are mixed into the water as this Utterance is recited:

I give you essential water, a tide in your time.
I bring the flood waters to purify your sanctuary.
I bring you the flood waters
to purify your Temple and your statue in its place,
the primordial water that purifies as in the First Time!

The Ritualist places an index finger into the water and moves it in a circular direction four times as the following is said:

Bastet, the Daughter of Ra, does purify this water;
Bastet, the Mistress of Radiance, does cleanse this water;
Bastet, Brow Serpent of Horakhty, does sanctify this water;
Bastet herself does endow this water with power and with life.

The Bowl of Natron-infused water is then taken up and the Ritualist sprinkles this lightly in front of and around the statue or image of

Bastet, applying some water to the base of the image, as the Utterance is recited:

> I come close to You, O Creatress of Sunbeams, Lady of Light.
> I bring the water of rejuvenation
> that flows from the Two Caverns.
> I sprinkle the water,
> purifying your image and your Temple from all impurity!

*The Ritualist picks up the bowl of **Natron** and **sprinkles a small amount in each of the four directions** as the following is recited:*

> The *Netjeret* Bastet herself does cleanse and purify this,
> her Temple to the South.
> The *Netjeret* Bastet herself does cleanse and purify this,
> her Temple to the North.
> The *Netjeret* Bastet herself does cleanse and purify this,
> her Temple to the West.
> The *Netjeret* Bastet herself does cleanse and purify this,
> her Temple to the East.

*Replacing the Natron on the altar, the Ritualist takes up the **bowl of water, sprinkling a small amount in each of the four directions**. The following Utterance is recited:*

> The *Netjeret* Bastet herself does sanctify and consecrate this,
> her Temple to the South.
> The *Netjeret* Bastet herself does sanctify and consecrate this,
> her Temple to the North.
> The *Netjeret* Bastet herself does sanctify and consecrate this,
> her Temple to the West.
> The *Netjeret* Bastet herself does sanctify and consecrate this,
> her Temple to the East.

The Temple of the *Netjeret* Bastet is established.
It is established for millions of years.

*The Ritualist returns to the altar and **lights the candle or oil lamp** while the following is said:*

Come, come in peace, O glorious Eye of Heru,
Be strong and renew your youth in peace.
For the flame shines like Ra on the double horizon.
The enemies are Ra are defeated. They are defeated.
I am pure, I am pure, I am pure, I am pure.

*The Ritualist **places incense on the burner** and **censes each sacred image beginning with the statue** of the Netjeret while the following is recited:*

The fire is laid, the fire shines;
The incense is laid on the fire, the incense shines.
    Your perfume comes to me, O Incense;
    May my perfume come to you, O Incense.
Your perfume comes to me, you Netjeru;
May my perfume come to you, You Netjeru.
    May I be with you, you Netjeru;
    May you be with me, you Netjeru.
May I live with you, you Netjeru;
May you live with me, you Netjeru.
    I love you, you Netjeru;
    May you love me, you Netjeru.

*Standing in front of the image of Bastet the Ritualist **offers the burning incense** and says:*

Take the incense,

Its essence is for you.
Its smoke permeates your shrine, bringing life!
Take the incense,
Its essence is for you.
Your Majesty is appeased with the incense.
This Eye of Heru,
This essence of the Eye of Heru comes to you.

At this point the following is said:

Homage to you, O Bastet, Daughter of Ra. At the Sight of Your Face the *Netjeru* rejoice. O Splendid and Mighty One, you burn the rebels with your fiery breath. Protect us your servants as you protect the *Netjeru*. O Lady of the Red Apparel Whose Flame Goes Forth Against the Enemies of Sokar, protect us and shelter us as we serve the Lord of Heaven, Ra, your Father.

Mistress of Radiance Who Drives Away Darkness, we shake the sistra so that it pleases your ears. We beat the hand drum for the Lady of Joy. We pacify with our sistra the Lady of Terror. O Mighty One, hear the sistra that we shake for you. Hear the sistra that delight your heart. Lady of Jubilation we praise you. Lady of Joy we honor you. You are the One with Numerous Festivals. You are the One with the Beautiful Face. Hear us play, O *Netjeret*. Hear us shake the sistra for you.

Praise be to you, O Bastet, Mistress of All the *Netjeru*. Words of adoration rise up to you, O Lady of the *Wedjat* Eye. You are the One with Many Faces. You are the One with Many Forms. Be with us as we shake the sistra for you. O Great Brow-Serpent, at Whose Sight both *Netjeru* and Humans Rejoice, we clap our hands for you, O Sweet One of Love. We shake the sistra for the Sole Mistress. Bless us who honor you. Protect us who bow before you.

Adoration to the Lady of Jubilation!
Adoration to the Lady of Light!
Adoration to the Lady of Joy!
Adoration to the Golden One!

*The Ritualist **places more incense on the charcoal** and again and again **slowly raises and lowers the incense cup** as the following is recited:*

O Bastet, may you advance with your *Ka*.
O Luminous One, the arm of your *Ka* is before you,
The arm of your *Ka* is behind you.
O Lady of Heaven, the foot of your *Ka* is before you,
The foot of your *Ka* is behind you.
O Beautiful Bastet, this incense is offered to you,
May your face be filled as this essence spreads itself over you.

*All present **perform the Henu Rite**—Embrace the Earth, the Fourfold Salute to the God, Embrace the Earth. The bodily gestures are performed alternately four times.*

For Embracing the Earth, all present prostrate themselves, face down, upon the floor. During the Fourfold Salute, all present rise upon one knee, and alternately raise their hands and arms into the *Dua* (praise) position with palms facing outward, followed by the *Sahu* (obedience) gesture, made by striking the chest with a closed fist and raising the other arm (also with closed fist) at a ninety-degree angle. The *Dua* position is accompanied by the words **"Adoration be to Bastet,"** followed by the *Sahu* gesture

accompanied with the words, **"Hail to the Lady of Heaven!"** The
bodily gestures are performed alternately four times.

*Following this **all present again prostrate themselves** before the
Netjeret. This is a sign and symbol of total submission and adoration
before the Netjeret. The following is said:*

> Homage to Bastet, Eye of Ra, Lady of Light,
> who is established on the Great Seat!
> I have placed myself on the floor in awe of you.
> I embrace the earth before you as before the Lady of All Powers.
> I have come that I might kiss the earth,
> that I might worship my Mistress,
> For I have seen her Beauty;
> I give praise to Bastet,
> For I have seen her Power.
> Her form is more distinguished than the *Netjeru*;
> Her arm is more powerful than the *Netjeru*.
> I am pure, I am pure, I am pure, I am pure!

Everyone stands up.
*The Ritualist **holds in the palm of one hand the image of Ma'at** and
with **the other hand open and raised over the image as if sheltering
it,** repeats the following:*

> I have come to you as Djehuty, whose two hands are joined
> together under Ma'at. She comes to be with you, for she is
> everywhere. You are provided with Ma'at. You move in Ma'at,
> you live in Ma'at. She fills your body, she rests in your head, she
> makes her seat upon your brow; the breath of your body is of
> Ma'at, your heart does live in Ma'at. All that you eat, all that you
> drink, all that you breathe is of Ma'at. Djehuty presents Ma'at to
> you, his two hands are upon her beauty before your face.

111

Richard J. Reidy

The Ritualist places the image of Ma'at near the divine statue. Then he/ she holds up before the image of Bastet **a pitcher of water** *and* **pours the water slowly into an offering bowl** *as the following Utterance is recited:*

> This libation is for you, O Luminous One.
> This libation is for you, O Bastet.
> I have brought to you this offering of water,
> That your heart may be refreshed.
> I have brought to you this Eye of Heru,
> Placing this at your feet.
> I present to you that which flows forth from you,
> That your heart shall continue to beat.
> For it is with you
> that all comes forth at the sound of the voice.

The offering bowl is placed on the altar. At this point the Ritualist **lightly sprinkles sand on the floor in front of the altar** *as the following is recited:*

> O Bastet, who resides in *Per Bastet,*[90]
> Take to yourself the Eye of Heru.
> You have rescued it, O Protectress of the Divine Order.
> You have sprinkled with sand the Eye pf Heru.

Lifting the wine offering *before the sacred image, the Ritualist repeats the following:*

> mn n.t irp irt ḥrw wȝdt
> [*"mán-niṯ 'úrip írat ḥáru wá'ḏat"*; approximately pronounced *MAHN-neetch OO-rip EE-raht HAH-roo WAH-jat*]

---

[90] The Egyptian name for the city of Bubastis.

Take to yourself wine, the green Eye of Heru,
which I offer to your *Ka*.
O Ruler, how beautiful is your beauty!
May you drink it; may your heart rejoice;
may anger be removed from your face.
It is pure.
[*iw.w wˁb* pronounced *"uwú wáˁib"*; approximately *oo-WOO WAH-ib*]

*The Ritualist **places myrrh on the fire** and **lifts up the smoking incense while at the same time he lifts up the meat-offering** before the Netjeret, and says the following:*

The scent of myrrh is for your nose. It fills your nostrils; your heart receives the meat-portions on its scent.[91]

*Slowly **elevating the food offerings four times** before the image of the Netjeret, the Ritualist repeats the following:*

I offer to Bastet, Creatress of Sunbeams.
All life emanates from you,
All health emanates from you,
All stability emanates from you,
All good fortune emanates from you,
O Lady of Light, Bastet, forever.

*The Ritualist **places the food offering before the divine image**, and then all present **extend one hand, palm down, over the offerings** and recite the following:*

---

[91] Quoted in "Worship and Festivals in an Egyptian Temple," by H. W. Fairman (publ. by The John Rylands Library, 1954), p. 191.

May offerings of every kind come forth in abundance,
like the things which come forth from the mouth of the
Netjeret.

piryá pírit ar ḥiráw mi purú:riat ma rá' ni naṯárat. (4 times)
[approximately pronounced *peer-YA PEER-it ar khi-RAU mee pu-
ROOR-iat ma RA nee nah-TCHAR-at*]

May offerings of every kind come forth in abundance, like
the things that come forth from the mouth of the Netjeret.

Holding the **Ankh** before Bastet, the Ritualist says:

Live, O Bastet, Eye of Ra, live for all time and for eternity!

ʿánaḫ niḥáḥ ḏát.
[approximately pronounced *AH-nakh nee-HAH JAHT*]

*The **Ankh** is placed next to the image of Bastet.*

*Holding the **Ib** (the golden heart) before the Netjeret, the Ritualist says:*

Hail to you, Bastet, Lady of the Breath of Life. I have brought
to you your heart to set it in its place. Let me draw near to you
with your heart, so that you may have pleasure through me, and
so that by means of me you may have power over your body.
Ascend, O Great One of *Bau*, radiant, rejuvenating, equipped as
a *Netjeret*. Live, O Eye of Ra, live forever and ever!

*After placing the **Ib** near the sacred image, **everyone sings or chants**
the hymn to Bastet. Participants may wish to alternate the singing of
verses.*

THE HYMN TO BASTET

I praise the Lady of Light, I worship her majesty. I exalt the Daughter of Ra. Adoration to Bastet, praise be to my mistress! O Lady of Life who drives away the darkness! All hail, jubilation to you, the mistress of all!

O Young Lioness, Devourer, Eye of Ra! Great of Strength and Quick of Stride, your Flame goes forth against your enemies! You make protection for your father Ra, as you make protection for the child in his nest. Powerful in battle and Mighty of Heart, your defeat does not exist.

Splendid One with Secret Form, Lady of the Breath of Life, grant long life to us who worship you. You, the Protector, are the One Who Protects the *Netjeru*. May you protect us who honor you. O Lady of Foods Who Opens a Perfect Year, grant us abundance in all the years of our lives. You give life to whomever walks upon your Way. Your people who love you see the faces of their loved ones through the rays of your Solar Disk.

I revere you, Bastet, Enrapturing One, Enlightener! O Mother of the *Netjeru*, from sky, from earth, from south, from north, from west, from east, from each land, from each place, where your majesty shines forth! See what is in my heart, what is in my inmost; my heart is blameless, my inmost open, no darkness is in my breast!

I bow in worship before you, O Queen of the *Netjeru*! You sit in truth and beauty upon your throne: Lady of Cities and Mistress of All Lands, who resides within the Oasis! Lady of Adornments and sweet fragrance! Lady of Jubilation and Joy, Greatly Beloved! It is the Protector of the divine entities who comes forth. Heaven exalts, the earth is full of gladness, Bastet the Great rejoices!

*At this point **perform the meditation or magical action** or, if it is a special feast, add the appropriate prayers.*

*Afterwards **all present back out of the Temple Chamber with heads slightly bowed** while the Ritualist performs the "removing the foot."*

*With the **broom** the Ritualist, as the last person to exit, **ritually sweeps the area beginning at the altar**. (This is known as "removing the foot.") While performing this action the Ritualist recites the following:*

The distress that causes confusion has been driven away, and all the Netjeru are in harmony. I have given Heru his Eye; I have placed the Wedjat-Eye in the correct position. I have given Setekh his Testicles, so that the two lords are content through the work of my hands.

I know the sky, I know the earth;
I know Heru, I know Setekh.
Heru is appeased with his Eyes;
Setekh is appeased with his Testicles.
I am Djehuty, who reconciles the Netjeru,
who makes offerings in their correct form.

*The **double doors are solemnly closed** as the Ritualist says the following:*

Djehuty has come.
He has filled the Eye of Heru;
He has restored the Testicles of Setekh.

No evil shall enter this Temple.
Ptah has closed the door,
Djehuty has set it fast.
The door is closed, the door is set fast with the bolt.

*All **bow, touching the palms of their hands to their knees.***

THE REVERSION OF OFFERINGS

*One priest or priestess and as many assistants as necessary enter the Temple Chamber a final time. While he/she and any assistants **lift up the offerings** before the sacred image the ritualist shall say:*

O Bastet, your enemy[92] withdraws for you. Heru has turned himself to his Eye in its name of 'Reversion-of-Offerings.' I am Djehuty. I come to perform this rite for Bastet, Queen of the Netjeru. These, your divine offerings revert, they revert to your servants for life, for stability, for health and for joy! O that the Eye of Heru may flourish for you eternally!

Everyone withdraws, **carrying away all food offerings except for one loaf of bread and a bowl of pure water.** These last items remain until evening. If this ritual is celebrated after sunset, these items would also be removed.

*After the candle has burned down, a servant-priest enters and closes the doors of the Kar-shrine. **Extinguishing the candle or oil lamp,** he/she exclaims:*

---

[92] Meat offerings held a two-fold meaning for the ancient priesthood. Since meat necessarily came from slain animals, it signified the defeated or slain enemies of the Netjeret. At the same time, the meat offering represented the produce of the land which ultimately was a gift of the Netjeru.

117

Richard J. Reidy

This is the Eye of Heru by which you have become great, by which you live, and by which you have power, O Bastet. This is the Eye of Heru which you consume and through which you enchant your body. The *Wedjat*-Eye now enters into the West, into *Manu*, but it shall return. Truly, the Eye of Heru returns in peace![93]

---

[93] It is important to consume the food offerings after the ceremony. Water used should either be drunk or poured onto the earth. If it is mixed with Natron, dilute it very greatly and then you can pour in onto the bare earth.

The General Ritual for Djehuty

The epithets for Djehuty come from the Rev. Patrick Boylan's classic scholarly work, *Thoth, the Hermes of Egypt* (reprint 2012), and C. J. Bleeker's *Hathor and Thoth: Two Key Figures of the Ancient Egyptian Religion* (Leiden: E. J. Brill, 1973).

Special offering for the Feast of Djehuty on the 19th day of the first month of the year (season of Akhet, month of Tekhy, day 19): dates and honey, as well as the traditional offerings of bread, beer, wine, and meat.

Like members of the ancient priesthood, participants should be clothed in white linen. No item made of animal products such as leather or wool is to be worn. Linen represents a pristine product of the earth whereas leather and wool come from humankind's domination of the animals, a domination that becomes part of the "natural order" only *after* the First Time when the *Netjeru* and humans and animals lived in peace and harmony. Just as the Morning Ritual harkens back to that First Time (*Zep Tepi*), so every temple rite re-presents mythic prototypes that occurred "in the beginning," that is, in that time before time. Even the sandals worn by the god's servants were made of white papyrus. This avoidance of animal products by the priesthood fits well with the fact that the ritualist acts as a *Netjer* and verbally asserts that he or she is a *Netjer*.

As with all Egyptian rituals begin with your purification—washing of hands and cleansing of mouth with Natron. This preliminary rite helps us to lay aside the cares of the day and to become mindful of the fact that we will encounter a divine being. If Natron is not available, then use a natural sea salt in its place until you make your own Natron.

If two or more persons are participating, then one person, impersonating the Netjer *Djehuty,* **purifies each person by sprinkling each with water while exclaiming:**

I purify you with the water of all life and good fortune, all stability, all health and happiness.[94]

Afterwards each person **rinses his mouth** *and* **places a small amount of Natron or sea salt in his mouth** *while saying:*

I wash my mouth; I chew natron so that I may extol the might of Djehuty, Heart of Ra and Judge of Ma'at.[95]

Participants **assemble outside the Temple Chamber** *and begin by* **softly rattling sistra.**

This time—several minutes or more—is used to focus minds and intention so that distracting thoughts are left behind. The sound of the sistrum was said to placate the deity, purifying the atmosphere in preparation for encountering divinity. The sistrum was associated with Hutheru and also with her and Heru's son Ihy, and thus has connotations of joy, celebration, and dancing.

---

[94] Taken from Aylward M. Blackman's article "Purification (Egyptian)" in Hastings Encyclopedia 10/1918/ 476-82. This article is reprinted in Gods, Priests, and Men, Studies in the Religion of Pharaonic Egypt, edited by Alan B. Lloyd (Kegan Paul International, 1998), p. 9.

[95] Modeled on a temple inscription taken from "The Myth of Horus at Edfu—II" by A. M. Blackman and H. W. Fairman, appearing in Gods, Priests and Men, Studies in the Religion of Pharaonic Egypt (Kegan Paul International, 1998) p. 283.

According to Plutarch (A.D. 46-120), the sound of sistra was also reputed to drive away Setekh. But this was of very late date. It may have been that since by that time Setekh had been demonized, the general apotropaic function of the sistrum against evil entities was extended to include this *Netjer* as well.

*Standing **before the closed doors,** the Ritualist **recites the entrance spell:***

UTTERANCE BEFORE THE CLOSED DOORS OF THE TEMPLE

*The ritualist **raises hands in adoration** (dua position-arms stretched out in front of the body and raised up to face level, with palms facing outward). The following shall be said:*

O you *Netjeru* of this Temple, you guardians of the great portal, great *Netjeru* of mysterious abode, who sanctify the god in his shrine, who consecrate his oblation, who receive the offerings in his presence in the Hall of the Ennead: I have made my way and I enter into your presence. I am one of you. I am Shu, the eldest son of his father, the senior *wab* servant-priest of Djehuty. Do not repulse me on the *Netjer's* path. My feet are not impeded. I am not turned back from the court of the great portal so that I may conduct the divine service, that I may present offerings to him that made them, that I may give bread to Djehuty. I have come on the way of the god. I have not shown partiality in judgment. I have not consorted with the strong. I have not reproached the lowly. I have not stolen things. I have not diminished the constituents of the Eye of Ra. I have not disturbed the Balance. I have not tampered with the requirements of the Sacred Eye. O Council of the Great *Netjer* in this Temple, behold, I have come to you to offer

Ma'at to the Lord of Ma'at, to content the Sound Eye for its lord. I am Shu; I flood his offering table. I present his offerings, Sekhmet consorting with me, that I may adore Djehuty at his festivals, that I may kiss the earth so great is his majesty, that I may endow his image with life. I am pure. I am purified.

*At this point the ritualist **opens the doors to the Temple Chamber,** or, if there are no doors, **makes a gesture of opening unseen doors,** and **steps forward as if crossing over a threshold.** The following is said:*

O you *Ba*-souls of *Khemenu* (Hermopolis) if you are strong, I am strong. If I am strong, you are strong. If your *Ka*-spirits are strong, my *Ka*-spirit is strong at the head of the living. As they are living so shall I live . . . . Djehuty, Lord of Divine Formulae, has given to me life, stability, and serenity round about my members, which Djehuty has gathered together for life. I am Heru in the height of heaven, the beautiful one of awe, Lord of Victory, mighty one of awe, exalted one of the two plumes, great one in *Waset* (Thebes), I am pure.

All temple members chant:

Awake in peace, O Djehuty, Lord of Divine Words,
may you awaken in peace.
Awake in peace, O Djehuty, Thrice Great of *Heka*-power,
may you awaken in peace.
Awake in peace, O Djehuty, Lord of Wisdom,
may you awaken in peace.
Awake in peace, O Djehuty, Lord of Judging,
may you awaken in peace.

May you awake beautifully at the top of the morning,
through that which the entirety of *Netjeru* say to you.

Enter, close the double doors and stand in front of the Kar-shrine and altar. All bow, touching their hands to their knees.

The ritualist slowly opens the two doors of the Kar-shrine housing the sacred image. All others bow, touching their hands to their knees. The following is said:

The doors of the sky are open; the doors of the earth are unlocked. This House is open for its Lord. Let me come forth as he shall come forth. Let me enter in as he shall enter in. Djehuty, the Bull of Ma'at, is exalted upon his Great Seat. The Great Company of the *Netjeru are exalted upon their seat.*

I have seen the *Netjer,* and the *Netjer* sees me. The *Netjer* rejoices at seeing me. I have gazed upon the statue of the Lord of Kindliness, the sacred image of the Ibis Splendid in *Heka.*[96]

Right hand on left shoulder of statue; left hand on right wrist of statue:

Heka has come to you. Awake when you hear his words. I have come as the envoy of Atum. My two arms are upon you like those of Heru. My two hands are upon you like those of Heka. My fingers are upon you like those of Anpu. Homage be to you. I am a living servant of Djehuty.

---

[96] Based on the temple text found in "Worship and Festivals in an Egyptian Temple," a lecture by H. W. Fairman (publ. by The John Rylands Library, 1954), p. 180.

Richard J. Reidy

All present recite the **Hymn to Djehuty:**

> Praise to Djehuty, the son of Ra,
> the Moon beautiful in his rising,
> Lord of Bright Appearings who illumines the *Netjeru.*
> Hail to you, Moon, Djehuty, Bull of *Iunu*
> who spreads out the seat of the *Netjeru,*
> who knows their mysteries and establishes their commands;
> He who sifts evidence,
> who makes the evil deed rise up against the doer,
> Who judges all humankind.
>
> Praise to Djehuty,
> exact Plummet in the Scales from whom evil flees,
> Who accepts him who avoids evil,
> the Vizier who gives judgment,
> Who vanquishes crime and recalls all that is forgotten,
> The one who remembers both time and eternity.
> Praise to Djehuty whose words endure forever![97]

The Ritualist holds up the **bowl of water** *in which he/she will be mixing the Natron. The following is said:*

> O water may you remove all evil,
> As Ra who bathes in the Lake of Rushes.
> May Heru wash my flesh;
> may Djehuty cleanse my feet.
> May Shu lift me up and Nut take my hand!
> May Setekh be my strength, and may Sekhmet be my healing!

---

[97] From a 'Hymn to Thoth' in Margaret A. Murray's Egyptian Religious Poetry (London, 19490, p. 99. This hymn is also found in the Journal of Egyptian Archaeology, vol. x, p. 3.

124

And may Amun-Ra be my life and my prospering!

*The bowl of water is set aside and the container of **Natron** is lifted up. The following is said:*

It is pure, it is pure.
My Natron is the Natron of Heru
and the Natron of Heru is my Natron.
My Natron is the Natron of Setekh
and the Natron of Setekh is my Natron.
My Natron is the Natron of Djehuty
and the Natron of Djehuty is my Natron.
My Natron is the Natron of Geb
and the Natron of Geb is my Natron.

My mouth is the mouth of a milking calf on the day that I
was born.

*Four pinches of **Natron** are mixed into the water as this Utterance is recited:*

I give you essential water, a tide in your time.
I bring the flood waters to purify your sanctuary.
I bring you the flood waters
to purify your Temple and your statue in its place,
the primordial water that purifies as in the First Time!

The Ritualist places an index finger into the water and moves it in a circular direction four times as the following is said:

Djehuty, the Heart of Ra, does purify this water;
Djehuty, the Tongue of Ptah, does cleanse this water;
Djehuty, the Throat of Him of the Hidden Name,

even Atum, does sanctify this water;
Djehuty, Mighty in His Words and Lord of *Heka*-power,
does endow this water with power and with life.

*The **Bowl of Natron-infused water** is then taken up and the Ritualist sprinkles this lightly in front of and around the statue or image of Djehuty, applying some water to the base of the image, as the Utterance is recited:*

I come close to You, O Judge of Ma'at, who sets all things in their proper places. I bring the water of rejuvenation that flows from the Two Caverns. I sprinkle the water, purifying your image and your Temple from all impurity!

*The Ritualist picks up the bowl of **Natron** and **sprinkles a small amount in each of the four directions** as the following is recited:*

The *Netjer* Djehuty himself does cleanse and purify this, his Temple to the South.
The *Netjer* Djehuty himself does cleanse and purify this, his Temple to the North.
The *Netjer* Djehuty himself does cleanse and purify this, his Temple to the West.
The *Netjer* Djehuty himself does cleanse and purify this, his Temple to the East.

*Replacing the Natron on the altar, the Ritualist takes up the bowl of **water, sprinkling a small amount in each of the four directions**. The following Utterance is recited:*

The *Netjer* Djehuty himself does sanctify and consecrate this, his Temple to the South.
The *Netjer* Djehuty himself does sanctify and consecrate this,

his Temple to the North.
The *Netjer* Djehuty himself does sanctify and consecrate this,
his Temple to the West.
The *Netjer* Djehuty himself does sanctify and consecrate this,
his Temple to the East.

The Temple of the *Netjer* Djehuty is established.
It is established for millions of years.

*The Ritualist returns to the altar and **lights the candle or oil lamp**
while the following is said:*

Come, come in peace, O glorious Eye of Heru;
be strong and renew your youth in peace,
for the flame shines like Ra on the double horizon.
The enemies of Ra are defeated. They are defeated.
I am pure, I am pure, I am pure, I am pure.

*The Ritualist **places incense on the burner** and **censes each sacred
image beginning with the statue** of the Netjer while the following is
recited:*

The fire is laid, the fire shines;
The incense is laid on the fire, the incense shines.
   Your perfume comes to me, O Incense;
   May my perfume come to you, O Incense.
Your perfume comes to me, you Netjeru;
May my perfume come to you, You Netjeru.
   May I be with you, you Netjeru;
   May you be with me, you Netjeru.
May I live with you, you Netjeru;
May you live with me, you Netjeru.

I love you, you Netjeru;
May you love me, you Netjeru.

*Standing in front of the image of Djehuty the Ritualist **offers the
burning incense** and says:*

Take the incense,
Its essence is for you, O Ibis Splendid in *Heka.*
Its smoke permeates your shrine, bringing life!
Take the incense,
Its essence is for you.
Your Majesty is appeased with the incense.
This Eye of Heru,
This essence of the Eye of Heru comes to you.

At this point the following is said:

Excellent One of Magic, homage be to you! Lord of Divine
Words, adoration be to you! O Djehuty, you repeat to us
what Ra has declared. You are Master of Divine Words
which put all things in their proper place. You give offerings
to the *Netjeru* and to the blessed dead. You are Djehuty who
puts *ma'at* into writing for the Ennead. Everything that
comes out of your mouth takes on existence as if you were
Ra. You are he who cannot be driven from the sky or earth
because you know what is concealed in the sky, inaccessible
on earth, and hidden in the Primeval Ocean. You are the
recorder and preserver of knowledge.

O Lord of Kindliness, leader of the entire multitude, I give
praise to you, O Djehuty, Straight Plummet in the Scales,
who repulses evil, who accepts him who leans not on crime;
I make rejoicing to you every day.

You are he who gives breath to the weary-hearted one and vindicates him against his enemies. Vindicate me against my enemies and adversaries. You are the Vizier who settles cases, who changes turmoil to peace, the Scribe of the *ma'at* who keeps the book, who punishes crime, who accepts the submissive, who is sound of arm, wise among the Ennead, who relates what was forgotten. Relate to me the secrets of magic, O *Netjer* of the Moon! Speak with me the words of power so the magic I enact is your own invincible magic, O Lord of Magic!

O creator of written language, Lord of the Divine Books, guide my hand in all my magical writings so the words are alive with your own divine power. O Ibis Splendid in *Heka*, Tongue of Ra and Lord of Divine Words, speak through my mouth the words of power; O Heart of Ra, mighty in his words, empower my words as utterance coming forth from your own heart so they at once take place. Encircle my workings with your protective presence, O Lord of Wisdom. Adoration be to you, O Djehuty!

The Ritualist **places more incense on the charcoal** *and again and again* **slowly raises and lowers the incense cup** *as the following is recited:*

O Djehuty, may you advance with your *Ka*.
O Tongue of Ra, the arm of your *Ka* is before you,
The arm of your *Ka* is behind you.
O Lord of Spells, the foot of your *Ka* is before you,
The foot of your *Ka* is behind you.
O Ibis Splendid in *Heka*, Djehuty, this incense is offered to you,

May your face be filled as this essence spreads itself over you.

*All present **perform the Henu Rite** — Embrace the Earth, the Fourfold Salute to the God, Embrace the Earth. The bodily gestures are performed alternately four times.*

For Embracing the Earth, all present prostrate themselves, face down, upon the floor. During the Fourfold Salute, all present rise upon one knee, and alternately raise their hands and arms into the *Dua* (praise) position with palms facing outward, followed by the *Sahu* (obedience) gesture, made by striking the chest with a closed fist and raising the other arm (also with closed fist) at a ninety-degree angle. The *Dua* position is accompanied by the words **"Adoration be to Djehuty,"** followed by the *Sahu* gesture accompanied with the words, **"Hail to the Vizier of Ra!"** The bodily gestures are performed alternately four times.

*Following this **all present again prostrate themselves** before the god. This is a sign and symbol of total submission and adoration before the Netjer. The following is said:*

Homage to Djehuty, Thrice Great of *Heka*-power,
who is established on the Great Seat
in the Mansion of the Moon!
I have placed myself on the floor in awe of you.
I embrace the earth before you as before the Bull of Ma'at.
I have come that I might kiss the earth,
that I might worship my Lord,
For I have seen his Strength;
I give praise to Djehuty,
For I have seen his Power.

His form is more distinguished than the *Netjeru*;
His arm is more powerful than the *Netjeru*.
I am pure, I am pure, I am pure, I am pure!

Everyone stands up.

*The Ritualist **holds in the palm of one hand the image of Ma'at**
and **with the other hand open and raised over the image as if
sheltering it,** repeats the following:*

I have come to you as Heka, whose two hands are joined
together under Ma'at. She comes to be with you, for she
is everywhere. You are provided with Ma'at. You move in
Ma'at, you live in Ma'at. She fills your body, she rests in
your head, she makes her seat upon your brow; the breath
of your body is of Ma'at, your heart does live in Ma'at. All
that you eat, all that you drink, all that you breathe is of
Ma'at. Heka presents Ma'at to you, his two hands are upon
her beauty before your face.

*The Ritualist places the image of Ma'at near the divine statue. Then he/
she holds up before the image of Djehuty **a pitcher of water** and **pours
the water slowly into a libation bowl** as the following Utterance is
recited:*

This libation is for you, O Lord of Magic.
This libation is for you, O Djehuty,
who reconciles the brother gods.
I have brought to you this offering of water,
That your heart may be refreshed.
I have brought to you this Eye of Heru,
Placing this at your feet.

I present to you that which flows forth from you,
That your heart shall continue to beat.
For it is with you
that all comes forth at the sound of the voice.

The libation bowl is placed on the altar. At this point the Ritualist **lightly sprinkles sand on the floor in front of the altar** *as the following is recited:*

O Djehuty, who resides in *Khemenu* (Hermopolis),
Take to yourself the Eye of Heru.
You have rescued it, O Lord of Triumph and Orderer of Fate.
You have sprinkled with sand the Eye of Heru.

On the **Festival of Djehuty** *the Ritualist* **offers a basket of figs and honey** *as the following is said:*

Take the figs and the White Eye of Heru (i.e., honey). You nourish yourself with it. Your heart is joyful for truly 'Sweet is the Truth.'[98]

All present respond,

Sweet is the Truth!

Lifting the wine offering *before the sacred image, the Ritualist repeats the following:*

---

[98] Adapted from Sylvie Cauville, L'Offrande aux dieux dans le temple égyptien (Leuven, Belgique: Peeters, 2011), p. 108. In ancient times Egyptians exchanged the greeting, "Sweet is the Truth" during the festival of Djehuty.

mn n.k irp irt ḥrw wȝḏt

["*mán-nik 'úrip írat ḥáru wá'ḏat*"; approximately pronounced *MAHN-neek OO-rip EE-raht HAH-roo WAH-jat*]

Take to yourself wine, the green Eye of Heru,
which I offer to your Ka.[99]
O Bull of Ma'at, how mighty is your strong arm!
May you drink it; may you be powerful through it;
may your mouth be opened by means of it.
It is pure.
[*iw.w wʿb* pronounced "*uwú wáʿib*"; approximately *oo-WOO WAH-ib*]

The Ritualist places myrrh on the fire and lifts up the smoking incense while at the same time he lifts up the meat-offering before the Netjer, and says the following:

The scent of myrrh is for your nose. It fills your nostrils; your heart receives the meat-portions on its scent.[100]

Slowly elevating the food offerings four times before the image of Djehuty, the Ritualist repeats the following:

I offer to Djehuty, Bull of Ma'at.
All life emanates from you,
All health emanates from you,

---

[99] Refer to pp. 92, 93, 99, and 105 in Mu-Chou Poo's Wine and Wine Offerings in Ancient Egypt (London & New York: Kegan Paul International, 1995).

[100] Quoted in "Worship and Festivals in an Egyptian Temple," by H. W. Fairman (publ. by The John Rylands Library, 1954), p. 191.

All stability emanates from you,
All good fortune emanates from you,
Lord of Judging who drives away evil, Djehuty forever.

*The Ritualist **places the food offering before the divine image**, and then all present **extend one hand, palm down, over the offerings** and recite the following:*

May offerings of every kind come forth in abundance,
like the things which come forth from the mouth of the
Netjer.

piryá pírit ar ḫiráw mi purú:riat ma rá' ni náṯar. (4 times)
[approximately pronounced *peer-YA PEER-it ar khi-RAU mee pu-ROOR-iat ma RA nee NAH-tchar*]

May offerings of every kind come forth in abundance, like
the things that come forth from the mouth of the Netjer.

*Holding the **Ankh** before Djehuty, the Ritualist says:*

Live, O Djehuty, lord of the *Netjeru,*
live for all time and for eternity!

ʿánaḫ niḥáḥ ḏát.
[approximately pronounced *AH-nakh nee-HAH JAHT*]

*The **Ankh** is placed next to the image of the Netjer.*

*Holding the **Ib** (**the golden heart**) before Djehuty, the Ritualist says:*

Hail to you, O Djehuty, Lord of the Moon. I have brought
to you your heart to set it in its place. Let me draw near to

you with your heart, so that you may have pleasure through me, and that by means of me you may have power over your body. Ascend, O Silver Sun, radiant one, who illumine the darkness with your light. Live, O Chief of Nut,[101] live forever and ever!

*After placing the **Ib** near the sacred image, **everyone sings or chants** the **Hymn to Djehuty**[102]. Participants may wish to alternate the singing of verses.*

I praise Djehuty, thrice great, Lord of *Khemenu* (Hermopolis), the glorious Ibis, presiding over the Two Lands, sprung from Ra, born at the beginning [(1)]; I worship his majesty, I exalt the Lord of Heaven.

Adoration to Djehuty, Praise to the Heart of Atum which has fashioned all things![(2)] O Djehuty who loves Ma'at, who looks into hearts, the Knowing One who searches out the hidden things of the body![(3)]

All hail, jubilation to you, Djehuty the Great, the Bau of Ra, the representative of Atum![(4)] You are the god sprung from the sun-god himself, for whom the gates of the horizon opened on the day of his birth. Every Netjer came forth at his command; his word passes into being. You are Khonsu-Djehuty.[(5)] Heaven rests upon your hands; the earth is under your feet. What you command, takes place. May you bless

---

[101] The epithet "chief of Nut" comes from the Pyramid Text 2150C and refers to the brightness of the moon in the night sky.

[102] 1) From a Denderah text quoted in Patrick Boylan's Thoth: The Hermes of Egypt (London: Oxford Univ. Press, 1922), p. 118; 2) 120; 3) 101; 4) 114; 5) 121; 6) 84; 7) 125-128; 8) 131-134; 9) 135; 10) 185, 188, and 214; 11) 65; 12) 40 and 192; 13) 139; 14) 94-95.

me with life and strength and health. O Lord of Strength, hear me!

Hail to you, Djehuty, Reckoner of Time, who divides seasons, months, and years, who increases time and multiplies years, grant me long life![6]

Hail to you, Djehuty, Great in Magic and Lord of Divine Formulae, dreaded of demons, the Peaceful One who knows how to repel evil, assist me in speaking the words of power![7]

Hail to you, Djehuty, Lord of Terror, strong of arm, who bathes in the blood of the enemies of the god, come to me when I call and be a shield round about me, defending me from every assault.[8] Grant that no evil being, male or female, can enter into my house.[9]

Hail to you, Djehuty, mighty in his words, Lord of Speech, fill my words with your effective power, and grant that I, like you, may be called 'excellent in counsel' and 'mighty in his words.'[10]

O Beautiful One of the Night, O Silver Sun, go forth in your name Ausir-Iooh-Djehuty that you may illumine the Two Lands, and make full the Eye on the 15th of the month.[11]

Advance, O Lord of Judging; you have made Heru glad; you have appeased the Rivals in the hour of their trouble. . . You have put away every evil thing.[12]

O Djehuty, Lord of the Balance, Judge of *ma'at,* stretch out your hand from heaven and lead me when I go into the presence of the Lords of Ma'at.[13]

O Lord of the effective word, Author of the formulae of power[14]; when my life here shall have come to its end, may you yourself speak the Divine words that cause me to ascend, even to the stars, to the stars. O Lord of gladness, hear me!

At this point perform the **meditation or magical action** *or, if it is a special feast, add the appropriate prayers.*

Afterwards **all present back out of the Temple Chamber with heads slightly bowed** *while the Ritualist performs the* **"removing the foot."**

With the **broom** *the Ritualist, as the last person to exit,* **ritually sweeps the area beginning at the altar.** *(This is known as* **"removing the foot."***) While performing this action the Ritualist recites the following:*

The distress that causes confusion has been driven away, and all the Netjeru are in harmony. I have given Heru his Eye; I have placed the Wedjat-Eye in the correct position. I have given Setekh his Testicles, so that the two lords are content through the work of my hands.

I know the sky, I know the earth;
I know Heru, I know Setekh.
Heru is appeased with his Eyes;
Setekh is appeased with his Testicles.
I am Djehuty, who reconciles the Netjeru,
who makes offerings in their correct form.

*The **double doors are solemnly closed** as the Ritualist says the following:*

> Djehuty has come.
> He has filled the Eye of Heru;
> He has restored the Testicles of Setekh.
> No evil shall enter this Temple.
> Ptah has closed the door,
> Djehuty has set it fast.
> The door is closed, the door is set fast with the bolt.

All **bow, touching the palms of their hands to their knees.**

THE REVERSION OF OFFERINGS

*One priest or priestess and as many assistants as necessary enter the Temple Chamber a final time. While he/she and any assistants **lift up the offerings** before the sacred image the ritualist shall say:*

> O Djehuty, your enemy[103] withdraws for you. Heru has turned himself to his Eye in its name of 'Reversion-of-Offerings.' I am Djehuty. I come to perform this rite for Djehuty, might of *Heka*-power. These, your divine offerings revert, they revert to your servants for life, for stability, for health and for joy! O that the Eye of Heru may flourish for you eternally!

---

[103] Meat offerings held a two-fold meaning for the ancient priesthood. Since meat necessarily came from slain animals, it signified the defeated or slain enemies of the Netjeret. At the same time, the meat offering represented the produce of the land which ultimately was a gift of the Netjeru.

*Everyone withdraws, **carrying away all food offerings except for one loaf of bread and a bowl of pure water**. These last items remain until evening. If this ritual is celebrated after sunset, these items would also be removed.*

*After the candle has burned down, a servant-priest enters and closes the doors of the Kar-shrine. **Extinguishing the candle or oil lamp**, he/she exclaims:*

This is the Eye of Heru by which you have become great, by which you live, and by which you have power, O Djehuty. This is the Eye of Heru which you consume and through which you enchant your body. The *Wedjat-*Eye now enters into the West, into *Manu*, but it shall return. Truly, the Eye of Heru returns in peace![104]

---

[104] It is important to consume the food offerings after the ceremony. Water used should either be drunk or poured onto the earth. If it is mixed with Natron, dilute it very greatly and then you can pour in onto the bare earth.

The General Ritual for Hat-Hór

The goddess's name is pronounced Hat-Hár or Hat-Hór. The 'th' is not sounded as in the word 'third.' The stress is on the second syllable. The name means 'House of Heru.'

All epithets of the goddess are based on those found in the *Lexikon der ägyptischen Götter und Götterbezeichnungen* (Dictionary of Egyptian Gods and God-Names), eight volumes. The epithets are capitalized in order to facilitate identification.

Offerings to Hat-Hór: two mirrors, pure oil of galbanum[105], beer, and the regular food offerings. For festivals of this goddess a special offering of oil of myrrh and oil of lotus may be made.

Like members of the ancient priesthood, participants should be clothed in white linen. No item made of animal products such as leather or wool is to be worn. Linen represents a pristine product of the earth whereas leather and wool come from humankind's domination of the animals, a domination that becomes part of the "natural order" only *after* the First Time when the *Netjeru* and humans and animals lived in peace and harmony. Just as the Morning Ritual harkens back to that First Time (*Zep Tepi*), so every temple rite re-presents mythic prototypes that occurred "in the beginning," that is, in that time before time. Even the sandals worn by the god's servants were made of white papyrus. This avoidance of animal products by the priesthood fits well with the fact that the ritualist acts as a *Netjer* and verbally asserts that he or she is a *Netjer*.

---

[105] Oil of galbanum is available as an essential oil. It was regarded as a sacred oil by the Egyptians.

As with all Egyptian rituals begin with your purification—washing of hands and cleansing of mouth with Natron. This preliminary rite helps us to lay aside the cares of the day and to become mindful of the fact that we will encounter a divine being. If Natron is not available, then use a natural sea salt in its place until you make your own Natron.

If two or more persons are participating, then one person, impersonating the Netjer *Djehuty,* **purifies each person by sprinkling each with water while exclaiming:**

I purify you with the water of all life and good fortune, all stability, all health and happiness.[106]

Afterwards each person **rinses his mouth** *and* **places a small amount of Natron or sea salt in his mouth** *while saying:*

I wash my mouth; I chew natron so that I may extol the might of Hat-Hór, Mistress of All that Exists, the Golden One.[107]

Participants **assemble outside the Temple Chamber** *and begin by softly rattling sistra.*

This time—several minutes or more—is used to focus minds and intention so that distracting thoughts are left behind. The

---

[106] Taken from Aylward M. Blackman's article "Purification (Egyptian)" in Hastings Encyclopedia 10/1918/ 476-82. This article is reprinted in Gods, Priests, and Men, Studies in the Religion of Pharaonic Egypt, edited by Alan B. Lloyd (Kegan Paul International, 1998), p. 9.

[107] Adapted from a temple inscription taken from "The Myth of Horus at Edfu—II" by A. M. Blackman and H. W. Fairman, appearing in Gods, Priests and Men, Studies in the Religion of Pharaonic Egypt, p. 283.

sound of the sistrum was said to placate the deity, purifying the atmosphere in preparation for encountering divinity. The sistrum was associated with Hutheru and also with her and Heru's son Ihy, and thus has connotations of joy, celebration, and dancing. According to Plutarch (A.D. 46-120), the sound of sistra was also reputed to drive away Setekh. But this was of very late date. It may have been that since by that time Setekh had been demonized, the general apotropaic function of the sistrum against evil entities was extended to include this *Netjer* as well.

*Standing **before the closed doors,** the Ritualist **recites the entrance spell:***

UTTERANCE BEFORE THE CLOSED DOORS OF THE TEMPLE

*The ritualist **raises hands in adoration** (dua position-arms stretched out in front of the body and raised up to face level, with palms facing outward). The following shall be said:*

O you *Netjeru* of this temple, you guardians of the great portal, great *Netjeru* of mysterious abode, who sanctify the *Netjeret* in her shrine, who consecrate her oblation, who receive the offerings in her presence in the Hall of the Ennead: I have made my way and I enter into your presence. I am one of you. I am Shu, the eldest son of his father, the senior wab servant-priest of Hat-Hór. Do not repulse me on the *Netjeret's* path. My feet are not impeded. I am not turned back from the court of the great portal so that I may conduct the divine service, that I may present offerings to her that made them, that I may give bread to Hat-Hór. I have come on the way of the *Netjeret*. I have not shown partiality in judgment. I have not consorted with the strong. I have not reproached the lowly. I have not stolen things. I have not diminished the constituents of the Eye of Ra. I have not disturbed the balance. I have not tampered with the requirements of the Sacred Eye. O Council of the Great *Netjeret* in this temple, behold, I have come to you to offer Ma'at to the Lady of Ma'at, to content the Sound Eye for its mistress. I am Shu; I flood her offering table. I present her offerings, Sekhmet consorting with me, that I may adore Hat-Hór at her festivals, that I may kiss the earth so great is her majesty, that I may endow her image with life. I am pure. I am purified.

At this point the ritualist **opens the doors to the Temple Chamber,** *or, if there are no doors,* **makes a gesture of opening unseen doors,** *and* **steps forward as if crossing over a threshold.** *The following is said:*

O you *Ba*-souls of *Iunet* (Dendera) if you are strong, I am strong. If I am strong, you are strong. If your *Ka*-spirits are strong, my *Ka*-spirit is strong at the head of the living. As they are living so shall I live . . . . Sekhmet, the great *Netjeret*, beloved of Ptah, has given to me life, stability, and serenity round about my members, which Djehuty has gathered together for life. I am Heru in the height of heaven, the beautiful one of awe, Lord of Victory, mighty one of awe, exalted one of the two plumes, great one in *Waset* (Thebes), I am pure.

All temple members chant:

Awake in peace, O Hat-Hór, Foremost of *Iunet*,
may you awaken in peace.
Awake in peace, O Hat-Hór, Golden One,
may you awaken in peace.

Awake in peace, O Hat-Hór, Possessor of Abundance,
may you awaken in peace.
Awake in peace, O Hat-Hór, Mistress of the Sycamore,
may you awaken in peace.

May you awake beautifully at the top of the morning,
through that which the entirety of *Netjeru* say to you.

*Enter, close the double doors and stand in front of the Kar-shrine
and altar. All bow, touching their hands to their knees.*

*The ritualist slowly opens the two doors of the Kar-shrine housing
the sacred image. All others bow, touching their hands to their
knees. The following is said:*

The doors of the sky are open; the doors of the earth are
unlocked. This House is open for its Mistress. Let me come
forth as she shall come forth. Let me enter in as she shall
enter in. Hat-Hór, the Golden One, the Lady of Intoxication,
is exalted upon her Great Seat. The Great Company of the
Netjeru are exalted upon their seat.

I have seen the *Netjeret,* and the *Netjeret* sees me. The *Netjeret*
rejoices at seeing me. I have gazed upon the statue of the
Lady of Life, the sacred image of Queen of the Stars.[108]

Right hand on left shoulder of statue; left hand on right wrist of statue:

---

[108] Based on the temple text found in "Worship and Festivals in an Egyptian
Temple," a lecture by H. W. Fairman (publ. by The John Rylands Library,
1954), p. 180.

Djehuty has come to you. Awake when you hear his words. I have come as the envoy of Atum. My two arms are upon you like those of Heru. My two hands are upon you like those of Djehuty. My fingers are upon you like those of Anpu. Homage be to you. I am a living servant of Hat-Hór.

*All present begin softly **playing their sistra** as the following is said:*

I play the sistrum before your beautiful face,
Hat-Hór the Great.
You are the One in the Temple-of-the-Phoenix,
ruler of *Waset* (Thebes),
Mistress of *Iunu* whose appearance is beautiful
in *Ipet-Sut* ('Most-Select-of-Places'; i.e., Karnak).
May you be at peace with me.
May you not launch your curse at me.[109]

How beautiful it is!
This sistrum that you desire, O Mistress of the Sistrum,
which your heart loves.
We shake the sistra for you to appease your *Ka*.
Your heart rejoices at their sound.
Welcome, O Lady of the Sistrum!
The *Netjeru* make music for you
and the *Netjerut* dance to appease your heart.[110]

---

[109] Émile Chassinat, et al., Le temple de Dendara, Vol. IV (Cairo: Institut francçais d'archéologie orientale), 75-76.

[110] Amr Gaber, The Central Hall in the Egyptian Temples of the Ptolemaic Period (2009), Durham theses, Durham University. Available at Durham E-Theses Online: http://etheses.dur.ac.uk/88/ Based on one of the ancient formulae for offering the sistrum: from the Central Hall in the Temple at Edfu; see p. 470 in the dissertation.

Praise to you, O Lady of Names in the Two Lands, Unique One,

Lady of Terror among the Guardian-*Netjeru*,

Great Uraeus on the horns of Atum

The *Netjeru* come to you prostrating themselves before you,

the *Netjerut* come to you bowing their heads before you.

Your Father Ra adores you,

his face rejoices when hearing your name.

Djehuty satisfies you with his glorifications,

and he raises his arms to you, carrying the sistrum.

The *Netjeru* rejoice for you when you appear.

You illuminate the Two Lands with the rays of your Eye.

The South, the North, the West, and the East

pay homage to you,

they make adorations to you.

Hat-Hór, Lady of *Iunet*,

may your beautiful face be pleased by this,

our service to you.[111]

Continue shaking the sistra as the Ritualist holds up a bowl of pure **water** *in which he/she will be mixing the Natron. The following is said:*

O water may you remove all evil,

As Ra who bathes in the Lake of Rushes,

May Heru wash my flesh,

May Djehuty cleanse my feet,

May Shu lift me up and Nut take my hand!

May Setekh be my strength, and may Sekhmet be my healing!

And may Amun-Ra be my life and my prospering!

---

[111] Émile Chassinat, et al., *Le temple de Dendara*, Vol. I (Cairo: Institut francçais d'archéologie orientale), p. 80.

*The bowl of water is set aside and the container of **Natron** is lifted up. The following is said:*

> It is pure, it is pure.
> My Natron is the Natron of Heru
> and the Natron of Heru is my Natron.
> My Natron is the Natron of Sutekh
> and the Natron of Sutekh is my Natron.
> My Natron is the Natron of Djehuty
> and the Natron of Djehuty is my Natron.
> My Natron is the Natron of Geb
> and the Natron of Geb is my Natron.
>
> My mouth is the mouth of a milking calf
> on the day that I was born.

*Sprinkle four pinches of **Natron** into the water as you recite the spell:*

> I give you essential water, a tide in your time.
> I bring the flood waters to purify your sanctuary.
> I bring you the flood waters
> to purify your Temple and your statue in its place,
> the primordial water that purified as in the First Time!

*Place your **index finger into the water** and **move it in a circular direction four times** as you say:*

> Hat-Hór, Daughter of Ra, does purify this water;
> Hat-Hór, Beloved of Heru, does cleanse this water;
> Hat-Hór, Lady of Jubilation, does sanctify this water;
> Hat-Hór herself does endow this water with power and with life.

Richard J. Reidy

*The **Bowl of Natron-infused water is then taken** up and the Ritualist*
***sprinkles this lightly in front of and around the statue** or image of*
Hat-Hór, applying some water to the base of the image, as the Utterance
is recited:

> I come close to you, O Pure One, Lady of the Waters of Life.
> I bring the water of rejuvenation
> that flows from the Two Caverns.
> I sprinkle the water, purifying your Temple from all
> impurity!

*The Ritualist picks up the bowl of **Natron** and **sprinkles a small***
***amount in each of the four directions** as the following is recited:*

> The *Netjeret* Hat-Hór herself does cleanse and purify this,
> her temple to the South.
> The *Netjeret* Hat-Hór herself does cleanse and purify this,
> her temple to the North.
> The *Netjeret* Hat-Hór herself does cleanse and purify this,
> her temple to the West.
> The *Netjeret* Hat-Hór herself does cleanse and purify this,
> her temple to the East.

*Replacing the Natron on the altar, the Ritualist takes up the **bowl of***
water, sprinkling a small amount in each of the four directions.
The following Utterance is recited:

> The *Netjeret* Hat-Hór herself does sanctify and consecrate this,
> her Temple to the South.
> The *Netjeret* Hat-Hór herself does sanctify and consecrate this,
> her Temple to the North.
> The *Netjeret* Hat-Hór herself does sanctify and consecrate this,

her Temple to the West.

The *Netjeret* Hat-Hór herself does sanctify and consecrate this, her Temple to the East.

The Temple of the *Netjeret* Hat-Hór is established.

It is established for millions of years!"

*The Ritualist returns to the altar and **lights the candle or oil lamp** while the following is said:*

Come, come in peace, O glorious Eye of Heru,

Be strong and renew your youth in peace.

For the flame shines like Ra on the double horizon.

The enemies of Ra are defeated. They are defeated.

I am pure, I am pure, I am pure, I am pure.

*The Ritualist places **incense** on the burner and **censes each sacred image** beginning with the statue of Hat-Hór while the following is recited:*

The fire is laid, the fire shines;

The incense is laid on the fire, the incense shines.

Your perfume comes to me, O Incense;

May my perfume come to you, O Incense.

Your perfume comes to me, you *Netjeru*;

May my perfume come to you, you *Netjeru*.

May I be with you, you *Netjeru*;

May you be with me, you *Netjeru*.

May I live with you, you *Netjeru*;

May you live with me, you *Netjeru*.

I love you, you *Netjeru*;

May you love me, you *Netjeru*.

Richard J. Reidy

Standing in front of the image of Hat-Hór, the Ritualist offers the burning incense and addresses the Netjeret:

Take the incense, O Mistress of Jubilation. Its essence is for you.
Its smoke permeates your shrine, bringing life!
Take the incense. Its essence is for you.
Your Majesty is appeased with the incense.
This Eye of Heru,
This essence of the Eye of Heru comes to you.

*At this point **the sistra are shaken again** as the following is said:*

Homage to Hat-Hór, Mistress of the Two Lands, Hat-Hór who resides in *Iunet*. Your headdress is of shining gold. It is radiant with electrum. When you shine the people rejoice in your light. Every living being, and every *Netjer* is in awe of you when you burst open the double doors, for you are the Queen of All. All do dance, and all do sing, *Nebet-Hetepet*! She who draws the hearts of the Company of the *Netjeru*. Advance, O Female Falcon, far-striding Mistress of the *Netjeru*, may your beautiful face be gracious to us. O Mistress of Music and Queen of the Dance, we pay homage to you! O Mistress of Inebriety without End, we rejoice in you.

Place more incense on the burner and hold it up as you repeat the following:

O Hat-Hór, may you advance with your *Ka*.
O Golden One, the arm of your *Ka* is before you,
The arm of your *Ka* is behind you.
O Lady of Heaven, the foot of your *Ka* is before you,

The foot of your *Ka* is behind you.

O Beautiful Hat-Hór, this incense is offered to you,

May your face be filled as this essence spreads itself over you.

*All present **perform the Henu Rite** — Embrace the Earth, the Fourfold Salute to the God, Embrace the Earth. The bodily gestures are performed alternately four times.*

For Embracing the Earth, all present prostrate themselves, face down, upon the floor. During the Fourfold Salute, all present rise upon one knee, and alternately raise their hands and arms into the *Dua* (praise) position with palms facing outward, followed by the *Sahu* (obedience) gesture, made by striking the chest with a closed fist and raising the other arm (also with closed fist) at a ninety-degree angle. The *Dua* position is accompanied by the words **"Adoration be to Hat-Hór,"** followed by the *Sahu* gesture accompanied with the words, **"Hail to the Lady of Life!"** The bodily gestures are performed alternately four times.

*Following this **all present again prostrate themselves** before the goddess. This is a sign and symbol of total submission and adoration before the Netjer. The following is said:*

Homage to Hat-Hór, Eye of Ra,

Daughter of Atum, Rait[112] in the sky,

Ruler of the Stars

who rises in gold together with him (i.e., Ra) who shines in gold,

who is established on the Great Seat!

I have placed myself on the floor in awe of you.

---

[112] Rait is the female form of Ra.

> I embrace the earth before you as before the Lady of Heaven.
> I have come that I might kiss the earth,
> that I might worship my Mistress,
> For I have seen her Beauty;
> I give praise to Hat-Hór,
> For I have seen her Power.
> Her form is more distinguished than the *Netjeru*;
> Her arm is more powerful than the *Netjeru*.
> I am pure, I am pure, I am pure, I am pure!

Everyone stands up.

The **offering of oil of galbanum** *as the following is recited:*

> Take the ointment that beautifies your flesh; the divine flow emanating from the *Netjer,* prepared by Shesmu with his own fingers and in a state of absolute purity. It makes your body healthy; it permeates your bones; its perfume is sweet for your body.[113]

For special festivals of this great goddess **the offering of oil of myrrh and oil of lotus** may be offered and the following is said:

> Presenting the container of essence of myrrh and of lotus. I carry the container filled with essence of myrrh provided with all its ingredients, fashioned of gold by the Ram, Master of the Vault of Heaven. I offer this to your beautiful face, sweet oil of myrrh of the highest quality and oil of

---

[113] From an inscription in the temple of Hathor at Dendara found in Sylvie Cauville, Dendara II Traduction (Leuven: Peeters, 1999), Section 20.

lotus for your hair. You reveal yourself through it. Thanks to it you are more divine than even the *Netjeru*.[114]

*The **offering of the two mirrors** as the following is recited:*

Take these mirrors fashioned by Ptah. Their disks are the sun and the moon. May you contemplate your perfect image. May you rejoice to see your beauty.[115]

*The Ritualist **holds in the palm of one hand the image of Ma'at** and **with the other hand open and raised over the image as if sheltering it,** repeats the following:*

I have come to you as Djehuty, whose two hands are joined together under Ma'at. She comes to be with you, for she is everywhere. You are provided with Ma'at. You move in Ma'at, you live in Ma'at. She fills your body, she rests in your head, she makes her seat upon your brow; the breath of your body is of Ma'at, your heart does live in Ma'at. All that you eat, all that you drink, all that you breathe is of Ma'at. Djehuty presents Ma'at to you, his two hands are upon her beauty before your face.

*The Ritualist places the image of Ma'at near the divine statue. Then he/ she holds up before the image of Hat-Hór **a pitcher of water** and **pours the water slowly into an offering bowl** as the following Utterance is recited:*

This libation is for you, O Gold,

---

[114] This beautiful text comes from Sylvie Cauville, Dendara IV Traduction (Leuven: Peeters, 2001), Section 70, p. 137.
[115] É. Chassinat, Le temple de Dendara, Vol. III, p. 17.

This libation is for you, O Hat-Hór.
I have brought to you this offering of water,
That your heart may be refreshed.
I have brought to you this offering of water,
Placing this at your feet.
I present to you that which flows forth from you,
That your heart shall continue to beat.
For it is with you that all comes forth at the sound of the
voice.

The offering bowl is placed on the altar. At this point the Ritualist **lightly sprinkles sand on the floor** *in front of the altar as the following is recited:*

O Hat-Hór, Who resides in *Iunet.*
Take to Yourself the Eye of Heru.
You have rescued it, O Mistress of exultation.
You have sprinkled with sand the Eye of Heru.

Lifting the **beer offering** *and* **playing the sistrum** *the Ritualist repeats the following:*

How beautiful is this! This beer of the Mistress of Magical
Spells, Hat-Hór, Lady of the Fields. The Shining One is more
than the shining ones, wine *Netjeret* more than the wine
Netjerut (goddesses), Hat-Hór, Lady of the Two Lands, Lady
of Bread. It is she who makes beer as the creation of her
heart, as one who makes as her handiwork this beer from
beautiful plants coming from Geb, as the grain which comes
from Nepit.[116] How beautiful it is! This container of beer

---

[116] Nepit is the goddess of grain which would be used in the production
of beer.

as well as this sistrum that you desire, O Mistress of the Sistrum, the sistrum which your heart loves. I shake the sistrum for you to appease your *Ka*. Your heart rejoices at its sound. Welcome, Lady of the Sistrum. The *Netjeru* make music to you. This *Netjeret* dances to appease her heart.[117]

Lifting the wine offering before the sacred image, the Ritualist repeats the following:

mn n.t̲ irp irt ḥrw w₃d̲t
["*mán-nit̲ 'úrip írat ḥáru wá'd̲at*"; approximately pronounced *MAHN-neetch OO-rip EE-raht HAH-roo WAH-jat*]

Take to yourself wine, the green Eye of Heru,
which I offer to your *Ka*.[118]
O Mistress of Inebriation, how beautiful is your beauty!
May you drink it; may your Majesty rejoice over that which you desire;
May your face be radiant with happiness because of that which you love.
May your mouth be opened by means of it.
It is pure.
[*iw.w w'b* pronounced "*uwú wá'ib*"; approximately *oo-WOO WAH-ib*]

---

[117] Amr Gaber, The Central Hall in the Egyptian Temples of the Ptolemaic Period, Durham theses, Durham University. Available at Durham E-Theses Online: http://etheses.dur.ac.uk/88/ based on one of the ancient formulae for offering beer: from the Central Hall in the Temple at Edfu; see p. 470 in the dissertation.

[118] Refer to pp. 92, 93, 99, and 105 in Mu-Chou Poo's Wine and Wine Offerings in Ancient Egypt (London & New York: Kegan Paul International, 1995).

Richard J. Reidy

*The Ritualist **places myrrh on the fire** and **lifts up the smoking incense** while at the same time he **lifts up the meat-offering** before the Netjeret, and says the following:*

> The scent of myrrh is for your nose. It fills your nostrils; your heart receives the meat-portions on its scent.[119]

*Slowly **elevating the food offerings four times** before the image of Hat-Hór, the Ritualist repeats the following:*

> I offer to Hat-Hór, Lady of Heaven and Mistress of the Offering.
> Take this food,
> That your *Ka* may be satisfied with this, the Eye of Heru.
> Take these offerings,
> That they may satisfy your heart each day.
> All life emanates from you,
> All health emanates from you,
> All stability emanates from you,
> All good fortune emanates from you,
> *Nebet Hetepet,* Hat-Hór forever!

*The Ritualist **places the food offering before the divine image**, and then all present **extend one hand, palm down, over the offerings** and recite the following:*

> May offerings of every kind come forth in abundance,
> like the things which come forth from the mouth of the Netjeret.

---

[119] Quoted in "Worship and Festivals in an Egyptian Temple," by H. W. Fairman (publ. by The John Rylands Library, 1954), p. 191.

piryá pírit ar ḫiráw mi purú:riat ma rá' ni naṯárat. (4 times)
[approximately pronounced *peer-YA PEER-it ar khi-RAU mee pu-ROOR-iat ma RA nee nah-TCHAR-at*]

May offerings of every kind come forth in abundance, like the things that come forth from the mouth of the Netjeret.

Holding up the Ankh say:

Live, O Golden One, live for all time and for eternity!

ʿánaḫ niḥáḫ ḏát.
[approximately pronounced *AH-nakh nee-HAH JAHT*]

*The **Ankh** is placed next to the image of the Netjeret.*

*Holding the **Ib (the golden heart)** before Hat-Hór, the Ritualist says:*

Hail to you, O Hat-Hór, Lady of Life. I have brought to you your heart to set it in its place. Let me draw near to you with your heart, so that you may have pleasure through me, and so that by means of me you may have power over your body. Ascend, O Lady of the double crown, radiant, rejuvenating, equipped as a *Netjeret*.

I come as Aset had, bringing the heart of her son Heru to him, placing it in its seat! I come as Heru had, bringing the heart of his mother Aset to her, placing it in its seat! I come as Djehuty had, Bringing the heart of the Flaming One to her, and this great Netjeret was appeased by Djehuty. I bring to you your heart, Hat-Hór, Placing it in its seat! Live, O Golden One, live forever and ever!

*After placing the **Ib** near the sacred image, **everyone sings or chants** the hymn to Hat-Hór while **sistra are softly played**. Participants may wish to alternate the singing of verses.*

I praise the Golden One, I worship her majesty, I exalt the Lady of Heaven! Adoration be to Hat-Hór, praise be to our mistress! O Golden One, breath of our life, Lady of Stars who enfolds us! All hail, jubilation to you, the Mistress of All!

O beauteous One, O nurturing Cow, O great One! O Great Magician, O splendid lady, Mistress of the *Netjeru*! We revere you; grant that we live! O Queen of the *Netjeru*, we revere you; grant that we live!

We revere you, Hat-Hór, Mistress from Heaven, Mistress from Lightland! O Queen of the *Netjeru*, from sky, from earth, from south, from west, from north, from east, from each land, from each place, where your majesty shines! See what is in our hearts, what is in our inmost, our hearts are straight, our inmost open. No darkness is in our breast. We revere you, O Mistress of the *Netjeru*. Grant that we may live![120]

O Golden One! Lady of Drunkenness, Lady of Music and Dance, Lady of Frankincense, of young women whom men acclaim because they love you! It is the Golden One who comes forth. Heaven makes merry, the earth is filled with life, heaven and earth rejoice!

---

[120] Miriam Lichtheim, Ancient Egyptian Literature, Volume III: The Late Period (Univ. of California Press, 1980), p. 108.

Praise to you, O Possessor of Abundance!
Praise to you, Queen of the Stars!
Praise to you, Eye of Ra!
Praise to you, Possessor of Ma'at!
Praise to you, Mistress of the Sycamore!
Praise to you, Mistress of the Vulva!
Praise to you, Mistress of Love!
Praise to you, Mistress of Inebriety![121]

We praise you with the sound of the sistra for you are the Mistress of Jubilation. You are the Queen of the Dance and Mistress of Music. You are the Mistress of Harp-playing, the Lady of the Choral Dance, the Queen of Wreath-weaving. You are the Mistress of Inebriety without end! Praise be to you![122]

At this point perform the meditation or magical action or, if it is a special feast, add the appropriate prayers.

*Afterwards **all present back out of the Temple Chamber with heads slightly bowed** while the Ritualist performs the "**removing the foot.**"*

*With the **broom** the Ritualist, as the last person to exit, **ritually sweeps the area beginning at the altar**. (This is known as "removing the foot.") While performing this action the Ritualist recites the following:*

The distress that causes confusion has been driven away, and all the Netjeru are in harmony. I have given Heru his

---

[121] This series of epithets for the goddess come from C. J. Bleeker's excellent work, Hathor and Thoth: Two Key Figures of the Ancient Egyptian Religion (Leiden: E. J. Brill, 1973). See especially pp. 27, 29, 36, 39, 40, 54.
[122] Ibid. p. 83.

Eye; I have placed the Wedjat-Eye in the correct position.
I have given Setekh his Testicles, so that the two lords are
content through the work of my hands.

I know the sky, I know the earth;
I know Heru, I know Setekh.
Heru is appeased with his Eyes;
Setekh is appeased with his Testicles.
I am Djehuty, who reconciles the Netjeru,
who makes offerings in their correct form.

*The **double doors are solemnly closed** as the Ritualist says the
following:*

Djehuty has come.
He has filled the Eye of Heru;
He has restored the Testicles of Setekh.
No evil shall enter this Temple.
Ptah has closed the door,
Djehuty has set it fast.
The door is closed, the door is set fast with the bolt.

*All **bow, touching the palms of their hands to their knees.***

THE REVERSION OF OFFERINGS

*One priest or priestess and as many assistants as necessary enter the
Temple Chamber a final time. While he/she and any assistants **lift up
the offerings** before the sacred image the ritualist shall say:*

O Hat-Hór, **your enemy**[123] **withdraws for you. Heru has turned himself to his Eye in its name of 'Reversion-of-Offerings.' I am Djehuty. I come to perform this rite for Hat-Hór, Mistress of the Netjeru. These, your divine offerings revert, they revert to your servants for life, for stability, for health and for joy! O that the Eye of Heru may flourish for you eternally!**

Everyone withdraws, **carrying away all food offerings except for one loaf of bread and a bowl of pure water.** These last items remain until evening. If this ritual is celebrated after sunset, these items would also be removed.

After the candle has burned down, a servant-priest enters and closes the doors of the Kar-shrine. **Extinguishing the candle or oil lamp, he/she exclaims:**

This is the Eye of Heru by which you have become great, by which you live, and by which you have power, O Hat-Hór. This is the Eye of Heru which you consume and through which you enchant your body. The Wedjat-Eye now enters into the West, into Manu, but it shall return. Truly, the Eye of Heru returns in peace![124]

---

[123] Meat offerings held a two-fold meaning for the ancient priesthood. Since meat necessarily came from slain animals, it signified the defeated or slain enemies of the Netjeret. At the same time, the meat offering represented the produce of the land which ultimately was a gift of the Netjeru.

[124] It is important to consume the food offerings after the ceremony. Water used should either be drunk or poured onto the earth. If it is mixed with Natron, dilute it very greatly and then you can pour in onto the bare earth.

The General Ritual for Heka

Like members of the ancient priesthood, participants should be clothed in white linen. No item made of animal products such as leather or wool is to be worn. Linen represents a pristine product of the earth whereas leather and wool come from humankind's domination of the animals, a domination that becomes part of the "natural order" only *after* the First Time when the *Netjeru* and humans and animals lived in peace and harmony. Just as the Morning Ritual harkens back to that First Time (*Zep Tepi*), so every temple rite re-presents mythic prototypes that occurred "in the beginning," that is, in that time before time. Even the sandals worn by the god's servants were made of white papyrus. This avoidance of animal products by the priesthood fits well with the fact that the ritualist acts as a *Netjer* and verbally asserts that he or she is a *Netjer*.

As with all Egyptian rituals begin with your purification—washing of hands and cleansing of mouth with Natron. This preliminary rite helps us to lay aside the cares of the day and to become mindful of the fact that we will encounter a divine being. If Natron is not available, then use a natural sea salt in its place until you make your own Natron.

If two or more persons are participating, then one person, impersonating the Netjer *Djehuty,* **purifies each person by sprinkling each with water while exclaiming**:

I purify you with the water of all life and good fortune, all stability, all health and happiness.[125]

---

[125] Taken from Aylward M. Blackman's article "Purification (Egyptian)" in Hastings Encyclopedia 10/1918/ 476-82. This article is reprinted in Gods,

Afterwards each person rinses his mouth and places a small amount of Natron or sea salt in his mouth while saying:

I wash my mouth; I chew natron so that I may extol the might of Heka, Lord of the House of Life, the Great God.[126]

Participants **assemble outside the Temple Chamber** *and begin by softly rattling sistra.*

This time—several minutes or more—is used to focus minds and intention so that distracting thoughts are left behind. The sound of the sistrum was said to placate the deity, purifying the atmosphere in preparation for encountering divinity. The sistrum was associated with Hutheru and also with her and Heru's son Ihy, and thus has connotations of joy, celebration, and dancing. According to Plutarch (A.D. 46-120), the sound of sistra was also reputed to drive away Setekh. But this was of very late date. It may have been that since by that time Setekh had been demonized, the general apotropaic function of the sistrum against evil entities was extended to include this *Netjer* as well.

Standing **before the closed doors,** *the Ritualist* **recites the entrance spell:**

UTTERANCE BEFORE THE CLOSED DOORS OF THE TEMPLE

The ritualist **raises hands in adoration** *(*dua *position-arms stretched out in front of the body and raised up to face level, with palms facing outward). The following shall be said:*

Priests, and Men, Studies in the Religion of Pharaonic Egypt, edited by Alan B. Lloyd (Kegan Paul International, 1998), p. 9.

[126] Adapted from a temple inscription taken from "The Myth of Horus at Edfu—II" by A. M. Blackman and H. W. Fairman, appearing in Gods, Priests and Men, Studies in the Religion of Pharaonic Egypt, p. 283.

O you *Netjeru* of this Temple, you guardians of the great portal, great *Netjeru* of mysterious abode, who sanctify the *Netjer* in his shrine, who consecrate his oblation, who receive the offerings in his presence in the Hall of the Ennead: I have made my way and I enter into your presence. I am one of you. I am Shu, the eldest son of his father, the senior *wab* servant-priest of Heka. Do not repulse me on the *Netjer*'s path. My feet are not impeded. I am not turned back from the court of the great portal so that I may conduct the divine service, that I may present offerings to him that made them, that I may give bread to Heka. I have come on the way of the god. I have not shown partiality in judgment. I have not consorted with the strong. I have not reproached the lowly. I have not stolen things. I have not diminished the constituents of the Eye of Ra. I have not disturbed the Balance. I have not tampered with the requirements of the Sacred Eye. O Council of the Great *Netjer* in this Temple, behold, I have come to you to offer Ma'at to the Lord of Ma'at, to content the Sound Eye for its lord. I am Shu; I flood his offering table. I present his offerings, Sekhmet consorting with me, that I may adore Heka at his festivals, that I may kiss the earth so great is his majesty, that I may endow his image with life. I am pure. I am purified.

At this point the ritualist **opens the doors to the Temple Chamber,** *or, if there are no doors,* **makes a gesture of opening unseen doors,** *and* **steps forward as if crossing over a threshold.** *The following is said:*

O you *Ba*-souls of *Ta-Senet* (Esna), if you are strong, I am strong. If I am strong, you are strong. If your *Ka*-spirits are strong, my *Ka*-spirit is strong at the head of the living. As they are living so shall I live . . . . Heka, Lord of Heaven, has given to me life, stability, and serenity round about my members, which Djehuty has gathered together for life. I am Heru in the height of heaven, the beautiful one of awe, Lord of Victory, mighty one of awe, exalted one of the two plumes, great one in *Waset* (Thebes), I am pure.

All temple members chant:

Awake in peace, O Heka, Foremost of the Ennead,
may you awaken in peace.
Awake in peace, O Heka, Great of Magic,
may you awaken in peace.
Awake in peace, O Heka, Oldest of the Kas of Ra,
may you awaken in peace.
Awake in peace, O Heka, Ruler of Action,
may you awaken in peace.

May you awake beautifully at the top of the morning, through that which the entirety of *Netjeru* say to you.

*Enter, **close the double doors** and **stand in front of the Kar-shrine** **and altar**. All bow, touching their hands to their knees.*

The ritualist **slowly opens the two doors of the Kar-shrine** *housing the sacred image. All others bow, touching their hands to their knees. The following is said:*

The doors of the sky are open; the doors of the earth are unlocked. This House is open for its Lord. Let me come forth as he shall come forth. Let me enter in as he shall enter in. Heka, the Sublime Power, is exalted upon his Great Seat. The Great Company of the *Netjeru* are exalted upon their seat.

I have seen the *Netjer,* and the *Netjer* sees me. The *Netjer* rejoices at seeing me. I have gazed upon the statue of the Lord of Magic, the sacred image of Eldest of the *Netjeru.*[127]

Right hand on left shoulder of statue; left hand on right wrist of statue:

Djehuty has come to you. Awake when you hear his words. I have come as the envoy of Atum. My two arms are upon you like those of Heru. My two hands are upon you like those of Djehuty. My fingers are upon you like those of Anpu. Homage be to you. I am a living servant of Heka.

*The Ritualist **holds up the bowl of water** in which he/she will be mixing the Natron. The following is said:*

O water may you remove all evil,
As Ra who bathes in the Lake of Rushes,
May Heru wash my flesh,
May Djehuty cleanse my feet,
May Shu lift me up and Nut take my hand!
May Setekh be my strength, and may Sekhmet be my healing!
And may Amun-Ra be my life and my prospering!

*The bowl of water is set aside and the container of **Natron** is lifted up. The following is said:*

It is pure, it is pure.
My Natron is the Natron of Heru,
and the Natron of Heru is my Natron.

---

[127] Based on the temple text found in "Worship and Festivals in an Egyptian Temple," a lecture by H. W. Fairman (publ. by The John Rylands Library, 1954), p. 180.

My Natron is the Natron of Setekh,
and the Natron of Setekh is my Natron.
My Natron is the Natron of Djehuty,
and the Natron of Djehuty is my Natron.
My Natron is the Natron of Geb,
and the Natron of Geb is my Natron.

My mouth is the mouth of a milking calf
on the day that I was born.

Four pinches of Natron are mixed into the water as this Utterance
is recited:

I give you essential water, a tide in your time.
I bring the flood waters to purify your sanctuary.
I bring you the flood waters
to purify your Temple and your statue in its place,
the primordial water that purifies as in the First Time!

*The Ritualist places an index finger into the water and moves it in
a circular direction four times* as the following is said:

Heka, Lord of Heaven,
does purify this water;
Heka, Foremost of the House of Eternity,
does cleanse this water;
Heka, Who Engenders All Things,
does sanctify this water;
Heka himself
does endow this water with power and with life.

*The Bowl of Natron-infused water is then taken up and the Ritualist
sprinkles this lightly in front of and around the statue or image*

of Heka, applying some of this water to the base of the image, as the Utterance is recited:

> I come close to you, O Lord of Growth, Whose Equal Does Not Exist. I bring the water of rejuvenation that flows from the Two Caverns. I sprinkle the water, purifying your image and your Temple from all impurity!

The Ritualist picks up the bowl of **Natron** and **sprinkles a small amount in each of the four directions** as the following is recited:

> The *Netjer* Heka himself does cleanse and purify this,
> his Temple to the South.
> The *Netjer* Heka himself does cleanse and purify this,
> his Temple to the North.
> The *Netjer* Heka himself does cleanse and purify this,
> his Temple to the West.
> The *Netjer* Heka himself does cleanse and purify this,
> his Temple to the East.

Replacing the Natron on the altar, the Ritualist takes up the bowl of **water, sprinkling a small amount in each of the four directions**. The following Utterance is recited:

> The *Netjer* Heka himself does sanctify and consecrate this,
> his Temple to the South.
> The *Netjer* Heka himself does sanctify and consecrate this,
> his Temple to the North.
> The *Netjer* Heka himself does sanctify and consecrate this,
> his Temple to the West.
> The *Netjer* Heka himself does sanctify and consecrate this,
> his Temple to the East.

The Temple of the *Netjer Heka* is established. It is established for millions of years.

*The Ritualist returns to the altar and **lights the candle or oil lamp** while the following is said:*

Come, come in peace, O glorious Eye of Heru,
Be strong and renew your youth in peace.
For the flame shines like Ra on the double horizon.
The enemies of Ra are defeated. They are defeated.
I am pure, I am pure, I am pure, I am pure.

*The Ritualist **places incense on the burner** and **censes each sacred image** beginning with the statue of Heka while the following is recited:*

The fire is laid, the fire shines;
The incense is laid on the fire, the incense shines.
　　Your perfume comes to me, O Incense;
　　May my perfume come to you, O Incense.
Your perfume comes to me, you *Netjeru*;
May my perfume come to you, you *Netjeru*.
　　May I be with you, you *Netjeru*;
　　May you be with me, you *Netjeru*.
May I live with you, you *Netjeru*;
May you live with me, you *Netjeru*.
　　I love you, you *Netjeru*;
　　May you love me, you *Netjeru*.

*Standing in front of the image of Heka the Ritualist **offers the burning incense** and says:*

Take the incense, O Sublime Power.
Its essence is for you.

Its smoke permeates your shrine, bringing life!
Take the incense,
Its essence is for you.
Your Majesty is appeased with the incense.
This Eye of Heru,
This essence of the Eye of Heru comes to you.

At this point the following is said:

We come before you, O Heka. We revere you in accordance to what we know. You are he whom the Sole Lord made before duality came into being, when he sent his Sole Eye while he was still alone, at the enunciation of his mouth when his Ka became a million-fold to protect his companions; when he spoke with Khopri but was mightier than he; when he (the Sole Lord) put **Authoritative Utterance** (i.e., the god Hu) upon his mouth.

You are indeed the son of Atum, having been born before any mother existed. You are the protection of what the Sole Lord commanded. You are he who caused the Ennead to live. Truly you are 'If-he-wishes-he does,' the father of the *Netjeru.*

Your standard is raised high. The *Netjeru* are endowed in accordance with what you, the Eldest *Netjer,* commanded. May you seat yourself in the presence of the Bulls of the Sky in this, your dignity of 'Greatest-of-the-Owners-of-*Kas*,' truly the heir of Atum.

Come to us, O Heka, that you may take possession of your throne and receive your dignity, for to you belonged everything before the *Netjeru* had come into being. We bow down and kneel before you, for truly you are Heka.[128]

The Ritualist places more incense on the charcoal and again and again slowly raises and lowers the incense cup as the following is recited:

O Heka, Lord of *Kas*, may you advance with your *Ka*.
The arm of your *Ka* is before you,
The arm of your *Ka* is behind you.
O Great Secret Lion, the foot of your *Ka* is before you,
The foot of your *Ka* is behind you.
O Sacred One Who Cannot Be Known, Heka,
this incense is offered to you,
May your face be filled as this essence spreads itself over you.

All present perform the Henu Rite—Embrace the Earth, the Fourfold Salute to the God, Embrace the Earth. The bodily gestures are performed alternately four times.

For Embracing the Earth, all present prostrate themselves, face down, upon the floor. During the Fourfold Salute, all present rise upon one knee, and alternately raise their hands and arms into the *Dua* (praise) position with palms facing outward, followed by the *Sahu* (obedience) gesture, made by striking the chest with a closed fist and raising the other arm (also with closed fist) at a ninety-degree angle. The *Dua* position is accompanied by the words

---

[128] This entire Utterance is based on Coffin Text 261, a deeply theological statement regarding this god. See Spell 261 in *The Ancient Egyptian Coffin Texts* by R. O. Faulkner (reprint with corrections, 1973), pp. 199-200. Also see *Myth and Symbol in Ancient Egypt* by R. T. Rundle Clark (London: Thames & Hudson, 1959), pp. 77-78.

"Adoration be to Heka," followed by the *Sahu* gesture accompanied with the words, **"Hail to the Lord of Life!"** The bodily gestures are performed alternately four times.

*Following this all present again **prostrate themselves before the god**. This is a sign and symbol of total submission and adoration before the Netjer. The following is said:*

> Homage to Heka, Great of Magic,
> who is established on the Great Seat!
> I have placed myself on the floor in awe of you.
> I embrace the earth before you
> as before the Father of the *Netjeru.*
> I have come that I might kiss the earth,
> that I might worship my Lord,
> For I have seen his Strength;
> I give praise to Heka,
> For I have seen his Power.
> His form is more distinguished than the *Netjeru;*
> His arm is more powerful than the *Netjeru.*
> I am pure, I am pure, I am pure, I am pure!

Everyone stands up.

*The Ritualist holds in the palm of one hand **the image of Ma'at** and **with the other hand open and raised over the image as if sheltering it**, repeats the following:*

> I have come to you as Djehuty, whose two hands are joined together under Ma'at. She comes to be with you, for she is everywhere. You are provided with Ma'at. You move in Ma'at, you live in Ma'at. She fills your body, she rests in

your head, she makes her seat upon your brow; the breath of your body is of Ma'at, your heart does live in Ma'at. All that you eat, all that you drink, all that you breathe is of Ma'at. Djehuty presents Ma'at to you, his two hands are upon her beauty before your face.

*The Ritualist places the image of Ma'at near the divine statue. Then he/ she holds up before the image of Heka **a pitcher of water** and **pours the water slowly into an offering bowl** as the following Utterance is recited:*

This libation is for you, O Oldest of the Netjeru.
This libation is for you, O Heka,
Who Brings the Plants to Fruition.
You are the One
Who Opens His Eyes so that the Two Lands Might See.[129]
I have brought to you this offering of water,
That your heart may be refreshed.
I have brought to you this Eye of Heru,
Placing this at your feet.
I present to you that which flows forth from you,
That your heart shall continue to beat.
For it is with you that all comes forth at the sound of the voice.

*The offering bowl is placed on the altar. At this point the Ritualist **lightly sprinkles sand on the floor in front of the altar** as the following is recited:*

O Heka, who resides in the 'Mansion of Heka'

---

[129] Robert Ritner, *The Mechanics of Ancient Egyptian Magical Practice* (Univ. of Chicago, 3rd Printing), p.27.

Richard J. Reidy

which is in *Iunu* (Heliopolis),[130]
Take to yourself the Eye of Heru.
You have rescued it, O Protector of the Divine Order.
You have sprinkled with sand the Eye of Heru.

Lifting the wine offering before the sacred image, the Ritualist repeats the following:

mn n.k irp irt ḥrw wꜣḏt
["*mán-nik 'úrip írat ḥáru wá'ḏat*"; approximately pronounced *MAHN-neek OO-rip EE-raht HAH-roo WAH-jat*]

Take to yourself wine, the green Eye of Heru,
which I offer to your *Ka*.[131]
O Ruler, how beautiful is your beauty!
May you drink it; may your heart rejoice;
may anger be removed from your face.
It is pure.
[*iw.w wꜥb* pronounced "*uwú wáꜥib*"; approximately oo-WOO WAH-ib]

The Ritualist places myrrh on the fire and lifts up the smoking incense while at the same time he lifts up the meat-offering before the Netjer, and says the following:

---

[130] Op. Cit. p. 26. A temple of Heka was associated with Heliopolis.
[131] **Refer to pp. 92, 93, 99, and 105 in Mu-Chou Poo's *Wine and Wine Offerings in Ancient Egypt* (London & New York: Kegan Paul International, 1995).**

174

The scent of myrrh is for your nose. It fills your nostrils; your heart receives the meat-portions on its scent.[132]

*Slowly **elevating the food offerings four times before the image** of Heka, the Ritualist repeats the following:*

I offer to Heka, Lord of Offerings.
All life emanates from you,
All health emanates from you,
All stability emanates from you,
All good fortune emanates from you,
O Lord of Nourishment, Heka, forever.

*The Ritualist **places the food offering before the divine image**, and then all present **extend one hand, palm down, over the offerings** and recite the following:*

May offerings of every kind come forth in abundance,
like the things which come forth from the mouth of the
Netjer.

piryá pírit ar ḫiráw mi purú:riat ma rá' ni náṭar. (4 times)
[approximately pronounced *peer-YA PEER-it ar khi-RAU mee pu-ROOR-iat ma RA nee NAH-tchar*]

May offerings of every kind come forth in abundance, like the things that come forth from the mouth of the Netjer.

*Holding the **Ankh** before Heka, the Ritualist says:*

---

[132] Quoted in "Worship and Festivals in an Egyptian Temple," by H. W. Fairman (publ. by The John Rylands Library, 1954), p. 191.

Live, O Heka, Who Comes Forth from the Lotus Flower, live for all time and for eternity!

ʿánaḫ niḥáḫ ḏát.
[approximately pronounced *AH-nakh nee-HAH JAHT*]

*The **Ankh** is placed next to the image of the Netjer.*

*Holding the **Ib** (**the golden heart**) before Heka, the Ritualist says:*

Hail to you, O Heka, Who Engenders All Things. I have brought to you your heart to set it in its place. Let me draw near to you with your heart, so that you may have pleasure through me, and so that by means of me you may have power over your body. Ascend, O Eldest of the *Kas* of Ra, radiant, rejuvenating, equipped as a *Netjer*. Live, O Youthful Aged One, live forever and ever!

*After placing the **Ib** near the sacred image, **everyone sings or chants the hymn** to Heka. Participants may wish to alternate the singing of verses.*

Hail to you, Heka, come forth from Atum! Your powers put fear into the Netjeru who came into being after you. Your myriad of *Ka*-spirits is within your mouth, O Lord of *Kas*. It was you who came into being of yourself, at seeing whom the Netjeru rejoiced, and through your sweet savor the Netjeru live—you who created the mountains and knit the firmament together.[133]

---

[133] Based on Coffin Text spell 648 quoted in Robert K. Ritner, *The Mechanics of Ancient Egyptian Magical Practice* (The Oriental Institute of the University of Chicago, 3rd printing with corrections, 1997), p. 17. Also see p. 25.

May you recite for me by means of your magic; may you
speak for me by means of your words for I have spoken
by means of your spells. I have recited by means of your
magic. I have spoken by means of your utterances. I have
made spells by means of your spells. I have enchanted by
means of your incantations which you created by means of
this magic which is in your mouth.[134]

Be not far from me, but be in me so my words are your
words. Be not far from me, but be in me so my incantations
are your own incantations. Be within me and around me so
my voice is your voice. May your heka be my heka. May my
enchantments be effective as I serve ma'at and defeat the foe.

Your name is a protection for us who serve you, O Heka.
(2 times)

At this point perform the **meditation or magical action** *or, if it is a
special feast, add the appropriate prayers.*

Afterwards **all present back out of the Temple Chamber with heads
slightly bowed** *while the Ritualist performs the* **"removing the foot."**

With the **broom** *the Ritualist, as the last person to exit,* **ritually sweeps
the area beginning at the altar.** *(This is known as* **"removing the
foot."***) While performing this action the Ritualist recites the following:*

The distress that causes confusion has been driven away,
and all the Netjeru are in harmony. I have given Heru his
Eye; I have placed the Wedjat-Eye in the correct position.
I have given Setekh his Testicles, so that the two lords are
content through the work of my hands.

---

[134] Op. Cit., based on Text "A" of the Horus Cippi, p. 41.

I know the sky, I know the earth;
I know Heru, I know Setekh.
Heru is appeased with his Eyes;
Setekh is appeased with his Testicles.
I am Djehuty, who reconciles the Netjeru,
who makes offerings in their correct form.

*The **double doors are solemnly closed** as the Ritualist says the following:*

Djehuty has come.
He has filled the Eye of Heru;
He has restored the Testicles of Setekh.
No evil shall enter this Temple.
Ptah has closed the door,
Djehuty has set it fast.
The door is closed, the door is set fast with the bolt.

*All **bow, touching the palms of their hands to their knees.***

THE REVERSION OF OFFERINGS

*One priest or priestess and as many assistants as necessary enter the Temple Chamber a final time. While he/she and any assistants **lift up the offerings** before the sacred image the ritualist shall say:*

O Heka, **your enemy**[135] **withdraws for you. Heru has turned himself to his Eye in its name of 'Reversion-of-Offerings.' I**

---

[135] Meat offerings held a two-fold meaning for the ancient priesthood. Since meat necessarily came from slain animals, it signified the defeated or slain enemies of the Netjeret. At the same time, the meat offering represented the produce of the land which ultimately was a gift of the Netjeru.

am Djehuty. I come to perform this rite for Heka, Lord of the Netjeru. **These, your divine offerings revert, they revert to your servants for life, for stability, for health and for joy! O that the Eye of Heru may flourish for you eternally!**

Everyone withdraws, **carrying away all food offerings except for one loaf of bread and a bowl of pure water.** These last items remain until evening. If this ritual is celebrated after sunset, these items would also be removed.

After the candle has burned down, a servant-priest enters and closes the doors of the Kar-shrine. ***Extinguishing the candle or oil lamp, he/she exclaims:***

This is the Eye of Heru by which you have become great, by which you live, and by which you have power, O Heka. This is the Eye of Heru which you consume and through which you enchant your body. The *Wedjat*-Eye now enters into the West, into *Manu,* but it shall return. Truly, the Eye of Heru returns in peace![136]

---

[136] It is important to consume the food offerings after the ceremony. Water used should either be drunk or poured onto the earth. If it is mixed with natron, dilute it very greatly and then you can pour in onto the earth without harming any plantings.

The General Rite for Heru Behdety

The 'Awake in Peace' section and most of the epithets appearing in this ritual come from Treffpunkt der Götter: Inschriften aus dem Tempel des Horus von Edfu, *by Dieter Kurth (Artemis Verlag, 1994). We gratefully acknowledge the arduous translation work of Temple of Ra member, Matthew Whealton, without whose extensive efforts both in translating the German text of the book as well as working with the difficult Ptolemaic hieroglyphic texts this present work would not have been possible. Thank you, Matt!*

In addition, a number of epithets come from the PhD. Dissertation of Randy L. Shonkwiler titled The Behdetite: A Study of Horus the Behdetite from the Old Kingdom to the Conquest of Alexander (University of Chicago, 21014). For the full text of this dissertation please see: https://oi.uchicago.edu/sites/oi.uchicago.edu/files/ uploads/shared/docs/SHONKWILERDISSERTATION.pdf

Offerings for Heru Behdety: a representation of the Eye of Heru, and the traditional offerings of bread, beer, wine, and meat

Like members of the ancient priesthood, participants should be clothed in white linen. No item made of animal products such as leather or wool is to be worn. Linen represents a pristine product of the earth whereas leather and wool come from humankind's domination of the animals, a domination that becomes part of the "natural order" only *after* the First Time when the *Netjeru* and humans and animals lived in peace and harmony. Just as the Morning Ritual harkens back to that First Time (*Zep Tepi*), so every temple rite re-presents mythic prototypes that occurred "in the beginning," that is, in that time before time. Even the sandals worn by the god's servants were made of white papyrus. This avoidance of animal products by the priesthood fits well with the fact that the ritualist acts as a *Netjer* and verbally asserts that he or she is a *Netjer*.

As with all Egyptian rituals begin with your purification – washing of hands and cleansing of mouth with Natron. This preliminary rite helps us to lay aside the cares of the day and to become mindful of the fact that we will encounter a divine being. If Natron is not available, then use a natural sea salt in its place until you make your own Natron.

If two or more persons are participating, then one person, impersonating the Netjer *Djehuty,* **purifies each person by sprinkling each with water while exclaiming***:

I purify you with the water of all life and good fortune, all stability, all health and happiness.[137]

Afterwards each person **rinses his mouth** *and places a* **small amount of Natron or sea salt in his mouth** *while saying:*

I wash my mouth; I chew natron that I may extol the might of Heru son of Aset, the Perfect Youth who came forth from Aset, son of Ausir, the Loveable One.[138]

---

[137] Taken from Aylward M. Blackman's article "Purification (Egyptian)" in Hastings Encyclopedia 10/1918/ 476-82. This article is reprinted in Gods, Priests, and Men, Studies in the Religion of Pharaonic Egypt, edited by Alan B. Lloyd (Kegan Paul International, 1998), p. 9.

[138] Based on a temple inscription taken from "The Myth of Horus at Edfu—II" by A. M. Blackman and H. W. Fairman, appearing in Gods, Priests and Men, Studies in the Religion of Pharaonic Egypt (Kegan Paul International, 1998) p. 283.

*Participants **assemble outside the Temple Chamber** and begin by softly rattling sistra.*

This time—several minutes or more—is used to focus minds and intention so that distracting thoughts are left behind. The sound of the sistrum was said to placate the deity, purifying the atmosphere in preparation for encountering divinity. The sistrum was associated with Hutheru and also with her and Heru's son Ihy, and thus has connotations of joy, celebration, and dancing. According to Plutarch (A.D. 46-120), the sound of sistra was also reputed to drive away Setekh. But this was of very late date. It may have been that since by that time Setekh had been demonized, the general apotropaic function of the sistrum against evil entities was extended to include this *Netjer* as well.

*Standing **before the closed doors**, the Ritualist **recites the entrance spell:***

UTTERANCE BEFORE THE CLOSED DOORS OF THE TEMPLE

*The ritualist **raises hands in adoration** (dua position-arms stretched out in front of the body and raised up to face level, with palms facing outward). The following shall be said:*

O you *Netjeru* of this Temple, you guardians of the great portal, great *Netjeru* of mysterious abode, who sanctify the *Netjer* in his shrine, who consecrate his oblation, who receive the offerings in his presence in the Hall of the Ennead: I have made my way and I enter into your presence. I am one of you. I am Shu, the eldest son of his father, the senior *wab* servant-priest of Heru Behdety. Do not repulse me on the *Netjer's* path. My feet are not impeded. I am not turned back from the court of the great portal so that I may conduct the divine service, that I may present offerings to him that made them, that I may give bread to Heru Behdety. I have come on the way of the *Netjer*. I have not shown partiality in judgment. I have not consorted with the strong. I have not reproached the lowly. I have not stolen things. I have not diminished the constituents of the Eye of Ra. I have not disturbed the Balance. I have not tampered with the requirements of the Sacred Eye. O Council of the Great *Netjer* in this Temple, behold, I have come to you to offer Ma'at to the Lord of Ma'at, to content the Sound Eye for its lord. I am Shu; I flood his offering table. I present his offerings, Sekhmet consorting with me, that I may adore Heru Behdety at his festivals, that I may kiss the earth so great is his majesty, that I may endow his image with life. I am pure. I am purified.

*At this point the ritualist **opens the doors to the Temple Chamber**, or, if there are no doors, **makes a gesture of opening unseen doors**, and steps forward as if crossing over a threshold. The following is said:*

O you *Ba-souls* of *Wetjeset-Hor* (Edfu[139]), if you are strong, I am strong. If I am strong, you are strong. If your *Ka-spirits* are strong, my *Ka-spirit* is strong at the head of the living. As they are living so shall I live . . . . Sekhmet, the great *Netjeret*, beloved of Ptah, has given to me life, stability, and serenity round about my members, which Djehuty has gathered together for life. I am Heru in the height of heaven, the beautiful one of awe, Lord of Victory, mighty one of awe, exalted one of the two plumes, great one in Wetjeset-Hor (Edfu) I am pure.

---

[139] Wetjeset-Hor (Greek, Edfu) is the cult center for Heru Behdety and his consort Hwt-Hrw.

Enter, **close the double doors** *and* **stand in front of the Kar-shrine and altar.** *All bow, touching their hands to their knees.*

PART 1 (Heru is awakened in his different manifestations and qualities.)

*rassáta! ḥatpáta! [approximately **rass-SAH-ta haht-PAH-ta**]*
*rassák náfir ma ḥátap! [approximately **rass-SAK NAH-fir mah HA-tap**]*
*rassá ḥáru baḥdáti: ma ʿánaḥ! [approximately **rass-SAH HAH-roo bah-DAH-tee mah AH-nakh**]*[140]

Be Awake! Be at peace!
May you awake well and in peace!
Awake Heru Behdety in life!

Be Awake! Be at peace! May you awake well and in peace! Awake Heru Behdety in life! The *Netjeru* are up early in the morning to revere your *Ba* (the sun), the Magnificent Winged Scarab that shines in heaven; for it is you who begins creation with the dawn sky and fills the Two Lands with Gold Dust, who rises in the Eastern Mountain, falls down in the Western Mountain, and sleeps day after day in *Wetjeset-Hor.*

Awake. . . . *(This word should precede each of the following stanzas)*

---

[140] This pronunciation key is the courtesy of Matthew Whealton from The Kemetic Temple of Ra, San Francisco. By pronouncing the words in ancient Egyptian, we invoke their original power and honor the ancient Priests who crafted the beautiful rituals we now celebrate.

1) Heru Behdety, Highly Respected One, equipped with power, King of the *Netjeru,* Ruler of *Wetjeset-Hor,* in peace. May you awake in peace.

2) Heru Behdety, Great *Netjer,* Lord of Heaven, Lord of Ma'at, with powerful throat, in peace. May you awake in peace.

3) Heru Behdety, Great *Netjer,* Lord of Heaven, under whose wings lie the circuit of heaven, in peace. May you awake in peace.

4) Behdety, *Gemehsu*-Falcon with Secret Form, Protected by his mother as the Vulture *Netjeret* (of El Kab), in peace. May you awake in peace.

5) Heru Behdety, who causes the inundation to come at the right time, who preserves *Netjeru* and people in life with his Efflux, in peace. May you awake in peace.

6) Heru Behdety, King of Upper Kemet, Ruler of Lower Kemet, for whom the Two Lands are unified, in peace. May you awake in peace.

7) Heru Behdety, Highly Respected One, Greatly Praised upon the Secret Mountain of Behdet, in peace. May you awake in peace.

8) Heru Behdety, *Gemehsu*-Falcon, Joyously Fertile Bull, Greatly Splendid in the magnificent chamber, in peace. May you awake in peace.

9) Heru Behdety, Lord of Mankind, Very Respected and more glorious than all the *Netjeru,* in peace. May you awake in peace.

10) Heru Behdety, Attacking *Ba,* Great of Strength, Who tramples and fully annihilates the enemies, in peace. May you awake in peace.

11) Heru Behdety, whose true name remains hidden from the *Netjeru*, whose statue is hidden, in peace. May you awake in peace.

12) Heru Behdety, who begins creation in the morning sky, who brings back the heavens with light, in peace. May you awake in peace.

13) Heru Behdety, Protector of His Father in *Wetjeset-Hor,* in peace. May you awake in peace.

Awake. . . . *(This word should precede each of the following stanzas)*

1) Your two living eyes (sun and moon) that emit fire, your two undamaged eyes that make the darkness bright, in peace. May you awake in peace.

2) Your eyebrows that awake perfectly, that make the face happy and are unacquainted with anger, in peace. May you awake in peace.

3) Your nose, the nest of air, from which the nostrils of a creature breathe, in peace. May you awake in peace.

4) Your speaking lips, the double doors of Heaven, which you open so that the land might live, in peace. May you awake in peace.

5) Your speaking tongue that continuously pronounces life, your tongue that also judges according to Ma'at, in peace. May you awake in peace.

6) Your incisors together with your molars, who are your Ennead, brightly shining, in peace. May you awake in peace.

7) Your esophagus that directs nourishment to your body, your throat, through which you live, in peace. May you awake in peace.

8) Two Female Falcons (the collarbone), the two harriers, your Daughters who sit on the wall of your shrine, in peace. May you awake in peace.

9) Your arms, your Sons, the Two Lions that envelope protectively the body of their Creator, in peace. May you awake in peace.

10) Your forearms, that strike the Opponent, that drive the Enemy from your Shrine, in peace. May you awake in peace.

11) Your hands, which crush the Evil One, that terrify our Enemy, in peace. May you awake in peace.

12) Your two body supports (the legs), that know no fatigue, Aset and Nebet-Het, that carry Their Father, in peace. May you awake in peace.

13) Both rows of your toes, the Two Great *Netjeru*, who are reconciled and joined with Your Majesty, in peace. May you awake in peace.

14) Your feet, which arrive at both heavens that do not tire when they walk along on their way, in peace. May you awake in peace.

15) Your hands, which crush the Evil One, that terrify your Enemy, in peace. May you awake in peace.

16) Your wings of Behdety, with which you fly over the sky *Netjeret* Nut, in peace. May you awake in peace.

17) Your body with what is in it, (that is) Heaven, equipped with its stars, in peace. May you awake in peace.

rassáta! ḥatpáta!
rassák náfir ma ḥátap!
rassá ḥáru baḥdáti: ma ʿánaḥ!

Be Awake! Be at peace! May you awake well and in peace! Awake Heru Behdety in life!

*The ritualist **slowly opens the two doors of the Kar-shrine** housing the sacred image. All others bow, touching their hands to their knees. The following is said:*

The doors of the sky are open; the doors of the earth are unlocked. This House is open for its lord. Let me come forth as he shall come forth. Let me enter in as he shall enter in. Heru Behdety is exalted upon his Great Seat. The Great Company of the *Netjeru* are exalted upon their seats.

I have seen the Netjer, and the Netjer sees me. The *Netjer* rejoices at seeing me. I have gazed upon the statue of the Divine Winged Beetle, the sacred image of the Falcon of Gold.[141]

The priest/priestess places his/her right hand on the arm of the statue, with the left hand placed on the wrist of the statue. The following is said:

Djehuty has come to you. Awake when you hear his words.
I have come as the envoy of Atum.
My two arms are upon you like those of Heru.
My two hands are upon you like those of Djehuty.
My fingers are upon you like those of Anpu. Homage be to you.
I am a living servant of Heru Behdety.

---

[141] Quoted in "Worship and Festivals in an Egyptian Temple," a lecture by H. W. Fairman (publ. by The John Rylands Library, 1954), p. 180.

I adore your majesty with choice expressions and prayers that magnify your prestige, in all your great names and in all the sacred forms of manifestation in which you revealed yourself in the First Time (of creation).[142]

*The Ritualist holds up the **bowl of water** in which he/she will be mixing the Natron. The following is said:*

O water may you remove all evil,
As Ra who bathes in the Lake of Rushes,
May Heru wash my flesh,
May Djehuty cleanse my feet,
May Shu lift me up and Nut take my hand!
May Setekh be my strength, and may Sekhmet be my healing!
And may Amun-Ra be my life and my prospering!

*The bowl of water is set aside and the container of **Natron** is lifted up. The following is said:*

It is pure, it is pure.
My Natron is the Natron of Heru,
and the Natron of Heru is my Natron.
My Natron is the Natron of Setekh,
and the Natron of Setekh is my Natron.
My Natron is the Natron of Djehuty,
and the Natron of Djehuty is my Natron.
My Natron is the Natron of Geb,
and the Natron of Geb is my Natron.

---

[142] Maurice Alliot, *Le Culte d'Horus à Edfou au temps des Ptolémées*, Vol. I (Cairo, 1941), p. 80.

My mouth is the mouth of a milking calf
on the day that I was born.

Four pinches of Natron are mixed into the water as this Utterance
is recited and raises the bowl before the Netjer:

I give you essential water, a tide in your time.
I bring the flood waters to purify your sanctuary.
I bring you the flood waters
to purify your Temple and your statue in its place,
the primordial water that purifies as in the First Time!

*The Ritualist places an index finger into the water and moves it in
a circular direction four times* as the following is said:

Heru, Pillar of His Mother,
does purify this water;
Heru, the Saviour of His Father,
does cleanse this water;
Heru, Who is Upon His Papyrus Plants,
does sanctify this water;
Heru Behdety himself
does endow this water with power and with life.

*The **Bowl of Natron-infused water** is then taken up and the Ritualist
sprinkles this lightly in front of and around the statue or image
of Heru Behdety, applying some water to the base of the image,* as the
Utterance is recited:

I come close to you, O Lord of Heaven. I bring the water of
rejuvenation that flows from the Two Caverns. I sprinkle
the water, purifying your image and your Temple from all
impurity!

The Ritualist picks up the bowl of **Natron** *and* **sprinkles** *a small amount in each of the four directions as the following is recited:*

The *Netjer* Heru Behdety himself does cleanse and purify this, his Temple to the South.
The *Netjer* Heru Behdety himself does cleanse and purify this, his Temple to the North.
The *Netjer* Heru Behdety himself does cleanse and purify this, his Temple to the West.
The *Netjer* Heru Behdety himself does cleanse and purify this, his Temple to the East.

Replacing the Natron on the altar, the Ritualist takes up the bowl of **water, sprinkling a small amount in each of the four directions.** *The following Utterance is recited:*

The *Netjer* Heru Behdety himself
does sanctify and consecrate this, his Temple to the South.
The *Netjer* Heru Behdety himself
does sanctify and consecrate this, his Temple to the North.
The *Netjer* Heru Behdety himself
does sanctify and consecrate this, his Temple to the West.
The *Netjer* Heru Behdety himself
does sanctify and consecrate this, his Temple to the East.
The Temple of the *Netjer* Heru Behdety is established.
It is established for millions of years.

The Ritualist returns to the altar and **lights the candle or oil lamp** *while the following is said:*

Come, come in peace, O glorious Eye of Heru,
Be strong and renew your youth in peace.
For the flame shines like Ra on the double horizon.

191

The Lie is abolished!
I am pure, I am pure, I am pure, I am pure.

*The Ritualist **places incense on the burner** and **censes each sacred image** beginning with the statue of the Netjer while the following is recited:*

The fire is laid, the fire shines;
The incense is laid on the fire, the incense shines.
    Your perfume comes to me, O Incense;
    May my perfume come to you, O Incense.
Your perfume comes to me, you *Netjeru*;
May my perfume come to you, you *Netjeru*.
    May I be with you, you *Netjeru*;
    May you be with me, you *Netjeru*.
May I live with you, you *Netjeru*;
May you live with me, you *Netjeru*.
    I love you, you *Netjeru*;
    May you love me, you *Netjeru*.

*Standing in front of the image of Heru Behdety the Ritualist **offers the burning incense** and says:*

Take the incense,
Its essence is for you, O Great *Netjer* of Multicolored Plumage.
Its smoke permeates your shrine, bringing life!
Take the incense,
Its essence is for you.
Your Majesty is appeased with the incense.
This Eye of Heru,
This essence of the Eye of Heru comes to you.

At this point the following is said:

Your heaven belongs to you, O Behdety, Brightly Colored One. You fly therein as the Winged Disk. You alight on the prow of the barque of Ra Horakhty, your two Uraei protect you. You are like Shu who lifts up heaven.[143]

Homage to you, O Heru Behdety, for you truly are Lord of Heaven. As you defeated the enemies of Ra, so may you now grant this temple and your servants victory against every adversary and adversity. May you protect us and shelter us under your wings. Place courage in our hearts in the knowledge that you are powerful of arm and swift of gait against every adversary. You are the Attacking *Ba*, Great of Strength. May you trample the enemies of Ra and the enemies of Ma'at. Praise be to you, Heru Behdety!

*The Ritualist **places more incense on the charcoal** and again and again **slowly raises and lowers the incense cup** as the following is recited:*

O Heru Behdety, may you advance with your *Ka*.
O Luminous One, the arm of your *Ka* is before you,
The arm of your *Ka* is behind you.
O Lord of Heaven, the foot of your *Ka* is before you,
The foot of your *Ka* is behind you.
O Golden Falcon, this incense is offered to you,
May your face be filled as this essence spreads itself over you.

---

[143] Words inscribed on the second register of the inner face of the west enclosure wall of the temple at Wetjeset-Hor (see Cassinat, vol. ii, p. 8).

Richard J. Reidy

*All present **perform the Henu Rite**—Embrace the Earth, the Fourfold Salute to the God, Embrace the Earth. The bodily gestures are performed alternately four times.*

For Embracing the Earth, all present prostrate themselves, face down, upon the floor. During the Fourfold Salute, all present rise upon one knee, and alternately raise their hands and arms into the *Dua* (praise) position with palms facing outward, followed by the *Sahu* (obedience) gesture, made by striking the chest with a closed fist and raising the other arm (also with closed fist) at a ninety-degree angle. The *Dua* position is accompanied by the words **"Adoration be to Heru Behdety,"** followed by the *Sahu* gesture accompanied with the words, **"Hail to the Lord of Heaven!"** The bodily gestures are performed alternately four times.

*Following this all present again **prostrate themselves before the divine image**. This is a sign and symbol of total submission and adoration before the Netjer. The following is said:*

> Homage to Heru Behdety, Great *Netjer*, Lord of Heaven,
> who is established on the Great Seat!
> I have placed myself on the floor in awe of you.
> I embrace the earth before you as before the Lord of Life.
> I have come that I might kiss the earth,
> that I might worship my Master,
> For I have seen his Beauty;
> I give praise to Heru Behdety,
> For I have seen his Power.
> His form is more distinguished than the *Netjeru*;
> His arm is more powerful than the *Netjeru*.
> I am pure, I am pure, I am pure, I am pure!

Everyone stands up.

*The Ritualist **holds in the palm of one hand the image of Ma'at** and with **the other hand open and raised over the image as if sheltering it**, repeats the following:*

> I have come to you as Djehuty, whose two hands are joined together under Ma'at. She comes to be with you, for she is everywhere. You are provided with Ma'at. You move in Ma'at, you live in Ma'at. She fills your body, she rests in your head, she makes his seat upon your brow; the breath of your body is of Ma'at, your heart does live in Ma'at. All that you eat, all that you drink, all that you breathe is of Ma'at. Djehuty presents Ma'at to you, his two hands are upon her beauty before your face.

*The Ritualist places the image of Ma'at near the divine statue. Then he/she holds up before the image of Heru Behdety a **pitcher of water** and **pours the water slowly into an offering bowl** as the following Utterance is recited:*

> This libation is for you, O Noble Winged Scarab.
> This libation is for you, Heru Behdety.
> I have brought to you this offering of pure water,
> That your heart may be refreshed.
> I have brought to you this Eye of Heru,
> Placing this at your feet.
> I present to you that which flows forth from you,
> That your heart shall continue to beat.
> For it is with you that all comes forth at the sound of the voice.

Richard J. Reidy

The offering bowl is placed on the altar.

*The Ritualist presents **an image of the Eye of Heru** and recites the following:*

> Take to yourself the *Wedjat*-Eye provided and equipped with its parts. There is no injury in it. This is the Eye at the sight of which you rejoice and your heart expands on account of it each day. Your right Eye (the sun) moves rapidly, and your left Eye (the moon) is counted, and your two Eyes are glorious in their place.[144]

*At this point the Ritualist **lightly sprinkles sand on the floor in front of the altar** as the following is recited:*

> O Heru Behdety, who resides in *Wetjeset-Hor* (Edfu),
> Take to yourself the Eye of Heru.
> You have rescued it, O Falcon Great of Strength.
> You have sprinkled with sand your Eye.

***Lifting the wine offering** before the sacred image, the Ritualist repeats the following:*

> mn n.k irp irt ḥrw wꜣḏt
> ["*mán-nik 'úrip írat ḥáru wá'ḏat*"; approximately
> pronounced *MAHN-neek OO-rip EE-raht HAH-roo WAH-jat*]

---

[144] C. Traunecker, *COPTOS: Hommes et Dieux sur le parvis de Geb* (Leuven, Belgium: Peeters Press, 1992), p. 185—187. There are thirty-five examples of this particular offering scene at Edfou, according to Traunecker.(v. p. 187)

Take to yourself wine, the green Eye of Heru,
which I offer to your Ka.
O Ruler, how beautiful is your beauty!
May you drink it; may your heart rejoice;
may anger be removed from your face.
It is pure.
[*iw.w w'b* pronounced *"uwú wá'ib"*; approximately *oo-WOO WAH-ib*]

*The Ritualist **places myrrh on the fire** and **lifts up the smoking incense** while at the same time he **lifts up the meat-offering** before the Netjer, and says the following:*

The scent of myrrh is for your nose. It fills your nostrils; your heart receives the meat-portions on its scent.[145]

*Slowly **elevating the food offerings four times** before the image of the Netjer, the Ritualist repeats the following:*

I offer to Heru Behdety, Lord of Humankind.
All life emanates from you,
All health emanates from you,
All stability emanates from you,
All good fortune emanates from you,
O Heru Behdety, Rich in Heka, forever and ever.

*The Ritualist **places the food offering before the divine image**, and then all present **extend one hand, palm down**, over the offerings and recite the following:*

---

[145] Quoted in "Worship and Festivals in an Egyptian Temple," by H. W. Fairman (publ. by The John Rylands Library, 1954), p. 191.

May offerings of every kind come forth in abundance, like the things which come forth from the mouth of the *Netjer.*

piryá pírit ar ḫiráw mi purú:riat ma rá' ni náṭar. (4 times) [approximately pronounced *peer-YA PEER-it ar khi-RAU mee pu-ROOR-iat ma RA nee NAH-tchar*]

May offerings of every kind come forth in abundance, like the things that come forth from the mouth of the Netjer.

Holding the **Ankh** *before Heru, the Ritualist says:*

Take the sign of life, Living Lord, venerable Ba who makes infinity live. You are the one who gives life to all people. You make the living live by your work.[146]

ʿánaḫ niḥáḫ ḏát.
[approximately pronounced *AH-nakh nee-HAH JAHT*]

The **Ankh** *is placed next to the divine image.*

Holding the **Ib** *(the golden heart) before Heru, the Ritualist says:*

Hail to you, O Heru Behdety, Lord of Awe. I have brought to you your heart to set it upon its seat, even as your mother Aset brought your heart to you and set it upon its seat, and as you brought the heart of Aset, your mother, to set it upon its seat, and as Djehuty brought the heart to the Flaming One, even Sekhmet, and as this *Netjeret* was appeased by

---

[146] Sylvie Cauville, *L'Offrande aux dieux dans le temple égyptien* (Leuven,,Belgium: Peeters, 2012), p. 161. This recitation is specified for Heru Behdety.

Djehuty. Let me draw near to you with your heart, so that you may have pleasure through me, and so that by means of me you may have power over your body. Ascend, O Lord of the Sky, radiant, rejuvenating, equipped as a *Netjer*. Live, O Highly Revered One, live forever and ever!

*After placing the **Ib** near the sacred image, **everyone sings or chants** the hymn to Heru Behdety. Participants may wish to alternate the singing of verses.*

1) The *Netjeru* in the Sky revere you, Heru Behdety, Great *Netjer*, Lord of Heaven with Dappled Plumage, because you are the perfect Sun Disk of gold who enables their *Bas* to remain in the heavens.

2) The *Netjeru* on the Earth revere you, Heru Behdety, because you are their king who protects the temples with their divine images.

3) The *Netjeru* in the *Duat* revere you, Heru Behdety, because you are their prince who has created their forms, making the Kingdom of the Departed Ones glorious with the Blessed Dead, caring for their divine corpses.

4) The *Netjeru* in the Primeval Waters (Nun), revere you, Heru Behdety, because you are their father from whom they have gone forth, having slain the enemies of Ra.

5) The *Netjeru* of the South, North, West, and East revere you, Heru Behdety, because you are the Living One from whose life one lives, the Lifter who raises up the sky.

6) Men and women revere you, Heru Behdety, because you have made joyful their hearts as the Caregiver who cares for his people.

7) All creatures—animals, birds, and fish—revere you, Heru Behdety, because you are the Bright One who illuminates the living with your light, giving the breath of life to all living things.

8) The plants of the field revere you, Heru Behdety, Great *Netjer*, Lord of Heaven with dappled plumage, because you are the Lord of Life who rejoices in all life.[147]

*At this point **perform the meditation or magical action** or, if it is a special feast, add the appropriate prayers.*

*Afterwards **all present back out of the Temple Chamber with heads slightly bowed** while the Ritualist performs the **"removing the foot."***

*With the **broom** the Ritualist, as the last person to exit, **ritually sweeps the area beginning at the altar**. (This is known as "removing the foot.") While performing this action the Ritualist recites the following:*

The distress that causes confusion has been driven away, and all the Netjeru are in harmony. I have given Heru his Eye; I have placed the Wedjat-Eye in the correct position.

---

[147] Notes: This English version is translated and modified from Dieter Kurth, *Treffpunkt der Götter: Inschriften aus dem Tempel des Horus von Edfu* (Artemis Verlag, 1994) pp. 282-284.The text is located on the base of the Gateway in the southern section of the mud-brick enclosure wall that leads to the Mammisi.

I have given Setekh his Testicles, so that the two lords are
content through the work of my hands.

I know the sky, I know the earth;
I know Heru, I know Setekh.
Heru is appeased with his Eyes;
Setekh is appeased with his Testicles.
I am Djehuty, who reconciles the Netjeru,
who makes offerings in their correct form.

*The **double doors are solemnly closed** as the Ritualist says the
following:*

Djehuty has come.
He has filled the Eye of Heru;
He has restored the Testicles of Setekh.
No evil shall enter this Temple.
Ptah has closed the door,
Djehuty has set it fast.
The door is closed, the door is set fast with the bolt.

*All **bow, touching the palms of their hands to their knees.***

THE REVERSION OF OFFERINGS

*One priest or priestess and as many assistants as necessary enter the
Temple Chamber a final time. While he/she and any assistants **lift up
the offerings** before the sacred image the ritualist shall say:*

O Heru Behdety, your enemy[148] withdraws for you. Heru has turned himself to his Eye in its name of 'Reversion-of-Offerings.' I am Djehuty. I come to perform this rite for the Lord of the Double Crown. These, your divine offerings revert, they revert to your servants for life, for stability, for health and for joy! O that the Eye of Heru may flourish for you eternally!

*Everyone withdraws, **carrying away all food offerings except for one loaf of bread and a bowl of pure water.** These last items remain until evening. If this ritual is celebrated after sunset, these items would also be removed.*

*After the candle has burned down, a servant-priest enters and closes the doors of the Kar-shrine. **Extinguishing the candle or oil lamp,** he/she exclaims:*

This is the Eye of Heru by which you have become great, by which you live, and by which you have power, O Heru Behdety. This is the Eye of Heru which you consume and through which you enchant your body. The Wedjat-Eye now enters into the West, into Manu, but it shall return. Truly, the Eye of Heru returns in peace![149]

---

[148] Meat offerings held a two-fold meaning for the ancient priesthood. Since meat necessarily came from slain animals, it signified the defeated or slain enemies of the Netjeret. At the same time, the meat offering represented the produce of the land which ultimately was a gift of the Netjeru.

[149] It is important to consume the food offerings after the ceremony. Water used should either be drunk or poured onto the earth. If it is mixed with Natron, dilute it very greatly and then you can pour in onto the bare earth.

The General Ritual for Khnum

Many thanks go to HiC Luttmers for the many long hours spent in translating important ritual texts from the Temple of Khnum at Esna. In addition, the ancient epithets for Khnum come from several selections found in Ancient Egyptian Literature, Volume III, *by Egyptologist Miriam Lichtheim. These include* The Famine Stela *(p. 90ff), and* Two Hymns to Khnum in the Temple of Esna *(pp. 109-115 and 150).*

Offerings for Khnum: flowers, a model or representation of a Potter's Wheel and the traditional offerings of bread, beer, wine, and meat

Annual Festival for Khnum: On the first day of Rekh Wer, the third month of the season of Peret—February on our own civil calendar. It is called the Festival of the Installation of the Potter's Wheel and is intertwined with the Festival of Raising the Heaven. Women presented the Potter's Wheel to the god; men were not allowed. [150]This was a fertility ritual whose goal was to call forth the god's creative energy for themselves as well as for the Two Lands (i.e., Egypt).

Like members of the ancient priesthood, participants should be clothed in white linen. No item made of animal products such as

---

[150] For further information on these festivals see Serge Sauneron's *Esna V: Les fêtes religieuses d'Esna aux derniers siècles du paganisme* (Cairo: Institut français d'archéologie orientale, 1962), 71-244. See also for a Secondary Source Jochen Hallof's article "Esna" available on line at https://escholarship.org/uc/item/6k78t4w9#page-1, part of the excellent series UCLA Encyclopedia of Egyptology.

leather or wool is to be worn. Linen represents a pristine product of the earth whereas leather and wool come from humankind's domination of the animals, a domination that becomes part of the "natural order" only *after* the First Time when the *Netjeru* and humans and animals lived in peace and harmony. Just as the Morning Ritual harkens back to that First Time (*Zep Tepi*), so every temple rite re-presents mythic prototypes that occurred "in the beginning," that is, in that time before time. Even the sandals worn by the god's servants were made of white papyrus. This avoidance of animal products by the priesthood fits well with the fact that the ritualist acts as a *Netjer* and verbally asserts that he or she is a *Netjer*.

As with all Egyptian rituals begin with your purification—washing of hands and cleansing of mouth with Natron. This preliminary rite helps us to lay aside the cares of the day and to become mindful of the fact that we will encounter a divine being. If Natron is not available, then use a natural sea salt in its place until you make your own Natron.

If two or more persons are participating, then one person, impersonating the Netjer *Djehuty,* **purifies each person by sprinkling each with water while exclaiming**:

I purify you with the water of all life and good fortune, all stability, all health and happiness.[151]

Afterwards each person rinses his mouth and places a small amount of Natron or sea salt in his mouth while saying:

----

[151] Taken from Aylward M. Blackman's article "Purification (Egyptian)" in Hastings Encyclopedia 10/1918/ 476-82. This article is reprinted in Gods, Priests, and Men, Studies in the Religion of Pharaonic Egypt, edited by Alan B. Lloyd (Kegan Paul International, 1998), p. 9.

I wash my mouth; I chew natron so that I may extol the might of Khnum, Lord of the Wheel Who Models All Things Between His Hands.[152]

*Participants **assemble outside the Temple Chamber** and begin by **softly rattling sistra**.*

This time—several minutes or more—is used to focus minds and intention so that distracting thoughts are left behind. The sound of the sistrum was said to placate the deity, purifying the atmosphere in preparation for encountering divinity. The sistrum was associated with Hutheru and also with her and Heru's son Ihy, and thus has connotations of joy, celebration, and dancing. According to Plutarch (A.D. 46-120), the sound of sistra was also reputed to drive away Setekh. But this was of very late date. It may have been that since by that time Setekh had been demonized, the general apotropaic function of the sistrum against evil entities was extended to include this *Netjer* as well.

*Standing **before the closed doors**, the Ritualist **recites the entrance spell**:*

UTTERANCE BEFORE THE CLOSED DOORS OF THE TEMPLE

*The ritualist **raises hands in adoration** (dua position-arms stretched out in front of the body and raised up to face level, with palms facing outward). The following shall be said:*

---

[152] Based on a temple inscription taken from "The Myth of Horus at Edfu—II" by A. M. Blackman and H. W. Fairman, appearing in Gods, Priests and Men, Studies in the Religion of Pharaonic Egypt (Kegan Paul International, 1998) p. 283.

O you *Netjeru* of this Temple, you guardians of the great portal, great *Netjeru* of mysterious abode, who sanctify the *Netjer* in his shrine, who consecrate his oblation, who receive the offerings in his presence in the Hall of the Ennead: I have made my way and I enter into your presence. I am one of you. I am Shu, the eldest son of his father, the senior *wab* servant-priest of Khnum. Do not repulse me on the *Netjer's* path. My feet are not impeded. I am not turned back from the court of the great portal so that I may conduct the divine service, that I may present offerings to him that made them, that I may give bread to Khnum. I have come on the way of the god. I have not shown partiality in judgment. I have not consorted with the strong. I have not reproached the lowly. I have not stolen things. I have not diminished the constituents of the Eye of Ra. I have not disturbed the Balance. I have not tampered with the requirements of the Sacred Eye. O Council of the Great *Netjer* in this Temple, behold, I have come to you to offer Ma'at to the Lord of Ma'at, to content the Sound Eye for its lord. I am Shu; I flood his offering table. I present his offerings, Sekhmet consorting with me, that I may adore Khnum at his festivals, that I may kiss the earth so great is his majesty, that I may endow his image with life. I am pure. I am purified.

At this point the ritualist **opens the doors to the Temple Chamber,** *or, if there are no doors,* **makes a gesture of opening unseen doors,** *and* **steps forward as if crossing over a threshold.** *The following is said:*

O you *Ba*-souls of *Ta-Senet* [Esna] if you are strong, I am strong. If I am strong, you are strong. If your *Ka*-spirits are strong, my *Ka*-spirit is strong at the head of the living.

As they are living so shall I live . . . . Khnum, Great in *Abu* [Elephantine], has given to me life, stability, and serenity round about my members, which Djehuty has gathered together for life. I am Heru in the height of heaven, the beautiful one of awe, Lord of Victory, mighty one of awe, exalted one of the two plumes, great one in *Ta-Senet*, I am pure.

Enter, **close the double doors** *and* **stand in front of the Kar-shrine and altar.** *All bow, touching their hands to their knees.*

All present recite or sing the Morning Hymn for this Netjer:

Awaken beautifully, Khnum, Lord of *Ta-Senet* [Esna], visible form amidst the visible forms of the Netjeru in their temples!

Awaken beautifully, Khnum, radiant of form, visible form above visible forms, *Netjer* of Eminent Manifestations!

Awaken beautifully, Khnum, Lord of Esna, eternal in his aspect, *Netjer* renewing his radiance each day, Living Ram who knows not how to perish!

Awaken beautifully, Khnum, protector of the *Netjeru*, Great pf Flame, who consumes the rebels in his fire!

Awaken beautifully, Khnum, visible form in the western mountains after you have awakened the departed, perfect of body, Lord of Humankind!

Awaken beautifully, Khnum, who gives life to the young being, male who sets the marrow inside the bones, Lord

207

of *Ta-Senet* [Esna], who breathes air into the interior of the egg!

Awaken beautifully, Khnum, Great Potter, architect of life who organizes the country by the action of his arms!

Awaken beautifully, Khnum, Lord of the Countryside, who models the egg on the wheel, who gives life to the chick, who makes breath for all nostrils, so that they are alive to see him, and who puts the son in the place that the father occupies!

Awaken beautifully, Khnum, *Netjer* of the Wheel, who shapes the *Netjeru* and molds all the world on his wheel, at the head of the House of Life, the *Netjer* who weaves his web of light, brings light to the darkness, whose clarity dispels obscurity, and who nourishes all stomachs with his fingertips, in this his name Khnum-Ra, Lord of *Ta-Senet* [Esna]!

Awaken beautifully, Khnum, Ram Warrior, who overthrows the rebels and triumphs over the insurgents in victory!

Awaken beautifully, Khnum, *Netjer* who maintains the egg in good condition, in this your name of Shu, breath of life within all things!

Awaken beautifully, Khnum. Awaken pacified, awaken in peace![153]

---

[153] The twelve verses for this Morning Hymn above are recorded in the great temple of Khnum at Esna. Those here are a portion of a much longer Morning Hymn. For the complete twenty-six verse hymn the reader is

*The ritualist slowly **opens the two doors of the Kar-shrine** housing the sacred image. All others bow, touching their hands to their knees. The following is said:*

> The doors of the sky are open; the doors of the earth are unlocked. This House is open for its Lord. Let me come forth as he shall come forth. Let me enter in as he shall enter in. Khnum, the Veil-faced One, is exalted upon his Great Seat. The Great Company of the *Netjeru* are exalted upon their seat.

The Netjer is now visible. All recite the following at the revelation of the Netjer's face:

> How beautiful is your face, O Khnum, Divine Potter, Regent of the Wheel, who provides the land with the seeds of life!
>
> How beautiful is your face, when your arms are on your wheel, occupied with fashioning every egg, every day!
>
> How beautiful is your face, when you mold humankind, give birth to the *Netjeru,* and in the same way create all animals!
>
> How beautiful is your face, when you are within the mother's body, giving wellbeing to all your creatures at the moment when they are going to come out into the world!

---

referred to *Les Fetê Religieuses d'Esna,* by Egyptologist Serge Sauneron (Cairo, 1962), pp. 87-90.

How beautiful is your face, when you are the air that gives breath in the nostrils, imbuing the flesh of all living substance!

How beautiful is your face, when you are manifest through the wind, and when your sister, the wind of the North, is at your side!

How beautiful is your face, in the flood season, when the nutritive earth is impregnated with grains and vegetation!

How beautiful is your face, when you are lord of the countryside, busy creating all the living things for the entire world!

How beautiful is your face, when you navigate the sky, and when your *Ba*-soul provides for the *Netjeru* that come forth from your wheel!

How beautiful is your face, when you are in the House of Books, inscribing the orders for whom you want, in the hieroglyphs of the *Netjer* Djehuty!

How beautiful is your face, when you are in the Mansion of Life, healing the sick, eliminating evil from those who call to you!

How beautiful is your face, when you are in every temple, engaged in filling the Eye of Heru with its elements, in your role of *souadj*-soul!

How beautiful is your face, wherever you are, good shepherd
of all the land![154]

*The Ritualist holds up the **bowl of water** in which he/she will be mixing
the Natron. The following is said:*

O water may you remove all evil,
As Ra who bathes in the Lake of Rushes,
May Heru wash my flesh,
May Djehuty cleanse my feet,
May Shu lift me up and Nut take my hand!
May Sutekh be my strength, and may Sekhmet be my healing!
And may Amun-Ra be my life and my prospering!

*The bowl of water is set aside and the container of **Natron** is lifted up.
The following is said:*

It is pure, it is pure.
My Natron is the Natron of Heru,
and the Natron of Heru is my Natron.
My Natron is the Natron of Setekh,
and the Natron of Setekh is my Natron.
My Natron is the Natron of Djehuty,
and the Natron of Djehuty is my Natron.
My Natron is the Natron of Geb,
and the Natron of Geb is my Natron.

My mouth is the mouth of a milking calf

---

[154] The verses for these exclamations at the Revelation of the Face above
are recorded in the great temple of Khnum at Esna. See *Les Fetê Religieuses
d'Esna*, by Egyptologist Serge Sauneron (Cairo, 1962), pp. 158-161. This
selection of the exclamations is only a portion of those extent on the
temple walls.

on the day that I was born.

Four pinches of Natron are mixed into the water as this Utterance
is recited:

> I give you essential water, a tide in your time.
> I bring the flood waters to purify your sanctuary.
> I bring you the flood waters
> to purify your Temple and your statue in its place,
> the primordial water that purifies as in the First Time!

*The Ritualist places an index finger into the water and moves it in
a circular, clockwise direction four times as the following is said:*

> Khnum, Whose Sandals Rest on the Flood,
> does purify this water;
> Khnum, Lord of the Cataract Region,
> does cleanse this water;
> Khnum, Exalted Nun,
> does sanctify this water;
> Khnum, Lord of Life,
> does endow this water with power and with life.

*The **Bowl of Natron-infused water** is then taken up and the Ritualist
sprinkles this lightly in front of and around the statue or image of
Khnum, applying some water to the base of the image, as the Utterance
is recited:*

> I come close to you, Ram Great of Majesty,
> Tall-plumed and great of horn.
> I bring the water of rejuvenation
> that flows from the Two Caverns.
> I sprinkle the water,

purifying your image and your Temple from all impurity!

The Ritualist picks up the bowl of **Natron** *and* **sprinkles a small amount in each of the four directions** *as the following is recited:*

The *Netjer* Khnum himself does cleanse and purify this,
his Temple to the South.
The *Netjer* Khnum himself does cleanse and purify this,
his Temple to the North.
The *Netjer* Khnum does cleanse and purify this,
his Temple to the West.
The *Netjer* Khnum does cleanse and purify this,
his Temple to the East.

Replacing the Natron on the altar, the Ritualist takes up the **bowl of water, sprinkling a small amount in each of the four directions.** *The following Utterance is recited:*

The *Netjer* Khnum does sanctify and consecrate this,
his Temple to the South.
The *Netjer* Khnum himself does sanctify and consecrate this,
his Temple to the North.
The *Netjer* Khnum himself does sanctify and consecrate this,
his Temple to the West.
The *Netjer* Khnum himself does sanctify and consecrate this,
his Temple to the East.

The Temple of the Netjer Khnum is established.
It is established for millions of years.

The Ritualist returns to the altar and **lights the candle or oil lamp** *while the following is said:*

Come, come in peace, O glorious Eye of Heru,
Be strong and renew your youth in peace.
For the flame shines like Ra on the double horizon.
The Lie is abolished! It is abolished!
I am pure, I am pure, I am pure, I am pure.

*The Ritualist **places incense on the burner** and **censes each sacred image** beginning with the statue of the goddess while the following is recited:*

The fire is laid, the fire shines;
The incense is laid on the fire, the incense shines.
    Your perfume comes to me, O Incense;
    May my perfume come to you, O Incense.
Your perfume comes to me, you *Netjeru*;
May my perfume come to you, You *Netjeru*.
    May I be with you, you *Netjeru*;
    May you be with me, you *Netjeru*.
May I live with you, you *Netjeru*;
May you live with me, you *Netjeru*.
    I love you, you *Netjeru*;
    May you love me, you *Netjeru*.

*Standing in front of the image of Khnum the Ritualist **offers the burning incense** and says:*

Take the incense, Fighting Ram Who Chases His Foes.
Its essence is for you.
Its smoke permeates your shrine, bringing life!
Take the incense,
Its essence is for you.
Your Majesty is appeased with the incense.

This Eye of Heru,
This essence of the Eye of Heru comes to you.

*At this point the following verses from the **Great Hymn to Khnum** is said:*

Adoration be to Khnum who molds the *Netjeru* and Humankind;
who fashions the animals, small and large.
He makes the birds as well as the fish.
He forms the breeding males, and puts on earth the fair female.
He devises the flow of blood in the bones,
molding all in his workshop by the strength of his arms.
And suddenly the breath of life permeated all things.

He causes women to give birth
when her womb has achieved the right moment,
in order for it to open of its own accord.
He diminishes suffering as his heart sees fit.
He relieves the throats,
giving air to those who breathe.
He makes grow the locks of hair,
molding the skin on the members of the body.

In every way, the nations were formed on his wheel, with vocal cords of each nation designed to obtain another language, compared to that of Kemet. This great *Netjer* created the exotic products within the diverse countries because the Lord of the Wheel is also their father, he who is Tatenen who gave birth to all that exists on every soil and who made for them their sustenance.

O Lord of the Wheel, all your creatures show you their appreciation, because you are Ptah-Tatenen, the Creator among the Creators, who brought into existence all that is. You nourish the young inside the mother's womb until the right time comes; then you cause the mother's body to eject the young when the moment arrives.

You have fashioned all humankind,
sent all the *Netjeru* to the world.
You made the animals, small and large.
You created birds, fish, and all crawling animals.
By your command you caused there to be fish
in the waters of Nun
in order to nourish both humans and *Netjeru*.
You caused vegetation to be born,
coloring the shores with their flowers.
You caused the fruit trees to produce their fruits
in order to furnish a means of subsistence
for humans and *Netjeru*.

You are creator of all that is, and creator of all beings.
You are true *Netjer*.
You are *Netjer* of the untroubled heart,
and *Netjer* who unites the limbs.
May your beautiful face be ever gracious towards us.
May you grant us to live forever![155]

---

[155] The verses for this Great Hymn to Khnum are closely modeled on a longer three-part hymn recorded in the great temple of Khnum at Esna. See *Les Fetê Religieuses d'Esna*, by Egyptologist Serge Sauneron (Cairo, 1962), pp. 95-106.

*The Ritualist places **more incense on the charcoal** and again and again **slowly raises and lowers the incense cup** as the following is recited:*

O Khnum, Lord of Life, may you advance with your *Ka*.

O Herdsman of His Followers, the arm of your *Ka* is before you,

The arm of your *Ka* is behind you.

O Great Power in Kemet, the foot of your *Ka* is before you,

The foot of your *Ka* is behind you.

O Lord of *Netjeru* and Humans, this incense is offered to you,

May your face be filled as this essence spreads itself over you.

*All present **perform the Henu Rite**—Embrace the Earth, the Fourfold Salute to the God, Embrace the Earth. The bodily gestures are performed alternately four times.*

For Embracing the Earth, all present prostrate themselves, face down, upon the floor. During the Fourfold Salute, all present rise upon one knee, and alternately raise their hands and arms into the *Dua* (praise) position with palms facing outward, followed by the *Sahu* (obedience) gesture, made by striking the chest with a closed fist and raising the other arm (also with closed fist) at a ninety-degree angle. The *Dua* position is accompanied by the words **"Adoration be to Khnum,"** followed by the *Sahu* gesture accompanied with the words, **"Hail to the Lord of Heaven!"** The bodily gestures are performed alternately four times.

*Following this **all present again prostrate themselves** before the divine image. This is a sign and symbol of total submission and adoration before the Netjer. The following is said:*

Homage be to Khnum
Who is established on the Great Seat!
I have placed myself on the floor in awe of you.
I embrace the earth before you as before the Lord of Life.
I have come that I might kiss the earth,
That I might worship my Lord,
Who illuminates by means of his flame,
For I have seen his Strength;
I give praise to Khnum,
For I have seen his Power.
His form is more distinguished than the *Netjeru*;
His arm is more powerful than the *Netjeru*.
I am pure, I am pure, I am pure, I am pure!

Everyone stands up.

*The Ritualist **holds in the palm of one hand the image of Ma'at** and with **the other hand open and raised over the image as if sheltering it**, repeats the following:*

I have come to you as Djehuty, whose two hands are joined together under Ma'at. She comes to be with you, for she is everywhere. You are provided with Ma'at. You move in Ma'at, you live in Ma'at. She fills your body, she rests in your head, she makes her seat upon your brow; the breath of your body is of Ma'at, your heart does live in Ma'at. All that you eat, all that you drink, all that you breathe is of Ma'at. Djehuty presents Ma'at to you, his two hands are upon her beauty before your face.

*The Ritualist places the image of Ma'at near the divine statue. Then he/ she holds up before the image of Khnum **a pitcher of water** and **pours*** *the water slowly into an offering bowl as the following Utterance is recited:*

> This libation is for you,
> Mighty Victor Who Conquers as He Wishes.
> This libation is for you, O Khnum.
> I have brought to you this offering of water,
> That your heart may be refreshed.
> I have brought to you this Eye of Heru,
> Placing this at your feet.
> I present to you that which flows forth from you,
> That your heart shall continue to beat.
> For it is with you
> That all comes forth at the sound of the voice.

The offering bowl is placed on the altar. At this point the Ritualist lightly sprinkles sand on the floor in front of the altar as the following is recited:

> O Khnum, who resides in *Ta-Senet* [Esna],
> Take to yourself the Eye of Heru.
> You have rescued it, O Beneficent *Netjer*.
> You have sprinkled with sand the Eye of Heru.

*Presenting **a bouquet of flowers,** the following is said:*

> O Khnum, Lord of *Ta-Senet,*
> accept the bouquet made of pleasing flowers.
> I come close to you, may you accept them.
> They bloom before your beautiful face,
> and the Lord of the Countryside breathes their perfume.

Richard J. Reidy

They are pure![156]

Lifting the wine offering before the sacred image, the Ritualist repeats the following:

mn n.k irp irt ḥrw wȝḏt
["*mán-nik 'úrip írat ḥáru wá'ḏat*"; approximately pronounced *MAHN-neek OO-rip EE-raht HAH-roo WAH-jat*]

> **Take to yourself wine, the green Eye of Heru,**
> **which I offer to your Ka.**
> **O Contenting** *Netjer*, **how beautiful is your beauty!**
> **May you drink it; may your heart rejoice;**
> **may anger be removed from your face.**
> *It is pure.*
> [*iw.w w'b* pronounced "*uwú wá'ib*"; approximately *oo-WOO WAH-ib*]

*The Ritualist **places myrrh on the fire** and **lifts up the smoking incense** while at the same time he **lifts up the meat-offering** before the Netjer, and says the following:*

> **The scent of myrrh is for your nose. It fills your nostrils;**
> **your heart receives the meat-portions on its scent.**[157]

*Slowly **elevating the food offerings** four times before the image of the goddess, the Ritualist repeats the following:*

[156] This Offering Formula for a bouquet is from *Les Fetê Religieuses d'Esna*, p. 139.
[157] Quoted in "Worship and Festivals in an Egyptian Temple," by H. W. Fairman (publ. by The John Rylands Library, 1954), p. 191.

I offer to Khnum, Who Models All Things between His
Hands.
All life emanates from you,
All health emanates from you,
All stability emanates from you,
All good fortune emanates from you,
O Lord of Life, Beneficent *Netjer.*

*The Ritualist places the food offering before the divine image, and
then all present extend one hand, palm down, over the offerings
and recite the following:*

May offerings of every kind come forth in abundance,
like the things which come forth from the mouth of the
Netjer.

piryá pírit ar ẖiráw mi purú:riat ma rá' ni náṭar. (4 times)
[approximately pronounced *peer-YA PEER-it ar khi-RAU mee pu-
ROOR-iat ma RA nee NAH-tchar*]

May offerings of every kind come forth in abundance, like
the things that come forth from the mouth of the Netjer.

Holding the Ankh before Khnum, the Ritualist says:

Live, O Khnum, live for all time and for eternity!

ʿánaẖ niḥáḥ ḏát.
[approximately pronounced *AH-nakh nee-HAH JAHT*]

The Ankh is placed next to the divine image.

Holding the Ib (the golden heart) before the statue, the Ritualist says:

Hail to you, O Khnum, Great Lion, Slayer of Rebels. I have brought to you your heart to set it in its place. Let me draw near to you with your heart, so that you may have pleasure through me, and so that by means of me you may have power over your body. Ascend, O Ram Great of Majesty, radiant, rejuvenating, equipped as a god. Live, O Mighty Victor, live forever and ever!

*After placing the **Ib** near the sacred image, **everyone sings or chants** the hymn to Khnum. Participants may wish to alternate the singing of verses.*

The sky is in celebration; the earth rejoices.
The Master of Life is satisfied.
Each one among us knows joy of the heart,
because they see Khnum established on his throne
in the center of the Mansion of Khnum.
His two arms are positioned on his wheel
in order to mold both *Netjeru* and humankind,
the animals small and large,
birds, fish, and reptiles of every species
in order to supply this land for us.[158]

*The Ritualist presents the **Nehep** **Potter's Wheel** to Khnum, **holding the** Nehep *with one hand and with **the other hand extended over this offering in a sign of protection** while reciting the following:*

I bring the Potter's Wheel to your Majesty, O Craftsman-Potter Khnum. You are the one who establishes the life-span. Shay (Destiny) and Ma'at establish that which needs to

---

[158] This Hymn of Joy is from Serge Sauneron's *Les fêtes religieuses d'Esna,* Vol. V (Cairo: 1962; 2012 edition), p. 150.

be done. You are the *Netjer* who exorcises misfortune. You set the seed to produce an heir; you create the embryo for the woman. On your Potter's Wheel you craft humankind. You are truly Lord of Life.[159]

At this point perform the **meditation or magical action** *or, if it is a special feast, add the appropriate prayers.*

Afterwards **all present back out of the Temple Chamber with heads slightly bowed** *while the Ritualist performs the "removing the foot."*

With the **broom** *the Ritualist, as the last person to exit,* **ritually sweeps the area beginning at the altar.** *(This is known as "removing the foot.") While performing this action the Ritualist recites the following:*

The distress that causes confusion has been driven away, and all the Netjeru are in harmony. I have given Heru his Eye; I have placed the Wedjat-Eye in the correct position. I have given Setekh his Testicles, so that the two lords are content through the work of my hands.

I know the sky, I know the earth;
I know Heru, I know Setekh.
Heru is appeased with his Eyes;
Setekh is appeased with his Testicles.
I am Djehuty, who reconciles the Netjeru,
who makes offerings in their correct form.

---

[159] Based on offering texts inscribed at the temple in Esna. See *L'Offrande aux dieux dans le temple égyptien* by Sylvie Cauville (Leuven, Belgium: Peeters, 2012), pp. 193-194.

*The **double doors are solemnly closed** as the Ritualist says the following:*

> Djehuty has come.
> He has filled the Eye of Heru;
> He has restored the Testicles of Setekh.
> No evil shall enter this Temple.
> Ptah has closed the door,
> Djehuty has set it fast.
> The door is closed, the door is set fast with the bolt.

*All **bow, touching the palms of their hands to their knees**.*

THE REVERSION OF OFFERINGS

*One priest or priestess and as many assistants as necessary enter the Temple Chamber a final time. While he/she and any assistants **lift up the offerings** before the sacred image the ritualist shall say:*

> O Khnum, your enemy[160] withdraws for you. Heru has turned himself to his Eye in its name of 'Reversion-of-Offerings.' I am Djehuty. I come to perform this rite for Khnum, the Bounty Giver. These, your divine offerings revert, they revert to your servants for life, for stability, for health and for joy! O that the Eye of Heru may flourish for you eternally!

---

[160] Meat offerings held a two-fold meaning for the ancient priesthood. Since meat necessarily came from slain animals, it signified the defeated or slain enemies of the Netjeret. At the same time, the meat offering represented the produce of the land which ultimately was a gift of the Netjeru.

Everyone withdraws, **carrying away all food offerings except for one loaf of bread and a bowl of pure water.** *These last items remain until evening. If this ritual is celebrated after sunset, these items would also be removed.*

After the candle has burned down, a servant-priest enters and closes the doors of the Kar-shrine. **Extinguishing the candle or oil lamp,** *he/she exclaims:*

> This is the Eye of Heru by which you have become great, by which you live, and by which you have power, O Khnum. This is the Eye of Heru which you consume and through which you enchant your body. The Wedjat-Eye now enters into the West, into Manu, but it shall return. Truly, the Eye of Heru returns in peace![161]

---

[161] It is important to consume the food offerings after the ceremony. Water used should either be drunk or poured onto the earth. If it is mixed with Natron, dilute it very greatly and then you can pour in onto the bare earth.

The General Ritual for Khonsu

Epithets for this *Netjer* come from *Lexikon der ägyptischen Götter und Götterbezeichnungen* ("Dictionary of Egyptian Gods and God-Names"), often abbreviated LGG in scholarly works. See also "The Khonsu Cosmogony," by Richard A. Parker and Leonard H. Lesko, in *Pyramid Studies and Other Essays presented to I. E. S. Edwards,* ed. by John Baines (The Egypt Exploration Society, 1988), 168-175. No attempt has been made to fabricate or "make up" epithets for this great *Netjer.*

Please do not feel that you must either do the entire ritual or nothing at all. If certain elements of the ritual speak to you and have special meaning, then please just do those particular elements. However, in my own experience I have found that as I repeat the ritual a few times, I am pleasantly surprised with 'aha!' moments where some new insight comes to light. The ritual's words have special meaning and power, and so may not be evident on first reading. Be patient and I believe the *Netjeru* will reward your effort.

Offerings for Khonsu: the traditional offerings of bread, beer, wine, meat and any other wholesome foods.

Like members of the ancient priesthood, participants should be clothed in white linen. No item made of animal products such as leather or wool is to be worn. Linen represents a pristine product of the earth whereas leather and wool come from humankind's domination of the animals, a domination that becomes part of the "natural order" only *after* the First Time when the *Netjeru* and humans and animals lived in peace and harmony. Just as the

Morning Ritual harkens back to that First Time (*Zep Tepi*), so every temple rite re-presents mythic prototypes that occurred "in the beginning," that is, in that time before time. Even the sandals worn by the god's servants were made of white papyrus. This avoidance of animal products by the priesthood fits well with the fact that the ritualist acts as a *Netjer* and verbally asserts that he or she is a *Netjer*.

As with all Egyptian rituals begin with your purification—washing of hands and cleansing of mouth with Natron. This preliminary rite helps us to lay aside the cares of the day and to become mindful of the fact that we will encounter a divine being. If Natron is not available, then use a natural sea salt in its place until you make your own Natron.

If two or more persons are participating, then one person, impersonating the Netjer *Djehuty,* **purifies each person by sprinkling each with water while exclaiming**:

I purify you with the water of all life and good fortune, all stability, all health and happiness.[162]

Afterwards each person **rinses his mouth** *and* **places a small amount of Natron or sea salt in his mouth** *while saying:*

I wash my mouth; I chew natron so that I may extol the might of Khonsu, Son of Amun, the Shining One.[163]

---

[162] Taken from Aylward M. Blackman's article "Purification (Egyptian)" in Hastings Encyclopedia 10/1918/ 476-82. This article is reprinted in Gods, Priests, and Men, Studies in the Religion of Pharaonic Egypt, edited by Alan B. Lloyd (Kegan Paul International, 1998), p. 9.

[163] Based on a temple inscription taken from "The Myth of Horus at Edfu—II" by A. M. Blackman and H. W. Fairman, appearing in Gods,

*Participants **assemble outside the Temple Chamber** and begin by softly rattling sistra.*

This time—several minutes or more—is used to focus minds and intention so that distracting thoughts are left behind. The sound of the sistrum was said to placate the deity, purifying the atmosphere in preparation for encountering divinity. The sistrum was associated with Hutheru and also with her and Heru's son Ihy, and thus has connotations of joy, celebration, and dancing. According to Plutarch (A.D. 46-120), the sound of sistra was also reputed to drive away Setekh. But this was of very late date. It may have been that since by that time Setekh had been demonized, the general apotropaic function of the sistrum against evil entities was extended to include this *Netjer* as well.

*Standing **before the closed doors**, the Ritualist **recites the entrance spell**:*

UTTERANCE BEFORE THE CLOSED DOORS OF THE TEMPLE

*The ritualist **raises hands in adoration** (dua position-arms stretched out in front of the body and raised up to face level, with palms facing outward). The following shall be said:*

O you *Netjeru* of this temple, you guardians of the great portal, great *Netjeru* of mysterious abode, who sanctify the *Netjer* in his shrine, who consecrate his oblation, who receive the offerings in his presence in the Hall of the Ennead: I have made my way and I enter into your presence. I am one of you. I am Shu, the eldest son of his

---

Priests and Men, Studies in the Religion of Pharaonic Egypt (Kegan Paul International, 1998) p. 283.

father, the senior *wab* servant priest of Khonsu. Do not repulse me on the *Netjer*'s path. My feet are not impeded. I am not turned back from the court of the great portal so that I may conduct the divine service, that I may present offerings to him that made them, that I may give bread to Khonsu. I have come on the way of the *Netjer*. I have not shown partiality in judgment. I have not consorted with the strong. I have not reproached the lowly. I have not stolen things. I have not diminished the constituents of the Eye of Ra. I have not disturbed the balance. I have not tampered with the requirements of the Sacred Eye. O Council of the Great *Netjer* in this temple, behold, I have come to you to offer Ma'at to the Pendulum of Heaven, to content the Sound Eye for its Lord. I am Shu; I flood his offering table. I present his offerings, Sekhmet consorting with me, that I may adore Khonsu at his festivals, that I may kiss the earth so great is his majesty, that I may endow his image with life. I am pure. I am purified.

At this point the ritualist **opens the doors to the Temple Chamber,** *or, if there are no doors,* **makes a gesture of opening unseen doors,** *and steps forward as if crossing over a threshold. The following is said:*

O you *Ba*-souls of *Waset* (Thebes), if you are strong, I am strong. If I am strong, you are strong. If your *Ka*-spirits are strong, my *Ka*-spirit is strong at the head of the living. As they are living so shall I live . . . . Sekhmet, the great *Netjeret*, beloved of Ptah, has given to me life, stability, and serenity round about my members, which Djehuty has gathered together for life. I am Heru in the height of heaven, the beautiful one of awe, Lord of Victory, Mighty

One of awe, exalted one of the two plumes, great one in *Abdju* (Abydos) I am pure.

All temple members chant:

Awake in peace,
O Khonsu, Son of Amun,
may you awaken in peace.
Awake in peace,
O Khonsu, The Provider,
Awake in peace,
O Khonsu, in Thebes, Greatly Pleased,
may you awaken in peace.
Awake in peace,
O Khonsu, Decider of the Life-Span,
may you awaken in peace.

Enter, **close the double doors** *and* **stand in front of the Kar-shrine and altar.** *All bow, touching their hands to their knees.*

The ritualist slowly **opens the two doors of the Kar-shrine** *or lifts the veil covering the sacred image. The following is said:*

The doors of the sky are open; the doors of the earth are unlocked. This House is open for its Lord. Let me come forth as he shall come forth. Let me enter in as he shall enter in. Khonsu, He Who Traverses the Sky, is exalted upon his Great Seat. The Great Company of the *Netjeru* are exalted upon their Seats.

I have seen the *Netjer*, and the *Netjer* sees me. The *Netjer* rejoices at seeing me. I have gazed upon the statue of the Luminous One, the sacred image of the Lord of Time.[164]

Right hand on left shoulder of statue; Left hand on right wrist of statue:

Djehuty has come to you. Awake when you hear his words. I have come as the envoy of Atum. My two arms are upon you like those of Heru. My two hands are upon you like those of Djehuty. My fingers are upon you like those of Anpu. Homage be to you. I am a living servant of Khonsu.

*The Ritualist holds up the **bowl of water** in which he/she will be mixing the Natron. The following is said:*

O water may you remove all evil,
As Ra who bathes in the Lake of Rushes,
May Heru wash my flesh.
May Djehuty cleanse my feet.
May Shu lift me up and Nut take my hand!
May Setekh be my strength, and may Sekhmet be my healing!
May Amun-Ra be my life and my prospering!

*The bowl of water is set aside and the container of **Natron** is lifted up. The following is said:*

It is pure, it is pure.
My Natron is the Natron of Heru,
and the Natron of Heru is my Natron.

---

[164] Based on the temple text found in "Worship and Festivals in an Egyptian Temple," a lecture by H. W. Fairman (publ. by The John Rylands Library, 1954) p. 180.

My Natron is the Natron of Setekh,
and the Natron of Setekh is my Natron.
My Natron is the Natron of Djehuty,
and the Natron of Djehuty is my Natron.
My Natron is the Natron of Geb,
and the Natron of Geb is my Natron.
My mouth is the mouth of a milking calf
on the day that I was born.

Four pinches of Natron are mixed into the water as this Utterance
is recited:

I give you essential water, a tide in your time.
I bring the flood waters to purify your sanctuary.
I bring you the flood waters
to purify your Temple and your statue in its place,
the primordial water that purifies as in the First Time!

The Ritualist **places an index finger into the water** and **moves it in
a circular, clockwise direction four times** *as the following is said:*

Khonsu, The Traveler,
does purify this water;
Khonsu, The Provider,
does cleanse this water;
Khonsu, in Thebes, Greatly Pleased,
does sanctify this water;
Khonsu, Decider of the Life-Span,
does endow this water with power and with life.[165]

---

[165] Note that it is the god himself, not his servant-priest, who cleanses and
then empowers the water.

*The **Bowl of Natron-infused water** is then taken up and the Ritualist sprinkles this lightly in front of and around the statue or image of Khonsu, applying some water to the base of the image, as the Utterance is recited:*

> I come close to you, O Son of Amun.
> I bring the water of rejuvenation
> that flows from the Two Caverns.
> I sprinkle the water,
> purifying your image and your Temple from all impurity!

*Pick up the **bowl of Natron** and **sprinkle a small amount in each of the four directions:***

> The *Netjer* Khonsu himself does cleanse and purify this,
> his Temple to the South.
> The *Netjer* Khonsu himself does cleanse and purify this,
> his Temple to the North.
> The *Netjer* Khonsu himself does cleanse and purify this,
> his Temple to the West.
> The *Netjer* Khonsu himself does cleanse and purify this,
> his Temple to the East.

*Pick up the **bowl of water** and **sprinkle a small amount in each of the four directions:***

> The *Netjer* Khonsu himself does sanctify and consecrate this,
> his Temple to the South.
> The *Netjer* Khonsu himself does sanctify and consecrate this,
> his Temple to the North.
> The *Netjer* Khonsu himself does sanctify and consecrate this,
> his Temple to the West.

The *Netjer* Khonsu himself does sanctify and consecrate this, his Temple to the East.
The Temple of the *Netjer* Khonsu is established.
It is established for millions of years.

*The Ritualist returns to the altar and **lights the candle or oil lamp** while the following is said:*

Come, come in peace, O glorious Eye of Heru,
Be strong and renew your youth in peace;
for the flame shines like Ra on the double horizon
and the enemies of Ra are defeated. They are defeated.
The lie is abolished!
I am pure, I am pure, I am pure, I am pure.

*The Ritualist **places incense on the burner** and **censes each sacred image**, beginning with the statue of the Netjer Khonsu, while the following is recited:*

The fire is laid, the fire shines;
The incense is laid on the fire, the incense shines.
    Your perfume comes to me, O Incense;
    May my perfume come to you, O Incense.
Your perfume comes to me, you *Netjeru*;
May my perfume come to you, you *Netjeru*.
    May I be with you, you *Netjeru*;
    May you be with me, you *Netjeru*.
May I live with you, you *Netjeru*;
May you live with me, you *Netjeru*.
    I love you, you *Netjeru*;
    May you love me, you *Netjeru*.

Standing in front of the image of Khonsu, the Ritualist **offers the burning incense** *and says:*

Take the incense, O Khonsu, *Nefer* Hotep,
its essence is for you.
Its smoke permeates your shrine, bringing life!
Take the incense,
its essence is for you.
Your Majesty is appeased with the incense.
This Eye of Heru,
this essence of the Eye of Heru comes to you.

All temple members recite the ancient prayer below:

Homage to you,
O Khonsu in *Waset* (Thebes), Beautiful-of-Setting,
Noble Child who came forth from the lotus.
Lord of Time,
Lord of Silver,
Lord of the circuit of the underworld.
The Great *Netjer*,
Vigorous Bull,
Son of Amun.
Come to me, O Noble Child,
Great *Netjer* in the disk of the moon,
The One Who pleases,
Coming forth from the four elements.
The avenger of flesh,
Whose true name cannot be known,
Whose form cannot be known,
Whose manner cannot be known.
But I know all these things,

For Great, Beneficial, Hidden is your name.
Your form is the lunar month.
Your woods are the vine and the persea tree.
Your herb, the herb of Amun.
Your bird, the heron.
Your fish, the black Nile fish.
Heaven is your shrine,
The earth is your forecourt.
You are the One who appears Shining and Enduring.

The Ritualist **places more incense on the charcoal** *and again and again* **slowly raises and lowers the incense cup** *as the following is recited:*

O Khonsu, may you advance with Your *Ka*.
O Vigorous Bull, the arm of Your *Ka* is before you,
The arm of Your *Ka* is behind you.
O Lord of Time, the foot of your *Ka* is before you,
The foot of your *Ka* is behind you.
O Great *Netjer*, this incense is offered to you,
May your face be filled as this essence spreads itself over you.

All present **perform the Henu Rite**—*Embrace the Earth, the Fourfold Salute to the God, Embrace the Earth. The bodily gestures are performed alternately four times.*

For Embracing the Earth, all present prostrate themselves, face down, upon the floor. During the Fourfold Salute, all present rise upon one knee, and alternately raise their hands and arms into the *Dua* (praise) position with palms facing outward, followed by the *Sahu* (obedience) gesture, made by striking the chest with a closed fist and raising the other arm (also with closed fist) at a ninety-degree angle. The *Dua* position is accompanied by the words **"Adoration be to Khonsu,"** followed by the *Sahu* gesture accompanied with the words, **"Hail to the Provider!"** The bodily gestures are performed alternately four times.

Following this all present again prostrate themselves before the sacred image. This is a sign and symbol of total submission and adoration before the Netjer. The following is said:

> **Homage be to Khonsu, the Shining One,**
> **who is established on the Great Seat!**
> **I have placed myself on the floor in awe of you.**
> **I embrace the earth before you as before the Lord of Time.**
> **I have come that I might kiss the earth,**
> **that I might worship my Master,**
> **For I have seen his Beauty;**
> **I give praise to Khonsu, *Nefer-Hotep*,**
> **For I have seen his Power.**
> **He rounds out his form and repeats his former form**
> **in his name of Moon.**
> **His form is more distinguished than the *Netjeru*;**
> **His arm is more powerful than the *Netjeru*.**
> **I am pure, I am pure, I am pure, I am pure!**

Everyone stands up.

*The Ritualist **holds in the palm of one hand the image of Ma'at** and with **the other hand open and raised over the image as if sheltering it**, repeats the following:*

> **I have come to you as Djehuty, whose two hands are joined together under Ma'at. She comes to be with You, for she**

is everywhere. You are provided with Ma'at. You move in Ma'at, You live in Ma'at. She fills your body, she rests in your head, she makes her seat upon your brow; the breath of your body is of Ma'at, your heart does live in Ma'at. All that you eat, all that you drink, all that you breathe is of Ma'at. Djehuty presents Ma'at to you, his two hands are upon her beauty before your face.

*The Ritualist places the image of Ma'at near the divine statue. Then he/ she holds up before the image of Khonsu a **pitcher of water** and **pours the water slowly into an offering bowl** as the following Utterance is recited:*

This libation is for you, O Heart of Eternity,
This libation is for you, O Khonsu.
I have brought to you this offering of water,
That your heart may be refreshed.
I have brought to you this Eye of Heru,
Placing this at your feet.
I present to you that which flows forth from you,
That your heart shall continue to beat.
For it is with you that all comes forth at the sound of the voice.

*The offering bowl is placed on the altar. At this point the Ritualist **lightly sprinkles sand on the floor in front of the altar** as the following is recited:*

O Khonsu, Falcon, Lord of Joy in *Ipet Sut* (Karnak),
Take to yourself the Eye of Heru.
You have rescued it,
O Great Disk which illuminates the Two Lands.
You have sprinkled with sand the Eye of Heru.

Lifting the wine offering before the sacred image, the Ritualist repeats the following:

mn n.k irp irt ḥrw w³ḏt

[*"mán-nik 'úrip írat ḥáru wá'ḏat"*; approximately pronounced *MAHN-neek OO-rip EE-raht HAH-roo WAH-jat*]

Take to yourself wine, the Green Eye of Heru,
which I offer to your Ka.
O Ruler, how beautiful is your beauty!
May you drink it; may your heart rejoice;
may anger be removed from your face.
It is pure.
[*iw.w w'b* pronounced *"uwú wá'ib"*; approximately *oo-WOO WAH-ib*]

The Ritualist places myrrh on the fire and lifts up the smoking incense while at the same time he lifts up the meat-offering before the Netjer, and says the following:

The scent of myrrh is for your nose. It fills your nostrils;
your heart receives the meat-portions on its scent.[166]

Slowly elevating the food offerings **four** times, the Ritualist exclaims:

I offer to Khonsu,
Who causes the moon to go round in accordance with Ma'at.
All life emanates from you,
All health emanates from you,
All stability emanates from you,

---

[166] Quoted in "Worship and Festivals in an Egyptian Temple," by H. W. Fairman (publ. by The John Rylands Library, 1954), p. 191.

All good fortune emanates from you,
O Greatly Pleased One, Khonsu, forever.

*The Ritualist **places the food offering before the divine image**, and then all present **extend one hand, palm down, over the offerings** and recite the following:*

May offerings of every kind come forth in abundance, like the things which come forth from the mouth of the **Netjer.**

piryá pírit ar ḫiráw mi purú:riat ma rá' ni náṯar. (4 times)
[approximately pronounced *peer-YA PEER-it ar khi-RAU mee pu-ROOR-iat ma RA nee NAH-tchar*]

May offerings of every kind come forth in abundance, like the things that come forth from the mouth of the Netjer.

*Holding the **Ankh** before the Netjer, the Ritualist says:*

Live, O Khonsu, Lord of Joy in *Ipet Sut (Karnak),* live for all time and for eternity!

ꜥánaḫ niḥáḥ ḏát.
[approximately pronounced *AH-nakh nee-HAH JAHT]*

*The **Ankh** is placed next to the statue of Khonsu.*

*Holding the **Ib (the golden heart)** before the Netjer, the Ritualist says:*

Hail to You, O Khonsu, Heart of Eternity. I have brought to you your heart to set it in its place. Let me draw near to

you with your heart, so that you may have pleasure through
me, and so that by means of me you may have power over
your body. Ascend, O Luminous One, equipped as a *Netjer*.
Live, O Great *Netjer* in the moon disk, live forever and ever!

*After placing the **Ib** near the sacred image, **everyone sings or chants**
the hymn to Khonsu. Begin by slowly playing the sistra. Participants
may wish to alternate the singing of verses.*

We sing praises to Khonsu, Pendulum of Heaven in His Fullness,
We prostrate ourselves before the Luminous One.

We praise you in the Sky and honor your perfection.
Look with favor upon us!
May we see your mercy without ceasing,
so that we might see your great strength.

Shine for us that we might see you.
For you are the Decider of the Life-Span,
All health and life are in your hands.
You are the Keeper of the Books of the End of the Year,
And all shall live by your command.

*At this point perform the **meditation or magical action** or, if it is a
special feast, add the appropriate prayers.*

*Afterwards **all present back out of the Temple Chamber with heads
slightly bowed** while the Ritualist performs the "**removing the foot.**"*

*With the **broom** the Ritualist, as the last person to exit, **ritually sweeps
the area beginning at the altar**. (This is known as "**removing the
foot.**") While performing this action the Ritualist recites the following:*

The distress that causes confusion has been driven away, and all the Netjeru are in harmony. I have given Heru his Eye; I have placed the Wedjat-Eye in the correct position. I have given Setekh his Testicles, so that the two lords are content through the work of my hands.

I know the sky, I know the earth;
I know Heru, I know Setekh.
Heru is appeased with his Eyes;
Setekh is appeased with his Testicles.
I am Djehuty, who reconciles the Netjeru,
who makes offerings in their correct form.

*The **double doors are solemnly closed** as the Ritualist says the following:*

Djehuty has come.
He has filled the Eye of Heru;
He has restored the Testicles of Setekh.
No evil shall enter this Temple.
Ptah has closed the door,
Djehuty has set it fast.
The door is closed, the door is set fast with the bolt.

*All **bow, touching the palms of their hands to their knees.***

THE REVERSION OF OFFERINGS

*One priest or priestess and as many assistants as necessary enter the Temple Chamber a final time. While he/she and any assistants **lift up the offerings** before the sacred image the ritualist shall say:*

O Khonsu, your enemy[167] withdraws for you. Heru has turned himself to his Eye in its name of 'Reversion-of-Offerings.' I am Djehuty. I come to perform this rite for Khonsu, Lord in *Waset* (Thebes). **These, your divine offerings revert; they revert to your servants for life, for stability, for health, and for joy! O that the Eye of Heru may flourish for you eternally!**

Everyone withdraws, **carrying away all food offerings except for one loaf of bread and a bowl of pure water.** These last items remain until evening. If this ritual is celebrated after sunset, these items would also be removed.

After the candle has burned down, a servant-priest enters and closes the doors of the Kar-shrine. **Extinguishing the candle or oil lamp,** *he/she exclaims:*

This is the Eye of Heru by which you have become great, by which you live, and by which you have power, O Khonsu. This is the Eye of Heru which you consume and through which you enchant your body. The *Wedjat*-Eye now enters into the West, into *Manu*, but it shall return. Truly, the Eye of Heru returns in peace![168]

---

[167] Meat offerings held a two-fold meaning for the ancient priesthood. Since meat necessarily came from slain animals, it signified the defeated or slain enemies of the Netjer. At the same time, the meat offering represented the produce of the land which ultimately was a gift of the Netjeru.

[168] It is important to consume the food offerings after the ceremony. Water used should either be drunk or poured onto the earth. If it is mixed with Natron, dilute it very greatly and then you can pour in onto the bare earth.

The General Ritual for Ma'at

Like members of the ancient priesthood, participants should be clothed in white linen. No item made of animal products such as leather or wool is to be worn. Linen represents a pristine product of the earth whereas leather and wool come from humankind's domination of the animals, a domination that becomes part of the "natural order" only *after* the First Time when the *Netjeru* and humans and animals lived in peace and harmony. Just as the Morning Ritual harkens back to that First Time (*Zep Tepi*), so every temple rite re-presents mythic prototypes that occurred "in the beginning," that is, in that time before time. Even the sandals worn by the god's servants were made of white papyrus. This avoidance of animal products by the priesthood fits well with the fact that the ritualist acts as a *Netjer* and verbally asserts that he or she is a *Netjer*.

Special offering for Ma'at: a floral 'Bouquet of Eternity', and the traditional offerings of bread, beer, wine, and fruit.

As with all Egyptian rituals begin with your purification – washing of hands and cleansing of mouth with Natron. This preliminary rite helps us to lay aside the cares of the day and to become mindful of the fact that we will encounter a divine being. If Natron is not available, then use a natural sea salt in its place until you make your own Natron.

If two or more persons are participating, then one person, impersonating the Netjer *Djehuty,* **purifies each person by sprinkling each with water while exclaiming**:

I purify you with the water of all life and good fortune, all stability, all health and happiness.[169]

*Afterwards each person **rinses his mouth** and **places a small amount of Natron or sea salt in his mouth** while saying:*

I wash my mouth; I chew natron so that I may extol the might of Ma'at, Lady of Protection Who Banishes Evil.[170]

*Participants **assemble outside the Temple Chamber** and begin by softly rattling sistra.*

This time—several minutes or more—is used to focus minds and intention so that distracting thoughts are left behind. The sound of the sistrum was said to placate the deity, purifying the atmosphere in preparation for encountering divinity. The sistrum was associated with Hutheru and also with her and Heru's son Ihy, and thus has connotations of joy, celebration, and dancing. According to Plutarch (A.D. 46-120), the sound of sistra was also reputed to drive away Setekh. But this was of very late date. It may have been that since by that time Setekh had been demonized, the general apotropaic function of the sistrum against evil entities was extended to include this *Netjer* as well.

---

[169] Taken from Aylward M. Blackman's article "Purification (Egyptian)" in Hastings Encyclopedia 10/1918/ 476-82. This article is reprinted in Gods, Priests, and Men, Studies in the Religion of Pharaonic Egypt, edited by Alan B. Lloyd (Kegan Paul International, 1998), p. 9.

[170] Based on a temple inscription taken from "The Myth of Horus at Edfu—II" by A. M. Blackman and H. W. Fairman, appearing in Gods, Priests and Men, Studies in the Religion of Pharaonic Egypt, Blackman and Lloyd, p. 283.

Richard J. Reidy

*Standing **before the closed doors**, the Ritualist **recites the entrance spell**:*

UTTERANCE BEFORE THE CLOSED DOORS OF THE TEMPLE

*The ritualist **raises hands in adoration** (dua position-arms stretched out in front of the body and raised up to face level, with palms facing outward). The following shall be said:*

O you *Netjeru* of this Temple, you guardians of the great portal, great *Netjeru* of mysterious abode, who sanctify the *Netjeret* in her shrine, who consecrate her oblation, who receive the offerings in her presence in the Hall of the Ennead: I have made my way and I enter into your presence. I am one of you. I am Shu, the eldest son of her father, the senior *wab* servant-priest of Ma'at. Do not repulse me on the *Netjeret's* path. My feet are not impeded. I am not turned back from the court of the great portal so that I may conduct the divine service, that I may present offerings to her that made them, that I may give bread to Ma'at. I have come on the way of the *Netjeret*. I have not shown partiality in judgment. I have not consorted with the strong. I have not reproached the lowly. I have not stolen things. I have not diminished the constituents of the Eye of Ra. I have not disturbed the Balance. I have not tampered with the requirements of the Sacred Eye. O Council of the Great *Netjeret* in this Temple, behold, I have come to you to offer Ma'at to the Lady of Heaven, to content the Sound Eye for its lord. I am Shu; I flood her offering table. I present her offerings, Sekhmet consorting with me, that I may adore Ma'at at her festivals, that I may kiss the earth so great is her majesty, that I may endow her image with life. I am pure. I am purified.

246

*At this point the ritualist **opens the doors to the Temple Chamber**, or, if there are no doors, **makes a gesture of opening unseen doors**, and steps forward as if crossing over a threshold. The following is said:*

O you *Ba*-souls of *Ipet-Sut* [Karnak] if you are strong, I am strong. If I am strong, you are strong. If your *Ka*-spirits are strong, my *Ka*-spirit is strong at the head of the living. As they are living so shall I live . . . . Ma'at, She Through Whom One Lives, has given to me life, stability, and serenity round about my members, which Djehuty has gathered together for life. I am Heru in the height of heaven, the beautiful one of awe, Lord of Victory, mighty one of awe, exalted one of the two plumes, great one in *Ipet-Sut*, I am pure.

*Enter, **close the double doors** and **stand in front of the Kar-shrine and altar**. All bow, touching their hands to their knees.*

All recite the following:

Awake, awake in peace,
O Greatly Beloved One.
May you awake in peace.
Awake, awake in peace,
O Lady of Protection.
May you awake in peace.
Awake, awake in peace,
O Ma'at Who Opens the Nostrils of the Living.
May you awake in peace.
Awake, awake in peace,
Gracious Daughter of Ra.
May you awake in peace.

Richard J. Reidy

*The ritualist **slowly opens the two doors of the Kar-shrine** housing
the sacred image. All others bow, touching their hands to their knees.
The following is said:*

> The doors of the sky are open; the doors of the earth are
> unlocked. This House is open for the Living One. Let me
> come forth as she shall come forth. Let me enter in as she
> shall enter in. Ma'at, Great One of the Throne Who Causes
> the *Netjeru* to Live, is exalted upon her Great Seat. The
> Great Company of the *Netjeru* are exalted upon their seat.
>
> I have seen the *Netjeret,* and the *Netjeret* sees me. The
> Netjeret rejoices at seeing me. I have gazed upon the statue
> of the Daughter of Ra, the sacred image of the Beloved of
> the *Netjeru.*[171]

*The priest/priestess places the right hand on the arm of the statue, with
the left hand placed on the wrist of the statue. The following is said:*

> Djehuty has come to you. Awake when you hear his words.
> I have come as the envoy of Atum.
> My two arms are upon you like those of Heru.
> My two hands are upon you like those of Djehuty.
> My fingers are upon you like those of Anpu.
> Homage be to you. I am a living servant of Ma'at.

*The Ritualist holds up the **bowl of water** in which he/she will be mixing
the Natron. The following is said:*

---

[171] Based on the temple text found in "Worship and Festivals in an Egyptian
Temple," a lecture by H. W. Fairman (publ. by The John Rylands Library,
1954; p. 180).

O water may you remove all evil,
As Ra who bathes in the Lake of Rushes,
May Heru wash my flesh,
May Djehuty cleanse my feet,
May Shu lift me up and Nut take my hand!
May Setekh be my strength, and may Sekhmet be my healing!
And may Amun-Ra be my life and my prospering!

*The bowl of water is set aside and the container of **Natron** is lifted up. The following is said:*

It is pure, it is pure.
My Natron is the Natron of Heru,
and the Natron of Heru is my Natron.
My Natron is the Natron of Setekh,
and the Natron of Setekh is my Natron.
My Natron is the Natron of Djehuty,
and the Natron of Djehuty is my Natron.
My Natron is the Natron of Geb,
and the Natron of Geb is my Natron.

My mouth is the mouth of a milking calf
on the day that I was born.

***Four pinches of Natron are mixed into the water** as this Utterance is recited:*

I give you essential water, a tide in your time.
I bring the flood waters to purify your sanctuary.
I bring you the flood waters
to purify your Temple and your divine statue in its place,

the primordial water that purifies as in the First Time!

*The Ritualist **places an index finger into the water** and **moves it in a circular, clockwise direction four times*** *as the following is said:*

Ma'at, Who Banishes Evil,
does purify this water;
Ma'at, Lady of Protection,
does cleanse this water;
Ma'at, Powerful One,
does sanctify this water;
Ma'at, Great of Heka-power,
does endow this water with power and with life.

*The **Bowl of Natron-infused water** is then taken up and the Ritualist **sprinkles this lightly in front of and around the statue** or image of Ma'at, lightly applying some water to the base of the image, as the Utterance is recited:*

I come close to you, O Beloved of All *Netjeru.*
I bring the water of rejuvenation
that flows from the Two Caverns.
I sprinkle the water,
purifying your image and your Temple from all impurity!

*The Ritualist picks up the bowl of **Natron** and **sprinkles a small amount in each of the four directions** as the following is recited:*

The *Netjeret,* Ma'at herself, does cleanse and purify this,
her Temple to the South.
The *Netjeret,* Ma'at herself, does cleanse and purify this,
her Temple to the North.
The *Netjeret,* Ma'at herself, does cleanse and purify this,

her Temple to the West.
The *Netjeret*, Ma'at herself, does cleanse and purify this,
her Temple to the East.

Replacing the Natron on the altar, the Ritualist takes up the bowl of **water,** *sprinkling a small amount in each of the four directions. The following Utterance is recited:*

The *Netjeret*, Ma'at herself, does sanctify and consecrate this,
her Temple to the South.
The *Netjeret*, Ma'at herself, does sanctify and consecrate this,
her Temple to the North.
The *Netjeret*, Ma'at herself, does sanctify and consecrate this,
her Temple to the West.
The *Netjeret*, Ma'at herself, does sanctify and consecrate this,
her Temple to the East.
The Temple of the *Netjeret* Ma'at is established.
It is established for millions of years.

The Ritualist returns to the altar and **lights the candle or oil lamp** *while the following is said:*

Come, come in peace, O glorious Eye of Heru,
Be strong and renew your youth in peace.
For the flame shines like Ra on the double horizon.
The lie is abolished. It is abolished.
I am pure, I am pure, I am pure, I am pure.

The Ritualist **places incense on the burner** *and* **censes each sacred image** *beginning with the statue of the goddess while the following is recited:*

The fire is laid, the fire shines;

The incense is laid on the fire, the incense shines.
  Your perfume comes to me, O Incense;
  May my perfume come to you, O Incense.
Your perfume comes to me, you *Netjeru*;
May my perfume come to you, You *Netjeru*.
  May I be with you, you *Netjeru*;
  May you be with me, you *Netjeru*.
May I live with you, you *Netjeru*;
May you live with me, you *Netjeru*.
  I love you, you *Netjeru*;
  May you love me, you *Netjeru*.

Standing in front of the image of Ma'at the Ritualist **offers the burning incense** *and says:*

Take the incense,
Its essence is for you.
Its smoke permeates your shrine, bringing life!
Take the incense,
Its essence is for you.
Your Majesty is appeased with the incense.
This Eye of Heru,
This essence of the Eye of Heru comes to you.

At this point the following is said:

Praise to you, Ma'at, Lady of the North Wind,
who opens the nostrils of the living
and who gives air to the One in the Midst of His Barque.
Allow us, your servants, to breathe the breezes born of heaven
just as the Lady of Punt, even Hat-Hór [Hathor],
breathes her aromas from the Lake of Myrrh.

May you allow our entry and departure from the Field of
Reeds,
and let us be provided there from the Field of Offerings,
and receive the daily gifts
from the altars of the Lords of *Iunu* [Heliopolis].

Let our hearts be in the water-crossing
from the Sacred Land [the necropolis]
to the pure islands of the Field of Reeds.
May you open wide to us the blessed path
and spread our road before us,
and may you place us, your servants,
in the retinue of Sokar
before the gates of the Beyond. [172]

The Ritualist places more incense on the charcoal and again and again
slowly raises and lowers the incense cup as the following is recited:

O Ma'at, may you advance with your *Ka*.
Magnificent and Powerful One,
the arm of your *Ka* is before you,
The arm of your *Ka* is behind you.
O Ma'at from Whom the *Netjeru* Come Forth,
the foot of your *Ka* is before you,
The foot of your *Ka* is behind you.
O Splendid One, this incense is offered to you,
May your face be filled as this essence spreads itself
over you.

---

[172] This hymn is adapted from the "Hymn to Thoth and Ma'at" (British
Museum Stele 551). It is available in *Hymns, Prayers, and Songs: An
Anthology of Ancient Egyptian Lyric Poetry*, by John L. Foster (Atlanta,
Georgia: Scholars Press, 1995), pp. 113-14.

*All present **perform the Henu Rite**—Embrace the Earth, the Fourfold Salute to the God, Embrace the Earth. The bodily gestures are performed alternately four times.*

For Embracing the Earth, all present prostrate themselves, face down, upon the floor. During the Fourfold Salute, all present rise upon one knee, and alternately raise their hands and arms into the *Dua* (praise) position with palms facing outward, followed by the *Sahu* (obedience) gesture, made by striking the chest with a closed fist and raising the other arm (also with closed fist) at a ninety-degree angle. The *Dua* position is accompanied by the words **"Adoration be to Ma'at,"** followed by the *Sahu* gesture accompanied with the words, **"Hail to the One Who Banishes Evil!"** The bodily gestures are performed alternately four times.

*Following this **all present again prostrate themselves** before the sacred image. This is a sign and symbol of total submission and adoration before the Netjer. The following is said:*

> **Homage to Ma'at Who Adorns the Chest of Djehuty,**
> **who is established on the Great Seat!**
> **I have placed myself on the floor in awe of you.**
> **I embrace the earth before you as before the Lady of Heaven.**
> **I have come that I might kiss the earth,**
> **that I might worship my Mistress,**
> **For I have seen her Strength;**
> **I give praise to Ma'at,**
> **For I have seen her Power.**
> **Her form is more distinguished than the *Netjeru*;**
> **her arm is more powerful than the *Netjeru*.**
> **I am pure, I am pure, I am pure, I am pure!**

Everyone stands up.

*The Ritualist **holds in the palm of one hand the image of Ma'at** and with **the other hand open and raised over the image as if sheltering it**, repeats the following:*

I have come to you as Djehuty, whose two hands are joined together under Ma'at. I present to you your own beautiful image for truly you are She Who Creates Her Own Mode-of-Action. Your Father Ra jubilates when he sees you. You are the protection of your Father. Truly you are the Greatly Beloved One. I come to be with you in this, the Temple of Truth. You cause the *Netjeru* to live. The *Netjeru* move in Ma'at, they live in Ma'at. You fill their bodies, you rest in their heads, you make your seat upon the brow of your Father; the breath of your body gives life to all; their hearts do live in Ma'at. All that they eat, all that they drink, all that they breathe is of Ma'at. I, Djehuty, present Ma'at to you, Greatly Beloved One, my two hands are upon your beauty before your face.

*The Ritualist places the image of Ma'at near the divine statue. Then he/she holds up before the image of Amon **a pitcher of water** and **pours the water slowly into an offering bowl** as the following Utterance is recited:*

This libation is for you, Who Allots Nourishment to the Kas.
This libation is for you, O Ma'at,
Who Opens the Nostrils of the Living.
I have brought to you this offering of water,
That your heart may be refreshed.
I have brought to you this Eye of Heru,
Placing this at your feet.
I present to you that which flows forth from you,

So that your heart shall continue to beat.
For it is with you
that all comes forth at the sound of the voice.

The offering bowl is placed on the altar. At this point the Ritualist lightly sprinkles sand on the floor in front of the altar as the following is recited:

O Ma'at, who resides in *Ipet Sut* [Karnak],
Take to yourself the Eye of Heru.
You have rescued it,
O You Who Are at the Head of the Hall of Judgment.
You have sprinkled with sand the Eye of Heru.

The Ritualist presents the floral 'Bouquet of Eternity' as the following is said:

Take the Bouquet of Eternity endowed with its years, countless years in the orb of the sun. These are the bouquets of your father Ra. You receive them; you hold them to your nose.[173]

Lifting the wine offering before the sacred image, the Ritualist repeats the following:

mn n.ṯ irp irt ḥrw wȝḏt
[*"mán-niṯ 'úrip írat ḥáru wá'ḏat"*; approximately pronounced *MAHN-neetch OO-rip EE-raht HAH-roo WAH-jat*]

Take to yourself wine, the green Eye of Heru,

---

[173] Sylvie Cauville, *Dendara IV: Traduction* (Leuven, Belgium: Peeters, 2001), Section 21.

which I offer to your *Ka*.

O Unique One in the House of Ma'at, how beautiful is your beauty!

May you drink it; may your heart rejoice;

may anger be removed from your face.

It is pure.

[*iw.w w'b* pronounced *"uwú wá'ib"*; approximately *oo-WOO WAH-ib*]

The Ritualist places myrrh on the fire and lifts up the smoking incense while at the same time he lifts up the meat-offering before the Netjeret, and says the following:

The scent of myrrh is for your nose. It fills your nostrils; your heart receives the meat-portions on its scent.[174]

Slowly elevating the food offerings four times before the image of Ma'at, the Ritualist repeats the following:

I offer to Ma'at, Ruler of Eternity.

All life emanates from you,

All health emanates from you,

All stability emanates from you,

All good fortune emanates from you,

O Throat of *Shai* [Fate], Most Splendid One, forever.

The Ritualist places the food offering before the divine image, and then all present extend one hand, palm down, over the offerings and recite the following:

---

[174] Quoted in "Worship and Festivals in an Egyptian Temple," by H. W. Fairman (publ. by The John Rylands Library, 1954), p. 191.

May offerings of every kind come forth in abundance,
like the things which come forth from the mouth of the
Netjeret.

piryá pírit ar ḫiráw mi purú:riat ma rá' ni naṯárat. (4 times)
[approximately pronounced *peer-YA PEER-it ar khi-RAU mee pu-ROOR-iat ma RA nee nah-TCHAR-at*]

May offerings of every kind come forth in abundance, like
the things that come forth from the mouth of the Netjeret.

*Holding the **Ankh** before the Netjeret, the Ritualist says:*

Live, O Ma'at, You Who Pacify the Hearts of the Ennead, live
for all time and for eternity!

ʿánaḫ niḥáḫ ḏát.
[approximately pronounced *AH-nakh nee-HAH JAHT*]

The Ankh is placed next to the Netjeret.

*Holding the **Ib (the golden heart)** before the Netjeret, the Ritualist says:*

Hail to you, O Ma'at Who Banishes Evil. I have brought to
you your heart to set it in its place. Let me draw near to you
with your heart, so that you may have pleasure through me,
and so that by means of me you may have power over your
body. Ascend, Sublime of Place in the Barque of Millions,
radiant, rejuvenating, equipped as a *Netjeret*. Live, Mistress
of Worthiness, live forever and ever!

*After placing the **Ib** near the sacred image, **everyone sings or chants**
the hymn to Ma'at. Participants may wish to alternate the singing of
verses.*

> Praise to you, Ma'at, daughter of Ra,
> consort of the *Netjer*, whom Ptah loves,
> The one who adorns the breast of Djehuty,
> who fashioned her own nature,
> foremost of the *Ba*-Souls of *Iunu* [Heliopolis];
> who pacified the two falcon gods through her good will,
> filled the *Per-Wer* shrine[175] with life and dominion;
> Skilled One who brought forth the *Netjeru* from herself
> and brought low the heads of the enemies;
> Who herself provides for the House of the Lord of All,
> and brings daily offerings for those who are on duty.
>
> Magnificent her throne before the judges—
> and she consumes the enemies of Atum.
> She is just; may there be no injustice in me,
> a son/daughter of Ra.
> Shu commingles with Djehuty
> his body is filled, through her, with humankind
> which he offers to Amun-Ra, Ptah, and Amun of Hibis.
> And the Great Ennead is powerful
> in the House of the Prince in *Iunu* [Heliopolis].
>
> Rise splendidly, O Ra,
> how beautiful you are because of Ma'at!

---

[175] The Per-Wer [Great House] shrine originally was the shrine
for Upper Egypt, with a recognizable shape. The Per-Neser [Flame
House] was the shrine for Lower Egypt. Eventually the Per-Wer came
to symbolize heaven and divinity. It is this shape that was used for
Tutankhamun's golden shrine, found in his tomb.

Richard J. Reidy

As Ma'at shines splendid from the heart of Ra,
so may I be splendid and live forever as a child of Ra.
May I be resplendent because of Ma'at
she who comes to the servants of Ra who live forever!

O Ma'at, build your throne in this your servant's head,
in my mouth, so that this child of Ra may live forever!
May you make heaven and earth rejoice in Ra, our father,
from whom we have come forth.
May you rise splendid from Ra on this beautiful day
in this your name of She-Who-Appears-in-Beauty.
May your beautiful face give peace to these, your servants,
so that we may live forever, like Ra.[176]

*At this point perform the **meditation or magical action** or, if it is a special feast, add the appropriate prayers.*

*Afterwards **all present back out of the Temple Chamber with heads slightly bowed** while the Ritualist performs the **"removing the foot."***

*With the **broom** the Ritualist, as the last person to exit, **ritually sweeps the area beginning at the altar.** (This is known as **"removing the foot."**) While performing this action the Ritualist recites the following:*

The distress that causes confusion has been driven away, and all the Netjeru are in harmony. I have given Heru his Eye; I have placed the Wedjat-Eye in the correct position. I have given Setekh his Testicles, so that the two lords are content through the work of my hands.

---

[176] This beautiful hymn is inscribed in the temple of Amun at Hibis. It is available in *Hymns, Prayers, and Songs: An Anthology of Ancient Egyptian Lyric Poetry*, tranlated by John L. Foster (Scholars Press, 1995), pp. 122-23.

I know the sky, I know the earth;
I know Heru, I know Setekh.
Heru is appeased with his Eyes;
Setekh is appeased with his Testicles.
I am Djehuty, who reconciles the Netjeru,
who makes offerings in their correct form.

*The **double doors are solemnly closed** as the Ritualist says the following:*

Djehuty has come.
He has filled the Eye of Heru;
He has restored the Testicles of Setekh.
No evil shall enter this Temple.
Ptah has closed the door,
Djehuty has set it fast.
The door is closed, the door is set fast with the bolt.

*All **bow, touching the palms of their hands to their knees.***

THE REVERSION OF OFFERINGS

*One priest or priestess and as many assistants as necessary enter the Temple Chamber a final time. While he/she and any assistants **lift up the offerings** before the sacred image the ritualist shall say:*

O Ma'at, Who Brings Low the Heads of the Enemies, your enemy[177] withdraws for you. Heru has turned himself to his Eye in its name of 'Reversion-of-Offerings.' I am Djehuty.

---

[177] Meat offerings held a two-fold meaning for the ancient priesthood. Since meat necessarily came from slain animals, it signified the defeated or slain enemies of the Netjer. At the same time, the meat offering represented the produce of the land which ultimately was a gift of the Netjeru.

I come to perform this rite for Ma'at, Who Banishes Evil. These, your divine offerings revert, they revert to your servants for life, for stability, for health and for joy! O that the Eye of Heru may flourish for you eternally!

Everyone withdraws, **carrying away all food offerings except for one loaf of bread and a bowl of pure water.** These last items remain until evening. If this ritual is celebrated after sunset, these items would also be removed.

After the candle has burned down, a servant-priest enters and closes the doors of the Kar-shrine. **Extinguishing the candle or oil lamp,** *he/she exclaims:*

This is the Eye of Heru by which you have become great, by which you live, and by which you have power, O Ma'at. This is the Eye of Heru which you consume and through which you enchant your body. The *Wedjat*-Eye now enters into the West, into *Manu*, but it shall return. Truly, the Eye of Heru returns in peace![178]

---

[178] It is important to consume the food offerings after the ceremony. Water used should either be drunk or poured onto the earth. If it is mixed with Natron, dilute it very greatly and then you can pour in onto the bare earth.

The General Ritual for Min

Min is traditionally shown with erect phallus in that he is a god closely associated with fertility. ". . . wherever he was worshipped lettuces were offered to him, for these vegetables, whose white sap is reminiscent of semen, were considered to have aphrodisiac qualities. . . . His cult placed great emphasis on procreation and fecundity. . . ." [179]

Offerings to Min: lettuce, a model or representation of the Eye of Heru.
and the traditional offerings (bread, beer, wine, and meat)

As with all Egyptian rituals begin with your purification—washing of hands and cleansing of mouth with Natron. This preliminary rite helps us to lay aside the cares of the day and to become mindful of the fact that we will encounter a divine being. If Natron is not available, then use a natural sea salt in its place until you make your own Natron.

If two or more persons are participating, then one person, impersonating the *Netjer* Djehuty, *purifies each person by sprinkling each with water while exclaiming:*

I purify you with the water of all life and good fortune, all stability, all health and happiness. [180]

---

[179] Barbara Watterson, *Gods of Ancient Egypt* (London, 1984), p. 195. Also see A. Badawy, "Min, the Cosmic Fertility God of Egypt," *MIO* 7 (1959), 163-179. (*MIO* abbrev. for *Mitteilungen des Instituts für Orientforschung*)
[180] Taken from Aylward M. Blackman's article "Purification (Egyptian)" in Hastings Encyclopaedia 10/1918/ 476-82. This article is reprinted in

Afterwards each person rinses his mouth and places a small amount of Natron or sea salt in his mouth while saying:

I wash my mouth; I chew natron so that I may extol the might of Min, Victorious Bull, Mighty One of Strength. [181]

*Participants **assemble outside the Temple Chamber** and begin by softly rattling sistra.*

This time—several minutes or more—is used to focus minds and intention so that distracting thoughts are left behind. The sound of the sistrum was said to placate the deity, purifying the atmosphere in preparation for encountering divinity. The sistrum was associated with Hutheru and also with her and Heru's son Ihy, and thus has connotations of joy, celebration, and dancing. According to Plutarch (A.D. 46-120), the sound of sistra was also reputed to drive away Setekh. But this was of very late date. It may have been that since by that time Setekh had been demonized, the general apotropaic function of the sistrum against evil entities was extended to include this *Netjer* as well.

*Standing **before the closed doors,** the Ritualist **recites the entrance spell:***

Gods, Priests, and Men, Studies in the Religion of Pharaonic Egypt, edited by Alan B. Lloyd (Kegan Paul International, 1998), p. 9.

[181] Adapted from a temple inscription taken from "The Myth of Horus at Edfu—II" by A. M. Blackman and H. W. Fairman, appearing in Gods, Priests and Men, Studies in the Religion of Pharaonic Egypt, p. 283.

UTTERANCE BEFORE THE CLOSED DOORS OF THE TEMPLE

The ritualist **raises hands** *in adoration (dua position-arms stretched out in front of the body and raised up to face level, with palms facing outward). The following shall be said:*

O you *Netjeru* of this Temple, you guardians of the great portal, great *Netjeru* of mysterious abode, who sanctify the *Netjer* in his shrine, who consecrate his oblation, who receive the offerings in his presence in the Hall of the Ennead: I have made my way and I enter into your presence. I am one of you. I am Shu, the eldest son of his father, the senior *wab* servant-priest of Min. Do not repulse me on the god's path. My feet are not impeded. I am not turned back from the court of the great portal so that I may conduct the divine service, that I may present offerings to him that made them, that I may give bread to Min. I have come on the way of the *Netjer*. I have not shown partiality in judgment. I have not consorted with the strong. I have not reproached the lowly. I have not stolen things. I have not diminished the constituents of the Eye of Ra. I have not disturbed the Balance. I have not tampered with the requirements of the Sacred Eye. O Council of the Great *Netjer* in this Temple, behold, I have come to you to offer Ma'at to the Lord of Ma'at, to content the Sound Eye for its lord. I am Shu; I flood his offering table. I present his offerings, Sekhmet consorting with me, that I may adore Min at his festivals, that I may kiss the earth so great is his majesty, that I may endow his image with life. I am pure. I am purified.

At this point the ritualist **opens the doors to the Temple Chamber**, *or, if there are no doors,* **makes a gesture of opening unseen doors,** *and* **steps forward as if crossing over a threshold.** *The following is said:*

O you *Ba*-souls of *Gebtu* (Coptos) if you are strong, I am strong. If I am strong, you are strong. If your *Ka*-spirits are strong, my *Ka*-spirit is strong at the head of the living. As they are living so shall I live . . . . Min, Bull of his Mother, *Kamutef,* has given to me life, stability, and serenity round about my members, which Djehuty has gathered together for life. I am Heru in the height of heaven, the beautiful one of awe, Lord of Victory, mighty one of awe, exalted one of the two plumes, great one in *Waset* (Thebes), I am pure.

All temple members chant:

Awake in peace, O Min, Great One with Uplifted Arm,
may you awaken in peace.
Awake in peace, O Min, Beautiful of Face,
may you awaken in peace.
Awake in peace, O Min, Lord of the Phallus,
may you awaken in peace.
Awake in peace, O Min, Who Endures on the Throne of Amun,
may you awaken in peace.

May you awake beautifully at the top of the morning,
through that which the entirety of *Netjeru* say to you.

Enter, **close the double doors** *and* **stand in front of the Kar-shrine and altar. All bow,** *touching their hands to their knees.*

The ritualist *slowly* **opens the two doors of the Kar-shrine** *housing the sacred image. All others bow, touching their hands to their knees. The following is said:*

The doors of the sky are open; the doors of the earth are unlocked. This House is open for its Lord. Let me come forth as he shall come forth. Let me enter in as he shall enter in. Min, Lord of Humankind and Great of Appearances, is exalted upon his Great Seat. The Great Company of the *Netjeru* are exalted upon their seat.

I have seen the *Netjer*, and the *Netjer* sees me. The *Netjer* rejoices at seeing me. I have gazed upon the statue of the Lord of Perfection, the sacred image of the Lord of Heaven.[182]

Right hand on left shoulder of statue; left hand on right wrist of statue:

Djehuty has come to you. Awake when you hear his words. I have come as the envoy of Atum. My two arms are upon you like those of Heru. My two hands are upon you like those of Djehuty. My fingers are upon you like those of Anpu. Homage be to you. I am a living servant of Min.

Rise up, O Min, my master. Appear, O Min, my master, for you are justified before Ra-Atum. Those who acclaim you are in adoration of you. They say to you, 'Raise yourself for your countenance is most comely among the *Netjeru*.' Djehuty rejoices and the spirits of the East are in joy, O Lord of Eternity. Arise on behalf of the spirits of the East while you protect us who honor you. [183]

---

[182] Based on the temple text found in "Worship and Festivals in an Egyptian Temple," a lecture by H. W. Fairman (publ. by The John Rylands Library, 1954), p. 180.

[183] Henri Gauthier, *Les Fêtes du dieu Min* (Cairo, Institut Français d'Archéologie Orientale, 1931), pp.179-184. The reference to the spirits of the East serves as a means of linking Min with Ra rising in the East.

Richard J. Reidy

*The Ritualist holds up the **bowl of water** in which he/she will be mixing the Natron. The following is said:*

O water may you remove all evil,
As Ra who bathes in the Lake of Rushes,
May Heru wash my flesh,
May Djehuty cleanse my feet,
May Shu lift me up and Nut take my hand!
May Set be my strength, and may Sekhmet be my healing!
And may Min-Ra be my life and my prospering!

*The bowl of water is set aside and the container of **Natron** is lifted up. The following is said:*

It is pure, it is pure.
My Natron is the Natron of Heru and the Natron of Heru is my Natron.
My Natron is the Natron of Setekh and the Natron of Setekh is my Natron.
My Natron is the Natron of Djehuty, and the Natron of Djehuty is my Natron.
My Natron is the Natron of Geb and the Natron of Geb is my Natron
My mouth is the mouth of a milking calf on the day that I was born.

***Four pinches of Natron** are mixed into the water as this Utterance is recited:*

I give you essential water, a tide in your time.

This solar identification compliments Min's role as the ithyphallic god of generation and renewal (v. p. 183).

I bring the flood waters to purify your sanctuary.

I bring you the flood waters to purify your Temple and your statue in its place, the primordial water that purifies as in the First Time!

*The Ritualist places an **index finger** into the water and moves it in a circular direction four times as the following is said:*

Min, Lord of Perfection, does purify this water;
Min, Foremost One of His Fields, does cleanse this water;
Min, With Powerful Arm, does sanctify this water;
Min himself does endow this water with power and with life.

*The **Bowl of Natron-infused water** is then taken up and the Ritualist sprinkles this lightly in front of and around the statue or image of Min, applying some water to the base of the image, as the Utterance is recited:*

I come close to You, O Great and Effective *Netjer*.
I bring the water of rejuvenation that flows from the Two Caverns.
I sprinkle the water, purifying your image and your Temple from all impurity!

*The Ritualist picks up the bowl of **Natron** and **sprinkles a small amount in each of the four directions** as the following is recited:*

The *Netjer* Min himself does cleanse and purify this, his Temple to the South.
The *Netjer* Min himself does cleanse and purify this, his Temple to the North.

The *Netjer* Min himself does cleanse and purify this, his Temple to the West.

The *Netjer* Min himself does cleanse and purify this, his Temple to the East.

*Replacing the Natron on the altar, the Ritualist **takes up the bowl of water, sprinkling a small amount in each of the four directions.** The following Utterance is recited:*

The *Netjer* Min himself does sanctify and consecrate this, his Temple to the South.

The *Netjer* Min himself does sanctify and consecrate this, his Temple to the North.

The *Netjer* Min himself does sanctify and consecrate this, his Temple to the West.

The *Netjer* Min himself does sanctify and consecrate this, his Temple to the East.

The Temple of the *Netjer* Min is established. It is established for millions of years.

*The Ritualist returns to the altar and **lights the candle or oil lamp** while the following is said:*

Come, come in peace, O glorious Eye of Heru,
Be strong and renew your youth in peace.
For the flame shines like Ra on the double horizon.
The enemies of Ra are defeated. They are defeated.
I am pure, I am pure, I am pure, I am pure.

*The Ritualist places **incense on the burner** and **censes each sacred image** beginning with the statue of Min while the following is recited:*

The fire is laid, the fire shines;
The incense is laid on the fire, the incense shines.
Your perfume comes to me, O Incense;
May my perfume come to you, O Incense.
Your perfume comes to me, you *Netjeru*;
May my perfume come to you, You *Netjeru*.
May I be with you, you *Netjeru*;
May you be with me, you *Netjeru*.
May I live with you, you *Netjeru*;
May you live with me, you *Netjeru*.
I love you, you *Netjeru*;
May you love me, you *Netjeru*.

*Standing in front of the image of Min the Ritualist **offers the burning
incense** and says:*

Take the incense,
Its essence is for you.
Its smoke permeates your shrine, bringing life!
Take the incense,
Its essence is for you.
Your Majesty is appeased with the incense.
This Eye of Heru,
This essence of the Eye of Heru comes to you.

At this point the following is said:

Greetings to you, O Min!
Greetings to you, O Copulating Bull!

Upraised of Arm, Tall of Plumes, Chief of the *Netjeru*.
Upraised of Arm, Lord of the Double-Crown,

Richard J. Reidy

Mighty of Prestige and Lord of Respect.
Kamutef, foremost of his fields,
Vaunted of his beauty, Lord of the Phallus.
Turquoise and black of beard,
With sparkling faces, the Beloved,
Lord of the *Wedjat*-Eyes, equipped with amulets.
He of *Gebtu* (Coptos), Foremost of the Garden,
He of *Ipy* (Achmim), who is upon his platform. [184]

*The Ritualist places **more incense on the charcoal** and again and again **slowly raises and lowers the incense cup** as the following is recited:*

O Min, may you advance with your *Ka*.
O Mighty One of Strength, the arm of your *Ka* is before you,
The arm of your *Ka* is behind you.
O Lord of Heaven, the foot of your *Ka* is before you,
The foot of your *Ka* is behind you.
O Min, great Lord of Perfume, this incense is offered to you,
May your face be filled as this essence spreads itself over you.

*All present **perform the Henu Rite**—Embrace the Earth, the Fourfold Salute to the God, Embrace the Earth.*

For Embracing the Earth, all present prostrate themselves, face down, upon the floor. During the Fourfold Salute, all present rise upon one knee, and alternately raise their hands and arms into the *Dua* (praise) position with palms facing outward, followed by the *Sahu* (obedience) gesture, made by striking the chest with a closed fist and raising the other arm (also with closed fist) at a

------

[184] David Klotz, *Adoration of the Ram: Five Hymns to Amun-Re from Hibis Temple* (New Haven, CT: Yale Egyptological Studies, 2003), p. 125.

ninety-degree angle. The *Dua* position is accompanied by the words **"Adoration be to Min,"** followed by the *Sahu* gesture accompanied with the words, **"Hail to the Lord of Heaven!"** The bodily gestures are performed alternately four times.

*Following this **all present again prostrate themselves** before the sacred image. This is a sign and symbol of total submission and adoration before the Netjer. The following is said:*

Homage to Min, Chief of the *Netjeru,*
who is established on the Great Seat!
I have placed myself on the floor in awe of you.
I embrace the earth before you as before the Lord of Fear.
I have come that I might kiss the earth,
that I might worship my Lord,
For I have seen his Strength;
I give praise to Min, the Mighty One of Strength;
For I have seen his Power.
His form is more distinguished than the *Netjeru;*
His arm is more powerful than the *Netjeru.*
I am pure, I am pure, I am pure, I am pure!

Everyone stands up.

*The Ritualist **holds in the palm of one hand the image of Ma'at** and with **the other hand open and raised over the image as if sheltering it**, repeats the following:*

I have come to you as Djehuty, whose two hands are joined together under Ma'at. She comes to be with you, for she is everywhere. You are provided with Ma'at. You move in Ma'at, you live in Ma'at. She fills your body, she rests in your head, she makes her seat upon your brow; the breath of your body is

273

of Ma'at, your heart does live in Ma'at. All that you eat, all that you drink, all that you breathe is of Ma'at. Djehuty presents Ma'at to you, his two hands are upon her beauty before your face.

*The Ritualist places the image of Ma'at near the divine statue. Then he/she holds up before the image of Min **a pitcher of water and pours the water slowly into an offering bowl** as the following Utterance is recited:*

This libation is for you, O Foremost One of His Fields.
This libation is for you, O Min, you of the Green Field at the New Year Season.
I have brought to you this offering of water,
That your heart may be refreshed.
I have brought to you this Eye of Heru,
Placing this at your feet.
I present to you that which flows forth from you,
That your heart shall continue to beat.
For it is with you that all comes forth at the sound of the voice.

The offering bowl is placed on the altar.

The Ritualist presents an image of **the Eye of Heru** and recites the following:

"Take to yourself the *Wedjat*-Eye provided and equipped with its parts. There is no injury in it. This is the Eye at the sight of which you rejoice and your heart expands on account of it each day. Your right Eye (the sun) moves rapidly, and your left

Eye (the moon) is counted, and your two Eyes are glorious in
their place." [185]

*At this point the Ritualist lightly sprinkles **sand on the floor in front
of the altar** as the following is recited:*

O Min, who resides in *Gebtu* (Coptos),
Take to yourself the Eye of Heru.
You have rescued it, O Mighty One of Strength.
You have sprinkled with sand the Eye of Heru.

Lifting the wine offering *before the sacred image, the Ritualist repeats
the following:*

mn n.k irp irt ḥrw w³d̲t
["***mán-nik 'úrip írat ḥáru wá'd̲at***"; approximately pronounced
MAHN-neek OO-rip EE-raht HAH-roo WAH-jat]

Take to Yourself wine, the green Eye of Heru, which I offer to
your *Ka.*
O Ruler, how beautiful is your beauty!
May you drink it; may your heart rejoice;
may anger be removed from your face.
It is pure. [***iw.w w'b*** pronounced "***uwú wá'ib***"; approximately *oo-
WOO WAH-ib*]

Lettuce *is now offered as the Ritualist recites the following:*

---

[185] Claude Traunecker, *COPTOS: Hommes et Dieux sur le parvis de Geb*
(Leuven, Belgium: Peeters Press, 1992), p. 185. This offering of the *Wedjat-
Eye* was made to Min-Ra, Lord of Coptos (see p. 186).

[*mn n.k ʿbw smw.k pn nfr m-ḥr.k* [186] pronounced *"mán-nik ʿábu símuk pin náfir ma ḥarúk"* (Approximately "MAHN-neek AH-boo SEEM-ook pin NAH-fir ma hah-OOK")]

Take to yourself lettuce. This, your perfect herb, is before your face.

It is seepage from your body, its discharge comes from your flesh. It is the seminal fluid of your Majesty. This beautiful plant is before you, being held by Djehuty. It is your living phallus. You ejaculate and thus you facilitate births." [187] This lettuce is for you, O Bull of Bulls and Lord of Sexual Desire. Take it to yourself and do that which you wish. You are the joyfully procreating Bull who makes the young pregnant and puts seed into the womb in order to create the egg. [188]

The Ritualist **places myrrh on the fire** *and* **lifts up the smoking incense** *while at the same time he* **lifts up the meat-offering** *before the Netjer, and says the following:*

---

[186] Adapted from: Secondary Source (for translation): André Block, *Die verborgene Konigsmythos von Edfu: Wiederentdeckung eines Konzepts dreidimensionaler Literatur* (Gladbeck: PeWe Verlag, 2014), pp. 220 and 216. Primary Source (for the text's hieroglyphs): Chassinat, *Le temple d'Edfou* volume IV, page 297, line 13 and page 270, lines 6-7.

[187] Sylvie Cauville, L'Offrande aux dieux dans le temple égyptien (Paris: Peeters, 2011), p. 98.

[188] Émile Chassinat, *Le temple d'Edfou* Vol. VII (Cairo), p. 115, line 16, to p. 116, line 4. This book is a primary source; that is, it contains the actual hieroglyphs, not a translation of the texts. A secondary source for the text in translation is Dieter Kurth. *Edfou VII: Die Inschriften des Tempels von Edfu*: Abteilung I, Übersetzungen: Band (i.e., Volume) 2 (Wiesbaden: Harrassowitz Verlag, 2004), p 206.

The scent of myrrh is for your nose. It fills your nostrils; your heart receives the meat-portions on its scent.[189]

*Slowly **elevating the remaining food offerings four times** before the image of Min, the Ritualist repeats the following:*

I offer to Min, Tall of Plumes, Lord of Humankind.
All life emanates from you,
All health emanates from you,
All stability emanates from you,
All good fortune emanates from you,
O Copulating Bull, Min, forever.

*The Ritualist **places the food offering before the divine image,** and then all present **extend one hand, palm down, over the offerings** and recite the following:*

May offerings of every kind come forth in abundance,
like the things which come forth from the mouth of the *Netjer*.

piryá pírit ar ḥiráw mi purú:riat ma rá' ni nátar. (4 times)
[approximately pronounced: peer-YA PEER-it ar khi-RAU mee pu-ROOR-iat ma RA nee NAH-tchar]

May offerings of every kind come forth in abundance, like the things that come forth from the mouth of the *Netjer*.

*Holding the **Ankh** before Min, the Ritualist says:*

Live, O Min, Lord of the *Netjeru*, live for all time and for eternity!

---

[189] Quoted in "Worship and Festivals in an Egyptian Temple," by H. W. Fairman (publ. by The John Rylands Library, 1954), p. 191.

Richard J. Reidy

ʿánaḫ niḥáḫ ḏát.

[approximately pronounced *AH-nakh nee-HAH JAHT*]

*The **Ankh** is placed next to the image of the Netjer.*

*Holding the **Ib (the golden heart)** before Min, the Ritualist says:*

Hail to you, O Min, Lord of the Two Uraei. I have brought to you your heart to set it in its place. Let me draw near to you with your heart, so that you may have pleasure through me, and so that by means of me you may have power over your body. Ascend, O Lord of the New Moon Festival, radiant, rejuvenating, equipped as a *Netjer*. Live, O Lord of the Phallus, live forever and ever!

*After placing the **Ib** near the sacred image, **everyone sings or chants** the hymn to Min. Participants may wish to alternate the singing/chanting of verses.*

I worship Min; I extoll arm-raising Heru.
Hail to you, Min in his procession!
Tall-plumed, son of Ausir,
Born of divine Aset.
Great in *Senut*, mighty in *Ipu*,[190]

---

[190] Senut was a sanctuary of Min in Upper Egypt, and Ipu was the name of the city the Greeks called Panopolis. It was one of two principal cult centers for Min, with the other being Coptos. Medja-land is a district thought to be located just east of the Second Cataract in Nubia. Utent was a region south of Egypt. We remember these ancient cities and areas in honor and commemoration of the ancient author of this hymn as well as in remembrance of these major centers for the worship of Min. His worship was widespread, thus showing the importance of this great Netjer.

You of *Gebtu* (Coptos), Heru strong-armed.
Lord of Awe who silences pride,
Sovereign of all the *Netjeru*!
Fragrance-laden when he comes from *Medja*-land,
Awe inspiring in Nubia,
You of *Utent*, hail and praise! [191]

*Everyone present **now recites** the following:*

Glory to you, Min of *Gebtu* (Coptos), Heru raising the arm, great of love, piercing the sky with his double plume, Lord of Joy in his shrine, Chief of the *Netjeru*, Sweet of Love, full of his mother, upon his great throne, great *Netjer* in the two hemispheres, surmounting his staircase, male of the *Netjeru*, prince of the desert, loving humankind he has created youths. His abomination is to say, 'Cut short the breath of life by which one lives;' causing to breathe him who follows his current. Fair of face, beautiful beyond the *Netjeru*, his excellence is beyond the divine cycle, traveling upon his current, healing the sick, making the distressed to live, good physician to him that places him in his heart. I am your servant, traveling upon your current. [192]

Praise to you, Great Fierce Lion!
Praise to you, Victorious Bull!
Praise to you, Primordial One!
Praise to you, Foremost One of His Fields!
Praise to you, Whose Phallus is Praised!
Praise to you, Lord of the Two Uraei!

---

[191] Miriam Lichtheim, *Ancient Egyptiam Literature*, Volume I, (Univ. of California Press, 1975), "Hymn to Min", p. 204.

[192] W. M. Flinders Petrie, *Koptos* (London, 1896), p. 20.

Praise to you, for Whose Fragrance the *Netjerut* (goddesses) rejoice!

Praise to you, the One Who Begets *Netjeru*!

Praise to you, the Bull Who Ejaculates *Nun*! [193]

Praise to you, Min, in all your Names.

Praise to you, Min, in all your Forms.

Praise to you, Min, in all your Aspects.

Praise to you, Min in all your Shrines.

Praise to you, O Min, in all places where your *Ka* desires to be!

May he give all life, all stability and all power to each of us, his servants, as to a Son/Daughter of Ra. Dominion be to the Lord of Life, Min!

*At this point perform the **meditation or magical action** or, if it is a special feast, add the appropriate prayers.*

*Afterwards **all present back out of the Temple Chamber with heads slightly bowed** while the Ritualist performs the **"removing the foot."***

*With the **broom** the Ritualist, as the last person to exit, **ritually sweeps the area beginning at the altar**. (This is known as "removing the foot.") While performing this action the Ritualist recites the following:*

The distress that causes confusion has been driven away, and all the *Netjeru* are in harmony. I have given Heru his Eye; I have placed the *Wedjat*-Eye in the correct position. I have given Setekh his Testicles, so that the two lords are content through the work of my hands.

---

[193] David Klotz, **Adoration of the Ram** (Yale Egyptological Studies, 2006), p. 24.

I know the sky, I know the earth;
I know Heru, I know Setekh.
Heru is appeased with his Eyes;
Setekh is appeased with his Testicles.
I am Djehuty, who reconciles the *Netjeru,*
who makes offerings in their correct form.

*The **double doors are solemnly closed** as the Ritualist says the following:*

Djehuty has come.
He has filled the Eye of Heru;
He has restored the Testicles of Setekh.
No evil shall enter this Temple.
Ptah has closed the door,
Djehuty has set it fast.
The door is closed, the door is set fast with the bolt.

*All **bow, touching the palms of their hands to their knees**.*

THE REVERSION OF OFFERINGS

*One priest or priestess and as many assistants as necessary enter the Temple Chamber a final time. While he/she and any assistants **lift up the offerings** before the sacred image the ritualist shall say:*

O Min, your enemy[194] withdraws for you. Heru has turned himself to his Eye in its name of 'Reversion-of-Offerings.' I am Djehuty. I come to perform this rite for Min, Lord of Humankind.

---

[194] Meat offerings held a two-fold meaning for the ancient priesthood. Since meat necessarily came from slain animals, it signified the defeated or slain enemies of the Netjer. At the same time, the meat offering represented the produce of the land which ultimately was a gift of the Netjeru.

These, your divine offerings revert, they revert to your servants for life, for stability, for health and for joy! O that the Eye of Heru may flourish for you eternally!

*Everyone withdraws, **carrying away all food offerings except for one loaf of bread together with a bowl of pure water.** These last items will remain until evening. If this ritual is celebrated after sunset, these items would also be removed.*

*After the candle has burned down, a servant-priest enters and closes the doors of the Kar-shrine **Extinguishing the candle or oil lamp,** he/she exclaims:*

This is the Eye of Heru by which you have become great, by which you live, and by which you have power, O Min. This is the Eye of Heru which you consume and through which you enchant your body. The *Wedjat*-Eye now enters into the West, into *Manu*, but it shall return. Truly, the Eye of Heru returns in peace!

It is important to consume the food offerings after the ceremony. Water used should either be drunk or poured onto the earth. If it is mixed with natron, dilute it very greatly and then you can pour in onto the earth without harming any plantings.

The General Ritual for Montu

The *Netjer* Montu is *the* war god *par excellence* whose aggressive nature serves ma'at. He was worshipped in four major cult centers: Armant, Medamud, Tod, and Thebes. The Buchis bull was recognized as the earthly manifestation of this god. Upon its death it was buried with great pomp in the Bucheum, a special cemetery for these bulls and their mothers. The last burial occurred in 340 CE.

The main hymn and epithets for Montu come from both the dissertation *The God Montu: From the Earliest Attestations to the End of the New Kingdom* by Edward Karl Werner (Yale University Dissertation, December 1985) as well as from the *Lexikon der ägyptischen Götter und Götterbezeichnungen* ("Dictionary of Egyptian gods and god-forms"), abbreviated LGG.

Many thanks to Matthew Whealton from the Temple of Ra for his essential work on researching the epithets appearing in this important ritual for the great *Netjer* Montu.

In ancient Egypt a festival for Montu occurred on days 16-18 of the third month of the Inundation[195] known as *Hwt-Hrw* (Hathor) which today typically happens in November-December. In years with the extra intercalary month this festival would occur in the ancient month of *Menhet* (also known as Phaophi).

---

[195] Edward Karl Werner, *The God Montu: From the Earliest Attestations to the End of the New Kingdom* (Yale University Dissertation, December 1985), p. 89; also see Note 51 in Chapter Three in the same dissertation.

In this case this feast would occur in October-November. For more on the subject of the ancient calendar and how to calculate whether an extra month occurs, please visit our temple's website http://kemetictemple.org/articles.html and click on 'Religious Calendar of Ancient KMT.'

Special offerings for Montu: the sickle-shaped weapon (known as a khepesh sword), and the traditional food offerings of bread, beer, wine, and meat. As a warrior god Montu receives the khepesh sword.

As with all Egyptian rituals begin with your purification—washing of hands and cleansing of mouth with Natron. This preliminary rite helps us to lay aside the cares of the day and to become mindful of the fact that we will encounter a divine being. If Natron is not available, then use a natural sea salt in its place until you make your own Natron.

If two or more persons are participating, then one person, impersonating the Netjer Djehuty, **purifies each person by sprinkling each with water while exclaiming:**

I purify you with the water of all life and good fortune, all stability, all health and happiness.[196]

Afterwards each person **rinses his mouth** *and places a small amount of Natron or sea salt in his mouth while saying:*

---

[196] Taken from Aylward M. Blackman's article "Purification (Egyptian)" in Hastings Encyclopaedia 10/1918/ 476-82. This article is reprinted in Gods, Priests, and Men, Studies in the Religion of Pharaonic Egypt, edited by Alan B. Lloyd (Kegan Paul International, 1998), p. 9.

I wash my mouth; I chew natron so that I may extol the might of Montu, Lord of Everlastingness, the Bull Who Dwells in *Iuny* (Armant).[197]

*Participants **assemble outside the Temple Chamber** and begin by softly rattling sistra.*

This time—several minutes or more—is used to focus minds and intention so that distracting thoughts are left behind. The sound of the sistrum was said to placate the deity, purifying the atmosphere in preparation for encountering divinity. The sistrum was associated with Hutheru and also with her and Heru's son Ihy, and thus has connotations of joy, celebration, and dancing. According to Plutarch (A.D. 46-120), the sound of sistra was also reputed to drive away Setekh. But this was of very late date. It may have been that since by that time Setekh had been demonized, the general apotropaic function of the sistrum against evil entities was extended to include this *Netjer* as well.

*Standing **before the closed doors**, the Ritualist **recites the entrance spell:***

UTTERANCE BEFORE THE CLOSED DOORS OF THE TEMPLE

*The ritualist **raises hands in adoration** (dua position-arms stretched out in front of the body and raised up to face level, with palms facing outward). The following shall be said:*

---

[197] Adapted from a temple inscription taken from "The Myth of Horus at Edfu—II" by A. M. Blackman and H. W. Fairman, appearing in Gods, Priests and Men, Studies in the Religion of Pharaonic Egypt, p. 283.

O you *Netjeru* of this Temple, you guardians of the great portal, great *Netjeru* of mysterious abode, who sanctify the *Netjer* in his shrine, who consecrate his oblation, who receive the offerings in his presence in the Hall of the Ennead: I have made my way and I enter into your presence. I am one of you. I am Shu, the eldest son of his father, the senior *wab* servant-priest of Montu. Do not repulse me on the *Netjer*'s path. My feet are not impeded. I am not turned back from the court of the great portal so that I may conduct the divine service, that I may present offerings to him that made them, that I may give bread to Montu. I have come on the way of the god. I have not shown partiality in judgment. I have not consorted with the strong. I have not reproached the lowly. I have not stolen things. I have not diminished the constituents of the Eye of Ra. I have not disturbed the Balance. I have not tampered with the requirements of the Sacred Eye. O Council of the Great *Netjer* in this Temple, behold, I have come to you to offer Ma'at to the Lord of Heaven, to content the Sound Eye for its lord. I am Shu; I flood his offering table. I present his offerings, Sekhmet consorting with me, that I may adore Montu at his festivals, that I may kiss the earth so great is his majesty, that I may endow his image with life. I am pure. I am purified.

At this point the ritualist **opens the doors to the Temple Chamber,** *or, if there are no doors,* **makes a gesture of opening unseen doors,** *and* **steps forward as if crossing over a threshold.** *The following is said:*

O you *Ba*-souls of *Iuny* (Armant) if you are strong, I am strong. If I am strong, you are strong. If your *Ka*-spirits are strong, my *Ka*-spirit is strong at the head of the living. As they are living so shall I live . . . . Montu, Great Wild Bull, has given to me life, stability, and serenity round about my members, which

Djehuty has gathered together for life. I am Heru in the height of heaven, the beautiful one of awe, Lord of Victory, mighty one of awe, exalted one of the two plumes, Great One in *Waset* (Thebes), I am pure.

*All temple members **chant**:*

Awake in peace, O Montu, Who Lives in Ma'at,
may you awaken in peace.
Awake in peace, O Montu, Lord of Strength Who Fights Victoriously,
may you awaken in peace.
Awake in peace, O Montu, Lord of the Firmament,
may you awaken in peace.
Awake in peace, O Montu, Lord of Bravery,
may you awaken in peace.

May you awake beautifully at the top of the morning,
through that which the entirety of *Netjeru* say to you.

*Enter, **close the double doors** and **stand in front of the Kar-shrine and altar. All bow**, touching their hands to their knees.*

*The ritualist slowly **opens the two doors of the Kar-shrine** housing the sacred image. All others bow, touching their hands to their knees. The following is said:*

The doors of the sky are open; the doors of the earth are unlocked. This House is open for its Lord. Let me come forth as he shall come forth. Let me enter in as he shall enter in. Montu, Who Overthrows the Rebels, is exalted upon his Great Seat. The Great Company of the *Netjeru* are exalted upon their seat.

I have seen the *Netjer*, and the *Netjer* sees me. The *Netjer* rejoices at seeing me. I have gazed upon the statue of the Lord of Victory, the sacred image of the Fighter.[198]

Right hand on left shoulder of statue; left hand on right wrist of statue:

Djehuty has come to you. Awake when you hear his words. I have come as the envoy of Atum. My two arms are upon you like those of Heru. My two hands are upon you like those of Djehuty. My fingers are upon you like those of Anpu. Homage be to you. I am a living servant of Montu.

*The Ritualist holds up the **bowl of water** in which he/she will be mixing the Natron. The following is said:*

O water may you remove all evil,
As Ra who bathes in the Lake of Rushes,
May Heru wash my flesh,
May Djehuty cleanse my feet,
May Shu lift me up and Nut take my hand!
May Set be my strength, and may Sekhmet be my healing!
And may Montu-Ra be my life and my prospering!

*The bowl of water is set aside and the container of **Natron is lifted up**. The following is said:*

It is pure, it is pure.
My Natron is the Natron of Heru and the Natron of Heru is my Natron.

---

[198] Based on the temple text found in "Worship and Festivals in an Egyptian Temple," a lecture by H. W. Fairman (publ. by The John Rylands Library, 1954; p. 180).

My Natron is the Natron of Setekh and the Natron of Setekh is my Natron.
My Natron is the Natron of Djehuty, and the Natron of Djehuty is my Natron.
My Natron is the Natron of Geb and the Natron of Geb is my Natron.

My mouth is the mouth of a milking calf on the day that I was born.

Four pinches of Natron are mixed into the water as this Utterance is recited:

I give you essential water, a tide in your time.
I bring the flood waters to purify your sanctuary.
I bring you the flood waters to purify your Temple and your statue in its place, the primordial water that purifies as in the First Time!

The Ritualist places an index finger into the water and moves it in a circular direction four times as the following is said:

Montu, Great of *Bas*, does purify this water;
Montu, Whose Flames are His Two Eyes, does cleanse this water;
Montu, Who Drives off Evil, does sanctify this water;
Montu himself does endow this water with power and with life.

The Bowl of Natron-infused water is then taken up and the Ritualist sprinkles this lightly in front of and around the statue or image of Montu, applying some of this water to the base of the image, as the Utterance is recited:

I come close to you, O Bull with Enduring Heart. I bring the water of rejuvenation that flows from the Two Caverns. I sprinkle the water, purifying your image and your Temple from all impurity!

The Ritualist picks up the bowl of **Natron** *and* **sprinkles a small amount in each of the four directions** *as the following is recited:*

The *Netjer* Montu himself does cleanse and purify this, his Temple to the South.
The *Netjer* Montu himself does cleanse and purify this, his Temple to the North.
The *Netjer* Montu himself does cleanse and purify this, his Temple to the West.
The *Netjer* Montu himself does cleanse and purify this, his Temple to the East.

Replacing the Natron on the altar, the Ritualist **picks up the bowl of water, sprinkling a small amount in each of the four directions.** *The following Utterance is recited:*

The *Netjer* Montu himself does sanctify and consecrate this, his Temple to the South.
The *Netjer* Montu himself does sanctify and consecrate this, his Temple to the North.
The *Netjer* Montu himself does sanctify and consecrate this, his Temple to the West.
The *Netjer* Montu himself does sanctify and consecrate this, his Temple to the East.

The Temple of the *Netjer* Montu is established. It is established for millions of years.

*The Ritualist returns to the altar and **lights the candle or oil lamp**
while the following is said:*

Come, come in peace, O glorious Eye of Heru,
Be strong and renew your youth in peace.
For the flame shines like Ra on the double horizon.
The enemies of Ra are defeated. They are defeated.
I am pure, I am pure, I am pure, I am pure.

*The Ritualist **places incense on the burner** and **censes each sacred
image** beginning with the statue of Montu while the following is recited:*

The fire is laid, the fire shines;
The incense is laid on the fire, the incense shines.
Your perfume comes to me, O Incense;
May my perfume come to you, O Incense.
Your perfume comes to me, you *Netjeru*;
May my perfume come to you, You *Netjeru*.
May I be with you, you *Netjeru*;
May you be with me, you *Netjeru*.
May I live with you, you *Netjeru*;
May you live with me, you *Netjeru*.
I love you, you *Netjeru*;
May you love me, you *Netjeru*.

*Standing in front of the image of Montu the Ritualist **offers the burning
incense** and says:*

Take the incense, O Great of Strength,
Its essence is for you.
Its smoke permeates your shrine, bringing life!
Take the incense,

Its essence is for you.

Your Majesty is appeased with the incense.

This Eye of Heru,

This essence of the Eye of Heru comes to you.

At this point the following is said:

Greetings Montu, Who Fells Enemies on the Battlefield,

Father of the Fathers of the Primordial Gods,

Whose length and breadth are without limit,

Powerful and skilled, Who Lives by Ma'at.

Great Falcon, Great of Magic.

Lord of Flame and Great of Rage, truly Great of *Bas*. [199]

Yours is the sky,

Yours is the earth,

Yours is the netherworld,

Yours are the waters,

And yours is the air which is within them.

That which is made acclaims you without tiring,

For you are the Lord of Rulers, truly the Lord of Years.

O Perfect Protector of the *Netjeru* and *Netjerut*,

You are the Great Courageous One.

You are the One Who Gives Bravery to the One He Wishes.

May you give courage to us as we battle the enemies of Ra.

O Montu, aid us as we battle *Isfet* (evil),

Great of *Bas*, may you strike the enemies of Ma'at.

Great of Justification on the Throne of Ra,

---

[199] Modeled on David Klotz, *Adoration of the Ram: Five Hymns to Amun-Re from Hibis Temple* (Yale Egyptological Studies, 2006), p. 129.

Who Eats Raw Flesh, may you consume the enemy in all its places.

You are the One with Fury-Red Eyes
Who Clothes His Claws with the Skin of His Enemies,
May you inspire us to acts of courage as we strive to fight for Ma'at.
You are the One Who Makes His Enemies Non-existent.
Give us your determination to join the battle for Ra.

The Ritualist places **more incense** *on the charcoal and again and again slowly raises and lowers the incense cup as the following is recited:*

O Montu, may you advance with your *Ka.*
the arm of your *Ka* is before you,
The arm of your *Ka* is behind you.
O Strong One of Power, the foot of your *Ka* is before you,
The foot of your *Ka* is behind you.
O Bull of Bulls, Montu, this incense is offered to you,
May your face be filled as this essence spreads itself over you.

All present **perform the Henu Rite**—*Embrace the Earth, the Fourfold Salute to the God, Embrace the Earth.*

For Embracing the Earth, all present prostrate themselves, face down, upon the floor. During the Fourfold Salute, all present rise upon one knee, and alternately raise their hands and arms into the *Dua* (praise) position with palms facing outward, followed by the *Sahu* (obedience) gesture, made by striking the chest with a closed fist and raising the other arm (also with closed fist) at a ninety-degree angle. The *Dua* position is accompanied by the words **"Adoration be to Montu,"** followed by the *Sahu* gesture accompanied with the words, **"Hail to the Lord of Bravery!"** The bodily gestures are performed alternately four times.

*Following this **all present again prostrate themselves** before the god. This is a sign and symbol of total submission and adoration before the Netjer. The following is said:*

Homage to Montu, Great of Victories,
who is established on the Great Seat!
I have placed myself on the floor in awe of you.
I embrace the earth before you as before the Furious One.
I have come that I might kiss the earth,
that I might worship my Lord,
For I have seen his Strength;
I give praise to Montu,
For I have seen his Power.
His form is more distinguished than the *Netjeru*;
His arm is more powerful than the *Netjeru*.
I am pure, I am pure, I am pure, I am pure!

Everyone stands up.

*The Ritualist **holds in the palm of one hand** the image of Ma'at and **with the other hand open and raised over the image as if sheltering it**, repeats the following:*

I have come to you as Djehuty, whose two hands are joined together under Ma'at. She comes to be with you, for she is everywhere. You are provided with Ma'at. You move in Ma'at, you live in Ma'at. She fills your body, she rests in your head, she makes her seat upon your brow; the breath of your body is of Ma'at, your heart does live in Ma'at. All that you eat, all that you drink, all that you breathe is of Ma'at. Djehuty presents

Ma'at to you, his two hands are upon her beauty before your face.

*The Ritualist places the image of Ma'at near the divine statue. Then he/ she holds up before the image of Montu **a pitcher of water** and **pours the water slowly into an offering bowl** as the following Utterance is recited:*

This libation is for you, O Rejuvenated Youth.
This libation is for you, O Montu, Lord of Eternity.
I have brought to you this offering of water,
That your heart may be refreshed.
I have brought to you this Eye of Heru,
Placing this at your feet.
I present to you that which flows forth from you,
That your heart shall continue to beat.
For it is with you that all comes forth at the sound of the voice.

*The offering bowl is placed on the altar. At this point the Ritualist **lightly sprinkles sand on the floor in front of the altar** as the following is recited:*

O Montu, who resides in *Iuny* (Armant),
Take to yourself the Eye of Heru.
You have rescued it, O Protector of the Divine Order.
You have sprinkled with sand the Eye of Heru.

*The Ritualist **presents the sickle-shaped weapon** (or an image of it) known as the **khepesh sword** and exclaims:*

Take this, the scepter of courage; it strikes your enemies. May you bestow upon us both courage for our arms and strength for our flesh.[200]

Lifting the wine offering before the sacred image, the Ritualist repeats the following:

mn n.k irp irt ḥrw w³dt

[*"mán-nik 'úrip írat ḥáru wá'dat"*; approximately pronounced *MAHN-neek OO-rip EE-raht HAH-roo WAH-jat*]

Take to Yourself wine, the green Eye of Heru, which I offer to your *Ka.*[201]

O Ruler, how beautiful is your beauty!

May you drink it; may your heart rejoice;

may anger be removed from your face.

It is pure. [iw.w w'b pronounced *"uwú wá'ib"*; approximately oo-WOO WAH-ib]

The Ritualist places myrrh on the fire and lifts up the smoking incense while at the same time he lifts up the meat-offering before the Netjer, and says the following:

The scent of myrrh is for your nose. It fills your nostrils; your heart receives the meat-portions on its scent.[202]

---

[200] C. De Wit, *Les inscriptions du temple d'Opet à Karnak* I (Brussels, Belgium: Bibliotheca Aegyptiaca XI (1958), 252.

[201] Refer to pp. 92, 93, 99, and 105 in Mu-Chou Poo's *Wine and Wine Offerings in Ancient Egypt* (London & New York: Kegan Paul International, 1995).

[202] Quoted in "Worship and Festivals in an Egyptian Temple," by H. W. Fairman (publ. by The John Rylands Library, 1954), p. 191.

*Slowly elevating the **food offerings** four times before the image of Montu, the Ritualist repeats the following:*

I offer to Montu, Lord of Foods.
All life emanates from you,
All health emanates from you,
All stability emanates from you,
All good fortune emanates from you,
O Great of *Heka-u,* Montu, forever.

*The Ritualist **places the** food **offering before the divine image**, and then all present **extend one hand, palm down, over the offerings** and recite the following:*

May offerings of every kind come forth in abundance,
like the things which come forth from the mouth of the *Netjer.*

piryá pírit ar ḫiráw mi purú:riat ma rá' ni náṭar. (4 times)
[approximately pronounced: peer-YA PEER-it ar khi-RAU mee pu-ROOR-iat ma RA nee NAH-tchar]

May offerings of every kind come forth in abundance, like the things that come forth from the mouth of the *Netjer.*

*Holding the **Ankh** before Montu, the Ritualist says:*

Live, O Montu, Perfect Protector of the *Netjeru,* live for all time and for eternity!

ʿánaḫ niḥáḫ ḏát.
[approximately pronounced *AH-nakh nee-HAH JAHT*]

Richard J. Reidy

*The **Ankh** is placed next to the image of the Netjer.*

Holding the Ib (the golden heart) before Montu, the Ritualist says:

Hail to you, O Montu, Pacified Bull. I have brought to you your heart to set it in its place. Let me draw near to you with your heart, so that you may have pleasure through me, and so that by means of me you may have power over your body. Ascend, O Peaceful One, radiant, rejuvenating, equipped as a *Netjer*. Live, O Friendly of Heart, live forever and ever!

*After placing the Ib near the sacred image, **everyone sings or chants** this ancient hymn to Montu.*

Praise to you, Montu, Lord of *Iuny* (modern Armant), Youthful Bull, sharp of horns, he of the double uraeus, king of the *Netjeru*, the sovereign, Ruler of the Two Banks (of the Nile), Possessor of Strength who seizes his power, Lord of Majesty among the great ones, the Ennead; the Raging One who prevails over the serpent-demon Nik, his spear having been caused to overpower him.

Great of Strength in the Night Barque; his strength is high and wide, he who saves the Two Lands while enduring upon earth, Great Hawk, Mysterious of Countenances, the Bull, sharp of knife, equipped with horns, provided with his spear, who causes Ra to sail in his barque and who overthrows his serpent enemy for him (Ra), his crew rejoicing, they receiving joy; greatly esteemed *Netjer*, Great of Power, the Bowman who prevails over his opponent, fear of him being given to those greater than he, awe of him being at rest in their bodies, they rejoice in his approach, they act as he has ordained for them, he who is seated on the throne.

The *Netjeru* and *Netjerut* make way for him, he overawes those who are above, the faces of those who see him turn aside at the brightness of his beauty, according as he has commanded, landing in his heavenly fields, he who comes forth as the Oarsman of Nun, whose mother gives birth to him every day, he who is rejuvenated every month, the Unwearying Stars together with the Imperishable Stars; those two baboons are quiet for you, the Sleepers praise you, O Montu.[203]

Grant us strength as we also fight the serpent-demon. Grant that our Spear of Truth defeats the Lie. Guide our aim so that we strike down the serpent-enemy. May Ra live, and may his enemies die! (4 times)

At this point perform the **meditation or magical action** *or, if it is a special feast, add the appropriate prayers.*

---

[203] Edward Karl Werner, *The God Montu: From the Earliest Attestations to the End of the New Kingdom* (Yale University Dissertation, December 1985), pp. 153-154. This dissertation is available from U.M.I. Dissertation Service, Ann Arbor, Michigan. As of 8/14/15 it is also available online at https://yadi.sk/i/0-CaCst-htUVF
The ancient hymn is "typical of Egyptian hymns which consist mainly of honorific titles, epithets, and participial phrases. . . ." As Egyptologist H. M. Stewart observed, there is, to our eyes, "a confusing interchange of second and third person pronouns" in such hymns as "characteristic of Egyptian participial clauses." See his article, "Traditional Egyptian Sun Hymns of the New Kingdom," *Bulletin of the Institute of Archaeology*, No. 6 (1967), p.40. I have chosen to retain the majority of such grammatical constructions unless they negatively impacted the smooth flow of the words and meaning.

*Afterwards **all present back out of the Temple Chamber with heads slightly bowed** while the Ritualist performs the "removing the foot."*

*With the broom the Ritualist, as the last person to exit, **ritually sweeps the area beginning at the altar**. (This is known as "removing the foot.") While performing this action the Ritualist recites the following:*

The distress that causes confusion has been driven away, and all the *Netjeru* are in harmony. I have given Heru his Eye; I have placed the *Wedjat*-Eye in the correct position. I have given Setekh his Testicles, so that the two lords are content through the work of my hands.

I know the sky, I know the earth;
I know Heru, I know Setekh.
Heru is appeased with his Eyes;
Setekh is appeased with his Testicles.
I am Djehuty, who reconciles the *Netjeru,*
who makes offerings in their correct form.

The double doors are solemnly closed as the Ritualist says the following:

Djehuty has come.
He has filled the Eye of Heru;
He has restored the Testicles of Setekh.
No evil shall enter this Temple.
Ptah has closed the door,
Djehuty has set it fast.
The door is closed, the door is set fast with the bolt.

All bow, touching the palms of their hands to their knees.

THE REVERSION OF OFFERINGS

*One priest or priestess and as many assistants as necessary enter the Temple Chamber a final time. While he/she and any assistants **lift up the offerings** before the sacred image the* ritualist *shall say:*

O Montu, your enemy[204] withdraws for you. Heru has turned himself to his Eye in its name of 'Reversion-of-Offerings.' I am Djehuty. I come to perform this rite for Montu, the Fighter. These, your divine offerings revert, they revert to your servants for life, for stability, for health and for joy! O that the Eye of Heru may flourish for you eternally!

*Everyone withdraws, **carrying away all food offerings except for one loaf of bread together with a bowl of pure water**. These last items will remain until evening. If this ritual is celebrated after sunset, these items would also be removed.*

*After the candle has burned down, a servant-priest enters and closes the doors of the Kar-shrine. **Extinguishing the candle or oil lamp**, he/she exclaims:*

This is the Eye of Heru by which you have become great, by which you live, and by which you have power, O Montu. This is the Eye of Heru which you consume and through which you enchant your body. The *Wedjat*-Eye now enters into the West, into *Manu*, but it shall return. Truly, the Eye of Heru returns in peace!

---

[204] Meat offerings held a two-fold meaning for the ancient priesthood. Since meat necessarily came from slain animals, it signified the defeated or slain enemies of the Netjer. At the same time, the meat offering represented the produce of the land which ultimately was a gift of the Netjeru.

It is important to consume the food offerings after the ceremony. Water used should either be drunk or poured onto the earth. If it is mixed with natron, dilute it very greatly and then you can pour in onto the earth without harming any plantings.

The General Ritual for Mut

All epithets for this *Netjeret* (goddess) as well as both major hymns to her come from three sources: "A Crossword Hymn to Mut," by H. M. Stewart, *Journal of Egyptian Archaeology, Vol. 57 (1971), 87-104;* "Mut Enthroned," by Lana Troy, in *Essays on Ancient Egypt in Honour of Herman te Velde,* edited by Jacobus van Dijk (Groningen: Styx Publ., 1997), pp. 301-315; as well as the 8-volume *Lexikon der ägyptischen Götter und Götterbezeichnungen (Dictionary of Egyptian Gods and God-Epithets).* One other very helpful book is R. A. Fazzini and J. van Dijk's *The First Pylon of the Mut Temple, South Karnak: Architecture, Decoration, Inscriptions* (Leuven: Peeters Publishers, 2015).

No attempt has been made to fabricate or "make up" epithets for this great *Netjeret.* The ancient sources are sufficiently rich in themselves. Mut is magnificent enough on her own. She does not need an inflated, syncretistic approach in ritual.

Please do not feel that you must either do the entire ritual or nothing at all. If certain elements of the ritual speak to you and have special meaning, then please just do those particular elements. However, in my own experience I have found that as I repeat the ritual a few times, I am pleasantly surprised with 'aha!' moments where some new insight comes to light. The ritual's words have special meaning and power, and so may not be evident on first reading. Be patient and I believe the *Netjeru* will reward your effort.

Like members of the ancient priesthood, participants should be clothed in white linen or, if necessary, white cotton. No item made of animal products such as leather or wool is to be worn. Linen represents a pristine product of the earth whereas leather and wool come from humankind's domination of the animals, a domination that becomes part of the "natural order" only *after* the First Time when the *Netjeru* and humans and animals lived in peace and harmony. Just as the Morning Ritual harkens back to that First Time (*Zep Tepi*), so every temple rite re-presents mythic prototypes that occurred "in the beginning," that is, in that time before time. Even the sandals worn by the god's servants were made of white papyrus. This avoidance of animal products by the priesthood fits well with the fact that the ritualist acts as a *Netjer* and verbally asserts that he or she is a *Netjer.*

As with all Egyptian rituals begin with your purification—washing of hands and cleansing of mouth with Natron. This preliminary rite helps us to lay aside the cares of the day and to become mindful of the fact that we will encounter a divine being. If Natron is not available, then use a natural sea salt in its place until you make your own Natron.

If two or more persons are participating, then one person, impersonating the Netjer Djehuty, **purifies each person by sprinkling each with water** *while exclaiming:*

I purify you with the water of all life and good fortune, all stability, all health and happiness.[205]

---

[205] Taken from Aylward M. Blackman's article "Purification (Egyptian)" in Hastings Encyclopaedia 10/1918/ 476-82. This article is reprinted in

*Afterwards each person **rinses his mouth** and **places a small amount of Natron or sea salt in his mouth** while saying:*

I wash my mouth; I chew natron so that I may extol the might of Mut, Great of Sunlight and August One of Heaven.[206]

*Participants **assemble outside the Temple Chamber** and begin by softly rattling sistra.*

This time—several minutes or more—is used to focus minds and intention so that distracting thoughts are left behind. The sound of the sistrum was said to placate the deity, purifying the atmosphere in preparation for encountering divinity.

*Standing **before the closed doors**, the Ritualist **recites the entrance spell**:*

UTTERANCE BEFORE THE CLOSED DOORS OF THE TEMPLE

*The ritualist **raises hands in adoration** (dua position—arms stretched out in front of the body and raised up to face level, with palms facing outward). The following shall be said:*

O you *Netjeru* of this Temple, you guardians of the great portal, great *Netjeru* of mysterious abode, who sanctify the *Netjeret* (goddess) in her shrine, who consecrate her oblation, who

---

Gods, Priests, and Men, Studies in the Religion of Pharaonic Egypt, edited by Alan B. Lloyd (Kegan Paul International, 1998), p. 9.

[206] Based on a temple inscription taken from "The Myth of Horus at Edfu—II" by A. M. Blackman and H. W. Fairman, appearing in Gods, Priests and Men, Studies in the Religion of Pharaonic Egypt (Kegan Paul International, 1998) p. 283.

receive the offerings in her presence in the Hall of the Ennead:
I have made my way and I enter into your presence. I am one
of you. I am Shu, the eldest son of his father, the senior *wab*
servant-priest of Mut. Do not repulse me on the *Netjeret*'s path.
My feet are not impeded. I am not turned back from the court
of the great portal so that I may conduct the divine service,
that I may present offerings to her that made them, that I may
give bread to Mut. I have come on the way of the *Netjeret*. I
have not shown partiality in judgment. I have not consorted
with the strong. I have not reproached the lowly. I have not
stolen things. I have not diminished the constituents of the Eye
of Ra. I have not disturbed the Balance. I have not tampered
with the requirements of the Sacred Eye. O Council of the Great
Netjeret in this Temple, behold, I have come to you to offer
Ma'at to the Queen of the *Netjeru*, to content the Sound Eye for
its mistress. I am Shu; I flood her offering table. I present her
offerings, Sekhmet consorting with me, that I may adore Mut at
her festivals, that I may kiss the earth so great is her majesty,
that I may endow her image with life. I am pure. I am purified.

At this point the ritualist **opens the doors to the Temple Chamber,** *or,
if there are no doors,* **makes a gesture of opening unseen doors,** *and
steps forward as if crossing over a threshold. The following is said:*

O you *Ba*-souls of *Ipet-Sut* (i.e., "Most Select of Places,"
Karnak[207]), if you are strong, I am strong. If I am strong, you
are strong. If your *Ka*-spirits are strong, my *Ka*-spirit is strong
at the head of the living. As they are living so shall I live . . . .
Sekhmet, the great *Netjeret*, beloved of Ptah, has given to me
life, stability, and serenity round about my members, which

---

[207] Ipet-Sut, litetally "Most Select of Places," was the cult center for the
Theban Triad: Amun, Mut, and Khonsu.

Djehuty has gathered together for life. I am Heru in the height of heaven, the beautiful one of awe, Lord of Victory, mighty one of awe, exalted one of the two plumes, great one in Abdju (Abydos) I am pure.

Enter, close the double doors and stand in front of the Kar-shrine and altar. All bow, touching their hands to their knees.

All recite the following:

Awake, awake in peace, O Mut, Mistress of Heaven. May you awake in peace.
Awake, awake in peace, O Mighty Ruler in *Isheru*. May you awake in peace.
Awake, awake in peace, O Beloved of Amun. May you awake in peace.
Awake, awake in peace, O Mut, Lady of the Lotuses. May you awake in peace.

May you awake beautifully at the top of the morning, through that which the entirety of *Netjeru* say to you.

The ritualist *slowly* **opens the two doors of the Kar-shrine** *housing the sacred image. All others bow, touching their hands to their knees. The following is said:*

The doors of the sky are open; the doors of the earth are unlocked. This House is open for its Mistress. Let me come forth as she shall come forth. Let me enter in as she shall enter in. Mut, Lady of the Uraeus, is exalted upon her Great Seat. The Great Company of the *Netjeru* are exalted upon their seat.

I have seen the *Netjeret,* and the *Netjeret* sees me. The *Netjeret* rejoices at seeing me. I have gazed upon the statue of the Mighty One, the sacred image of the Mistress of Heaven.[208]

Right hand on left shoulder of statue; left hand on right wrist of statue:

Djehuty has come to you. Awake when you hear his words. I have come as the envoy of Atum. My two arms are upon you like those of Heru. My two hands are upon you like those of Djehuty. My fingers are upon you like those of Anpu. Homage be to you. I am a living servant of Mut.

The Ritualist **holds up the bowl of water** *in which he/she will be mixing the Natron. The following is said:*

O water may you remove all evil,
As Ra who bathes in the Lake of Rushes,
May Heru wash my flesh,
May Djehuty cleanse my feet,
May Shu lift me up and Nut take my hand!
May Setekh be my strength, and may Sekhmet be my healing!
And may Amun-Ra be my life and my prospering!

The bowl of water is set aside and the container of **Natron** *is* **lifted up***. The following is said:*

It is pure, it is pure.
My Natron is the Natron of Heru and the Natron of Heru is my Natron.

---

[208] Based on a passage in "Worship and Festivals in an Egyptian Temple," a lecture by H. W. Fairman (publ. by The John Rylands Library, 1954), p. 180.

My Natron is the Natron of Setekh and the Natron of Setekh is
my Natron.
My Natron is the Natron of Djehuty, and the Natron of Djehuty
is my Natron.
My Natron is the Natron of Geb and the Natron of Geb is my
Natron.

My mouth is the mouth of a milking calf on the day that I was
born.

*Four pinches of Natron are mixed into the water as this Utterance
is recited:*

I give you essential water, a tide in your time.
I bring the flood waters to purify your sanctuary.
I bring you the flood waters to purify your Temple and your
statue in its place, the primordial water that purifies as in the
First Time!

*The Ritualist places an index finger into the water and moves it in
a circular direction four times as the following is said:*

Mut, Great of Sunrays, does purify this water;
Mut, Mistress of the Seas, does cleanse this water;
Mut, Mistress of Peace, does sanctify this water;
Mut herself, Great and Powerful, does endow this water with
power and with life.

*The Bowl of Natron-infused water is then taken up and the Ritualist
sprinkles this lightly in front of and around the statue or image
of Mut, applying some water to the base of the image, as the Utterance
is recited:*

I come close to You, O Mistress of All That Exists.
I bring the water of rejuvenation that flows from the Two
Caverns.
I sprinkle the water, purifying your image and your Temple
from all impurity!

*The Ritualist picks up **the bowl of Natron** and **sprinkles a small
amount in each of the four directions** as the following is recited:*

The *Netjeret* Mut herself does cleanse and purify this, her
Temple to the South.
The *Netjeret* Mut herself does cleanse and purify this, her
Temple to the North.
The *Netjeret* Mut herself does cleanse and purify this, her
Temple to the West.
The *Netjeret* Mut herself does cleanse and purify this, her
Temple to the East.

*Replacing the Natron on the altar, the Ritualist **takes up the bowl of
water, sprinkling a small amount in each of the four directions**.
The following Utterance is recited:*

The *Netjeret* Mut herself does sanctify and consecrate this, her
Temple to the South.
The *Netjeret* Mut herself does sanctify and consecrate this, her
Temple to the North.
The *Netjeret* Mut herself does sanctify and consecrate this, her
Temple to the West.
The *Netjeret* Mut herself does sanctify and consecrate this, her
Temple to the East.
The Temple of the *Netjeret* Mut is established.
It is established for millions of years.

The Ritualist returns to the altar and **lights the candle or oil lamp**
while the following is said:

Come, come in peace, O glorious Eye of Heru,
Be strong and renew your youth in peace.
For the flame shines like Ra on the double horizon.
The enemies of Ra are defeated. They are defeated.
I am pure, I am pure, I am pure, I am pure.

The Ritualist **places incense on the burner** *and* **censes each sacred
image** *beginning with the statue of the Netjeret while the following is
recited:*

The fire is laid, the fire shines;
The incense is laid on the fire, the incense shines.
   Your perfume comes to me, O Incense;
   May my perfume come to you, O Incense.
Your perfume comes to me, you *Netjeru*;
May my perfume come to you, You *Netjeru*.
   May I be with you, you *Netjeru*;
   May you be with me, you *Netjeru*.
May I live with you, you *Netjeru*;
May you live with me, you *Netjeru*.
   I love you, you *Netjeru*;
   May you love me, you *Netjeru*.

Standing in front of the image of Mut the Ritualist **offers the burning
incense** *and says:*

Arise in glory, O Manifest One, being pleased with your going
forth on high even as Wadjet goes forth. The Great Ennead and
the Little Ennead are pleased with the perfume of her fragrance,
being joyful with that which the Eye of Heru, the Bright One,

did. The *Netjeru* came into being from her tears, and Atum is vivified in her flesh. This incense is for Mut, being our offering. May we be given life, stability, and good fortune.[209]

Take the incense,
Its essence is for you, O Lady of Joy.
Its smoke permeates your shrine, bringing life!
Take the incense,
Its essence is for you.
Your Majesty is appeased with the incense.
This Eye of Heru,
This essence of the Eye of Heru comes to you.

At this point the following is said:

THE GREAT HYMN TO MUT

The main Ritualist **reads the following inscription** *from the stela containing this hymn to the Netjeret Mut.*
As to this writing . . . never was its like seen before; never was it heard since the time of the *Netjer*. It is established in the temple of Mut, Mistress of *Isheru,* forever like Ra, eternally.
The following stanzas **can be recited alternately** *by all participants:*
Praise be to you, Mut, Great of Sunlight, who illumine the entire land with your rays. You cause the land to prosper, the glorious eye of Horakhty. You are the Ruler of What Exists, the Great and Powerful Mistress, life being in your possession. The hearts of the Ennead are glad because of you, the Mistress of Their Joy in this your name of 'Heaven.'

---

[209] "Certain Reliefs at Karnak and Medinet Habu and the Ritual of Amenophis I—continued," by Harold H. Nelson *JNES*, Vol. 8 (1949),pp. 310-345; quote on p. 341. *JNES* is the abbreviation for the *Journal of Near Eastern Studies.*

Ra sees her might just as she sees by means of him, since he knows her majesty's beauty. The *Netjerut* (goddesses) shout for her. She is a noble one. When she shines, the land possesses love of her. She is the mistress of the horizon at her beautiful rising at dawn. She has received the insignia of Ra, lord of the thrones.

Humans follow her likeness, she being like him who crosses the sky. Indeed she is his manifestation. She grants what she wishes. Mut has received these gifts. All animals rejoice at her. She rests between his brows (as the uraeus) while everyone worships him. All humankind is joyful of heart.

Ra traverses the Lakes of Fire[210] for his great daughter, Mistress of the *Netjeru*, this *Netjeret* who is upon his breast. Ra gives rejoicing to her who is with him—he who came into existence by himself. She is great of dignity, Mistress of Lower Kemet, Lady of the Uraeus. Humankind and the *Netjeru* are her offspring. She is the *Netjeret* who bore them. Their lives are of her giving. Mighty of Births, her *Ka*-spirit is in the sky. She gives sunlight. The sun-disk shines as her likeness. Khepera, Numerous of Forms, adores her; Heru praises her. There is prosperity under this *Netjeret*. Everyone is in praise of her. She is in their hearts. She has appeared and shown as the Woman of Gold. Everyone comes into existence through her. She shines as gold. The apes chatter to her because of her kindly face. She is the Beloved One, who has been exalted since primeval times in heaven. She is the noble Uraeus. May you protect us as we praise your name. The lotuses of this *Netjeret* are beautiful in her temple. She is the Great One. She is the noble *Wedjat*-Eye. Health and life are in the possession of her *Ka*-spirit. They have been given to her.

---

[210] The Lakes of Fire are in the Underworld. Those 'True-of-Voice' (the justified dead) experience the waters as refreshing, whereas the unworthy would only experience the burning fire.

May you, O Mut, give to us both health and life. All humankind and *Netjeru* belong to you. May you make our hearts content each day. Today is beautiful because of your beautiful face. The lord Khonsu is happy, and Ra as well, when you have appeared as both *Netjeret* and Mistress. We celebrate this day as a festival for you. Praise to you, O Mut! Praise to you, O Mistress of Heaven![211]

*The Ritualist places **more incense** on the charcoal and again and again **slowly raises and lowers the incense cup** as the following is recited:*

O Mut, may you advance with your *Ka*.
O Great One of the Sun Disk, the arm of your *Ka* is before you,
The arm of your *Ka* is behind you.
O Mistress of Heaven, the foot of your *Ka* is before you,
The foot of your *Ka* is behind you.
O Beautiful Mut, this incense is offered to you,
May your face be filled as this essence spreads itself over you.

*All present **perform the Henu Rite**—Embrace the Earth, the Fourfold Salute to the Goddess, Embrace the Earth.*

For Embracing the Earth, all present prostrate themselves, face down, upon the floor. During the Fourfold Salute, all present rise upon one knee, and alternately raise their hands and arms into the *Dua* (praise) position with palms facing outward, followed by the *Sahu* (obedience) gesture, made by striking the chest with a

---

[211] This hymn is based on the first eighteen stanzas of a much longer hymn to Mut found at Karnak. It dates to the reign of Ramesses VI. The interested reader may read the entire hymn in H. M. Stewart's article, "A Crossword Hymn to Mut," *Journal of Egyptian Archaeology* Vol. 57 (1971), 87-104.

closed fist and raising the other arm (also with closed fist) at a ninety-degree angle. The *Dua* position is accompanied by the words **"Adoration be to Mut,"** followed by the *Sahu* gesture accompanied with the words, **"Hail to the Mighty One!"** The bodily gestures are performed alternately four times.

Following this **all present again prostrate themselves** *before the sacred image. This is a sign and symbol of total submission and adoration before the Netjeret. The following is said:*

Homage be to Mut, Great of Dread,
who is established on the Great Seat!
I have placed myself on the floor in awe of you.
I embrace the earth before you as before the Mistress of Heaven
and Earth.
I have come that I might kiss the earth,
that I might worship my Mistress,
For I have seen her beauty;
I give praise to Mut,
For I have seen her Power.
Her form is more distinguished than the *Netjeru*;
Her arm is more powerful than the *Netjeru*.
I am pure, I am pure, I am pure, I am pure!

Everyone stands up.

The Ritualist **holds in the palm of one hand** *the image of Ma'at and with* **the other hand open and raised over the image as if sheltering it,** *repeats the following:*

I have come to you as Djehuty, whose two hands are joined together under Ma'at. She comes to be with you, for she is

everywhere. You are provided with Ma'at. You move in Ma'at, you live in Ma'at. She fills your body, she rests in your head, she makes her seat upon your brow; the breath of your body is of Ma'at, your heart does live in Ma'at. All that you eat, all that you drink, all that you breathe is of Ma'at. Djehuty presents Ma'at to you, his two hands are upon her beauty before your face.

*The Ritualist places the image of Ma'at near the divine statue. Then he/she holds up before the image of Mut **a pitcher of water** and **pours the water slowly into an offering bowl** as the following Utterance is recited:*

This libation is for you, O Mistress of the Seas.
This libation is for you, O Mut.
I have brought to you this offering of water,
That your heart may be refreshed.
I have brought to you this Eye of Heru,
Placing this at your feet.
I present to you that which flows forth from you,
That your heart shall continue to beat.
For it is with you that all comes forth at the sound of the voice.

*The offering bowl is placed on the altar. At this point the Ritualist lightly **sprinkles sand on the floor in front of the altar** as the following is recited:*

O Mut, who resides in *Ipet-Sut,* [i.e., *Karnak*]
Take to yourself the Eye of Heru.
You have rescued it, O Great of Magic.
You have sprinkled with sand the Eye of Heru.

Lifting the wine offering before the sacred image, the Ritualist repeats the following:

mn n.t irp irt ḥrw wȝdt
[*"mán-nit 'úrip írat ḥáru wá'ḏat"*; approximately pronounced *MAHN-neetch OO-rip EE-raht HAH-roo WAH-jat*]

Take to Yourself wine, the green Eye of Heru, which I offer to your **Ka.**
O Queen, how beautiful is your beauty!
May you drink it; may your heart rejoice;
may anger be removed from your face.
It is pure.
[*iw.w w'b* pronounced *"uwú wá'ib"*; approximately *oo-WOO WAH-ib*]

*The Ritualist **places myrrh on the fire** and **lifts up the smoking incense** while at the same time he **lifts up the meat-offering** before the Netjeret, and says the following:*

The scent of myrrh is for your nose. It fills your nostrils; your heart receives the meat-portions on its scent. [212]

*Slowly **elevating the food offerings** four times before the image of the Netjeret, the Ritualist repeats the following:*

I offer to Mut, Mistress of All That Exists.
All life emanates from you,
All health emanates from you,
All stability emanates from you,
All good fortune emanates from you,

---

[212] *Quoted in "Worship and Festivals in an Egyptian Temple," by H. W. Fairman (publ. by The John Rylands Library, 1954), p. 191.*

O Mut, Lady of Contentment, forever.

The Ritualist places the food offering before the divine image, and then all present extend one hand, palm down, over the offerings and recite the following:

May offerings of every kind come forth in abundance,
like the things which come forth from the mouth of the *Netjeret*.

piryá pírit ar ḫiráw mi purú:riat ma rá' ni naṯárat. (4 times)
[approximately pronounced: peer-YA PEER-it ar khi-RAU mee pu-ROOR-iat ma RA nee nah-TCHAR-at]

May offerings of every kind come forth in abundance, like the things that come forth from the mouth of the *Netjeret*.

*Holding the **Ankh** before the Netjeret, the Ritualist says:*

Live, O Mut, Lady of Love, live for all time and for eternity!

ʿánaḫ niḥáḥ ḏát.
[approximately pronounced *AH-nakh nee-HAH JAHT*]

*The **Ankh** is placed next to the Netjeret.*

*Holding the **Ib (the golden heart)** before the Netjeret, the Ritualist says:*

Hail to you, O Mut, Lady of Joy. I have brought to you your heart to set it in its place. Let me draw near to you with your heart, so that you may have pleasure through me, and so that by means of me you may have power over your body. Ascend,

O Great of Magic, radiant, rejuvenating, equipped as a *Netjeret*.
Live, O Lady of the Uraeus, live forever and ever!

*After placing the Ib near the sacred image, everyone sings or chants the
hymn to Mut. Begin by* **slowly playing the sistra**. *Participants may
wish to alternate the singing of verses.*

A HYMN TO MUT

Praise to you, O Mut. Praise to you, O Great One, Kindly of Face.
You have appeared in *Waset* (ancient Thebes, modern Luxor). The
lords of *Iunu* (Heliopolis) are glad at seeing you. You are Lady of
the *Per-wer*[213] shrine in Upper Kemet in the company of Neith.
You distribute that which Ra gives, he who is the leader of
humankind. You satisfy the heart with offerings given by you.
You are great in heaven like the horizon. Sunrays belong to
you, since power has been given to you, the Mistress of Heaven.
Praise to you, O Mistress of the Throne of *Isheru*[214]. You are
the August One of Heaven. You are the Likeness of the Lady
of Justice, even Ma'at. You are truly the Lady of Joy, Great of
Dread. Joy appears among people when you appear, shining in
your temple. Joy arises wherever you live. Grant us joy of heart
to us who serve you.

Praise to you, Mut in *Isheru*; to you belongs a million years of
health. He whom you love is one possessing health because of

---

[213] The Per-wer (literally, 'House of Greatness') "was the holy shrine into
which the king stepped at his coronation to have the uraeus officially
affixed to his brow." Barbara Lesko, The Great Goddesses of Egypt, p. 67.
[214] Isheru is the name of the horseshow-shaped lake by the temple of Mut
at Karnak. This manmade body of water served ritual purposes connected
with this goddess. It became the name for the entire temple complex
of Mut.

your love. May we be worthy of your love, O You Who Shine in the Sun-Disk.

To you belongs the Red Crown. To you belongs the White Crown. Truly you are Lady of the Two Lands. May you also be the lady of this land. Your enemies have been defeated. Your enemies have been destroyed by Ra, your father. May Ra himself defeat our enemies.

O Beloved of Amun and Mother of Khonsu, great *Netjeret* of the Uraeus, you are mistress of all that exists under you. You are Mut, Mistress of Heaven, Great of Dread, Foremost in the Ennead. Mistress of Power, Great of Majesty, Lady of the War-Cry, protect us who worship you.

O Mistress of the Sea, you travel the seas and the ocean of Ra in order that praise of you may endure in all places. This day we bow before your image. We bow before you, Mistress of the Land. Gracious are you, O Mistress, who bear with your hand the supports of the sky. Your home is filled with the breath of life. May you be present in our homes and fill them with the breath of life.

The mouths of the people utter praise to you with an eternity of festivals.

Praise to you, Mut, in all your Names!

Praise to you, Mut, in all your Forms!

Praise to you, Mut, in all your Aspects!

Praise to you, Mut, in all your Houses!

Praise to you, Mut, in all places where you are pleased to be![215]

At this point perform the meditation or magical action or, if it is a special feast, add the appropriate prayers.

---

[215] This hymn is based on stanzas nineteen through seventy-seven in "A Crossword Hymn to Mut," *Journal of Egyptian Archaeology* Vol. 57 (1971), 92-97.

*Afterwards **all present back out of the Temple Chamber with heads slightly bowed** while the Ritualist performs the "removing the foot."*

*With the **broom** the Ritualist, as the last person to exit, **ritually sweeps the area beginning at the altar.** (This is known as "removing the foot.") While performing this action the Ritualist recites the following:*

The distress that causes confusion has been driven away, and all the *Netjeru* are in harmony. I have given Heru his Eye; I have placed the *Wedjat*-Eye in the correct position. I have given Setekh his Testicles, so that the two lords are content through the work of my hands.

I know the sky, I know the earth;
I know Heru, I know Setekh.
Heru is appeased with his Eyes;
Setekh is appeased with his Testicles.
I am Djehuty, who reconciles the *Netjeru*,
who makes offerings in their correct form.

*The **double doors are solemnly closed** as the Ritualist says the following:*

Djehuty has come.
He has filled the Eye of Heru;
He has restored the Testicles of Setekh.
No evil shall enter this Temple.
Ptah has closed the door,
Djehuty has set it fast.
The door is closed, the door is set fast with the bolt.

All bow, touching the palms of their hands to their knees.

THE REVERSION OF OFFERINGS

*One priest or priestess and as many assistants as necessary enter the Temple Chamber a final time. While he/she and any assistants **lift up the offerings** before the sacred image the ritualist shall say:*

O Mut, your enemy[216] withdraws for you. Heru has turned himself to his Eye in its name of 'Reversion-of-Offerings.' I am Djehuty. I come to perform this rite for Mut, Mistress of the *Netjeru*. These, your divine offerings revert, they revert to your servants for life, for stability, for health and for joy! O that the Eye of Heru may flourish for you eternally!

Everyone withdraws, carrying away all food offerings except for one loaf of bread together with a bowl of pure water. These last items will remain until evening. If this ritual is celebrated after sunset, these items would also be removed.

It is important to consume the food offerings after the ceremony. Water used should either be drunk or poured onto the earth. If it is mixed with natron, dilute it very greatly and then you can pour in onto the earth without harming any plantings.

*After the candle has burned down, a servant-priest **enters and closes the doors of the Kar-shrine**.*

***Extinguishing the candle or oil lamp,** he/she exclaims:*

---

[216] Meat offerings held a two-fold meaning for the ancient priesthood. Since meat necessarily came from slain animals, it signified the defeated or slain enemies of the Netjeret. At the same time, the meat offering represented the produce of the land which ultimately was a gift of the Netjeru.

This is the Eye of Heru by which you have become great, by which you live, and by which you have power, O Mut. This is the Eye of Heru which you consume and through which you enchant your body. The *Wedjat*-Eye now enters into the West, into *Manu*, but it shall return. Truly, the Eye of Heru returns in peace!

The General Ritual for Nebet-Hut

All epithets for this *Netjeret* (goddess) come from *Lexikon der ägyptischen Götter und Götterbezeichnungen (Dictionary of Egyptian Gods and God-Epithets)*. No attempt has been made to fabricate or "make up" epithets for this great *Netjeret*. The ancient sources are sufficiently rich in themselves.

Please do not feel that you must either do the entire ritual or nothing at all. If certain elements of the ritual speak to you and have special meaning, then please just do those particular elements. However, in my own experience I have found that as I repeat the ritual a few times, I am pleasantly surprised with 'aha!' moments where some new insight comes to light. The ritual's words have special meaning and power, and so may not be evident on first reading. Be patient and I believe the *Netjeru* will reward your effort.

Like members of the ancient priesthood, participants should be clothed in white linen or, if necessary, white cotton. No item made of animal products such as leather or wool is to be worn. Linen represents a pristine product of the earth whereas leather and wool come from humankind's domination of the animals, a domination that becomes part of the "natural order" only *after* the First Time when the *Netjeru* and humans and animals lived in peace and harmony. Just as the Morning Ritual harkens back to that First Time (*Zep Tepi*), so every temple rite re-presents mythic prototypes that occurred "in the beginning," that is, in that time before time. Even the sandals worn by the god's servants were made of white papyrus. This avoidance of animal products by the priesthood fits well with the fact that the ritualist acts as a *Netjer* and verbally asserts that he or she is a *Netjer*.

Special Food Offering for Nebet-Hut: milk. The offerings also should include the regular food and beverage offerings.

As with all Egyptian rituals begin with your purification – washing of hands and cleansing of mouth with Natron. This preliminary rite helps us to lay aside the cares of the day and to become mindful of the fact that we will encounter a divine being. If Natron is not available, then use a natural sea salt in its place until you make your own Natron.

If two or more persons are participating, then one person, impersonating the Netjer Djehuty, **purifies each person by sprinkling each with water** *while exclaiming:*

I purify you with the water of all life and good fortune, all stability, all health and happiness.[217]

Afterwards each person **rinses his mouth** *and* **places a small amount of Natron or sea salt in his mouth** *while saying:*

---

[217] Taken from Aylward M. Blackman's article "Purification (Egyptian)" in Hastings Encyclopaedia 10/1918/ 476-82. This article is reprinted in Gods, Priests, and Men, Studies in the Religion of Pharaonic Egypt, edited by Alan B. Lloyd (Kegan Paul International, 1998), p. 9.

I wash my mouth; I chew natron so that I may extol the might of Nebet-Hut, the Beautiful Radiant One and Daughter of Nut.[218]

*Participants **assemble outside the Temple Chamber** and begin by softly rattling sistra.*

This time—several minutes or more—is used to focus minds and intention so that distracting thoughts are left behind. The sound of the sistrum was said to placate the deity, purifying the atmosphere in preparation for encountering divinity. The sistrum was associated with Hutheru and also with her and Heru's son Ihy, and thus has connotations of joy, celebration, and dancing. According to Plutarch (A.D. 46-120), the sound of sistra was also reputed to drive away Setekh. But this was of very late date. It may have been that since by that time Setekh unfortunately had been demonized, the general apotropaic function of the sistrum against evil entities was extended to include this *Netjer* as well.

*Standing **before the closed doors**, the Ritualist **recites the entrance spell**:*

UTTERANCE BEFORE THE CLOSED DOORS OF THE TEMPLE

*The ritualist **raises hands in adoration** (dua position—arms stretched out in front of the body and raised up to face level, with palms facing outward). The following shall be said:*

---

[218] Based on a temple inscription taken from "The Myth of Horus at Edfu—II" by A. M. Blackman and H. W. Fairman, appearing in Gods, Priests and Men, Studies in the Religion of Pharaonic Egypt (Kegan Paul International, 1998) p. 283.

O you *Netjeru* of this Temple, you guardians of the great portal, great *Netjeru* of mysterious abode, who sanctify the *Netjeret* (goddess) in her shrine, who consecrate her oblation, who receive the offerings in her presence in the Hall of the Ennead: I have made my way and I enter into your presence. I am one of you. I am Shu, the eldest son of his father, the senior *wab* servant-priest of Nebet-Hut. Do not repulse me on the *Netjeret's* path. My feet are not impeded. I am not turned back from the court of the great portal so that I may conduct the divine service, that I may present offerings to her that made them, that I may give bread to Nebet-Hut. I have come on the way of the *Netjeret*. I have not shown partiality in judgment. I have not consorted with the strong. I have not reproached the lowly. I have not stolen things. I have not diminished the constituents of the Eye of Ra. I have not disturbed the Balance. I have not tampered with the requirements of the Sacred Eye. O Council of the Great *Netjeret* in this Temple, behold, I have come to you to offer Ma'at to the Sister of Aset to content the Sound Eye for its mistress. I am Shu; I flood her offering table. I present her offerings, Sekhmet consorting with me, that I may adore Nebet-Hut at her festivals, that I may kiss the earth so great is her majesty, that I may endow her image with life. I am pure. I am purified.

At this point the ritualist **opens the doors to the Temple Chamber, or, if there are no doors,** makes a gesture of opening unseen doors, *and* steps forward as if crossing over a threshold. *The following is said:*

O you *Ba*-souls of *Sepermeru*[219], if you are strong, I am strong. If I am strong, you are strong. If your *Ka*-spirits are strong, my

---

[219] Sepermeru, a town in the Nineteenth Upper Egyptian nome, is the site with the only surviving remnants of a temple of Nebet-Hut. Her temple

Ka-spirit is strong at the head of the living. As they are living so shall I live . . . . Sekhmet, the great *Netjeret*, beloved of Ptah, has given to me life, stability, and serenity round about my members, which Djehuty has gathered together for life. I am Heru in the height of heaven, the beautiful one of awe, Lord of Victory, mighty one of awe, exalted one of the two plumes, great one in Abdju (Abydos) I am pure.

Enter, close the double doors and stand in front of the Kar-shrine and altar. All bow, touching their hands to their knees.

All recite the following:

Awake, awake in peace, O Nebet-Hut, Lady of the West. May you awake in peace.
Awake, awake in peace, O Excellent Sister Who Overthrows Darkness. May you awake in peace.
Awake, awake in peace, O Lady of Renewal. May you awake in peace.
Awake, awake in peace, O Nebet-Hut, Mistress of Women. May you awake in peace.

May you awake beautifully at the top of the morning, through that which the entirety of *Netjeru* say to you.

The ritualist *slowly opens the two doors of the Kar-shrine* housing *the sacred image. All others bow, touching their hands to their knees. The following is said:*

The doors of the sky are open; the doors of the earth are unlocked. This House is open for its Mistress. Let me come forth

---

was called the "House of Nebet-Hut of Ramesses-Meriamun.

as she shall come forth. Let me enter in as she shall enter in. Nebet-Hut, the Lady of Light, Sister of Ausir, is exalted upon her Great Seat. The Great Company of the *Netjeru* are exalted upon their seat.

I have seen the *Netjeret*, and the *Netjeret* sees me. The *Netjeret* rejoices at seeing me. I have gazed upon the statue of the Lady of Life, the sacred image of the Lamenter.[220]

Right hand on left shoulder of statue; left hand on right wrist of statue:

Djehuty has come to you. Awake when you hear his words. I have come as the envoy of Atum. My two arms are upon you like those of Heru. My two hands are upon you like those of Djehuty. My fingers are upon you like those of Anpu. Homage be to you. I am a living servant of Nebet-Hut.

*The Ritualist holds up the **bowl of water** in which he/she will be mixing the Natron. The following is said:*

O water may you remove all evil,
As Ra who bathes in the Lake of Rushes,
May Heru wash my flesh,
May Djehuty cleanse my feet,
May Shu lift me up and Nut take my hand!
May Setekh be my strength, and may Sekhmet be my healing!
And may Amun-Ra be my life and my prospering!

---

[220] Based on a passage in "Worship and Festivals in an Egyptian Temple," a lecture by H. W. Fairman (publ. by The John Rylands Library, 1954), p. 180.

*The bowl of water is set aside and the container of **Natron** is lifted up. The following is said:*

It is pure, it is pure.
My Natron is the Natron of Heru and the Natron of Heru is my Natron.
My Natron is the Natron of Setekh and the Natron of Setekh is my Natron.
My Natron is the Natron of Djehuty, and the Natron of Djehuty is my Natron.
My Natron is the Natron of Geb and the Natron of Geb is my Natron.

My mouth is the mouth of a milking calf on the day that I was born.

Four pinches of Natron are mixed into the water as this Utterance is recited:

I give you essential water, a tide in your time.
I bring the flood waters to purify your sanctuary.
I bring you the flood waters to purify your Temple and your statue in its place, the primordial water that purifies as in the First Time!

*The Ritualist **places an index finger** into the water and **moves it in a circular direction four times** as the following is said:*

Nebet-Hut, the Lady of Purification, does purify this water;
Nebet-Hut, the Pure One, does cleanse this water;
Nebet-Hut, Effective of Magic, does sanctify this water;

Nebet-Hut herself, the Female Magician, does endow this water with power and with life.

*The **Bowl of Natron-infused water** is then taken up and the Ritualist **sprinkles this lightly in front of and around the statue** or image of Nebet-Hut, applying some water to the base of the image, as the Utterance is recited:*

I come close to you, O Primordial One, Lady of Renewal.
I bring the water of rejuvenation that flows from the Two Caverns.
I sprinkle the water, purifying your image and your Temple from all impurity!

*The Ritualist **picks up the bowl of Natron** and **sprinkles a small amount in each of the four directions** as the following is recited:*

The *Netjeret* Nebet-Hut herself does cleanse and purify this, her Temple to the South.
The *Netjeret* Nebet-Hut herself does cleanse and purify this, her Temple to the North.
The *Netjeret* Nebet-Hut herself does cleanse and purify this, her Temple to the West.
The *Netjeret* Nebet-Hut herself does cleanse and purify this, her Temple to the East.

*Replacing the Natron on the altar, the Ritualist takes up the bowl of **water, sprinkling a small amount in each of the four directions.** The following Utterance is recited:*

The *Netjeret* Nebet-Hut herself does sanctify and consecrate this, her Temple to the South.

Richard J. Reidy

The *Netjeret* Nebet-Hut herself does sanctify and consecrate this, her Temple to the North.
The *Netjeret* Nebet-Hut herself does sanctify and consecrate this, her Temple to the West.
The *Netjeret* Nebet-Hut herself does sanctify and consecrate this, her Temple to the East.
The Temple of the *Netjeret* Nebet-Hut is established.
It is established for millions of years.

*The Ritualist returns to the altar and **lights the candle** or **oil lamp** while the following is said:*

Come, come in peace, O glorious Eye of Heru,
Be strong and renew your youth in peace.
For the flame shines like Ra on the double horizon.
The enemies of Ra are defeated. They are defeated.
I am pure, I am pure, I am pure, I am pure.

*The Ritualist **places incense on the burner and censes each sacred image,** beginning with the statue of the Netjeret, while the following is recited:*

The fire is laid, the fire shines;
The incense is laid on the fire, the incense shines.
    Your perfume comes to me, O Incense;
    May my perfume come to you, O Incense.
Your perfume comes to me, you *Netjeru*;
May my perfume come to you, You *Netjeru*.
    May I be with you, you *Netjeru*;
    May you be with me, you *Netjeru*.
May I live with you, you *Netjeru*;
May you live with me, you *Netjeru*.

I love you, you *Netjeru*;
May you love me, you *Netjeru*.

*Standing in front of the image of Nebet-Hut the Ritualist **offers the burning incense** and says:*

Take the incense,
Its essence is for you, O Daughter of Geb.
Its smoke permeates your shrine, bringing life!
Take the incense,
Its essence is for you.
Your Majesty is appeased with the incense.
This Eye of Heru,
This essence of the Eye of Heru comes to you.

At this point the following is said:

The Ritualist and all present alternate the following verses of this Utterance that combines prayer with a magical spell:

The doors of the sky are opened for me,
The doors of Nut are thrown open for me,
The doors of the sky are opened for me,
The doors of the firmament are thrown open for me.
May Aset say to me, 'Endure!'
May you, O Nebet-Hut, say to me, 'In peace! In peace!'[221]

---

[221] Adapted from PT 536, lines 1291-92. PT refers to Pyramid Text number 536 in R. O. *Faulkner's The Ancient Egyptian Pyramid Texts* (Oxford Univ. Press, 1969). As the author states in the Preface, "One of the great difficulties in translating the Pyramid Texts . . . is the ambiguity . . . as to whether a given sentence is to be understood as a statement or as a wish." (p. viii) It is commonly agreed that the Pyramid as well as the

May I ascend upon the thighs of Aset,
May I climb up upon the thighs of Nebet-Hut,
My father Atum will seize my hand for me,
and he will assign me to those excellent and wise *Netjeru*,
the Imperishable Stars.[222]

May Aset have my arm,
May Nebet-Hut take hold of my hand, so I shall go between them.
The sky is given to me,
The earth is given to me,
And the Fields of Rushes together with the Mounds of Heru
And the Mounds of Setekh are given to me by Atum,
and he who speaks about it is Geb.[223]

Grant that I awake to life, the earth being bright!
O Nebet-Hut, may you favor me so that I do not lose my House of Joy.
May Anpu be content with me,
May Khnum be content with me.
O Nebet-Hut, may you favor me
so that I do not lose my House of Life.[224]

Coffin Texts are magical spells for an individual in a postmortem state. However, a large number of these spells later occur in Books of the Dead where it states that the spells have been proven effective for the living as well as for the departed. In the present ritual, the Utterance combines a number of texts from both the Pyramid Texts as well as the Coffin Texts that serve simultaneously as both prayer and spell. Examples of this sort of combination also appear in other Egyptian magical texts.

[222] PT 269, lines 379-80

[223] PT 477, lines 960-61

[224] CT 53, lines 241-42, in Faulkner's companion volume, *The Ancient Egyptian Coffin Texts*: Spells 1-1185 & Indexes (Oxford: Aris & Phillips,

O Nebet-Hut, may you come and lay hold of me
and place my heart in my body.
May you bring me Heru and his Great-of-Magic.
May you bring me Setekh and his Great-of-Magic.[225]

For I am the redness which came forth from Aset,
I am the blood which issued from Nebet-Hut,
There is nothing the *Netjeru* can do to me,
For I am the representative of Ra and I do not die.
Hear, O Geb, chief of the *Netjeru*, and equip me with my shape;
Hear, O Djehuty, in whom is the peace of the *Netjeru*.
Open, O Heru; guard, O Setekh, that I may rise in the eastern
sky like Ra,
like Ra.[226]

All present recite the final stanza:

My mother is Aset,
My nurse is Nebet-Hut,
Neith is behind me,
And Selket is before me.[227]

*The Ritualist **places more incense** on the charcoal and again and
again **slowly raises and lowers the incense cup** as the following is
recited:*

O Nebet-Hut, may you advance with your *Ka*.
O Lady of Love, the arm of your *Ka* is before you,

1973).
[225] CT 526, line 118
[226] PT 570, lines 1464-65
[227] PT 555, lines 1375

Richard J. Reidy

The arm of your *Ka* is behind you.
O Queen of Heaven Who Protects Her Brother,
the foot of your *Ka* is before you,
The foot of your *Ka* is behind you.
O Beautiful Nebet-Hut, this incense is offered to you,
May your face be filled as this essence spreads itself over you.

*All present **perform the Henu Rite**—Embrace the Earth, the Fourfold Salute to the Goddess, Embrace the Earth.*

For Embracing the Earth, all present prostrate themselves, face down, upon the floor. During the Fourfold Salute, all present rise upon one knee, and alternately raise their hands and arms into the *Dua* (praise) position with palms facing outward, followed by the *Sahu* (obedience) gesture, made by striking the chest with a closed fist and raising the other arm (also with closed fist) at a ninety-degree angle. The *Dua* position is accompanied by the words **"Adoration be to Nebet-Hut,"** followed by the *Sahu* gesture accompanied with the words, **"Hail to the Perfect One of Transfiguration!"** The bodily gestures are performed alternately four times.

Following this all present again prostrate themselves before the sacred image. This is a sign and symbol of total submission and adoration before the Netjeret. The following is said:

Homage be to Nebet-Hut, the Beautiful One,
who is established on the Great Seat!
I have placed myself on the floor in awe of you.
I embrace the earth before you as before the Lady of Perfection.
I have come that I might kiss the earth,
that I might worship my Mistress,
for I have seen her Beauty;

I give praise to Nebet-Hut, She with Perfect Love,
for I have seen her Power.
Her form is more distinguished than the *Netjeru*;
Her arm is more powerful than the *Netjeru*.
I am pure, I am pure, I am pure, I am pure!

Everyone stands up.

*The Ritualist **holds in the palm of one hand the image of Ma'at** and with **the other hand open and raised over the image as if sheltering it**, repeats the following:*

I have come to you as Djehuty, whose two hands are joined together under Ma'at. She comes to be with you, for she is everywhere. You are provided with Ma'at. You move in Ma'at, you live in Ma'at. She fills your body, she rests in your head, she makes her seat upon your brow; the breath of your body is of Ma'at, your heart does live in Ma'at. All that you eat, all that you drink, all that you breathe is of Ma'at. Djehuty presents Ma'at to you, his two hands are upon her beauty before your face.

*The Ritualist places the image of Ma'at near the divine statue. Then he/she holds up before the image of Nebet-Hut **a pitcher of water and pours the water slowly into an offering bowl** as the following Utterance is recited:*

This libation is for you, O Lady of Love.
This libation is for you, O Nebet-Hut.
I have brought to you this offering of water,
That your heart may be refreshed.
I have brought to you this Eye of Heru,

Placing this at your feet.
I present to you that which flows forth from you,
That your heart shall continue to beat.
For it is with you that all comes forth at the sound of the voice.

The offering bowl is placed on the altar. At this point the Ritualist **lightly sprinkles sand on the floor in front of the altar** *as the following is recited:*

O Nebet-Hut, who resides in Sepermeru in the House of Nebet-Hut of Ramesses-Meriamun (the name of her temple in that city),
Take to yourself the Eye of Heru.
You have rescued it, O Mistress of the *Netjeru*.
You have sprinkled with sand the Eye of Heru.

Lifting the offering of milk, the following is said:

Take to yourself this white and sweet milk, created by your mother Nut.
May you live on it, may you be healthy on account of it. May your body be refreshed every day.[228]

Lifting the wine offering before the sacred image, the Ritualist repeats the following:

mn n.t irp irt ḥrw w³dt
[*"mán-niṯ 'úrip írat ḥáru wá'ḏat"*; approximately pronounced *MAHN-neetch OO-rip EE-raht HAH-roo WAH-jat*]

---

[228] Gaber, Amr, *The Central Hall in the Egyptian Temples of the Ptolemaic Period*, Durham theses, Durham University. (2009) Available at Durham E-Theses Online: http://etheses.dur.ac.uk/88/ This offering formula occurs in the central hall of the temple at Edfu. See p. 454 in the dissertation.

Take to Yourself wine, the green Eye of Heru, which I offer to
your *Ka.* [229]
O Queen, how beautiful is your beauty!
May you drink it; may your heart rejoice;
may anger be removed from your face.
It is pure.
[*iw.w w'b* pronounced *"uwú wá'ib"*; approximately *oo-WOO
WAH-ib*]

*The Ritualist places myrrh on the fire and lifts up the smoking
incense while at the same time he lifts up the meat-offering before
the Netjeret, and says the following:*

The scent of myrrh is for your nose. It fills your nostrils; your
heart receives the meat-portions on its scent.[230]

*Slowly elevating the food offerings four times before the image of
the Netjeret, the Ritualist repeats the following:*

I offer to Nebet-Hut, Mistress of the *Netjerut* (goddesses).
All life emanates from you,
All health emanates from you,
All stability emanates from you,
All good fortune emanates from you,
O Nebet-Hut, Lady of Life, forever.

---

[229] Refer to pp. 92, 93, 99, and 105 in Mu-Chou Poo's *Wine and Wine
Offerings in Ancient Egypt* (London & New York: Kegan Paul International,
1995).

[230] Quoted in "Worship and Festivals in an Egyptian Temple," by H. W.
Fairman (publ. by The John Rylands Library, 1954), p. 191.

*The Ritualist **places the food offering before the divine image,** and then all present **extend one hand, palm down, over the offerings** and recite the following:*

May offerings of every kind come forth in abundance, like the things which come forth from the mouth of the *Netjeret.*

piryá pírit ar ḫiráw mi purú:riat ma rá' ni naṯárat. (4 *times)*
[approximately pronounced: peer-YA PEER-it ar khi-RAU mee pu-ROOR-iat ma RA nee nah-TCHAR-at]

May offerings of every kind come forth in abundance, like the things that come forth from the mouth of the *Netjeret.*

*Holding the **Ankh** before the Netjeret, the Ritualist says:*

Live, O Nebet-Hut, Sweetly Beloved, live for all time and for eternity!

ꜥánaḫ niḥáḫ ḏát.
[approximately pronounced *AH-nakh nee-HAH JAHT]*

*The **Ankh** is placed next to the Netjeret.*

*Holding the **Ib (the golden heart)** before the Netjeret, the Ritualist says:*

Hail to you, O Nebet-Hut, Companion of *Wennefer.* I have brought to you your heart to set it in its place. Let me draw near to you with your heart, so that you may have pleasure through me, and so that by means of me you may have power over your body. Ascend, O Lady of Judgment, radiant, rejuvenating, equipped as a *Netjeret*. Live, O Female Kite, live forever and ever!

*After placing the **Ib** near the sacred image, **everyone sings or chants** the hymn to Nebet-Hut. Begin by **slowly playing the sistra**. Participants may wish to alternate the singing of verses.*

I play the sistra before your beautiful face,
Nebet-Hut, Lady of the Sistrum,
Who Drives the Rebels from Where Her Brother is.
You are the Brave One, Powerful of Arm.

I play the sistra for you,
Lady of Love, Mistress of Women,
Who fills heaven and earth with your beauty,
Wet Nurse of the Falcon-of-Gold,
Great Sister of *Wennefer.*
We play our sistra for you.

Female Magician Who Foretells Events,
Reveal to us all evils for us to avoid.
We play our sistra for you for you are the One Who Drives Away Darkness.
Drive far from us the Rebels and those who would work *isfet* (evil).
You are the Panther. May you strike fear in the hearts of the enemies.
You are Mafdet. May you deliver the doers of evil into your claws.
For truly you are the One Effective of Magic.

May your beautiful face be gracious to us who honor you.

**O Lady of Festivals, Lady of the Sistrum, you With Hidden Form,
Whose face enjoys the trickling of fresh myrrh.**[231]
O Mighty One, be gracious, be gracious to us who serve you.

At this point perform the **meditation or magical action** *or, if it is a special feast, add the appropriate prayers.*

Afterwards **all present back out of the Temple Chamber with heads slightly bowed** *while the Ritualist performs the* **"removing the foot."**

With the broom the Ritualist, as the last person to exit, **ritually sweeps the area beginning at the altar.** *(This is known as "removing the foot.") While performing this action the Ritualist recites the following:*

The distress that causes confusion has been driven away,
and all the *Netjeru* are in harmony.
I have given Heru his Eye;
I have placed the *Wedjat*-Eye in the correct position.
I have given Setekh his Testicles,
so that the two lords are content through the work of my hands.

I know the sky, I know the earth;
I know Heru, I know Setekh.
Heru is appeased with his Eyes;
Setekh is appeased with his Testicles.
I am Djehuty, who reconciles the *Netjeru,*
who makes offerings in their correct form.

The **double doors are solemnly closed** *as the Ritualist says the following:*

231

Djehuty has come.

He has filled the Eye of Heru;

He has restored the Testicles of Setekh.

No evil shall enter this Temple.

Ptah has closed the door,

Djehuty has set it fast.

The door is closed, the door is set fast with the bolt.

All bow, touching the palms of their hands to their knees.

THE REVERSION OF OFFERINGS

One priest or priestess and as many assistants as necessary enter the Temple Chamber a final time. While he/she and any assistants lift up the offerings before the sacred image the ritualist shall say:

O Nebet-Hut, your enemy[232] withdraws for you. Heru has turned himself to his Eye in its name of 'Reversion-of-Offerings.' I am Djehuty. I come to perform this rite for Nebet-Hut, queen of the *Netjeru* Who Lights Up the Horizon. These, your divine offerings revert, they revert to your servants for life, for stability, for health and for joy! O that the Eye of Heru may flourish for you eternally!

Everyone withdraws, carrying away all food offerings except for one loaf of bread together with a bowl of pure water. These last items

---

[232] Meat offerings held a two-fold meaning for the ancient priesthood. Since meat necessarily came from slain animals, it signified the defeated or slain enemies of the Netjeret. At the same time, the meat offering represented the produce of the land which ultimately was a gift of the Netjeru.

will remain until evening. If this ritual is celebrated after sunset, these items would also be removed[233].

After the candle has burned down, a servant-priest enters and closes the doors of the Kar-shrine.

Extinguishing the candle or oil lamp, *he/she exclaims:*

This is the Eye of Heru by which you have become great, by which you live, and by which you have power, O Nebet-Hut. This is the Eye of Heru which you consume and through which you enchant your body. The *Wedjat*-Eye now enters into the West, into *Manu*, but it shall return. Truly, the Eye of Heru returns in peace!

---

[233] It is important to consume the food offerings after the ceremony. Water used should either be drunk or poured onto the earth. If it is mixed with natron, dilute it very greatly and then you can pour in onto the earth without harming any plantings.

The General Ritual for Nefertum

All epithets of the god are based on those found in the *Lexikon der ägyptischen Götter und Götterbezeichnungen* (Dictionary of Egyptian Gods and God-Epithets"), eight volumes. The epithets are capitalized in order to facilitate identification.

Like members of the ancient priesthood, participants should be clothed in white linen or cotton. No item made of animal products such as leather or wool is to be worn.

As with all Egyptian rituals begin with your purification—washing of hands and cleansing of mouth with Natron. This preliminary rite helps us to lay aside the cares of the day and to become mindful of the fact that we will encounter a divine being. If Natron is not available, then use a natural sea salt in its place until you make your own Natron.

If two or more persons are participating, then one person, impersonating the Netjer Djehuty, **purifies each person by sprinkling each with water** *while exclaiming:*

I purify you with the water of all life and good fortune, all stability, all health and happiness.[234]

---

[234] Taken from Aylward M. Blackman's article "Purification (Egyptian)" in Hastings Encyclopaedia 10/1918/ 476-82. This article is reprinted in Gods, Priests, and Men, Studies in the Religion of Pharaonic Egypt, edited by Alan B. Lloyd (Kegan Paul International, 1998), p. 9.

*Afterwards each person **rinses his mouth** and places **a small amount of Natron or sea salt in his mouth** while saying:*

I wash my mouth; I chew natron so that I may extol the might of Nefertum Who Comes Forth from the Horizon, the Great Protector.[235]

*Participants **assemble outside the Temple Chamber** and begin by softly rattling sistra.*

This time—several minutes or more—is used to focus minds and intention so that distracting thoughts are left behind. The sound of the sistrum was said to placate the deity, purifying the atmosphere in preparation for encountering divinity. The sistrum was associated with Hutheru and also with her and Heru's son Ihy, and thus has connotations of joy, celebration, and dancing. According to Plutarch (A.D. 46-120), the sound of sistra was also reputed to drive away Setekh. But this was of very late date. It may have been that since by that time Setekh had been demonized, the general apotropaic function of the sistrum against evil entities was extended to include this *Netjer* as well.

*Standing **before the closed doors**, the Ritualist **recites the entrance spell:***

---

[235] Based on a temple inscription taken from "The Myth of Horus at Edfu—II" by A. M. Blackman and H. W. Fairman, appearing in Gods, Priests and Men, Studies in the Religion of Pharaonic Egypt (Kegan Paul International, 1998) p. 283.

UTTERANCE BEFORE THE CLOSED DOORS OF THE TEMPLE

The ritualist *raises hands in adoration (dua position-arms stretched out in front of the body and raised up to face level, with palms facing outward). The following shall be said:*

O you *Netjeru* of this Temple, you guardians of the great portal, great *Netjeru* of mysterious abode, who sanctify the god in his shrine, who consecrate his oblation, who receive the offerings in his presence in the Hall of the Ennead: I have made my way and I enter into your presence. I am one of you. I am Shu, the eldest son of his father, the senior *wab* servant-priest of Nefertum. Do not repulse me on the *Netjer's* path. My feet are not impeded. I am not turned back from the court of the great portal so that I may conduct the divine service, that I may present offerings to him that made them, that I may give bread to Nefertum. I have come on the way of the god. I have not shown partiality in judgment. I have not consorted with the strong. I have not reproached the lowly. I have not stolen things. I have not diminished the constituents of the Eye of Ra. I have not disturbed the Balance. I have not tampered with the requirements of the Sacred Eye. O Council of the Great *Netjer* in this Temple, behold, I have come to you to offer Ma'at to the Lord of Ma'at, to content the Sound Eye for its lord. I am Shu; I flood his offering table. I present his offerings, Sekhmet consorting with me, that I may adore Nefertum at his festivals, that I may kiss the earth so great is his majesty, that I may endow his image with life. I am pure. I am purified.

At this point the ritualist *opens the doors to the Temple Chamber, or, if there are no doors, makes a gesture of opening unseen doors, and steps forward as if crossing over a threshold. The following is said:*

O you *Ba*-souls of *Mennefer* (Memphis) if you are strong, I am strong. If I am strong, you are strong. If your *Ka*-spirits are strong, my *Ka*-spirit is strong at the head of the living. As they are living so shall I live . . . . Nefertum, Lord of *Ka*-spirits, has given to me life, stability, and serenity round about my members, which Djehuty has gathered together for life. I am Heru in the height of heaven, the beautiful one of awe, Lord of Victory, mighty one of awe, exalted one of the two plumes, great one in Thebes, I am pure.

All temple members chant:

Awake in peace, O Nefertum, Foremost of the Temple of Ptah,
may you awaken in peace.
Awake in peace, O Nefertum, Son of Sekhmet,
may you awaken in peace.
Awake in peace, O Nefertum, Lord of Eternity,
may you awaken in peace.
Awake in peace, O Nefertum, Great Protector,
may you awaken in peace.

May you awake beautifully at the top of the morning,
through that which the entirety of the *Netjeru* say to you.

Enter, **close the double doors** *and* **stand in front of the Kar-shrine and altar.** *All bow, touching their hands to their knees.*

The ritualist *slowly* **opens the two doors of the Kar-shrine** *housing the sacred image. All others bow, touching their hands to their knees. The following is said:*

The doors of the sky are open; the doors of the earth are unlocked. This House is open for its Lord. Let me come forth as he shall come forth. Let me enter in as he shall enter in. Nefertum, the Lord of *Ka*-spirits, Great of Strength, is exalted upon his Great Seat. The Great Company of the *Netjeru* are exalted upon their seat.

I have seen the *Netjer,* and the *Netjer* sees me. The *Netjer* rejoices at seeing me. I have gazed upon the statue of the Great Lotus, the sacred image of the Great Protector.[236]

Right hand on left shoulder of statue; left hand on right wrist of statue:

Djehuty has come to you. Awake when you hear his words. I have come as the envoy of Atum. My two arms are upon you like those of Heru. My two hands are upon you like those of Djehuty. My fingers are upon you like those of Anpu. Homage be to you. I am a living servant of Nefertum.

*The Ritualist holds up the **bowl of water** in which he/she will be mixing the Natron. The following is said:*

O water may you remove all evil,
As Ra who bathes in the Lake of Rushes,
May Heru wash my flesh,
May Djehuty cleanse my feet,
May Shu lift me up and Nut take my hand!
May Set be my strength, and may Sekhmet be my healing!
And may Amun-Ra be my life and my prospering!

---

[236] Based on the temple text found in "Worship and Festivals in an Egyptian Temple," a lecture by H. W. Fairman (publ. by The John Rylands Library, 1954), p. 180.

Richard J. Reidy

*The bowl of water is set aside and the container of **Natron** is lifted up. The following is said:*

It is pure, it is pure.
My Natron is the Natron of Heru and the Natron of Heru is my Natron.
My Natron is the Natron of Setekh and the Natron of Setekh is my Natron.
My Natron is the Natron of Djehuty, and the Natron of Djehuty is my Natron.
My Natron is the Natron of Geb and the Natron of Geb is my Natron.

My mouth is the mouth of a milking calf on the day that I was born.

Four pinches of Natron are mixed into the water as this Utterance is recited:

I give you essential water, a tide in your time.
I bring the flood waters to purify your sanctuary in the Temple of Ptah.
I bring you the flood waters to purify your Temple and your statue in its place, the primordial water that purifies as in the First Time!

*The Ritualist places an **index finger into the water** and **moves it in a circular direction four times** as the following is said:*

Nefertum, Divine *Netjer*, does purify this water;
Nefertum, Who Comes Forth from the Horizon, does cleanse this water;
Nefertum, the Lotus at the Nose of Ra, does sanctify this water;

Nefertum himself does endow this water with power and with life.

*The **Bowl of Natron-infused water** is then taken up and the **Ritualist** sprinkles this lightly in front of and around the statue or image of Nefertum, applying some of the water to the base of the image, as the Utterance is recited:*

I come close to you, O Divine *Netjer* and Protector.
I bring the water of rejuvenation that flows from the Two Caverns.
I sprinkle the water, purifying your image and your Temple from all impurity!

*The Ritualist picks up the bowl of **Natron** and **sprinkles a small amount in each of the four directions** as the following is recited:*

The *Netjer* Nefertum himself does cleanse and purify this, his Temple to the South.
The *Netjer* Nefertum himself does cleanse and purify this, his Temple to the North.
The *Netjer* Nefertum himself does cleanse and purify this, his Temple to the West.
The *Netjer* Nefertum himself does cleanse and purify this, his Temple to the East.

*Replacing the Natron on the altar, the Ritualist **takes up the bowl of water, sprinkling a small amount in each of the four directions**. The following Utterance is recited:*

The *Netjer* Nefertum himself does sanctify and consecrate this, his Temple to the South.

The *Netjer* Nefertum himself does sanctify and consecrate this, his Temple to the North.

The *Netjer* Nefertum himself does sanctify and consecrate this, his Temple to the West.

The *Netjer* Nefertum himself does sanctify and consecrate this, his Temple to the East.

The Temple of the *Netjer* Nefertum is established. It is established for millions of years.

*The Ritualist returns to the altar and **lights the candle or oil lamp** while the following is said:*

Come, come in peace, O glorious Eye of Heru,
Be strong and renew your youth in peace.
For the flame shines like Ra on the double horizon.
The enemies of Ra are defeated. They are defeated.
I am pure, I am pure, I am pure, I am pure.

*The Ritualist **places incense** on the burner and **censes each sacred image** beginning with the statue of Nefertum while the following is recited:*

The fire is laid, the fire shines;
The incense is laid on the fire, the incense shines.
    Your perfume comes to me, O Incense;
    May my perfume come to you, O Incense.
Your perfume comes to me, you *Netjeru*;
May my perfume come to you, You *Netjeru*.
    May I be with you, you *Netjeru*;
    May you be with me, you *Netjeru*.
May I live with you, you *Netjeru*;

May you live with me, you *Netjeru*.
I love you, you *Netjeru*;
May you love me, you *Netjeru*.

Standing in front of the image of Nefertum the Ritualist **offers the burning incense** *and says:*

Take the incense,
Its essence is for you.
Its smoke permeates your shrine, bringing life!
Take the incense,
Its essence is for you.
Your Majesty is appeased with the incense.
This Eye of Heru,
This essence of the Eye of Heru comes to you.

At this point the following is said:

Greeting to you, O Nefertum, who comes forth as the Lotus revealing the divine sun. Truly you are the Beautiful Lotus at the Nose of Ra. Each sunrise you are the Praise Giver. You are the Protector and Leader of the People. Grant us now your protection. You are the One Who Makes the People Live. Grant us life, strength, and health so that we may praise you, O Flourishing *Ka*-spirit. Praise be to you, Nefertum!

The Ritualist places **more incense** *on the charcoal and again and again* **slowly raises and lowers the incense cup** *as the following is recited:*

O Nefertum, may you advance with your *Ka*.
O Great of Strength, the arm of your *Ka* is before you,
The arm of your *Ka* is behind you.
O Perfect Power, the foot of your *Ka* is before you,

The foot of your *Ka* is behind you.
O Nefertum, Lord of Protection, this incense is offered to you,
May your face be filled as this essence spreads itself over you.

All present perform the **Henu Rite**—*Embrace the Earth, the Fourfold Salute to the God, Embrace the Earth.*

For Embracing the Earth, all present prostrate themselves, face down, upon the floor. During the Fourfold Salute, all present rise upon one knee, and alternately raise their hands and arms into the *Dua* (praise) position with palms facing outward, followed by the *Sahu* (obedience) gesture, made by striking the chest with a closed fist and raising the other arm (also with closed fist) at a ninety-degree angle. The *Dua* position is accompanied by the words **"Adoration be to Nefertum,"** followed by the *Sahu* gesture accompanied with the words, **"Hail to the Lord of Eternity!"** The bodily gestures are performed alternately four times.

Following this **all present again prostrate themselves** *before the god. This is a sign and symbol of total submission and adoration before the Netjer. The following is said:*

Homage to Nefertum, the Perfect Powerful One,
who is established on the Great Seat!
I have placed myself on the floor in awe of you.
I embrace the earth before you as before the Lord of Terror.
I have come that I might kiss the earth,
that I might worship my Lord,
For I have seen his Strength;
I give praise to Nefertum,
For I have seen his Power.
His form is more distinguished than the *Netjeru*;
His arm is more powerful than the *Netjeru*.

I am pure, I am pure, I am pure, I am pure!

*Everyone stands up. The Ritualist **holds in the palm of one hand the image of Ma'at** and with **the other hand open and raised over the image as if sheltering it**, repeats the following:*

I have come to you as Djehuty, whose two hands are joined together under Ma'at. She comes to be with you, for she is everywhere. You are provided with Ma'at. You move in Ma'at, you live in Ma'at. She fills your body, she rests in your head, she makes her seat upon your brow; the breath of your body is of Ma'at, your heart does live in Ma'at. All that you eat, all that you drink, all that you breathe is of Ma'at. Djehuty presents Ma'at to you, his two hands are upon her beauty before your face.

*The Ritualist places the image of Ma'at near the divine statue. Then he/she holds up before the image of Nefertum **a pitcher of water** and **pours the water slowly into an offering bowl** as the following Utterance is recited:*

This libation is for you, O Son of Sekhmet and Ptah.
This libation is for you, O Nefertum, Lord of Eternity.
I have brought to you this offering of water,
That your heart may be refreshed.
I have brought to you this Eye of Heru,
Placing this at your feet.
I present to you that which flows forth from you,
That your heart shall continue to beat.
For it is with you that all comes forth at the sound of the voice.

The offering bowl is placed on the altar. At this point the Ritualist **lightly sprinkles sand on the floor in front of the altar** *as the following is recited:*

O Nefertum, who resides in **Mennefer** (Memphis),
Take to yourself the Eye of Heru.
You have rescued it, O Perfect Power.
You have sprinkled with sand the Eye of Heru.

Lifting the wine offering *before the sacred image, the Ritualist repeats the following:*

mn n.k irp irt ḥrw w3ḏt
[*"mán-nik 'úrip írat ḥáru wá'ḏat"*; approximately pronounced *MAHN-neek OO-rip EE-raht HAH-roo WAH-jat*]

"Take to Yourself wine, the green Eye of Heru, which I offer to your **Ka**.
O Ruler, how beautiful is your beauty!
May you drink it; may your heart rejoice;
may anger be removed from your face.
It is pure." [*iw.w w'b* pronounced *"uwú wá'ib"*; approximately *oo-WOO WAH-ib*]

Calling the Netjer to his meal:

Come to me, Nefertum, my **Netjer,** Adjudicator of the **Netjeru,** who brings his **heka,** his **Ba,** his **Sekhem**-power, and his acclaim, to this your bread, to this your beer, to these offerings of many kinds. The Eye of **Heru** has been brought for you! Furnish yourself with it! Come to me, Nefertum, adjudicator of the **Netjeru,** for every good and fresh thing has entered for you into your temple. I appease you, Nefertum. I am Djehuty and I appease you with the Eye of Heru, having brought you your meal of what is in heaven, and what is on earth. Your meal is the meal of Heru with his Eye. Your meal is the meal of Setekh with his Testicles. You have satisfied Heru with his Eye. You have satisfied Setekh with his Testicles. What you have sought is brought to you. What you have requested is brought to you.[237]

The Ritualist **places myrrh on the fire** *and* **lifts up the smoking incense** *while at the same time* **he lifts up the meat-offering** *before the Netjer, and says the following:*

The scent of myrrh is for your nose. It fills your nostrils; your heart receives the meat-portions on its scent[238].

Slowly elevating the **food offerings** *four times before the image of Nefertum, the Ritualist repeats the following:*

I offer to Nefertum, Lord of Nourishment and Leader of the People.
All life emanates from you,
All health emanates from you,
All stability emanates from you,
All good fortune emanates from you,
O Nefertum, Flourishing of Appearances, forever.

---

[237] From the Nefertum Chapel of Sety I at Abydos: North Wall, Lower Register, Middle. Translated from Auguste Mariette's *Abydos: description des fouilles executees sur l'emplacement de cette ville,* Vol. I, (Paris, 1869).
[238] Quoted in "Worship and Festivals in an Egyptian Temple," by H. W. Fairman (publ. by The John Rylands Library, 1954), p. 191.

The Ritualist **places the food offering before the divine image,** *and then* **all present extend one hand, palm down, over the offerings** *and recite the following:*

May offerings of every kind come forth in abundance, like the things which come forth from the mouth of the Netjer.

piryá pírit ar ḫiráw mi purú:riat ma rá' ni náṯar. (4 times)
[approximately pronounced: peer-YA PEER-it ar khi-RAU mee pu-ROOR-iat ma RA nee NAH-tchar]

May offerings of every kind come forth in abundance, like the things that come forth from the mouth of the Netjer.

Holding the **Ankh** *before Nefertum, the Ritualist says:*

Live, O Nefertum, lord of the Netjeru, **live for all time and for eternity!**

ꜥánaḫ niḥáḥ ḏát.
[approximately pronounced *AH-nakh nee-HAH JAHT*]

The **Ankh** *is placed next to the image of the Netjer.*

Holding the **Ib (the golden heart)** *before Nefertum, the Ritualist says:*

Hail to you, O Nefertum, Lord of Protection. I have brought to you your heart to set it in its place. Let me draw near to you with your heart, so that you may have pleasure through me, and so that by means of me you may have power over your body. Ascend, O Perfect Powerful One, radiant, rejuvenating, equipped as a Netjer. **Live, O Lord of the Phallus, live forever and ever!**

*After placing the **Ib** near the sacred image, **everyone sings or chants** the hymn to Nefertum. Participants may wish to alternate the singing of verses.*

I invoke Nefertum, in the following of Ptah. You are the guardian and protector of the perfume and oil makers, protector and **Netjer** of the sacred lotus. Ausir is the body of the plants; you, O Nefertum, are the soul of the plants, the plants purified. The divine perfume belongs to you, O Nefertum, living forever.[239]

Praise be to you O Son of Sekhmet and Ptah. Praise to you, Nefertum, for you are He Who Causes Ill Health to be Distant from Bodies. May you drive away from us who honor you every illness and affliction.

O Lord of Terror, you are the Great Protector. Protect us from everything that can harm us. You are the One over His Flame. May you drive away from us every harmful thing. O Perfect Power, defend us. As you are He Who Protects Sokar by Your Own Perfection, protect us and those whom we love from all harmful things.

Praise be to you, O Lord of Flourishing Appearances. You are the One Clad in the Green Fabric of Heru. Place the strong arms of your protection around us, O Lord of the **Ka**. Praise be to you, O Nefertum!

*At this point perform the **meditation or magical action** or, if it is a special feast, add the appropriate prayers.*

---

[239] Steve Van Toller, G. H. Todd, "Hymn to Nefertem," *Fragrance: Psychology and Biology of Perfume* (Springer, 1992), p. 290.

Richard J. Reidy

*Afterwards **all present back out of the Temple Chamber with heads slightly bowed** while the Ritualist performs the **"removing the foot."***

*With the **broom** the Ritualist, as the last person to exit, **ritually sweeps the area beginning at the altar**. (This is known as "removing the foot.") While performing this action the Ritualist recites the following:*

The distress that causes confusion has been driven away, and all the *Netjeru* are in harmony. I have given Heru his Eye; I have placed the *Wedjat*-Eye in the correct position. I have given Setekh his Testicles, so that the two lords are content through the work of my hands.

I know the sky, I know the earth;
I know Heru, I know Setekh.
Heru is appeased with his Eyes;
Setekh is appeased with his Testicles.
I am Djehuty, who reconciles the *Netjeru*,
who makes offerings in their correct form.

The double doors are solemnly closed as the Ritualist says the following:

Djehuty has come.
He has filled the Eye of Heru;
He has restored the Testicles of Setekh.
No evil shall enter this Temple.
Ptah has closed the door,
Djehuty has set it fast.
The door is closed, the door is set fast with the bolt.

All bow, touching the palms of their hands to their knees.

THE REVERSION OF OFFERINGS

*One priest or priestess and as many assistants as necessary enter the Temple Chamber a final time. While he/she and any assistants **lift up the offerings** before the sacred image the ritualist shall say:*

O Nefertum, your enemy[240] withdraws for you. Heru has turned himself to his Eye in its name of 'Reversion-of-Offerings.' I am Djehuty. I come to perform this rite for Nefertum, Lord of the *Netjeru*. These, your divine offerings revert, they revert to your servants for life, for stability, for health and for joy! O that the Eye of Heru may flourish for you eternally!

*Everyone withdraws, **carrying away all food offerings except for one loaf of bread together with a bowl of pure water.** These last items will remain until evening. If this ritual is celebrated after sunset, these items would also be removed.*

After the candle has burned down, a servant-priest enters and closes the doors of the Kar-shrine.

***Extinguishing the candle or oil lamp,** he/she exclaims:*

This is the Eye of Heru by which you have become great, by which you live, and by which you have power, O Nefertum.

---

[240] Meat offerings held a two-fold meaning for the ancient priesthood. Since meat necessarily came from slain animals, it signified the defeated or slain enemies of the Netjer. At the same time, the meat offering represented the produce of the land which ultimately was a gift of the Netjeru.

This is the Eye of Heru which you consume and through which you enchant your body. The *Wedjat*-Eye now enters into the West, into *Manu*, but it shall return. Truly, the Eye of Heru returns in peace![241]

---

[241] It is important to consume the food offerings after the ceremony. Water used should either be drunk or poured onto the earth. If it is mixed with natron, dilute it very greatly and then you can pour in onto the earth without harming any plantings.

The General Ritual for Neith

The general ritual for Neith also forms the first part of the Brilliant Festival of Lights of Neith and is incorporated into that ritual as well.

Like members of the ancient priesthood, participants should be clothed in white linen, or, if necessary, white cotton. No items made of animal products such as leather or wool are to be worn.

As with all Egyptian rituals begin with your purification—washing of hands and cleansing of mouth with Natron. This preliminary rite helps us to lay aside the cares of the day and to become mindful of the fact that we will encounter a divine being. If Natron is not available, then use a natural sea salt in its place until you make your own Natron.

If two or more persons are participating, then one person, impersonating the Netjer Djehuty, **purifies each person by sprinkling each with water** *while exclaiming:*

I purify you with the water of all life and good fortune, all stability, all health and happiness.[242]

Afterwards each person **rinses his mouth** *and* **places a small amount of Natron or sea salt** *in his mouth while saying the following:*

---

[242] Taken from Aylward M. Blackman's article "Purification (Egyptian)" in Hastings Encyclopaedia 10/1918/ 476-82. This article is reprinted in Gods, Priests, and Men, Studies in the Religion of Pharaonic Egypt, edited by Alan B. Lloyd (Kegan Paul International, 1998), p. 9.

I wash my mouth; I chew natron so that I may extol the might of Neith, Mother of Ra, She Who Comes Forth from Nun.[243]

*Participants **assemble outside the Temple Chamber** and begin by softly rattling sistra.*

This time—several minutes or more—is used to focus minds and intention so that distracting thoughts are left behind. The sound of the sistrum was said to placate the deity, purifying the atmosphere in preparation for encountering divinity. The sistrum was associated with Hutheru and also with her and Heru's son Ihy, and thus has connotations of joy, celebration, and dancing. According to Plutarch (A.D. 46-120), the sound of sistra was also reputed to drive away Setekh. But this was of late date. It may have been that since by that time Setekh had been demonized, the general apotropaic function of the sistrum against evil entities was extended to include this *Netjer* as well.

*Standing **before the closed doors,** the Liturgist **recites the entrance spell:***

UTTERANCE BEFORE THE CLOSED DOORS OF THE TEMPLE

*The ritualist **raises hands in adoration** (dua position—arms stretched out in front of the body and raised up to face level, with palms facing outward). The following shall be said:*

O you *Netjeru* of this Temple, you guardians of the great portal, great *Netjeru* of mysterious abode, who sanctify the *Netjeret* in her shrine, who consecrate her oblation, who receive the

---

[243] Adapted from a temple inscription taken from "The Myth of Horus at Edfu—II" by A. M. Blackman and H. W. Fairman, appearing in Gods, Priests and Men, Studies in the Religion of Pharaonic Egypt, p. 283.

offerings in her presence in the Hall of the Ennead: I have made my way and I enter into your presence. I am one of you. I am Shu, the eldest son of his father, the senior *wab* servant-priest of Neith. Do not repulse me on the *Netjeret's* path. My feet are not impeded. I am not turned back from the court of the great portal so that I may conduct the divine service, that I may present offerings to her that made them, that I may give bread to Neith. I have come on the way of the *Netjeret*. I have not shown partiality in judgment. I have not consorted with the strong. I have not reproached the lowly. I have not stolen things. I have not diminished the constituents of the Eye of Ra. I have not disturbed the Balance. I have not tampered with the requirements of the Sacred Eye. O Council of the Great *Netjeret* in this Temple, behold, I have come to you to offer Ma'at to the Lady of Ma'at,

to content the Sound Eye for its mistress. I am Shu; I flood her offering table. I present her offerings, Sekhmet consorting with me, that I may adore Neith at her festivals, that I may kiss the earth so great is her majesty, that I may endow her image with life. I am pure. I am purified.

At this point the ritualist **opens the doors to the Temple Chamber, or, if there are no doors, makes a gesture of opening unseen doors, and steps forward as if crossing over a threshold.** *The following is said:*

O you *Ba*-souls of *Sau* (i.e., Sais[244]), if you are strong, I am strong. If I am strong, you are strong. If your *Ka*-spirits are strong, my *Ka*-spirit is strong at the head of the living. As they are living so shall I live . . . . Sekhmet, the great *Netjeret*, beloved of Ptah, has given to me life, stability, and serenity round about my members, which Djehuty has gathered together for life. I am

---

[244] Sau (Greek, Sais) is the cult center for Neith.

Heru in the height of heaven, the beautiful one of awe, Lord of Victory, mighty one of awe, exalted one of the two plumes, great one in *Abdju* (Abydos) I am pure.

All temple members chant:

Awake in peace, O Neith, Ruler of Heaven,
may you awaken in peace.
Awake in peace, O Neith, Mistress of Life,
may you awaken in peace.
Awake in peace, O Neith, Lady of Perfection,
may you awaken in peace.
Awake in peace, O Neith, Lady of Jubilation,
may you awaken in peace.

Enter, **close the double doors** *and* **stand in front of the Kar-shrine and altar. All bow, touching their hands to their knees.**

The ritualist **slowly opens the two doors of the Kar-shrine** *housing the sacred image. All others bow, touching their hands to their knees. The following is said:*

The doors of the sky are open; the doors of the earth are unlocked. This House is open for its Mistress. Let me come forth as she shall come forth. Let me enter in as she shall enter in. Neith, Ruler of the *Netjeru* of the earth, is exalted upon her Great Seat. The Great Company of the *Netjeru* are exalted upon their seat.

I have seen the *Netjeret*, and the *Netjeret* sees me. The *Netjeret* rejoices at seeing me. I have gazed upon the statue of the

Greatly Secret One, the sacred image of the Greatly Sublime One.[245]

Right hand on left shoulder of the sacred image; Left hand on right wrist:

Djehuty has come to you. Awake when you hear his words. I have come as the envoy of Atum. My two arms are upon you like those of Heru. My two hands are upon you like those of Djehuty. My fingers are upon you like those of Anpu. Homage be to you. I am a living servant of Neith.

*The Liturgist holds up the **bowl of water** in which he/she will be mixing the Natron. The following is said:*

O water may you remove all evil,
As Ra who bathes in the Lake of Rushes,
May Heru wash my flesh,
May Djehuty cleanse my feet,
May Shu lift me up and Nut take my hand!
May Setekh be my strength, and may Sekhmet be my healing!
And may Amun-Ra be my life and my prospering!

*The bowl of water is set aside and the container of **Natron** is lifted up. The following is said:*

It is pure, it is pure.
My Natron is the Natron of Heru and the Natron of Heru is my Natron.

---

[245] Based on a passage in "Worship and Festivals in an Egyptian Temple," a lecture by H. W. Fairman (publ. by The John Rylands Library, 1954), p.180.

My Natron is the Natron of Setekh and the Natron of Setekh is my Natron.

My Natron is the Natron of Djehuty, and the Natron of Djehuty is my Natron.

My Natron is the Natron of Geb and the Natron of Geb is my Natron.

My mouth is the mouth of a milking calf on the day that I was born.

Four pinches of Natron are mixed into the water as this Utterance is recited:

I give you essential water, a tide in your time.

I bring the flood waters to purify your sanctuary.

I bring you the flood waters to purify your Temple and your statue in its place, the primordial water that purifies as in the First Time!

The Liturgist places an index finger into the water and moves it in a circular direction four times as the following is said:

Neith, Who Raises up What Exists, does purify this water;

Neith, Who Created Nun, does cleanse this water;

Neith, the One Who Brings to Life, the Vivifier, does sanctify this water;

Neith herself does endow this water with power and with life.

The Bowl of Natron-infused water is then taken up and the Ritualist sprinkles this lightly in front of and around the statue or image of Neith, applying some water to the base of the image, as the Utterance is recited:

I come close to You, O Protectress of the First Primordial Order.
I bring the water of rejuvenation that flows from the Two Caverns.
I sprinkle the water, purifying your image and your Temple from all impurity!

*The Liturgist picks up the bowl of **Natron** and **sprinkles a small amount in each of the four directions** as the following is recited:*

The *Netjeret* Neith herself does cleanse and purify this, her Temple to the South.
The *Netjeret* Neith herself does cleanse and purify this, her Temple to the North.
The *Netjeret* Neith herself does cleanse and purify this, her Temple to the West.
The *Netjeret* Neith herself does cleanse and purify this, her Temple to the East.

*Replacing the Natron on the altar, the Liturgist **takes up the bowl of water, sprinkling a small amount in each of the four directions**. The following Utterance is recited:*

The *Netjeret* Neith herself does sanctify and consecrate this, her Temple to the South.
The *Netjeret* Neith herself does sanctify and consecrate this, her Temple to the North.
The *Netjeret* Neith herself does sanctify and consecrate this, her Temple to the West.
The *Netjeret* Neith herself does sanctify and consecrate this, her Temple to the East.
The Temple of the *Netjeret* Neith herself is established.
It is established for millions of years.

Richard J. Reidy

*The Liturgist returns to the altar and **lights the candle or oil lamp** while the following is said:*

Come, come in peace, O glorious Eye of Heru,
Be strong and renew your youth in peace.
For the flame shines like Ra on the double horizon.
The enemies of Ra are defeated. They are defeated.
I am pure, I am pure, I am pure, I am pure.

*The Liturgist **places incense on the burner** and **censes each sacred image** beginning with the statue of the Netjeret while the following is recited:*

The fire is laid, the fire shines;
The incense is laid on the fire, the incense shines.
　Your perfume comes to me, O Incense;
　May my perfume come to you, O Incense.
Your perfume comes to me, you *Netjeru*;
May my perfume come to you, You *Netjeru*.
　May I be with you, you *Netjeru*;
　May you be with me, you *Netjeru*.
May I live with you, you *Netjeru*;
May you live with me, you *Netjeru*.
　I love you, you *Netjeru*;
　May you love me, you *Netjeru*.

*Standing in front of the image of Neith the Liturgist **offers the burning incense** and says:*

Take the incense,
Its essence is for you.
Its smoke permeates your shrine, bringing life!
Take the incense,

Its essence is for you.
Your Majesty is appeased with the incense.
This Eye of Heru,
This essence of the Eye of Heru comes to you.

At this point the following hymn of joy from the temple at Esna is recited:

The sky is in celebration,
the earth rejoices,
the temples are entranced in joy,
the *Netjeru* (gods) cheer,
the *Netjerut* (goddesses) show their joy,
and humankind venerates her appearance:
Neith, the great, the powerful,
who creates the beings
and spreads joy in her city,
makes her morning appearance in her palace,
accompanied by all life, all time, all power.
Nut the Great pushes back the storm clouds,
drives away the rain before Neith,
so that the sky shines brightly,
and the earth is luminescent,
because as Nut Neith the Great rises,
in order to form from it the heavens.
We enact our celebration once again,
the day of the celebration of 'raising the sky,'
because as Tatenen she appears another time.

Eternity is the name one gives to her majesty:
It is, in fact, Tatenen,
two thirds of her being masculine,

one third is feminine;
she created the rays of light,
drives away obscurity,
covering the solar disk with its luminous brilliance,
and concealing it in its pupil [eye].
At its rising,
she places its light in the world,
in order that each one be able to distinguish himself from his companion.
Appearing in the form of the moon,
she drives away obscurity.
Because it is as if she is Nut, in whom the *Netjer* of the horizon rises and sets,
the *Netjeret* who has no [physical] limits,
and through whom one can know the temporal limits.
Brilliant like the sun,
rising as the moon,
she illumines the shores with her splendor.
She created what is,
she created the beings,
giving birth to all things endowed with life.
Sky [Heaven] is the name one gives to her Majesty;
she gave a beginning to the earth according to her plans,
and she made all things as a creation of her heart.
When she traverses the sky by following her heart,
her son, Ra, is jubilant before her,
the two arms raised in adoration before the mistress of the *Netjeru*,
making up hymns as an act of grace for his powerful mother,
[as when she gives birth to him] like a child in the morning.
Ra himself presents the morning song to her person.
Young man having passed a certain age,

it is (from then on) **Ra-Horakhty who hails her glory;**
Man having attained the strength of age,
it is [finally] **Atum who kisses the earth before her face.**
Netjeru and *Netjerut* are in adoration
and the First Ancestors bow down before her intensity.
The Great Ennead is present and the Little Ennead bows its
head.
The Great Horizon, solemnly clouds in itself,
because the Lady of Awe has illuminated the earth.
The *Netjeru* of the South are bowed down,
the *Netjeru* of the North bow down their heads,
those of the West make the gesture of welcome to her,
and the East is in adoration.
The inhabitants of the horizon worship her glory;
the Souls of the East praise and cry out, 'Praise!'
And the great *Netjeru*, reunited in a single group,
gaze upon their mother,
who is at the same time *Netjer* and *Netjeret*
and each *Netjer* says to his consort:[246]

UNION OF THE SUN / 2 HYMNS OF JOY

'Let us sing praises to the queen of the *Netjeru*,
let us exalt the great of prestige;
let us show our joy to the lady of love,
let us reconcile ourselves with the graces of the All Powerful
in her shrine:
let us cry out in a loud roar in honor of the Cow (of the Sky);
let us satisfy with our praises
the heart of the Lady of the Sky and of the Earth,

---

[246] Serge Sauneron, *Les fêtes religieuses d'Esna*, (=*Esna* Vol. V) (Cairo, 1962), pp. 151-152.

let us satisfy the desires of the divine mother of Ra,
let us prostrate ourselves in honor of the Lady of the South and
the North,
let us sanctify the ground for the worthy and powerful *Netjeret,*
when she comes on the horizon of the sky.

That which the perfume fills the air from Punt,
whose odor is that of dry oliban [a variety of frankincense].
The sun *Netjeret* who shines at her appearance,
whose fine jewels shine brighter than the finery of the South
and the North,
or that of the sky when a great rainstorm has cleansed it.
That which has no equal,
such that there is no other that resembles it,
that illumines the sky with the light of her eyes,
that lights up the desert with her glance.
Her barque is made of beautiful gold, sparkling with decorations,
and all manner of truly precious stones;
every *Netjer* stands ready to be of service;
the crew of her barque is in joy,
her holy cabin is in joy,
while we tow its owner;
the *Netjeru* who find themselves there are in delight,
the musician *Netjerut* [goddesses] of the South and the North
raise their arms in adoration;
the Souls of Pé and of Nekhen gesture with their arms
before her greatness,
and her barque progresses, without navigation,
in one direction or another, being interrupted,
in the Mansion of Neith,
and the whole of Kemet is in celebration,
because she, the divine being, is at once *Netjer* and *Netjeret,*

their mistress shines above their heads,
and every eye sees grace in her rays,
all the land is illuminated by her brilliant radiance.
Her shrine also spreads light for those who are in the *Duat,*
and the inhabitants of the world of the Blessed Ones delight at
the sight of her.'[247]

Hail Neith in all her Names!
Hail Neith in all her Forms!
Hail Neith in all her Aspects!
Hail Neith in all her Houses!
Hail Neith in all places where she pleases to be![248]

*The Liturgist **places more incense** on the charcoal and again and
again **slowly raises and lowers the incense cup** as the following is
recited:*

O Neith, may you advance with your *Ka.*
O Great of Might, the arm of your *Ka* is before you,
The arm of your *Ka* is behind you.
O Powerful One, the foot of your *Ka* is before you,
The foot of your *Ka* is behind you.
O Brave One, Neith, this incense is offered to you,
May your face be filled as this essence spreads itself over you.

*All present perform the **Henu Rite**—Embrace the Earth, the Fourfold
Salute to the Goddess, Embrace the Earth.*

---

[247] Ibid., pp. 153-154.

[248] Adapted from Serge Sauneron, *L'écriture figurative dans les textes d'Esna,*
(=Esna Vol. VIII) (Cairo, 1982). "The Litany of Neith", pp. 39.

For Embracing the Earth, all present prostrate themselves, face down, upon the floor. During the Fourfold Salute, all present rise upon one knee, and alternately raise their hands and arms into the *Dua* (praise) position with palms facing outward, followed by the *Sahu* (obedience) gesture, made by striking the chest with a closed fist and raising the other arm (also with closed fist) at a ninety-degree angle. The *Dua* position is accompanied by the words **"Adoration be to Neith,"** followed by the *Sahu* gesture accompanied with the words, **"Hail to the Divine Creatress!"** The bodily gestures are performed alternately four times.

Following this **all present again prostrate themselves** *before the divine image. This is a sign and symbol of total submission and adoration before the Netjeret. The following is said:*

Homage to Neith, Lady of Might in the Mansion of the Bee [the name of Neith's temple in Sais],
who is established on the Great Seat!
I have placed myself on the floor in awe of you.
I embrace the earth before you as before the Great One of Trembling.
I have come that I might kiss the earth,
that I might worship my Mistress,
For I have seen her Beauty;
I give praise to Neith,
For I have seen her Power.
Her form is more distinguished than the *Netjeru*;
Her arm is more powerful than the *Netjeru*.
I am pure, I am pure, I am pure, I am pure!

Everyone stands up.

*The Liturgist **holds in the palm of one hand the image of Ma'at** and **with the other hand open and raised over the image as if sheltering it,** repeats the following:*

I have come to you as Djehuty, whose two hands are joined together under Ma'at. She comes to be with you, for she is everywhere. You are provided with Ma'at. You move in Ma'at, you live in Ma'at. She fills your body, she rests in your head, she makes her seat upon your brow; the breath of your body is of Ma'at, your heart does live in Ma'at. All that you eat, all that you drink, all that you breathe is of Ma'at. Djehuty presents Ma'at to you, his two hands are upon her beauty before your face.

*The Liturgist places the image of Ma'at near the divine statue. Then he/ she holds up before the image of Neith **a pitcher of water** and **pours the water slowly into an offering bowl** as the following Utterance is recited:*

This libation is for you, O Great Golden One.
This libation is for you, O Neith.
I have brought to you this offering of water,
That your heart may be refreshed.
I have brought to you this Eye of Heru,
Placing this at your feet.
I present to you that which flows forth from you,
That your heart shall continue to beat.
For it is with you
that all comes forth at the sound of the voice.

The offering bowl is placed on the altar. At this point the Liturgist lightly sprinkles sand on the floor in front of the altar as the following is recited:

O Neith, who resides in *Sau,* *(The Egyptian name for Sais).*
Take to yourself the Eye of Heru.
You have rescued it, O Protectress of the Divine Order.
You have sprinkled with sand the Eye of Heru.

Lifting the wine offering before the sacred image, the Liturgist repeats the following:

You, O Neith, are She Who Rises from Nun and fills Heaven and Earth with your Beauty—Parent of Thousands, Mother of Millions, who peopled the earth with excellent seed. Your son is the Sun, illuminating the Two Lands.[249]

The Liturgist continues to elevate the wine offering while saying:

mn n.t irp irt ḥrw wꜣḏt
[*"mán-nit 'úrip írat ḥáru wá'ḏat"*; approximately pronounced *MAHN-neetch OO-rip EE-raht HAH-roo WAH-jat*]

Take to yourself wine, the green Eye of Heru, which I offer to your *Ka.*
O You Without Equal, how beautiful is your beauty!
May you drink it; may your heart rejoice;
may anger be removed from your face.

---

[249] From the wine offering scene in the temple at Esna, cited in David Klotz, *Articulata Forma Dei,* "A Cosmic Epithet from Esna and Medinet Habu, ENIM 5, 2012, pp. 31-32. See also *ESNA* II, 28,14.
See http://www.enim-egyptologie.fr/revue/2012/4/Klotz_ENIM5_p31-37.pdf

It is pure. [iw.w w'b pronounced *"uwú wá'ib";* approximately *oo-WOO WAH-ib*]

The Ritualist **places myrrh on the fire** *and* **lifts up the smoking incense** *while at the same time he* **lifts up the meat-offering** *before the Netjeret, and says the following:*

The scent of myrrh is for your nose. It fills your nostrils; your heart receives the meat-portions on its scent.[250]

Slowly elevating the **food offerings** *four times before the image of the Netjeret, the Liturgist repeats the following:*

I offer to Neith, Magnificent and Powerful.
All life emanates from you,
All health emanates from you,
All stability emanates from you,
All good fortune emanates from you,
The One Without Equal, Neith, forever.

The Liturgist **places the food offering before the divine image,** *and then all present* **extend one hand, palm down, over the offerings** *and recite the following:*

May offerings of every kind come forth in abundance,
like the things which come forth from the mouth of the *Netjeret*.

piryá pírit ar ḫiráw mi purú:riat ma rá' ni naṯárat. (4 times)
[approximately pronounced: peer-YA PEER-it ar khi-RAU mee pu-ROOR-iat ma RA nee nah-TCHAR-at]

---

[250] Quoted in "Worship and Festivals in an Egyptian Temple," by H. W. Fairman (publ. by The John Rylands Library, 1954), p. 191.

May offerings of every kind come forth in abundance, like the things that come forth from the mouth of the *Netjeret.*

*Holding the **Ankh** before the Netjeret, the Liturgist says:*

Live, O Neith, Whose Perfection Fills Heaven, live for all time and for eternity!

'ánaḫ niḫáḫ ḏát.
[approximately pronounced *AH-nakh nee-HAH JAHT]*

*The **Ankh** is placed next to the image of Neith.*

*Holding the **Ib** (the golden heart) before the Netjeret, the Liturgist says:*

Hail to you, O Neith, Mother at the Beginning. I have brought to you your heart to set it in its place. Let me draw near to you with your heart, so that you may have pleasure through me, and so that by means of me you may have power over your body. Ascend, O Lady of Eternity and Everlastingness, radiant, rejuvenating, equipped as a *Netjeret*. Live, O Nourishing One, live forever and ever!

*After placing the **Ib** near the sacred image, **everyone recites** this prayer to Neith.*

Giving praise to your *Ka*, kissing the earth for your name. Calling to you in the hours of trouble. [251] **Father of Fathers and Mother of Mothers, you are the divinity who came into being**

---

[251] David Klotz, "Between Heaven and Earth in Deir el-Medina: Stela MMA 21.2.6," *SAK* 34, p. 272. (*SAK* is abbrev. for the journal *Studien zur altägyptischen Kultur.*)

in the midst of the primeval waters. She is the one having appeared out of herself while the land was in twilight and no land had yet come forth and no plant had yet grown. She illuminated the rays with her two eyes and dawn came into being.[252]

O Neith, divine Creatress, we thank you. We praise you. We bow down before you. O Unique *Netjeret*, mysterious and great, be with us with your powerful arm to defeat the enemies of Ra. May you be a protection for us forever!

At this point perform the **meditation or magical action** *or, if it is a special feast, add the appropriate prayers.*

Afterwards **all present back out of the Temple Chamber with heads slightly bowed** *while the Ritualist performs the* **"removing the foot."**

With the **broom** *the Liturgist, as the last person to exit,* **ritually sweeps the area beginning at the altar.** *(This is known as* **"removing the foot.")** *While performing this action the Liturgist recites the following:*

The distress that causes confusion has been driven away, and all the *Netjeru* are in harmony. I have given Heru his Eye; I have placed the *Wedjat*-Eye in the correct position. I have given Setekh his Testicles, so that the two lords are content through the work of my hands.

I know the sky, I know the earth;
I know Heru, I know Setekh.
Heru is appeased with his Eyes;
Setekh is appeased with his Testicles.

---

[252] From Serge Sauneron, *Le Temple d'Esna*, Vol. V, p. 28.

I am Djehuty, who reconciles the *Netjeru*,
who makes offerings in their correct form.

*The **double doors are solemnly closed** as the Liturgist says the following:*

Djehuty has come.
He has filled the Eye of Heru;
He has restored the Testicles of Setekh.
No evil shall enter this Temple.
Ptah has closed the door,
Djehuty has set it fast.
The door is closed, the door is set fast with the bolt.

All bow, touching the palms of their hands to their knees.

THE REVERSION OF OFFERINGS

*One priest or priestess and as many assistants as necessary enter the Temple Chamber a final time. While he/she and any assistants **lift up the offerings** before the sacred image the ritualist shall say:*

O Neith, your enemy[253] withdraws for you. Heru has turned himself to his Eye in its name of 'Reversion-of-Offerings.' I am Djehuty. I come to perform this rite for Neith, Mother and Father at the Beginning. These, your divine offerings revert, they revert to your servants for life, for stability, for health and for joy! O that the Eye of Heru may flourish for you eternally!

---

[253] Meat offerings held a two-fold meaning for the ancient priesthood. Since meat necessarily came from slain animals, it signified the defeated or slain enemies of the Netjer. At the same time, the meat offering represented the produce of the land which ultimately was a gift of the Netjeru.

*Everyone withdraws, **carrying away all food offerings except for one loaf of bread together with a bowl of pure water.** These last items will remain until evening. If this ritual is celebrated after sunset, these items would also be removed*[254].

After the candle has burned down, a servant-priest enters and closes the doors of the Kar-shrine.

Extinguishing the candle or oil lamp, *he/she exclaims:*

This is the Eye of Heru by which you have become great, by which you live, and by which you have power, O Neith. This is the Eye of Heru which you consume and through which you enchant your body. The *Wedjat*-Eye now enters into the West, into *Manu,* but it shall return. Truly, the Eye of Heru returns in peace!

---

[254] It is important to consume the food offerings after the ceremony. Water used should either be drunk or poured onto the earth. If it is mixed with Natron, dilute it very greatly and then you can pour in onto the bare earth.

The General Ritual for Nekhbet

All epithets for this *Netjeret* (goddess) come from the eight-volume *Lexikon der ägyptischen Götter und Götterbezeichnungen (Dictionary of Egyptian Gods and God-Names)*. No attempt has been made to fabricate or "make up" epithets for this great *Netjeret*. The ancient sources are sufficiently rich in themselves.

Please do not feel that you must either do the entire ritual or nothing at all. If certain elements of the ritual speak to you and have special meaning, then please just do those particular elements. However, in my own experience I have found that as I repeat the ritual a few times, I am pleasantly surprised with 'aha!' moments where some new insight comes to light. The ritual's words have special meaning and power, and so may not be evident on first reading. Be patient and I believe the *Netjeru* will reward your effort.

Like members of the ancient priesthood, participants should be clothed in white linen or, if necessary, white cotton.

Special offering: milk. Other offerings for Nekhbet should include the regular food and beverage offerings of bread, beer, wine, and meat. Other healthy foods may also be included.

As with all Egyptian rituals begin with your purification—washing of hands and cleansing of mouth with Natron. This preliminary rite helps us to lay aside the cares of the day and to become mindful of the fact that we will encounter a divine being. If Natron is not available, then use a natural sea salt in its place until you make your own Natron.

If two or more persons are participating, then one person, impersonating the Netjer Djehuty, purifies each person by sprinkling each with water while exclaiming:

I purify you with the water of all life and good fortune, all stability, all health and happiness.[255]

Afterwards each person rinses his mouth and places a small amount of Natron or sea salt in his mouth while saying:

I wash my mouth; I chew natron so that I may extol the might of Nekhbet, the Noble Female Vulture and Lady of Protection.[256]

Participants assemble outside the Temple Chamber and begin by softly rattling sistra.

This time—several minutes or more—is used to focus minds and intention so that distracting thoughts are left behind.

Standing before the closed doors, the Ritualist recites the entrance spell:

---

[255] Taken from Aylward M. Blackman's article "Purification (Egyptian)" in Hastings Encyclopaedia 10/1918/ 476-82. This article is reprinted in Gods, Priests, and Men, Studies in the Religion of Pharaonic Egypt, edited by Alan B. Lloyd (Kegan Paul International, 1998), p. 9.

[256] Based on a temple inscription taken from "The Myth of Horus at Edfu—II" by A. M. Blackman and H. W. Fairman, appearing in Gods, Priests and Men, Studies in the Religion of Pharaonic Egypt (Kegan Paul International, 1998) p. 283.

Richard J. Reidy

UTTERANCE BEFORE THE CLOSED DOORS OF THE TEMPLE

The ritualist **raises hands in adoration** *(dua position—arms stretched out in front of the body and raised up to face level, with palms facing outward). The following shall be said:*

O you *Netjeru* of this Temple, you guardians of the great portal, great *Netjeru* of mysterious abode, who sanctify the *Netjeret* (goddess) in her shrine, who consecrate her oblation, who receive the offerings in her presence in the Hall of the Ennead: I have made my way and I enter into your presence. I am one of you. I am Shu, the eldest son of his father, the senior *wab* servant-priest of Nekhbet. Do not repulse me on the *Netjeret's* path. My feet are not impeded. I am not turned back from the court of the great portal so that I may conduct the divine service, that I may present offerings to her that made them, that I may give bread to Nekhbet. I have come on the way of the *Netjeret*. I have not shown partiality in judgment. I have not consorted with the strong. I have not reproached the lowly. I have not stolen things. I have not diminished the constituents of the Eye of Ra. I have not disturbed the Balance. I have not tampered with the requirements of the Sacred Eye. O Council of the Great *Netjeret* in this Temple, behold, I have come to you to offer Ma'at to the Queen of the *Netjeru*, to content the Sound Eye for its mistress. I am Shu; I flood her offering table. I present her offerings, Sekhmet consorting with me, that I may adore Nekhbet at her festivals, that I may kiss the earth so great is her majesty, that I may endow her image with life. I am pure. I am purified.

At this point the ritualist **opens the doors to the Temple Chamber,** *or, if there are no doors,* **makes a gesture of opening unseen doors,** *and* **steps forward as if crossing over a threshold.** *The following is said:*

O you *Ba*-souls of *Nekheb* (i.e., Eleithiapolis[257]), if you are strong, I am strong. If I am strong, you are strong. If your *Ka*-spirits are strong, my *Ka*-spirit is strong at the head of the living. As they are living so shall I live . . . . Sekhmet, the great *Netjeret*, beloved of Ptah, has given to me life, stability, and serenity round about my members, which Djehuty has gathered together for life. I am Heru in the height of heaven, the beautiful one of awe, Lord of Victory, mighty one of awe, exalted one of the two plumes, great one in *Abdju* (Abydos) I am pure.

Enter, **close the double doors** *and* **stand in front of the Kar-shrine and altar. All bow, touching their hands to their knees.**

All recite the following:

Awake, awake in peace, O Nekhbet, Lady of Light Beams. May you awake in peace.
Awake, awake in peace, O Right Eye of the Sun Disk. May you awake in peace.
Awake, awake in peace, O Lady of the Horizon. May you awake in peace.
Awake, awake in peace, O Nekhbet, Who Floods the Land with Gold Dust. May you awake in peace.

---

[257] Nekheb (Greek, Eleithiapolis) is the cult center for Nekhbet, the principle goddess for Upper Egypt, the living embodiment of the White Crown. In her vulture form she adorned the forehead of the pharaoh.

May you awake beautifully at the top of the morning, through that which the entirety of *Netjeru* say to you.

The ritualist *slowly* **opens the two doors of the Kar-shrine** *housing the sacred image.* **All others bow, touching their hands to their knees.** *The following is said:*

The doors of the sky are open; the doors of the earth are unlocked. This House is open for its Mistress. Let me come forth as she shall come forth. Let me enter in as she shall enter in. Nekhbet, She of Burning Light, is exalted upon her Great Seat. The Great Company of the *Netjeru* are exalted upon their seat.

I have seen the *Netjeret*, and the *Netjeret* sees me. The *Netjeret* rejoices at seeing me. I have gazed upon the statue of the Lady of Life, the sacred image of the Female Vulture of Upper Kemet.[258]

Right hand on left shoulder of statue; left hand on right wrist of statue:

Djehuty has come to you. Awake when you hear his words. I have come as the envoy of Atum. My two arms are upon you like those of Heru. My two hands are upon you like those of Djehuty. My fingers are upon you like those of Anpu. Homage be to you. I am a living servant of Nekhbet.

The Ritualist recites the ancient Hymn to Nekhbet:

---

[258] Based on a passage in "Worship and Festivals in an Egyptian Temple," a lecture by H. W. Fairman (publ. by The John Rylands Library, 1954), p. 180.

Homage to you, Lady of the Mouth of the Valley, Lady of Heaven. Mistress of the *Netjeru*, Beautiful Tiller for him who has no rudder, judge in heaven and on earth, Beautiful Star unseen save in time of good. I have come to you. Grant that my mouth may speak, my feet may walk, my eyes may see your brightness every day, so that I may enjoy the good things that are presented to me. Grant then to us that our praises may be pleasing to you this day.[259]

*The Ritualist holds up the **bowl of water** in which he/she will be mixing the Natron. The following is said:*

O water may you remove all evil,
As Ra who bathes in the Lake of Rushes,
May Heru wash my flesh,
May Djehuty cleanse my feet,
May Shu lift me up and Nut take my hand!
May Setekh be my strength, and may Sekhmet be my healing!
And may Amun-Ra be my life and my prospering!

*The bowl of water is set aside and the container of **Natron** is lifted up. The following is said:*

It is pure, it is pure.
My Natron is the Natron of Heru and the Natron of Heru is my Natron.

---

[259] From the Hymn to Nekhbet in the tomb of Paheri as quoted by Margaret A. Murray in *Egyptian Religious Poetry* (Westport, Connecticut: Greenwood Press, 1980; reprint of the 1949 ed.), p. 100. Paheri is buried in El-Kab, the ancient city of Nekheb, a city dedicated to Nekhbet. Paheri was nomarch (governor) for the city of Nekheb and superintendent of the priests of Nekhbet. For this hymn's Primary Source see J. J. Tylor and F. L. Griffith's *The Tomb of Paheri at El-Kab* (The Egypt Exploration Fund, 11, 1894).

My Natron is the Natron of Setekh and the Natron of Setekh is my Natron.
My Natron is the Natron of Djehuty, and the Natron of Djehuty is my Natron.
My Natron is the Natron of Geb and the Natron of Geb is my Natron.

My mouth is the mouth of a milking calf on the day that I was born.

Four pinches of Natron are mixed into the water as this Utterance is recited:

I give you essential water, a tide in your time.
I bring the flood waters to purify your sanctuary.
I bring you the flood waters to purify your Temple and your statue in its place, the primordial water that purifies as in the First Time!

The Ritualist places an index finger into the water and moves it in a circular direction four times as the following is said:

Nekhbet, the Primordial One, does purify this water;
Nekhbet, Mother of Mothers, does cleanse this water;
Nekhbet, Who Shoots Out Rays, does sanctify this water;
Nekhbet herself, the Lady of Life, does endow this water with power and with life.

The Bowl of Natron-infused water is then taken up and the Ritualist sprinkles this lightly in front of and around the statue or image of Nekhbet, applying some water to the base of the image, as the Utterance is recited:

I come close to You, O Beautiful Star, Who Brightens the Two Lands.

I bring the water of rejuvenation that flows from the Two Caverns.

I sprinkle the water, purifying your image and your Temple from all impurity!

*The Ritualist picks up the **bowl of Natron** and **sprinkles a small amount in each of the four directions** as the following is recited:*

The *Netjeret* Nekhbet herself does cleanse and purify this, her Temple to the South.

The *Netjeret* Nekhbet herself does cleanse and purify this, her Temple to the North.

The *Netjeret* Nekhbet herself does cleanse and purify this, her Temple to the West.

The *Netjeret* Nekhbet herself does cleanse and purify this, her Temple to the East.

*Replacing the Natron on the altar, the Ritualist takes up the **bowl of water, sprinkling a small amount in each of the four directions.** The following Utterance is recited:*

The *Netjeret* Nekhbet herself does sanctify and consecrate this, her Temple to the South.

The *Netjeret* Nekhbet herself does sanctify and consecrate this, her Temple to the North.

The *Netjeret* Nekhbet herself does sanctify and consecrate this, her Temple to the West.

The *Netjeret* Nekhbet herself does sanctify and consecrate this, her Temple to the East.

The Temple of the *Netjeret* Nekhbet is established.

Richard J. Reidy

It is established for millions of years.

*The Ritualist returns to the altar and **lights the candle or oil lamp** while the following is said:*

Come, come in peace, O glorious Eye of Heru,
Be strong and renew your youth in peace.
For the flame shines like Ra on the double horizon.
The enemies of Ra are defeated. They are defeated.
I am pure, I am pure, I am pure, I am pure.

*The Ritualist **places incense on the burner** and **censes each sacred image** beginning with the statue of the Netjeret while the following is recited:*

The fire is laid, the fire shines;
The incense is laid on the fire, the incense shines.
    Your perfume comes to me, O Incense;
    May my perfume come to you, O Incense.
Your perfume comes to me, you *Netjeru*;
May my perfume come to you, You *Netjeru*.
    May I be with you, you *Netjeru*;
    May you be with me, you *Netjeru*.
May I live with you, you *Netjeru*;
May you live with me, you *Netjeru*.
    I love you, you *Netjeru*;
    May you love me, you *Netjeru*.

*Standing in front of the image of Nekhbet the Ritualist **offers the burning incense** and says:*

Take the incense,

Its essence is for you, O Magnificent Female Vulture.
Its smoke permeates your shrine, bringing life!
Take the incense,
Its essence is for you.
Your Majesty is appeased with the incense.
This Eye of Heru,
This essence of the Eye of Heru comes to you.

At this point the following is said:

Hail to you, Nekhbet, Great One of Massacre,
Who Kills the Rebels with Her Sharp Claws,
Mighty in Heaven before Ra.

Adoration to you in the night-barque,
Jubilation to you in the day-barque,
Greatly Beloved in the Hearts of the *Netjeru* and *Netjerut*.

I have come before you, Lady of Life,
On this day on which you have gloriously appeared,
For you are the One Who Brightens the Palace with Her
Perfection.
You, the Bejeweled One, are she Who Drives off Sorrow after
You are Called.

May your *Ka* be in peace, O Lady of Life,
On this day on which you have gloriously appeared,
You whom the *Netjeru* have propitiated.

O Mistress of Flame who are in the barque of Ra,
Repelling A/pep, for you are the Lady of Scorching Heat,
At Whose Sight One Trembles,
Behold, I have come before you,

So that, purified, I may adore your beauty.[260]

May you come to your House to join your Image,
Your radiance inundating our faces,
Like the radiance of Ra when he shows himself in the morning.

You are the Beloved One of Ra, the White Eye of Heru,
Who, as Leader of People, Gives Sweet Breath,
Who Hears Prayers,
Truly you are the Lady of Protection.

O Nekhbet the Great, Who Crosses the Sky with Her Wings,
Lady of Perfect Fields, Lady of All Lands,
Foremost of Stars on Her Throne,
Worshipped in your sanctuaries.

Make enduring our years.
Establish us like the Falcon upon the *Serekh.*
Make us to endure eternally, like Ra.[261]

The Ritualist places more incense on the charcoal and again and again slowly raises and lowers the incense cup as the following is recited:

O Nekhbet, may you advance with your *Ka.*
O Lady of Love, the arm of your *Ka* is before you,
The arm of your *Ka* is behind you.
O Sovereign, the foot of your *Ka* is before you,
The foot of your *Ka* is behind you.

---

[260] Adapted from and modeled on Hymn VIII, in *Hymns to Isis in Her Temple at Philae,* by Louis V. Zabkar (Brandeis University Press, 1988), p. 119.

[261] Op. Cit., from Hymn V, pp. 58-59.

O Beautiful Nekhbet, this incense is offered to you,
May your face be filled as this essence spreads itself over you.

All present perform the **Henu Rite** *—Embrace the Earth, the Fourfold Salute to the Goddess, Embrace the Earth.*

For Embracing the Earth, all present prostrate themselves, face down, upon the floor. During the Fourfold Salute, all present rise upon one knee, and alternately raise their hands and arms into the *Dua* (praise) position with palms facing outward, followed by the *Sahu* (obedience) gesture, made by striking the chest with a closed fist and raising the other arm (also with closed fist) at a ninety-degree angle. The *Dua* position is accompanied by the words **"Adoration be to Nekhbet,"** followed by the *Sahu* gesture accompanied with the words, **"Hail to the Female Vulture!"** The bodily gestures are performed alternately four times.

All present perform the **Henu Rite** *—Embrace the Earth, the Fourfold Salute to Nekhbet, Embrace the Earth—and then the following is said:*

Homage be to Nekhbet, the One of Many Forms,
who is established on the Great Seat!
I have placed myself on the floor in awe of you.
I embrace the earth before you as before the Great One in Heaven.
I have come that I might kiss the earth,
that I might worship my Mistress,
for I have seen her Beauty;
I give praise to Nekhbet,
for I have seen her Power.
Her form is more distinguished than the *Netjeru*;
Her arm is more powerful than the *Netjeru.*

I am pure, I am pure, I am pure, I am pure!

Everyone stands up.

*The Ritualist holds in the palm of one hand **the image of Ma'at** and **with the other hand open and raised over the image as if sheltering it**, repeats the following:*

I have come to you as Djehuty, whose two hands are joined together under Ma'at. She comes to be with you, for she is everywhere. You are provided with Ma'at. You move in Ma'at, you live in Ma'at. She fills your body, she rests in your head, she makes her seat upon your brow; the breath of your body is of Ma'at, your heart does live in Ma'at. All that you eat, all that you drink, all that you breathe is of Ma'at. Djehuty presents Ma'at to you, his two hands are upon her beauty before your face.

*The Ritualist places the image of Ma'at near the divine statue. Then he/she holds up before the image of Nekhbet **a pitcher of water** and **pours the water slowly into an offering bowl** as the following Utterance is recited:*

This libation is for you, O Lady of Love.
This libation is for you, O Nekhbet.
I have brought to you this offering of water,
That your heart may be refreshed.
I have brought to you this Eye of Heru,
Placing this at your feet.
I present to you that which flows forth from you,
That your heart shall continue to beat.
For it is with you that all comes forth at the sound of the voice.

*The offering bowl is placed on the altar. At this point the Ritualist lightly **sprinkles sand on the floor in front of the altar** as the following is recited:*

O Nekhbet, who resides in **Nekheb,**
Take to yourself the Eye of Heru.
You have rescued it, O Beloved One of Ra.
You have sprinkled with sand the Eye of Heru.

Lifting the offering of milk, the following is said:

Take to yourself this white and sweet milk, created by Nut. May you live on it, may you be healthy on account of it. May your body be refreshed every day.[262]

Lifting the wine offering before the sacred image, the Ritualist repeats the following:

mn n.t irp irt ḥrw w3ḏt
[*"mán-niṯ 'úrip írat ḥáru wá'ḏat"*; approximately pronounced *MAHN-neetch OO-rip EE-raht HAH-roo WAH-jat*]

Take to yourself wine, the green Eye of Heru, which I offer to your **Ka.** [263]
O Queen, how beautiful is your beauty!
May you drink it; may your heart rejoice;

---

[262] Amr, Aber, *The Central Hall in the Egyptian Temples of the Ptolemaic Period*, Durham theses, Durham University. (2009) Available at Durham E-Theses Online: http://etheses.dur.ac.uk/88/ This offering formula occurs in the central hall of the temple at Edfu. See p. 454 in the dissertation.
[263] Refer to pp. 92, 93, 99, and 105 in Mu-Chou Poo's *Wine and Wine Offerings in Ancient Egypt* (London & New York: Kegan Paul International, 1995).

may anger be removed from your face.

It is pure. [*iw.w w'b* pronounced *"uwú wá'ib"*; approximately *oo-WOO WAH-ib*]

The Ritualist **places myrrh** *on the fire and* **lifts up the smoking incense** *while at the same time he* **lifts up the meat-offering** *before the Netjeret, and says the following:*

The scent of myrrh is for your nose. It fills your nostrils; your heart receives the meat-portions on its scent.[264]

Slowly **elevating the food offerings four times** *before the image of the Netjeret, the Ritualist repeats the following:*

I offer to Nekhbet, Foremost of the *Netjerut* (goddesses).
All life emanates from you,
All health emanates from you,
All stability emanates from you,
All good fortune emanates from you,
O Nekhbet, Lady of Life, forever.

The Ritualist **places the food offering** *before the divine image, and then all present* **extend one hand, palm down, over the offerings** *and recite the following:*

May offerings of every kind come forth in abundance,
like the things which come forth from the mouth of the *Netjeret*.

piryá pírit ar ḫiráw mi purú:riat ma rá' ni naṯárat. (4 times)

---

[264] Quoted in "Worship and Festivals in an Egyptian Temple," by H. W. Fairman (publ. by The John Rylands Library, 1954), p. 191.

[approximately pronounced: peer-YA PEER-it ar khi-RAU mee pu-ROOR-iat ma RA nee nah-TCHAR-at]

May offerings of every kind come forth in abundance, like the things that come forth from the mouth of the *Netjeret*.

*Holding the **Ankh** before the Netjeret, the Ritualist says:*

Live, O Nekhbet, Lady of Love, live for all time and for eternity!
ʿánaḫ niḥáḫ ḏát.
[approximately pronounced *AH-nakh nee-HAH JAHT*]

*The **Ankh** is placed next to the Netjeret.*

*Holding the **Ib (the golden heart)** before the Netjeret, the Ritualist says:*

Hail to you, O Nekhbet, Mistress of All. I have brought to you your heart to set it in its place. Let me draw near to you with your heart, so that you may have pleasure through me, and so that by means of me you may have power over your body. Ascend, O Great of Magic, radiant, rejuvenating, equipped as a *Netjeret*. Live, O Excellent of Tongue whose speech cannot fail, live forever and ever!

*After placing the **Ib** near the sacred image, **everyone sings or chants** the hymn to Nekhbet. Begin by **slowly playing the sistra**. Participants may wish to alternate the singing of verses.*

I play the sistra before your beautiful face,
Nekhbet, Mistress of Sistra, residing in *Nekheb*,
Who has no equal in heaven.

I play the sistra for you,
Lady of Scorching Heat, Great of Terror,
You are the One Who Severs the Heads of Her Enemies with
her Claws.

O Protector, may you protect us as you protect Ra.
You are she Who Prepares Protection for the Weary of Heart
(Ausir).
May you protect us as you protect him.

August one, Great Secret One, Who Gives Life like Ra,
The Mother Who Spreads Her Wings,
Mighty One with Cutting Beak,
One who moves freely in the barque of millions,
Pilot of the Night Barque.[265]

May your beautiful face be gracious to us who honor you.
O Lady of the Lotus Plants, Lady of Love, great of praise,
Whose face enjoys the trickling of fresh myrrh.[266]
O Lady of Life, be gracious, be gracious to us who honor you.

*At this point perform the **meditation or magical action** or, if it is a
special feast, add the appropriate prayers.*

*Afterwards **all present back out of the Temple Chamber with heads
slightly bowed** while the Ritualist performs the **"removing the foot."***

*With the **broom** the Ritualist, as the last person to exit, **ritually sweeps
the area beginning at the altar.** (This is known as **"removing the
foot"**). While performing this action the Ritualist recites the following:*

---

[265] Op. Cit., modeled on Hymn VII, p. 107.
[266] Op. Cit., modeled on Hymn III, p. 42.

The distress that causes confusion has been driven away,
and all the *Netjeru* are in harmony.
I have given Heru his Eye;
I have placed the *Wedjat*-Eye in the correct position.
I have given Setekh his Testicles,
so that the two Lords are content through the work of my hands.

I know the sky, I know the earth;
I know Heru, I know Setekh.
Heru is appeased with his Eyes;
Setekh is appeased with his Testicles.
I am Djehuty, who reconciles the *Netjeru,*
who makes offerings in their correct form.

*The double doors are **solemnly closed** as the Ritualist says the following:*

Djehuty has come.
He has filled the Eye of Heru;
He has restored the Testicles of Setekh.
No evil shall enter this Temple.
Ptah has closed the door,
Djehuty has set it fast.
The door is closed, the door is set fast with the bolt.

All bow, touching the palms of their hands to their knees.

THE REVERSION OF OFFERINGS

*One priest or priestess and as many assistants as necessary enter the Temple Chamber a final time. While he/she and any assistants **lift up the offerings** before the sacred image the ritualist shall say:*

O Nekhbet, your enemy[267] withdraws for you. Heru has turned himself to his Eye in its name of 'Reversion-of-Offerings.' I am Djehuty. I come to perform this rite for Nekhbet, queen of the *Netjeru*. These, your divine offerings revert, they revert to your servants for life, for stability, for health and for joy! O that the Eye of Heru may flourish for you eternally!

*Everyone withdraws, **carrying away all food offerings except for one loaf of bread together with a bowl of pure water.** These last items will remain until evening. If this ritual is celebrated after sunset, these items would also be removed.*[268]

After the candle has burned down, a servant-priest enters and closes the doors of the Kar-shrine.

Extinguishing the candle or oil lamp, *he/she exclaims:*

This is the Eye of Heru by which you have become great, by which you live, and by which you have power, O Nekhbet. This is the Eye of Heru which you consume and through which you enchant your body. The *Wedjat*-Eye now enters into the West, into *Manu*, but it shall return. Truly, the Eye of Heru returns in peace!

---

[267] Meat offerings held a two-fold meaning for the ancient priesthood. Since meat necessarily came from slain animals, it signified the defeated or slain enemies of the Netjeret. At the same time, the meat offering represented the produce of the land which ultimately was a gift of the Netjeru.

[268] It is important to consume the food offerings after the ceremony. Water used should either be drunk or poured onto the earth. If it is mixed with natron, dilute it very greatly and then you can pour in onto the earth without harming any plantings.

The General Rite for Ptah

All epithets of Ptah are sourced from quoted hymn texts or from Lexikon der ägyptischen Götter und Götterbezeichnungen, Band [Volume] III, pp. 168-180.

Like members of the ancient priesthood, participants should be clothed in white linen. No items made of animal products such as leather or wool are to be worn.

As with all Egyptian rituals begin with your purification—washing of hands and cleansing of mouth with Natron. This preliminary rite helps us to lay aside the cares of the day and to become mindful of the fact that we will encounter a divine being. If Natron is not available, then use a natural sea salt in its place until you make your own Natron.

*If two or more persons are participating, then one person, impersonating the Netjer Djehuty, **purifies each person by sprinkling each with water** while exclaiming:*

I purify you with the water of all life and good fortune, all stability, all health and happiness.[269]

*Afterwards each person **rinses his mouth** and **places a small amount of Natron or sea salt in his mouth** while saying:*

---

[269] Taken from Aylward M. Blackman's article "Purification (Egyptian)" in Hastings Encyclopaedia 10/1918/ 476-82. This article is reprinted in Gods, Priests, and Men, Studies in the Religion of Pharaonic Egypt, edited by Alan B. Lloyd (Kegan Paul International, 1998), p. 9.

I wash my mouth; I chew natron so that I may extol the might of Ptah the Great, the Gracious Creator.[270]

Participants **assemble outside the Temple Chamber** *and begin by* *softly rattling sistra.*

This time—several minutes or more—is used to focus minds and intention so that distracting thoughts are left behind. The sound of the sistra dispels negative energy, purifying the atmosphere in preparation for encountering divinity.

Standing before the closed doors, the Liturgist **recites the entrance** **spell:**

UTTERANCE BEFORE THE CLOSED DOORS OF THE TEMPLE

The ritualist **raises hands in adoration** *(dua position—arms stretched* *out in front of the body and raised up to face level, with palms facing* *outward). The following shall be said:*

O you *Netjeru* **of this Temple, you guardians of the great portal, great** *Netjeru* **of mysterious abode, who sanctify the** *Netjer* **in his shrine, who consecrate his oblation, who receive the offerings in his presence in the Hall of the Ennead: I have made my way and I enter into your presence. I am one of you. I am Shu, the eldest son of his father, the senior** *wab* **servant-priest of Ptah. Do not repulse me on the** *Netjer's* **path. My feet are not impeded. I am not turned back from the court of the great portal so that I may conduct the divine service, that I**

---

[270] Based on a temple inscription taken from "The Myth of Horus at Edfu—II" by A. M. Blackman and H. W. Fairman, appearing in Gods, Priests and Men, Studies in the Religion of Pharaonic Egypt, Blackman and Lloyd, p. 283.

may present offerings to him that made them, that I may give bread to Ptah. I have come on the way of the *Netjer*. I have not shown partiality in judgment. I have not consorted with the strong. I have not reproached the lowly. I have not stolen things. I have not diminished the constituents of the Eye of Ra. I have not disturbed the Balance. I have not tampered with the requirements of the Sacred Eye. O Council of the Great *Netjer* in this Temple, behold, I have come to you to offer Ma'at to the Lord of Ma'at, to content the Sound Eye for its master. I am Shu; I flood his offering table. I present his offerings, Sekhmet consorting with me, that I may adore Ptah at his festivals, that I may kiss the earth so great is his majesty, that I may endow his image with life. I am pure. I am purified.

At this point the ritualist **opens the doors to the Temple Chamber, or, if there are no doors, makes a gesture of opening unseen doors,** *and* **steps forward as if crossing over a threshold.** *The following is said:*

O you *Ba*-souls of *Mennefer* (i.e., Memphis[271]), if you are strong, I am strong. If I am strong, you are strong. If your *Ka*-spirits are strong, my *Ka*-spirit is strong at the head of the living. As they are living so shall I live . . . . Ptah, the great *Netjer*, Creator with his heart and tongue, has given to me life, stability, and serenity round about my members, which Djehuty has gathered together for life. I am Heru in the height of heaven, the beautiful one of awe, Lord of Victory, mighty one of awe, exalted one of the two plumes, great one in *Abdju* (Abydos). I am pure.

All temple members chant:

---

[271] Mennefer (Greek, Memphis) is the cult center for Ptah and his consort Sekhmet.

Awake in peace, O Ptah, Lord of Life,
may you awaken in peace.
Awake in peace, O Ptah, Hearer of Prayers,
may you awaken in peace.
Awake in peace, O Ptah, Tatenen,
may you awaken in peace.
Awake in peace, O Ptah, great Lord of Ma'at,
may you awaken in peace.

May you awake beautifully at the top of the morning,
through that which the entirety of *Netjeru* say to you.

Enter, **close the double doors** *and* **stand in front of the Kar-shrine and altar.** *All bow, touching their hands to their knees.*

The ritualist *slowly* **opens the two doors of the Kar-shrine** *housing the sacred image. All others bow, touching their hands to their knees. The following is said:*

The doors of the sky are open; the doors of the earth are unlocked. This House is open for its Master. Let me come forth as he shall come forth. Let me enter in as he shall enter in. Ptah, the Great One, Lord of Ma'at, is exalted upon his Great Seat. The Great Company of the *Netjeru* are exalted upon their seat.

I have seen the *Netjer,* and the *Netjer* sees me. The *Netjer* rejoices at seeing me. I have gazed upon the statue of the Great *Netjer* of Noble Forms, the sacred image of the Lord of Ma'at.[272]

---

[272] Based on the temple text found in "Worship and Festivals in an Egyptian Temple," a lecture by H. W. Fairman (publ. by The John Rylands Library, 1954), p. 180.

Right hand on left shoulder of statue; left hand on right wrist of statue:

Djehuty has come to you. Awake when you hear his words. I have come as the envoy of Atum. My two arms are upon you like those of Heru. My two hands are upon you like those of Djehuty. My fingers are upon you like those of Anpu. Homage be to you. I am a living servant of Ptah.

*The Ritualist holds up the **bowl of water** in which he/she will be mixing the Natron. The following is said:*

O water, may you remove all evil,
as Ra who bathes in the Lake of Rushes,
may Heru wash my flesh,
may Djehuty cleanse my feet,
may Shu lift me up and Nut take my hand!
May Setekh be my strength, and may Sekhmet be my healing!
And may Amun-Ra be my life and my prospering!

*The bowl of water is set aside and the container of **Natron** is lifted up. The following is said:*

It is pure, it is pure.
My Natron is the Natron of Heru and the Natron of Heru is my Natron.
My Natron is the Natron of Setekh and the Natron of Setekh is my Natron.
My Natron is the Natron of Djehuty, and the Natron of Djehuty is my Natron.
My Natron is the Natron of Geb and the Natron of Geb is my Natron.

My mouth is the mouth of a milking calf on the day that I was born.

Four pinches of Natron are mixed into the water as this Utterance is recited:

I give you essential water, a tide in your time.
I bring the flood waters to purify your sanctuary.
I bring you the flood waters to purify your Temple and your statue in its place, the primordial water that purifies as in the First Time!

The Ritualist places an index finger into the water and moves it in a circular, clockwise direction four times as the following is said:

Ptah, South of His Wall, does purify this water;
Ptah, upon the Great Seat, does cleanse this water;
Ptah, for whom the Cavern of Nun opens, does sanctify this water;
Ptah himself does endow this water with power and with life.

The Bowl of Natron-infused water is then taken up and the Ritualist sprinkles this lightly in front of and around the statue or image of Ptah, and applying the water to the base of the image, as the Utterance is recited:

I come close to you, Lord of Ma'at, Handsome of Face upon your Great Seat.
I bring the water of rejuvenation that flows from the Two Caverns.
I sprinkle the water, purifying your image and your Temple from all impurity!

The Ritualist picks up the bowl of Natron and sprinkles a small amount in each of the four directions as the following is recited:

The *Netjer* Ptah himself does cleanse and purify this, his Temple to the South.
The *Netjer* Ptah himself does cleanse and purify this, his Temple to the North.
The *Netjer* Ptah himself does cleanse and purify this, his Temple to the West.
The *Netjer* Ptah himself does cleanse and purify this, his Temple to the East.

Replacing the Natron on the altar, the Ritualist takes up the bowl of water, sprinkling a small amount in each of the four directions. The following Utterance is recited:

The *Netjer* Ptah himself does sanctify and consecrate this, his Temple to the South.
The *Netjer* Ptah himself does sanctify and consecrate this, his Temple to the North.
The *Netjer* Ptah himself does sanctify and consecrate this, his Temple to the West.
The *Netjer* Ptah himself does sanctify and consecrate this, his Temple to the East.
The Temple of the *Netjer* Ptah is established.
It is established for millions of years.

The Ritualist returns to the altar and lights the candle or oil lamp while the following is said:

Come, come in peace, O glorious Eye of Heru,
be strong and renew your youth in peace,
for the flame shines like Ra on the double horizon.

Richard J. Reidy

The enemies of Ra are defeated. They are defeated.
I am pure, I am pure, I am pure, I am pure.

*The Ritualist **places incense on the burner** and **censes each sacred image** beginning with the statue of the Netjer while the following is recited:*

The fire is laid, the fire shines;
The incense is laid on the fire, the incense shines.
Your perfume comes to me, O Incense;
May my perfume come to you, O Incense.
Your perfume comes to me, you *Netjeru*;
May my perfume come to you, you *Netjeru*.
May I be with you, you *Netjeru*;
May you be with me, you *Netjeru*.
May I live with you, you *Netjeru*;
May you live with me, you *Netjeru*.
I love you, you *Netjeru*;
May you love me, you *Netjeru*.

*Standing in front of the image of Ptah the Ritualist **offers the burning incense** and says:*

Take the incense,
its essence is for you.
Its smoke permeates your shrine, bringing life!
Take the incense,
its essence is for you.
Your Majesty is appeased with the incense.
This Eye of Heru,
this essence of the Eye of Heru comes to you.

At this point the following is said:

Homage to you, exalted Ancient One, O Tatenen, father of the *Netjeru*, eldest *Netjer* of the First Occasion, you shaped mankind and formed the *Netjeru*;

You initiated Becoming as the first primeval *Netjer*—the very event that occurred came after you. You created the sky according to what your heart imagined and raised it up like one lifts up a feather;

You founded the world as your own creation, circled it about with Nun and the Great Green Sea. You made the underworld, provided for the dead, and enabled Ra to sail across the *Duat* to comfort them as Ruler of Eternity and Lord of Forever.

Lord of Life, you cause throats to breathe, you offer air to every nostril, you let all people live through your provisions. Time, fate, and fortune are under your dominion—we live by that which issues from your mouth.

You created the offerings for all the *Netjeru* when you embodied yourself as Nun, the primal waters. Lord of Eternity, the everlasting is under your care, you breathe out life for everyone.

I am your child, whom you installed in my place, peacefully;
I am upon your waters; your good counsel is with me.
May you double good things for me while I am upon the earth.
May you draw me toward rest at your side in the West of heaven just as you do for all the hidden gods of the *Duat*—so that I might be a friend of your Enneads in your secret precinct like Apis, your splendid *Ba* (soul), who is at your side.

411

Richard J. Reidy

Let me swallow contentment from your offerings –
the bread, incense, beer, and wine.
Let me live again within the Sacred Realm;
And let me see you daily as your two Enneads do.
But while I am upon earth, let me not keep my heart from zealousness for you—seeking out all that is useful for your splendid dwelling,
behaving well before you in your City of the Wall.[273]

*The Ritualist **places more incense** on the charcoal and again and again **slowly raises and lowers the incense cup** as the following is recited:*

O Ptah, may you advance with your *Ka.*
O Lord of Ma'at, the arm of your *Ka* is before you,
the arm of your *Ka* is behind you.
O Hearer of Prayers, the foot of your *Ka* is before you,
the foot of your *Ka* is behind you.
O Ptah, South of your Wall, this incense is offered to you,
may your face be filled as this essence spreads itself over you.

*All present perform the **Henu Rite**—Embrace the Earth, the Fourfold Salute to the God, Embrace the Earth.*

For Embracing the Earth, all present prostrate themselves, face down, upon the floor. During the Fourfold Salute, all present rise upon one knee, and alternately raise their hands and arms into the *Dua* (praise) position with palms facing outward, followed by the *Sahu* (obedience) gesture, made by striking the chest with a

---

[273] John L. Foster. Hymn and Prayer to Ptah from Papyrus Harris I, modified excerpt. *Hymns, Prayers, and Songs: An Anthology of Ancient Egyptian Lyric Poetry* (Scholars Press, Atlanta, 1996), 109-110.

closed fist and raising the other arm (also with closed fist) at a ninety-degree angle. The *Dua* position is accompanied by the words **"Adoration be to Ptah,"** followed by the *Sahu* gesture accompanied with the words, **"Hail to the Lord of Ma'at!"** The bodily gestures are performed alternately four times.

Following this all present again prostrate themselves before the sacred image. This is a sign and symbol of total submission and adoration before the Netjer. The following is said:

Homage to Ptah, Great One, you are in every place you wish to be;
you are established on the Great Seat!
I have placed myself on the floor in awe of you.
I embrace the earth before you, Creator by means of your heart and tongue.
I have come that I might kiss the earth,
that I might worship my Master,
for I have seen his Beauty;
I give praise to Ptah,
for I have seen his Power.
His form is more distinguished than the *Netjeru*;
His arm is more powerful than the *Netjeru*.
I am pure, I am pure, I am pure, I am pure!

Everyone stands up.

*The Ritualist **holds in the palm of one hand the image of Ma'at and with the other hand open and raised over the image as if sheltering it,** repeats the following:*

I have come to you as Djehuty, whose two hands are joined together under Ma'at. She comes to be with you, for she is everywhere. You are provided with Ma'at. You move in Ma'at, you live in Ma'at. She fills your body, she rests in your head, she makes her seat upon your brow; the breath of your body is of Ma'at, your heart does live in Ma'at. All that you eat, all that you drink, all that you breathe is of Ma'at. Djehuty presents Ma'at to you, his two hands are upon her beauty before your face.

*The Ritualist places the image of Ma'at near the divine statue. Then he/ she holds up before the image of Ptah **a pitcher of water** and **pours the water slowly into an offering bowl** as the following Utterance is recited:*

This libation is for you, O Lord of Life.
This libation is for you, O Ptah.
I have brought to you this offering of water,
that your heart may be refreshed.
I have brought to you this Eye of Heru,
placing this at your feet.
I present to you that which flows forth from you,
that your heart shall continue to beat.
For it is with you that all comes forth at the sound of the voice.

*The offering bowl is placed on the altar. At this point the Ritualist **lightly sprinkles sand on the floor in front of the altar** as the following is recited:*

O Ptah, residing in Mennefer, [the Egyptian name for Memphis]
take to yourself the Eye of Heru.
You have rescued it, O Lord of Truth.

You have sprinkled with sand the Eye of Heru.

*Lifting the **wine offering** before the sacred image, the Ritualist repeats the following:*

mn n.k irp irt ḥrw wĳdt

[*"mán-nik 'úrip írat ḥáru wá'ḏat"*; approximately pronounced *MAHN-neek OO-rip EE-raht HAH-roo WAH-jat*]

Take to yourself wine, the green Eye of Heru, which I offer to your **Ka.**
O Ruler, how beautiful is your beauty!
May you drink it; may your heart rejoice;
May anger be removed from your face.
It is pure. [iw.w w'b pronounced *"uwú wá'ib"*; approximately *oo-WOO WAH-ib*]

*The Ritualist **places myrrh** on the fire and **lifts up the smoking incense** while at the same time he **lifts up the meat-offering** before the Netjer, and says the following:*

The scent of myrrh is for your nose. It fills your nostrils; your heart receives the meat-portions on its scent.[274]

Slowly elevating the **food offerings** four times before the image of the *Netjer*, the Ritualist repeats the following:

I offer to Ptah, the Great One.
All life emanates from you,
all health emanates from you,

---

[274] Quoted in "Worship and Festivals in an Egyptian Temple," by H. W. Fairman (publ. by The John Rylands Library, 1954), p. 191.

all stability emanates from you,
all good fortune emanates from you,
O Hearer of Prayers, Ptah, forever.

The Ritualist places the food offering before the divine image, and then all present extend one hand, palm down, over the offerings and recite the following:

May offerings of every kind come forth in abundance,
like the things which come forth from the mouth of the *Netjer*.

piryá pírit ar ḫiráw mi purú:riat ma rá' ni náṯar. (4 times)
[approximately pronounced: peer-YA PEER-it ar khi-RAU mee pu-ROOR-iat ma RA nee NAH-tchar]

May offerings of every kind come forth in abundance, like the things that come forth from the mouth of the *Netjer*.

*Holding the **Ankh** before the sacred image, the Ritualist says:*

Live, O Ptah, Lord of Ma'at, live for all time and for eternity!

ʿánaḫ niḥáḫ ḏát.
[approximately pronounced *AH-nakh nee-HAH JAHT]*

*The **Ankh** is placed next to the statue of image of the Netjer.*

*Holding the **Ib (the golden heart)** before the Netjer, the Ritualist says:*

Hail to you, Ptah. You are in Heaven and upon the Earth. I have brought to you your heart to set it in its place. Let me draw near to you with your heart, so that you may have pleasure through me, and so that by means of me you may have power over your body. Ascend, O Giver of Shape and Form, radiant, rejuvenating, equipped as a *Netjer*. Live, you who are in every place you wish to be, live forever and ever!

*After placing the **Ib** near the sacred image, **everyone sings or chants** the hymn to Ptah. Participants may wish to alternate the singing of verses.*

I praise Ptah, Lord of Ma'at, King of the Two Lands, Handsome of Face on the Great Seat, Great *Netjer* among the Ennead, [275] Beloved One who hears prayers! O Great One, who is in every place you wish to be, in all your temples, in all your times!

O Ptah Tatenen, the Very Great, you have given life to all the *Netjeru* and their *Kas* through your heart and tongue, from which Heru has come forth as Ptah comes forth, and from which Djehuty has come forth as Ptah comes forth. You placed the *Netjeru* in their shrines, settled their offerings, and made their bodies according to their wishes. Thus the *Netjeru* entered into their bodies, of every wood, every stone, every kind of clay, everything that grows upon you in which they came to be. Thus were gathered to you all the *Netjeru* and their *Kas*, united with the Lord of the Two Lands.[276]

Homage to you, Ptah, Father of the *Netjeru*, Tatenen, eldest of the primordial *Netjeru*, Great *Netjer* of Noble Forms. Greatly

---

[275] Miriam Lichtheim. Stela of Neferabu with Hymn to Ptah, British Museum 589. *Ancient Egyptian Literature Volume II: The New Kingdom* (University of California Press, 1976), 109.

[276] Adapted from Miriam Lichtheim. Memphite Theology. British Museum No. 498 (Shabaka Stone). **Ancient Egyptian Literature, Volume I: The Old and Middle Kingdoms**, (University of California Press, 1973), 54-55.

Feared One, on the Great Seat, your authority is powerful, your manifestations noble. Your Force is mighty and you carry all by your strength!

I come to you, O Ptah! I come to you, whose forms are distinguished! Homage to you! Divine embodiment, you created the *Netjeru* after you came into existence. You modeled your own body when the sky and the earth did not exist, before the Flood (i.e., Nun) burst forth. You assembled your flesh, enumerated your members, and found yourself unique. You have no father who had begotten you when you came into existence, and no mother gave birth to you!

Come, sing hymns to Ptah! He who created the *Netjeru*, humankind and all animals, who created all countries, shorelines, and the Sea, in his name of He Who Forms the Land!

Come sing hymns to Ptah! He who led the Nile out of its cave, who makes the fruit tree flourish, who creates what we need without ceasing, in his name of Nun the Venerable![277]

*At this point perform the **meditation or magical action** or, if it is a special feast, add the appropriate prayers.*

*Afterwards **all present back out of the Temple Chamber with heads slightly bowed** while the Ritualist performs the **"removing the foot."***

---

[277] André Barucq, François Daumas. Hymn from Papyrus Berlin 3048. *Hymnes et prières de l'Égypte ancienne*, (Les Éditions du Cerf, 1980), 390-391, 394, 399-400.

*With the **broom** the Ritualist, as the last person to exit, **ritually sweeps the area beginning at the altar.** (This is known as "**removing the foot.**")*

While performing this action the Liturgist recites the following:

The distress that causes confusion has been driven away, and all the *Netjeru* are in harmony. I have given Heru his Eye; I have placed the *Wedjat*-Eye in the correct position. I have given Setekh his Testicles, so that the two lords are content through the work of my hands.

I know the sky, I know the earth;
I know Heru, I know Setekh.
Heru is appeased with his Eyes;
Setekh is appeased with his Testicles.
I am Djehuty, who reconciles the *Netjeru*,
who makes offerings in their correct form.

The double doors are solemnly closed as the Ritualist says the following:

Djehuty has come.
He has filled the Eye of Heru;
He has restored the Testicles of Setekh.
No evil shall enter this Temple.
Ptah has closed the door,
Djehuty has set it fast.
The door is closed, the door is set fast with the bolt.

*All **bow, touching the palms of their hands to their knees.***

THE REVERSION OF OFFERINGS

Richard J. Reidy

*One priest or priestess and as many assistants as necessary enter the Temple Chamber a final time. While he/she and any assistants **lift up the offerings** before the sacred image the* ritualist *shall say:*

O Ptah, your enemy[278] withdraws for you. Heru has turned himself to his Eye in its name of 'Reversion-of-Offerings.' I am Djehuty. I come to perform this rite for Ptah, father of the *Netjeru*. These, your divine offerings revert, they revert to your servants for life, for stability, for health and for joy! O that the Eye of Heru may flourish for you eternally!

*Everyone withdraws, **carrying away all food offerings except for one loaf of bread together with a bowl of pure water.** These last items will remain until evening. If this ritual is celebrated after sunset, these items would also be removed.*

*After the candle has burned down, a servant-priest enters and **closes the doors of the Kar-shrine**.*

***Extinguishing the candle or oil lamp,** he/she exclaims:*

This is the Eye of Heru by which you have become great, by which you live, and by which you have power, O Ptah. This is the Eye of Heru which you consume and through which you enchant your body. The *Wedjat*-Eye now enters into the West, into *Manu*, but it shall return. Truly, the Eye of Heru returns in peace![279]

---

[278] Meat offerings held a two-fold meaning for the ancient priesthood. Since meat necessarily came from slain animals, it signified the defeated or slain enemies of the Netjer. At the same time, the meat offering represented the produce of the land which ultimately was a gift of the Netjeru.

[279] It is important to consume the food offerings after the ceremony. Water used should either be drunk or poured onto the earth. If it is mixed with

The General Ritual for Sebek

All epithets and hymns appearing within this rite are taken from the article "Hymns to Sobk in a Ramesseum Papyrus," by Sir Alan Gardiner, published in Revue d'Egyptologie, *Tome 11, 1957, pages 44-56. The Egyptian priests perceived that any deity had many and varied aspects, and, hence, they used the literary device of epithets referring to those aspects in their litanies and ritual texts. Theirs was a highly liturgical theology which sought to express the reality of the Netjeru [gods] in poetic expression rather than in the dry "reasoned" explanations found in so much Western theology.*

Like members of the ancient priesthood, participants should be clothed in white linen. No items made of animal products such as leather or wool are to be worn. Linen represents a pristine product of the earth whereas leather and wool come from humankind's domination of the animals, a domination that becomes part of the "natural order" only *after* the First Time when the *Netjeru* and humans and animals lived in peace and harmony. Just as the Morning Ritual harkens back to that First Time (*Zep Tepi*), so every temple rite re-presents mythic prototypes that occurred "in the beginning," that is, in that time before time. Even the sandals worn by the *Netjer's* servants were made of white papyrus. This avoidance of animal products by the priesthood fits well with the fact that the ritualist acts as a *Netjer* and verbally asserts that he or she is a *Netjer.*

As with all Egyptian rituals begin with your purification—washing of hands and cleansing of mouth with Natron. This preliminary rite

---

natron, dilute it very greatly and then you can pour in onto the earth without harming any plantings.

helps us to lay aside the cares of the day and to become mindful of the fact that we will encounter a divine being. If Natron is not available, then use a natural sea salt in its place until you make your own Natron.

If two or more persons are participating, then one person, impersonating the Netjer Djehuty, **purifies each person by sprinkling each with water** *while exclaiming:*

I purify you with the water of all life and good fortune, all stability, all health and happiness.[280]

Afterwards each person **rinses his mouth** *and* **places a small amount of Natron or sea salt in his mouth** *while saying:*

I wash my mouth; I chew natron so that I may extol the might of Sebek, Master of Awe and Lord of Oracles.[281]

Participants **assemble outside the Temple Chamber** *and begin by* **softly rattling sistra.**

This time—several minutes or more—is used to focus minds and intention so that distracting thoughts are left behind. The sound of the sistra dispels negative energy, purifying the atmosphere in preparation for encountering divinity.

---

[280] Taken from Aylward M. Blackman's article "Purification (Egyptian)" in Hastings Encyclopaedia 10/1918/ 476-82. This article is reprinted in Gods, Priests, and Men, Studies in the Religion of Pharaonic Egypt, edited by Alan B. Lloyd (Kegan Paul International, 1998), p. 9.

[281] Based on a temple inscription taken from "The Myth of Horus at Edfu—II" by A. M. Blackman and H. W. Fairman, appearing in Gods, Priests and Men, Studies in the Religion of Pharaonic Egypt, Blackman and Lloyd, p. 283.

*Standing before the closed doors, the Ritualist **recites the entrance spell**:*

UTTERANCE BEFORE THE CLOSED DOORS OF THE TEMPLE

*The ritualist **raises hands in adoration** (dua position—arms stretched out in front of the body and raised up to face level, with palms facing outward). The following shall be said:*

O you Netjeru of this Temple, you guardians of the great portal, great *Netjeru* of mysterious abode, who sanctify the *Netjer* in his shrine, who consecrate his oblation, who receive the offerings in his presence in the Hall of the Ennead: I have made my way and I enter into your presence. I am one of you. I am Shu, the eldest son of his father, the senior *wab* servant-priest of Sebek. Do not repulse me on the *Netjer*'s path. My feet are not impeded. I am not turned back from the court of the great portal so that I may conduct the divine service, that I may present offerings to him that made them, that I may give bread to Sebek. I have come on the way of the *Netjer*. I have not shown partiality in judgment. I have not consorted with the strong. I have not reproached the lowly. I have not stolen things. I have not diminished the constituents of the Eye of Ra. I have not disturbed the Balance. I have not tampered with the requirements of the Sacred Eye. O Council of the Great *Netjer* in this Temple, behold, I have come to you to offer Ma'at to the Lord of Powers, to content the Sound Eye for its master. I am Shu; I flood his offering table. I present his offerings, Sekhmet consorting with me, that I may adore Sebek at his festivals, that I may kiss the earth so great is his majesty, that I may endow his image with life. I am pure. I am purified.

*At this point the ritualist **opens the doors to the Temple Chamber**, or, if there are no doors, **makes a gesture of opening unseen doors**, and **steps forward as if crossing over a threshold**. The following is said:*

O you *Ba*-souls of *Shedet* (i.e., Crocodilopolis[282]), if you are strong, I am strong. If I am strong, you are strong. If your *Ka*-spirits are strong, my *Ka*-spirit is strong at the head of the living. As they are living so shall I live . . . . Sekhmet, the great *Netjeret*, beloved of Ptah, has given to me life, stability, and serenity round about my members, which Djehuty has gathered together for life. I am Heru in the height of heaven, the beautiful one of awe, Lord of Victory, mighty one of awe, exalted one of the two plumes, great one in *Abdju* (Abydos) I am pure.

All temple members chant:

Awake in peace, O Sebek, Guardian of the Earth,
may you awaken in peace.
Awake in peace, O Sebek, Lord of Maat,
may you awaken in peace.
Awake in peace, O Sebek, Devourer of the Companions of Apep,
may you awaken in peace.
Awake in peace, O Sebek, Noble Powerful One,
may you awaken in peace.

May you awake beautifully at the top of the morning,
through that which the entirety of *Netjeru* say to you.

*Enter, **close the double doors** and **stand in front of the Kar-shrine and altar**. All bow, touching their hands to their knees.*

---

[282] Shedet (Greek, Crocodilopolis) is the major cult center for Sebek and his consort Renenutet.

The ritualist *slowly* **opens the two doors of the Kar-shrine** *housing the sacred image.* **All others bow, touching their hands to their knees.** *The following is said:*

The doors of the sky are open; the doors of the earth are unlocked. This House is open for its Lord. Let me come forth as he shall come forth. Let me enter in as he shall enter in. Sebek, Son of Neith, Beloved of Hat-Hór [Hathor], is exalted upon his Great Seat. The Great Company of the *Netjeru* are exalted upon their seat.

I have seen the *Netjer,* and the *Netjer* sees me. The *Netjer* rejoices at seeing me. I have gazed upon the statue of the Greatly Revered One, the sacred image of Sebek.[283]

Right hand on left shoulder of statue; left hand on right wrist of statue:

Djehuty has come to you. Awake when you hear his words. I have come as the envoy of Atum. My two arms are upon you like those of Heru. My two hands are upon you like those of Djehuty. My fingers are upon you like those of Anpu. Homage be to you. I am a living servant of Sebek.

The Ritualist holds up the **bowl of water** *in which he/she will be mixing the Natron. The following is said:*

O water may you remove all evil,
As Ra who bathes in the Lake of Rushes,
May Heru wash my flesh,

---

[283] Based on the temple text found in "Worship and Festivals in an Egyptian Temple," a lecture by H. W. Fairman (publ. by The John Rylands Library, 1954), p. 180.

Richard J. Reidy

May Djehuty cleanse my feet,
May Shu lift me up and Nut take my hand!
May Setekh be my strength, and may Sekhmet be my healing!
And may Amun-Ra be my life and my prospering!

*The bowl of water is set aside and the container of **Natron** is lifted up. The following is said:*

It is pure, it is pure.
My Natron is the Natron of Heru and the Natron of Heru is my Natron.
My Natron is the Natron of Setekh and the Natron of Setekh is my Natron.
My Natron is the Natron of Djehuty, and the Natron of Djehuty is my Natron.
My Natron is the Natron of Geb and the Natron of Geb is my Natron.

My mouth is the mouth of a milking calf on the day that I was born.

***Four pinches of Natron are mixed into the water** as this Utterance is recited:*

I give you essential water, a tide in your time.
I bring the flood waters to purify your sanctuary.
I bring you the flood waters to purify your Temple and your statue in its place. The primordial water that purifies as in the First Time!

*The Ritualist **places an index finger into the water** and **moves it in a circular, clockwise direction four times** as the following is said:*

Sebek, the Son of Neith, does purify this water;
Sebek, Beloved of Renenutet, does cleanse this water;
Sebek, Lord of Love, does sanctify this water;
Sebek himself does endow this water with power and with life.

*The **Bowl of Natron-infused water** is then taken up and the Ritualist sprinkles this lightly in front of and around the statue or image of Sebek, applying the water to the base of the image, as the Utterance is recited:*

I come close to you, O Powerful One, who did rise from the Primeval Waters. I bring the water of rejuvenation that flows from the Two Caverns. I sprinkle the water, purifying your image and your Temple from all impurity!

*The Ritualist picks up the bowl of **Natron** and **sprinkles a small amount in each of the four directions** as the following is recited:*

The *Netjer* Sebek himself does cleanse and purify this, his Temple to the South.
The *Netjer* Sebek himself does cleanse and purify this, his Temple to the North.
The *Netjer* Sebek himself does cleanse and purify this, his Temple to the West.
The *Netjer* Sebek himself does cleanse and purify this, his Temple to the East.

*Replacing the Natron on the altar, the Ritualist does the same with the **water, sprinkling a small amount in each of the four directions**. The following Utterance is recited:*

427

The *Netjer* Sebek himself does sanctify and consecrate this, his
Temple to the South.
The *Netjer* Sebek himself does sanctify and consecrate this, his
Temple to the North.
The *Netjer* Sebek himself does sanctify and consecrate this, his
Temple to the West.
The *Netjer* Sebek himself does sanctify and consecrate this, his
Temple to the East.
The Temple of the great *Netjer* Sebek is established.
It is established for millions of years.

The Ritualist returns to the altar and then **lights the candle or oil
lamp** *while the following is said:*

Come, come in peace, O glorious Eye of Heru,
Be strong and renew your youth in peace.
For the flame shines like Ra on the double horizon.
The enemies of Ra are defeated. They are defeated.
I am pure, I am pure, I am pure, I am pure.

The Ritualist **places incense** *on the burner and* **censes each sacred
image** *beginning with the statue of the Netjer while the following is
recited:*

The fire is laid, the fire shines;
The incense is laid on the fire, the incense shines.
    Your perfume comes to me, O Incense;
    May my perfume come to you, O Incense.
Your perfume comes to me, you *Netjeru*;
May my perfume come to you, You *Netjeru*.
    May I be with you, you *Netjeru*;
    May you be with me, you *Netjeru*.

May I live with you, you *Netjeru*;
May you live with me, you *Netjeru*.
I love you, you *Netjeru*;
May you love me, you *Netjeru*.

*Standing in front of the image of Sebek, the Ritualist **offers the burning incense** and says:*

Take the incense,
Its essence is for you, O Lord of Incense.
Its smoke permeates your shrine, bringing life!
Take the incense,
Its essence is for you, O Lord of Fear.
Your Majesty is appeased with the incense.
This Eye of Heru,
This essence of the Eye of Heru comes to you.

At this point the following is said:

Homage to You, O Sebek, Son of Neith,
Who did arise from the Primeval Waters,
Beautiful of Stature, Great Virile One,
Lord of *Shedet*. You make holy the Two Lands with your love.
Greater is the awe of you than that of the *Netjeru*.

Those who are in the *Duat* adore you,
those who are in the Flood pacify you.
How beautiful you are, O Sebek of *Shedet*,
being born, living, strong, alert, honored and enduring.

Appear gloriously, O Sebek.
The *Netjerut* (i.e., goddesses) praise you, they call upon you.
'Come, our Heru; Come, our *Netjer*,

Lord of Fear, Great of Terror, Whose onslaught is not repelled.'
Praised of the Western *Netjeru*, Revered of the Eastern *Netjeru*.
Foremost of Heart,
Welcome in peace, O Lord of Peace.

*The Ritualist **places more incense** on the charcoal and again and again **slowly raises and lowers the incense cup** as the following is recited:*

O Sebek, may you advance with your *Ka*.
O Lord of Love, the arm of your *Ka* is before you,
The arm of your *Ka* is behind you.
O Rutting Bull, the foot of your *Ka* is before you,
The foot of your *Ka* is behind you.
O Sebek, beautiful of stature, this incense is offered to you,
May your face be filled as this essence spreads itself over you.

*All present perform the **Henu Rite**—Embrace the Earth, the Fourfold Salute to the Netjer, Embrace the Earth.*

For Embracing the Earth, all present prostrate themselves, face down, upon the floor. During the Fourfold Salute, all present rise upon one knee, and alternately raise their hands and arms into the *Dua* (praise) position with palms facing outward, followed by the *Sahu* (obedience) gesture, made by striking the chest with a closed fist and raising the other arm (also with closed fist) at a ninety-degree angle. The *Dua* position is accompanied by the words **"Adoration be to Sebek,"** followed by the *Sahu* gesture accompanied with the words, **"Hail to the Lord of Oracles!"** The bodily gestures are performed alternately four times.

*Following this **all present again prostrate themselves** before the Netjer. This is a sign and symbol of total submission and adoration before the Netjer. The following is said:*

Homage to Sebek, Lord of Oracles, Power of Powers,
who is established on the Great Seat!
I have placed myself on the floor in awe of you.
I embrace the earth before you as before the Lord of Powers.
I have come that I might kiss the earth,
that I might worship my Master,
For I have seen his strength;
I give praise to Sebek,
For I have seen his Power.
His form is more distinguished than the *Netjeru*;
His arm is more powerful than the *Netjeru*.
I am pure, I am pure, I am pure, I am pure!

Everyone stands up.

*The Ritualist **holds in the palm of one hand the image of Ma'at** and with **the other hand open and raised over the image as if sheltering it**, repeats the following:*

I have come to you as Djehuty, whose two hands are joined together under Ma'at. She comes to be with you, for she is everywhere. You are provided with Ma'at. You move in Ma'at, you live in Ma'at. She fills your body, she rests in your head, she makes her seat upon your brow; the breath of your body is of Ma'at, your heart does live in Ma'at. All that you eat, all that you drink, all that you breathe is of Ma'at. Djehuty presents Ma'at to you, his two hands are upon her beauty before your face.

431

Richard J. Reidy

*The Ritualist places the image of Ma'at near the divine statue. Then he/ she holds up before the image of Sebek **a pitcher** of water and **pours all the water slowly into an offering bowl** as the following Utterance is recited:*

This libation is for you, O Gleaming One,
This libation is for you, O Sebek.
I have brought to you this offering of water,
That your heart may be refreshed.
I have brought to you this Eye of Heru,
Placing this at your feet.
I present to you that which flows forth from you,
That your heart shall continue to beat.
For it is with you that all comes forth at the sound of the voice.

*The offering bowl is placed on the altar. At this point the Ritualist lightly **sprinkles sand on the floor in front of the altar** as the following is recited:*

O Sebek, who resides in **Shedet.** [The Egyptian name for Crocodilopolis]
Take to yourself the Eye of Heru.
You have rescued it, O Foremost of Heart,
You have sprinkled with sand the Eye of Heru.

*Lifting the **wine offering** before the sacred image, the Ritualist repeats the following:*

mn n.k irp irt ḥrw wȝḏt
["**mán-nik 'úrip írat ḥáru wá'ḏat**"; approximately pronounced *MAHN-neek OO-rip EE-raht HAH-roo WAH-jat*]

Take to Yourself wine, the green Eye of Heru, which I offer to
your *Ka.*
O Ruler, how beautiful is your beauty!
May you drink it; may your heart rejoice;
may anger be removed from your face.
It is pure. [*iw.w wˁb* pronounced *"uwú wáˁib"*; approximately *oo-
WOO WAH-ib*]

*The Ritualist **places myrrh on the fire** and **lifts up the smoking
incense** while at the same time he **lifts up the meat-offering** before
the Netjer, and says the following:*

The scent of myrrh is for your nose. It fills your nostrils; your
heart receives the meat-portions on its scent.[284]

*Slowly **elevating the food offerings four times** before the image of
the Netjer, the Ritualist repeats the following:*

I offer to Sebek, O Powerful One.
All life emanates from you,
All health emanates from you,
All stability emanates from you,
All good fortune emanates from you,
O Greatly Revered One, Sebek, forever.

*The Ritualist **places the food offering before the divine image,** and
then all present **extend one hand, palm down, over the offerings**
and recite the following:*

May offerings of every kind come forth in abundance,

---

[284] Quoted in "Worship and Festivals in an Egyptian Temple," by H. W.
Fairman (publ. by The John Rylands Library, 1954), p. 191.

like the things which come forth from the mouth of the *Netjer*.

piryá pírit ar ḫiráw mi purú:riat ma rá' ni náṭar. (4 times)
[approximately pronounced: peer-YA PEER-it ar khi-RAU mee pu-ROOR-iat ma RA nee NAH-tchar]

May offerings of every kind come forth in abundance,
like the things which come forth from the mouth of the *Netjer*.

*Holding the **Ankh** before the divine image, the Ritualist says:*

Live, O Sebek, Duplicate of Ra, live for all time and for eternity!

ʿánaḫ niḥáḥ ḏát.
[approximately pronounced *AH-nakh nee-HAH JAHT*]

*The **Ankh** is placed next to the Netjer.*

*Holding the **Ib (the golden heart)** before the Sebek, the Ritualist says:*

Hail to you, O Sebek, Master of Awe. I have brought to you your heart to set it in its place. Let me draw near to you with your heart, so that you may have pleasure through me, and so that by means of me you may have power over your body. Ascend gloriously, O Ram greatly revered. You have taken rulership over heaven. You have filled the Two Lands with your power. Live, O Duplicate of Ra, live forever and ever!

*After placing the **Ib** near the sacred image, **everyone sings or chants** the hymn to Sebek. Participants may wish to alternate the singing of verses.*

I praise the Gleaming One, I worship his Majesty!

I exalt the Son of Neith.
Adoration be to Sebek. Praise be to my Master!
O Ruler of the river and streams, Controller of the winds,
Who enfolds me in your strong arms.
All hail! Jubilation to you, the Lord of Love.

O Lord of Attributes, Great Luminary, Duplicate of Ra!
As you delivered the four Sons of Heru in your net,
Deliver me from every snare of the enemy.
O Lord of Strength, Great of Fortitude,
Help me overcome all obstacles.

I revere you, Sebek, Lord of the Waters, Gleaming One!
Beloved of Renenutet.
from sky, from earth, from south, from north,
from west, from east, from each land, from each place,
where your Majesty shines forth!
See what is in my heart, see what is in my inmost.
My heart is blameless, my inmost is open.
No darkness is in my breast!

I adore you, Savage Lion, Great of Strength, Sharp of Teeth.
Bull of the Seven Hwt-Hrw's.
Grant me long life, health, and stability.
So that I might rejoice in the House of Jubilation.
Heaven and earth are opened.
The Gates of the two Beholding-Eyes are flung wide for Sebek.

Heaven exalts, the Earth is filled with gladness.
Sebek the Great rejoices! *(4 times)*

*At this point perform the **meditation or magical action** or, if it is a
special feast, add the appropriate prayers.*

*Afterwards **all present back out of the Temple Chamber with heads slightly bowed** while the Ritualist performs the "removing the foot."*

*With the **broom** the Ritualist, as the last person to exit, **ritually sweeps the area beginning at the altar**. (This is known as "removing the foot".) While performing this action the Ritualist recites the following:*

The distress that causes confusion has been driven away, and all the
Netjeru are in harmony. I have given Heru his Eye, I have placed the *Wedjat*-Eye in the correct position. I have given Setekh his Testicles, so that the two lords are content through the work of my hands.

I know the sky, I know the earth; I know Heru, I know Setekh. Heru is appeased with his Eyes, Setekh is appeased with his Testicles.
I am Djehuty, who reconciles the *Netjeru*, who makes offerings in their correct form.

*The double doors are **solemnly closed** as the Ritualist says the following:*

Djehuty has come.
He has filled the Eye of Heru;
He has restored the Testicles of Setekh.
No evil shall enter this Temple.
Ptah has closed the door,
Djehuty has set it fast.
The door is closed, the door is set fast with the bolt.

All bow, touching the palms of their hands to their knees.

THE REVERSION OF OFFERINGS

*One priest or priestess and as many assistants as necessary enter the Temple Chamber a final time. While he/she and any assistants **lift up the offerings** before the sacred image the ritualist shall say:*

O Sebek, your enemy withdraws for you. Heru has turned himself to his Eye in its name of 'Reversion-of-Offerings'. I am Djehuty. I come to perform this rite for Sebek, lord of *Shedet*. These, your divine offerings revert, they revert to your servants for life, for stability, for health and for joy! O that the Eye of Heru may flourish for you eternally![285]

*Everyone withdraws, **carrying away all food offerings except for one loaf of bread together with a bowl of pure water.** These last items will remain until evening. If this ritual is celebrated after sunset, these items would also be removed.*

*After the candle has burned down, a servant-priest enters and **closes the doors of the Kar-shrine.***

***Extinguishing the candle or oil lamp,** he/she exclaims:*

This is the Eye of Heru by which you have become great, by which you live, and by which you have power, O Sebek. This

---

[285] Meat offerings held a two-fold meaning for the ancient priesthood. Since meat necessarily came from slain animals, it signified the defeated or slain enemies of the Netjer. At the same time, the meat offering represented the produce of the land which ultimately was a gift of the Netjeru.

is the Eye of Heru which you consume and through which you enchant your body. The *Wedjat*-Eye now enters into the West, into *Manu,* but it shall return. Truly, the Eye of Heru returns in peace![286]

---

[286] It is important to consume the food offerings after the ceremony. Water used should either be drunk or poured onto the earth. If it is mixed with Natron, dilute it very greatly and then pour in onto the bare earth.

The General Ritual for Sekhmet

Like members of the ancient priesthood, participants should be clothed in white linen. No items made of animal products such as leather or wool are to be worn. Linen represents a pristine product of the earth whereas leather and wool come from humankind's domination of the animals, a domination that becomes part of the "natural order" only *after* the First Time when the *Netjeru* and humans and animals lived in peace and harmony. Just as the Morning Ritual harkens back to that First Time (*Zep Tepi*), so every temple rite re-presents mythic prototypes that occurred "in the beginning," that is, in that time before time. Even the sandals worn by the god's servants were made of white papyrus. This avoidance of animal products by the priesthood fits well with the fact that the ritualist acts as a *Netjer* and verbally asserts that he or she is a *Netjer*.

As with all Egyptian rituals begin with your purification—washing of hands and cleansing of mouth with Natron. This preliminary rite helps us to lay aside the cares of the day and to become mindful of the fact that we will encounter a divine being. If Natron is not available, then use a natural sea salt in its place until you make your own Natron.

Special offering: beer, as well as the traditional offerings of bread, wine, and meat. Beer is used to pacify this goddess. Other healthy foods may also be offered.

If two or more persons are participating, then one person, impersonating the Netjer Djehuty, **purifies each person by sprinkling each with water** *while exclaiming:*

I purify you with the water of all life and good fortune, all stability, all health and happiness.[287]

Afterwards each person rinses his mouth and places a small amount of Natron or sea salt in his mouth while saying:

I wash my mouth; I chew natron so that I may extol the might of Sekhmet, Lady of All Powers, the Mistress of Awe.[288]

Participants assemble outside the Temple Chamber and begin by softly rattling sistra.

This time—several minutes or more—is used to focus minds and intention so that distracting thoughts are left behind. The sound of the sistra dispels negative energy, purifying the atmosphere in preparation for encountering divinity.

Standing before the closed doors, the Ritualist recites the entrance spell:

UTTERANCE BEFORE THE CLOSED DOORS OF THE TEMPLE

The ritualist raises hands in adoration (dua position—arms stretched out in front of the body and raised up to face level, with palms facing outward). The following shall be said:

---

[287] Taken from Aylward M. Blackman's article "Purification (Egyptian)" in Hastings Encyclopaedia 10/1918/ 476-82. This article is reprinted in Gods, Priests, and Men, Studies in the Religion of Pharaonic Egypt, edited by Alan B. Lloyd (Kegan Paul International, 1998), p. 9.

[288] Based on a temple inscription taken from "The Myth of Horus at Edfu—II" by A. M. Blackman and H. W. Fairman, appearing in Gods, Priests and Men, Studies in the Religion of Pharaonic Egypt (Kegan Paul International, 1998) p. 283.

O you *Netjeru* of this Temple, you guardians of the great portal, great *Netjeru* of mysterious abode, who sanctify the *Netjeret* in her shrine, who consecrate her oblation, who receive the offerings in her presence in the Hall of the Ennead: I have made my way and I enter into your presence. I am one of you. I am Shu, the eldest son of his father, the senior *wab* servant-priest of Sekhmet. Do not repulse me on the *Netjeret's* path. My feet are not impeded. I am not turned back from the court of the great portal so that I may conduct the divine service, that I may present offerings to her that made them, that I may give bread to Sekhmet. I have come on the way of the *Netjeret*. I have not shown partiality in judgment. I have not consorted with the strong. I have not reproached the lowly. I have not stolen things. I have not diminished the constituents of the Eye of Ra. I have not disturbed the Balance. I have not tampered with the requirements of the Sacred Eye. O Council of the Great *Netjeret* in this Temple, behold, I have come to you to offer Ma'at to the Lady of Ma'at, to content the Sound Eye for its mistress. I am Shu; I flood her offering table. I present her offerings, this great *Netjeret* consorting with me, that I may adore Sekhmet at her festivals, that I may kiss the earth so great is her majesty, that I may endow her image with life. I am pure. I am purified.

At this point the ritualist *opens the doors to the Temple Chamber, or, if there are no doors,* **makes a gesture of opening unseen doors,** *and* **steps forward as if crossing over a threshold.** *The following is said:*

O you *Ba*-souls of *Mennefer* (i.e., Memphis[289]), if you are strong, I am strong. If I am strong, you are strong. If your *Ka*-spirits are strong, my *Ka*-spirit is strong at the head of the living. As

---

[289] Mennefer (Greek, Memphis) is the cult center for Ptah and his consort Sekhmet.

they are living so shall I live . . . . Sekhmet, the great *Netjeret*, beloved of Ptah, has given to me life, stability, and serenity round about my members, which Djehuty has gathered together for life. I am Heru in the height of heaven, the beautiful one of awe, Lord of Victory, mighty one of awe, exalted one of the two plumes, great one in *Abdju* (Abydos) I am pure.

All temple members chant:

Awake in peace, O Sekhmet, may you awake in peace.
Awake in peace, O Lady of Life, may you awake in peace.
Awake in peace, O Lady of Protection, Who Hears Petitions, may you awake in peace.
Awake in peace, O Beautiful Sekhmet, may you awake in peace.

May you awake beautifully at the top of the morning, through that which the entirety of *Netjeru* say to you.

Enter, close the double doors and stand in front of the Kar-shrine and altar. All bow, touching their hands to their knees.

The ritualist *slowly opens the two doors of the Kar-shrine housing the sacred image. All others bow, touching their hands to their knees. The following is said:*

The doors of the sky are open; the doors of the earth are unlocked. This House is open for its Mistress. Let me come forth as she shall come forth. Let me enter in as she shall enter in. Sekhmet, Daughter of the Limitless One, Beloved of Ptah, is exalted upon her Great Seat. The Great Company of the *Netjeru* are exalted upon their seat.

I have seen the *Netjeret,* and the *Netjeret* sees me. The *Netjeret* rejoices at seeing me. I have gazed upon the statue of the Luminous One, the sacred image of the Eye of Ra.[290]

Right hand on left shoulder of statue; left hand on right wrist of statue:

Djehuty has come to you. Awake when you hear his words.
I have come as the envoy of Atum. My two arms are upon like those of Heru.
My two hands are upon you like those of Djehuty. My fingers are upon you like those of Anpu.
Homage be to you. I am a living servant of Sekhmet.

The Ritualist holds up the **bowl of water** *in which he/she will be mixing the Natron. The following is said:*

O water may you remove all evil,
As Ra who bathes in the Lake of Rushes,
May Heru wash my flesh,
May Djehuty cleanse my feet,
May Shu lift me up and Nut take my hand!
May Setekh be my strength, and may Sekhmet be my healing!
And may Amun-Ra be my life and my prospering!

The bowl of water is set aside and the container of **Natron** *is lifted up. The following is said:*

It is pure, it is pure.

---

[290] Based on the temple text found in "Worship and Festivals in an Egyptian Temple," a lecture by H. W. Fairman (publ. by The John Rylands Library, 1954) p. 180.

My Natron is the Natron of Heru and the Natron of Heru is my Natron.

My Natron is the Natron of Setekh and the Natron of Setekh is my Natron.

My Natron is the Natron of Djehuty, and the Natron of Djehuty is my Natron.

My Natron is the Natron of Geb and the Natron of Geb is my Natron.

My mouth is the mouth of a milking calf on the day that I was born.

Four pinches of Natron are mixed into the water as this Utterance is recited:

I give you essential water, a tide in your time.
I bring the flood waters to purify your sanctuary.
I bring you the flood waters to purify your Temple and your statue in its place, the primordial water that purifies as in the First Time!

The Ritualist places an index finger into the water and moves it in a circular, clockwise direction four times as the following is said:

Sekhmet, the Daughter of Ra, does purify this water;
Sekhmet, the Beloved of Ptah, does cleanse this water;
Sekhmet, Sweet One of Heru and Setekh, does sanctify this water;
Sekhmet herself does endow this water with power and with life.

*The **Bowl of Natron-infused water** is then taken up and the Ritualist **sprinkles this lightly in front of and around the statue** or image of Sekhmet, applying the water to the base of the image, as the Utterance is recited:*

I come close to You, O Pure One, Lady of the Waters of Life.
I bring the water of rejuvenation that flows from the Two Caverns.
I sprinkle the water, purifying your image and your Temple from all impurity!

*The Ritualist picks up **the bowl of Natron** and **sprinkles a small amount in each of the four directions** as the following is recited:*

The *Netjeret* Sekhmet herself does cleanse and purify this, her Temple to the South.
The *Netjeret* Sekhmet herself does cleanse and purify this, her Temple to the North.
The *Netjeret* Sekhmet herself does cleanse and purify this, her Temple to the West.
The N*etjeret* Sekhmet herself does cleanse and purify this, her Temple to the East.

*Replacing the Natron on the altar, the Ritualist takes up **the bowl of water, sprinkling a small amount in each of the four directions.** The following Utterance is recited:*

The *Netjeret* Sekhmet herself does sanctify and consecrate this, her Temple to the South.
The *Netjeret* Sekhmet herself does sanctify and consecrate this, her Temple to the North.
The *Netjeret* Sekhmet herself does sanctify and consecrate this, her Temple to the West.

The *Netjeret* Sekhmet herself does sanctify and consecrate this,
her Temple to the East.
The Temple of the *Netjeret* Sekhmet is established.
It is established for millions of years.

*The Ritualist returns to the altar and lights the candle or oil lamp
while the following is said:*

Come, come in peace, O glorious Eye of Heru,
Be strong and renew your youth in peace.
For the flame shines like Ra on the double horizon.
The enemies are Ra are defeated. They are defeated.
I am pure, I am pure, I am pure, I am pure.

*The Ritualist places incense on the burner and censes each sacred
image beginning with the statue of the Netjeret while the following is
recited:*

The fire is laid, the fire shines;
The incense is laid on the fire, the incense shines.
Your perfume comes to me, O Incense;
May my perfume come to you, O Incense.
Your perfume comes to me, you *Netjeru*;
May my perfume come to you, You *Netjeru*.
May I be with you, you *Netjeru*;
May you be with me, you *Netjeru*.
May I live with you, you *Netjeru*;
May you live with me, you *Netjeru*.
I love you, you *Netjeru*;
May you love me, you *Netjeru*.

*Standing in front of the image of Sekhmet the Ritualist offers the
burning incense and says:*

Take the incense, O Lady of Flame.
Its essence is for you.
Its smoke permeates your shrine, bringing life!
Take the incense,
Its essence is for you.
Your Majesty is appeased with the incense.
This Eye of Heru,
This essence of the Eye of Heru comes to you.

At this point the following is said:

Homage to you, O Sekhmet, Daughter of Ra, mistress of the *Netjeru*, bearer of wings, Lady of the Red Apparel, queen of the crowns of the South and North, Only One, Chief One of her Father, superior to whom the *Netjeru* cannot be, Mighty One of Enchantments in the Boat-of-Millions-of-Years, you who are preeminent, you who rise in the Seat of Silence, mother of the god Nefertum, smiter of the enemies of Ra, mistress and lady of the tomb, Mother in the horizon of heaven, gracious one, beloved, destroyer of rebellion, offerings are in your grasp— offerings are in your grasp—and you are standing in the boat of your divine Father to overthrow the fiend Qetu.

You have placed Ma'at in the bows of His boat. You are the fire *Netjeret* Ammi-seshet, whose opportunity escapes her not . . . Praise be to you, O Lady, who are mightier than the *Netjeru*. Words of adoration rise up to you from the Eight *Netjeru* of *Khemenu* (Hermopolis).

The living *Ba*-souls who are in their hidden places praise the mystery of you, O you who are their mother; you the Source from which they sprang, who make for them a place in the hidden Underworld, who make sound their bones and preserve them from every terror, you who make them strong in the Abode-of-Everlastingness, who preserve them from the evil Chamber of the souls of HES'-HER, you who are among the company of the *Netjeru*. Your name is *zfy pr m Hs Hr hApu Dt.f* (pronounced "seh-fee per em Hes' Her h'poo jet-ef").[291] **Your name is "Lady-of-Life.**[292]

*The Ritualist **places more incense** on the charcoal and again and again **slowly raises and lowers the incense cup** as the following is recited:*

O Sekhmet, may you advance with your *Ka*.
O Luminous One, the arm of your *Ka* is before you,
The arm of your *Ka* is behind you.
O Lady of Heaven, the foot of your *Ka* is before you,
The foot of your *Ka* is behind you.
O Beautiful Sekhmet, this incense is offered to you,

---

[291] This epithet translates as "Child Who comes of/from 'Fierce-of-Face,' mysterious of His forms." 'Fierce-of-Face' may refer to the scorching heat of the sun and thus to the god Ra, or it may refer to a netherworld deity called 'Fierce of Face.' In either case this epithet may be regarded as a 'name of power' for invoking this Netjeret in her capacity as powerful Protectress of those in the Duat (Netherworld or Afterlife Realm). This entire paragraph refers specifically to those "in the hidden Underworld."

[292] Adapted from an ancient prayer in E. A. Wallis Budge, The Gods of the Egyptians, Vol. 1 (London, 1904), pp. 518-519. Primary Source is Book of the Dead Chapter clxiv. There exist many revisions of editions of the Book of the Dead. Not every Chapter is in every copy of the Book. The best source for locating every known Chapter is Egyptologist Stephen Quirke's comprehensive Going out in Daylight - prt m hrw: The Ancient Egyptian Book of the Dead—translation, sources, meanings (Golden House Publications, 2013).

May your face be filled as this essence spreads itself over you.

All present perform the **Henu Rite** *—Embrace the Earth, the Fourfold Salute to Sekhmet, and again Embrace the Earth.*

For Embracing the Earth, all present prostrate themselves, face down, upon the floor. During the Fourfold Salute, all present rise upon one knee, and alternately raise their hands and arms into the *Dua* (praise) position with palms facing outward, followed by the *Sahu* (obedience) gesture, made by striking the chest with a closed fist and raising the other arm (also with closed fist) at a ninety-degree angle. The *Dua* position is accompanied by the words **"Adoration be to Sekhmet,"** followed by the *Sahu* gesture accompanied with the words, **"Hail to the Lady of Protection!"**. The bodily gestures are performed alternately four times.

Following this **all present again prostrate themselves** *before the Netjeret. This is a sign and symbol of total submission and adoration before the Netjeret. The following is said:*

Homage to Sekhmet, Eye of Ra, Great of Flame,
who is established on the Great Seat!
I have placed myself on the floor in awe of you.
I embrace the earth before you as before the Lady of All Powers.
I have come that I might kiss the earth,
that I might worship my Mistress,
For I have seen her Beauty;
I give praise to Sekhmet,
For I have seen her Power.
Her form is more distinguished than the *Netjeru*;
Her arm is more powerful than the *Netjeru*.
I am pure, I am pure, I am pure, I am pure!

Richard J. Reidy

Everyone stands up.

*The Ritualist **holds in the palm of one hand the image of Ma'at** and with **the other hand open and raised over the image as if sheltering it**, repeats the following:*

I have come to you as Djehuty, whose two hands are joined together under Ma'at. She comes to be with you, for she is everywhere. You are provided with Ma'at. You move in Ma'at, you live in Ma'at. She fills your body, she rests in your head, she makes her seat upon your brow; the breath of your body is of Ma'at, your heart does live in Ma'at. All that you eat, all that you drink, all that you breathe is of Ma'at. Djehuty presents Ma'at to you, his two hands are upon her beauty before your face.

*The Ritualist places the image of Ma'at near the divine statue. Then he/she holds up before the image of Sekhmet **a pitcher of water** and **pours the water slowly into an offering bowl** as the following Utterance is recited:*

This libation is for you, O Sparkling One.
This libation is for you, O Sekhmet.
I have brought to you this offering of water,
That your heart may be refreshed.
I have brought to you this Eye of Heru,
Placing this at your feet.
I present to you that which flows forth from you,
That your heart shall continue to beat.
For it is with you
that all comes forth at the sound of the voice.

*The offering bowl is placed on the altar. At this point the Ritualist lightly **sprinkles sand on the floor in front of the altar** as the following is recited:*

O Sekhmet, who resides in **Mennefer,** [The Egyptian name for the city of Memphis]
Take to yourself the Eye of Heru.
You have rescued it, O Protectress of the Divine Order.
You have sprinkled with sand the Eye of Heru.
The Eye of Heru is healed. It is restored whole and complete.
It is Djehuty who has done this with his fingers.

Lifting the beer offering, the Ritualist recites the following:

This beer Menqet brings to you, Menqet, the *Netjeret* who prepares the beer with her own recipes, inspired by her heart, these pitchers of beer are with her, overflowing with her beverage and filled with good herbs coming forth from the soil, filled with the goodness extracted from cereals, mixed by herself with her own hands in order to invigorate your heart with it.[293]

Lifting the wine offering before the sacred image, the Ritualist repeats the following:

mn n.t irp irt ḥrw wȝdt

---

[293] Quoted in Sylvie Cauville, *Dendara IV: Traduction* (Leuven, Belgium: Peeters, 2001), p. 333. The goddess Menqet is a little-known deity, appearing perhaps only at Dendara. We can restore her place in our own era. In the *LÄGG* her epithets include the following: 'She Who Brews Beer', 'Lady of Red Beer', 'She Who Originated Beer Brewing', 'She Who Makes the Golden One Drunk by Her Daily Task,' and 'Mistress of Beer'. She is also identified with another beer goddess, Tchenemit (Tnmyt).

[*"mán-niṯ 'úrip írat ḥáru wá'ḏat"*; approximately pronounced *MAHN-neetch OO-rip EE-raht HAH-roo WAH-jat*]

Take to Yourself wine, the green Eye of Heru, which I offer to your *Ka*.
O Ruler, how beautiful is your beauty!
May you drink it; may your heart rejoice;
may anger be removed from your face.
It is pure. [*iw.w w'b* pronounced *"uwú wá'ib"*; approximately oo-WOO WAH-ib]

The Ritualist **places myrrh on the fire** *and* **lifts up the smoking incense** *while at the same time he* **lifts up the meat-offering** *before the Netjeret, and says the following:*

The scent of myrrh is for your nose. It fills your nostrils; your heart receives the meat-portions on its scent.[294]

Slowly **elevating the food offerings four times** *before the image of the Netjeret, the Ritualist repeats the following:*

I offer to Sekhmet, O Powerful One.
All life emanates from you,
All health emanates from you,
All stability emanates from you,
All good fortune emanates from you,
O Great One of *Heka-u*, Sekhmet, forever.

---

[294] Quoted in "Worship and Festivals in an Egyptian Temple," by H. W. Fairman (publ. by The John Rylands Library, 1954), p. 191.

The Ritualist places the food offering before the divine image, and then all present extend one hand, palm down, over the offerings and recite the following:

May offerings of every kind come forth in abundance, like the things which come forth from the mouth of the Netjeret.

piryá pírit ar ḫiráw mi purú:riat ma rá' ni naṯárat. (4 times)
[approximately pronounced: peer-YA PEER-it ar khi-RAU mee pu-ROOR-iat ma RA nee nah-TCHAR-at]

May offerings of every kind come forth in abundance, like the things that come forth from the mouth of the Netjeret.

*Holding the **Ankh** before Sekhmet, the Ritualist says:*

Live, O Sekhmet, Eye of Ra, live for all time and for eternity!

ʿánaḫ niḥáḫ ḍát.
[approximately pronounced *AH-nakh nee-HAH JAHT*]

*The **Ankh** is placed next to the image of Sekhmet.*

*Holding the **Ib** (the golden heart) before the Netjeret, the Ritualist says:*

Hail to you, O Sekhmet, Mistress of Awe. I have brought to you your heart to set it in its place. Let me draw near to you with your heart, so that you may have pleasure through me, and so that by means of me you may have power over your body. Ascend, O Solar Feminine Disk, radiant, rejuvenating, equipped as a Netjeret. Live, O Eye of Ra, live forever and ever!

Richard J. Reidy

*After placing the **Ib** near the sacred image, **everyone sings or chants** the hymn to Sekhmet. Participants may wish to alternate the singing of verses.*

I praise the Gleaming One, I worship her majesty. I exalt the Daughter of Ra. Adoration to Sekhmet, praise be to my mistress! O Golden One, breath of my life, Lady of All Powers who enfolds me! All hail, jubilation to you, the mistress of all!

O Golden One, Sole Ruler, Eye of Ra! Bountiful One who gives birth to divine entities, forms the animals, models them as she pleases, who fashions humanity. O Mother! Luminous One who thrusts back the darkness, illuminating every human being with her light!

I revere you, Sekhmet, Enrapturing One, Enlightener! O Mother of the *Netjeru*, from sky, from earth, from South, from North, from West, from East, from each land, from each place, where your majesty shines forth! See what is in my heart, what is in my inmost; my heart is blameless, my inmost open, no darkness is in my breast!

I adore you, O Queen of the *Netjeru*! O Golden One! Lady of Intoxications, Lady of Jubilation, Adorable One! It is the Gold of the divine entities who comes forth.

Heaven exalts, the earth is full of gladness, Sekhmet the Great rejoices!

*At this point perform the **meditation or magical action** or, if it is a special feast, add the appropriate prayers.*

*Afterwards **all present back out of the Temple Chamber with heads slightly bowed** while the Ritualist performs the "removing the foot."*

*With the **broom** the Ritualist, as the last person to exit, **ritually sweeps the area beginning at the altar.** (This is known as "removing the foot.") While performing this action the Ritualist recites the following:*

The distress that causes confusion has been driven away, and all the *Netjeru* are in harmony. I have given Heru his Eye; I have placed the *Wedjat*-Eye in the correct position. I have given Setekh his Testicles, so that the two lords are content through the work of my hands.

I know the sky, I know the earth;
I know Heru, I know Setekh.
Heru is appeased with his Eyes;
Setekh is appeased with his Testicles.
I am Djehuty, who reconciles the *Netjeru*,
who makes offerings in their correct form.

*The double doors are **solemnly closed** as the Ritualist says the following:*

Djehuty has come.
He has filled the Eye of Heru;
He has restored the Testicles of Setekh.
No evil shall enter this Temple.
Ptah has closed the door,
Djehuty has set it fast.
The door is closed, the door is set fast with the bolt.

All bow, touching the palms of their hands to their knees.

Richard J. Reidy

THE REVERSION OF OFFERINGS

One priest or priestess and as many assistants as necessary enter the Temple Chamber a final time. While he/she and any assistants **lift up the offerings before the sacred image** the ritualist shall say:

O Sekhmet, your enemy[295] withdraws for you. Heru has turned himself to his Eye in its name of 'Reversion-of-Offerings.' I am Djehuty. I come to perform this rite for Sekhmet, queen of the _Netjeru_. These, your divine offerings revert, they revert to your servants for life, for stability, for health and for joy! O that the Eye of Heru may flourish for you eternally!

Everyone withdraws, **carrying away all food offerings except for one loaf of bread together with a bowl of pure water**. These last items will remain until evening. If this ritual is celebrated after sunset, these items would also be removed.

After the candle has burned down, a servant-priest enters and **closes the doors of the Kar-shrine**.

**Extinguishing the candle or oil lamp,** he/she exclaims:

This is the Eye of Heru by which you have become great, by which you live, and by which you have power, O Sekhmet. This

---

[295] Meat offerings held a two-fold meaning for the ancient priesthood. Since meat necessarily came from slain animals, it signified the defeated or slain enemies of the Netjeret. At the same time, the meat offering represented the produce of the land which ultimately was a gift of the Netjeru.

456

is the Eye of Heru which you consume and through which you enchant your body. The *Wedjat*-Eye now enters into the West, into *Manu*, but it shall return. Truly, the Eye of Heru returns in peace![296]

---

[296] It is important to consume the food offerings after the ceremony. Water used should either be drunk or poured onto the earth. If it is mixed with natron, dilute it very greatly and then you can pour in onto the earth without harming any plantings.

The General Ritual for Seshat

Like members of the ancient priesthood, participants should be clothed in white linen. No item made of animal products such as leather or wool is to be worn. Linen represents a pristine product of the earth whereas leather and wool come from humankind's domination of the animals, a domination that becomes part of the "natural order" only after the First Time when the *Netjeru* and humans and animals lived in peace and harmony. Just as the Morning Ritual harkens back to that First Time (*Zep Tepi*), so every temple rite re-presents mythic prototypes that occurred "in the beginning," that is, in that time before time. Even the sandals worn by the god's servants were made of white papyrus. This avoidance of animal products by the priesthood fits well with the fact that the ritualist acts as a *Netjer* and verbally asserts that he or she is a *Netjer*.

As with all Egyptian rituals begin with your purification-washing of hands and cleansing of mouth with Natron.

As with all Egyptian rituals begin with your purification—washing of hands and cleansing of mouth with Natron. This preliminary rite helps us to lay aside the cares of the day and to become mindful of the fact that we will encounter a divine being. If Natron is not available, then use a natural sea salt in its place until you make your own Natron.

*If two or more persons are participating, then one person, impersonating the Netjer Djehuty, **purifies each person by sprinkling each with water** while exclaiming:*

I purify you with the water of all life and good fortune, all stability, all health and happiness.[297]

Afterwards each person **rinses his mouth** *and places a small amount of Natron or sea salt in his mouth* *while saying:*

I wash my mouth; I chew natron so that I may extol the might of Seshat, Magnificent One in the House of Life.[298]

Participants **assemble outside the Temple Chamber** *and begin by* **softly rattling sistra.**

This time—several minutes or more—is used to focus minds and intention, so that distracting thoughts are left behind. The sound of the sistrum was said to placate the deity, purifying the atmosphere in preparation for encountering divinity. The sistrum was associated with Hat-Hór (Hathor) and also with her and Heru's son Ihy, and thus has connotations of joy, celebration, and dancing. According to Plutarch (A.D. 46-120), the sound of sistra was also reputed to drive away Setekh. But this was of very late date. It may have been that since by that time Setekh had been demonized, the general apotropaic function of the sistrum against evil entities was extended to include this *Netjer* as well.

---

[297] Taken from Aylward M. Blackman's article "Purification (Egyptian)" in Hastings Encyclopaedia 10/1918/ 476-82. This article is reprinted in Gods, Priests, and Men, Studies in the Religion of Pharaonic Egypt, edited by Alan B. Lloyd (Kegan Paul, 1998), p. 9.

[298] Based on a temple inscription taken from "The Myth of Horus at Edfu—II" by A. M. Blackman and H. W. Fairman, appearing in Gods, Priests and Men, Studies in the Religion of Pharaonic Egypt (Kegan Paul International, 1998) p. 283.

Richard J. Reidy

Standing before the closed doors, the Ritualist **recites the entrance spell:**

UTTERANCE BEFORE THE CLOSED DOORS OF THE TEMPLE

The ritualist **raises hands in adoration** *(dua position-arms stretched out in front of the body and raised up to face level, with palms facing outward). The following shall be said:*

O you *Netjeru* of this Temple, you guardians of the great portal, great *Netjeru* of mysterious abode, who sanctify the *Netjeret* in her shrine, who consecrate her oblation, who receive the offerings in her presence in the Hall of the Ennead: I have made my way and I enter into your presence. I am one of you. I am Shu, the eldest son of his father; the senior *wab* servant-priest of Seshat. Do not repulse me on the *Netjeret's* path. My feet are not impeded. I am not turned back from the court of the great portal so that I may conduct the divine service, that I may present offerings to her that made them, that I may give bread to Seshat. I have come on the way of the *Netjeret* Seshat. I have not shown partiality in judgment. I have not consorted with the strong. I have not reproached the lowly. I have not stolen things. I have not diminished the constituents of the Eye of Ra. I have not disturbed the Balance. I have not tampered with the requirements of the Sacred Eye. O Council of the Great *Netjeret* in this Temple, behold, I have come to you to offer Ma'at to the Judge of Ma'at, to content the Sound Eye for its Lord. I am Shu; I flood her offering table. I present her offerings, the great *Netjeret* Sekhmet consorting with me, that I may adore Seshat at her festivals, that I may kiss the earth so great is her majesty, that I may endow her image with life. I am pure. I am purified.

At this point the ritualist **opens the doors to the Temple Chamber,** *or,* *if there are no doors,* **makes a gesture of opening unseen doors,** *and* **steps forward as if crossing over a threshold.** *The following is said:*

O you *Ba*-souls of *Wetjeset-Hor* (Edfu), if you are strong, I am strong. If I am strong, you are strong. If your *Ka*-spirits are strong, my *Ka*-spirit is strong at the head of the living. As they are living so shall I live, Sekhmet, the great *Netjeret*, beloved of Ptah, has given to me life, stability, and serenity round about my members, which Djehuty has gathered together for life. I am Heru in the height of heaven, the beautiful one of awe, Lord of Victory, mighty one of awe, exalted one of the two plumes, great one in *Abdju* (Abydos). I am pure.

Enter, **close the double doors** *and* **stand in front of the Kar-shrine and altar. All bow, touching their hands to their knees.**

All recite the following:

Awake, awake in peace, O Lady of the House of Books.
May you awake in peace.
Awake, awake in peace, O Magnificent One in the House of Life.
May you awake in peace.
Awake, awake in peace, O Sovereign of *Netjeru*.
May you awake in peace.
Awake, awake in peace, O Perfect *Netjeret*, Seshat. May you awake in peace.

The ritualist **slowly opens the two doors of the Kar-shrine** *housing the sacred image.* **All others bow, touching their hands to their knees.** *The following is said:*

The doors of the sky are open; the doors of the earth are unlocked. This House is open for its Mistress Seshat. Let me come forth as she shall come forth. Let me enter in as she shall enter in. Seshat, beloved of Djehuty, first born of Amun-Re, is exalted upon her Great Seat. The Great Company of the *Netjeru* are exalted upon their seat.

I have seen the *Netjeret*, and the *Netjeret* sees me. The *Netjeret* rejoices at seeing me. I have gazed upon the statue of the Daughter of Amun-Ra, the sacred image of the Magnificent One.

Right hand on the left shoulder of statue; left hand on the right wrist of statue:

Djehuty has come to you. Awake when you hear his words.
I have come as the envoy of Atum.
My two arms are upon you like those of Heru.
My two hands are upon you like those of Djehuty.
My fingers are upon you like those of Anpu.
Homage be to you. I am a living servant of Seshat.

*The Ritualist **holds up the bowl of water** in which he/she will mix the Natron. The following is said:*

O water, may you remove all evil
As Ra who bathes in the Lake of Rushes.
May Heru wash my flesh,
May Djehuty cleanse my feet,
May Shu lift me up and Nut take my hand!
May Setekh be my strength, and may Sekhmet be my healing!
May Amun-Ra be my life and my prospering!

*The bowl of water is set aside and the container of **Natron is lifted up**. The following is said:*

It is pure, it is pure.
My Natron is the Natron of Heru and the Natron of Heru is my Natron.
My Natron is the Natron of Setekh and the Natron of Setekh is my Natron.
My Natron is the Natron of Djehuty, and the Natron of Djehuty is my Natron.
My Natron is the Natron of Geb and the Natron of Geb is my Natron.
My mouth is the mouth of a milking calf on the day that I was born.

*Four pinches of **Natron are mixed into the water** as this Utterance is recited:*

I give you essential water, a tide in your time.
I bring the flood waters to purify your sanctuary.
I bring you the flood waters to purify your Temple and your statue in its place, the primordial water that purifies as in the First Time!

*The Ritualist **places an index finger into the water** and **moves it in a circular direction four times** as the following is said:*

Seshat, who brings the Nile forth from its Cavern, does purify this water.
Seshat, Lady of Life in the Evening Barque, does cleanse this water;
Seshat, Lady of Years, does sanctify this water;

Seshat herself does endow this water with power and with life.

The Bowl of Natron-infused water is then taken up and the Ritualist **sprinkles this lightly in front of and around the statue** *or image of Seshat, applying the water to the base of the image, as the Utterance is recited:*

I come close to You, O Seshat, Who Passes Eternity Repeatedly, I bring the water of rejuvenation that flows from the Two Caverns. I sprinkle the water, purifying your image and your Temple from all impurity!

The Ritualist **picks up the bowl of Natron** *and sprinkles a small amount in each of the four directions* *as the following is recited:*

The *Netjeret* Seshat herself does cleanse and purify this, her Temple to the South.
The *Netjeret* Seshat herself does cleanse and purify this, her Temple to the North.
The *Netjeret* Seshat herself does cleanse and purify this, her Temple to the West.
The *Netjeret* Seshat herself does cleanse and purify this, her Temple to the East.

Replacing the Natron on the altar, the Ritualist takes up the **bowl of water, sprinkling a small amount in each of the four directions.** *The following Utterance is recited:*

The *Netjeret* Seshat herself does sanctify and consecrate this, her Temple to the South.
The *Netjeret* Seshat herself does sanctify and consecrate this, her Temple to the North.

The *Netjeret* Seshat herself does sanctify and consecrate this, her Temple to the West.
The *Netjeret* Seshat herself does sanctify and consecrate this, her Temple to the East.

The Temple of the *Netjeret* Seshat is established. It is established for millions of years.

*The Ritualist returns to the altar and **lights the candle or oil lamp** while the following is said:*

Come, come in peace, O glorious Eye of Heru,
Be strong and renew your youth in peace
For the flame shines like Ra on the double horizon.
The enemies of Ra are defeated. They are defeated.
I am pure, I am pure, I am pure, I am pure.

*The Ritualist **places incense on the burner** and **censes each sacred image** beginning with the statue of Seshat while the following is recited:*

The fire is laid, the fire shines;
The incense is laid on the fire, the incense shines.
Your perfume comes to me, O Incense;
May my perfume come to you, O Incense.

Your perfume comes to me, you *Netjeru*;
May my perfume come to you, you *Netjeru*.
May I be with you, you *Netjeru*;
May you be with me, you *Netjeru*.

May I live with you, you *Netjeru*;
May you live with me, you *Netjeru*.

I love you, you *Netjeru*;
May you love me, you *Netjeru*.

*Standing in front of the image of Seshat the Ritualist **offers the burning incense** and says:*

Take the incense,
Its essence is for you.
Its smoke permeates your shrine, bringing life!
Take the incense,
Its essence is for you.
Your Majesty is appeased with the incense.
This Eye of Heru,
This essence of the Eye of Heru comes to you.

At this point, the following is said to the Netjeret:

GREAT HYMN TO SESHAT

Seshat, Great of Heka,
Daughter of Nut,
open the Door of Heaven to us.
Daughter of Amun-Ra,
record our names in the scrolls of life.
Shining One, Seshat, Consort of Sokar,
we honor you as the Guardian of the Mansions of the West
and Protectress of the Body of Ausir.
Along with Nebet Hut, and Djehuty, with Hu and Sia assisting,
you restore the members of the blessed dead.
You are the Recorder of all things in the *Duat*.
You are the Gleaming One in the Chamber of Darkness.
May you restore us when we enter the *Duat*,
and may you protect us as you protected the Body of Ausir.

Seshat, Enumerator,
Foremost of Builders,
You inscribe the floor plan according to the correct stars,
Holding the stake and the mallet.
You stretch the cords in the Place of Beginnings,
you begin the foundation of every temple,
may you grant our temple a firm foundation.
Seshat, Mistress of the House of Architects,
Lady of the Wall,
N*etjeret* of Construction, we praise you.
Star-Sighting One, we honor you.
Your clarity illumines the House of the *Netjer*.
Your *heka* makes firm the foundation of the Two Lands.
May you make firm the foundation of this land.
May you make firm this your temple and these your servants.
May you guide us in the up-building of your holy temple.

Seshat, you are the Magnificent One in the House of Life.
Netjeret of Speech, Books and Secret Writings,
may you help us in our sacred writings;
Lady of Sacred Writing.
Seshat Who Gives to Those She Loves,
may you guide us who honor you.
Praise to you Who Stand Before the Library.
You are the One of Exquisite Works,
You are Lady of the Word of the *Netjer*.

Eye of Ra, Great *Netjeret* Seshat,
As you recorded the *Sed* and Jubilee Festivals, may you measure
out for us long lives.
You are She Who Rejuvenates the Year.
May the sight of you rejuvenate our spirits.

467

You are the Recorder Who Repulses the Fierce Ones,
You are She Who Chronicles the Lifespan
and Lifetime of the Nine (the Ennead).
Seshat, record for us long lives and strength and good health.
Repulse for us the Fierce Ones and grant us your protection.
Truly you are the One Who Fixes the Decrees of the *Netjeru*.
May you fix for us who worship you a long lifetime with joy of heart.
We rejoice when we see your beautiful image, O Magnificent One.
Truly you are the Lady of All the *Netjeru*.
Praise to you, Seshat. Praise to you, Great *Netjeret*.

The Ritualist places more incense on the charcoal and again and again slowly raises and lowers the incense cup as the following is recited:

O Seshat May you advance with your *Ka*.
O Lady of Palaces, the arm of your *Ka* is before you,
The arm of your *Ka* is behind you.
Seshat, the One with Great Magical Power, the foot of your *Ka* is before you,
The foot of your *Ka* is behind you.
Lady of The Two Lands, this incense is offered to you,
May your face be filled as this essence spreads itself over you.

All present perform the **Henu Rite** *—Embrace the Earth, the Fourfold Salute to the Goddess, Embrace the Earth.*

For Embracing the Earth, all present prostrate themselves, face down, upon the floor. During the Fourfold Salute, all present rise upon one knee, and alternately raise their hands and arms into the *Dua* (praise) position with palms facing outward, followed by the *Sahu* (obedience) gesture, made by striking the chest with a closed fist and raising the other arm (also with closed fist) at a ninety-degree angle. The *Dua* position is accompanied by the words **"Adoration be to Seshat,"** followed by the *Sahu* gesture accompanied with the words, **"Hail to the Lady of Sacred Writing!"** The bodily gestures are performed alternately four times.

*Following this **all present again prostrate themselves** before the sacred image. This is a sign and symbol of total submission and adoration before the Netjeret. The following is said:*

Homage to Seshat, the Shining One,
who is established on the Great Seat!
I have placed myself on the floor in awe of you.
I embrace the earth before you, the Magnificent One.
I have come that I might kiss the earth,
that I might worship my Lady,
For I have seen her beauty;
I give praise to Seshat,
for I have seen her Power.
Her form is more perfect than the *Netjeru*;
Her arm is more powerful than the *Netjeru*.
I am pure, I am pure, I am pure, I am pure!

Everyone stands up.

*The Ritualist **holds in the palm of one hand the image of Ma'at** and with **the other hand open and raised over the image as if sheltering it**, repeats the following:*

I have come to you as Djehuty, whose two hands are joined together under Ma'at. She comes to be with you, for she is everywhere. You are provided with Ma'at. You move in Ma'at, you live in Ma'at. She fills your body, she rests in your head,

she makes her seat upon your brow; the breath of your body is of Ma'at, your heart does live in Ma'at. All that you eat, all that you drink, all that you breathe is of Ma'at. Djehuty presents Ma'at to you, his two hands are upon her beauty before your face.

*The Ritualist places the image of Ma'at near the divine statue. Then he/she holds up before the image of Seshat a **pitcher of water and pours the water slowly into an offering bowl** as the following Utterance is recited:*

This libation is for you, O Seshat.
This libation is for you, Lady of Engravings,
who lays out the decree of the *Netjeru*.
I have brought to you this offering of water,
That your heart may be refreshed.
I have brought to you this Eye of Heru,
Placing this at your feet.
I present to you that which flows forth from you,
That your heart shall continue to beat.
For it is with you that all comes forth at the sound of the voice.

*The libation bowl is placed on the altar. At this point the Ritualist **lightly sprinkles sand on the floor in front of the altar** as the following is recited:*

O Seshat who resides in *Wetjeset-Hor* (Edfu),
take to yourself the Eye of Heru.
You have rescued it, O Lady of the Library.
You have sprinkled with sand the Eye of Heru.
The Eye of Heru is healed. It is restored whole and complete.
It is Djehuty who has done this with his fingers.

Lifting the wine offering before the sacred image, the Ritualist repeats the following:

mn n.t irp irt ḥrw w₃dt

[*"mán-nit 'úrip írat ḥáru wá'dat"*; approximately pronounced *MAHN-neetch OO-rip EE-raht HAH-roo WAH-jat*]

"Take to yourself the green Eye of Heru, which I offer to your *Ka.* O Lady of Cities, how beautiful is your beauty! You are she who founds the sanctuaries of Divine Powers according to your directions. May you drink it. May your heart rejoice. May anger be removed from your face. *It is pure."* [*iw.w w'b* pronounced *"uwú wá'ib"*; approximately *oo-WOO WAH-ib*]

*The Ritualist **places myrrh on the fire and lifts up the smoking incense** while at the same time he **lifts up the meat-offering** before the Netjeret, and says the following:*

The scent of myrrh is for your nose. It fills your nostrils; your heart receives the meat-portions on its scent.[299]

*Slowly, **elevating** the food offerings **four** times before the image of the Netjeret, the Ritualist repeats the following:*

I offer to Seshat, the One with Great *Heka*-Power.
All life emanates from you,
All health emanates from you,
All stability emanates from you,
All good fortune emanates from you,

---

[299] Quoted in "Worship and Festivals in an Egyptian Temple," by H. W. Fairman (publ. by The John Rylands Library, 1954), p. 191.

You are the one who lengthens the lifetime of those who do ma'at, forever.

The Ritualist places the food offering before the divine image, and then all present extend one hand, palm down, over the offerings and recite the following:

May offerings of every kind come forth in abundance, like the things which come forth from the mouth of the *Netjeret*.

piryá pírit ar ḫiráw mi purú:riat ma rá' ni naṯárat. **(4 times)**
[approximately pronounced: peer-YA PEER-it ar khi-RAU mee pu-ROOR-iat ma RA nee nah-TCHAR-at]

May offerings of every kind come forth in abundance, like the things that come forth from the mouth of the *Netjeret*.

Holding the Ankh before the Netjeret, the Ritualist says:

Live, O Seshat, Sentry of the Birthing Place. Live for all time and for eternity!

ʿánaḫ niḫáḫ ḏát.
[approximately pronounced *AH-nakh nee-HAH JAHT]*

The Ankh is placed next to the image of the Netjeret.

Holding the Ib (the golden heart) before Seshat, the Ritualist says:

Hail to you, O Seshat, you who lay out Decrees. I have brought to you your heart to set it in its place. Let me draw near to you with your heart, so that you may have pleasure through me, and so that by means of me you may have power over your body. Ascend, Lady of Books, Sovereign of the *Netjeru*, who stretch the cord in Edfu. Live, O Great *Netjeret*, Lady Seshat, live forever and ever!

*After placing the Ib near the sacred image, **everyone sings or chants** the hymn to Seshat. Participants may wish to alternate the singing of verses.*

Homage be to Seshat, Guardian of the House of Life!
Homage be to the perfect Renenutet of the House of Heru!

Praise be to Seshat who fixes the decrees of the *Netjeru*! Praise to the One who records the Jubilee Festivals!
Praise be to Seshat who stretches the cords in the place of the beginning!
Praise to the Lady of the Measuring Cords!

Praise to the Lady of Holy Writing! Praise to the Lady of Secret Writing!
We worship Seshat, we extol the Mistress of the House of Life!
Born of Amun-Ra, great in *Wetjeset-Hor*.
You give to those you love; may you love us who honor you.
You lead all the *Netjer*'s servant-priests, may you lead us who serve you.

All the *Netjeru* of the South, North, West, and East—all do praise you!
All do extol you!

Establish this our temple! Make firm its foundation that we may make offerings to you and to the *Netjeru* forever!

*At this point, perform the **meditation or magical action** or if it is a special feast, add the appropriate prayers.*

REMOVING THE FOOT

*With the broom the Ritualist, as the last person to exit, **ritually sweeps the area beginning at the altar**. (This is known as "removing the foot.") While performing this action, the Ritualist recites the following:*

The distress that causes confusion has been driven away, and all the *Netjeru* are in harmony. I have given Heru his Eye; I have placed the *Wedjat*-Eye in the correct position. I have given Setekh his Testicles, so that the two lords are content through the work of my hands.

I know the sky, I know the earth;
I know Heru, I know Setekh.
Heru is appeased with his Eyes;
Setekh is appeased with his Testicles.
I am Djehuty, who reconciles the *Netjeru*,
who makes offerings in their correct form.

*The double doors are **solemnly closed** as the Ritualist says the following:*

Djehuty has come.
He has filled the Eye of Heru;
He has restored the Testicles of Setekh.
No evil shall enter this Temple.
Ptah has closed the door;
Djehuty has set it fast.
The door is closed, the door is set fast with the bolt.

All bow, touching the palms of their hands to their knees.

THE REVERSION OF OFFERINGS

One priest or priestess and as many assistants as necessary enter the Temple Chamber a final time. While ritualist *and any assistants* **lift up the offerings** *before the sacred image, the* ritualist *shall say:*

O Seshat, your enemy[300] withdraws for you. Heru has turned himself to his Eye in its name of 'Reversion-of-Offerings.' I am Djehuty. I come to perform this rite for Seshat, Lady of Measuring Cords. These, your divine offerings revert, they revert to your servants for life, for stability, for health and for joy! O that the Eye of Heru may flourish for you eternally!

Everyone withdraws, **carrying away all food offerings except for one loaf of bread together with a bowl of pure water.** *These last items will remain until evening. If this ritual is celebrated after sunset, these items would also be removed.*

After the candle has burned down, a servant-priest enters and **closes the doors of the Kar-shrine.**

Extinguishing the candle or oil lamp, he/she exclaims:

This is the Eye of Heru by which you have become great, by which you live, and by which you have power, O Seshat. This

---

[300] Meat offerings held a two-fold meaning for the ancient priesthood. Since meat necessarily came from slain animals, it signified the defeated or slain enemies of the Netjer. At the same time, the meat offering represented the produce of the land which ultimately was a gift of the Netjeru.

is the Eye of Heru which you consume and through which you enchant your body. The *Wedjat*-Eye now enters into the West, into *Manu,* but it shall return. Truly, the Eye of Heru returns in peace![301]

---

[301] It is important to consume the food offerings after the ceremony. Water used should either be drunk or poured onto the earth. If it is mixed with natron, dilute it very greatly and then you can pour in onto the earth without harming any plantings.

The General Ritual for Setekh

The various epithets for Setekh can each be found in Herman te Velde's important work, Seth, God of Confusion *(Leiden: E. J. Brill, 1977) as well as in the Lexikon (LÄGG).*

Special offerings for Setekh: a representation of the Testicles, a WAS scepter, and an Adze. *The Was scepter symbolizes power; the Adze is a ritual tool used in the Opening of the Mouth as well as representing the seven stars of the constellation of Setekh, i.e. what we today call Ursa Major; and the Testicles are that which is healed by Djehuty when Heru and Setekh fought and injured each other.*

Like members of the ancient priesthood, participants should be clothed in white linen. No item made of animal products such as leather or wool is to be worn. Linen represents a pristine product of the earth whereas leather and wool come from humankind's domination of the animals, a domination that becomes part of the "natural order" only *after* the First Time when the *Netjeru* and humans and animals lived in peace and harmony. Just as the Morning Ritual harkens back to that First Time (*Zep Tepi*), so every temple rite re-presents mythic prototypes that occurred "in the beginning," that is, in that time before time. Even the sandals worn by the god's servants were made of white papyrus. This avoidance of animal products by the priesthood fits well with the fact that the ritualist acts as a *Netjer* and verbally asserts that he or she is a *Netjer*.

Richard J. Reidy

As with all Egyptian rituals begin with your purification—washing of hands and cleansing of mouth with Natron. This preliminary rite helps us to lay aside the cares of the day and to become mindful of the fact that we will encounter a divine being. If Natron is not available, then use a natural sea salt in its place until you make your own Natron.

If two or more persons are participating, then one person, impersonating the Netjer Djehuty, **purifies each person by sprinkling each with water** *while exclaiming:*

I purify you with the water of all life and good fortune, all stability, all health and happiness.[302]

Afterwards each person **rinses his mouth** *and* **places a small amount of Natron or sea salt in his mouth** *while saying:*

I wash my mouth; I chew natron so that I may extol the might of Setekh, Chosen One of Ra, Defender of the Barque of Millions-of-Years.[303]

Participants **assemble outside the Temple Chamber** *and begin by softly rattling sistra.*

---

[302] Taken from Aylward M. Blackman's article "Purification (Egyptian)" in Hastings Encyclopaedia 10/1918/ 476-82. This article is reprinted in Gods, Priests, and Men, Studies in the Religion of Pharaonic Egypt, edited by Alan B. Lloyd (Kegan Paul International, 1998), p. 9.

[303] Based on a temple inscription taken from "The Myth of Horus at Edfu—II" by A. M. Blackman and H. W. Fairman, appearing in Gods, Priests and Men, Studies in the Religion of Pharaonic Egypt (Kegan Paul International, 1998) p. 283.

This time—several minutes or more—is used to focus minds and intention so that distracting thoughts are left behind. The sound of the sistrum was said to placate the deity, purifying the atmosphere in preparation for encountering divinity. The sistrum was associated with Hutheru and also with her and Heru's son Ihy, and thus has connotations of joy, celebration, and dancing. According to Plutarch (A.D. 46-120), the sound of sistra was also reputed to drive away Setekh. But this was of very late date. It may have been that since by that time Setekh had been demonized, the general apotropaic function of the sistrum against evil entities was extended to include this *Netjer* as well.

*Standing **before the closed doors**, the Ritualist recites the entrance spell:*

UTTERANCE BEFORE THE CLOSED DOORS OF THE TEMPLE

*The ritualist **raises hands in adoration** (dua position-arms stretched out in front of the body and raised up to face level, with palms facing outward). The following shall be said:*

O you *Netjeru* of this Temple, you guardians of the great portal, great *Netjeru* of mysterious abode, who sanctify the god in his shrine, who consecrate his oblation, who receive the offerings in his presence in the Hall of the Ennead: I have made my way and I enter into your presence. I am one of you. I am Shu, the eldest son of his father, the senior *wab* servant-priest of Setekh. Do not repulse me on the god's path. My feet are not impeded. I am not turned back from the court of the great portal so that I may conduct the divine service, that I may present offerings to him that made them, that I may give bread to Setekh. I have come on the way of the god. I have not shown partiality in judgment. I have not consorted with the strong. I have not reproached the lowly. I have not stolen things. I have not diminished the constituents of the Eye of Ra. I have not disturbed the Balance. I have not tampered with the requirements of the Sacred Eye. O Council of the Great *Netjer* in this Temple, behold, I have come to you to offer Ma'at to the Lord of Ma'at, to content the Sound Eye for its lord. I am Shu; I flood his offering table. I present his offerings, Sekhmet consorting with me, that I may adore Setekh at his festivals, that I may kiss the earth so great is his majesty, that I may endow his image with life. I am pure. I am purified.

At this point the ritualist **opens the doors to the Temple Chamber**, *or, if there are no doors,* **makes a gesture of opening unseen doors,** *and* **steps forward as if crossing over a threshold.** *The following is said:*

O you *Ba*-souls of *Nubt* (Ombos) if you are strong, I am strong. If I am strong, you are strong. If your *Ka*-spirits are strong, my *Ka*-spirit is strong at the head of the living. As they are living so shall I live . . . . Setekh, Bull of his Mother, has given to me life, stability, and serenity round about my members, which Djehuty has gathered together for life. I am Heru in the height of heaven, the beautiful one of awe, Lord of Victory, mighty one of awe, exalted one of the two plumes, great one in Thebes, I am pure.

All temple members chant:

Awake in peace, O Setekh, Great in Strength,
may you awaken in peace.
Awake in peace, O Setekh, Powerful of Heart,
may you awaken in peace.

Awake in peace, O Setekh, Great Lord of the Seven Stars,
may you awaken in peace.
Awake in peace, O Setekh, Slayer of the Serpent-Foe,
may you awaken in peace.

May you awake beautifully at the top of the morning,
through that which the entirety of *Netjeru* say to you.

*Enter, close the double doors and stand in front of the Kar-shrine
and altar. All bow, touching their hands to their knees.*

The ritualist *slowly opens the two doors of the Kar-shrine* housing
*the sacred image. **All others bow, touching their hands to their
knees.** The following is said:*

The doors of the sky are open; the doors of the earth are
unlocked. This House is open for its Lord. Let me come forth as
he shall come forth. Let me enter in as he shall enter in. Setekh,
Lord of the Land of Sedges, is exalted upon his Great Seat. The
Great Company of the *Netjeru* are exalted upon their seat.

I have seen the *Netjer*, and the *Netjer* sees me. The *Netjer* rejoices
at seeing me. I have gazed upon the statue of the Defender of
the Barque of Millions-of-Years, truly the Chosen One of Ra.[304]

Right hand on left shoulder of statue; left hand on right wrist of statue:

Djehuty has come to you. Awake when you hear his words. I
have come as the envoy of Atum. My two arms are upon you

---

[304] Based on the temple text found in "Worship and Festivals in an Egyptian
Temple," a lecture by H. W. Fairman (publ. by The John Rylands Library,
1954), p. 180.

like those of Heru. My two hands are upon you like those of
Djehuty. My fingers are upon you like those of Anpu. Homage
be to you. I am a living servant of Setekh.

*The Ritualist holds up the **bowl of water** in which he/she will be mixing
the Natron. The following is said:*

O water may you remove all evil,
as Ra who bathes in the Lake of Rushes.
May Heru wash my flesh;
may Djehuty cleanse my feet.
May Shu lift me up and Nut take my hand!
May Setekh be my strength, and may Sekhmet be my healing!
And may Amun-Ra be my life and my prospering!

*The bowl of water is set aside and the container of **Natron** is lifted up.
The following is said:*

It is pure, it is pure.
My Natron is the Natron of Heru and the Natron of Heru is my
Natron.
My Natron is the Natron of Setekh and the Natron of Setekh is
my Natron.
My Natron is the Natron of Djehuty, and the Natron of Djehuty
is my Natron.
My Natron is the Natron of Geb and the Natron of Geb is my
Natron.

My mouth is the mouth of a milking calf on the day that I was
born.

Four pinches of Natron *are mixed into the water as this Utterance
is recited:*

I give you essential water, a tide in your time.

I bring the flood waters to purify your sanctuary.

I bring you the flood waters to purify your Temple and your statue in its place, the primordial water that purifies as in the First Time!

The Ritualist places an index finger into the water and moves it in a circular direction four times as the following is said:

Setekh, Great of Strength in the Barque of Millions, does purify this water;

Setekh, the Mighty One, does cleanse this water;

Setekh, Lord of Life, does sanctify this water;

Setekh himself does endow this water with power and with life.

The Bowl of Natron-infused water is then taken up and the Ritualist sprinkles this lightly in front of and around the statue or image of Setekh, applying the water to the base of the image, as the Utterance is recited:

I come close to you, O Son of Nut.

I bring the water of rejuvenation that flows from the Two Caverns.

I sprinkle the water, purifying your image and your Temple from all impurity!

The Ritualist picks up the bowl of Natron and sprinkles a small amount in each of the four directions as the following is recited:

The *Netjer* Setekh himself does cleanse and purify this, his Temple to the South.

Richard J. Reidy

The *Netjer* Setekh himself does cleanse and purify this, his Temple to the North.

The *Netjer* Setekh himself does cleanse and purify this, his Temple to the West.

The *Netjer* Setekh himself does cleanse and purify this, his Temple to the East.

*Replacing the Natron on the altar, the Ritualist takes up the **bowl of water**, sprinkling a small amount in each of the four directions. The following Utterance is recited:*

The *Netjer* Setekh himself does sanctify and consecrate this, his Temple to the South.

The *Netjer* Setekh himself does sanctify and consecrate this, his Temple to the North.

The *Netjer* Setekh himself does sanctify and consecrate this, his Temple to the West.

The *Netjer* Setekh himself does sanctify and consecrate this, his Temple to the East.

The Temple of the *Netjer* Setekh is established. It is established for millions of years.

*The Ritualist returns to the altar and **lights the candle or oil lamp** while the following is said:*

Come, come in peace, O glorious Eye of Heru,
Be strong and renew your youth in peace.
For the flame shines like Ra on the double horizon.
The enemies of Ra are defeated. They are defeated.
I am pure, I am pure, I am pure, I am pure.

The Ritualist places incense on the burner and censes each sacred image beginning with the statue of Setekh while the following is recited:

The fire is laid, the fire shines;
The incense is laid on the fire, the incense shines.
 Your perfume comes to me, O Incense;
 May my perfume come to you, O Incense.
Your perfume comes to me, you *Netjeru*;
May my perfume come to you, You *Netjeru*.
 May I be with you, you *Netjeru*;
 May you be with me, you *Netjeru*.
May I live with you, you *Netjeru*;
May you live with me, you *Netjeru*.
 I love you, you *Netjeru*;
 May you love me, you *Netjeru*.

Standing in front of the image of Setekh the Ritualist offers the burning incense and says:

Take the incense,
Its essence is for you.
Its smoke permeates your shrine, bringing life!
Take the incense,
Its essence is for you.
Your Majesty is appeased with the incense.
This Eye of Heru,
This essence of the Eye of Heru comes to you.

At this point the following is said:

Hail to you, O Setekh, Son of Nut, Great of Strength in the Barque of Millions, felling the enemy, the snake, at the prow of the Barque of Ra, Great of Battle-Cry. May you give me a good lifetime.[305]

O Setekh, Lord of Life, who is upon the prow of the Barque of Ra, save me from all evil clamor of this year.[306]

*The Ritualist **places more incense on the charcoal** and again and again **slowly raises and lowers the incense cup** as the following is recited:*

O Setekh, may you advance with your *Ka*.
O Chosen One of Ra, the arm of your *Ka* is before you,
the arm of your *Ka* is behind you.
O Instigator of Confusion fighting against the serpent-foe,
the foot of your *Ka* is before you,
the foot of your *Ka* is behind you.
O powerful Setekh, this incense is offered to you,
May your face be filled as this essence spreads itself over you.

*All present perform the **Henu Rite**—Embrace the Earth, the Fourfold Salute to the God, Embrace the Earth.*

For Embracing the Earth, all present prostrate themselves, face down, upon the floor. During the Fourfold Salute, all present rise upon one knee, and alternately raise their hands and arms into the *Dua* (praise) position with palms facing outward, followed

---

[305] Four Hundred Years-stela. Cf. K. Sethe, *Der Denkstein mit dem Datum des Jahres 400 der Ära von Tanis, ZÄS,*65 (1930), p. 87. (*ZÄS* abbrev. for the journal *Zeitschrift für Ägyptische Sprache und Altertumskunde.*)

[306] *Pap. Leiden I,* 346 II, 12; cf. B. H. Stricker, *Spreuken tot beveiliging gedurende de schrikkeldagen naar Pap.I,* 346, *OMRO NR* 29 (1948), p. 68. (*OMRO,* abbrev. *for the journal Oudheidkundige Mededeelingen uit het Rijksmuseum van Oudheden te Leiden.*)

by the *Sahu* (obedience) gesture, made by striking the chest with a closed fist and raising the other arm (also with closed fist) at a ninety-degree angle. The *Dua* position is accompanied by the words **"Adoration be to Setekh,"** followed by the *Sahu* gesture accompanied with the words, **"Hail to the Lord of Life!"** The bodily gestures are performed alternately four times.

Following this all present again prostrate themselves before the god. This is a sign and symbol of total submission and adoration before the Netjer. The following is said:

Homage to Setekh, Chosen One of Ra,
who is established on the Great Seat!
I have placed myself on the floor in awe of you.
I embrace the earth before you as before the Great Wild Bull.
I have come that I might kiss the earth,
that I might worship my Lord,
For I have seen his Strength.
I give praise to Setekh,
for I have seen his Power.
His form is more distinguished than the *Netjeru*;
his arm is more powerful than the *Netjeru*.
I am pure, I am pure, I am pure, I am pure!

Everyone stands up.

*The Ritualist **holds in the palm of one hand the image of Ma'at** and with **the other hand open and raised over the image as if sheltering it,** repeats the following:*

I have come to you as Djehuty, whose two hands are joined together under Ma'at. She comes to be with you, for she is

everywhere. You are provided with Ma'at. You move in Ma'at, you live in Ma'at. She fills your body, she rests in your head, she makes her seat upon your brow; the breath of your body is of Ma'at, your heart does live in Ma'at. All that you eat, all that you drink, all that you breathe is of Ma'at. Djehuty presents Ma'at to you, his two hands are upon her beauty before your face.

*The Ritualist places the image of Ma'at near the divine statue. Then he/ she holds up before the image of Setekh **a pitcher of water** and **pours the water slowly into an offering bowl** as the following Utterance is recited:*

This libation is for you, O Lord of Life.
This libation is for you, Setekh, *Nubti* [He of Gold Town, i.e., Ombos].
I have brought to you this offering of water,
That your heart may be refreshed.
I have brought to you this your appendage,
Placing this at your feet.
I present to you that which flows forth from you,
That your heart shall continue to beat.
For it is with you that all comes forth at the sound of the voice.

*The offering bowl is placed on the altar. At this point the Ritualist **lightly sprinkles sand on the floor in front of the altar** as the following is recited:*

O Setekh, who resides in *Nubt* (Ombos),
Take to yourself your Testicles.
Djehuty has rescued them,
He has restored them whole and sound.

He has sprinkled with sand your Testicles.

The next three items offered are specific to Setekh: 1) the Testicles, symbol of virile strength; 2) the *Was* scepter; and 3) the sculptor's Adze.

*The Ritualist **takes in his hands the symbol of the Testicles**[307] **and holds it forth before the god's statue**. After reciting the following text, the Ritualist places the symbol to one side of the sacred image.*

I come as Djehuty. Your Testicles which were injured are restored, whole and intact. I, Djehuty, have healed them. May your *Ka* be content with this healing of your injury.

*The Ritualist **holds in one hand the WAS scepter** and **extends his arm** as he recites the following:*

The scepter of power is yours, O Setekh. You conquer every enemy with your might. May you defeat the enemies of Ra with your strong arm. May you pierce them with your lance of iron. I present to you your scepter of power.

*The Ritualist **takes in his hands the Adze** and **extends his arms toward the god's image** as he recites the following:*

I present to you the Adze by which you opened the mouths of *Netjeru* and humankind. The *Meshkhetyu* instrument of iron

---

[307] The hieroglyph for testicles resembles an inverted Valentine's heart, with tip pointing up and the two rounded halves below. They can easily be crafted from clay and afterwards gilt. I have also seen small heart-shaped stones or paper weights that might serve the purpose.

wherewith you make firm the mouth and by which you open the two eyes. It is yours for all time and for eternity.

Lifting the wine offering before the sacred image, the Ritualist repeats the following:

mn n.k irp irt ḥrw w₃dt

[*"mán-nik 'úrip írat ḥáru wá'ḏat"*; approximately pronounced *MAHN-neek OO-rip EE-raht HAH-roo WAH-jat*]

Take to yourself wine, the sweat of Ra, which I offer to your *Ka.*
O Ruler, how beautiful is your beauty!
May you drink it; may your heart rejoice;
may anger be removed from your face.
It is pure. [*iw.w w'b* pronounced *"uwú wá'ib"*; approximately *oo-WOO WAH-ib*]

The Ritualist **places myrrh on the fire** *and* **lifts up the smoking incense** *while at the same time he* **lifts up the meat-offering** *before the Netjer, and says the following:*

The scent of myrrh is for your nose. It fills your nostrils; your heart receives the meat-portions on its scent.[308]

Slowly **elevating the food offerings four times** *before the image of Setekh, the Ritualist repeats the following:*

I offer to Setekh, Powerful of Forefoot.
All life emanates from you,
All health emanates from you,

---

[308] Quoted in "Worship and Festivals in an Egyptian Temple," by H. W. Fairman (publ. by The John Rylands Library, 1954), p. 191.

All stability emanates from you,
All good fortune emanates from you,
Lord of Life, Great in Strength, Setekh, forever.

The Ritualist places the food offering before the divine image, and then all present extend one hand, palm down, over the offerings and recite the following:

May offerings of every kind come forth in abundance,
like the things which come forth from the mouth of the *Netjer*.

piryá pírit ar ḫiráw mi purú:riat ma rá' ni náṯar. (4 times)
[approximately pronounced: peer-YA PEER-it ar khi-RAU mee pu-ROOR-iat ma RA nee NAH-tchar]

May offerings of every kind come forth in abundance, like the things that come forth from the mouth of the *Netjer*.

*Holding the **Ankh** before Setekh, the Ritualist says:*

Live, O Setekh, Chosen One of Ra, live for all time and for eternity!

ʿánaḫ niḥáḫ ḏát.
[approximately pronounced *AH-nakh nee-HAH JAHT*]

*The **Ankh** is placed next to the image of the Netjer.*

*Holding the **Ib (the golden heart)** before Setekh, the Ritualist says:*

Hail to you, Setekh, Powerful of Heart, great *Netjer* of this Temple, lord of *Nubt* (Ombos)! I have brought to you your

491

heart to set it in its place, even as your sister Aset brought the heart of her son Heru to him and set it in its place, and even as Heru brought the heart of his mother Aset to her and set it in its place.

Keep silence, you *Netjeru,* and listen, you Ennead. Attend to the good words which I speak to my father Setekh, so that he thereby might have greatness, glory, and power, that he thereby might be present with me, and that he might be here as Great-in-Strength.

A way is given to you, O Setekh, like Ra in his horizons, and you have honor therein even as Ra has honor. A way is given to you like Geb, your father, made for Amun-Ra. A way is given to you like Ra in his horizons.

You, being in heaven, O Master of the Seven Stars, great Lord of *Meskhet,* [309] come in your glory.

---

[309] The constellation of Setekh is the Bull's Foreleg, the seven stars currently referred to as the Big Dipper, and referred to as the Great Bear (Ursa Major) by the Greeks. This constellation in ancient times was visible throughout the entire night, hence these stars were called the "Imperishable Ones." The Egyptians saw in these stars two patterns: the foreleg of a bull, and also an adze, the important ritual instrument used to "Open the Mouth" of statues and mummies. Meteors appear to fall from the northern sky, the location of this constellation. Hence, meteoric iron – the only type of iron available to the ancient Egyptians – was regarded as the metal of Setekh. Notice in the following hymn to Setekh the reference, "Mysterious One who opens the mouths of the Netjeru with the metal that came forth from you." Setekh as Lord of Meskhet (the Adze) is therefore intimately connected with the central ceremony of Opening the Mouth.

You, being upon earth, O Lord of Victories, come in your triumph. Come, your mother Nut opens for you the gates of heaven. Come, your father Geb has opened for you the gates of the earth—south, north, west, and east.

Come, let me draw near to you with your heart, that you may have pleasure through me, and that by means of me you may have power over your body.

Ascend, glorious as Ra, powerful and equipped as a *Netjer*. Live, Powerful-of-Heart[310], live forever and ever![311]

*After placing the **Ib** (the golden heart) near the sacred image, **everyone sings or chants** the hymn to Setekh. Participants may wish to alternate the singing of verses.*

I praise the Son of Nut, I worship his majesty, I exalt the Lord of Heaven. Adoration be to Setekh, praise be to my master! O Powerful One, breath of my life, Lord of the Seven Stars who enfolds me! All hail, jubilation to you, the master of all! Heaven rests upon your hands; the earth is under your feet. What you command, takes place. May you bless me with life and strength and health. O Father, hear me!

---

[310] This honorific title is based on 'Djed medu' ("Words to be said") on the third epagomenal day of the year, the birthday of Setekh: "O Setekh, son of Nut, great in strength . . . Protection is at the hands of your holiness. I am your son. The name of this day is 'Powerful of Heart.'"

[311] This Utterance for presenting the *Ib* to the god is closely based on a similar recitation in The Ritual of Amenophis I, Chester Beatty Papyrus No. IX, in *Hieratic Papyri in the British Museum*, Alan H. Gardiner, editor. Vol. I. Text. (London, 1935), p. 86.

O Dark One, Thunderer, Chosen of Ra! Mysterious One who opens the mouths of the *Netjeru* with the metal that came forth from you. Strong One who destroys the serpent, thundering in heaven, the Feared One! O Setekh, powerful of magic in driving away enemies.

I revere you, Setekh, Lord of Winds! O Defender of the *Netjeru*, throughout the sky and earth, in the south, the north, the west, the east, in each land, in each place where your powerful voice thunders forth!

See what is in my heart, what is in my inmost; my heart is blameless, my inmost open, no evil is in my breast! I adore you, O Thunderer! O Dark One! Lord of unbridled forces, Strong Bull of erotic energy, most virile among the Ennead!

It is the Iron of the divine entities which comes forth from you. With it the mouths of the *Netjeru* were opened; with it the mouths of men are able to speak before the great Ennead.

"Heaven makes merry, the earth is filled with life, Setekh rejoices!"
[*Repeat this final acclamation four times.*]

*At this point perform the **meditation or magical action** or, if it is a special feast, add the appropriate prayers.*

*Afterwards **all present back out of the Temple Chamber with heads slightly bowed** while the Ritualist performs the **"removing the foot."***

*With the **broom** the Ritualist, as the last person to exit, **ritually sweeps the area beginning at the altar**. (This is known as "removing the foot.") While performing this action the Ritualist recites the following:*

The distress that causes confusion has been driven away, and all the *Netjeru* are in harmony. I have given Heru his Eye; I have placed the *Wedjat*-Eye in the correct position. I have given Setekh his Testicles, so that the two lords are content through the work of my hands.

I know the sky, I know the earth;
I know Heru, I know Setekh.
Heru is appeased with his Eyes;
Setekh is appeased with his Testicles.
I am Djehuty, who reconciles the *Netjeru*,
who makes offerings in their correct form.

*The **double doors are solemnly closed** as the Ritualist says the following:*

Djehuty has come.
He has filled the Eye of Heru;
He has restored the Testicles of Setekh.
No evil shall enter this Temple.
Ptah has closed the door,
Djehuty has set it fast.
The door is closed, the door is set fast with the bolt.

Richard J. Reidy

All bow, touching the palms of their hands to their knees.

THE REVERSION OF OFFERINGS

*One priest or priestess and as many assistants as necessary enter the Temple Chamber a final time. While he/she and any assistants **lift up the offerings** before the sacred image the ritualist shall say:*

O Setekh, your enemy[312] withdraws for you. Heru has turned himself to his Eye in its name of 'Reversion-of-Offerings.' I am Djehuty. I come to perform this rite for Setekh, the Chosen One of Ra. These, your divine offerings revert, they revert to your servants for life, for stability, for health and for joy! O that the Eye of Heru may flourish for you eternally!

*Everyone withdraws, **carrying away all food offerings except for one loaf of bread together with a bowl of pure water.** These last items will remain until evening. If this ritual is celebrated after sunset, these items would also be removed.*

*After the candle has burned down, a servant-priest enters and **closes the doors of the Kar-shrine.***

Extinguishing the candle or oil lamp, he/she exclaims:

This is the Eye of Heru by which you have become great, by which you live, and by which you have power, O Setekh. This

---

[312] Meat offerings held a two-fold meaning for the ancient priesthood. Since meat necessarily came from slain animals, it signified the defeated or slain enemies of the Netjer. At the same time, the meat offering represented the produce of the land which ultimately was a gift of the Netjeru.

is the Eye of Heru which you consume and through which you enchant your body. The *Wedjat*-Eye now enters into the West, into *Manu,* but it shall return. Truly, the Eye of Heru returns in peace![313]

---

[313] It is important to consume the food offerings after the ceremony. Water used should either be drunk or poured onto the earth. If it is mixed with natron, dilute it very greatly and then you can pour in onto the earth without harming any plantings.

The General Ritual for Sokar
Together with the Nighttime Ritual of Bringing in Sokar

Very special thanks go to Lisa Pedersen from the Kemetic Temple of Sacramento for her many long hours translating the hundreds of epithets for this god.

The following text includes both a general ritual for this god as well as a special rite called 'The Ritual of Bringing in Sokar.' The latter rite occurs toward the end of the general ritual just before the "Removing the Foot" ritual action.

The **Ritual of Bringing in Sokar** occurs on the night of the 26th day of the fourth month of the Inundation Season (*Akhet*); that is, the final day for the Commemorations of the Mysteries of Ausir in the ancient month of *Ka-Hr-Ka* (i.e. also known as Koiak). Egyptologist R. O. Faulkner speculates that this ritual would have followed the Lamentation Songs of Aset and Nebet-Hut in the aforementioned Mysteries of Ausir. In today's calendar, this would occur in or around December depending on whether or not, based on various astrological events, the year has an extra month as customarily occurred every three or four years in ancient Egypt.

Items needed: statues or images of Sokar, Ausir, and Hat-Hór. The traditional food offerings are presented along with a bouquet of five green-stemmed onions or scallions. Scallions are the closest in appearance to Egyptian onions and are readily available in markets.

The green-stemmed onion had many uses in ancient Egypt—in numerous medicinal formulations, as an antiseptic, as a snake repellent and a snake-bite remedy, and in magic. In mummification, such onions have been found in various sections of the body: near the heart, in the abdomen, in the ears, on the eyelids, in the mouth, and in the thorax. They also were placed inside the mummy wrappings. Since these onions repelled serpents, it was seen as being able to repel Apep, the Serpent Enemy.[314]

For the Feast of Bringing in Sokar each celebrant should **wear a necklace or collar with five onion bulbs**. These bulbs represent the five body orifices: two eyes, two ears, and the mouth. These onions evoke the opening of the five orifices in the Opening of the Mouth ceremony performed on the deceased.[315]

In as much as Sokar is a chthonian or underworld deity, he is closely involved in the renewal and protection of the dead. This ritual honors that aspect of the god. His ritual follows immediately after the mysteries of Ausir and the lamentations of Aset and Nebet-Hut.

In addition to wearing the necklace of green-stemmed onions, the ritualist offers a bouquet of five onions with their green stems still attached. The recitation for this offering appears later in the ritual.

---

[314] "Les oignons de Sokar," by Catherine Graindorge, in *Revue d'Egyptologie*, Volume 43 (1992), pp. 87-105. See p. 89 for list of body cavities with onions.

[315] Op. Cit., p. 98-99. See also Jean-Claude Goyon, 'Le Cérémonial pour faire sortir Sokar: Papyrus Louvre I. 3079," in *Revue d'Egyptologie* Volume 20 (1968), pp. 63-96. Also see G. A. Gaballa's two articles "New Light on the Cult of Sokar," in Orientalia Vol. 41 (1972), pp.178-79, and "The Festival of Sokar," in Orientalia Vol. 38, Issue 1 (1969), pp. 1-76.

After the regular presentation of the *Ib* (the golden heart), participants form a procession that ideally moves around the exterior of the building. If this is not possible, then the procession moves around the interior of the home, all the while carrying aloft the statue or image of Sokar and one of *Hat-Hór* as the litany of praises is recited or chanted (see litany beginning **"O you who wore the White Crown even when coming forth from the womb!** *Praise be to you!")*

* * * * *

As with all Egyptian rituals begin with your purification—washing of hands and cleansing of mouth with Natron. This preliminary rite helps us to lay aside the cares of the day and to become mindful of the fact that we will encounter a divine being. If Natron is not available, then use a natural sea salt in its place until you make your own Natron.

If two or more persons are participating, then one person, impersonating the Netjer Djehuty, **purifies each person by sprinkling each with water** *while exclaiming:*

I purify you with the water of all life and good fortune, all stability, all health and happiness.[316]

Afterwards each person **rinses his mouth** *and places a small amount* **of Natron or sea salt in his mouth** *while saying:*

---

[316] Taken from Aylward M. Blackman's article "Purification (Egyptian)" in Hastings Encyclopaedia 10/1918/ 476-82. This article is reprinted in Gods, Priests, and Men, Studies in the Religion of Pharaonic Egypt, edited by Alan B. Lloyd (Kegan Paul International, 1998), p. 9.

I wash my mouth; I chew natron so that I may extol the might of Sokar, Lord of the Caverns, the Hidden One.[317]

*Participants **assemble outside the Temple Chamber** and begin by softly rattling sistra.*

This time—several minutes or more—is used to focus minds and intention so that distracting thoughts are left behind. The sound of the sistrum was said to placate the deity, purifying the atmosphere in preparation for encountering divinity. The sistrum was associated with Hutheru and also with her and Heru's son Ihy, and thus has connotations of joy, celebration, and dancing. According to Plutarch (A.D. 46-120), the sound of sistra was also reputed to drive away Setekh. But this was of very late date. It may have been that since by that time Setekh had been demonized, the general apotropaic function of the sistrum against evil entities was extended to include this *Netjer* as well.

*Standing **before the closed doors**, the Ritualist recites the entrance spell:*

UTTERANCE BEFORE THE CLOSED DOORS OF THE TEMPLE

*The ritualist **raises hands in adoration** (dua position-arms stretched out in front of the body and raised up to face level, with palms facing outward). The following shall be said:*

---

[317] Adapted from a temple inscription taken from "The Myth of Horus at Edfu—II" by A. M. Blackman and H. W. Fairman, appearing in Gods, Priests and Men, Studies in the Religion of Pharaonic Egypt, p. 283.

O you *Netjeru* of this Temple, you guardians of the great portal, great *Netjeru* of mysterious abode, who sanctify the *Netjer* in his shrine, who consecrate his oblation, who receive the offerings in his presence in the Hall of the Ennead: I have made my way and I enter into your presence. I am one of you. I am Shu, the eldest son of his father, the senior *wab* servant-priest of Sokar. Do not repulse me on the *Netjer*'s path. My feet are not impeded. I am not turned back from the court of the great portal so that I may conduct the divine service, that I may present offerings to him that made them, that I may give bread to Sokar. I have come on the way of the god. I have not shown partiality in judgment. I have not consorted with the strong. I have not reproached the lowly. I have not stolen things. I have not diminished the constituents of the Eye of Ra. I have not disturbed the Balance. I have not tampered with the requirements of the Sacred Eye. O Council of the Great *Netjer* in this Temple, behold, I have come to you to offer Ma'at to the Lord of Ma'at, to content the Sound Eye for its lord. I am Shu; I flood his offering table. I present his offerings, Sekhmet consorting with me, that I may adore Sokar at his festivals, that I may kiss the earth so great is his majesty, that I may endow his image with life. I am pure. I am purified.

At this point the ritualist **opens the doors to the Temple Chamber,** *or, if there are no doors,* **makes a gesture of opening unseen doors,** *and* **steps forward as if crossing over a threshold.** *The following is said:*

O you *Ba*-souls of **Mennefer** (Memphis) if you are strong, I am strong. If I am strong, you are strong. If your *Ka*-spirits are strong, my *Ka*-spirit is strong at the head of the living. As they are living so shall I live . . . . Sokar, the Possessor of Everlasting Life, has given to me life, stability, and serenity round about my members, which Djehuty has gathered together for life. I am Heru in the height of heaven, the beautiful one of awe, Lord of Victory, mighty one of awe, exalted one of the two plumes, great one in Thebes, I am pure.

All temple members chant:

Awake in peace, O Sokar, Possessor of Many Faces,
may you awaken in peace.
Awake in peace, O Sokar, Well-beloved of the *Netjeru,*
may you awaken in peace.
Awake in peace, O Sokar, Lord of Time,
may you awaken in peace.
Awake in peace, O Sokar, Who Dwell in the Netherworld,
may you awaken in peace.

May you awake beautifully at the top of the morning,
through that which the entirety of *Netjeru* say to you.

Enter, close the double doors and stand in front of the Kar-shrine and altar. All bow, touching their hands to their knees.

The ritualist *slowly* **opens the two doors of the Kar-shrine** housing *the sacred image.* **All others bow, touching their hands to their knees.** *The following is said:*

The doors of the sky are open; the doors of the earth are unlocked. This House is open for its Lord. Let me come forth as he shall come forth. Let me enter in as he shall enter in. Sokar, the Lord of Fear, the *Ba* of Ausir, is exalted upon his Great Seat. The Great Company of the *Netjeru* are exalted upon their seat.

I have seen the *Netjer,* and the *Netjer* sees me. The *Netjer* rejoices at seeing me. I have gazed upon the statue of the Lord of the *Henu*-barque, the sacred image of the Possessor of Everlasting Life.[318]

Right hand on left shoulder of statue; left hand on right wrist of statue:

Djehuty has come to you. Awake when you hear his words. I have come as the envoy of Atum. My two arms are upon you like those of Heru. My two hands are upon you like those of Djehuty. My fingers are upon you like those of Anpu. Homage be to you. I am a living servant of Sokar.

A garland of onions is presented and placed before the god's image:

You are adored, O Sokar who resides in the *Sheteyet* Shrine. See, I have come close to you; I have brought to you this garland of onions on this the Feast of Going Around the Walls. These onions which purify are a protection against the serpent enemy. He is repelled! He is repelled![319]

*The Ritualist now holds up the **bowl of water** in which he/she will be mixing the Natron. The following is said:*

O water may you remove all evil,
As Ra who bathes in the Lake of Rushes,
May Heru wash my flesh,
May Djehuty cleanse my feet,

---

[318] Based on the temple text found in "Worship and Festivals in an Egyptian Temple," a lecture by H. W. Fairman (publ. by The John Rylands Library, 1954; p. 180).

[319] Catherine Graindorge-Hereil, Le Dieu Sokar à Thèbes au Nouvel Empire, Tome 1: Textes (Wiesbaden, Harrassowitz Verlag, 1994), pp. 152 & 395.

May Shu lift me up and Nut take my hand!
May Setekh be my strength, and may Sekhmet be my healing!
And may Amun-Ra be my life and my prospering!

*The bowl of water is set aside and the container of **Natron** is lifted up. The following is said:*

It is pure, it is pure.
My Natron is the Natron of Heru and the Natron of Heru is my Natron.
My Natron is the Natron of Setekh and the Natron of Setekh is my Natron.
My Natron is the Natron of Djehuty, and the Natron of Djehuty is my Natron.
My Natron is the Natron of Geb and the Natron of Geb is my Natron.

My mouth is the mouth of a milking calf on the day that I was born.

Four pinches of Natron are mixed into the water as this Utterance is recited:

I give you essential water, a tide in your time.
I bring the flood waters to purify your sanctuary.
I bring you the flood waters to purify your Temple and your statue in its place, the primordial water that purifies as in the First Time!

The Ritualist places an index finger into the water and moves it in a circular direction four times as the following is said:

Sokar, Whose Waters of Life are Great, does purify this water;

Sokar, the Living One, does cleanse this water;
Sokar, the Rejuvenator, does sanctify this water;
Sokar himself does endow this water with power and with life.

*The **Bowl of Natron-infused water** is then taken up and the Ritualist sprinkles this lightly in front of and around the statue or image of Sokar, applying some of this water to the base of the image, as the Utterance is recited:*

I come close to you, O Weary of Heart. I bring the water of rejuvenation that flows from the Two Caverns. I sprinkle the water, purifying your image and your Temple from all impurity!

*The Ritualist picks up the bowl of **Natron** and **sprinkles a small amount in each of the four directions** as the following is recited:*

The *Netjer* Sokar himself does cleanse and purify this, his Temple to the South.
The *Netjer* Sokar himself does cleanse and purify this, his Temple to the North.
The *Netjer* Sokar himself does cleanse and purify this, his Temple to the West.
The *Netjer* Sokar himself does cleanse and purify this, his Temple to the East.

*Replacing the Natron on the altar, the Ritualist takes up the **bowl of water**, sprinkling a small amount in each of the four directions. The following Utterance is recited:*

The *Netjer* Sokar himself does sanctify and consecrate this, his Temple to the South.

The *Netjer* Sokar himself does sanctify and consecrate this, his
Temple to the North.
The *Netjer* Sokar himself does sanctify and consecrate this, his
Temple to the West.
The *Netjer* Sokar himself does sanctify and consecrate this, his
Temple to the East.

The Temple of the *Netjer* Sokar is established. It is established
for millions of years.

*The Ritualist returns to the altar and **lights the candle or oil lamp**
while the following is said:*

Come, come in peace, O glorious Eye of Heru,
Be strong and renew your youth in peace.
For the flame shines like Ra on the double horizon.
The enemies of Ra are defeated. They are defeated.
I am pure, I am pure, I am pure, I am pure.

*The Ritualist **places incense on the burner and censes each sacred
image** beginning with the statue of Sokar while the following is recited:*

The fire is laid, the fire shines;
The incense is laid on the fire, the incense shines.
     Your perfume comes to me, O Incense;
        May my perfume come to you, O Incense.
Your perfume comes to me, you *Netjeru;*
May my perfume come to you, You *Netjeru.*
     May I be with you, you *Netjeru;*
        May you be with me, you *Netjeru.*
May I live with you, you *Netjeru;*
May you live with me, you *Netjeru.*

I love you, you *Netjeru;*
May you love me, you *Netjeru.*

Standing in front of the image of Sokar the Ritualist **offers the burning incense** *and says:*

Take the incense, O Lord of Time Who Grants Years.
Its essence is for you.
Its smoke permeates your shrine, bringing life!
Take the incense,
Its essence is for you.
Your Majesty is appeased with the incense.
This Eye of Heru,
This essence of the Eye of Heru comes to you.

At this point the following is said:

Hail to you, Sokar, Lord of the *Sheteyet* Shrine[320] and Ruler of the Realm of the Dead. You are He Who Comes as the Rejuvenator, truly the Lord of Joy. May you rejuvenate us who serve you.

Hail to you, Sokar, of Great Esteem, Great *Netjer* in the House of Purification, Lord of the Holy Land (i.e., the necropolis) **and Living** *Ba.* **You are He for Whom One Creates the Transfiguration. May you transfigure us when we enter the realm of the Living Ones** (i.e., the dead).

Hail to you, Sokar-Ausir, for Whom the Mourning Women Cry with Their Songs of Sorrow. O you of the Black Wrappings, may our sadness be turned to joy, O Lord of Joy.

---

[320] The Sheteyet Shrine is the shrine or burial site of Sokar. It can also mean the Underworld.

Hail to you, Sokar-Ausir, Lord of the Sixth Day Festival[321]. Truly you are He of the Pleasant Splendor of the Left Eye. May you place the strong arms of your protection around us who bow down before your image.

*The Ritualist **places more incense on the charcoal** and again and again **slowly raises and lowers the incense cup** as the following is recited:*

O Sokar, may you advance with your *Ka*.
O Excellent Power in the Realm of the Blessed Ones,
the arm of your *Ka* is before you,
The arm of your *Ka* is behind you.
O Lord of the Necropolis, the foot of your *Ka* is before you,
The foot of your *Ka* is behind you.
O Sokar, this incense is offered to you,
May your face be filled as this essence spreads itself over you.

*All present perform the **Henu Rite**—Embrace the Earth, the Fourfold Salute to the God, Embrace the Earth.*

For Embracing the Earth, all present prostrate themselves, face down, upon the floor. During the Fourfold Salute, all present rise upon one knee, and alternately raise their hands and arms into the *Dua* (praise) position with palms facing outward, followed by the *Sahu* (obedience) gesture, made by striking the chest with a closed fist and raising the other arm (also with closed fist) at a ninety-degree angle. The *Dua* position is accompanied by the words **"Adoration**

---

[321] On the Sixth Day of each lunar month (i.e., the First Quarter Moon), temples commemorated the 'Filling of the Eye" as a time when the six segments of the Eye of Heru were ritually brought together and made complete.

be to Sokar," followed by the *Sahu* gesture accompanied with the words, **"Hail to the Ruler of Eternity!"** The bodily gestures are performed alternately four times.

*Following this **all present again prostrate themselves** before the god. This is a sign and symbol of total submission and adoration before the Netjer. The following is said:*

Homage to Sokar, Foremost of the Barque of Ma'at,
who is established on the Great Seat!
I have placed myself on the floor in awe of you.
I embrace the earth before you as before the Lord of Terror.
I have come that I might kiss the earth,
that I might worship my Lord,
For I have seen his Strength;
I give praise to Sokar,
For I have seen his Power.
His form is more distinguished than the *Netjeru*;
His arm is more powerful than the *Netjeru*.
I am pure, I am pure, I am pure, I am pure!

Everyone stands up.

*The Ritualist **holds in the palm of one hand the image of Ma'at** and with **the other hand open and raised over the image as if sheltering it**, repeats the following:*

I have come to you as Djehuty, whose two hands are joined together under Ma'at. She comes to be with you, for she is everywhere. You are provided with Ma'at. You move in Ma'at, you live in Ma'at. She fills your body, she rests in your head, she makes her seat upon your brow; the breath of your body is of Ma'at, your heart does live in Ma'at. All that you eat, all that you drink, all that you breathe is of Ma'at. Djehuty presents Ma'at to you, his two hands are upon her beauty before your face.

*The Ritualist places the image of Ma'at near the divine statue. Then he/ she holds up before the image of Sokar **a pitcher of water and pours the water slowly into an offering bowl** as the following Utterance is recited:*

This libation is for you, O Living One.
This libation is for you, O Sokar, Lord of Eternity.
I have brought to you this offering of water,
That your heart may be refreshed.
I have brought to you this Eye of Heru,
Placing this at your feet.
I present to you that which flows forth from you,
That your heart shall continue to beat.
For it is with you that all comes forth at the sound of the voice.

*The offering bowl is placed on the altar. At this point the Ritualist **lightly sprinkles sand on the floor in front of the altar** as the following is recited:*

O Sokar, who resides in *Mennefer* (Memphis),
Take to yourself the Eye of Heru.
You have rescued it, O Divine Regenerator.
You have sprinkled with sand the Eye of Heru.

***Lifting the wine offering** before the sacred image, the Ritualist repeats the following:*

mn n.k irp irt ḥrw wȝḏt

[*"mán-nik 'úrip írat ḥáru wá'ḏat"*; approximately pronounced *MAHN-neek OO-rip EE-raht HAH-roo WAH-jat*]

Take to yourself wine, the green Eye of Heru, which I offer to your *Ka.* [322]

O Foremost of the *Duat* (Underworld), how beautiful is your beauty!

May you drink it; may your heart rejoice;

may anger be removed from your face.

It is pure. [*iw.w w'b* pronounced *"uwú wá'ib"*; approximately oo-WOO WAH-ib]

The Ritualist **places myrrh on the fire** *and* **lifts up the smoking incense** *while at the same time he* **lifts up the meat-offering** *before the Netjer, and says the following:*

The scent of myrrh is for your nose. It fills your nostrils; your heart receives the meat-portions on its scent.[323]

Slowly **elevating the food offerings four times** *before the image of Sokar, the Ritualist repeats the following:*

I offer to Sokar, Who Restrains the Serpent-Enemy in the Fifth Hour of the Night.

All life emanates from you,

All health emanates from you,

All stability emanates from you,

---

[322] Refer to pp. 92, 93, 99, and 105 in Mu-Chou Poo's *Wine and Wine Offerings in Ancient Egypt* (London & New York: Kegan Paul International, 1995).

[323] Quoted in "Worship and Festivals in an Egyptian Temple," by H. W. Fairman (publ. by The John Rylands Library, 1954), p. 191.

All good fortune emanates from you,
O Foremost of the Netherworld, Sokar, forever.

The Ritualist places the food offering before the divine image, and then all present extend one hand, palm down, over the offerings and recite the following:

May offerings of every kind come forth in abundance,
like the things which come forth from the mouth of the *Netjer*.

piryá pírit ar ḥiráw mi purú:riat ma rá' ni náṯar. (4 times)
approximately pronounced: peer-YA PEER-it ar khi-RAU mee pu-ROOR-iat ma RA nee NAH-tchar

May offerings of every kind come forth in abundance, like the things that come forth from the mouth of the *Netjer*.

Holding the Ankh before Sokar, the Ritualist says:

Live, O Sokar, Lord of the *Netjeru*, live for all time and for eternity!

ʿánaḫ niḥáḫ ḏát.
[approximately pronounced *AH-nakh nee-HAH JAHT*]

The Ankh is placed next to the image of the Netjer.

Holding the Ib (the golden heart) before Sokar, the Ritualist says:

Hail to you, O Sokar, Old One of *Neheh* Time. I have brought to you your heart to set it in its place. Let me draw near to you with your heart, so that you may have pleasure through me, and so that by means of me you may have power over your body. Ascend, O Beautiful Young One, radiant, rejuvenating, equipped as a *Netjer*. Live, O Bull of the West, live forever and ever!

*After placing the **Ib** near the sacred image, **everyone sings or chants the hymn to Sokar**. Participants may wish to alternate the singing of verses.*

Sokar, Lord of the *heh-Netjeru* (i.e., the eight Ogdoad gods) who support the *Netjeru*, Most Primeval of the *Netjeru*, Eldest of the primeval ones, we give praise to you on this your feast.

The following praises are addressed to Sokar on the Feast of Bringing in Sokar. A statue or image of this god is carried in procession around the exterior of the temple building. If this is not feasible, then the image should be carried around the inside of the home as an accommodation to the specific situation. In ancient times the statue of this god was placed on a ritual barque carried on the shoulders of priests. Again, if this is not possible, then simply carry the statue raised up on high above the heads of participants.

O you who wore the White Crown even when coming forth from the womb! *Praise be to you!*
O Eldest Son of the First Primeval One! *Praise be to you!*
O Possessor of Many Faces, manifold of forms! *Praise be to you!*
O Medicine of Gold in the Temples! *Praise be to you!*
O Lord of Time who grants years! *Praise be to you!*
O Possessor of everlasting life! *Praise be to you!*
O Lord of Millions, rich in myriads! *Praise be to you!*
O you who shine when rising peacefully! *Praise be to you!*
O you who heals for yourself your throat! *Praise be to you!*

O Lord of Fear, at whom humans greatly tremble! *Praise be to you!*

O Possessor of Many Faces, rich in Uraei! *Praise be to you!*

O you who appears with the White Crown, Lord of the *Ureret-crown*! *Praise be to you!*

O august offspring of *Har-hekenu*! *Praise be to you!*

O *Ba* (soul) of Ra in the Bark of Millions! *Praise be to you!*

O weary Leader, come to your *Sheteyet* Shrine! *Praise be to you!*

O Lord of Fear, who came into being of himself! *Praise be to you!*

O Weary of Heart, come to your city! *Praise be to you!*

O you who rejoice, come to your city! *Praise be to you!*

O you, well-beloved of the *Netjeru* and *Netjerut*! *Praise be to you!*

O you whose waters of life are great, come to your Temple! *Praise be to you!*

O you who dwell in the Netherworld, come to your offerings! *Praise be to you!*

O you who protect yourself, come to your Temples! *Praise be to you!*

O you whose darkness is more enduring than the light of the sun! *Praise be to you!*

O august *kiki*-plant[324] (the medicinal castor-oil plant) of the Great Temple! *Praise be to you!*

O august rope-maker of the Night-barque! *Praise be to you!*

O Lord of the *Henu*-barque, youthful in the *Sheteyet* Shrine! *Praise be to you!*

O Excellent Power who are in the Realm of the Blessed Ones! *Praise be to you!*

O august controller of Upper and Lower Kemet! *Praise be to you!*

---

[324] For more on the extensive medical uses of the castor-oil plant, please refer to Lise Manniche's *An Ancient Egyptian Herbal* (Austin: University of Texas Press, 1989), pp. 142-143. By identifying the god with a healing plant, the ancient author is stressing the great healing power of Sokar.

O Hidden One whom the common folk do not know! *Praise be to you!*

O you who blindfold him who is in the Netherworld from seeing the sun! *Praise be to you!*

O Lord of the *Atef*-Crown, great in the Temple of *Hwt-nen-nesu* ("house of the royal child", i.e., Herakleopolis)! *Praise be to you!*

O you who art greatly majestic beside the *naaret*-tree! *Praise be to you!*

O you who art in *Waset*, who flourish forever! *Praise be to you!*

O you who increase offerings and sacrifices in *Rosetau* (the Netherworld)! *Praise be to you!*

O you who place the Uraeus on the head of its Lord! *Praise be to you!*

O you who establish the earth in its place! *Praise be to you!*

O you who open the mouths of the four Great *Netjeru* who are in the Realm of the Blessed Ones! *Praise be to you!* O Living *Ba* (soul) of Ausir when he appears as the Moon! *Praise be to you!*

O you whose body is hidden in the Great *Sheteyet* Shrine in *Iunu* (Heliopolis)! *Praise be to you!*

O Divine One who hide Ausir in the Realm of the Blessed Ones! *Praise be to you!*

O you whose *Ba* (soul) rests in Heaven, whose foe is fallen! *Praise be to you!*

*The procession concludes as the **statue of Sokar is placed once again in its central place** in the shrine.*

*The **statue or image of Hat-Hór** carried in procession **is now placed in the shrine next to Sokar** while the following is said:*

The Divine Aset speaks to you with joyful voice from the river which the pure a*bed*-fish cleaves in front of the bark of Ra.

The Lady of Horns (Hathor) is come into being with joy, the egg is come into being in the canal.

The heads of the impious-ones are cut off in this her name of Lady of *Per Hat-Hór* (House of Hathor) (i.e., called by the Greeks Aphroditopolis).

The Lady of Horns is come in peace in this her name of *Hat-Hór*, Lady of *Mefkat* (the Sinai).

The Lady of *Waset* (Thebes) is come in peace in this her name of *Hat-Hór*, Lady of *Waset*.

She is come in peace as Tayt comes in her name Lady of *Hetepet*. She is come in peace to overthrow her foe in her name of *Hat-Hór*, Lady of the Temple of *Hwt-nen-nesu* (i.e., House of the Royal Child) (Herakleopolis).

The Golden One is come in peace in that her name of *Hat-Hór*, Lady of *Mennefer* (Memphis), ...

You being at peace in the presence of the Lord of All (Ra) in this your name of *Hat-Hór*, Lady of the Red Mountain (near *Iunu*-Heliopolis); the Golden One rises beside her father (Ra).

*At this point in the ritual all present turn toward those who are bringing in the statue of Ausir **preceded by a celebrant carrying burning incense**. Those present **address this Netjer** with the following exclamations:*

O you Nine Companions, come with your hands bearing your father Ausir.

The revered *Netjer* comes! *(4 times)*

Hail, Crowned One, Crowned One, Sovereign! Hail! How sweet is the smell that you love! Hail! Live forever and forever! Hail!

Be festal in spirit forever! Hail! Be enduring in Upper *Djedu* (Abydos)! Hail! O *Netjer*! Hear the joyous worship!
Hail! Hear the worship in the *Netjer*'s region (the Netherworld)!
Hail! You are protected according to your word!

Hail! We on earth do what you desire.
Hail! We on earth do what you praise. Hail, Enthroned One!
Come, O Weary-hearted One!
Hail, you Divine One for whom this ritual is recited!
Hail, you whose name endures in *Djedu*[325] (the town of Busiris)!
Hail, you who are the sweet-savoured one in *Djedu*! Hail! Come, you who crush the rebels against Ma'at. Hail! Come, O you youthful Adored One!
Hail! The fear of whom is put into the impious ones!
Hail, Ausir! The awe of you is in our hearts! Hail, Ausir!

THE HYMN TO SOKAR FROM
SCENE V OF THE "FEAST OF SOKAR"

[From the II Court of the "Temple of Millions of Years" of King Ramses III, West Waset (Thebes)]

RUBRIC: The Chief Lector Priest recites the words, and the other celebrants reply to him.

*Words that the **Chief Lector Priest** utters when conducting Sokar:*

Hail! Be triumphant, triumphant, O Sovereign!
Hail! How sweet is the fragrance which you love!
Hail! Behold, I perform the things which you love!

---

[325] The town of Djedu (Busiris) was regarded as the birthplace of Ausir. Upper Djedu was the town of Abydos, another cult center for Ausir and Sokar.

Hail! I shall do what you do praise!

Hail! I kiss the earth, I open the way, O Favored-Ones of *Abdju* (Abydos)!

Hail! Fiery of Eye!

Hail! Protection is according to what you say!

Hail! I love your face when you rest in the God's broad hall within the Temple!

Hail! How pleasant is the fragrance of *Abdju*. *Abdju* is protected, protected!

Hail! My *Netjer*, hearken to the worship!

Hail! Be joyous, and hearken to the worship that comes from our mouths!

Hail! As for a devotee who follows his Lord, Bastet shall not have power over him because the priests of Bastet punish in their rituals the impious ones, but she is gracious and favorable to the devotees of the *Netjeru*!

Hail! We pray to you, come, drive out the rebels against Ma'at!

Hail! Put the fear of you into the rebels against the Gods!

Hail! Be pleased and come, O Weary-hearted One!

Hail! Enduring of Name in *Djedu* (Busiris)!

Hail! May you live, may you live forever!

Hail! Your festivals shall be everlasting.

Hail! The Lord of Upper *Djedu* (Sokar-Osiris) has come. He has smitten the rebels against Ma'at!

For the beautiful, good, and perfect God, beloved of Sokar, that he may grant very numerous jubilees to us who honor him!

THE LITANY OF OFFERINGS TO SOKAR IN ALL HIS NAMES

[from the III scene of the "Feast of Sokar", II Court of the "Temple of Millions of Years" of King Ramses III, West *Waset* (Thebes)]

Praise to Sokar in *Sheteyet* (the Cult-Shrine of Sokar in the necropolis of Memphis)

Praise to Sokar in Rosetau![326]
Praise to Sokar presiding over Rosetau!
Praise to Sokar upon the desert hills!
Praise to Sokar upon his sand!
Praise to Sokar in his place within Rosetau!
Praise to Sokar in Tjanenet (Memphite Sanctuary)!
Praise to Sokar presiding over the Divine Booth of the craftsmen!
Praise to Sokar in the Land of Sokar!
Praise to Sokar presiding over his city!
Praise to Sokar in the barque of the Two Ma'at-Goddesses!
Praise to Sokar in all his places within Upper Kemet!
Praise to Sokar in all his places within Lower Kemet!
Praise to Sokar in the foreign countries!
Praise to Sokar in Heaven!
Praise to Sokar on Earth!
Praise to Sokar in all his Names!
Praise to Sokar in all his Temples!
Praise to Sokar in all his establishments!
Praise to Sokar in all his shrines!
Praise to Sokar in all his Divine Booths!
Praise to Sokar in every place in which he desires to be!

---

[326] Rosetau is the name of a region in the underworld. According to Erik Hornung in *The Ancient Egyptian Books of the Afterlife,* p. 11, this region "lies 'at the boundary of the sky' and contains the corpse of Osiris; according to Coffin Text spell 1,080, it is 'locked in darkness and surrounded by fire.' The deceased wishes to reach this place, for whoever gazes on the deceased Osiris cannot die (Coffin Text VII 302e)."

This concludes the recitations for the Feast of Bringing in Sokar.

*At this point **all present back out of the Temple Chamber with heads slightly bowed** while the Ritualist performs the "removing the foot."*

*With the broom the Ritualist, as the last person to exit, **ritually sweeps the area beginning at the altar**. (This is known as "removing the foot.") While performing this action the Ritualist recites the following:*

The distress that causes confusion has been driven away, and all the *Netjeru* are in harmony. I have given Heru his Eye; I have placed the *Wedjat*-Eye in the correct position. I have given Setekh his Testicles, so that the two lords are content through the work of my hands.

I know the sky, I know the earth;
I know Heru, I know Setekh.
Heru is appeased with his Eyes;
Setekh is appeased with his Testicles.
I am Djehuty, who reconciles the *Netjeru*,
who makes offerings in their correct form.

*The double doors are **solemnly closed** as the Ritualist says the following:*

Djehuty has come.
He has filled the Eye of Heru;
He has restored the Testicles of Setekh.
No evil shall enter this Temple.
Ptah has closed the door,

Djehuty has set it fast.
The door is closed, the door is set fast with the bolt.

All bow, touching the palms of their hands to their knees.

THE REVERSION OF OFFERINGS

*One priest or priestess and as many assistants as necessary enter the Temple Chamber a final time. While he/she and any assistants **lift up the offerings** before the sacred image the ritualist shall say:*

O Sokar, your enemy[327] withdraws for you. Heru has turned himself to his Eye in its name of 'Reversion-of-Offerings.' I am Djehuty. I come to perform this rite for Sokar, the One Who Provides Foods for the Sanctuaries. These, your divine offerings revert, they revert to your servants for life, for stability, for health and for joy! O that the Eye of Heru may flourish for you eternally!

*Everyone withdraws, **carrying away all food offerings except for one loaf of bread together with a bowl of pure water.** These last items will remain until evening. If this ritual is celebrated after sunset, these items would also be removed.*

*After the candle has burned down, a servant-priest enters **and closes the doors of the Kar-shrine.***

Extinguishing the candle or oil lamp, he/she exclaims:

---

[327] Meat offerings held a two-fold meaning for the ancient priesthood. Since meat necessarily came from slain animals, it signified the defeated or slain enemies of the Netjer. At the same time, the meat offering represented the produce of the land which ultimately was a gift of the Netjeru.

This is the Eye of Heru by which you have become great, by which you live, and by which you have power, O Sokar. This is the Eye of Heru which you consume and through which you enchant your body. The *Wedjat*-Eye now enters into the West, into *Manu*, but it shall return. Truly, the Eye of Heru returns in peace![328]

---

[328] It is important to consume the food offerings after the ceremony. Water used should either be drunk or poured onto the earth. If it is mixed with natron, dilute it very greatly and then you can pour in onto the earth without harming any plantings.

The General Ritual for Tutu

"Known cult centres of Tutu are Sais, Athribis, Middle Egypt (the region of Antaeopolis), Koptos, Shenhur, Luxor, Esna, the region of the First Cataract, and Ismant el-Kharab (Kellis) in the Dakhla Oasis." [329]

This great god holds the unique position of being the "Master of the Executioners (ḫ3tyw pronounced 'khatyu') of Sekhmet and the Wandering Demons (šm3yw) of Bastet." These forces were seen as bringing sickness, misfortune, and death. Tutu was perceived as the one god who had absolute control of these entities. Many of his epithets relate to this role as protector of humans from these negative forces.

As Egyptologist Panagiotis Kousoulis explains, "The words 'demon' and 'demonology' as it is used in contemporary English . . . are drawing on our own, Judaeo-Christian, cultural heritage and are seen as negative aspects of cultural conceptualization and practice." [330] Kousoulis later states, "Egyptian demons are usually understood by Egyptologists as 'minor divinities', assistants to superior powers, or agents of chaos and evil." [331] Therefore, when we encounter a reference to the demons of Sekhmet or Bastet, we can understand those particular beings as both minor divinities as well as assistants to these goddesses—all in the

---

[329] Olaf E. Kaper, *The Egyptian God Tutu: A Study of the Sphinx-God and Master of Demons with a Corpus of Monuments* (Leuven, Belgium: Peeters Publishers, 2003), p. 205.

[330] Panagiotis Kousoulis, "The Demonic Lore of Ancient Egypt," in *Ancient Egyptian Demonology: Studies on the Boundaries between the Demonic and the Divine in Egyptian Magic*; ed/ by P. Kousoulis (Leuven: Peeters, 2011), p. X.

[331] Op./ Cit., p. XI.

service of ma'at. *Rather than seeing sickness, misfortune, and death itself as divine punishments, these conditions have the potential to help us reevaluate our own priorities and values so that when we cross from this life to the next, we can be found "justified" and "true-of-voice," entering into that new life as a transfigured, luminous spirit—our divine destiny.*

In the temple calendar at Esna a festival of Tutu occurred on the 14th day of the first month of the religious year and again a festival for him and his divine mother Neith on the 10th of the third month of the year.[332]

Special offerings for Tutu: the sickle-shaped weapon (known as a khepesh sword), the sistrum, and the traditional food offerings of bread, beer, wine, and meat. In ancient Egyptian, this ritual weapon is called 'the sword of valor' (ḫpš n ḵnw). As a warrior god Tutu receives the khepesh, and as a potentially aggressive god he receives the calming sound of the sistrum.

Like members of the ancient priesthood, participants should be clothed in white linen. No item made of animal products such as leather or wool is to be worn.

As with all Egyptian rituals begin with your purification—washing of hands and cleansing of mouth with Natron. This preliminary rite helps us to lay aside the cares of the day and to become mindful of the fact that we will encounter a divine being. If Natron is not available, then use a natural sea salt in its place until you make your own Natron.

---

[332] Op. Cit., p. 130.

If two or more persons are participating, then one person, impersonating the Netjer Djehuty, **purifies each person by sprinkling each with water** *while exclaiming:*

I purify you with the water of all life and good fortune, all stability, all health and happiness.[333]

Afterwards each person **rinses his mouth** *and* **places a small amount of Natron or sea salt in his mouth** *while saying:*

I wash my mouth; I chew natron so that I may extol the might of Tutu, Great of Strength, Lord of Victories.[334]

Participants **assemble outside the Temple Chamber** *and begin by softly rattling sistra.*

This time—several minutes or more—is used to focus minds and intention so that distracting thoughts are left behind. The sound of the sistrum was said to placate the deity, purifying the atmosphere in preparation for encountering divinity. The sistrum was associated with Hutheru and also with her and Heru's son Ihy, and thus has connotations of joy, celebration, and dancing. According to Plutarch (A.D. 46-120), the sound of sistra was also reputed to drive away Setekh. But this was of very late date. It may have been that since by that time

---

[333] Taken from Aylward M. Blackman's article "Purification (Egyptian)" in Hastings Encyclopaedia 10/1918/ 476-82. This article is reprinted in Gods, Priests, and Men, Studies in the Religion of Pharaonic Egypt, edited by Alan B. Lloyd (Kegan Paul International, 1998), p. 9.

[334] Adapted from a temple inscription taken from "The Myth of Horus at Edfu—II" by A. M. Blackman and H. W. Fairman, appearing in Gods, Priests and Men, Studies in the Religion of Pharaonic Egypt, p. 283.

Setekh had been demonized, the general apotropaic function of the sistrum against evil entities was extended to include this *Netjer* as well.

*Standing before the closed doors, the Ritualist **recites the entrance spell**:*

UTTERANCE BEFORE THE CLOSED DOORS OF THE TEMPLE

*The ritualist **raises hands in adoration** (dua position-arms stretched out in front of the body and raised up to face level, with palms facing outward). The following shall be said:*

O you *Netjeru* of this Temple, you guardians of the great portal, great *Netjeru* of mysterious abode, who sanctify the *Netjer* in his shrine, who consecrate his oblation, who receive the offerings in his presence in the Hall of the Ennead: I have made my way and I enter into your presence. I am one of you. I am Shu, the eldest son of his father, the senior *wab* servant-priest of Tutu. Do not repulse me on the *Netjer's* path. My feet are not impeded. I am not turned back from the court of the great portal so that I may conduct the divine service, that I may present offerings to him that made them, that I may give bread to Tutu. I have come on the way of the god. I have not shown partiality in judgment. I have not consorted with the strong. I have not reproached the lowly. I have not stolen things. I have not diminished the constituents of the Eye of Ra. I have not disturbed the Balance. I have not tampered with the requirements of the Sacred Eye. O Council of the Great *Netjer* in this Temple, behold, I have come to you to offer Ma'at to the Lord of Ma'at, to content the Sound Eye for its lord. I am Shu; I flood his offering table. I present his offerings, Sekhmet consorting with me, that I may adore Tutu at his festivals, that

I may kiss the earth so great is his majesty, that I may endow his image with life. I am pure. I am purified.

*At this point the ritualist **opens the doors to the Temple Chamber**, or, if there are no doors, **makes a gesture of opening unseen doors**, and **steps forward as if crossing over a threshold**. The following is said:*

O you *Ba*-souls of *Kellis* and *Gebtu* (Koptos)[335], if you are strong, I am strong. If I am strong, you are strong. If your *Ka*-spirits are strong, my *Ka*-spirit is strong at the head of the living. As they are living so shall I live . . . . Tutu, Bull of his Mother, has given to me life, stability, and serenity round about my members, which Djehuty has gathered together for life. I am Heru in the height of heaven, the beautiful one of awe, Lord of Victory, mighty one of awe, exalted one of the two plumes, great one in *Waset*, I am pure.

All temple members chant:

Awake in peace, O Tutu, Foremost in *Kellis*,
may you awaken in peace.
Awake in peace, O Tutu, Who Drives Away the Enemies,
may you awaken in peace.
Awake in peace, O Tutu, Who Overthrows A/pep,
may you awaken in peace.
Awake in peace, O Tutu, Strong *Netjer*,
may you awaken in peace.

May you awake beautifully at the top of the morning,
through that which the entirety of *Netjeru* say to you.

---

[335] Kellis and Gebtu are two of the cult centers for the god Tutu.

Enter, close the double doors and stand in front of the Kar-shrine and altar. All bow, touching their hands to their knees.

The ritualist *slowly opens the two doors of the Kar-shrine housing the sacred image. All others bow, touching their hands to their knees. The following is said:*

The doors of the sky are open; the doors of the earth are unlocked. This House is open for its Lord. Let me come forth as he shall come forth. Let me enter in as he shall enter in. Tutu, Mighty of Arm, the Great Fighting *Ba*, is exalted upon his Great Seat. The Great Company of the *Netjeru* are exalted upon their seat.

I have seen the *Netjer,* and the *Netjer* sees me. The *Netjer* rejoices at seeing me. I have gazed upon the statue of the One Who Comes to the One Calling Him, the sacred image of the Master of the Arrow Demons.[336]

Right hand on left shoulder of statue; left hand on right wrist of statue:

Djehuty has come to you. Awake when you hear his words. I have come as the envoy of Atum. My two arms are upon you like those of Heru. My two hands are upon you like those of Djehuty. My fingers are upon you like those of Anpu. Homage be to you. I am a living servant of Tutu.

*All present begin softly **playing their sistra** as the Ritualist **presents a sistrum** to Tutu as the following is said:*

---

[336] Based on the temple text found in "Worship and Festivals in an Egyptian Temple," a lecture by H. W. Fairman (publ. by The John Rylands Library, 1954; p. 180).

I come to you, Great Protector, lord of this sanctuary. I bring you the sistrum to satisfy your heart, for you are Tutu, Great of Strength, Master of the Arrow Demons and Lord of the Book, who judges in the Castle of the Benben in *Iunu* (Heliopolis), great messenger in the Netherworld. There is no other comparable to you.[337] May you be at peace with me. May you not launch your curse at me.[338]

How beautiful it is! This sistrum that you desire, O Lord of Kind Character, this music which your heart loves. We shake the sistra for you to appease your *Ka*. Your heart rejoices at their sound. Welcome, O Son of Neith! The *Netjeru* make music for you and the *Netjerut* dance to appease your heart.[339]

Praise to you, O Strong God, Unique One,
Great Guardian among the Guardian-*Netjeru*.
The *Netjeru* come to you prostrating themselves before you,
the *Netjerut* come to you bowing their heads before you.

Your Father Ra adores you, his face rejoices when hearing your name.
Djehuty satisfies you with his glorifications,
and he raises his arms to you, carrying the sistrum.

---

[337] Based on an inscription on Tutu's naos (shrine). See Olaf E. Kaper's *The Egyptian God Tutu*, p. 251. The epithet 'Lord of the Book' refers to the Book of Bad Things of Finishing the Lifetime (i.e., causing death).

[338] Émile Chassinat, et al., *Le temple de Dendara*, Vol. IV (Cairo: Institut francçais d'archéologie orientale), 75-76.

[339] Amr Gaber, *The Central Hall in the Egyptian Temples of the Ptolemaic Period* (2009), Durham theses, Durham University. Available at Durham E-Theses Online: http://etheses.dur.ac.uk/88/ Based on one of the ancient formulae for offering the sistrum: from the Central Hall in the Temple at Edfu; see p. 470 in the dissertation.

The *Netjeru* rejoice for you when you appear.

The South, the North, the West, and the East pay homage to you; they make adorations to you. Tutu, Lord of Heaven, may your powerful face be pleased by this, our service to you.[340]

*All present **recite the hymn** honoring Tutu:*

Happy is the temple and happy are the priests
And happy are the watchers of the day.
For the Great Protector has entered his shrine,
And the people bow down in homage.

For Tutu is Mighty of Arm and Kind of Character,
And he is the One Who Comes to the One Calling Him.
He shines like the sun in *Kellis*, his city.
He shines like the sun in this city.

O Guardian Who Lengthens the Lifespan,
Upon whom the *Netjeru* desire to look
As the Great of Strength comes forth from heaven.

All people, all people of Tutu's temple, come and adore,
For this *Netjer* is He Who Tramples the Cobra!
And the protection he extends to the one who calls him
Is because he is the One Who Saves Humans from All Evil.

Loud are the shouts that ascend to the sky,
That he hears as he passes on his way,
For happy are the people and happy are the priests,

---

[340] Émile Chassinat, et al., *Le temple de Dendara*, Vol. I (Cairo: Institut francçais d'archéologie orientale), p. 80.

And happy are the watchers of the day![341]

*The Ritualist holds up the **bowl of water** in which he/she will be mixing the Natron. The following is said:*

O water may you remove all evil,
As Ra who bathes in the Lake of Rushes,
May Heru wash my flesh,
May Djehuty cleanse my feet,
May Shu lift me up and Nut take my hand!
May Setekh be my strength, and may Sekhmet be my healing!
And may Amun-Ra be my life and my prospering!

*The bowl of water is set aside and the container of **Natron** is lifted up. The following is said:*

It is pure, it is pure.
My Natron is the Natron of Heru and the Natron of Heru is my Natron.
My Natron is the Natron of Setekh and the Natron of Setekh is my Natron.
My Natron is the Natron of Djehuty, and the Natron of Djehuty is my Natron.
My Natron is the Natron of Geb and the Natron of Geb is my Natron.

My mouth is the mouth of a milking calf on the day that I was born.

---

[341] Modeled on a hymn in Margaret A. Murray's *Egyptian Religious Poetry* (London, 1949), pp. 93-94. Original source, *The Journal of Egyptian Archaeology*, vol. xvi (1930), p. 57. All ancient epithets for Tutu are capitalized throughout this ritual.

Four pinches of Natron are mixed into the water as this Utterance is recited:

I give you essential water, a tide in your time.
I bring the flood waters to purify your sanctuary.
I bring you the flood waters to purify your Temple and your statue in its place, the primordial water that purifies as in the First Time!

*The Ritualist places an **index finger into the water** and **moves it in a circular direction four times** as the following is said:*

Tutu, the Son of Neith, does purify this water;
Tutu, Mighty of Arm, does cleanse this water;
Tutu, Who Dispels the Wandering Demons, does sanctify this water;
Tutu himself does endow this water with power and with life.

*The **Bowl of Natron-infused water** is then taken up and the Ritualist sprinkles this lightly in front of and around the statue or image of Tutu, applying some of this water to the base of the image, as the Utterance is recited:*

I come close to you, O Lord of Heaven Who Has No Equal, Strong *Netjer*. I bring the water of rejuvenation that flows from the Two Caverns.
I sprinkle the water, purifying your image and your Temple from all impurity!

*The Ritualist picks up the **bowl of Natron** and **sprinkles a small amount in each of the four directions** as the following is recited:*

The *Netjer* Tutu himself does cleanse and purify this, his Temple to the South.

The *Netjer* Tutu himself does cleanse and purify this, his Temple to the North.

The *Netjer* Tutu himself does cleanse and purify this, his Temple to the West.

The *Netjer* Tutu himself does cleanse and purify this, his Temple to the East.

*Replacing the Natron on the altar, the Ritualist takes up the **bowl of water, sprinkling a small amount in each of the four directions**. The following Utterance is recited:*

The *Netjer* Tutu himself does sanctify and consecrate this, his Temple to the South.

The *Netjer* Tutu himself does sanctify and consecrate this, his Temple to the North.

The *Netjer* Tutu himself does sanctify and consecrate this, his Temple to the West.

The *Netjer* Tutu himself does sanctify and consecrate this, his Temple to the East.

The Temple of the *Netjer* Tutu is established. It is established for millions of years.

*The Ritualist returns to the altar and **lights the candle or oil lamp** while the following is said:*

Come, come in peace, O glorious Eye of Heru,
Be strong and renew your youth in peace.
For the flame shines like Ra on the double horizon.
The enemies of Ra are defeated. They are defeated.

I am pure, I am pure, I am pure, I am pure.

The Ritualist places incense on the burner and censes each sacred image beginning with the statue of Tutu while the following is recited:

The fire is laid, the fire shines;
The incense is laid on the fire, the incense shines.
    Your perfume comes to me, O Incense;
    May my perfume come to you, O Incense.
Your perfume comes to me, you *Netjeru*;
May my perfume come to you, You *Netjeru*.
    May I be with you, you *Netjeru*;
    May you be with me, you *Netjeru*.
May I live with you, you *Netjeru*;
May you live with me, you *Netjeru*.
    I love you, you *Netjeru*;
    May you love me, you *Netjeru*.

Standing in front of the image of Tutu the Ritualist offers the burning incense and says:

Take the incense, O Guardian, the One Who Protects the Land.
Its essence is for you.
Its smoke permeates your shrine, bringing life!
Take the incense,
Its essence is for you.
Your Majesty is appeased with the incense.
This Eye of Heru,
This essence of the Eye of Heru comes to you.

At this point the following is said:

Hail to you, Tutu, for you are He Who Overthrows A/pep. You are the One Who overthrows the Messenger Demons, those bringers of death and misfortune. You are the Great Protector, Strong of Valor, Great Fighting *Ba*.

***Netjer* of the *Netjeru*, Great of Roaring, praise be to you! Leader of the Decan stars Khau (*ḫ³w*), adoration be to you! You are he Whose Astral Form is the Decan Ipdes (*ípds*), hear us who call to you![342]**

The Ritualist places more incense on the charcoal and again and again slowly raises and lowers the incense cup as the following is recited:

O Tutu, may you advance with your *Ka*.
O Strong of Valor, the arm of your *Ka* is before you,
The arm of your *Ka* is behind you.
O Swift of Pace, the foot of your *Ka* is before you,
The foot of your *Ka* is behind you.
O Strong God, Tutu, this incense is offered to you,
May your face be filled as this essence spreads itself over you.

---

[342] Op. Cit., p. 29. "Although we know the names of the decans, and in some cases can translate the names (*Hry-ib wiA* means 'in the centre of the boat') the locations of the decanal stars and their relationships to modern star names and constellations are not known. This is due to many factors, but key problems are the uncertainty surrounding the observation methods used to develop and populate the diagonal star tables, and the criteria used to select decans (brightness, position, relationship with other stars, and so on)" Sarah Simons, "A Star's Year: The Annual Cycle in the Ancient Egyptian Sky" in: Steele, J.M. (Ed.), *Calendars and Years: Astronomy and Time in the Ancient World.* Oxbow Books, Oxford, pp. 1-33

*All present perform the **Henu Rite**—Embrace the Earth, the Fourfold Salute to the God, Embrace the Earth.*

For Embracing the Earth, all present prostrate themselves, face down, upon the floor. During the Fourfold Salute, all present rise upon one knee, and alternately raise their hands and arms into the *Dua* (praise) position with palms facing outward, followed by the *Sahu* (obedience) gesture, made by striking the chest with a closed fist and raising the other arm (also with closed fist) at a ninety-degree angle. The *Dua* position is accompanied by the words **"Adoration be to Tutu,"** followed by the *Sahu* gesture accompanied with the words, **"Hail to the Lord of Strength!"** The bodily gestures are performed alternately four times.

*Following this **all present again prostrate themselves** before the god. This is a sign and symbol of total submission and adoration before the Netjer. The following is said:*

**Homage to Tutu, Who Drives Away the Enemies,
who is established on the Great Seat!
I have placed myself on the floor in awe of you.
I embrace the earth before you as before the Great *Netjer*, Who Has No Equal.
I have come that I might kiss the earth,
that I might worship my Lord,
For I have seen his Strength;
I give praise to Tutu,
For I have seen his Power.
His form is more distinguished than the *Netjeru*;
His arm is more powerful than the *Netjeru*.
I am pure, I am pure, I am pure, I am pure!**

Everyone stands up.

The Ritualist **holds in the palm of one hand the image of Ma'at** *and* **with the other hand open and raised over the image as if sheltering it,** *repeats the following:*

I have come to you as Djehuty, whose two hands are joined together under Ma'at. She comes to be with you, for she is everywhere. You are provided with Ma'at. You move in Ma'at, you live in Ma'at. She fills your body, she rests in your head, she makes her seat upon your brow; the breath of your body is of Ma'at, your heart does live in Ma'at. All that you eat, all that you drink, all that you breathe is of Ma'at. Djehuty presents Ma'at to you, his two hands are upon her beauty before your face.

The Ritualist places the image of Ma'at near the divine statue. Then he/ she holds up before the image of Tutu **a pitcher of water** *and* **pours the water slowly into an offering bowl** *as the following Utterance is recited:*

This libation is for you, O Free-Striding Lion.
This libation is for you, O Tutu, Fierce of Face.
I have brought to you this offering of water,
That your heart may be refreshed.
I have brought to you this Eye of Heru,
Placing this at your feet.
I present to you that which flows forth from you,
That your heart shall continue to beat.
For it is with you that all comes forth at the sound of the voice.

*The offering bowl is placed on the altar. At this point the **Ritualist lightly sprinkles sand on the floor in front of the altar** as the following is recited:*

O Tutu, who resides in *Sau* (i.e., Sais),
Take to yourself the Eye of Heru.
You have rescued it, O Protector of the Divine Order.
You have sprinkled with sand the Eye of Heru.

*The Ritualist **presents the sickle-shaped weapon** (or an image of it) known as the **Khepesh sword** and exclaims:*

Take this, the scepter of courage; it strikes your enemies. May you bestow upon us both courage for our arms and strength for our flesh.[343]

__Lifting the wine offering__ before the sacred image, the Ritualist repeats the following:

mn n.k irp irt ḥrw wȝḏt
["*mán-nik 'úrip írat ḥáru wá'ḏat*"; approximately pronounced *MAHN-neek OO-rip EE-raht HAH-roo WAH-jat*]

Take to yourself wine, the green Eye of Heru, which I offer to your *Ka*.[344]
O Ruler, how beautiful is your beauty!
May you drink it; may your heart rejoice;

---

[343] C. De Wit, *Les inscriptions du temple d'Opet à Karnak* I (Brussels, Belgium: Bibliotheca Aegyptiaca XI (1958), 252.

[344] Refer to pp. 92, 93, 99, and 105 in Mu-Chou Poo's *Wine and Wine Offerings in Ancient Egypt* (London & New York: Kegan Paul International, 1995).

may anger be removed from your face.
It is pure. [*iw.w w'b* pronounced *"uwú wá'ib"*; approximately *oo-WOO WAH-ib*]

*The Ritualist **places myrrh on the fire** and **lifts up the smoking incense** while at the same time he **lifts up the meat-offering** before the Netjer, and says the following:*

The scent of myrrh is for your nose. It fills your nostrils; your heart receives the meat-portions on its scent.[345]

*Slowly **elevating the food offerings four times** before the image of Tutu, the Ritualist repeats the following:*

I offer to Tutu, Who Gives Food Offerings and Victuals Which the Sky Gives and Which the Cultivated Land Produces.
All life emanates from you,
All health emanates from you,
All stability emanates from you,
All good fortune emanates from you,
O Great Protector, Tutu, forever.

*The Ritualist **places the food offering before the divine image**, and then all **present extend one hand, palm down**, over the offerings and recite the following:*

May offerings of every kind come forth in abundance,
like the things which come forth from the mouth of the *Netjer*.

piryá pírit ar ḫiráw mi purú:riat ma rá' ni náṯar. (4 times)

---

[345] Quoted in "Worship and Festivals in an Egyptian Temple," by H. W. Fairman (publ. by The John Rylands Library, 1954), p. 191.

[approximately pronounced: peer-YA PEER-it ar khi-RAU mee pu-ROOR-iat ma RA nee NAH-tchar]

May offerings of every kind come forth in abundance, like the things that come forth from the mouth of the *Netjer*.

*Holding the **Ankh** before Tutu, the Ritualist says:*

Live, O Tutu, Lord of Heaven, live for all time and for eternity!

ʿánaḫ niḥáḫ ḏát.
[approximately pronounced *AH-nakh nee-HAH JAHT]*
*The **Ankh** is placed next to the image of the Netjer.*

*Holding the **Ib (the golden heart)** before Tutu, the Ritualist says:*

Hail to you, O Tutu, Son of Neith. I have brought to you your heart to set it in its place. Let me draw near to you with your heart, so that you may have pleasure through me, and so that by means of me you may have power over your body. Ascend, O Lord of Victories, radiant, rejuvenating, equipped as a *Netjer*. Live, O Master of the Arrow Demons, live forever and ever!

*After placing the **Ib** near the sacred image, **everyone sings or chants** the hymn to Tutu. Participants may wish to alternate the singing of verses.*

I praise the Master of the Executioner (ḫ3tyw) Demons of Sekhmet and the Wandering (šm3yw) Demons of Bastet. I exalt the Son of Neith for it is you who controls the Seven Demons of Neith. [346] All hail, jubilation to you, the Lord of the Book

---

[346] Kaper, Op. Cit. p. 60.

Who Judges Words. Adoration be to you, the Lord of the Book of Death and Life.[347]

O Great of Strength and Great Protector! We revere you for truly you are the One Who Comes to the One Calling Him; grant that we live. O great Guardian, may you guard us from all demons for truly they must obey your commands.

You are the One 'Who Apportions the 'Book of Bad Things' to the Wandering Demons and to the Messengers who bring about massacre.' [348] May you send them against the enemies of your father Ra. May you send them against the enemies of Ma'at. For you are the Great Protector. May your name be a protection for us who serve you, O Tutu.

*At this point perform the **meditation or magical action** or, if it is a special feast, add the appropriate prayers.*

*Afterwards **all present back out of the Temple Chamber with heads slightly bowed** while the Ritualist performs the "removing the foot."*

*With the broom the Ritualist, as the last person to exit, **ritually sweeps the area beginning at the altar**. (This is known as "removing the foot.") While performing this action the Ritualist recites the following:*

The distress that causes confusion has been driven away, and all the *Netjeru* are in harmony. I have given Heru his Eye; I have placed the *Wedjat*-Eye in the correct position. I have given

---

[347] Op. Cit., p. 63.

[348] Op. Cit., p. 31. "The 'Book of Bad Things' is known from other sources. Its full title appears on the sarcophagus of Ankhnesneferibre as 'The Book of Bad Things of Finishing the Lifetime.'" (p. 63)

Setekh his Testicles, so that the two lords are content through the work of my hands.

I know the sky, I know the earth;
I know Heru, I know Setekh.
Heru is appeased with his Eyes;
Setekh is appeased with his Testicles.
I am Djehuty, who reconciles the *Netjeru*,
who makes offerings in their correct form.

The double doors are solemnly closed as the Ritualist says the following:

Djehuty has come.
He has filled the Eye of Heru;
He has restored the Testicles of Setekh.
No evil shall enter this Temple.
Ptah has closed the door,
Djehuty has set it fast.
The door is closed, the door is set fast with the bolt.

All bow, touching the palms of their hands to their knees.

THE REVERSION OF OFFERINGS

One priest or priestess and as many assistants as necessary enter the Temple Chamber a final time. While he/she and any assistants lift up the offerings before the sacred image the ritualist shall say:

O Tutu, your enemy[349] withdraws for you. Heru has turned himself to his Eye in its name of 'Reversion-of-Offerings.' I am

---

[349] Meat offerings held a two-fold meaning for the ancient priesthood. Since meat necessarily came from slain animals, it signified the defeated or slain

Djehuty. I come to perform this rite for Tutu, Who Lengthens the Lifespan. These, your divine offerings revert, they revert to your servants for life, for stability, for health and for joy! O that the Eye of Heru may flourish for you eternally!

*Everyone withdraws, **carrying away all food offerings except for one loaf of bread together with a bowl of pure water.** These last items will remain until evening. If this ritual is celebrated after sunset, these items would also be removed.*

*After the candle has burned down, a servant-priest enters and **closes the doors of the Kar-shrine.***

***Extinguishing the candle or oil lamp,** he/she exclaims:*

This is the Eye of Heru by which you have become great, by which you live, and by which you have power, O Tutu. This is the Eye of Heru which you consume and through which you enchant your body. The *Wedjat*-Eye now enters into the West, into *Manu,* but it shall return. Truly, the Eye of Heru returns in peace![350]

---

enemies of the Netjer. At the same time, the meat offering represented the produce of the land which ultimately was a gift of the Netjeru.

[350] It is important to consume the food offerings after the ceremony. Water used should either be drunk or poured onto the earth. If it is mixed with natron, dilute it very greatly and then you can pour in onto the earth without harming any plantings.

The General Ritual for Wadjet

Like members of the ancient priesthood, participants should be clothed in white linen or, if necessary, white cotton. No item made of animal products such as leather or wool is to be worn.

Please do not feel that you must either do the entire ritual or nothing at all. If certain elements of the ritual speak to you and have special meaning, then please just do those particular elements. However, in my own experience I have found that as I repeat the ritual a few times, I am pleasantly surprised with 'aha!' moments where some new insight comes to light. The ritual's words have special meaning and power, and so may not be evident on first reading. Be patient and I believe the *Netjeru* will reward your effort.

Special Offerings for Wadjet: a papyrus-shaped amulet and milk. The offerings also should include the regular food and beverage offerings.
A simple papyrus-shaped amulet can be fabricated from clay or a carefully made drawing of this amulet can suffice.

As with all Egyptian rituals begin with your purification—washing of hands and cleansing of mouth with Natron. This preliminary rite helps us to lay aside the cares of the day and to become mindful of the fact that we will encounter a divine being. If Natron is not available, then use a natural sea salt in its place until you make your own Natron.

Richard J. Reidy

*If two or more persons are participating, then one person, impersonating the Netjer Djehuty, **purifies each person by sprinkling each with water** while exclaiming:*

I purify you with the water of all life and good fortune, all stability, all health and happiness.[351]

*Afterwards each person **rinses his mouth** and **places a small amount of Natron or sea salt in his mouth** while saying:*

I wash my mouth; I chew natron so that I may extol the might of Wadjet, the Bright One Who Rises on the Head of Ra.[352]

*Participants **assemble outside the Temple Chamber** and begin by **softly rattling sistra.***

This time—several minutes or more—is used to focus minds and intention so that distracting thoughts are left behind. The sound of the sistrum was said to placate the deity, purifying the atmosphere in preparation for encountering divinity. The sistrum was associated with Hutheru and also with her and Heru's son Ihy, and thus has connotations of joy, celebration, and dancing. According to Plutarch (A.D. 46-120), the sound of sistra was also reputed to drive away Setekh. But this was of

---

[351] Taken from Aylward M. Blackman's article "Purification (Egyptian)" in Hastings Encyclopaedia 10/1918/ 476-82. This article is reprinted in Gods, Priests, and Men, Studies in the Religion of Pharaonic Egypt, edited by Alan B. Lloyd (Kegan Paul International, 1998), p. 9.

[352] Based on a temple inscription taken from "The Myth of Horus at Edfu—II" by A. M. Blackman and H. W. Fairman, appearing in Gods, Priests and Men, Studies in the Religion of Pharaonic Egypt (Kegan Paul International, 1998) p. 283.

very late date. It may have been that since by that time Setekh unfortunately had been demonized, the general apotropaic function of the sistrum against evil entities was extended to include this *Netjer* as well.

*Standing **before the closed doors**, the Ritualist recites the entrance spell:*

UTTERANCE BEFORE THE CLOSED DOORS OF THE TEMPLE

*The ritualist **raises hands in adoration** (dua position—arms stretched out in front of the body and raised up to face level, with palms facing outward). The following shall be said:*

O you *Netjeru* of this Temple, you guardians of the great portal, great *Netjeru* of mysterious abode, who sanctify the *Netjeret* (goddess) in her shrine, who consecrate her oblation, who receive the offerings in her presence in the Hall of the Ennead: I have made my way and I enter into your presence. I am one of you. I am Shu, the eldest son of his father, the senior *wab* servant-priest of Wadjet. Do not repulse me on the *Netjeret's* path. My feet are not impeded. I am not turned back from the court of the great portal so that I may conduct the divine service, that I may present offerings to her that made them, that I may give bread to Wadjet. I have come on the way of the *Netjeret*. I have not shown partiality in judgment. I have not consorted with the strong. I have not reproached the lowly. I have not stolen things. I have not diminished the constituents of the Eye of Ra. I have not disturbed the Balance. I have not tampered with the requirements of the Sacred Eye. O Council of the Great *Netjeret* in this Temple, behold, I have come to you to offer Ma'at to the Queen of the *Netjeru*, to content the Sound Eye for its mistress. I am Shu; I flood her offering table.

I present her offerings, Sekhmet consorting with me, that I may adore Wadjet at her festivals, that I may kiss the earth so great is her majesty, that I may endow her image with life. I am pure. I am purified.

At this point the ritualist **opens the doors to the Temple Chamber,** *or,* *if there are no doors,* **makes a gesture of opening unseen doors,** *and* **steps forward as if crossing over a threshold.** *The following is said:*

O you *Ba*-souls of *Per-Wadjet* (i.e., Buto[353]), if you are strong, I am strong. If I am strong, you are strong. If your *Ka*-spirits are strong, my *Ka*-spirit is strong at the head of the living. As they are living so shall I live . . . . Sekhmet, the great *Netjeret*, beloved of Ptah, has given to me life, stability, and serenity round about my members, which Djehuty has gathered together for life. I am Heru in the height of heaven, the beautiful one of awe, Lord of Victory, mighty one of awe, exalted one of the two plumes, great one in *Abdju* (Abydos) I am pure.

Enter, **close the double doors** *and* **stand in front of the Kar-shrine** *and* **altar. All bow, touching their hands to their knees.**

All recite the following:

Awake, awake in peace, O Wadjet, Lady of the Beams of Light. May you awake in peace.
Awake, awake in peace, O Serpent on the Brow of Ra. May you awake in peace.
Awake, awake in peace, O Lady of Flame. May you awake in peace.

---

[353] Per-Wadjet (Greek, Buto) is the cult center for Wadjet in Lower Egypt.

Awake, awake in peace, O Wadjet, She of the Solar Disk. May you awake in peace.

May you awake beautifully at the top of the morning, through that which the entirety of *Netjeru* say to you.

*The ritualist slowly **opens the two doors of the Kar-shrine** housing the sacred image. **All others bow, touching their hands to their knees.** The following is said:*

The doors of the sky are open; the doors of the earth are unlocked. This House is open for its Mistress. Let me come forth as she shall come forth. Let me enter in as she shall enter in. Wadjet, the Great One of Fear, is exalted upon her Great Seat. The Great Company of the *Netjeru* are exalted upon their seat.

I have seen the *Netjeret*, and the *Netjeret* sees me. The *Netjeret* rejoices at seeing me. I have gazed upon the statue of the Magnificent Cobra, the sacred image of the Great Maiden.[354]

Right hand on left shoulder of statue; left hand on right wrist of statue:

Djehuty has come to you. Awake when you hear his words. I have come as the envoy of Atum. My two arms are upon you like those of Heru. My two hands are upon you like those of Djehuty. My fingers are upon you like those of Anpu. Homage be to you. I am a living servant of Wadjet.

---

[354] Based on a passage in "Worship and Festivals in an Egyptian Temple," a lecture by H. W. Fairman (publ. by The John Rylands Library, 1954), p. 180.

***All present make a profound bow, placing their hands on their knees,** while the Ritualist exclaims:*

Hail to you, Wadjet, who cuts off the heads of those in the following of the enemies of Ra.
May you tread them down; may you besprinkle the *Netjeru* with that which came forth from you—in your name of Mistress of the *Atef*-crown.
Awe of you is greater than that of your foes—in your name of Mistress of Awe.
The fear of you is produced in them that conspire against you—in your name of Mistress of Fear.[355]

*The Ritualist holds up the **bowl of water** in which he/she will be mixing the Natron. The following is said:*

O water may you remove all evil,
As Ra who bathes in the Lake of Rushes,
May Heru wash my flesh,
May Djehuty cleanse my feet,
May Shu lift me up and Nut take my hand!
May Setekh be my strength, and may Sekhmet be my healing!
And may Amun-Ra be my life and my prospering!

*The bowl of water is set aside and the container of **Natron** is lifted up. The following is said:*

It is pure, it is pure.

---

[355] Modeled on a hymn in Adolf Erman's *Hymnen an das diadem der pharaonen, aus einem papyrus der sammlung Golenischeff* (Berlin, 1911), lines 2-4.

My Natron is the Natron of Heru and the Natron of Heru is my Natron.

My Natron is the Natron of Setekh and the Natron of Setekh is my Natron.

My Natron is the Natron of Djehuty, and the Natron of Djehuty is my Natron.

My Natron is the Natron of Geb and the Natron of Geb is my Natron.

My mouth is the mouth of a milking calf on the day that I was born.

Four pinches of Natron are mixed into the water as this Utterance is recited:

I give you essential water, a tide in your time.
I bring the flood waters to purify your sanctuary.
I bring you the flood waters to purify your Temple and your statue in its place, the primordial water that purifies as in the First Time!

The Ritualist places an index finger into the water and moves it in a circular direction four times as the following is said:

Wadjet, the Burning One, does purify this water;
Wadjet, Who Drives off Darkness, does cleanse this water;
Wadjet, Beautiful of Face, does sanctify this water;
Wadjet herself, Lady of Swimming, does endow this water with power and with life.

The Bowl of Natron-infused water is then taken up and the Ritualist sprinkles this lightly in front of and around the statue or image of

Wadjet, applying some water to the base of the image, as the Utterance is recited:

I come close to you, O Excellent One, the One Who Allots Life. I bring the water of rejuvenation that flows from the Two Caverns.
I sprinkle the water, purifying your image and your Temple from all impurity!

*The Ritualist picks up the bowl of **Natron** and **sprinkles a small amount in each of the four directions** as the following is recited:*

The *Netjeret* Wadjet herself does cleanse and purify this, her Temple to the South.
The *Netjeret* Wadjet herself does cleanse and purify this, her Temple to the North.
The *Netjeret* Wadjet herself does cleanse and purify this, her Temple to the West.
The *Netjeret* Wadjet herself does cleanse and purify this, her Temple to the East.

*Replacing the Natron on the altar, the Ritualist takes up the **bowl of water**, sprinkling a small amount in each of the four directions. The following Utterance is recited:*

The *Netjeret* Wadjet herself does sanctify and consecrate this, her Temple to the South.
The *Netjeret* Wadjet herself does sanctify and consecrate this, her Temple to the North.
The *Netjeret* Wadjet herself does sanctify and consecrate this, her Temple to the West.

The *Netjeret* Wadjet herself does sanctify and consecrate this, her Temple to the East.
The Temple of the *Netjeret* Wadjet is established.
It is established for millions of years.

*The Ritualist returns to the altar and **lights the candle or oil lamp** while the following is said:*

Come, come in peace, O glorious Eye of Heru,
Be strong and renew your youth in peace.
For the flame shines like Ra on the double horizon.
The enemies of Ra are defeated. They are defeated.
I am pure, I am pure, I am pure, I am pure.

*The Ritualist **places incense on the burner** and **censes each sacred image** beginning with the statue of the Netjeret while the following is recited:*

The fire is laid, the fire shines;
The incense is laid on the fire, the incense shines.
    Your perfume comes to me, O Incense;
    May my perfume come to you, O Incense.
Your perfume comes to me, you *Netjeru;*
May my perfume come to you, You *Netjeru.*
    May I be with you, you *Netjeru;*
    May you be with me, you *Netjeru.*
May I live with you, you *Netjeru;*
May you live with me, you *Netjeru.*
    I love you, you *Netjeru;*
    May you love me, you *Netjeru.*

*Standing in front of the image of Wadjet the Ritualist **offers the burning incense** and says:*

Take the incense,
Its essence is for you, O Great Protectress.
Its smoke permeates your shrine, bringing life!
Take the incense,
Its essence is for you.
Your Majesty is appeased with the incense.
This Eye of Heru,
This essence of the Eye of Heru comes to you.

At this point the following is said:

Hail to you, Wadjet,
Who Encircles the Sun Disk as Brow Serpent.
Mighty in Heaven before Ra.

Adoration to you in the night-barque,
Jubilation to you in the day-barque,
Lady of Dance and Lady of Joy,
At Whose Sight Everyone Rejoices.

I have come before you, Lady of Life,
On this day on which you have gloriously appeared,
You are the One Who Watches over Heru
For you are the Lady of Protection.

May your *Ka* be in peace, O Lady of Life,
On this day on which you have gloriously appeared,
You whom the *Netjeru* have propitiated.

O beloved of Ra who are in his barque,

Repelling Apep with the effectiveness of your flame,
Behold, I have come before you,
So that, purified, I may adore your beauty.[356]

May you come to your House to join your Image,
Your radiance inundating our faces,
Like the radiance of Ra when he shows himself in the morning.

O Wadjet the Great, Lady of *Per-Wadjet*,
Protector of Heru, Perfect of Character,
at Whose Sight the *Netjeru* Rejoice.
Lady of appearances,
Worshipped in your sanctuaries.

O Lady of the Devouring Flame,
Surround us with your protection.
As you protect Ra, so now protect us from the serpent-enemy.

Make enduring our years.
Establish us like the Falcon upon the *Serekh*.
Make us to endure eternally, like Ra.[357]

The Ritualist places more incense on the charcoal and again and again slowly raises and lowers the incense cup as the following is recited:

O Wadjet, may you advance with your *Ka*.
O Mistress of Stars, the arm of your *Ka* is before you,
The arm of your *Ka* is behind you.

---

[356] Modeled on Hymn VIII, in *Hymns to Isis in Her Temple at Philae*, by Louis V. Zabkar (Brandeis University Press, 1988), p. 119.
[357] Op. Cit., modeled on Hymn V, pp. 58-59.

O Lady of Protection, the foot of your *Ka* is before you,
The foot of your *Ka* is behind you.
O Beautiful Wadjet, this incense is offered to you,
May your face be filled as this essence spreads itself over you.

All present perform the **Henu Rite** *—Embrace the Earth, the Fourfold Salute to the Goddess, Embrace the Earth.*

For Embracing the Earth, all present prostrate themselves, face down, upon the floor. During the Fourfold Salute, all present rise upon one knee, and alternately raise their hands and arms into the *Dua* (praise) position with palms facing outward, followed by the *Sahu* (obedience) gesture, made by striking the chest with a closed fist and raising the other arm (also with closed fist) at a ninety-degree angle. The *Dua* position is accompanied by the words **"Adoration be to Wadjet,"** followed by the *Sahu* gesture accompanied with the words, **"Hail to the Living Uraeus!"** The bodily gestures are performed alternately four times.

Following this **all present again prostrate themselves before the sacred image***. This is a sign and symbol of total submission and adoration before the Netjeret. The following is said:*

Homage be to Wadjet, the Burning One,
who is established on the Great Seat!
I have placed myself on the floor in awe of you.
I embrace the earth before you as before the Mistress of the Earth.
I have come that I might kiss the earth,
that I might worship my Mistress,
for I have seen her Beauty;
I give praise to Wadjet,

for I have seen her Power.
Her form is more distinguished than the *Netjeru*;
Her arm is more powerful than the *Netjeru*.
I am pure, I am pure, I am pure, I am pure!

Everyone stands up.

*The Ritualist **holds in the palm of one hand the image of Ma'at** and with **the other hand open and raised over the image as if sheltering it**, repeats the following:*

I have come to you as Djehuty, whose two hands are joined together under Ma'at. She comes to be with you, for she is everywhere. You are provided with Ma'at. You move in Ma'at, you live in Ma'at. She fills your body, she rests in your head, she makes her seat upon your brow; the breath of your body is of Ma'at, your heart does live in Ma'at. All that you eat, all that you drink, all that you breathe is of Ma'at. Djehuty presents Ma'at to you, his two hands are upon her beauty before your face.

*The Ritualist places the image of Ma'at near the divine statue. Then he/ she holds up before the image of Wadjet **a pitcher of water** and **pours the water slowly into an offering bowl** as the following Utterance is recited:*

This libation is for you, O Lady of Life.
This libation is for you, O Wadjet.
I have brought to you this offering of water,
That your heart may be refreshed.
I have brought to you this Eye of Heru,
Placing this at your feet.

I present to you that which flows forth from you,
That your heart shall continue to beat.
For it is with you that all comes forth at the sound of the voice.

The offering bowl is placed on the altar. At this point the Ritualist **lightly sprinkles sand on the floor in front of the altar** *as the following is recited:*

O Wadjet, who resides in *Per-Wadjet* (i.e., Buto),
Take to yourself the Eye of Heru.
You have rescued it, O Mistress of the Sky.
You have sprinkled with sand the Eye of Heru.

Lifting up a **papyrus-shaped amulet,** *the Ritualist recites:*

I present the papyrus-shaped amulet to your *Ka*, O Wadjet. May this, your scepter of life, make this land prosperous, and may you keep our bodies healthy. May you give us the life span of Heru in *Per-Wadjet*. I am your Heru.[358]

Place the amulet in front of the Netjeret. Lifting the **offering of milk,** *the following is said:*

Take to yourself this white and sweet milk, created by Nut. May you live on it, may you be healthy on account of it. May your body be refreshed every day.[359]

---

[358] Sylvie Cauville, *L'offrande aux dieux dans le temple égyptien* (Leuven: Peeters, 2011), pp. 179-180. The temple at Edfu contains several inscriptions of the offering of this amulet to Wadjet.

[359] Amr, Aber, *The Central Hall in the Egyptian Temples of the Ptolemaic Period*, Durham theses, Durham University. (2009) Available at Durham E-Theses Online: http://etheses.dur.ac.uk/88/ This offering formula occurs in the central hall of the temple at Edfu. See p. 454 in the dissertation.

*Lifting the **wine offering** before the sacred image, the Ritualist repeats the following:*

mn n.ṯ irp irt ḥrw w³ḏt
[*"mán-niṯ 'úrip írat ḥáru wá'ḏat"*; approximately pronounced *MAHN-neetch OO-rip EE-raht HAH-roo WAH-jat*]

Take to Yourself wine, the green Eye of Heru, which I offer to your *Ka*.[360]
O Excellent One, Perfect of Character, how beautiful is your beauty!
May you drink it; may your heart rejoice; may anger be removed from your face.
It is pure. [*iw.w w'b* pronounced *"uwú wá'ib"*; approximately *oo-WOO WAH-ib*]

*The Ritualist **places myrrh on the fire** and **lifts up the smoking incense** while at the same time he **lifts up the meat-offering** before the Netjeret, and says the following:*

The scent of myrrh is for your nose. It fills your nostrils; your heart receives the meat-portions on its scent.[361]

*Slowly **elevating the food offerings four times** before the image of the Netjeret, the Ritualist repeats the following:*

I offer to Wadjet, the Living Uraeus.

---

[360] Refer to pp. 92, 93, 99, and 105 in Mu-Chou Poo's *Wine and Wine Offerings in Ancient Egypt* (London & New York: Kegan Paul International, 1995).

[361] Quoted in "Worship and Festivals in an Egyptian Temple," by H. W. Fairman (publ. by The John Rylands Library, 1954), p. 191.

All life emanates from you,
All health emanates from you,
All stability emanates from you,
All good fortune emanates from you,
O Wadjet, Lady of Life, forever.

*The Ritualist places the **food offering** before the divine image, and then **all present extend one hand, palm down, over the offerings** and recite the following:*

May offerings of every kind come forth in abundance,
like the things which come forth from the mouth of the *Netjeret.*

piryá pírit ar ḫiráw mi purú:riat ma rá' ni naṯárat. (4 times)
[approximately pronounced: peer-YA PEER-it ar khi-RAU mee pu-ROOR-iat ma RA nee nah-TCHAR-at]

May offerings of every kind come forth in abundance, like the things that come forth from the mouth of the *Netjeret.*

*Holding the **Ankh** before the Netjeret, the Ritualist says:*

Live, O Wadjet, Lady of Joy, live for all time and for eternity!

ʿánaḫ niḥáḫ ḏát.
[approximately pronounced *AH-nakh nee-HAH JAHT]*

*The **Ankh** is placed next to the Netjeret.*

*Holding the **Ib (the golden heart)** before the Netjeret, the Ritualist says:*

Hail to you, O Wadjet, at Whose Sight the *Netjeru* Rejoice! I have brought to you your heart to set it in its place. Let me draw near to you with your heart, so that you may have pleasure through me, and so that by means of me you may have power over your body. Ascend, O Mistress of the People, radiant, rejuvenating, equipped as a *Netjeret*. Live, O Burning One Who Drives off Darkness, live forever and ever!

*After placing the **Ib** near the sacred image, **everyone sings or chants the hymn to Wadjet. Begin by slowly playing the sistra.** Participants may wish to alternate the singing of verses.*

I play the sistra before your beautiful image,
Wadjet, Lady of Life, Who Pacifies the Eye of Heru with Your Milk,
For you are truly the Lady of Eternity, Atop Your Papyrus Column.

I play the sistra for you,
Great One of Fear, Lady of Flame,
Who fills heaven and earth with your beauty,
Body of Khepri, Mistress of the People,
Unique One on the Head of the Lord of All.

O Wadjet, come to us in your form of the Living Uraeus,
Anointing our heads with your protective flame.
May you appear on the left side of our forehead,
Rising up on the right side of our forehead every hour in silence!
In silence!
May you together with Nekhbet encircle us with your protection even as you both do for your father Ra.

May you establish yourself upon our heads even as on the brow of Ra.[362]

I play the sistra for you,
Lady of the Field, Lady of Every Land,
Brow Serpent of Your Father, Cobra Who Shines as Gold.
As you are the One Who Gives Joy in the Morning Barque,
So grant us joy who bow before you.

May your beautiful face be gracious to us who honor you.
O Lady of Joy, Sweet One of Love Who Has No Equal,
You are She Who Floods the House of Your Father with Your Perfection.
O Lady of Life, Lady of Protection, be gracious, be gracious to us who honor you.

At this point perform the **meditation or magical action** *or, if it is a special feast, add the appropriate prayers.*

Afterwards **all present back out of the Temple Chamber with heads slightly bowed** *while the Ritualist performs the* **"removing the foot."**

With the **broom** *the Ritualist, as the last person to exit,* **ritually sweeps the area beginning at the altar.** *(This is known as* **"removing the foot.")** *While performing this action the Ritualist recites the following:*

The distress that causes confusion has been driven away,
and all the *Netjeru* are in harmony.
I have given Heru his Eye;

---

[362] Adapted from Gaston Maspero, *Mémoire sur quelques papyrus du Louvre* (Paris: Imprimerie Nationale, 1875), pp. 81-82. Maspero quotes from a certain papyrus identified as papyrus no. 3, Rituel d'embaumement.

I have placed the *Wedjat*-Eye in the correct position.
I have given Setekh his Testicles,
so that the two lords are content through the work of my hands.

I know the sky, I know the earth;
I know Heru, I know Setekh.
Heru is appeased with his Eyes;
Setekh is appeased with his Testicles.
I am Djehuty, who reconciles the *Netjeru*,
who makes offerings in their correct form.

*The **double doors are solemnly closed** as the Ritualist says the following:*

Djehuty has come.
He has filled the Eye of Heru;
He has restored the Testicles of Setekh.
No evil shall enter this Temple.
Ptah has closed the door,
Djehuty has set it fast.
The door is closed, the door is set fast with the bolt.

All bow, touching the palms of their hands to their knees.

THE REVERSION OF OFFERINGS

*One priest or priestess and as many assistants as necessary enter the Temple Chamber a final time. While he/she and any assistants **lift up the offerings** before the sacred image the ritualist shall say:*

O Wadjet, your enemy[363] withdraws for you. Heru has turned himself to his Eye in its name of 'Reversion-of-Offerings.' I am Djehuty. I come to perform this rite for Wadjet, Who Burns up the Enemies of Her Father. These, your divine offerings revert, they revert to your servants for life, for stability, for health and for joy! O that the Eye of Heru may flourish for you eternally!

*Everyone withdraws, **carrying away all food offerings except for one loaf of bread together with a bowl of pure water**. These last items will remain until evening. If this ritual is celebrated after sunset, these items would also be removed.*[364]

*After the candle has burned down, a servant-priest enters and **closes the doors of the Kar-shrine**.*

Extinguishing the candle or oil lamp, he/she exclaims:

This is the Eye of Heru by which you have become great, by which you live, and by which you have power, O Wadjet. This is the Eye of Heru which you consume and through which you enchant your body. The *Wedjat*-Eye now enters into the West, into *Manu*, but it shall return. Truly, the Eye of Heru returns in peace!

---

[363] Meat offerings held a two-fold meaning for the ancient priesthood. Since meat necessarily came from slain animals, it signified the defeated or slain enemies of the Netjeret. At the same time, the meat offering represented the produce of the land which ultimately was a gift of the Netjeru.

[364] It is important to consume the food offerings after the ceremony. Water used should either be drunk or poured onto the earth. If it is mixed with natron, dilute it very greatly and then you can pour in onto the earth without harming any plantings.

The General Ritual for Wepwawet

The ancient Egyptian priesthood had an array of epithets for each *Netjer*, thereby showing the multi-aspected nature of each of their deities. These epithets are found in temple texts, funerary texts, tomb engravings, private stelae, and ostraca. They have been collected in the eight-volume *Lexikon der ägyptischen Götter und Götterbezeichnungen* (i.e., "Dictionary of Egyptian Gods and God-Epithets") (Leuven: Peeters, 2002). The epithets are capitalized in order to facilitate identification.

The following ritual for Wepwawet includes epithets found in the *Lexikon*. All epithets used in this ritual are of ancient origin. The hymns appearing toward the end of the rite are from ancient prayer texts. Wepwawet was/is the chief *Netjer* in the ancient city of Asyut, hence His title, Lord of Asyut.

Like members of the ancient priesthood, participants should be clothed in white linen. (If linen garments are not available, then white cotton is a good substitute.) No item made of animal products such as leather or wool is to be worn. Linen represents a pristine product of the earth whereas leather and wool come from humankind's domination of the animals, a domination that becomes part of the "natural order" only *after* the First Time when the *Netjeru* and humans and animals lived in peace and harmony. Just as the Morning Ritual harkens back to that First Time (*Zep Tepi*), so every temple rite re-presents mythic prototypes that occurred "in the beginning," that is, in that time before time. Even the sandals worn by the god's servants were made of white papyrus. This avoidance

Richard J. Reidy

of animal products by the priesthood fits well with the fact that the ritualist acts as a *Netjer* and verbally asserts that he or she is a *Netjer*.

As with all Egyptian rituals begin with your purification—washing of hands and cleansing of mouth with Natron. This preliminary rite helps us to lay aside the cares of the day and to become mindful of the fact that we will encounter a divine being. If Natron is not available, then use a natural sea salt in its place until you make your own Natron.

*If two or more persons are participating, then one person, impersonating the Netjer Djehuty, **purifies each person by sprinkling each with water** while exclaiming:*

I purify you with the water of all life and good fortune, all stability, all health and happiness.[365]

*Afterwards each person **rinses his mouth and places a small amount of Natron or sea salt in his mouth** while saying:*

I wash my mouth; I chew natron so that I may extol the might of Wepwawet, Lord of Strength and Power, the One Who Brings Forth Goodness.[366]

---

[365] Taken from Aylward M. Blackman's article "Purification (Egyptian)" in Hastings Encyclopaedia 10/1918/ 476-82. This article is reprinted in Gods, Priests, and Men, Studies in the Religion of Pharaonic Egypt, edited by Alan B. Lloyd (Kegan Paul International, 1998), p. 9.

[366] Based on a temple inscription taken from "The Myth of Horus at Edfu—II" by A. M. Blackman and H. W. Fairman, appearing in Gods, Priests and Men, Studies in the Religion of Pharaonic Egypt (Kegan Paul International, 1998) p. 283.

*Participants **assemble outside the Temple Chamber** and begin by softly rattling sistra.*

This time—several minutes or more—is used to focus minds and intention so that distracting thoughts are left behind. The sound of the sistrum was said to placate the deity, purifying the atmosphere in preparation for encountering divinity. The sistrum was associated with Hut-Heru and also with her and Heru's son Ihy, and thus has connotations of joy, celebration, and dancing. According to Plutarch (A.D. 46-120), the sound of sistra was also reputed to drive away Setekh. But this was of very late date, when the religious vision of Egypt had been clouded due to long term foreign domination. It may have been that since by that time Setekh had been demonized, the general apotropaic function of the sistrum against evil entities was extended to include this *Netjer* as well. To this day the Coptic Christian Church of Egypt as well as the Orthodox Church of Ethiopia still use the ancient sistrum in its religious rites. In the Coptic liturgical tradition, the priest directs the sistrum toward the four cardinal points.

Standing before the closed doors, the Ritualist recites the entrance spell:

UTTERANCE BEFORE THE CLOSED DOORS OF THE TEMPLE

*The ritualist **raises hands in adoration** (dua position-arms stretched out in front of the body and raised up to face level, with palms facing outward). The following shall be said:*

O you *Netjeru* of this Temple, you guardians of the great portal, great *Netjeru* of mysterious abode, who sanctify the *Netjer* in his shrine, who consecrate his oblation, who receive the offerings in his presence in the Hall of the Ennead: I have made my way and I enter into your presence. I am one of you. I am Shu, the eldest son of his father, the senior *wab* servant-priest of Wepwawet. Do not repulse me on the *Netjer*'s path. My feet are not impeded. I am not turned back from the court of the great portal so that I may conduct the divine service, that I may present offerings to him that made them, that I may give bread to Wepwawet. I have come on the way of the *Netjer*. I have not shown partiality in judgment. I have not consorted with the strong. I have not reproached the lowly. I have not stolen things. I have not diminished the constituents of the Eye of Ra. I have not disturbed the Balance. I have not tampered with the requirements of the Sacred Eye. O Council of the Great *Netjer* in this Temple, behold, I have come to you to offer Ma'at to him who loves Ma'at, to content the Sound Eye for its lord. I am Shu; I flood his offering table. I present his offerings, Sekhmet consorting with me, that I may adore Wepwawet at his festivals, that I may kiss the earth so great is his majesty, that I may endow his image with life. I am pure. I am purified.

At this point the ritualist **opens the doors to the Temple Chamber,** or, *if there are no doors,* **makes a gesture of opening unseen doors,** and **steps forward as if crossing over a threshold.** *The following is said:*

O you *Ba*-souls of *Asyut* if you are strong, I am strong. If I am strong, you are strong. If your *Ka*-spirits are strong, my *Ka*-spirit is strong at the head of the living. As they are living so shall I live . . . . Wepwawet, the Enduring One, has given to me life, stability, and serenity round about my members, which Djehuty has gathered together for life. I am Heru in the height of heaven, the beautiful one of awe, Lord of Victory, mighty one of awe, exalted one of the two plumes, great one in *Waset* (Thebes), I am pure.

Enter, close the double doors and stand in front of the Kar-shrine and altar. All bow, touching their hands to their knees.

All recite the following:

Awake, awake in peace, O Noble Jackal.
May you awake in peace.
Awake, awake in peace, O Wepwawet Who Separates the Sky from the Earth.
May you awake in peace.
Awake, awake in peace, O Sovereign, Divine King.
May you awake in peace.
Awake, awake in peace, Opener of the Way for the Gods and Goddesses.
May you awake in peace.

The ritualist slowly opens the two doors of the Kar-shrine housing the sacred image. All others bow, touching their hands to their knees. The following is said:

The doors of the sky are open; the doors of the earth are unlocked. This House is open for its Lord. Let me come forth as he shall come forth. Let me enter in as he shall enter in. Wepwawet, Opener of the Ways, He with the Great *Bas*, is exalted upon his Great Seat. The Great Company of the *Netjeru* are exalted upon their seats.

I have seen the *Netjer*, and the *Netjer* sees me. The *Netjer* rejoices at seeing me. I have gazed upon the statue of the Bull of Offerings, the sacred image of the Lord of Provisions.[367]

---

[367] Quoted in "Worship and Festivals in an Egyptian Temple," a lecture by H. W. Fairman (publ. by The John Rylands Library, 1954) p.180.

Right hand on left shoulder of statue; left hand on right wrist of statue:

Djehuty has come to you. Awake when you hear his words.
I have come as the envoy of Atum.
My two arms are upon you like those of Heru.
My two hands are upon you like those of Djehuty.
My fingers are upon you like those of Anpu. Homage be to you.
I am a living servant of Wepwawet.

*The Ritualist holds up the **bowl of water** in which he/she will be mixing the Natron. The following is said:*

O water may you remove all evil,
As Ra who bathes in the Lake of Rushes,
May Heru wash my flesh,
May Djehuty cleanse my feet,
May Shu lift me up and Nut take my hand!
May Setekh be my strength, and may Sekhmet be my healing!
And may Amun-Ra be my life and my prospering!

*The bowl of water is set aside and the container of **Natron** is lifted up. The following is said:*

It is pure, it is pure.
My Natron is the Natron of Heru and the Natron of Heru is my Natron.
My Natron is the Natron of Setekh and the Natron of Setekh is my Natron.
My Natron is the Natron of Djehuty, and the Natron of Djehuty is my Natron.
My Natron is the Natron of Geb and the Natron of Geb is my Natron.

My mouth is the mouth of a milking calf on the day that I was born.

Four pinches of Natron are mixed into the water as this Utterance is recited:

I give you essential water, a tide in your time.
I bring the flood waters to purify your sanctuary.
I bring you the flood waters to purify your Temple and your statue in its place, the primordial water that purifies as in the First Time!

The Ritualist places an index finger into the water and moves it in a circular direction four times as the following is said:

Wepwawet, the Enduring Primeval One, does purify this water;
Wepwawet, the Powerful One, does cleanse this water;
Wepwawet, Divine *Netjer*, does sanctify this water;
Wepwawet himself does endow this water with power and with life.

The Bowl of Natron-infused water is then taken up and the Ritualist sprinkles this lightly in front of and around the statue or image of Wepwawet, and also applying the water to the base of the image, as the Utterance is recited:

I come close to You, O Controller of the Two Lands, Great *Netjer*.
I bring the water of rejuvenation that flows from the Two Caverns.
I sprinkle the water, purifying your image and your Temple from all impurity!

*The Ritualist picks up the bowl of **Natron** and **sprinkles a small amount in each of the four directions** as the following is recited:*

The *Netjer* Wepwawet himself does cleanse and purify this, his Temple to the South.

The *Netjer* Wepwawet himself does cleanse and purify this, his Temple to the North.

The *Netjer* Wepwawet himself does cleanse and purify this, his Temple to the West.

The *Netjer* Wepwawet himself does cleanse and purify this, his Temple to the East.

*Replacing the Natron on the altar, the Ritualist takes up the **bowl of water, sprinkling a small amount in each of the four directions.** The following Utterance is recited:*

The *Netjer* Wepwawet himself does sanctify and consecrate this, his Temple to the South.

The *Netjer* Wepwawet himself does sanctify and consecrate this, his Temple to the North.

The *Netjer* Wepwawet himself does sanctify and consecrate this, his Temple to the West.

The *Netjer* Wepwawet himself does sanctify and consecrate this, his Temple to the East.

The Temple of the *Netjer* Wepwawet is established. It is established for millions of years.

*The Ritualist returns to the altar and **lights the candle or oil lamp** while the following is said:*

Come, come in peace, O glorious Eye of Heru,
Be strong and renew your youth in peace.

For the flame shines like Ra on the double horizon.
The enemies of Ra are defeated. They are defeated.
The lie is abolished!
I am pure, I am pure, I am pure, I am pure.

The Ritualist places incense on the burner and censes each sacred image beginning with the statue of the Netjer while the following is recited:

The fire is laid, the fire shines;
The incense is laid on the fire, the incense shines.
>Your perfume comes to me, O Incense;
>May my perfume come to you, O Incense.

Your perfume comes to me, you *Netjeru*;
May my perfume come to you, You *Netjeru*.
>May I be with you, you *Netjeru*;
>May you be with me, you *Netjeru*.

May I live with you, you *Netjeru*;
May you live with me, you *Netjeru*.
>I love you, you *Netjeru*;
>May you love me, you *Netjeru*.

Standing in front of the image of Wepwawet the Ritualist offers the burning incense and says:

Take the incense, O Opener-of-the-Ways.
Its essence is for you.
Its smoke permeates your shrine, bringing life!
Take the incense,
Its essence is for you.
O Lord of Incense, your Majesty is appeased with the incense.
This Eye of Heru,

This essence of the Eye of Heru comes to you.

At this point the following is said:

Hail to you, Wepwawet,
Bull of Offerings and Lord of Provisions, Great of *wereret*-crown,
who came forth from the womb of his mother Nut,
eldest *Netjer*, who came forth from his mother's womb already wise,
and to whom Geb has ordered his inheritance;
Great *Netjer*, lord of *Rosetau*,
may you place me among the followers and noble ones behind you![368]

Wepwawet, the Adored One, who is upon his standard,
lord of the *shedshed* (i.e., the protuberance on the standard)
exalted above the *Netjeru*,
the one with sharp arrows, lord of Asyut,
who is upon the thrones of Atum,
who is stronger and more powerful than the *Netjeru*,
who took possession of the Two Lands being triumphant,
to whom the heritage was given forever,
Wepwawet, the Upper Egyptian—*shemawy*—power of the two lands—*sekhem tawy*, controller of the *Netjeru*.[369]
May you protect me from evil ones,

---

[368] This prayer is from the 13th Dynasty stela of a court official, p. 105 in Detlef Franke's article, "Middle Kingdom Hymns, other Sundry Religious Texts—an Inventory," in **Egypt—Temple of the Whole World, Studies in Honour of Jan Assmann**, ed. by Sibylle Meyer (Brill: Leiden-Boston, 2003).

[369] This comes from an inscription in the tomb of Djefai-Hapi I, nomarch of Assyut, 12th Dynasty, in *Ancient Asyut: the First Synthesis after 300 Years of Research,* by Jochem Kahl (Wiesbaden, 2007), p. 40.

may you open the way for me in safety and in peace.

*The Ritualist **places more incense on the charcoal** and again and again **slowly raises and lowers the incense cup** as the following is recited:*

O Wepwawet, may you advance with your *Ka*.
O You Who open the Way for the *Netjeru*, the arm of your *Ka* is before you,
The arm of your *Ka* is behind you.
O You Who Bring Forth Goodness, the foot of your *Ka* is before you,
The foot of your *Ka* is behind you.
O Lord of Myrrh, Wepwawet, this incense is offered to you,
May your face be filled as this essence spreads itself over you.

*All present perform the **Henu Rite**—Embrace the Earth, the Fourfold Salute to the God, Embrace the Earth.*

For Embracing the Earth, all present prostrate themselves, face down, upon the floor. During the Fourfold Salute, all present rise upon one knee, and alternately raise their hands and arms into the *Dua* (praise) position with palms facing outward, followed by the *Sahu* (obedience) gesture, made by striking the chest with a closed fist and raising the other arm (also with closed fist) at a ninety-degree angle. The *Dua* position is accompanied by the words **"Adoration be to Wepwawet,"** followed by the *Sahu* gesture accompanied with the words, **"Hail to the Lord of Strength and Power!"** The bodily gestures are performed alternately four times.

*Following this **all present again prostrate themselves before the sacred image**. This is a sign and symbol of total submission and adoration before the Netjeret. The following is said:*

Homage be to Wepwawet, Lord of the Two Cobras,
who is established on the Great Seat!
I have placed myself on the floor in awe of you.
I embrace the earth before you as before Him
Who is Over the Thrones of Atum.
I have come that I might kiss the earth,
that I might worship my Lord,
who opens the Way to *Abdju* (Abydos),
For I have seen his Strength;
I give praise to Wepwawet,
For I have seen his Power.
His form is more distinguished than the *Netjeru*;
His arm is more powerful than the *Netjeru*.
I am pure, I am pure, I am pure, I am pure!

Everyone stands up.

*The Ritualist **holds in the palm of one hand the image of Ma'at** and with **the other hand open and raised over the image as if sheltering it**, repeats the following:*

I have come to you as Djehuty, whose two hands are joined together under Ma'at. She comes to be with you, for she is everywhere. You are provided with Ma'at. You move in Ma'at, you live in Ma'at. She fills your body, she rests in your head, she makes her seat upon your brow; the breath of your body is of Ma'at, your heart does live in Ma'at. All that you eat, all that you drink, all that you breathe is of Ma'at. Djehuty presents Ma'at to you, his two hands are upon her beauty before your face.

*The Ritualist places the image of Ma'at near the divine statue. Then he/she holds up before the image of Wepwawet **a pitcher of water*** and **pours the water slowly into an offering bowl as** *the following Utterance is recited:*

This libation is for you, O Foremost of the *Ba*-Souls of *Iunu* (Heliopolis).
This libation is for you, O Wepwawet, Who is over His Secrets.
I have brought to you this offering of water,
That your heart may be refreshed.
I have brought to you this Eye of Heru,
Placing this at your feet.
I present to you that which flows forth from you,
That your heart shall continue to beat.
For it is with you
that all comes forth at the sound of the voice.

The offering bowl is placed on the altar. At this point the Ritualist **lightly sprinkles sand on the floor in front of the altar** *as the following is recited:*

O Wepwawet, who resides in *Asyut*,
Take to yourself the Eye of Heru.
You have rescued it, O You Who abhor *Isfet* [evil/injustice].
You have sprinkled with sand the Eye of Heru.

Lifting the **wine offering** *before the sacred image, the Ritualist repeats the following:*

mn n.k irp irt ḥrw wꜣḏt
["*mán-nik 'úrip írat ḥáru wá'ḏat*"; approximately pronounced MAHN-neek OO-rip EE-raht HAH-roo WAH-jat]

Take to Yourself wine, the green Eye of Heru, which I offer to your *Ka.*
O Lord of the Feast, how beautiful is your beauty!
May you drink it; may your heart rejoice;
may anger be removed from your face.
It is pure. [*iw.w w'b* pronounced *"uwú wá'ib"*; approximately *oo-WOO WAH-ib*]

The Ritualist **places myrrh on the fire and lifts up the smoking incense** *while at the same time he* **lifts up the meat-offering** *before the Netjer, and says the following:*

The scent of myrrh is for your nose. It fills your nostrils; your heart receives the meat-portions on its scent.[370]

Slowly **elevating the food offerings** *four times before the image of the Netjer, the Ritualist repeats the following:*

I offer to Wepwawet, Bull of Offerings.
All life emanates from you,
All health emanates from you,
All stability emanates from you,
All good fortune emanates from you,
O Lord of the Feast, Who is Sublime on His Standard, forever and ever.

The Ritualist **places the food offering before the divine image,** *and then* **all present extend one hand, palm down, over the offerings** *and recite the following:*

---

[370] Quoted in "Worship and Festivals in an Egyptian Temple," by H. W. Fairman (publ. by The John Rylands Library, 1954), p. 191.

May offerings of every kind come forth in abundance,
like the things which come forth from the mouth of the *Netjer*.

piryá pírit ar ḫiráw mi purú:riat ma rá' ni náṭar. (4 times)
[approximately pronounced: peer-YA PEER-it ar khi-RAU mee pu-ROOR-iat ma RA nee NAH-tchar]

May offerings of every kind come forth in abundance, like the things that come forth from the mouth of the *Netjer*.

Holding the Ankh before the Netjer, the Ritualist says:

Live, O Wepwawet, Lord of Joy, live for all time and for eternity!"

ʿánaḫ niḥáḥ ḏát.
[approximately pronounced *AH-nakh nee-HAH JAHT*]

The Ankh is placed next to the sacred image.

Holding the Ib (the golden heart) before the Netjer, the Ritualist says:

Hail to you, O Wepwawet, Who Brings Forth Goodness. I have brought to you your heart to set it in its place. Let me draw near to you with your heart, so that you may have pleasure through me, and so that by means of me you may have power over your body. Ascend, O Bull of Offering, Powerful Phallus, radiant, rejuvenating, equipped as a *Netjer*. Live, O Beloved of the Lady of *Medjed*, even Hat-Hór, live forever and ever!

*After placing the Ib near the sacred image, **everyone sings or chants** the hymn to Wepwawet. Participants may wish to alternate the singing of verses.*

Please notice the transliterated word **'sab'**, which means 'canid.'
It covers a variety of canids including jackals, wolves, foxes, and
wild dogs. Wepwawet is called a **'sab.'** Other evidence, including
artefactual evidence, points to Him being a wolf, not a jackal. But
the conclusion is still tentative until further evidence emerges.

Hail to you, Wepwawet,
who separated heaven from earth!
'sab' of Upper Kemet, who came forth from Nut,
your face appears upon her thighs
in this your name of 'sab' of Upper Kemet;
the *Netjeru* tremble before you in your fury
in this your name of Wepwawet, Opener-of-the-Ways;
the *Netjeru* tremble before you in your rage
in this your name of Upbreaker-of-the-Heart;
the lords heading the land tremble before you,
the *Netjeru* tremble before you in the great House-of-Nobles
which is in *Iunu* (Heliopolis).

Lord of Slaughter, High of Neck,
who is in front, more than every *Netjer*!
You are strong in heaven,
powerful on earth.[371]

Open the way for me in peace and in safety.
Lord of Strength and Power,[372] push aside all obstacles for me
so that you may see me among the righteous who do ma'at.

---

[371] This hymn appears in the chapel of Wenemi, pp. 105-106 in Detlef
Franke's article, "Middle Kingdom Hymns, other Sundry Religious Texts—
an Inventory," in *Egypt—Temple of the Whole World, Studies in Honour of
Jan Assmann*, ed. by Sibylle Meyer (Brill: Leiden-Boston, 2003).
[372] This epithet appears in a hymn on a stela from the 13th Dynasty. Ibid.,
p. 107.

*At this point perform the **meditation or magical action** or, if it is a special feast, add the appropriate prayers.*

*Afterwards **all present back out of the Temple Chamber with heads slightly bowed** while the Ritualist performs the "removing the foot."*

*With the broom the Ritualist, as the last person to exit, **ritually sweeps the area beginning at the altar**. (This is known as "removing the foot.") While performing this action the Ritualist recites the following:*

The distress that causes confusion has been driven away, and all the *Netjeru* are in harmony. I have given Heru his Eye; I have placed the *Wedjat*-Eye in the correct position. I have given Setekh his Testicles, so that the two lords are content through the work of my hands.

I know the sky, I know the earth;
I know Heru, I know Setekh.
Heru is appeased with his Eyes;
Setekh is appeased with his Testicles.
I am Djehuty, who reconciles the *Netjeru*,
who makes offerings in their correct form.

*The **double doors are solemnly closed** as the Ritualist says the following:*

Djehuty has come.
He has filled the Eye of Heru;
He has restored the Testicles of Setekh.
No evil shall enter this Temple.
Ptah has closed the door,
Djehuty has set it fast.
The door is closed, the door is set fast with the bolt.

All bow, touching the palms of their hands to their knees.

THE REVERSION OF OFFERINGS:

*One priest or priestess and as many assistants as necessary enter the Temple Chamber a final time. While he/she and any assistants **lift up the offerings before the sacred image** the ritualist shall say:*

O Wepwawet, your enemy[373] withdraws for you. Heru has turned himself to his Eye in its name of 'Reversion-of-Offerings.' I am Djehuty. I come to perform this rite for Wepwawet, Bull of Offerings. These, your divine offerings revert, they revert to your servants for life, for stability, for health and for joy! O that the Eye of Heru may flourish for you eternally!

*Everyone withdraws, **carrying away all food offerings except for one loaf of bread together with a bowl of pure water.** These last items will remain until evening. If this ritual is celebrated after sunset, these items would also be removed.*

*After the candle has burned down, a servant-priest enters and **closes the doors of the Kar-shrine.***

Extinguishing the candle or oil lamp, he/she exclaims:

This is the Eye of Heru by which you have become great, by which you live, and by which you have power, O Wepwawet. This is the Eye of Heru which you consume and through which you enchant your body. The *Wedjat-* Eye now enters into the

---

[373] Meat offerings held a two-fold meaning for the ancient priesthood. Since meat necessarily came from slain animals, it signified the defeated or slain enemies of the Netjer. At the same time, the meat offering represented the produce of the land which ultimately was a gift of the Netjeru.

West, into *Manu*, but it shall return. Truly, the Eye of Heru returns in peace![374]

In addition to the sources already referenced above, the following texts are also useful.

DuQuesne, Terence. "Votive Stelae for Upwawet from the Salakhana Trove," in *Discussions in Egyptology,* Vol. 48 (2000), 5-47.

_____ "Documents on the Cult of the Jackal Deities at Asyut: Seven More Ramesside Stelae from the Salakhana Trove," in *Discussions in Egyptology,* Vol. 53 (2002), 9-30.

_____ "Hathor of Medjed," in *Discussions in Egyptology* Vol. 54 (2002), 39-60.

_____ "Exalting the God, Processions of Upwawet at Asyut in the New Kingdom," in *Discussions in Egyptology,* Vol. 57 (2003), 21-45.

_____ "Empowering the Divine Standard: an Unusual Motif on the Salakhana Stelae," in *Discussions in Egyptology,* Vol. 58 (2004), 29-59.

_____ *The Jackal Divinities of Egypt. I. From the Archaic Period to Dynasty X*
(London: Oxfordshire Communications in Egyptology VI, 2005).

_____ *Anubis, Upwawet, and Other Deities: Personal Worship and Official Religion in Ancient Egypt, Catalogue of the Exhibition of the Egyptian Museum Cairo 2007* (Cairo, 2007).

---

[374] It is important to consume the food offerings after the ceremony. Water used should either be drunk or poured onto the earth. If it is mixed with Natron, dilute it very greatly and then you can pour in onto the bare earth.

ANNUAL FESTIVAL RITUALS

Wep Renpet - New Year Rite for Sekhmet, Eye of Ra

Throughout ancient Egypt the celebration of *Wep Renpet* (New Year) was *the* major religious celebration of the entire year. Today it occurs in late July or early August, depending on the rising of the star Sirius in your area. Please refer to Appendix C at the end of this ritual for a step by step guide on how to determine the date for *Wep Renpet* in your locale.

This New Year rite should begin shortly before midday in order that the sacred image of this goddess may be lifted up when the sun is at its zenith. Two altars are required: the ritual begins at an indoor location, then a procession with the statue goes to an outside altar where direct sunlight can shine upon the sacred image. Participants may also carry statues of their special god or goddess and place them on the outside altar so that sunlight can shine down upon them.

Special offerings: wine, beer, bread, and an assortment of fruit. These items will be presented to Sekhmet at the outside altar. Each has a special recitation.

Two Supplemental Rites are attached: **The Thirty-Eight Invocations to Sekhmet**, and the **Anointing Rite**. The Invocations may be recited at the outside altar.
The Anointing Rite occurs after the image of Sekhmet is returned to the indoor altar. An appropriate solar oil such as a high-quality olive oil may be used for the anointing.

As with all Egyptian rituals begin with your purification – washing of hands and cleansing of mouth with Natron. This preliminary rite helps us to lay aside the cares of the day and to become mindful of the fact that we will encounter a divine being. If Natron is not available, then use a natural sea salt in its place until you make your own Natron.

If two or more persons are participating, then one person, impersonating the Netjer Djehuty, **purifies each person by sprinkling each with water** *while exclaiming:*

I purify you with the water of all life and good fortune, all stability, all health and happiness.[375]

Afterwards each person **rinses his mouth** *and* **places a small amount of Natron or sea salt in his mouth** *while saying:*

I wash my mouth; I chew natron so that I may extol the might of Sekhmet, Lady of All Powers, the Mistress of Awe.[376]

Participants **assemble outside the Temple Chamber** *and begin by softly rattling sistra.*

This time—several minutes or more—is used to focus minds and intention so that distracting thoughts are left behind. The sound

---

[375] Taken from Aylward M. Blackman's article "Purification (Egyptian)" in Hastings Encyclopaedia 10/1918/ 476-82. This article is reprinted in Gods, Priests, and Men, Studies in the Religion of Pharaonic Egypt, edited by Alan B. Lloyd (Kegan Paul International, 1998), p. 9.

[376] Based on a temple inscription taken from "The Myth of Horus at Edfu—II" by A. M. Blackman and H. W. Fairman, appearing in Gods, Priests and Men, Studies in the Religion of Pharaonic Egypt (Kegan Paul International, 1998), p. 283.

of the sistra dispels negative energy, purifying the atmosphere in preparation for encountering divinity.

Standing before the closed doors, the Liturgist recites the entrance spell:

UTTERANCE BEFORE THE CLOSED DOORS OF THE TEMPLE

*The ritualist **raises hands in adoration** ('dua' position—arms stretched out in front of the body and raised up to face level, with palms facing outward). The following shall be said:*

O you *Netjeru* of this temple, you guardians of the great portal, great *Netjeru* of mysterious abode, who sanctify this *Netjeret* in her shrine, who consecrate her oblation, who receive the offerings in her presence in the Hall of the Ennead: I have made my way and I enter into your presence. I am one of you. I am Shu, the eldest son of his father, the senior *wab* servant-priest of Sekhmet. Do not repulse me on the *Netjeret*'s path. My feet are not impeded. I am not turned back from the court of the great portal so that I may conduct the divine service, that I may present offerings to her that made them, that I may give bread to Sekhmet. I have come on the way of the *Netjeret*. I have not shown partiality in judgement. I have not consorted with the strong. I have not reproached the lowly. I have not stolen things. I have not diminished the constituents of the Eye of Ra. I have not disturbed the balance. I have not tampered with the requirements of the Sacred Eye. O Council of the Great *Netjeret* in this temple, behold, I have come to you to offer Ma'at to the Lady of Ma'at, to content the Sound Eye for its mistress. I am Shu; I flood her offering table. I present her offerings, this great *Netjeret* consorting with me, that I may adore Sekhmet at her festivals, that I may kiss the earth so great is her majesty, that I may endow her image with life. I am pure. I am purified.

At this point the ritualist **opens the doors to the Temple Chamber, or,** *if there are no doors,* **makes a gesture of opening unseen doors,** *and* **steps forward as if crossing over a threshold.** *The following is said:*

O you *Ba*-souls of *Mennefer* (i.e., Memphis), if you are strong, I am strong. If I am strong, you are strong. If your *Ka*-spirits are strong, my *Ka*-spirit is strong at the head of the living. As they live so shall I live. . . . Sekhmet, the great *Netjeret*, beloved of Ptah, has given me life, stability, and serenity round about my members, which Djehuty has gathered together for life. I am Heru in the height of heaven, the beautiful one of awe, Lord of Victory, mighty one of awe, exalted one of the two plumes, great one in *Abdju* (Abydos). I am pure.

All temple members chant:

Awake in peace, O Sekhmet, Eye of Ra,
may you awaken in peace.
Awake in peace, O Sekhmet, the Powerful One,
may you awaken in peace.
Awake in peace, O Sekhmet, Lady of Flame,
may you awaken in peace.
Awake in peace, O Sekhmet, Luminous One,
may you awaken in peace.

May you awake beautifully at the top of the morning, through that which the entirety of *Netjeru* say to you.

The ritualist *slowly opens the two doors of the Kar-shrine housing the sacred image. All others bow, touching their hands to their knees. The following is said:*

The doors of the sky are open; the doors of the earth are unlocked. This House is open for its Mistress. Let me come forth as she shall come forth. Let me enter in as she shall enter in. Sekhmet, Daughter of the Limitless One, Beloved of Ptah, is exalted upon her Great Seat. The Great Company of the *Netjeru* are exalted upon their seat.

I have seen the *Netjeret,* and the *Netjeret* sees me. The *Netjeret* rejoices at seeing me. I have gazed upon the statue of the Luminous One, the sacred image of the Eye of Ra.[377]

Right hand on left shoulder of statue; left hand on right wrist of statue:

Djehuty has come to you. Awake when you hear his words. I have come as the envoy of Atum. My two arms are upon you like those of Heru. My two hands are upon you like those of Djehuty. My fingers are upon you like those of Anpu. Homage be to you. I am a living servant of Sekhmet.

The Ritualist holds up the **bowl of water** *in which he/she will be mixing the Natron. The following is said:*

O water, may you remove all evil,
As Ra who bathes in the Lake of Rushes,
May Heru wash my flesh,

---

[377] Based on the temple text found in "Worship and Festivals in an Egyptian Temple," a lecture by H. W. Fairman (publ. by The John Rylands Library, 1954) p. 183.

May Djehuty cleanse my feet,
May Shu lift me up and Nut take my hand.
May Setekh be my strength, and may Sekhmet be my healing.
And may Amun-Ra be my life and my prospering!

*Set aside the bowl of water and **lift up the Natron** as you say:*

It is pure, it is pure. My Natron is the Natron of Heru, and the Natron of Heru is my Natron.
My Natron is the Natron of Setekh, and the Natron of Setekh is my Natron.
My Natron is the Natron of Djehuty, and the Natron of Djehuty is my Natron.
My Natron is the Natron of Geb, and the Natron of Geb is my Natron.

My mouth is the mouth of a milking calf on the day that I was born.

*Four pinches of **Natron** are **mixed into the water** and the bowl is lifted up before the Netjeret as this Utterance is recited:*

I give you essential water, a tide in your time.
I bring the flood waters to purify your sanctuary.
I bring you the flood waters to purify your temple and your statue in its place, the primordial water that purifies as in the First Time!

*The Ritualist **places an index finger into the water and moves it in a circular direction four times** as the following is said:*

Sekhmet, the Daughter of Ra, does purify this water;

Sekhmet, the Beloved of Ptah, does cleanse this water;
Sekhmet, Sweet One of Heru and Setekh, does sanctify this water;
Sekhmet herself does endow this water with power and with life.

The bowl of Natron-infused water is then taken up and the Ritualist sprinkles this lightly in front of the statue of Sekhmet and also anoints with water the base of her image as this Utterance is recited:

I come close to You, O Pure One, Lady of the Waters of Life.
I bring the water of rejuvenation that flows from the Two Caverns.
I sprinkle the water, purifying your image and your temple from all impurity!

The Ritualist picks up the bowl of Natron and sprinkles a small amount in each of the four directions as the following is recited:

The *Netjeret* Sekhmet herself does cleanse and purify this, her temple to the South.
The *Netjeret* Sekhmet herself does cleanse and purify this, her temple to the North.
The *Netjeret* Sekhmet herself does cleanse and purify this, her temple to the West.
The *Netjeret* Sekhmet herself does cleanse and purify this, her temple to the East.

Replacing the Natron on the altar, the Ritualist does the same with the water, sprinkling it in each of the four directions. The following is said:

The *Netjeret* Sekhmet herself does sanctify and consecrate this, her temple to the South.

The N*etjeret* Sekhmet herself does sanctify and consecrate this, her temple to the North.

The *Netjeret* Sekhmet herself does sanctify and consecrate this, her temple to the West.

The *Netjeret* Sekhmet herself does sanctify and consecrate this, her temple to the East.

The temple of the *Netjeret* Sekhmet is established.

It is established for millions of years.

*The Ritualist returns to the altar and then **lights the candle or oil lamp** while the following is said:*

Come, come in peace, O glorious Eye of Heru,
Be strong and renew Your youth in peace.
For the flame shines like Ra on the double horizon.
I am pure, I am pure, I am pure, I am pure.

***Place incense on the burner and cense each sacred image** while the following is said:*

The fire is laid, the fire shines;
The incense is laid on the fire, the incense shines.
Your perfume comes to me, O Incense;
May my perfume come to you, O Incense.
Your perfume comes to me, you *Netjeru*;
May my perfume come to you, you *Netjeru*.
May I be with you, you *Netjeru*;
May you be with me, you *Netjeru*.
May I live with you, you *Netjeru*;
May you live with me, you *Netjeru*.

I love you, you *Neteru*;
May you love me, you *Netjeru*.

At this point recite the following:

Homage to you, O Sekhmet, Daughter of Ra, Mistress of the *Netjeru*, Bearer of Wings, Lady of the Red Apparel, Queen of the Crowns of the South and North, Only One, sovereign of her Father, superior to whom the *Netjeru* cannot be, mighty one of enchantments in the Boat of Millions of Years, you who art preeminent, who rise in the seat of silence, mother of the god Nefertum, Smiter of the enemies of Ra, Mistress and Lady of the tomb, Mother in the horizon of heaven, gracious one, beloved, destroyer of rebellion, offerings are in your grasp—offerings are in your grasp—and you are standing in the boat of your divine Father to overthrow (the fiend) *Qetu*.

You have placed Ma'at in the bows of his boat. You are the fire *Netjeret* Ammi-seshet, whose opportunity escapes her not . . . Praise be unto you, O Lady, who are mightier than the *Netjeru*. Words of adoration rise unto you from the Eight *Netjeru* of *Khemenu* (Hermopolis).

The living *Ba*-souls who are in their hidden places praise the mystery of you, O you who are their mother, you Source from which they sprang, who make for them a place in the hidden Underworld, who make sound their bones and preserve them from terror, who make them strong in the Abode of Everlastingness, who preserve them from the evil chamber of the souls of HES' HER, you who are among the company of the *Netjeru*. Your name is *zfy pr m Hs Hr hApu Dt.f* (pronounced "seh-fee per em Hes' Her h'poo jet-ef"). Your name is "Lady-of-life."

*The Ritualist **places more incense on the charcoal** and again and again **slowly raises and lowers the incense cup** as the following Utterance is recited:*

O Sekhmet, May you advance with your *Ka*.
O Golden One, the arm of your *Ka* is before you,
The arm of your *Ka* is behind you.
O Lady of Heaven, the foot of your *Ka* is before you,
The foot of your *Ka* is behind you.
O Beautiful Sekhmet, this incense is offered to you,
May your face be filled
As this essence spreads itself over you.

*All present perform the **Henu Rite**—Embrace the Earth, the Fourfold Salute to Sekhmet, and again Embrace the Earth.*

For Embracing the Earth, all present prostrate themselves, face down, upon the floor. During the Fourfold Salute, all present rise upon one knee, and alternately raise their hands and arms into the *Dua* (praise) position with palms facing outward, followed by the *Sahu* (obedience) gesture, made by striking the chest with a closed fist and raising the other arm (also with closed fist) at a ninety-degree angle. The *Dua* position is accompanied by the words **"Adoration be to Sekhmet,"** followed by the *Sahu* gesture accompanied with the words, **"Hail to the Lady of Protection!"** The bodily gestures are performed alternately four times.

*Following this **all present again prostrate themselves** before the Netjeret. This is a sign and symbol of total submission and adoration before the Netjeret. The following is said:*

Homage to Sekhmet, Eye of Ra, Great of Flame,
who is established on the Great Seat!

I have placed myself on the floor in awe of you.
I embrace the earth before you as before the Lady of All Powers.
I have come that I might kiss the earth,
that I might worship my Mistress,
For I have seen her beauty;
I give praise to Sekhmet,
For I have seen her power.
Her form is more distinguished than the *Netjeru*;
Her arm is more powerful than the *Netjeru*.
I am pure, I am pure, I am pure, I am pure!

Everyone stands up.

*The Ritualist **holds in the palm of one hand the statue of Ma'at** and with **the other hand open and raised over the image as if sheltering it**, repeats the following:*

I have come to you as Djehuty, whose two hands are joined together under Ma'at. She comes to be with you, for she is everywhere. You are provided with Ma'at. You move in Ma'at, you live in Ma'at. She fills your body, she rests in your head, she makes her seat upon your brow; the breath of your body is of Ma'at, your heart does live in Ma'at. All that you eat, all that you drink, all that you breathe is of Ma'at. Djehuty presents Ma'at to you, his two hands are upon her beauty before your face.

*The Ritualist **places the image of Ma'at near the divine statue.***

*The Ritualist picks up the **Ankh** and holds it before the divine image, and says:*

Live, O Sekhmet, Eye of Ra, live for all time and for eternity!

ʿánaḫ niḥáḫ ḏát.
[approximately pronounced *AH-nakh nee-HAH JAHT]*

*The Ritualist holds up the **Ib (the golden heart)** before the Netjeret
and says:*

Hail to you, O Sekhmet, Mistress of Awe. I have brought to you
your heart to set it in its place. Let me draw near to you with
your heart, so that you may have pleasure through me, and
so that by means of me you may have power over your body.
Ascend, O Solar Feminine Disk, radiant, rejuvenating, equipped
as *Netjeret*. Live, O Eye of Ra, live for all time and for eternity!

*After placing the **Ib** near the sacred image, **everyone sings or chants**
the hymn to Sekhmet. Participants may wish to alternate the singing
of verses.*

I praise the Gleaming One, I worship her majesty. I exalt the
Daughter of Ra. Adoration to Sekhmet, Praise to my mistress! O
Golden One, breath of my life, Lady of All Powers who enfolds
me! All hail, jubilation to you, the Mistress of All!

O Golden One, sole ruler, Eye of Ra! Bountiful One who gives
birth to divine entities, forms the animals, models them as
she pleases, fashions humanity. O Mother! Luminous One who
thrusts back the darkness, illuminating every human being
with her light!

I revere you, Sekhmet, Enrapturing One, Enlightener! O Mother
of the Netjeru, from sky, from earth, from south, from west,
from north, from east, from each land, from each place, where
your majesty shines!

See what is in my heart, what is in my inmost; my heart is blameless, my inmost open, no darkness is in my breast! I adore you, O Queen of the Netjeru! O Golden One! Lady of Intoxications, Lady of Jubilation, Adorable One! It is the Gold of the divine entities who comes forth.

Heaven exalts, the earth is full of gladness, Sekhmet the Great rejoices! (4 times)

*With care and reverence the Liturgist **lifts the image of Sekhmet from the altar** while reciting the following:*

Let us go to the heavenly vault,
that Sekhmet may unite with her Father,
and humanity might see her beauty!

*If others are participating in the rite **they should state:***

Let us gather close following behind you to the sanctuary!
May we follow Djehuty on the beautiful day of the beginning of the Inundation!
Hear the jubilation in the temple when the Golden One appears to show her love!

The person carrying the image shall say:

I proceed as Djehuty to the sanctuary,
On the beautiful day of the beginning of the Inundation!
Hearing the jubilation in the temple,
When the Gleaming One appears to show her love!

Place incense on the charcoal and carry the censer in front of the image.

Once at the outdoor location, **lay out a white linen** *where the image is to rest.*

Place the statue on the linen in the sunlight. Begin the invocation:

The sky is clear, *Sopdet* (the star Sirius, or Isis) **lives!**
She comes clad in her brilliance!
Radiantly, above her Father's forehead,
the Daughter of Ra, the Golden One, rises.
Her Mysterious form occupies the bow of his solar boat.

Her light unites with the light of the brilliant *Netjer,*
On the beautiful day of the birth of the Sun Disk!
This New Year's Feast, *Wep-Renpet!*
Radiant rises the Golden One above the forehead of her Father;
Her mysterious form at the head of his solar boat.

As her fellow *Netjeru* unite with her Father's light,
Merging with the brilliance of the Sun Disk,
Mennefer (the city of Memphis) **is joyful!**
There is a festive mood as all behold the Great One,
The firmly striding creator of feasts in the holy city,
On the beautiful day of *Wep-Renpet.*

Sekhmet, the Beautiful One who appears in heaven,
The truth which regulates the world at the head of the Sun barge,
The Queen and Mistress of Awe,
The ruler of the *Netjeru.*

Sekhmet the Great,
The Mother of the *Netjeru*,
Be with me (us) from this day!" [*repeat 4 times*]

Gently pick up the statue, raise it high while facing the sun and repeat:

Sekhmet is the Gleaming One,
Beautiful Eye which gives life to the Two Lands,
With her Father she is announced with joy by the star that rises at the beginning of the year! She of radiant perfection!

Sekhmet, Shining-of-Countenance, appears as a Great Serpent on the head of her Father before the Ennead,
She unites with Ra in the barge,
She is the one who arouses perfection.

She who was with Ra causing creation to happen!
Sekhmet the Great;
The Mistress of the Sky;
Sovereign of all the *Netjeru*;
Sekhmet is brilliant in her sanctuary on the *Wep-Renpet*!

She unites with the rays of her Father!
She pleases Ra who is joyous in his city!

Place the sacred image on the linen cloth, and then, *looking to the sky, say:*

Praise to you Ra! Praise to you Khepera! Praise to you Ra Horakhty!
The Sun disk illuminating the land with his rays!
The Sole One felling the enemies of her Lord of the two horizons!

Praise to you Heru who protects by burning his enemies!
Praise to you, Ennead in the Barque of the Morning, and Ennead in the Barque of the Evening, the followers who are in the horizon, appeasing his majesty Ra!
Praise to you who created yourself, you who live in Ma'at, you who abide no Isfet,
He shines upon the land. He shines upon all faces.

How perfect is your rising Ra, Ram of the *Netjeru*.
How perfect is your rising Ra, sailing without becoming weary.
How perfect is your rising Ra, you who are Hapy, equipped with two wings.
How perfect is your rising Ra, Apep is massacred before the *Mandjet* boat.
How perfect is your rising Ra, the serpent-enemy is burnt with the flame.

How perfect is your rising Ra, you rise as Horakhty.
How perfect is your rising Ra, your barque sails with a good breeze.
How perfect is your rising Ra, you fell the turtle [symbol of the enemy].
How perfect is your rising Ra, you are the Great Disk creating light.
How perfect is your rising Ra, you cut off the heads of your enemies.
How perfect is your rising Ra, there stands no enmity in your path.
How perfect is your rising Ra, you fill the globe with rays.
How perfect is your rising Ra, you illuminate the two lands.
How perfect is your rising Ra, you join the Sun Disk to the living.

How perfect is your rising Ra, you shine upon the beings with your Eyes.

How perfect is your sailing, Illuminating One, you massacre the rebels.
How perfect is your sailing, Heh, you cross the sky with the breeze.
How perfect is your sailing, Behedet, your enemies are slaughtered.
How perfect is your sailing, Horsamtu, there is no enemy upon the path.
How perfect is your sailing, Hapy, dual King, you fly in the sky as the winged disk.
How perfect is your sailing, Hor-Akhty, the sky rises for you in joy, in joy!

Then face the image of Sekhmet, with arms in the dua position.

At this point offer a libation of water by pouring it into a bowl as you repeat the following:

I give to you the Water of Renewal, abundant in its time.
Sopdet calls forth the rising flood at the debut of the year,
Dispensing life to the living ones;
I give to you the life that is in this water.

Now **four offerings**—representing "All Things Good and Pure"—are made:
1) wine; 2) beer; 3) bread; 4) fruit.

*The **wine is offered** as the following is recited:*

I come close to you, Flaming One,

Sekhmet, powerful one without equal.
I bring you wine as that of the south and north,
I bring you wine as that of west and east,
All the wine from the Land of *Netjer*,
For you are the Lady of Intoxications,
The Giver of Ecstasies.
Sekhmet, who delights in joy.
I, myself, offer this libation.
It is pure.
I give this wine to you,
That you may enjoy drunkenness, intoxication,
And merry making ceaselessly!

Beer is offered and the following is said:

Take this sweet beer, Sacred Mistress,
Taste how pleasing it is!
I come close to you, Golden Mistress of *Mennefer* (Memphis),
In the place of drunkenness,
I bring the beer that it may delight your heart,
For you are the Lady of Intoxications,
The Enrapturing One,
You whose face is beautiful,
You whose love is pleasing.
I offer this beer to you, O *Netjeret*,
That your heart may rejoice each day.

Bread is offered and the following is said:

I bring you bread,
That you may consume,
That you may eat,

601

That you may sustain your body,
You invoke your *Ka*,
You are satisfied with the Eye of Heru,
You dispense life to those who follow you,
You are generous with the food of the divine living forces.

*The **fruit offerings** are presented while repeating the following:*

I offer to Sekhmet, Eye of Ra, Sweet One of Heru and Setekh.
Take this food,
That your *Ka* may be satisfied with this Eye of Heru,
Take these offerings,
That they may satisfy your heart each day.

For you are the Beautiful Eye which gives life to the Two Lands,
The Lady of Transformations in the Great Seat!
All life emanates from you,
All health emanates from you,
All stability emanates from you,
All good fortune emanates from you, Sekhmet the Great forever!

*Having **placed the food offerings** before the divine image, all present point an open, outstretched hand toward the offering and say:*

May offerings of every kind come forth in abundance,
like the things which come forth from the mouth of the *Netjeret*.

piryá pírit ar ḫiráw mi purú:riat ma rá' ni naṯárat. (4 times)
[approximately pronounced: peer-YA PEER-it ar khi-RAU mee pu-ROOR-iat ma RA nee nah-TCHAR-at]

May offerings of every kind come forth in abundance,

like the things which come forth from the mouth of the *Netjeret*.

Shaking the Sistrum, chant the following as you visualize the flow of light from the Sun into the statue. Continue chanting until you feel that a climax of energy has been reached merging with the statue:

Clad in her brilliance,
Merging with the Sun,
Sekhmet and Ra
Now become One! (*repeat 7 times*)

Pick up the statue and then ceremonially return Sekhmet to your normal ritual area. Pick up all the food offerings and carry them in procession into the temple area. Place them on a table before the image of Sekhmet.

This is time for **quiet meditation**, the full **The Thirty-Eight Invocations to Sekhmet, Invocation Against the Seven Arrows of the Year** and/or the **Anointing Rite** for each temple member (see below for these Supplemental Rites).

*Then, with the broom, **ritually sweep the area beginning at the altar** as you back out of the temple area. This is known as "removing the foot".* *Upon leaving the ritual area **set the broom aside, bow** and then say:*

The distress that causes confusion has been driven away, and all the *Netjeru* are in harmony. I have given Heru his Eye, I have placed the *Wedjat*-Eye in the correct position. I have given Setekh his Testicles, so that the two lords are content through the work of my hands.

I know the sky, I know the earth; I know Heru, I know Setekh. Heru is appeased with his Eyes, Setekh is appeased with his Testicles.
I am Djehuty, who reconciles the *Netjeru*, who makes offerings in their correct form.

Closing the double doors, say:

Djehuty has come.
He has filled the Eye of Heru; He has restored the testicles of Setekh.
No evil shall enter this temple.
Ptah has closed the door,
Djehuty has set it fast.
The door is closed, the door is set fast with the bolt.

Bow, touching the palms of your hands to your knees.

THE REVERSION OF OFFERINGS

One priest or priestess and as many assistants as necessary enter the Temple Chamber a final time. While he/she and any assistants **lift up the offerings before the sacred image** the ritualist shall say:

O Sekhmet, your enemy[378] withdraws for you. Heru has turned himself to his Eye in its name of 'Reversion-of-Offerings'. I am Djehuty. I come to perform this rite for Sekhmet, queen of the *Netjeru*. These, your divine offerings, revert, they revert to

---

[378] Meat offerings held a two-fold meaning for the ancient priesthood. Since meat necessarily came from slain animals, it signified the defeated or slain enemies of the Netjeret. At the same time, the meat offering represented the produce of the land which ultimately was a gift of the Netjeru.

your servants for life, for stability, for health, and for joy! O that the Eye of Heru may flourish for you eternally!

*Everyone withdraws, **carrying away all food offerings except for one loaf of bread together with a bowl of pure water.** These last items will remain until evening.*

*After the candle has burned down, a servant-priest enters and **closes the doors of the Kar-shrine.***

***Extinguishing the candle or oil lamp,** he/she exclaims:*

This is the Eye of Heru by which you have become great, by which you live, and by which you have power, O Sekhmet. This is the Eye of Heru which you consume and through which you enchant your body. The *Wedjat*-Eye now enters into the West, into *Manu*, but it shall return. Truly, the Eye of Heru returns in peace![379]

The ancient Egyptians greeted one another with the wish, *"Renpet Neferet"* (good year!)[380]

Supplemental Rite 1: The Thirty-Eight Invocations to Sekhmet

All thirty-eight Invocations are my translation and adaptation from the French text found in Philippe Germond's *Sekhmet et la protection du monde* (1981). Although originally written for the protection of the ruling pharaoh, the following adaptations are written for personal use in our contemporary world. The Kemetic

---

[379] It is important to consume the food offerings after the ceremony. Water should either be drunk or poured out onto the earth.

[380] Christian Jacq, Fascinating Hieroglyphs, p. 68.

religion has outgrown the geographical boundaries of Kemet and, as a consequence, the need for one terrestrial ruler. Our need for protection, however, remains. Sekhmet is uniquely qualified to protect us from both physical as well as spiritual evils.

1. O Sekhmet, Eye of Ra, Great of Flame, Lady of Protection who surrounds her creator! Come toward me as you came toward the King of Upper and Lower Kemet [Egypt], the Master of the Double Land, the Son of Ra, the Lord of Crowns, the Living Image! Protect me and preserve me from every arrow and every impurity of this year, because it is Ra himself from whom you are descended.

2. O Sekhmet, You who illumine the Double Land with your flame and give the faculty of sight to all! Come toward me as you came toward the Living Image, the Living Falcon! Free me, preserve me from all the evil contagions of this year, so that they never hold ascendancy over me.

3. O Sekhmet, Lady of Flame, Great of Flame, Great of Terror, in fear of whom the Double Land trembles! Come toward me as you came toward the Living Image, the Living Falcon! Make me pass far from every fever, from every pestilence of the year, for you are my Sole Protectress!

4. O Sekhmet, with red heart toward him from whom she issues forth, when He brought her back after imploring her! Come toward me as you came toward the Living Image! Protect me, save me, deliver me; protect me from the massacre of slaughtering spirits so that I will not die because of them.

5. O Sekhmet, Uraeus on the head of her master, who protects him with her flame! Come towards me as you came toward the

Living Image! Liberate me; put your protection around me! Protect me from every arrow and from every pestilence of the year! Preserve me from the one who plots against me, for I am like unto him who in his name of Ra is eternally in the sky.

6. O Sekhmet, the one who makes every eye to see without blindness happening! Come to me as you came to the Living Image, the Living Falcon! For it is Ra from whom you issue forth, I am like unto him who is the Protected One of the year . . . . Grant that I will be preserved from every arrow, from every contagion, from every bitterness, and from every fever, because I am like unto Heru, the Offspring.

7. O Sekhmet, when you rise, the Light appears; when you go back, darkness comes! Grant that I do not die from your arrow, and grant that your fever does not catch me, for I am like unto the great *Netjer* from whom you come forth. I am like unto Heru, the Offspring.

8. O Sekhmet, who clothes her master in her light, and who conceals him inside her pupil! Come to me as you came to the Living Image, the Living Falcon! Protect me from every evil fly of this year, so that it does not cling to me, ...

9. O Sekhmet, Ardent Flame, who lights a fire when she takes the torch! Come to me as you came to the Living Image, the Living Falcon! Preserve me from every evil . . . Because I am like unto Ra who cannot go toward your slaughtering spirits!

10. O Sekhmet, whose flame is well-respected among mankind! Who causes her flame to rise. Preserve me as you preserved the Living Image, the Living Falcon! Protect me and deliver me

from the pestilence of the year which reigns in the land, for I am like unto the Unique One who is indestructible . . . .

11. O Sekhmet, for whom the two skies open at once after she shows herself in splendor! Preserve me as you preserved the Living Image, the Living Falcon! Free me, protect me as well as my loved ones and my children from every terror, from every evil arrow of this year, and from all difficulties, . . .

12. O Sekhmet, Lady of Slaughter the way you like, the one who turns her face toward the south, the north, the west, and the east, in such a way that mankind is in fear! Come toward me as you came toward the King of Upper and Lower Kemet, Master of the Double Land, Son of Ra, the Lord of crowns, the Living Image, the Living Falcon! Protect me. . . .

13. O Sekhmet, who enters in the opening of the mountains, she from which the flame fills for him (i.e., Ra) the Double Land, who inspires fear in the *Netjeru*! She from which the flame fills for him the Double Land; (and which) she places among the *Netjeru*. Come toward me even as you came toward the Living Image, the Living Falcon! Preserve me, deliver me, and make me to pass well away from harm, for I am like unto the Protected One of your arm of this year.

14. O Sekhmet, who fashions her Lord on herself, whose place is preeminent in front of him! Do not send your messengers against me who am like unto the Living Image! . . . In order that I cannot go in front of any of your evil arrows.

15. O Sekhmet, the one who spreads out your terror upon everything, the one who has been asked for life by those who rest in your hand! Preserve me as you preserved the Living

Image, the Living Falcon, from your Slaughtering Spirits, because he was the only recourse of his people, the only recourse of his mates and of his children . . . .

16. O Sekhmet, Eater of Blood, the one who does not push away the arm's grip, the one who establishes her domination in the house of the *Netjeru*! Come toward me as you came toward the Living Image, the Living Falcon! Deliver me from the impurity which you have spread out in this year, so that I do not go toward this impurity, because I am like unto the one to whom the two Eyes have been sent . . . .

17. O Sekhmet, more divine than the *Netjeru* [the gods], more glorious than the Ennead, Lady of Light, whose place is preeminent on the head of her Lord! Come toward me as you came toward the Living Image, the Living Falcon! Make me pass far from all contagion, from every evil arrow, every pernicious fever, so that they do not penetrate into me, for I am like unto Atum, the night, who cannot die for all eternity.

18. O Sekhmet, Lady of Flame, the one who is in her moment (of rage), who grasps hearts for herself! Preserve me as you preserved the Living Image, the Living Falcon; deliver me from every disastrous death of this year . . . .

19. O Sekhmet, the one who presides as the Power for capturing the Wanderers, Lady of Life of the Double Land, who can be the cause of death! Make me to pass far from all evil even as you accomplished this for the Living Image, the Living Falcon! Protect me, for I am like unto he who has the name *spty.f(y)*, the one who must exist on earth.

20. O Sekhmet the Great, Lady of the Uraeus, the one whom we fear around the shrine! Come toward me as you came toward the Living Image, the Living Falcon! Protect me, place your protection around me, for I am like unto Heru [Horus] the Offspring. May I live, may I live eternally, for ever and ever!

21. O Sekhmet, the one who opens the mountains, the one for whom the desert animals have been killed on account of the fear which she inspires! Come to me as you came to the Living Image, the Living Falcon! Save me; do not permit that your massacre is exercised on me; do not strike me, for I am like the one who is protected by his Eye.

22. O Sekhmet, the sight of whom reduces all things to ashes, while humans throw themselves down upon their faces! Come toward me as you came toward the Son of Ra, the Lord of Crowns, the Living Image, the Living Falcon! Save me, protect me from this your terror, for I am like unto the One sheltered from your arm.

23. O Sekhmet, woman who plays the role of the male, and whom every *Netjer* fears! Come toward me even as you came toward the Living Image, the Living Falcon! May I be possessor of your protection, and if you live, I live; if you are in good health, I am in good health, (and) I will not be destroyed, no, not ever!

24. O Sekhmet, the one who is at the head of all things, thanks to whom what every eye sees can be contemplated! Come toward me as toward the Living Image, the Living Falcon! Make me to pass well away from harm, for I am like unto Ra,

even like he who is the Venerable Falcon, in this his name of Ra, each day.

25. O Sekhmet, the one who shines, on account of whom one jubilates when it is ordered that her flame advances! When you shine, one jubilates because of you; when you are kind, the flame is pacified. Come toward me as you indeed came toward the Living Image, the Living Falcon! Push away your messengers; do not permit them to be sent against me, so that they cannot have power against me.

26. O Sekhmet, at whose setting the darkness appears, in such a way that if someone nods his head to his neighbor, they will not see one another! Come toward me as toward the Living Image, the Living Falcon! Control every contagion, every arrow . . . . (and) all malicious things . . . so that they cannot be sent against me, not ever.

27. O Sekhmet, Lady of Flame, Great One who causes all to tremble, the power of any other god turns out to be non-existent when he is handed over to her. Come toward me as toward the Son of Ra, the Living Image, the Living Falcon! Protect me and save me . . . . from harmful things issuing from you, in order that I do not die because of them.

28. O Sekhmet, Lady of Ma'at, the one who hates the thief, the one who devours him to satiation, in accordance with your desire! Come toward me as toward the Living Image, the Living Falcon! Save me, make me to pass far away from the bodily diseases of this year, for like him may I be the ultimate protected body.

29. O Sekhmet, for whom heads are severed by her messengers, the one who is at the head of her wandering spirits. Come toward me as toward the Living Image, the Living Falcon! Keep me away from all harm. . . . . . For I am like unto this one whom one does not attack . . . .

30. O Sekhmet, the one who fills the ways with blood and who slays to the limit of all she sees! Come toward me as you came toward the Living Image, the Living Falcon! Protect me, and save me from every contagion and from every arrow of this year hurled against my faculty of sight.

31. O Sekhmet, the one who opens and one lives; the one who seals, and one dies; Lady of Life who awards according to her desire! Come toward me as you came to the Son of Ra, the Living Image, the Living Falcon! Grant me to live, for I am like unto that Son of Ra, who survives every evil arrow of this year, of this month, of this instant.

Supplemental Rite 1, Partial: Invocation Against the Seven Arrows of the Year

32. O Sekhmet, the one who presides over the country, Lady of Vegetation, Generous One, Sekhmet who protects the Double Land! Come toward me even as you came to the King of Upper and Lower Kemet, the Lord of the Double Land, the Son of Ra, Lord of crowns, the Living Image, the Living Falcon! Save me, protect me, and preserve me from the First Arrow of the year!

33. O Sekhmet, the Curled One, Lady of Obscurity, Wadjet the Great! Come toward me even as you came toward the King of Upper and Lower Kemet, the Lord of the Double Land, the Son

of Ra, Lord of crowns, the Living Image, the Living Falcon! Save me, protect me, and preserve me from the Second Arrow of the year!

34. O Sekhmet, the one who moves in light, the one who terrifies the *Netjeru* by her massacre! Come toward me even as you came toward the King of Upper and Lower Kemet, the Lord of the Double Land, the Son of Ra, Lord of crowns, the Living Image, the Living Falcon! Save me, protect me, and preserve me from the Third Arrow of the year!

35. O Sekhmet, the one who guides mankind, Lady of the Two Shores, and Lady of humanity! Come toward me as you came to the King of Upper and Lower Kemet, the Lord of the Double Land, the Son of Ra, Lord of crowns, the Living Image, the Living Falcon! Save me, protect me, and preserve me from the Fourth Arrow of the year!

36. O Sekhmet, Luminous One, the Great, preeminent in the Mansion of Fire, who terrorizes the Double Land by her fear! Come toward me as you came to the King of Upper and Lower Kemet, the Lord of the Double Land, the Son of Ra, Lord of crowns, the Living Image, the Living Falcon! Save me, protect me, and preserve me from the Fifth Arrow of the year!

37. O Sekhmet, the one who loves Ma'at and who detests Evil, Lady of the people (*rekhyt*). Come toward me as you came to the King of Upper and Lower Kemet, the Lord of the Double Land, the Son of Ra, Lord of crowns, the Living Image, the Living Falcon! Save me, protect me, and preserve me from the Sixth Arrow of the year!

38. O Sekhmet, Uraeus who opens the acacia[381], Sovereign One, the Great! Come toward me as you came to the King of Upper and Lower Kemet, the Lord of the Double Land, the Son of Ra, the Lord of Crowns, the Living Image, the Living Falcon! Save me, protect me, and preserve me from the Seventh Arrow of the year!"

Supplemental Rite 2: Anointing Rite

Using Solar Oil or olive oil, the priest/priestess **dips the small finger of his/her power hand into the oil** *and* **touches it to the appropriate part of the one being anointed.**

1) *Anointing the* **lids of both eyes, say one time:**

I come to you as Djehuty, whose words are truly effective. They are effective.

Through the power of Sekhmet, protected be your eyes so that you
may see your path with clarity and insight. Like Ra you are protected.

2) *Anointing* **the nostrils, say:**

Through the power of Sekhmet, protected be your nostrils so that
you may breathe your essence in peace. Like Ra you are protected.

---

[381] Possibly in the sense of "who causes the acacia to bloom" as the warmth of the sun brings forth the blossoms on a tree.

3) *Anointing **the mouth**, say:*

Through the power of Sekhmet, protected be your lips that you may
recite the words of HEKA with effectiveness and strength. Like Ra
you are protected.

4) *Anointing **the ears**, say:*

Through the power of Sekhmet, protected be your ears that you may
hear the counsel of the gods with openness from whatever quarter
it may come. Like Ra you are protected.

5) *Anointing the **chest over the heart**, say:*

Through the power of Sekhmet, protected be your heart that it may be found justified in the Balance. Like Ra you are protected.

6) *Anointing **the palms of the two hands**, say:*

Through the power of Sekhmet, protected be your hands that all your works may be fruitful and in union with Ma'at. Like Ra you are protected.

7) ***Anointing the feet**, say:*

Through the power of Sekhmet, protected be your feet that you may walk in your ways in safety and in peace. Like Ra you are protected.

Place your hands on the shoulders of the one who has been anointed and **with a strong sweeping motion** as if brushing off something negative from the person, say:

The seven arrows of Sekhmet are averted from you; they are averted from you.

The slaughtering spirits of Sekhmet do not approach you; they do not approach you.

The *khatiu* demons of Sekhmet do not attack you; they do not attack you.

Sekhmet herself protects you;
She preserves you.

You are the possessor of her protection.
Like Ra, you are the possessor of her protection.

Addendum: The Religious Calendar

The religious calendar of ancient Kemet is both lunar–with each month starting on the day of the New Moon—as well as sidereal—with the New Year—called 'Wep Renpet' or the Opening of the Year – celebrated on the morning of the visible rise of Sopdet (Sirius) just prior to sunrise.

To determine the date for the beginning of the New Year we need to calculate the precise date that the star Sirius (called 'Sopdet' in

Egyptian) rises just before sunrise. Sirius had been invisible for some 70 days – which means it arose when the sun had already risen and hence could not be seen by the naked eye due to the illuminated atmosphere.

Today we can utilize a government astronomical website that provides us with the necessary information. Here's what to do:

Go to http://www.usno.navy.mil

• In top toolbar click on 'Astronomy'
• Then click on Data Services
• Click on Rise/Set/Transit Times for Major Solar System Objects and Bright Stars
• Fill out the required fields, including your location, the star Sirius, and dates from late July to August 14 or later.
• Print a copy of the resulting table of Rise/Set/Transit Times.
• Then go back and fill out the form again, but this time you will select Sun so you can get Rise/Set/Transit Times for the sun.
• Finally, compare the two sets of Times, remembering that you are looking for the first date when Sirius appears BEFORE Civil Twilight.

For example, in the city of San Francisco for 2009, on the date of August 6 Sirius rises at 5.45 a.m. and the time for beginning Civil Twilight is 5.49. That means that on that date the human eye will see Sirius just 4 minutes before Twilight begins. Once the sun actually rises at 6.18am it will be far too bright to see the star.

The date of New Year will vary considerably, depending on latitude and longitude in our very large country.

For example, in Miami, Florida, the date for New Year 2009 will be July 27 – and not August 6 as in San Francisco – because Civil Twilight begins at 6.20 a.m. and Sirius rises at 6.16 a.m., just four minutes prior. That means Sirius will be visible for the first time in this season. On dates prior to July 27 Sirius will be rising after the start of Civil Twilight and Sunrise and hence will not be seen by the naked eye because the sky will be too bright.

This does raise some issues that could to be explored by the various Kemetic temples. Would it be "within the Tradition" to have such variation in celebrating the New Year across this country? Would it be better to select one date for the nation or for a fellowship of affiliated temples, even though they are geographically far apart?

Might we use the date based on calculations for Egypt instead of the United States? And, if so, which location in Egypt—since Egypt is also a very large country? You see, the questions multiply.

My sense of things is that we are not wrong to use our own location in determining the date for *Wep Renpet*. Humans' experience of their world is in fact local, not global. The sun rises for us in our location at a certain time, and for other folks in their locations at different times. On the other hand, perhaps we Kemetics should select one location—let's say, the nation's capital—to calculate the date of *Wep Renpet*. At this very early stage in our development as Kemetic Reconstructionists I think we can begin a period of reflection and discussion on the topic in a spirit of mutual respect for the varying insights and opinions that will likely emerge. Just as in ancient Kemet there were a number of differing creation myths, and all were honored, so today we can learn from their example to honor diversity of opinion.

You may like to read Jeremy Naydler's *Temple of the Cosmos*, pages 67-73, about Sirius's role. Several thousand years ago I believe the rising of Sopde (or Sopdet, i.e. Sirius) would have occurred earlier, in late June or July. Due to celestial movements, however, today it occurs in late July or early August.

Determining if there will be an extra intercalary month in any given year

We know that the ancient Egyptian religious calendar placed the beginning of a new year on the day where the heliacal rising of Sopdet (the star Sirius) occurs just before sunrise after a period of invisibility lasting approximately seventy days. We also know that the religious calendar was a lunar calendar, with the New Moon being regarded as the first day of the month. The following question comes up: how did the ancient Egyptians coordinate the rising of Sopdet with the waxing and waning of the moon? Rarely does the rising of Sopdet fall precisely on the day of the New Moon. In fact, such an occurrence would be quite rare. That means Wep Renpet (new year day) would most likely occur some days before a New Moon. What becomes of those days? The solution apparently employed by the ancient Egyptian priesthood was to add a thirteenth lunar month—rather than the standard twelve—to the new year. Today this is referred to as an 'intercalary month.' If New Moon occurs within less than 11 days of the heliacal rising of Sopdet then that extra intercalary month becomes the first lunar month of the new year. The Egyptologist Richard Parker thought that this extra month occurred just about every three years. The ancient Egyptians dedicated it to Djehuty and it continues to bear this god's name.

Richard J. Reidy

Today, as we attempt to restore and revive an authentic Kemetic festival calendar we need to keep these two factors in mind: 1) the appearance of Sopdet immediately before sunrise; and 2) the accurate periodic inclusion of that extra month at the start of the year. Once we determine those two conditions we will then be able to create our annual religious calendar beginning with the four-month cycles of Akhet (*3ḥt*), followed by the four months of Peret (*prt*), and the four months of Shomu (*šmw*). In 2009, for example, in the San Francisco Bay Area the feast of *Wep Renpet* occurred on August 6, with another 14 days before New Moon. Consequently, that year did not have that extra intercalary month, but instead began with the month of Tekhy, considered the first lunar month of the new year.[382]

For anyone interested in learning more about the calendars of ancient Egypt the following books will be helpful:

Sherif El-Sabban, *Temple Festival Calendars of Ancient Egypt* (Liverpool Univ. Press, 2000).

Richard A. Parker, *The Calendars of Ancient Egypt* (Chicago, 1950).

Anthony J. Spalinger, ed., *Revolutions in Time: Studies in Ancient Egyptian Calendrics* (San Antonio, TX, 1994).

---

[382] This article appears on our temples' website, kemetictemple.org under Articles.

The Brilliant Festival of the Lights of Neith

The General Ritual for Neith

Following the General Ritual, the Brilliant Festival of the Lights of Neith is celebrated. On the ancient calendar, this takes place on the 26th of the month of Hnt-htj (called 'Payni' by the Greeks). On our modern calendar, it occurs in June or July, depending on the previous date for Wep Renpet (New Year). Lights were lit in the evening in each room of the home and lights were placed on little papyrus boats and put afloat on the Nile and on the sacred lake next to the goddess's great temple at Sais.

For this special feast, each participant shall bring a floating votive candle. Also needed are two essential oils: frankincense and myrrh. In front of the image of Neith, place a shallow bowl of water in which the candles will be floated after being anointed in the ritual.

Like members of the ancient priesthood, participants should be clothed in white linen, or, if necessary, white cotton. No items made of animal products such as leather or wool are to be worn.

As with all Egyptian rituals begin with your purification—washing of hands and cleansing of mouth with Natron. This preliminary rite helps us to lay aside the cares of the day and to become mindful of the fact that we will encounter a divine being. If Natron is not available, then use a natural sea salt in its place until you make your own Natron.

*If two or more persons are participating, then one person, impersonating the Netjer Djehuty, **purifies each person by sprinkling each with water** while exclaiming:*

I purify you with the water of all life and good fortune, all stability, all health and happiness.[383]

*Afterwards each person **rinses his mouth** and **places a small amount of Natron or sea salt in his mouth** while saying the following:*

I wash my mouth; I chew natron so that I may extol the might of Neith, Mother of Ra, She Who Comes Forth from Nun.[384]

*Participants **assemble outside the Temple Chamber** and begin by softly rattling sistra.*

This time—several minutes or more—is used to focus minds and intention so that distracting thoughts are left behind. The sound of the sistrum was said to placate the deity, purifying the atmosphere in preparation for encountering divinity. The sistrum was associated with Hutheru and also with her and Heru's son Ihy, and thus has connotations of joy, celebration, and dancing. According to Plutarch (A.D. 46-120), the sound of sistra was also reputed to drive away Setekh. But this was of late date. It may have been that since by that time Setekh had been demonized, the

---

[383] Taken from Aylward M. Blackman's article "Purification (Egyptian)" in Hastings Encyclopaedia 10/1918/ 476-82. This article is reprinted in Gods, Priests, and Men, Studies in the Religion of Pharaonic Egypt, edited by Alan B. Lloyd (Kegan Paul International, 1998), p. 9.

[384] Adapted from a temple inscription taken from "The Myth of Horus at Edfu—II" by A. M. Blackman and H. W. Fairman, appearing in Gods, Priests and Men, Studies in the Religion of Pharaonic Egypt, p. 283.

general apotropaic function of the sistrum against evil entities was extended to include this *Netjer* as well. Our temples do not subscribe to this idea regarding the great *Netjer*, Setekh.

Standing before the closed doors, the Liturgist recites the entrance spell:

UTTERANCE BEFORE THE CLOSED DOORS OF THE TEMPLE

*The ritualist **raises hands in adoration** (dua position—arms stretched out in front of the body and raised up to face level, with palms facing outward). The following shall be said:*

O you *Netjeru* of this Temple, you guardians of the great portal, great *Netjeru* of mysterious abode, who sanctify the *Netjeret* in her shrine, who consecrate her oblation, who receive the offerings in her presence in the Hall of the Ennead: I have made my way and I enter into your presence. I am one of you. I am Shu, the eldest son of his father, the senior *wab* servant-priest of Neith. Do not repulse me on the *Netjeret's* path. My feet are not impeded. I am not turned back from the court of the great portal so that I may conduct the divine service, that I may present offerings to her that made them, that I may give bread to Neith. I have come on the way of the *Netjeret*. I have not shown partiality in judgment. I have not consorted with the strong. I have not reproached the lowly. I have not stolen things. I have not diminished the constituents of the Eye of Ra. I have not disturbed the Balance. I have not tampered with the requirements of the Sacred Eye. O Council of the Great *Netjeret* in this Temple, behold, I have come to you to offer Ma'at to the Lady of Ma'at, to content the Sound Eye for its mistress. I am Shu; I flood her offering table. I present her offerings, Sekhmet consorting with me, that I may adore Neith at her festivals, that

I may kiss the earth so great is her majesty, that I may endow her image with life. I am pure. I am purified.

At this point the ritualist *opens the doors to the Temple Chamber, or, if there are no doors, makes a gesture of opening unseen doors, and steps forward as if crossing over a threshold. The following is said:*

O you *Ba*-souls of *Sau* (i.e., Sais[385]), if you are strong, I am strong. If I am strong, you are strong. If your *Ka*-spirits are strong, my *Ka*-spirit is strong at the head of the living. As they are living so shall I live . . . . Sekhmet, the great *Netjeret*, beloved of Ptah, has given to me life, stability, and serenity round about my members, which Djehuty has gathered together for life. I am Heru in the height of heaven, the beautiful one of awe, Lord of Victory, mighty one of awe, exalted one of the two plumes, great one in *Abdju* (Abydos) I am pure.

All temple members chant:

Awake in peace, O Neith, Ruler of Heaven,
may you awaken in peace.
Awake in peace, O Neith, Mistress of Life,
may you awaken in peace.
Awake in peace, O Neith, Lady of Perfection,
may you awaken in peace.
Awake in peace, O Neith, Lady of Jubilation,
may you awaken in peace.

Enter, close the double doors and stand in front of the Kar-shrine and altar. All bow, touching their hands to their knees.

---

[385] Sau (Greek, Sais) is the cult center for Neith.

The ritualist slowly **opens the two doors of the Kar-shrine** *housing the sacred image. All others bow, touching their hands to their knees. The following is said:*

The doors of the sky are open; the doors of the earth are unlocked. This House is open for its Mistress. Let me come forth as she shall come forth. Let me enter in as she shall enter in. Neith, Ruler of the *Netjeru* of the earth, is exalted upon her Great Seat. The Great Company of the *Netjeru* are exalted upon their seat.

I have seen the *Netjeret,* and the *Netjeret* sees me. The *Netjeret* rejoices at seeing me. I have gazed upon the statue of the Greatly Secret One, the sacred image of the Greatly Sublime One.[386]

Right hand on left shoulder of the sacred image; Left hand on right wrist:

Djehuty has come to you. Awake when you hear his words. I have come as the envoy of Atum. My two arms are upon you like those of Heru. My two hands are upon you like those of Djehuty. My fingers are upon you like those of Anpu. Homage be to you. I am a living servant of Neith.

The Liturgist holds up the **bowl of water** *in which he/she will be mixing the Natron. The following is said:*

O water may you remove all evil,
As Ra who bathes in the Lake of Rushes,

---

[386] Based on a passage in "Worship and Festivals in an Egyptian Temple," a lecture by H. W. Fairman (publ. by The John Rylands Library, 1954), p.180.

May Heru wash my flesh,
May Djehuty cleanse my feet,
May Shu lift me up and Nut take my hand!
May Setekh be my strength, and may Sekhmet be my healing!
And may Amun-Ra be my life and my prospering!

*The bowl of water is set aside and the container of **Natron** is lifted up. The following is said:*

It is pure, it is pure.
My Natron is the Natron of Heru and the Natron of Heru is my Natron.
My Natron is the Natron of Setekh and the Natron of Setekh is my Natron.
My Natron is the Natron of Djehuty, and the Natron of Djehuty is my Natron.
My Natron is the Natron of Geb and the Natron of Geb is my Natron.

My mouth is the mouth of a milking calf on the day that I was born.

*Four pinches of **Natron** are mixed into the water as this Utterance is recited:*

I give you essential water, a tide in your time.
I bring the flood waters to purify your sanctuary.
I bring you the flood waters to purify your Temple and your statue in its place, the primordial water that purifies as in the First Time!

*The Liturgist **places an index finger into the water** and **moves it in a circular direction four times** as the following is said:*

Neith, Who Raises up What Exists, does purify this water;
Neith, Who Created Nun, does cleanse this water;
Neith, the One Who Brings to Life, the Vivifier, does sanctify
this water;
Neith herself does endow this water with power and with life.

*The **Bowl of Natron-infused water** is then taken up and the Ritualist
sprinkles this lightly in front of and around the statue or image of
Neith, applying some water to the base of the image, as the Utterance
is recited:*

I come close to You, O Protectress of the First Primordial Order.
I bring the water of rejuvenation that flows from the Two
Caverns.
I sprinkle the water, purifying your image and your Temple
from all impurity!

*The Liturgist picks up the bowl of **Natron** and **sprinkles a small
amount in each of the four directions** as the following is recited:*

The *Netjeret* Neith herself does cleanse and purify this, her
Temple to the South.
The *Netjeret* Neith herself does cleanse and purify this, her
Temple to the North.
The *Netjeret* Neith herself does cleanse and purify this, her
Temple to the West.
The *Netjeret* Neith herself does cleanse and purify this, her
Temple to the East.

*Replacing the Natron on the altar, the Liturgist takes up the **bowl of
water**, sprinkling a small amount in each of the four directions.
The following Utterance is recited:*

The *Netjeret* Neith herself does sanctify and consecrate this, her Temple to the South.
The *Netjeret* Neith herself does sanctify and consecrate this, her Temple to the North.
The *Netjeret* Neith herself does sanctify and consecrate this, her Temple to the West.
The *Netjeret* Neith herself does sanctify and consecrate this, her Temple to the East.
The Temple of the *Netjeret* Neith herself is established.
It is established for millions of years.

*The Liturgist returns to the altar and **lights the candle or oil lamp** while the following is said:*

Come, come in peace, O glorious Eye of Heru,
Be strong and renew your youth in peace.
For the flame shines like Ra on the double horizon.
The enemies of Ra are defeated. They are defeated.
I am pure, I am pure, I am pure, I am pure.

*The Liturgist **places incense on the burner** and **censes each sacred image** beginning with the statue of the Netjeret while the following is recited:*

The fire is laid, the fire shines;
The incense is laid on the fire, the incense shines.
   Your perfume comes to me, O Incense;
   May my perfume come to you, O Incense.
Your perfume comes to me, you *Netjeru*;
May my perfume come to you, You *Netjeru*.
   May I be with you, you *Netjeru*;
   May you be with me, you *Netjeru*.

May I live with you, you *Netjeru*;
May you live with me, you *Netjeru*.
   I love you, you *Netjeru*;
   May you love me, you *Netjeru*.

Standing in front of the image of Neith the Liturgist **offers the burning incense** *and says:*

Take the incense,
Its essence is for you.
Its smoke permeates your shrine, bringing life!
Take the incense,
Its essence is for you.
Your Majesty is appeased with the incense.
This Eye of Heru,
This essence of the Eye of Heru comes to you.

At this point the following hymn of joy from the temple at Esna is recited:

The sky is in celebration,
the earth rejoices,
the temples are entranced in joy,
the *Netjeru* (gods) cheer,
the *Netjerut* (goddesses) show their joy,
and humankind venerates her appearance:
Neith, the great, the powerful,
who creates the beings
and spreads joy in her city,
makes her morning appearance in her palace,
accompanied by all life, all time, all power.
Nut the Great pushes back the storm clouds,

drives away the rain before Neith,
so that the sky shines brightly,
and the earth is luminescent,
because as Nut Neith the Great rises,
in order to form from it the heavens.
We enact our celebration once again,
the day of the celebration of 'raising the sky,'
because as Tatenen she appears another time.

Eternity is the name one gives to her majesty:
It is, in fact, Tatenen,
two thirds of her being masculine,
one third is feminine;
she created the rays of light,
drives away obscurity,
covering the solar disk with its luminous brilliance,
and concealing it in its pupil [eye].
At its rising,
she places its light in the world,
in order that each one be able to distinguish himself from his
companion.
Appearing in the form of the moon,
she drives away obscurity.
Because it is as if she is Nut, in whom the *Netjer* of the horizon
rises and sets,
the *Netjeret* who has no [physical] limits,
and through whom one can know the temporal limits.
Brilliant like the sun,
rising as the moon,
she illumines the shores with her splendor.
She created what is,
she created the beings,

giving birth to all things endowed with life.
Sky [Heaven] is the name one gives to her Majesty;
she gave a beginning to the earth according to her plans,
and she made all things as a creation of her heart.
When she traverses the sky by following her heart,
her son, Ra, is jubilant before her,
the two arms raised in adoration before the mistress of the *Netjeru*,
making up hymns as an act of grace for his powerful mother,
[as when she gives birth to him] like a child in the morning.
Ra himself presents the morning song to her person.
Young man having passed a certain age,
it is (from then on) Ra-Horakhty who hails her glory;
Man having attained the strength of age,
it is [finally] Atum who kisses the earth before her face.
Netjeru and *Netjerut* are in adoration
and the First Ancestors bow down before her intensity.
The Great Ennead is present and the Little Ennead bows its head.
The Great Horizon, solemnly clouds in itself,
because the Lady of Awe has illuminated the earth.
The *Netjeru* of the South are bowed down,
the *Netjeru* of the North bow down their heads,
those of the West make the gesture of welcome to her,
and the East is in adoration.
The inhabitants of the horizon worship her glory;
the Souls of the East praise and cry out, 'Praise!'
And the great *Netjeru*, reunited in a single group,
gaze upon their mother,
who is at the same time *Netjer* and *Netjeret*

and each *Netjer* says to his consort:[387]

UNION OF THE SUN / 2 HYMNS OF JOY

'Let us sing praises to the queen of the *Netjeru*,
let us exalt the great of prestige;
let us show our joy to the lady of love,
let us reconcile ourselves with the graces of the All Powerful
in her shrine:
let us cry out in a loud roar in honor of the Cow (of the Sky);
let us satisfy with our praises
the heart of the Lady of the Sky and of the Earth,
let us satisfy the desires of the divine mother of Ra,
let us prostrate ourselves in honor of the Lady of the South and
the North,
let us sanctify the ground for the worthy and powerful *Netjeret*,
when she comes on the horizon of the sky.

That which the perfume fills the air from Punt,
whose odor is that of dry oliban [a variety of frankincense].
The sun *Netjeret* who shines at her appearance,
whose fine jewels shine brighter than the finery of the South
and the North,
or that of the sky when a great rainstorm has cleansed it.
That which has no equal,
such that there is no other that resembles it,
that illumines the sky with the light of her eyes,
that lights up the desert with her glance.
Her barque is made of beautiful gold, sparkling with decorations,
and all manner of truly precious stones;

---

[387] Serge Sauneron, *Les fêtes religieuses d'Esna*, (=*Esna* Vol. V) (Cairo, 1962), pp. 151-152.

every *Netjer* stands ready to be of service;
the crew of her barque is in joy,
her holy cabin is in joy,
while we tow its owner;
the *Netjeru* who find themselves there are in delight,
the musician *Netjerut* [goddesses] of the South and the North
raise their arms in adoration;
the Souls of Pé and of Nekhen gesture with their arms
before her greatness,
and her barque progresses, without navigation,
in one direction or another, being interrupted,
in the Mansion of Neith,
and the whole of Kemet is in celebration,
because she, the divine being, is at once *Netjer* and *Netjeret*,
their mistress shines above their heads,
and every eye sees grace in her rays,
all the land is illuminated by her brilliant radiance.
Her shrine also spreads light for those who are in the *Duat*,
and the inhabitants of the world of the Blessed Ones delight at
the sight of her.'[388]

Hail Neith in all her Names!
Hail Neith in all her Forms!
Hail Neith in all her Aspects!
Hail Neith in all her Houses!
Hail Neith in all places where she pleases to be![389]

---

[388] Ibid., pp. 153-154.

[389] Adapted from Serge Sauneron, *L'écriture figurative dans les textes d'Esna*, (=Esna Vol. VIII) (Cairo, 1982). "The Litany of Neith", pp. 39.

*The Liturgist **places more incense on the charcoal** and again and again **slowly raises and lowers the incense cup as the following is recited:***

O Neith, may you advance with your *Ka*.
O Great of Might, the arm of your *Ka* is before you,
The arm of your *Ka* is behind you.
O Powerful One, the foot of your *Ka* is before you,
The foot of your *Ka* is behind you.
O Brave One, Neith, this incense is offered to you,
May your face be filled as this essence spreads itself over you.

*All present perform the **Henu Rite**—Embrace the Earth, the Fourfold Salute to the Goddess, Embrace the Earth.*

For Embracing the Earth, all present prostrate themselves, face down, upon the floor. During the Fourfold Salute, all present rise upon one knee, and alternately raise their hands and arms into the *Dua* (praise) position with palms facing outward, followed by the *Sahu* (obedience) gesture, made by striking the chest with a closed fist and raising the other arm (also with closed fist) at a ninety-degree angle. The *Dua* position is accompanied by the words **"Adoration be to Neith,"** followed by the *Sahu* gesture accompanied with the words, **"Hail to the Divine Creatress!"** The bodily gestures are performed alternately four times.

*Following this **all present again prostrate themselves** before the divine image. This is a sign and symbol of total submission and adoration before the Netjeret. The following is said:*

Homage to Neith, Lady of Might in the Mansion of the Bee [the name of Neith's temple in Sais],
who is established on the Great Seat!

I have placed myself on the floor in awe of you.

I embrace the earth before you as before the Great One of Trembling.

I have come that I might kiss the earth,

that I might worship my Mistress,

For I have seen her Beauty;

I give praise to Neith,

For I have seen her Power.

Her form is more distinguished than the *Netjeru*;

Her arm is more powerful than the *Netjeru*.

I am pure, I am pure, I am pure, I am pure!

Everyone stands up.

*The Liturgist **holds in the palm of one hand the image of Ma'at** and with **the other hand open and raised over the image as if sheltering it**, repeats the following:*

I have come to you as Djehuty, whose two hands are joined together under Ma'at. She comes to be with you, for she is everywhere. You are provided with Ma'at. You move in Ma'at, you live in Ma'at. She fills your body, she rests in your head, she makes her seat upon your brow; the breath of your body is of Ma'at, your heart does live in Ma'at. All that you eat, all that you drink, all that you breathe is of Ma'at. Djehuty presents Ma'at to you, his two hands are upon her beauty before your face.

*The Liturgist places the image of Ma'at near the divine statue. Then he/ she holds up before the image of Neith a **pitcher of water** and **pours the water slowly into an offering bowl** as the following Utterance is recited:*

This libation is for you, O Great Golden One.
This libation is for you, O Neith.
I have brought to you this offering of water,
That your heart may be refreshed.
I have brought to you this Eye of Heru,
Placing this at your feet.
I present to you that which flows forth from you,
That your heart shall continue to beat.
For it is with you
that all comes forth at the sound of the voice.

*The offering bowl is placed on the altar. At this point the **Liturgist lightly sprinkles sand on the floor in front of the altar** as the following is recited:*

O Neith, who resides in *Sau*, *[The Egyptian name for Sais]*
Take to yourself the Eye of Heru.
You have rescued it, O Protectress of the Divine Order.
You have sprinkled with sand the Eye of Heru.

*Lifting the **wine offering** before the sacred image, the Liturgist repeats the following:*

You, O Neith, are She Who Rises from Nun and fills Heaven and Earth with your Beauty—Parent of Thousands, Mother of Millions, who peopled the earth with excellent seed. Your son is the Sun, illuminating the Two Lands.[390]

---

[390] From the wine offering scene in the temple at Esna, cited in David Klotz, *Articulata Forma Dei,* "A Cosmic Epithet from Esna and Medinet Habu, ENIM 5, 2012, pp. 31-32. See also *ESNA* II, 28,14.
See http://www.enim-egyptologie.fr/revue/2012/4/Klotz_ENIM5_p31-37.pdf

*The Liturgist **continues to elevate the wine offering** while saying:*

mn n.t irp irt ḥrw w³ḏt
[*"mán-niṯ 'úrip írat ḥáru wá'ḏat"*; approximately pronounced
MAHN-neetch OO-rip EE-raht HAH-roo WAH-jat]

Take to yourself wine, the green Eye of Heru, which I offer to
your **Ka.**
O You Without Equal, how beautiful is your beauty!
May you drink it; may your heart rejoice;
may anger be removed from your face.
It is pure. [*iw.w w'b* pronounced *"uwú wá'ib"*; approximately *oo-WOO WAH-ib*]

*The Ritualist **places myrrh on the fire and lifts up the smoking
incense** while at the same time he **lifts up the meat-offering** before
the Netjeret, and says the following:*

**The scent of myrrh is for your nose. It fills your nostrils; your
heart receives the meat-portions on its scent.**[391]

*Slowly **elevating the food offerings four times** before the image of
the Netjeret, the Liturgist repeats the following:*

I offer to Neith, Magnificent and Powerful.
All life emanates from you,
All health emanates from you,
All stability emanates from you,
All good fortune emanates from you,
The One Without Equal, Neith, forever.

---

[391] Quoted in "Worship and Festivals in an Egyptian Temple," by H. W.
Fairman (publ. by The John Rylands Library, 1954), p. 191.

Richard J. Reidy

*The Liturgist places the **food offering** before the divine image, and then **all present extend one hand, palm down, over the offerings** and recite the following:*

May offerings of every kind come forth in abundance,
like the things which come forth from the mouth of the *Netjeret*.

piryá pírit ar ḫiráw mi purú:riat ma rá' ni naṯárat. (4 times)
[approximately pronounced: peer-YA PEER-it ar khi-RAU mee pu-ROOR-iat ma RA nee nah-TCHAR-at]

May offerings of every kind come forth in abundance, like the things that come forth from the mouth of the *Netjeret*.

*Holding the **Ankh** before the Netjeret, the Liturgist says:*

Live, O Neith, Whose Perfection Fills Heaven, live for all time and for eternity!

ʿánaḫ niḥáḥ ḏát.
[approximately pronounced *AH-nakh nee-HAH JAHT]*

*The **Ankh** is placed next to the image of Neith.*

*Holding the **Ib (the golden heart)** before the Netjeret, the Liturgist says:*

Hail to you, O Neith, Mother at the Beginning. I have brought to you your heart to set it in its place. Let me draw near to you with your heart, so that you may have pleasure through me, and so that by means of me you may have power over your body. Ascend, O Lady of Eternity and Everlastingness, radiant, rejuvenating, equipped as a *Netjeret*. Live, O Nourishing One, live forever and ever!

*After placing the **Ib** near the sacred image, everyone recites this prayer to Neith.*

Giving praise to your *Ka*, kissing the earth for your name. Calling to you in the hours of trouble.[392] Father of Fathers and Mother of Mothers, you are the divinity who came into being in the midst of the primeval waters. She is the one having appeared out of herself while the land was in twilight and no land had yet come forth and no plant had yet grown. She illuminated the rays with her two eyes and dawn came into being.[393]

O Neith, divine Creatress, we thank you. We praise you. We bow down before you. O Unique *Netjeret*, mysterious and great, be with us with your powerful arm to defeat the enemies of Ra. May you be a protection for us forever!

THE BRILLIANT FESTIVAL OF THE LIGHTS OF NEITH

On the twenty-sixth day of the ancient month of Payni (today that would fall in June or July—approximately)—the tenth month of the Kemetic year—a beautiful festival in honor of Neith was held in her city of Sais. It makes a wonderful way today to celebrate this important divine creatress.

An image of Neith has been resting on the altar. A shallow four-sided dish or Pyrex glass baking dish is filled with fresh water. It is placed in front of the image of Neith. This container of water will

---

[392] David Klotz, "Between Heaven and Earth in Deir el-Medina: Stela MMA 21.2.6," *SAK* 34, p. 272. (*SAK* is abbrev. for the journal *Studien zur altägyptischen Kultur.*)

[393] From Serge Sauneron, *Le Temple d'Esna*, Vol. V, p. 28.

be used for **floating each anointed candle** offered to the *Netjeret.*
While gently shaking sistra the following is said:

Hail Great Mother, [the time of] **your birth has not been
uncovered** [i.e., discovered]! **Oh Eternal Enduring One!**

**Hail Great *Netjeret,* who lives in the *Duat* (Underworld] twice
hidden!
Oh Unknown One!**

**Hail, Divine Great One, whose cloak has not been loosened.
Unloose your cloak for me.**

**Hail, Hidden One. No man knows the way of entrance to her.
Come then, receive my *Ba* and protect it within your two
hands.**[394]

O great Mother!
'a mí'wat wúrrat! [approximately AH MI-wat WOOR-rat]

O great *Netjeret!*
'a naṯárat `á'at! [approximately AH na-TCHAH-rat AH-aht]

O Hidden One!
'a Há'pat! [approximately AH MI-wat HAH-pat]

**You are the Lady of *Sau (Sais)* . . . Whose two-thirds are masculine
and one-third is feminine. Unique *Netjeret,* mysterious and great,**

---

[394] A text quoted in Budge, *The Gods of the Egyptians,* pp. 459-460.
Although Budge's translations of hieroglyphic texts is very much outdated,
his books still contain much useful information, although he is heavily
influenced by the triumphalist Christianity of his own era.

who came to exist in the beginning, and caused everything to come to be . . . Divine Mother of Ra, who shines in the horizon, the mysterious one who radiates her brightness.[395]

O great Mother!
'a mí'wat wúrrat! [approximately AH MI-wat WOOR-rat]

"O great *Netjeret!*"
'a natjárat `á'at! [approximately AH na-TCHAH-rat AH-aht]

"O Hidden One!" [approximately AH MI-wat HAH-pat]
'a Há'pat!

O Neith, the mighty mother, who gave birth to Ra!
'a Níyit wúrrat mí'wat mísyat Ree`u! [approximately AH NEE-yit WOOR-rat MI-wat MISS-yat REE-oo]

Hail, Father of Fathers, and Mother of Mothers, Neith, the Great Cow who gave birth to the sun, who made the germ of the *Netjeru* and of humankind, the mother of Ra, who raised up Atum in primeval time, who existed when nothing else had being, and who created that which exists after she had come into being.[396]

We come today, great *Netjeret*, to celebrate the mystery of you. Great Creatress, Hidden One, we dedicate to you these lights [i.e., candles]. As they light up the darkness, as they illumine our dwellings, may you yourself repel from us who are your

---

[395] An inscription in the temple in Esna, quoted in Barbara Lesko's *The Great Goddesses of Egypt*, p. 61. See Serge Sauneron, *Le Temple d'Esna*, 3.137, lines 252.25-26.

[396] Adapted from a text in E. A. Wallis Budge, *The Gods of the Egyptians*, Vol. 1, p. 463.

children every dark force and every enemy, whether human or divine, whether manifest or hidden, which would hinder us or harm us in any way. As a token of our love, as a sign of our devotion, we anoint with fragrant oils of frankincense and myrrh each candle dedicated to you.

Anointing his/her candle with myrrh oil, each person says:

This oil of myrrh comes; it comes as the Eye of Heru to cleanse and to purify this candle for you, O Neith. It is well.

Anointing the candle with frankincense oil, say:

This oil of frankincense comes: it comes as the Testicles of Setekh to empower and to strengthen this candle for you, O Neith. It is well.

Lighting the candle, say:

The candle has come to your *Ka*, O Neith, Lady of *Sau* (Sais).
The Second Self of Ra has come; it has appeared gloriously in this sanctuary.
I present this candle to your *Ka*, O Neith.
The Eye of Heru is your strength. May it be my strength.
The Testicles of Setekh are your strength. May they be my strength.

After each person has anointed & lighted his candle, one person says:

O *Netjeret,* you are the Male who acts the role of the Female; you are the Female who acts the role of the Male. [397] As both male

---

[397] Lana Troy, *Patterns of Queenship in Ancient Egyptian Myths and History* (Stockholm, 1986), pp. 17-18.

and female, you are the font and source of duality, for truly you created it. Help us to reconcile every duality in ourselves, and help us to embrace it in others, and in our world. Give us light to see with a clear vision into the dark mystery of duality. We dedicate these candles to you, O mysterious, veiled One. We dedicate these lights to you, O Neith.

THE LITANY OF NEITH, LADY OF *SAU* (Greek SAIS)

Each participant shall recite a section of this beautiful litany. Make the offering of the Litany to Neith on this day, saying:

I/we offer this litany to Neith, the Great One, mother of the *Netjer*, Mistress of *Ta Senet* (Esna) in all her names. May she give me/us Life, Prosperity, and Health.

Hail Neith, the Great One, mother of the *Netjer*, Divine Mother, Mistress of *Ta-Senet*;
Hail Neith, the Great One, mother of the *Netjer*, Divine Mother, Mistress of *Sau* (Sais), Hail Neith of the Chapel within the Mansion of Neith; Hail Neith, Mistress of *Sau*, great sovereign of Kemet;
Hail Neith, the Flood who made everlastingness;
Hail Neith, who rose in Nun while the Earth was still in darkness;
Hail Neith, the Serpent of Life who raised her head out of Nun as Khnum lifted up Heaven.

Hail Neith, the Ancestor, who reared up at the beginning, the mother of primordial time who gave birth to all creatures;
Hail Neith, the Great Cobra, who touches the limits of eternity and everlastingness, with whose name all cobras are marked,

Hail Neith, the Serpent who rose at the beginning, the Serpent of Life who protects the Land;
Hail Neith, the Radiant!

Hail Neith, the Blazing Bull;
Hail Neith, who was at the beginning and who created those who are on high and those who are low;
Hail Neith, the Mysterious One who made all beings and created all that exists by her birth;
Hail Neith, who made Heaven for her *Ka*, and who placed her Son there as the Radiant Light.

Hail Neith, who made the concealing Underworld, in her form of the Concealing One;
Hail Neith, Father and Mother, who came into being at the beginning, who came from Nun before the birth of all other beings;
Hail Neith, the Father of Fathers, the Mother of Mothers, who was born before birth;
Hail Neith, Ancestor who created the Ancestors;
Hail Neith, the Great Cow *A-hat*, whose child is Ra, and who nurses the germination of *Netjeru* and of humanity;
Hail Neith, Mistress of the Land of Kemet, who shoots her arrows against all the enemies of Ra;
Hail Neith, Mistress of the Mansion of the Father, who protects her son Ra against his enemies;
Hail Neith, who grasps the bow, and who grabs the arrows to repulse the invaders;

Hail Neith, Mistress of the Mansion of the Bee, in whose honor the *Ba*-souls of Pé and Dep dance in acclamation;
Hail Neith, The Great One, the Powerful One, without equal amongst the *Netjeru*:

Hail Neith, the great cow *Mehet-Weret*, who created Ra;

Hail Neith, the Mother of the Unique *Netjer* who has no equal;

Hail Neith who raised her son Ra and put him between her two horns, who crossed Nun in the form of *Mehet-Weret*, the Great Swimmer, and pushed back the rebels against him on the water;

Hail Neith, who makes protection around Ra and who delights the heart of Ra between her horns.

Hail Neith, the Extensive Water who gave birth to all beings;

Hail Neith, who made the flood burst forth at the right time;

Hail Neith who gives back youth in the Waters of Renewal in her season;

Hail Neith, who provides Ausir the weary-hearted *Netjer* with life, who protects her son Heru;

Hail Neith, the Great One of Great Ones, the Ancestor of Ancestors.

Hail Neith, Mistress of the Mansion of the Mother, who suckles her two Crocodile Sons;

Hail Neith who watches over her Mansion, who embraces the neck of the crocodile in her two arms;

Hail Neith, The Great One of Great Ones, at the head of the Mansion of the Father;

Hail Neith, the Mother of Ra, who created Atum, who made the *Netjeru* and gave life to all humanity.

Hail Neith in all her Names.

Hail Neith in all her Forms.

Hail Neith in all her Aspects.

Hail Neith in all her Houses.

Hail Neith in all places where she pleases herself.[398]

May she give all life, all stability and all power to each of her servants as to the Son/Daughter of Ra. Dominion be to the Preserver, Neith!

Participants now should make themselves comfortable, and then focus on the candles' light. Repeat slowly:

O Hidden One, bless us. . . . O Veiled One, guide us.

After a period of silent prayer and meditation, **participants back out of the Temple Chamber with heads slightly bowed** *while the Ritualist performs the* **"removing the foot."**

With the broom the Liturgist, as the last person to exit, **ritually sweeps the area beginning at the altar.** *(This is known as* **"removing the foot."***) While performing this action the Liturgist recites the following:*

The distress that causes confusion has been driven away, and all the *Netjeru* are in harmony. I have given Heru his Eye; I have placed the *Wedjat*-Eye in the correct position. I have given Setekh his Testicles, so that the two lords are content through the work of my hands.

I know the sky, I know the earth;
I know Heru, I know Setekh.
Heru is appeased with his Eyes;
Setekh is appeased with his Testicles.

---

[398] This is only a portion of a longer Litany to Neith inscribed at the temple in Esna. For the full text see Serge Sauneron's multi-volume work Esna VIII, *L'écriture figurative dans les textes d'Esna*, (Cairo, 1982), pp. 35-39.

I am Djehuty, who reconciles the *Netjeru,*
who makes offerings in their correct form.

The double doors are solemnly closed as the Liturgist says the following:

Djehuty has come.
He has filled the Eye of Heru;
He has restored the Testicles of Setekh.
No evil shall enter this Temple.
Ptah has closed the door,
Djehuty has set it fast.
The door is closed, the door is set fast with the bolt.

All bow, touching the palms of their hands to their knees.

THE REVERSION OF OFFERINGS

One priest or priestess and as many assistants as necessary enter the Temple Chamber a final time. While he/she and any assistants lift up the offerings before the sacred image the ritualist *shall say:*

O Neith, your enemy[399] withdraws for you. Heru has turned himself to his Eye in its name of 'Reversion-of-Offerings.' I am Djehuty. I come to perform this rite for Neith, Mother and Father at the Beginning. These, your divine offerings revert, they revert to your servants for life, for stability, for health and for joy! O that the Eye of Heru may flourish for you eternally!

---

[399] Meat offerings held a two-fold meaning for the ancient priesthood. Since meat necessarily came from slain animals, it signified the defeated or slain enemies of the Netjer. At the same time, the meat offering represented the produce of the land which ultimately was a gift of the Netjeru.

*Everyone withdraws, **carrying away all food offerings except for one loaf of bread together with a bowl of pure water**. These last items will remain until evening. If this ritual is celebrated after sunset, these items would also be removed.*

*After the candle has burned down, a servant-priest enters **and closes the doors of the Kar-shrine**.*

***Extinguishing the candle or oil lamp**, he/she exclaims:*

This is the Eye of Heru by which you have become great, by which you live, and by which you have power, O Neith. This is the Eye of Heru which you consume and through which you enchant your body. The *Wedjat*-Eye now enters into the West, into *Manu*, but it shall return. Truly, the Eye of Heru returns in peace![400]

---

[400] It is important to consume the food offerings after the ceremony. Water used should either be drunk or poured onto the earth. If it is mixed with Natron, dilute it very greatly and then you can pour in onto the bare earth.

Spells for the Reconciliation of the Brother-Gods

This ritual can be preceded by either the General Ritual for Heru or the one for Setekh. The Reconciliation Rite below can be inserted toward the conclusion of the General Ritual where meditation or magical action is called for.

Items needed: representations of the Eye of Heru and the Testicles of Setekh[401];
a WAS scepter, a bowl of sand, cedar oil, two votive or tea candles for each participant; images of the two gods, Heru and Setekh.

At that point in the daily rite which is set aside for meditation, the main Ritualist raises the WAS sceptre and exclaims:

Open are the double doors of the horizon.
Unlocked are its bolts.
Clouds darken the sky. The stars rain down.
The constellations stagger.
The bones of the Earth God tremble.
All movements cease when they see the Brother-Gods arise.[402]

The heaven is agitated, the earth trembles.

---

[401] The hieroglyph for 'testicles' is shaped like an upside-down Valentine's heart. It can be made of any material—clay, stone, or wood.

[402] Adapted from Utterance 273-4 in *The Pyramid of Unas*. Bollingen Series XI: Volume 5, Egyptian Religious Texts and Representations (Princeton University Press, 1969) by Alexandre Piankoff, page 244. Please note that all the texts in this ritual come from ancient sources quoted by Piankoff, Griffiths, or te Velde. These secondary sources have collected and commented on important ancient texts to help readers understand them better within the ancient tradition.

Richard J. Reidy

Heru comes, Setekh approaches.[403]

*At this point **each person separately is to recite the following spell while touching his little finger to his mouth and applying spittle to the Eye of Heru** on the altar. Then each person is to **sprinkle a small amount of sand on the Testicles of Setekh.***

May I see the two inhabitants of the Palace;
may I see Heru and Setekh.
I place my spittle on the face of Heru for a healing;
I bandage the wound which is upon him.
I take in my hands the testicles of Sutekh;
I bandage his mutilation which is upon him.[404]

That One is born for me, this One is conceived for me.
You are born, O Heru, as the one whose name is He-before-Whom-the-Earth-Quakes.
You are conceived, O Setekh, as the one whose name is He-before-
Whom-the-Sky-Shakes.[405]

The reciters should continue alternating recitations as the next person recites:

Such a One has no mutilation (Heru);
such a One has no injury (Setekh).
So I have no injury; I have no mutilation.[406]

---

[403] Op. Cit., p. 8, quoting Pyramid Text 956a.
[404] Pyramid Text 141d-142d, as quoted in J. Gwyn Griffiths, *The Conflict of Horus and Seth* (Liverpool Univ. Press, 1960), p. 23.
[405] Pyramid Text 215, lines 142-143, quoted in Piankoff, p. 60.
[406] Ibid.

I have equipped myself as the Great-in-Magic who is in *Nubt* (Ombos), lord of Upper Kemet. I have equipped myself as Heru, son of Aset, lord of Lower Kemet. [407]

The doors of the sky are opened to Heru, the doors of the earth are opened to Setekh. . . . I go forth, and Heru goes forth. I speak, and Setekh speaks.[408]

I have filled the Eye when it was injured on this day of the conflict of the Two Rival Gods. What is that, the conflict of the Two Rival Gods?[409]

That is the day on which Heru fought with Setekh, when Setekh wounded the face of Heru, when Heru seized the testicles of Setekh. It was Djehuty who did this with his fingers.[410]

I am Djehuty. I have judged the Two Rival Gods. I have removed their strife. I have destroyed their lamentations.[411]

Having first wet his/her little finger with Cedar Oil, each person separately recites the following spell and touches that finger to the Eye of Heru and then to the Testicles of Setekh, saying:

O Heru, I make full your Eye for you with ointment. It is well. O Setekh, I make whole your Testicles for you with ointment. It is well.

Continue as formerly taking turns in reciting the following spells:

---

[407] Griffiths, Op. Cit., p. 23.

[408] Ibid.

[409] H. Grapow, *Religiöse Urkunden*. (Vol. 5), 32, quoted in Griffiths, p. 29.

[410] Ibid.

[411] Op.Cit., p. 82.

Hail to you, moon, Djehuty, in this your name of Reconciler.

Hail to you, moon, Djehuty, who did drive out the conflict from the western sky.

Hail to you, moon, Djehuty, who did quell the strife in the eastern sky.[412]

Heru and Setekh, may you take hold of my hand, may you conduct me daily.[413]

My Natron is the natron of Heru, my natron is the natron of Setekh.

My right side is Heru; my left side is Setekh.

Heru carries me. Setekh raises me.[414]

Hail to you, O Eye of Heru, to whom Ra has given glory before the Ennead. Protect me from every illness. I am that Djehuty, that physician of the Eye of Heru.

Hail to you, O Testicles of Setekh, to whom Ra has given glory before the Ennead. Protect me from every illness. I am that Djehuty, that physician of the Testicles of Setekh.

I am He-With-The-Two-*Bas*, who are in his two chicks. Those are the *Ba* of Heru and the *Ba* of Setekh, when he came to *Khem*

---

[412] From the Turin Magical Papyrus quotedin Griffith, p. 82.

[413] Griffith, p. 24.

[414] Ibid.

(Letopolis[415]). **Finally, they embraced one another and became He-With-The-Two-*Bas*.**[416]

O Amun-Ra, grant to me the portion of Heru as life, grant to me the years of Setekh as happiness!

The Brother-Gods are in peace! They are in peace! It is Djehuty who accomplishes these deeds.[417]

NOTE: The foregoing rite incorporates a number of spells that were first inscribed in the Pyramid of the Pharaoh Unas, last king of the Fifth Dynasty (c. 2345 BCE), as well as several spells found in various other burial sites of that era (i.e., the Old Kingdom). These are collectively referred to as the Pyramid Texts. Some come from Sixth Dynasty pyramids—those of Pepi I, Teti, Pepi II, Aba, Neith, and Apuit as well as others. There is also a passage from one version of the Book of the Dead, as well as from the Turin Magical Papyrus.

The conflict of the two Brother-Gods was always considered an extremely important event; hence, references to it are common. However, the Egyptians carefully avoided giving many details about it—unlike other stories involving the gods. References to it were typically oblique, indirect, and couched in non-specific

---

[415] Letopolis, city of the Falcon god Heru the Elder, whose right eye was the Sun and the left the Moon. When these two heavenly bodies are invisible (as on the night of the new moon) he goes blind and takes the name Mekhenty-er-irty, "He who has no eyes." When he recovers them, he becomes Khenty-irty, "He who has eyes." Khem was the capital of the second Nome of Lower Egypt.

[416] Hermann te Velde, *Seth, God of Confusion* ((Leiden: E. J. Brill, 1977), p. 70.

[417] K. Sethe and W. Helck *Urkunden des 18. Dynastie* (Urk. iv), 244, 16-17, quoted in Griffiths, p. 70.

language—completely unlike Greek or Roman myths. It is as if the Egyptians did not want to bring the event into existence once again by enfleshing it with details. That other crucial event, the slaying of Ausir, is similarly not detailed in any writings. For the Egyptians words had power—in fact, words *were* power.

Four magical actions accompany the recitation of the words: 1) the application of spittle to the Eye; 2) the sprinkling of sand over the Testicles; and 3 and 4) the twofold anointing with oil of cedar. Four is the number of completeness. The healing of the wounded members is complete. The reconciliation is accomplished. Peace and balance and harmony are restored, not by the two Combatants, but by the actions of the Lord of Spells, Djehuty, He-of-the-Balance.

Concluding Rite for the Feast of the Reconciliation of Heru and Setekh

Holding the two unlighted candles in his outstretched hands each reciter says:

Giving praise to Heru and Setekh,
paying homage to the Brother-Gods,
that they may give me a happy life-time, a body of joy,
and pleasure of heart in the course of each day.[418]

Each person first lights and then presents an inscribed votive candle to Heru. Holding the lighted candle up to the Netjer's image, say the following:

---

[418] Adapted from the standard offering formula inscribed on votive stelae presented at temples throughout Egypt. See <u>Votive Offerings to Hathor</u>, by Geraldine Pinch (Oxford: Ashmolean Museum, 1993), pp. 99 and 126.

The candle has come to your *Ka*, O Heru, lord of Lower Egypt. The second self of Ra has come; it has appeared gloriously in this sanctuary. I present this candle to your *Ka*, O Heru. The Eye of Heru is your protection. May it be my protection. The Eye of Heru sees the hidden word; it knows its meaning. It has power over it, to give or to take away. May you grant this, the desire of my heart. The protection of Heru is effective. It is effective.[419]

Place the candle in front of the image of Heru.

Then **light and present an inscribed votive candle to Setekh,** *saying:*

The candle has come to your *Ka*, O Setekh, lord of Upper Kemet. The second self of Ra has come; it has appeared gloriously in this sanctuary. I present this candle to your *Ka*, O Setekh. The Testicles of Setekh are your strength. May they be my strength. The Majesty of Setekh sees the hidden word; it knows its meaning. It has power over it, to give or to take away. May you grant this, the desire of my heart. The strength of Setekh is effective. It is effective.[420]

This concludes the Reconciliation Rite. Please **continue with the customary "removing the foot" action and recitation** *found at the end of every ritual for the Netjeru.*

---

[419] From a candle-lighting spell in the Ritual of Amenophis I in *Hieratic Papyri in the British Museum*, edited by Alan Gardiner, Vol 1 (London: Trustees of the British Museum, 1935), p. 90.
[420] Ibid.

Mysteries of Osiris (Ausir)

Preliminary Rite for Celebrating the Mysteries of Ausir

If possible, have a statue of Amun-Ra on a side table. (A picture may be substituted if no statue is available.)

Enter into the Temple and bow, touching your knees, before the images of
the Netjeru. *The Priest proclaims:*

Hail to you, Amun-Ra,
Lord of the Thrones of the Two Lands, presiding over Ipet-Isut (Karnak),
. . . Eldest of heaven, first-born of earth,
Lord of what is, enduring in all things, enduring in all things!
. . . . Lord of Ma'at and father of the Netjeru. . . .

"Hail to you, O Ra, Lord of Ma'at!
Amun hidden in His shrine, yet lord of the Netjeru,
Khepri in the midst of His barque,
Who gave commands and the Netjeru came into being.
Atum, who created humankind,
Distinguished their natures, made them alive,
And made their features differ, one from the other.
Who hears the prayer of him who is in captivity,
Gracious of Heart to whomever calls on him.
Saving the fearful from the terrible of heart,
Rendering judgment on behalf of the weak and the injured. . . .
Possessor of sweetness, greatly beloved.

O Lord of Life, even Amun-Ra, we come to recite the formula for making glorious the *Ka* of Ausir, Foremost of the Westerners. We come as your children to glorify you, King of the Netjeru, for by your life-giving power you rejuvenate nightly in the realm of the dead even the first-born of Geb. By your power, O Lord of Life, you bestow life upon those in the Mysterious Caverns. May you watch in peace!

Return to the altar. Then **light the candle/oil lamp** *as you say:*

The shining Eye of Heru comes.
The brilliant Eye of Heru comes.
It comes in peace, it sends forth rays of light unto Ra in the horizon, and it destroys the power of ʿApep according to the decree.
It leads on the serpent and it takes possession of him, and its flame is kindled against him.
Its flame comes and goes about, and it brings adoration;
it comes and goes about heaven in the train of Ra upon the two hands of your two sisters, O Ra.
The Eye of Heru lives! Truly, it lives!

Place incense on the burner and say:

The incense comes, the odor of the Netjer comes, the odor thereof comes to you, Amun-Ra, Lord of the Throne of the Two Lands. The odor of the Eye of Heru is for you, the odor of the Netjeret [goddess] Nekhbet is for you. It washes you, it ornaments you, it takes its place upon your two hands. O Amun-Ra, I have presented to you the Eye of Heru; the odor comes to you, the odor of the Eye of Heru is for you.

*Turning now to the image of Ausir, the Priest **lights the candle** while saying:*

The torch comes to your Ka, O Ausir, Foremost of the Westerners. The Eye of Heru is your protection. It spreads its protection over you;
it defeats all your adversaries. Truly your adversaries are fallen!

***Place incense on the burner** and say:*

Crossing the river you see heaven, while the fragrance of incense is in front of you and you ferry across heaven adorned. O Ausir, Chief of the Westerners, great Netjer, Lord of Abdju (Abydos), heaven is open for you. Earth is open for you. The ways of your resting place are open for you, so that you may go out and come in with Ra, so that you may walk freely as Lord of Eternity.

The Mysteries of Ausir, Part I

Throughout the temples of Egypt in the fourth month of the Inundation (*Akhet*), called *Ka-Hr-Ka* (Koiak)—what later would be called the 'Mysteries' of Osiris (Ausir)—the priests and people commemorated the death, rejuvenation and triumph of this great *Netjer*. The surviving documents show that the rituals enacted involved certain dramatic elements.

Although the rituals below call for several Ritualists, it can be celebrated even by just one person.

In addition to enacting this ritual for Ausir, participants are encouraged to bring photos of their blessed dead to be placed on the altar and used exclusively for rituals for the departed. The names of the blessed dead should be written on a piece of paper that then will be used in the ritual when calling the departed by name.

Items needed are
- [ ] *a statue or image of Ausir*
- [ ] *a pitcher of water for libations*
- [ ] *a lighted candle for Ausir*
- [ ] *a photo or drawing of a False Door[421]*
- [ ] *photos or mementos of the blessed dead along with their full names and, if possible the first name of their mother*
- [ ] *foods for offering including a small loaf of bread that will be divided into two*
- [ ] *a statue or image of Amun-Ra*

---

[421] The False Door is a traditional element in both tombs and temples. It is an artistic representation of a door which serves as the threshold between the two worlds. Photos or mementos of the blessed dead may be placed in front of the False Door. Traditionally the False Door is placed in the west, the direction associated with the realm of the blessed dead.

The Book Of Making The *Ka* Of Ausir [422]

The formula for making the *Ka* of Ausir in Akertet, which shall be recited for this *Netjer*, the Lord of *Abdju* (Abydos), at every festival of Ausir. . . . It shall make glorious his *Ba*; it shall establish his body, it shall make his *Ba* to shine in the sky, and shall make him to renew his youth each month. It shall establish his son Heru upon his seat . . . . It will benefit a man if he recite it, for he shall become a favored one of Ausir upon earth among the living . . . . It will cause the *Ba* of the deceased to live in Akertet every day. It will gladden his heart every day, and will overthrow all his enemies, and it shall be recited during the fourth month of the season of *Akhet* (Inundation) . . . .

Photos of members' beloved dead are arranged on the altar—each with a lighted candle in front of the photo and the name of the dead written on paper is placed by the photo.

A list of all the dead who are to be commemorated has been assembled for the servant-priests who will be reciting the names and calling forth their spirits. When possible, the name should be accompanied by the name of the individual's mother, as was customary in ancient Kemet.

---

[422] From a papyrus at Paris, a portion of which has been edited by Paul Pierret (*Études Égyptologiques*, 1873), also see Heinrich Brugsch, *Religion und Mythologie der Aegypter* (Religion and Mythology of the Egyptians) (Leipzig, 1887) p. 626 ff. An English translation is available in *Osiris and the Egyptian Resurrection*, by E. A. Wallis Budge, VOL. II, (publ. in 1911; reprint Dover Publ. 1975), p. 44 ff. The reader is warned that Budge's translation is somewhat outdated due to over a century of research into the ancient language.

1st PRIEST: **Come to your house, come to your house, O Ausir. Come to your house, O Beautiful Bull, Lord of men and women, Beloved One. . . . First of those in the Netherworld. Are not all hearts drunk through love of you, O Wennefer** (i.e., Ausir), **triumphant? . . . The hands of humankind and *Netjeru* are lifted on high seeking you, even as those of a child are stretched out after his mother. Come to them for their hearts are sad, and make them to appear as beings who rejoice.**

3rd PRIEST AS ASET: **Hail, Ausir! First of those in the Netherworld! I am your sister Aset. No *Netjer* has done for you what I have done, and no *Netjeret*. I made a man child, though I was a woman, because of my desire to make your name to live upon the earth. Your divine essence was in my body and I brought forth your child. He pleaded your case, he healed your suffering. . . . The throne of Geb belongs to you, O you who are his beloved Son!**

Hail, Sokar-Ausir! This calamity happened to you in the Primeval Time. The *Netjer* embalmed you and made sweet the odor of you. Anpu toiled for you in the place of purification, and performed all that he had to perform. I and my sister Nebet-Hut kindled a lamp at the door. . . . The mourners, male and female, made their lamentations for you. The *Netjeru* stand up and utter groans by reason of the great calamity which has happened to you, and they send forth their loud cries to heaven. Those who dwell in the horizon hear the *Netjeret* making lamentation over the Motionless One. Djehuty stands at the door of the pure chamber in order to recite his formulae which shall give life to the *Ba* each day. The sons of Heru are with you. Heru himself is before you. Your mouth is opened by the Book of Opening the Mouth. . . . Sokar has triumphed; your enemies are overthrown.

2nd PRIEST: Hail, Ausir Khenti-Amentiu, come to your sister, O Wennefer triumphant, come to your wife!

ALL: Hail, Ausir Khenti-Amentiu, the *Netjeru* and *Netjerut*, with their heads on their knees, await your coming. Men with outcry and shouting call out: 'O you who are invisible, come to us!' O *Ba*-Soul, perfect to all eternity, your members are in a state of well-being, your sufferings are relieved, every evil thing in you has been done away with. Your limbs are rejoined; you are protected. You have no defect.
Your limbs are rejoined, and not a member of yours is lacking.

1st PRIEST: Hail, Ausir Khenti-Amentiu! Rise up! Rise up! Do not be motionless. Your son Heru overthrows your enemies. Rise up to heaven and unite yourself to Ra. Those in the Divine Barque ascribe praises to you. The mouths of the *Netjeru* of the horizon utter words of joy. Acclamations follow you. Your love is in their hearts. Awe of you is in their breasts when you enter into the two Eyes and unite with it. Those who are on earth and those in the Netherworld flourish at the sight of you, O Moon. . . . When you rise in the sky, calamity departs.

2nd and 3rd PRIESTS AS ASET & NEBET-HUT: Hail, Ausir Khenti-Amentiu! There is health in your members; your wounds are done away with. Your suffering is relieved; your groaning shall never return. Come to us, the sisters, come to us; our hearts will live when you come. Men shall cry out to you, women shall weep for you with gladness when you come to them.

1st PRIEST: **Hail to you, Aset, Mourner of Ausir, who bewails the limp Great One, Bull of the West; at seeing whom the Westerners rejoice. Lady of All in the secret place; to whom Ausir turns his back in these his moments of inertness; Aset, who is in front of the Lord of Abydos; whose place on the paths of the Netherworld is hidden; who bewails her lord at the internment in this her name of She-who-bewails-her-lord. Hail to you, Mourner of Ausir, Companion of the Bull of Nedit, who makes the mummy-wrappings to breathe, who veils the limpness, to whom Ausir has turned his back, helper of the embalmer Anpu when treating the body of the Inert One.**

2nd PRIEST: **The glorious Aset was perfect in command and in speech, and she mourned her brother. She sought him without ceasing. She wandered throughout the land uttering cries of pain, and she did not rest until she had found him. She overshadowed him with her wings, and she uttered cries at the burial of her brother.**

1st PRIEST: **The screecher comes; the kite comes, namely Aset and Nebet-Hut. They have come seeking their brother Ausir, seeking their brother the King.**

3rd PRIEST: **Weep for your brother, O Aset; weep for your brother, O Nebet-Hut. Weep for your brother!**

1st PRIEST: **Aset sits down with her hands on her head. Nebet-Hut has clutched her breasts because of their brother the King, who crouches on his belly—an Ausir in his danger, an Anpu foremost of grip.**

3rd PRIEST: **You shall have no putrefaction, O Ausir! You shall have no cold sweat, O Ausir! You shall have no efflux. You shall have no dust.**

2nd PRIEST: **The starry sky serves your celestial serpent [Aset] whom you love. Your eyes have been given to you, O Ausir, as your two uraei because you are Wepwawet who is on his standard, and you are Anpu who presides over the *Netjer's* Booth.**

1st PRIEST: **Behold now, Aset speaks:**

3rd PRIEST AS ASET: **Come to your house, Oh You of *Iunu* [i.e., Ausir]! Come to your house for your enemies are not! Behold the excellent sistrum-bearer—come to your house! Lo, I, your sister, love you—do not depart from me! Behold Ausir, *Hennu*, the beautiful One! Come to your house immediately—come to your Temple immediately!**

Behold my heart which grieves for you; behold me seeking for you—I am searching for you to see you. Lo, I am prevented from beholding you, oh You of *Iunu*! I love you more than all the earth. And you love not another as you do love your sister!

1st PRIEST: **Behold now, Nebet-Hut speaks:**

2nd PRIEST AS NEBET-HUT: **Behold the excellent sistrum-bearer—come to your house! Cause your heart to rejoice, for your enemies are not! Both of your sister-*Netjerut* are at your side and behind your couch, calling upon you with weeping—yet you are prostrate upon your bed!**

Hearken to the beautiful words uttered by us and by every noble One among us. Subdue every sorrow which is in the hearts of your sisters, oh you strong One among the *Netjeru*—strong among men who behold you! We come before you, oh prince, our lord; do not turn your face away from us. Sweeten our hearts when we behold you, oh prince! Beautify our hearts when we behold you! I, Nebet-Hut, your sister, I love you: Your foes are subdued, there is not one remaining. Lo, I am with you; I shall protect your limbs forever, eternally.

1st PRIEST: Your right eye is like the *Sektet* Barque; your left eye is like the *Atet* Barque; your eyebrows are like Anpu; your fingers are like Djehuty; your hair is like Ptah-Sokar; they make a way for you, and they smite down for you your enemies.

3rd PRIEST AS ASET: I have come to protect you, O Ausir, with the north wind which comes forth from Tem; I have strengthened for you your throat; I have caused you to be with the *Netjer*; and I have placed all your enemies under your feet.

2nd PRIEST AS NEBET-HUT: I go round about behind my brother Ausir. I have come that I may protect you, and my strength which protects shall be behind you forever and forever. The *Netjer* Ra hears your cry. You, O son of Nut, are destined to triumph—your head shall never be taken away from you, and you shall be made to rise up in peace.

1st PRIEST: The earth is made waste; the sun does not rise. The moon does not appear—it no longer exists. The ocean sinks, the land spins round, the river is no longer navigable. The entire world moans and cries—*Netjeru* and *Netjerut*, humans, transfigured ones, and the dead, small and large cattle, they all cry out loud, 'The *Netjer* is dead!'

The ancestor-*Netjeru* who are in Pé are full of sorrow, and they come to Ausir the king at the sound of the weeping of Aset, at the cry of Nebet-Hut, at the wailing of these two spirits over this Great One who has come forth from the Netherworld. The ancestor-*Netjeru* of Pé clash sticks for you, O Ausir; they clap their hands for you, they tug their side-locks for you, they smack their thighs for you, and they say to you:

3rd PRIEST AS A SOUL OF PÉ: O Ausir the King, you have gone, but you will return. You have fallen asleep, but you will awake. You have died, but you will live. Stand up and see what your son Heru has done for you.

2nd PRIEST: Praise be to you, O Ausir, Lord of Eternity, Wennefer, Heru-khuti, whose forms are manifold, whose works are mighty. Ptah Sokar-Tem in *Iunu* [Heliopolis], the Lord of the Hidden Place, and the creator of *Het-ka-Ptah* [Memphis] and of the *Netjeru* therein, Guide of the Underworld, whom the *Netjeru* glorify when you set in Nut. Aset embraces you in peace, and she drives away the fiends from the entrance of your paths. You turn your face upon Amentet [i.e., the Underworld], and you make the earth to shine as with refined copper. The souls who are laying on their biers rise up to look upon you, they breathe the air and they look upon your face as the Disk rises on its horizon. Their hearts are content at the sight of you, O you who are Eternity and Everlastingness.

1st PRIEST: Homage to you, O Lord of the Netherworld, Foremost of the Westerners.

ALL: Grant to me a path whereon I may pass in peace, for I am just and true; I have not spoken lies willingly, nor have I done anything with deceit.

1st PRIEST: Homage to you, O Great *Netjer*, Lord of the Weighing of Words, Lord of Ma'at.

ALL: Grant to me a path whereon I may pass in peace, for I am just and true; I have not spoken lies willingly, nor have I done anything with deceit.

1st PRIEST: Homage to you, O Ausir, Wennefer, the great *Netjer* who dwells in *Abdju* [Abydos], king of eternity, lord of everlastingness, who passes through millions of years in his existence—the firstborn son.

ALL: Grant to me a path whereon I may pass in peace, for I am just and true; I have not spoken lies willingly, nor have I done anything with deceit.

1st PRIEST: Homage to you, O Lord of the Acacia Tree, the Boat of Sokar has been placed upon its sledge; you turn back the *Sebau* Fiend, the worker of evil, and you cause the *Wedj*at-Eye to rest upon its throne.

ALL: Grant to me a path whereon I may pass in peace, for I am just and true; I have not spoken lies willingly, nor have I done anything with deceit.

1st PRIEST: Homage to you, O you who are mighty in your hour, great and mighty Prince, dweller in *An-rut-ef*, Lord of Eternity and Creator of Everlastingness, you who are lord of Truth.

ALL: **Grant to me a path whereon I may pass in peace, for I am just and true; I have not spoken lies willingly, nor have I done anything with deceit.**

1st PRIEST: **Homage to you, O you who are founded upon Right and Truth; you are Lord of *Abdju* [Abydos], and your limbs are joined unto the Sacred Land; you are he to whom lies are abominations.**

ALL: **Grant to me a path whereon I may pass in peace, for I am just and true; I have not spoken lies willingly, nor have I done anything with deceit.**

1st PRIEST: **Homage to you, O you who dwell within your Boat; you bring the Nile forth from his cavern, and the light-*Netjer* rolls above your body. You are the dweller in Nekhen.**

ALL: **Grant to me a path whereon I may pass in peace, for I am just and true; I have not spoken lies willingly, nor have I done anything with deceit.**

1st PRIEST: **Homage to you, O creator of *Netjeru*, king of the South and North, Ausir, triumphant, overlord of the Two Lands in your gracious seasons.**

ALL: **Grant to me a path whereon I may pass in peace, for I am just and true; I have not spoken lies willingly, nor have I done anything with deceit.**

3rd PRIEST AS ASET: **Come to your house, come to your house! You of *Iunu* [Heliopolis], come to your house, your foes are not! O good musician, come to your house! Behold me, I am your beloved sister, you shall not part from me! O good youth, come** to your house! Long, long have I not seen you! My heart mourns you, my eyes seek you; I search for you to see you! Shall I not see you, shall I not see you, Good King, shall I not see you? It is good to see you, good to see you, you of *Iunu* [Heliopolis], it is good to see you! Come to your beloved, come to your beloved! Wennefer, Justified, come to your sister! Come to your wife, come to your wife, Weary Hearted; come to your house-mistress! I am you sister by your mother, you shall not leave me! *Netjeru* and men look for you, they weep for you together!

While I can see I call to you, weeping to the height of heaven! But you do not hear my voice, though I am your sister whom you loved on earth, you loved none but me, the sister, the sister!

2nd PRIEST AS NEBET-HUT:
O good King, come to your house! Please your heart, all your foes are not! Your two sisters beside you guard your bier, call for you in tears! Turn around on your bier! See the women, speak to us! King our lord, drive all pain from our hearts! Your court of *Netjeru* and men behold you, show them your face, King our lord! Our faces live by seeing your face! Let your face not shun our faces! Our hearts are glad to see you, King! Our hearts are happy to see you! I am Nebet-Hut, your beloved sister! . . . . I am with you, your body-guard, for all eternity!

3rd PRIEST AS ASET:
O you of *Iunu*, you rise for us daily in heaven! We cease not to see your rays! Djehuty, your guard, raises your *Ba*, in the day-bark in this your name of 'Moon.'

I have come to see your beauty in the Heru Eye, in your name of 'Lord-of-the-Sixth-Day-Feast.' Your courtiers beside you shall

Richard J. Reidy

not leave you, you conquered heaven by your majesty's might, in this your name of 'Lord of-the-fifteenth-day-feast.' You rise for us like Ra every day, you shine for us like Atum, *Netjeru* and men live by your sight. As you rise for us you light the Two Lands, Lightland is filled with your presence; *Netjeru* and men look to you, no evil befalls them when you shine. As you cross the sky your foes are not; I am your guard every day! You come to us as Child in moon and sun, we cease not to behold you! Your sacred image, *Sahu* [Orion] in heaven, rises and sets every day; I am *Sopdet* [Sirius] who follows him, I will not depart from him! The noble image issued from you nourishes *Netjeru* and men; reptiles and herds live by it. You flow from your cavern for us in your time, pouring out water to your *Ba*, making offerings to your *Ka*, to nourish *Netjeru* and men alike. Oh my lord! There is no *Netjer* like you! Heaven has your *Ba*; the earth has your form; the Netherworld is filled with your secrets. Your wife is your guard, your son Heru rules the lands!

2nd PRIEST AS NEBET-HUT:

"O good King, come to your house! Wennefer, justified, come to *Djedet* [the town of Mendes]. Hail, Bull, O fertile one, come to *Anpet* [another name for Mendes]! O lover of women, come to *Hat-mehyt*, come to *Djedet*, the place your *Ba* loves! The *Bau* of your fathers are your companions, your young son Heru, the sister's child, is before you; I am your protectress at dawn every day, I will not depart from you ever! O you of *Iunu* [Heliopolis], come to Sais, 'Saite' is your name; Come to Sais to see your mother Neith, good child, you shall not part from her! Come to her breasts that overflow, beautiful brother, you shall not part from her! O divine son, come to Sais! Your seat is in the Temple! Come to Sais, your city! Your place is the Palace, you shall repose near your mother forever! She protects your body,

670

she repels your foes; she will guard your body forever! Hail, beautiful Sovereign, come to your house! Lord of Sais, come to Sais!

3rd PRIEST AS ASET:
Come to your house, come to your house, Good King, come to your house!

Come, look upon your son Heru as King of *Netjeru* and men! He has conquered towns and nomes by the greatness of his glory. The heavens and earth are in awe of him, the bow-land is in dread of him. Your court of *Netjeru* and men is his in the Two Lands, in performing the rites that are to be performed for you; Your two sisters beside you pour out libations to your *Ka*, your son Heru presents you offerings which appear at the word—bread, beer, oxen and fowl. The *Netjer* Djehuty recites your liturgy, and calls you with his magical spells; the sons of Heru guard your body, and make offerings to your *Ka* every day. Your son Heru, champion of your name and your shrine, makes oblations to your *Ka*; The *Netjeru,* with *nemset* vases in their hands, pour water libations to your *Ka*. Come to your nobles, O sovereign King, our lord! Do not depart from them!

*The 1st Priest **holds up a vase filled with water, and walking around the image of Ausir four times, sprinkles a good quantity of it around the** Netjer, while the 2nd Priest announces:*

2nd PRIEST: Hail, Ausir! The Eye of Heru has purified you, and I have brought to you that which flows from Nun, which came forth in the primeval time from the *Netjer* Atum in the name of 'NEMSET,' which came forth from Ra.

*A second time the 1ˢᵗ Priest **liberally sprinkles water around the image of Ausir** while the 2ⁿᵈ Priest recites the following:*

In possessing the water, your heart is filled with joy. . . . The *nemset* vase of turquoise has performed the act of '*nemset*' on the *Netjeru* in its name of '*NEMSET.*' . . . The '*nemset*' vase comes! It comes as the Shining One! It comes as the Holy One! It comes as the uraeus! It comes as the Eye of Heru! Ra has opened your mouth, and he has opened for you your two eyes. The mouth of Ausir has been opened, and his heart is in his body forever.

*The 2ⁿᵈ priest as Anpu **stretches forth his hand and points to the False Door**, saying:*

2ⁿᵈ PRIEST: I am Anpu in the Divine Booth, Lord of the West; I open the way for those in the necropolis. The way is opened. The secret door is opened.

ALL: The way is opened. The secret door is opened.

3ʳᵈ PRIEST: I am Djehuty the perfect scribe, whose hands are pure. I am lord of holy words, Elder of the Magicians. I speak the spells that call forth the Shining Ones, even those in the West. . . . My heart is not weary to perform for you the service for the dead every day—on the feast of the month and half-month, throughout the duration of your years.

ALL: The way is opened. The secret door is opened.

*The 3ʳᵈ Priest as Djehuty **stretches forth his staff and points to the False Door**, saying:*

Come forth, O Ausir (name of deceased), **son/daughter of** (mother's name if known), **Justified. The door is opened for you in the West.**

ALL: **The way is opened. The secret door is opened.**

2nd PRIEST: **The way is opened for you. The secret door is opened. Come forth, O Ausir** (name of deceased), **justified.**

ALL: **The way is opened. The secret door is opened.**

The 1st Priest **points to the food offerings** *and says:*

1st PRIEST: *Hotep di nisoot*— **An offering-which-the-King-gives to Ausir, the Lord of Eternity, who quelled the warfare in the Two Lands, the again-born, the heir of Geb. May He grant to travel in the divine barque in the train of the great** *Netjer* . . . **for the** *Ka* **of** (name of deceased), **justified, and to receive a place among his followers, . . . and to come in peace and justification, (his/her) soul to the sky, (his/her) body to the Netherworld.**

The 2nd Priest **points to the food offerings** *and says:*

2nd PRIEST: *Hotep di nisoot*— **An offering-which-the-King-gives to Anpu in the Divine Booth, who is in Ut, Lord of the Sacred Land . . . May He grant the opening of the Netherworld, union with the burial chamber, to see rays in the place of darkness; for the** *Ka* **of** (name of deceased), **justified.**

The 3rd Priest **points to the food offerings** *and says:*

3rd PRIEST: *Hotep di nisoot*— **An offering-which-the-King-gives to Ma'at, mistress of the** *Netjeru*, **beautiful of appearances in**

673

the Bark of Millions, beloved of Ra every day, that She may grant offerings of bread and beer, oxen and geese, and all things good and pure to the *Ka* of (name of deceased), **justified.**

*The Priest **points to the food offerings** and says:*

PRIEST: *Hotep di nisoot*— An offering-which-the-King-gives to Amun-Ra, Lord of the Thrones of the Two Lands in 'Elect-of-Places' [Karnak], may he grant offerings and provisions, cloth, thread, incense and oil, gifts of all that grow, what heaven gives, what earth creates, what the waters bring; for the *Ka* of (name of deceased), **justified**; and that he/she be in the train of this great *Netjer* forever.

*The 2ⁿᵈ Priest offers this invocation to the Deceased. **First, he picks up a small offering loaf and divides it in half; holding the two halves in his outstretched hands,** he addresses the Deceased:*

2ⁿᵈ PRIEST: **Sit down now; the voice of the King goes forth. You are provided with every good thing that your *Ka* desires. May offerings of every kind come forth in abundance, like the things which come forth from the mouth of the *Netjer*.**

piryá pírit ar ḥiráw mi purú:riat ma rá' ni náṭar. (4 times)
[approximately pronounced: peer-YA PEER-it ar khi-RAU mee pu-ROOR-iat ma RA nee NAH-tchar]

May offerings of every kind come forth in abundance,
like the things which come forth from the mouth of the *Netjer*.

O Shining One(s), the Eye of Heru has been presented to you for your tasting. It has been presented to you that it may embrace you.

*The 1ˢᵗ Priest now **passes his hand four times around the image (picture) of the Deceased**. (The mysterious energy and life-giving power existing in the Netjeru is now transmitted to the Deceased through these magical passes of the hand.)*

1ˢᵗ PRIEST: **O Shining One(s), the** *Sa* [fluid of life] **shall not be separated from you, and you shall not be separated from it. Ra and Heru perform for you the passes by which you obtain the** *Sa* [fluid of life].

The *Ka* **of every Ausir called forth is satisfied. Return, then, refreshed. Return, then, rejuvenated. Return, Shining One(s), to the mysterious Cavern. Anpu opens the way for you. Djehuty recites with authoritative utterance his magical formulae protecting you. Return, O Shining One(s), in peace!**

*The priests **pick up the food-offerings and hold them up before the image of Amun-Ra**, they recite:*

O Ra, may the worship which you have in heaven, and the worship which is rendered to you of every kind, may it be rendered likewise to the Ausir, and may everything which is offered to your body be offered likewise to the *Ka* **of the Ausir, and may everything which is offered to his/her body be yours.**

*The priests **take the offerings and back out of the Temple while one priest performs the Removing the Foot** ceremony.*

The first part of the Mysteries of Ausir is at an end.

Works Consulted

Please note that the writings of Budge must be approached with considerable caution. His views reflect the colonialist triumphalism of his era and his translations are often problematic. His pronouncing key is outdated as a result of a century of linguistic scholarship since Budge's own time. However, the hieroglyphs he provides are generally accurate and make available to the English reader texts that are otherwise unavailable.

Budge, E.A.Wallis. *The Liturgy of Funerary Offerings*. New York: Dover Publ., 1994. (Originally published by Kegan Paul, Trench, Trubner & Co. Ltd., London, in 1909.)

The Mysteries of Ausir, Part II

The Raising of the *Djed* Pillar—A Ceremony of Resurrecting the *Netjer* [423]

Items needed are

- ☐ *a Djed Pillar;*
- ☐ *four black ribbon or strips of cloth;*
- ☐ *one red ribbon or strip of cloth;*
- ☐ *scissors (if needed to cut the black ribbons);*
- ☐ *statue of image of Ausir.*
- ☐ *Incense should already be burning throughout this rite.*
- ☐ *Photos of the Blessed Dead from the previous ritual can remain on the altar. Candles as well should continue burning. A broom for the 'removing of the foot' recitations should be available.*

*Participants begin by **shaking sistra slowly in front of the Djed Pillar,** which is lying on its side in front of the altar.*

Four black ribbons are tied around the *Djed* Pillar, symbolizing that the Pillar which contains the god is Death itself. But the bonds of Death will be loosed and thereby transform the god into a Living *Netjer* in the Realm of the Dead.

1ˢᵗ PRIEST: **Hail to you, Lady of Goodness. Those in the Netherworld rejoice as they behold you who remove the limpness of the Inert One. Because of you Ausir has the power of movement. Hail to you, Mistress of the Ancient Ones, Lady of many faces in the Secret Place, whose words affect the Bull**

---

[423] For more information on this important rite see L. B. Mikhail's article "Raising the *Djed*-Pillar. The Last Day of the Osirian Khoiak-Festival," in *Göttinger Miszellen* Vol. 83 (1984), pp. 51-70.

of *Djedu*. You guide the Lord of the West. Ausir rejoices at beholding you. Mistress of the hidden mysteries—the Inert One has turned his face to you in this your name of Mistress of Faces. Hail to you, Great One behind your lord; who raises him up after being limp . . . . Hail to you, you who attend to your lord, Mourner of Ausir, Great One, the Wailer.

4ᵗʰ PRIEST: The beneficent Aset who protected her brother and sought for him, she would take no rest until she had found him. She shaded him with her feathers and gave him air with her wings. She revived the weariness of the Listless One. She took his seed into her body, thereby giving him an heir. She suckled the child in secret, the place where he was being unknown.

PRIEST: Hail to you, O tree which encloses the god. O Ausir, behold your tomb, the shade of which is over you, the tree which repels the striking power of the one who did this to you in Gehesty.

The 3ʳᵈ Priest **picks up a pair of scissors** and **begins to cut each of the four black ribbons** *which have been tied around the Djed-pillar. Instead of cutting the ribbons, each one may simply be untied and set aside. The priest/priestess says:*

3ʳᵈ PRIEST: The *Djed*-pillar of the Day-barque is released for its lord. The *Djed*-pillar of the Day-barque is released for its protector. Aset comes and Nebet-Hut comes, one from the west and one from the east—one as a screecher, one as a kite. They have found Ausir, his brother Setekh having laid him low in Nedit.

The 3ʳᵈ Priestess **points her hand toward the** Djed *& says:*

3rd PRIESTESS AS ASET: **This is our brother. Come, let us lift up his head. Let us rejoin his bones. Come, let us re-assemble his limbs. Let us put an end to all his woe. Ausir, live! Ausir, let the great Listless One rise up! I am Aset.**

2nd PRIESTESS AS NEBET-HUT: **I am Nebet-Hut. Heru will embrace you. Djehuty will protect you. Then will your father Atum call 'Come! Ausir, live! Ausir, the great Listless One, rise up!'**

1st PRIEST: **The sky reels, the earth quakes, Heru comes, Djehuty appears. They raise Ausir from upon his side. They make him to stand up in front of the Two Enneads.**

Slowly at first, and then faster, begin shaking the sistra.

ALL: **Raise yourself O Ausir! . . . Aset has your arm, O Ausir! Nebet-Hut has your hand. The sky is given to you; the earth is given to you. The Field of Rushes, the Mounds of Heru, and the Mounds of Setekh are given to you. And he who issues commands is your father Geb. Rise up, O Still Heart! Place yourself upon your base. I bring to you a *Djed* of Gold so that you may rejoice therein. Rise up!**

The 2nd & 3rd Priestesses **stand the** Djed-*pillar upright. Continue to shake the sistra.*

1st PRIEST: **Your mother Nut has borne you; your father Geb has wiped your mouth for you. The Great Ennead protects you. Your foe is reconciled to you.**

4th PRIEST: **Your sister Aset comes to you, rejoicing for love of you. You have placed her on your phallus and your seed issues**

Richard J. Reidy

into her, she being ready as the star-*Netjeret* Sopdet, and Har-Sopd has come forth from you as Heru who is in Sopdet.

*The Priest **ties a red ribbon around the** Djed-pillar to represent the union of Aset and Ausir. **Shake the sistra.***

2ⁿᵈ PRIEST: **Hail, Lord of the Netherworld. You have repelled your disasters; you have driven away the evil event. Lord, come to us in peace!**

3ʳᵈ PRIEST: **You are more gentle than the *Netjeru*. The emanations of your body make the dead and the living to live, O Lord of food, prince of green herbs, O mighty Lord, you—the staff of life, the giver of offerings to the *Netjeru*, and of sepulchral meals to the blessed dead.**

4ᵗʰ PRIEST: **Anpu comes to you, and the two sisters come to you. They gather together your limbs for you, and they seek to put together the mutilated members of your body. Wipe the impurities which are on them upon our hair and come to us, having no remembrance of that which has caused you sorrow.**

ALL: **Come in your attribute of Prince-of-the-Earth. Lay aside your trepidation and be at peace with us, O lord. You shall be proclaimed heir of the world . . . . All the *Netjeru* invoke you; come, therefore, to your Temple and be not afraid.**

PRIEST: **O Ausir, you are beloved of Aset and Nebet-Hut; rest in your habitation forever! Praise be to you, O Setekh, for by your striking-power you have opened the way for the lordship of your brother forever. Praise be to you, O sisters, for by your love you have revived the Listless One forever! Praise be to you,**

O *Netjeru,* for because of your great deeds the Shining Ones shall live forever!

ALL: **They shall live forever!**

The normal concluding actions and recitations are repeated; that is, the **Reversion of Offerings** *and the* **Removal of the Foot.**

The candles can be left burning in front of the statues and photos until the attendees depart. At that time the attendees can take the candles and re-light them at home in front of their *Akhu* shrine. Any photo used should be returned to the home shrine and not be used in any other way.

MONTHLY LUNAR RITUALS

Hymn to the Crescent Moon

The following hymn comes from the article *Un hymne à la lune croissante* (François-René Herbin), appearing in BIFAO (82) 1982, pages 237-282, translated by HiC Luttmers from the Kemetic Temple of San Jose and edited by Richard Reidy from the Temple of Ra. BIFAO stands for *Bulletin de l'institut français d'archéologie orientale.*

One ritualist **holds up the image of the Lunar Eye above his/her head** *as the* **first person recites** *the following hymn. Following in succession,* **each participant recites one stanza.**

The sky is in celebration, bearing the mystery of the Left Eye.
The *Ba*-souls of the *Netjeru* appear in procession before him,
and Ausir shines forth as Iah (i.e., Moon).
Djehuty, by means of a net, gives his protection.

These are the *Netjeru* that together come in peace toward him.
Montu, at the beginning of the month, his heart is in exaltation.
Atum verily is at peace.
Shu and Tefnut shine within him (the Eye),
and exaltation rises through their limbs.

Geb and Nut are in jubilation;
Khenty-mekes is united in the Left Eye.
Ausir shines as a *Netjer* in him.
The Ancient Scarab fills him who is diminished,

and rejoices in mixing with him.
Netjer unites with *Netjer*.

The sky is distant and sanctified under his Majesty.
When he illuminated the Two Lands as Iah.
Aset the Divine came in jubilation
to give her protection and her figure when Iah began his cycle
anew.

Heru came in joy to give instructions concerning the Eye so
that it is renewed and rejuvenated.
Nebet Het came in joy to cleanse his body and to supply his
elements with the means of his light.

Hathor, mistress of Iunu, appeared in the Left Eye.
Heru of *Wetjeset-Hor*, great *Netjer*, master of the sky, shines
forth in the Left Eye.
Tananet and Iunyt[424] came to their place
so that each one of them occupied one day.

Djehuty the Great comes out victorious.
The Left Eye unites with the Right Eye, and Iah comes at the fixed
time without there being any irregularity in the celebration of
each of his phases, established from the rising to the setting.

You are the light that shines forth in the sky and upon the
earth.
Ra rejoices upon seeing your beauty.
The *Netjeru* of the Horizon, their hearts exult.

---

[424] Tananet and Iunyt are local goddesses of Hermonthis, the capital of
the fourth Nome of Upper Egypt prior to the 18th Dynasty.

Richard J. Reidy

Djehuty the Great comes forth triumphant; he takes inventory of the radiant *Wedjat* Eye for its owner after endowing it with its elements (the various phases of the moon as it progresses toward full visibility or Full Moon).

O beloved Sovereign of the *Netjeru*, grant that your name be stable for eternity!
Waset, Iunu, Mennefer, Nubt, Iunet, and Wetjeset-Hor[425], and all the temples that are found therein, were established for you for all time and for eternity.

All: **Ra in his Disk is triumphant against his enemies.** *(4 times)*
All: **Ausir, Iah, Djehuty, bull of the sky, prince of the Netjeru, is triumphant against his enemies.** *(4 times)*

I have incorporated the names of these six cities into this one recitation although they appear separately in the several variants that were used in their respective cities' temples. It seemed to me to be appropriate to combine into one list all the cities that used versions of this one great Hymn to the Moon.

---

[425] The towns named above are identified by their ancient Egyptian names. The Greek equivalents are as follows:
Waset: Thebes
Iunu: Heliopolis
Mennefer: Memphis
Nubt: Ombos
Iunet: Dendara
Wetjeset-Hor: Edfu

Two Rituals for Quarter Moon (the Sixth Day Feast)

Quarter Moon Rite For the Beloved Dead

In ancient Egypt Quarter Moon was occasion for the Sixth Day Feast (six days following the first visible lunar crescent). It is a day dedicated to making offerings to our departed ancestors, friends, and associates as well as to the *Netjeru* associated with the Afterlife—Ausir, Anpu, Sokar, and Ptah-Sokar.

As individuals, we can create a small shrine for our Beloved Dead with photos or even just their names. Place a candle in front of each photo and name card and make offerings of food and drink for their *Kas* (spirits). A statue or image of Ausir (Osiris) should also be placed on the altar.

Our ancient Egyptian predecessors knew well that death does not conquer love, but rather love conquers death itself. We are called to maintain their sacred traditions for our own Blessed Dead.

As the candle is lit the following is said:

The torch comes to your *Ka*, O Ausir, Foremost of the Westerners (the Blessed Dead)**, and the torch comes to your *Ka*, O Ausir** (Name of Deceased)**. There comes he who promises the night after the day; there come the Two Sisters** (Aset and Nebet-Hut) **from Ra; there comes she who was manifested in *Abdju*** (Abydos)**, for I cause it to come, even that Eye of Heru which was foretold to you, O Ausir, Foremost of the Westerners.**

*The Ritualist **pours a libation of fresh water** while the following is said:*

It is pure; it is pure, 'An-Offering-Which-the-King-Gives.' Accept this libation as a libation of the coolest water. May your *Ka* be refreshed, O Ausir (Name of Deceased). Accept this, the Eye of Heru; I offer the water which is in it, fresh water as of love and praise.

*An **offering of bread and other foods** are presented:*

'An-Offering-Which-the-King-Gives' to Ausir, Lord of Eternity. May he grant to travel in the divine barque in the train of the great *Netjer,* for the *Ka* of (Name of Deceased), **True-of-Voice.**

'An-Offering-Which-the-King-Gives' to Sokar and to Anpu upon his mountain, that they may grant to go forth on earth to see the sun in the heavens every day, for the *Ka* of (Name of Deceased), **True-of-Voice.**

'An-Offering-Which-the-King-Gives' to Amun-Ra and Atum, Lord of What Exists, remaining in everything, that they may give offerings of all things good and pure to the *Ka* of (Name of Deceased), **True-of-Voice.**

Addressing the Blessed Dead, *the Ritualist recites the following:*

Receive these offerings from my hands so that your *Ka* may flourish and endure forever.

*The Ritualist **may now wish to spend time conversing with the Blessed Dead.***

*The offerings **may remain on the altar for a time** and then **they revert for use by the Ritualist and any other family members.***

Quarter Moon Rite for the Left Lunar Eye

The ancient Egyptian priesthood commemorated the appearance of the Quarter Moon with a ritual of lunar restoration. The battle between the Two Combatants (Heru and Setekh) resulted in injuries to the Eye of Heru and the Testicles of Setekh. Both injuries are healed by Djehuty, the Divine Physician. At Quarter Moon the priesthood conducted a ritual reassembling the six fragments of the Lunar Eye, that is, the Eye of Heru. This commemoration was repeated monthly and is considered an important recurring ritual. In the ritual below, the rite calls for a bowl of fresh sand and a six-part model of the Eye of Heru. Each part should be shaped so it can contain an amount of sand for this ritual. If this is not available, then a drawing or large photo of the Eye of Heru can be used effectively. The sand can be carefully sprinkled along the lines of each lunar section depicted.

If you do not have a ceramic six-part Eye, then draw one on paper or paint it on a circle of wood. Make it large enough so that you can place a small amount of sand within each of the six sessions.

The six sections[426] of the Eye of Heru are placed on the altar. A bowl of fresh sand is set to its side. The ritualist will fill each of the six sections with sand in the following order:

The 1st section is the glyph for the fraction 1/64.
The 2nd section.........for the fraction 1/32.

---

[426] Mjwhealton note: The six sections may be found with a quick internet image search. These were also used to indicate fractions in Egyptian texts. The order of the sections, roughtly in words is 1: the 'tear-duct' marking, 2: the 'coil' marking, 3: rear sclera (furthest from the beak), 4: 'eyebrow' marking, 5: iris/pupil, 6: front sclera.

The 3rd section.........for the fraction 1/16.

The 4th section.........for the fraction 1/8.

The 5th section.........for the fraction ¼.

The 6th section.........for the fraction ½.

Taking sand in his/her hand the Ritualist sprinkles a small amount into the 1st section, saying:

Djehuty has come. The Divine Physician has come. He fills the 1st part of the Eye of Heru with sand from his hand for a healing.

Next the Ritualist places a small amount of sand into the 2nd section, saying:

Djehuty, Thrice Great of *Heka*-power, fills the 2nd part of the Eye with sand from his hand for a healing.

Filling the 3rd section with sand, the Ritualist says:

Djehuty, Who makes the Eye equipped with all that belongs to it, fills the 3rd part of the Eye with sand from his hand for a healing.

Filling the 4th section with sand, the Ritualist says:

Djehuty, Who soothes the heart of the *Netjeru* by His words, fills the 4th part of the Eye with sand from his hand for a healing.

Filling the 5th section with sand, the Ritualist says:

Djehuty, Who fills the *Wedjat*-Eye with what it needs, fills the 5th part of the Eye with sand from his hand for a healing.

Filling the 6th section with sand, the Ritualist says:

Djehuty, Who sets the *Wedjat*-Eye in its place, fills the 6th part of the Eye with sand from his hand for a healing.

It is Djehuty Who has done this. He has restored the Eye of Heru. He has healed the injury that was upon it. The Eye is restored, whole and complete. It is Djehuty Who has done this with His fingers.

The Combatants are pacified. They are at peace. At peace. It is Djehuty Who has done this for the Brother Gods.

The following hymn comes from the article Un hymne à la lune croissante (François-René Herbin), appearing in BIFAO (82) 1982, pages 237-282, translated by HiC Luttmers from the Kemetic Temple of San Jose and edited by Richard Reidy from the Temple of Ra. BIFAO stands for Bulletin de l'institut français d'archéologie orientale.

One ritualist **holds up the image of the Lunar Eye above his/her head** *as the first person recites the following hymn.* **Following in succession, each participant recites one stanza.**

The sky is in celebration, bearing the mystery of the Left Eye. The *Ba*-souls of the *Netjeru* appear in procession before him, and Ausir shines forth as Iah (i.e., Moon).
Djehuty, by means of a net, gives his protection.

These are the *Netjeru* that together come in peace toward him.

Montu, at the beginning of the month, his heart is in exaltation.
Atum verily is at peace.
Shu and Tefnut shine within him (the Eye),
and exaltation rises through their limbs.

Geb and Nut are in jubilation;
Khenty-mekes is united in the Left Eye.
Ausir shines as a *Netjer* in him.
The Ancient Scarab fills him who is diminished,
and rejoices in mixing with him.
Netjer unites with *Netjer.*

The sky is distant and sanctified under his Majesty
When he illuminated the Two Lands as Iah.
Aset the Divine came in jubilation
to give her protection and her figure when Iah began his cycle
anew.

Heru came in joy to give instructions concerning the Eye so
that it is renewed and rejuvenated.
Nebet Hut (Nephthys) came in joy to cleanse his body and to
supply his elements with the means of his light.

Hat-Hór (Hathor), mistress of *Iunu,* appeared in the Left Eye.
Heru of *Wetjeset-Hor,* great *Netjer,* master of the sky, shines
forth in the Left Eye.
Tananet and Iunyt came to their place so that each one of them
occupied one day.[427]

---

[427] Tananet and Iunyt are local goddesses of Hermonthis, the capital of
the fourth Nome of Upper Egypt prior to the 18th Dynasty.

Note: Epithets for Djehuty are taken from *Thoth: The Hermes of Egypt,* by Patrick Boylan (Oxford University Press, 1922). See especially pages 72, 129, 73, 128, 187, and 190 for the epithets in lunar sections 1, 2, 3, 4, 5, and 6 respectively.

Full Moon Rite

The text of this monthly ritual is based closely on inscriptions appearing in *The Temple of Khonsu, Volume 2: Scenes and Inscriptions in the Court and the First Hypostyle Hall: with translations of Texts and Glossary* (Univ. of Chicago, Oriental Institute Publications, 1981), vol. 2, p. 60.

On the feast of the Full Moon, **an image of the Eye of Heru, superimposed over a representation of a full moon,** *should be* **held over the incense burner.** *Begin by reciting the following:*

I bring the Eye to its Lord: I am Djehuty. I make full the Eye, equipping it with all that belongs to it.[428]

As fifteen grains of frankincense are placed, one by one, on the charcoal, the following words are recited:

Montu, entering the Left Eye on the First Lunar Day.
Atum, entering the Left Eye on the Second Lunar Day.
Shu, entering the Left Eye on the Third Lunar Day.
Tefnut, entering the Left Eye on the Fourth Lunar Day.
Geb, entering the Left Eye on the Fifth Lunar Day.
Nut, entering the Left Eye on the Sixth Lunar Day.
Djehuty, entering the Left Eye on the Seventh Lunar Day.
Nebet Het, entering the Left Eye on the Eighth Lunar Day.
Ausir, entering the Left Eye on the Ninth Lunar Day.
Aset, entering the Left Eye on the Tenth Lunar Day.

---

[428] From Patrick Boylan's *Thoth: the Hermes of Egypt* (Oxford University Press, 1922), p. 65.

Heru, entering the Left Eye on the Eleventh Lunar Day.
Hwt-Heru, entering the Left Eye on the Twelfth Lunar Day.
Sebek, entering the Left Eye on the Thirteenth Lunar Day.
Mut, entering the Left Eye on the Fourteenth Lunar Day.
Neith, entering the Left Eye on the Fifteenth Lunar Day.[429]

The Left Eye is filled. It is restored, whole and sound.
The sound Eye of Heru shines. It shines, resplendent in the heavens.

Continue holding the Eye of Heru above the ascending smoke of the incense:

O Moon, Pillar of Heaven! Illuminating the night!
May your kindly face be gracious to me and to my loved ones.
The sky is clear, and the horizon bears the form of the moon,
so that the Left Eye can make illumination for everyone.
The sky is clear for Egypt when the Sound Eye, born of Nut,
is elevated."
"The sky is clear for this nation and this city when the Sound
Eye, born of Nut, is elevated.[430]

---

[429] For the last two of the fifteen deities invoked, I have substituted Mut
and Neith for the originally named Tjenenet and Iunyt. Tjenenet are
goddesses associated with Hermonthis, a city in Upper Egypt. I substituted
Mut and Neith, both being very ancient mother-goddesses. Mut is mother
of Khonsu, and Neith gave birth to Ra, king of all deities. These goddesses
symbolize both lunar and solar aspects, the full cycle of time. In ancient
Egypt rituals were regularly modified and adapted to local conditions.
Hence, I felt free to make this change in goddesses named in order to
incorporate into the ritual two very important deities.

[430] The foregoing text comes from inscriptions appearing in *The Temple
of Khonsu, Volume 2: Scenes and Inscriptions in the Court and the First*

*Holding the Eye of Heru in your cupped hands, approach the image of Djehuty. **Offering the Eye to Djehuty**, recite:*

Receive the Eye, that you may go forth therein in your name Ausir-Iah-Djehuty, so that you may illumine the Two Lands, and make full the Eye on the 15th of the month.

In silence place the image on the altar. Then say:

O Khonsu, Lord of Joy, Great God of the Very Beginning, may you give to me all valor and all victory. May you give me eternity.

O Djehuty, may you inscribe for me the Jubilees of Ra and the years of Atum. May you give me life and dominion like Ra.[431]

Hypostyle Hall: with translations of Texts and Glossary (Univ. of Chicago, Oriental Institute Publications, 1981), vol. 2, p. 60.

[431] Boylan, p. 73.

Appendix 1: Pronunciation Key for Egyptian Reconstructed Vocalizations and Links to Vocalization of the Names of Gods and Goddesses

Pronunciation Key (MJWhealton):

Key to pronunciations of Egyptian words in the rituals in this book.

a, i, u = short pure vowels: the 'a' of "f<u>a</u>ther", 'ee' of "b<u>ee</u>t", 'u' of "L<u>u</u>ke" but short in duration.

′ = primary syllable stress, no vowel quality change, though perhaps a bit longer in duration

: = long vowel duration, hold the vowel preceding the colon longer – about twice as long

'= glottal stop, a catch in the throat that stops the sound momentarily, like the transition between the two syllables of English "<u>Uh-oh</u>" or the way a person speaking British Cockney slang would say the two 'tt' in "bo<u>tt</u>le"

ʿ = a consonant with the sound of the Arabic letter `ain – not present in English or related languages. It is common in languages of the Afro-Asiatic language phylum, to which Egyptian, Arabic, Aramaic, Syriac, Somali, and many others belong. It is made by constricting the throat and forcing air past the blockage. To give a rough idea of the sound, try saying 'ah' and slowly (carefully!) pushing your throat just above the Adam's apple with your fingers to restrict the airflow. Here is a video which may help: https://www.youtube.com/watch?v=Y0ro6b50-Lk

ḥ = an h stronger than English, sort of like a cat or iguana hissing, similar to the strong 'j' in Latin American Spanish "<u>J</u>uan" ḫ = like 'ch' in German "Aḫ", Scottish "Loḫ", or Hebrew "la-Ḫayim"

ḥ = a soft ch sound - like the 'ch' in southern German "iḥ"

ḳ = a sound like English 'k' but further back in the throat.

ḏ = dj like English "just"

ṯ = ch like English "ḥip"

A list of vocalizations of the names of gods and goddesses may be found on the blog Imperishable Stars:

https://imperishablestars.com/2016/05/18/names-of-gods-names-of-goddesses/

Appendix 2: Contacts and Links

Links:

Supplementary Information about this book and its contents, including background on rituals and vocalic reconstruction of Ancient Egyptian, and other Kemetic topics:
ImperishableStars.com

General Information on the Kemetic Temple Family of Temples (also known as the Kemetic Temple Collective or KTC):
Kemetictemple.org

Contacts:
General inquiries concerning the KTC):
Kemetictemple.org/contact.html

Inquiries concerning specific Temples in KTC):
Temple of Ra, San Francisco, CA
mwhealton@gmail.com

Kemetic Temple of San Jose, San Jose, CA
hic@kemetictemple.org

Kemetic Temple of Sacramento, Sacramento, CA
mbclewis@hotmail.com

Per Akhet Kemetic Temple, Denver, CO
Tree@perakhet.com

Printed in the United States
By Bookmasters